KV-015-742

LIVERPOOL JMU LIBRARY

3 1111 00734 3674

Aldham Robarts LRC

Liverpool John Moores University

LIVERPOOL
JOHN MOORES UNIVERSITY
TRUEMAN STREET LIBRARY
15-21 WEBSTER STREET
LIVERPOOL L3 2ET
TEL. 051 231 4022/4023

THE HISTORY
OF TRADE UNIONISM

AMS PRESS

NEW YORK

SIDNEY AND BEATRICE WEBB

THE HISTORY OF
TRADE UNIONISM

LONGMANS GREEN AND CO
LONDON · NEW YORK · TORONTO

1920

Library of Congress Cataloging in Publication Data

Passfield, Sidney James Webb, Baron, 1859-1947.
  The history of trade unionism.

    Reprint of the 1920 ed. published by Longmans Green,
London.
    Includes bibliographical references and index.
    1. Trade-unions—Great Britain—History. I. Webb, Beatrice
Potter, 1858-1943. II. Title.
HD6664.P3 1975   331.88'0941   75-173495
ISBN 0-404-06885-5

Reprinted from the edition of 1920, New York and London
First AMS edition published in 1975
Manufactured in the United States of America

AMS PRESS INC.
NEW YORK, N. Y. 10003

INTRODUCTION TO THE EDITION
OF 1920

THE thirty years that have elapsed since 1890, down to
which date we brought the first edition of this book, have
been momentous in the history of British Trade Unionism.
The Trade Union Movement, which then included scarcely
20 per cent of the adult male manual-working wage-earners,
now includes over 60 per cent. Its legal and constitutional
status, which was then indefinite and precarious, has now
been explicitly defined and embodied in precise and absolutely expressed statutes. Its internal organisation has
been, in many cases, officially adopted as part of the
machinery of public administration. Most important of
all, it has equipped itself with an entirely new political
organisation, extending throughout the whole of Great
Britain, inspired by large ideas embodied in a comprehensive
programme of Social Reconstruction, which has already
achieved the position of " His Majesty's Opposition," and
now makes a bid for that of " His Majesty's Government."
So great an advance within a single generation makes the
historical account of Trade Union development down to
1920 equivalent to a new book.

We have taken the opportunity to revise, and at some
points to amplify, our description of the origin and early
struggles of Trade Unionism in this country. We have
naturally examined the new material that has been made
accessible during the past quarter of a century, in order to

incorporate in our work whatever has thus been added to public knowledge. But we have not found it necessary to make any but trifling changes in our original interpretation of the historical development. The Home Office papers are now available in the Public Record Office for the troubled period at the beginning of the nineteenth century ; and these, together with the researches of Professor George Unwin, Mr. and Mrs. Hammond, Professor Graham Wallas, Mr. Mark Hovell, and Mr. M. Beer, have enabled us both to verify and to amplify our statements at certain points. For the recent history of Trade Unionism we have found most useful the collections and knowledge of the Labour Research Department, established in 1913 ; and we gratefully acknowledge the assistance in facts, suggestions, and criticisms that we have had from Mr. G. D. H. Cole and Mr. R. Page Arnot. We owe thanks, also, to Miss Ivy Schmidt for unwearied assistance in research.

The reader must not expect to find, in this historical volume, either an analysis of Trade Union organisation, policy, and methods, or any judgement upon the validity of its assumptions, its economic achievements, or its limitations. On these things we have written at great length, and very explicitly, in our *Industrial Democracy*, and in other books described in the pages at the end of this volume, to which we must refer those desirous of knowing whether the Trade Unionism of which we now write merely the story is a good or a bad element in industry and in the State.

SIDNEY AND BEATRICE WEBB.

41 GROSVENOR ROAD,
WESTMINSTER,
January 1920.

PREFACE TO THE ORIGINAL EDITION
OF 1894

It is not our intention to delay the reader here by a conventional preface. As every one knows, the preface is never written until the story is finished; and this story will not be finished in our time, or for many generations after us. A word or two as to our method of work and its results is all that we need say before getting to our main business.

Though we undertook the study of the Trade Union movement, not to prove any proposition of our own, but to discover what problems it had to present to us, our minds were not so blank on the subject that we had no preconception of the character of these problems. We thought they would almost certainly be economic, pointing a common economic moral; and that expectation still seems to us so natural, that if it had been fulfilled we should have accepted its fulfilment without comment. But it was not so. Our researches were no sooner fairly in hand than we began to discover that the effects of Trade Unionism upon the conditions of labour, and upon industrial organisation and progress, are so governed by the infinite technical variety of our productive processes, that they vary from industry to industry and even from trade to trade; and the economic moral varies with them. Where we expected to find an economic thread for a treatise, we found a spider's web; and from that moment we recognised that what we had first to write was not a treatise, but a history. And we saw that even a history would be impossible to follow unless we separated the general history of the whole movement from the particular histories of thousands of trade societies, some of which have maintained a continuous existence from the last century, whilst others have cropped up, run their brief course, and disappeared. Thus, when we had finished our labour of investigating the records of practically every important trade society from one end of the kingdom to the other, and accumulated piles of extracts, classified under endless trades and subdivisions of trades, we found that we must exclude from the first volume all but a small selection from those documents which appeared to us most significant with regard to the development of the general movement. Many famous strikes and lock-outs, many interesting trade disputes, many sensational prosecutions, and some furious outbursts of riot and crime, together with many drier matters relating to particular trades, have had either to be altogether omitted from our narrative, or else accorded a strictly subordinate reference in their relation to the history of Trade Unionism as a whole. All analysis of the economic effects of Trade Union action we reserve for a subsequent volume on the Problems of Trade Unionism, for which we shall draw more fully from the annals of the separate unions. And in that volume the most exacting seeker for economic morals will be more than satisfied ; for there will be almost as many economic morals drawn as societies described.

That history of the general movement, to which we have confined ourselves here, will be found to be part of the political history of England. In spite of all the pleas of modern historians for less history of the actions of governments, and more descriptions of the manners and customs of the governed, it remains true that history, however it may relieve and enliven itself with descriptions of the manners and morals of the people, must, if it is to be history at all, follow the course of continuous organisations. The history of a perfectly democratic State would be at once the history of a government and of a people. The history of Trade Unionism is the history of a State within our State, and one so jealously democratic that to know it well is to know the English working man as no reader of middle-class histories can know him. From the early years of the eighteenth century down to the present day, Democracy, Freedom of Association, *Laisser-faire*, Regulation of the Hours and Wages of Labour, Co-operative Production, Free Trade, Protection, and many other distinct and often contradictory political ideals, have from time to time seized the imagination of the organised wage-earners and made their mark on the course of the Trade Union move-ment. And, since 1867 at least, wherever the ideals have left their mark on Trade Unionism, Trade Unionism has left its mark on politics. We shall be able to show that some of those overthrows of our party governments which have caused most surprise in the middle and upper classes, and for which the most far-fetched reasons have been given by them and their journalists and historians after the event, carry their explanation on the surface for any one who knows what the Trade Unionists of the period were thinking. Such demonstrations, however, will be purely incidental, as we have written throughout of Trade Unionism for its own sake, and not for that of the innumerable sidelights which it throws on party politics.

In our concluding chapter, which we should perhaps offer as an appendix rather than as part of the regular plan of the volume, we have attempted to give a bird's-eye view of the Trade Union world of to-day, with its unequal distribution, its strong sectional organisation and defective political machinery, its new governing class of trade officials —above all, its present state of transition in methods, aims, and policy, in the face of the multitude of unsettled constitutional, economic, and political problems with which it stands confronted.

A few words upon the work of collecting materials for

our work may prove useful to those who may hereafter come to reap in the same field. In the absence of any exhaustive treatment of any period of Trade Union history we have to rely mainly upon our own investigations. But every student of the subject must acknowledge the value of Dr. Brentano's fertile researches into English working-class history, and of Mr. George Howell's thoroughly practical exposition of the Trade Unionism of his own school and his own time. Perhaps the most important published material on the subject is the *Report on Trade Societies and Strikes* issued by the Social Science Association in 1860, a compact storehouse of carefully sifted facts which compares favourably with the enormous bulk of scrappy and unverified information collected by the five historic official inquiries into Trade Unionism between 1824 and 1894. We have, moreover, found a great many miscellaneous facts about Trade Unions in periodical literature and ephemeral pamphlets in the various public libraries all over the country. To facilitate the work of future students we append to this volume a complete list of such published materials as we have been able to discover. For the early history of combinations we have had to rely upon the public records, old newspapers, and miscellaneous contemporary pamphlets. Thus, our first two chapters are principally based upon the journals of the House of Commons, the minutes of the Privy Council, the publications of the Record Office, and the innumerable broadsheet petitions to Parliament and old tracts relating to Trade which have been preserved in the British Museum, the Guildhall Library, and the invaluable collection of economic literature made by Professor H. S. Foxwell, St. John's College, Cambridge.[1] Most important of all, for the period prior to 1835, are the many volumes of manuscript commentaries, newspaper cuttings, rules, reports, pamphlets, etc., left by Francis Place, and now in the British Museum. This unique collection, formed by the busiest politician of his time, is indispensable, not

---

[1] Now in the Goldsmiths' Library at the University of London.

only to the student of working-class movements, but also to any historian of English political or social life during the first forty years of the century.[1]

But the greater part of our material, especially that relating to the present century, has come from the Trade Unionists themselves. The offices of the older unions contain interesting archives, sometimes reaching back to the eighteenth century—minute-books in which generations of diligent, if unlettered, secretaries, the true historians of a great movement, have struggled to record the doings of their committees, and files of Trade Union periodicals, ignored even by the British Museum, through which the plans and aspirations of ardent working-class politicians and administrators have been expounded month by month to the scattered branches of their organisations. We were assured at the outset of our investigation that no outsider would be allowed access to the inner history of some of the old-fashioned societies. But we have found this prevalent impression as to the jealous secrecy of the Trade Unions without justification. The secretaries of old branches or ancient local societies have rummaged for us their archaic chests with three locks, dating from the eighteenth century. The surviving leaders of a bygone Trade Unionism have ransacked their drawers to find for our use the rules and minutes of their long-forgotten societies. In many a working man's home in London and Liverpool, Newcastle and Dublin—above all, in Glasgow and Manchester—the descendants of the old skilled handicraftsmen have unearthed " grandfather's indentures," or " father's old card," or a tattered set of rules, to help forward the investigation of a stranger whom they dimly recognised as striving to record the annals of their class. The whole of the docu-

[1] Place's *Letter Books*, together with an unpublished autobiography, preserved by his family, are now in the custody of Mr. Graham Wallas, who is preparing a critical biography of this great reformer, which will throw much new light on all the social and political events of English history between 1798 and 1840 [published, 1st edition, 1898; 2nd edition, 1913].

ments in the offices of the great National and County Unions have been most generously placed at our disposal, from the printed reports and sets of rules to the private cash accounts and executive minute-books. In only one case has a General Secretary refused us access to the old books of his society, and then simply on the ground that he was himself proposing to write its history, and regarded us as rivals in the literary field.

Nor has this generous confidence been confined to the musty records of the past. In the long sojourns at the various industrial centres which this examination of local archives has necessitated, every facility has been afforded to us for studying the actual working of the Trade Union organisation of to-day. We have attended the sittings of the Trades Councils in most of the large towns ; we have sat through numerous branch and members' meetings all over the country ; and one of us has even enjoyed the exceptional privilege of being present at the private delibera-tions of the Executive Committees of various national societies, as well as at the special delegate meetings sum-moned by the great federal Unions of Cotton-spinners, Cotton-weavers, and Coalminers for the settlement of momentous issues of trade policy, and at the six weeks' sessions in 1892 in which sixty chosen delegates of the Amalgamated Society of Engineers overhauled the trade policy and internal administration of that world-wide organisation.

We have naturally not confined ourselves to the work-men's side of the case. In almost every industrial centre we have sought out representative employers in the different industries. From them we have received many useful hints and criticisms. But, as might have been expected, the great captains of industry are, for the most part, ab-sorbed in the commercial side of their business, and are seldom accurately acquainted with the details of the past, or even of the present, organisation of their workmen. Of more assistance in our task have been the secretaries of the various employers' associations. Especially in the ship-building ports have these gentlemen placed at our disposal their experience in collective negotiation with the different sections of labour, and the private statistics compiled by their associations. But of all the employing class we have found the working managers and foremen, who have themselves often been workmen, the best informed and most suggestive critics of Trade Union organisation and methods. We have often regretted that precisely this class is the most difficult of access to the investigator of industrial problems, and the least often called as witnesses before Royal Commissions.

The difficulty of welding into narrative form the innumerable details of the thousands of distinct organisations, and of constructing out of their separate chronicles anything like a history of the general movement, has, we need hardly say, been very great. We are painfully aware of the shortcomings of our work, both from a literary and from a historical point of view. We have been encouraged in our task by the conviction—strengthened as our investigation proceeded—that the Trade Union records contain material of the utmost value to the future historian of industrial and political organisation, and that these records are fast disappearing. Many of the older archives are in the possession of individual workmen, who are insensible of their historical value. Among the larger societies it is not uncommon to find only one complete set of rules, reports, circulars, etc., in existence. A fire, a removal to new premises, or the death of an old secretary frequently results in the disappearance of everything not actually in daily office use. The keen investigator or collector will appreciate the extremity of the vexation with which we have learnt on arriving at an ancient Trade Union centre that the "old rubbish" of the office had been "cleared out" six months before. The local public libraries, and even the British Museum, seldom contain any of the internal Trade Union records new or old. We have therefore not only collected every Trade Union document that we could acquire, but we have made lengthy extracts from, and abstracts of, the piles of minute-books, reports, rules, circulars, pamphlets, working-class newspapers, etc., which have been lent to us.

This collection of material, and, indeed, the wide scope of the investigation itself, would have been impossible if we had not had the good fortune to secure the help of a colleague exceptionally well qualified for the work. In Mr. F. W. Galton we have found a devoted assistant, to whose unwearied labours we owe the extensive range of our material and our statistics. Himself a skilled handi-craftsman, and for some time secretary to his Trade Union, he has brought to the task not only keen intelligence and unremitting industry, but also a personal acquaintance with the details of Trade Union life and organisation which has rendered his co-operation of inestimable value. We have incorporated in our last chapter a graphic sketch from his pen of the inner life of a Trade Union.

We have, moreover, received the most cordial assistance from all quarters. If we were to acknowledge by name all those to whom our thanks are due, we should set forth a list of nearly all the Trade Union officials in the kingdom. Individual acknowledgement is in their case the less neces-sary, in that many of them are our valued personal friends. Only second to this is our indebtedness to many of the great " captains of industry," notably to Mr. Hugh Bell, of Middlesboro', and Colonel Dyer, of Elswick, and the secretaries of employers' associations, whose time has been freely placed at our disposal. To Professor H. S. Foxwell, Mr. Frederic Harrison, Professor E. S. Beesly, Mr. Robert Applegarth, and Mr. John Burns, M.P., we are especially indebted for the loan of many scarce pamphlets and working-class journals, whilst Mr. John Burnett and Mr. Henry Crompton have been good enough to go through one or more of our chapters in proof, and to improve them by numerous suggestions. And there are two dear comrades and friends to whose repeated revision of every line of our manuscript the volume owes whatever approach to literary merit it may possess.

The bibliography has been prepared from our material by Mr. R. A. Peddie, to whom, as well as to Miss Appleyard for the laborious task of verifying nearly all the quotations, our thanks are due.

SIDNEY AND BEATRICE WEBB.

41 GROSVENOR ROAD,
WESTMINSTER,
April 1894.

CONTENTS

THE HISTORY

OF

TRADE UNIONISM

CHAPTER I

THE ORIGINS OF TRADE UNIONISM

A TRADE UNION, as we understand the term, is a continuous association of wage-earners for the purpose of maintaining or improving the conditions of their working lives.[1] This form of association has, as we shall see, existed in England for over two centuries, and cannot be supposed to have sprung at once fully developed into existence. But although we shall briefly discuss the institutions which have sometimes been described as the forerunners of Trade Unionism, our narrative will commence only from the latter part of the seventeenth century, before which date we have been unable to discover the existence in the British Isles of anything falling within our definition. Moreover, although it is suggested that analogous associations may have existed during the Middle Ages in various parts of the Continent of Europe, we have no reason to suppose that such institutions

[1] In the first edition we said " of their employment." This has been objected to as implying that Trade Unions have always contemplated a perpetual continuance of the capitalist or wage-system. No such implication was intended. Trade Unions have, at various dates during the past century at any rate, frequently had aspirations towards a revolutionary change in social and economic relations.

B

exercised any influence whatever upon the rise and development of the Trade Union Movement in this country. We feel ourselves, therefore, warranted, as we are indeed compelled, to limit our history exclusively to the Trade Unions of the United Kingdom.

We have, by our definition, expressly excluded from our history any account of the innumerable instances in which the manual workers have formed ephemeral combinations against their social superiors. Strikes are as old as history itself. The ingenious seeker of historical parallels might, for instance, find in the revolt, 1490 B.C., of the Hebrew brickmakers in Egypt against being required to make bricks without straw, a curious precedent for the strike of the Stalybridge cotton-spinners, A.D. 1892, against the supply of bad material for their work. But we cannot seriously regard, as in any way analogous to the Trade Union Movement of to-day, the innumerable rebellions of subject races, the slave insurrections, and the semi-servile peasant revolts of which the annals of history are full. These forms of the " labour war " fall outside our subject, not only because they in no case resulted in permanent associations, but because the " strikers " were not seeking to improve the conditions of a contract of service into which they voluntarily entered.

When, however, we pass from the annals of slavery or serfdom to those of the nominally free citizenship of the mediæval town, we are on more debatable ground. We make no pretence to a thorough knowledge of English town-life in the Middle Ages. But it is clear that there were at times, alongside of the independent master craftsmen, a number of hired journeymen and labourers, who are known to have occasionally combined against their rulers and governors. These combinations are stated sometimes to have lasted for months, and even for years. As early as 1383 we find the Corporation of the City of London prohibiting all " congregations, covins, and conspiracies of workmen." In 1387 the serving-men of the London cord-

wainers, in rebellion against the " overseers of the trade," [1]
are reported to be aiming at making a permanent fraternity.
Nine years later the serving-men of the saddlers, " called
yeomen," assert that they have had a fraternity of their
own, " time out of mind," with a livery and appointed
governors. The masters declared, however, that the
association was only thirteen years old, and that its object
was to raise wages.[2] In 1417 the tailors' " serving men
and journeymen " in London have to be forbidden to dwell
apart from their masters as they hold assemblies and have
formed a kind of association.[3] Nor were these fraternities
confined to London. In 1538 the Bishop of Ely reports to
Cromwell that twenty-one journeymen shoemakers of
Wisbech have assembled on a hill without the town, and
sent three of their number to summon all the master shoemakers to meet them, in order to insist upon an advance in
their wages, threatening that " there shall none come into
the town to serve for that wages within a twelve month and
a day, but we woll have an harme or a legge of hym, except
they woll take an othe as we have doon." [4]

These instances derived from the very fragmentary
materials as yet printed, suggest that a more complete
examination of the unpublished archives might possibly
disclose a whole series of journeymen fraternities, and
enable us to determine the exact constitution of these
associations. It is, for instance, by no means clear whether
the instances cited were strikes against employers, or revolts
against the authority of the gild. Our impression is that
the case of the Wisbech shoemakers, and possibly some of

[1] Riley's *Memorials of London and London Life in the Thirteenth,
Fourteenth, and Fifteenth Centuries* (1888), p. 495 (partly cited in *Trade
Unions*, by William Trant, 1884).

[2] *Ibid.* pp. 542-3.

[3] *Ibid.* p. 609 ; Clode's *Early History of the Merchant Taylors' Company*, vol. i. p. 63.

[4] *Calendars of State Papers : Letters and Papers, Foreign and Domestic,
Henry VIII.* vol. xiii. part i., 1538, No. 1454, p. 537. Compare the
ephemeral combinations cited by Fagniez, *Études sur l'industrie et la classe
industrielle à Paris* (Paris, 1877), pp. 76, 82, etc.

the others, represent the embryo stage of a Trade Union. Supposing, therefore, that further investigation were to prove that such ephemeral combinations by hired journey-men against their employers did actually pass into durable associations of like character, we should be constrained to begin our history with the fourteenth or fifteenth century. But, after detailed consideration of every published instance of a journeyman's fraternity in England, we are fully convinced that there is as yet no evidence of the existence of any such durable and independent combination of wage-earners against their employers during the Middle Ages.

There are certain other cases in which associations during the fifteenth and sixteenth centuries, which are sometimes assumed to have been composed of journeymen,[1] maintained

---

[1] It has been assumed that, in the company of " Bachelors " or " Yeomen Tailors " connected with the Merchant Taylors' Company of London between 1446 and 1661, we have " for the first time revealed to us the existence, and something of the constitution, of a journeyman's society which succeeded in maintaining itself for a prolonged period." More careful examination of the materials from which this vivid picture of this supposed journeyman's society has been drawn leads us to believe that it was not composed of journeymen at all, but of masters. This might, in the first place, have been inferred from the fact that in the ranks of the supposed journeymen were to be found opulent leaders like Richard Hilles, the friend of Cranmer and Bullinger, who " became a Bachelor in Budge of the Yeoman Company " in 1535 (Clode, *Early History of the Merchant Taylors' Company*, vol. ii. p. 64), and Sir Leonard Halliday, afterwards Lord Mayor, who was in the Bachelors' Company from 1572 to 1594, when " he was elected a member of the higher hierarchy of the Corporation " (*ibid.* p. 237). The Bachelors' Company, indeed, far from being composed of needy wage-earners, bore the greater part of the expense of the pageant in connection with the mayoralty, and managed the whole proceedings. The Bachelors " in Foynes " and those " in Budge " are all named as marching in the procession in " gownes to be welted with velvet, and there jackyttes, cassockes, and doublettes to be either of satten damaske, taffataye " (*ibid.* pp. 262-6). And when, in 1609, the Company was assessed to contribute to the Plantation of Ulster, the Bachelors contributed nearly as much as the merchants (£155, 10s. from ten members as compared with £187, 10s. from nine members (*ibid.* vol. i. pp. 327-9)). Whether the Bachelors' Company ever included any large proportion of hired journeymen appears extremely doubtful, though its object was clearly the regulation of the trade. The members, according to the Ordinance of 1613, paid a contribution of 2s. 2d. a quarter " for the poor of the fraternity." This may be contrasted with the quarterage of 8d. a year or 2d. per quarter, levied, according to order of August 1578, on every servant or journeyman free of the City. The

a continuous existence. But in all these cases, so far as we have been able to investigate them, the "Bachelors' Company," presumed to be a journeymen's fraternity, formed a subordinate department of the masters' gild, by the rulers of which it was governed. It will be obvious that associations in which the employers dispensed the funds and appointed the officers can bear no analogy to modern Trade Unions. Moreover, these "yeoman" organisations or

---

funds of the two companies were kept distinct, but frequent donations were made from one to the other, and not only from the inferior to the superior (*ibid.* vol. i. pp. 67-9). That the Bachelors' Company was by no means confined to journeymen is clear. Sir Leonard Halliday, for instance, became a freeman in April 1564 on completing his apprenticeship, and at once set up in business for himself, obtaining a charitable loan for the purpose. Yet, although he prospered in business, "in 1572 we find him assessed as in the Bachelors' Company," and he was not elected to the superior company until 1594 (*ibid.* vol. ii. p. 237). And in the Ordinance of 1507, "for all those persons that shall be abled by the maister and Wardeins to holde hous or shop open," it is provided that the person desiring to set up shop shall not only pay a licence fee, but also "for his incomyng to the bachelers' Company and to be broder with theym iijˢ iiiᵈ" (Clode, *Memorials of the Merchant Taylors' Company,* p. 209). Nor do the instances of its action imply that it had at heart the interest of the wage-earners, as distinguished from that of the employers. The hostility to foreigners, the desire to secure government clothing contracts, and the preference for a limitation of apprentices to two for each employer are all consistent with the theory that the Bachelors Company was, like its superior, composed of masters, probably less opulent than the governing clique, and perhaps occupied in tailoring rather than in the business of a clothier or merchant. It is not until 1675 and 1682 that can be traced in the MS. records of the Clothworkers' Company the existence of distinctively journeymen's combinations (*Industrial Organisation in the Sixteenth and Seventeenth Centuries,* by George Unwin, 1904, p. 199). The other instances of identification of "Bachelors' Companies" or "Yeomen" organisation with journeymen's societies are no more convincing than that of the Merchant Taylors. That the "valets," serving-men, or journeymen in many trades possessed some kind of "almsbox," or charitable funds of their own is indeed clear, but that this was ever used in trade disputes, or was independent of the masters' control, must at present be regarded as highly improbable. The strongest instance of independence is that of the Oxford cordwainers (*Selections from the Records of the City of Oxford,* by William H. Turner, Oxford, 1880). See. on the whole subject, the chapter on "Mediæval Journeymen's Clubs," in Sir William Ashley's *Surveys: Historic and Economic,* 1900; *Industrial Organisation in the Sixteenth and Seventeenth Centuries,* by Professor George Unwin, 1904; and an article on "The Origin of Trade Unionism," by Mr. W. A. S. Hewins, in the *Economic Review,* April 1895 (vol. v.).

" Bachelors' Companies " do not appear to have long survived the sixteenth century.

The explanation of the tardy growth of stable independent combination among hired journeymen is, we believe, to be found in the prospects of economic advancement which the skilled handicraftsman still possessed. We do not wish to suggest the existence of any Golden Age in which each skilled workman was his own master, and the wage system was unknown. The earliest records of English town history imply the presence of hired journeymen, who were not always contented with their wages. But the apprenticed journeyman in the skilled handicrafts belonged, until comparatively modern times, to the same social grade as his employer, and was indeed usually the son of a master in the same or an analogous trade. So long as industry was carried on mainly by small masters, each employing but one or two journeymen, the period of any energetic man's service as a hired wage-earner cannot normally have exceeded a few years, and the industrious apprentice might reasonably hope, if not always to marry his master's daughter, at any rate to set up in business for himself. Any incipient organisation would always be losing its oldest and most capable members, and would of necessity be confined, like the Coventry journeymen's Gild of St. George, to " the young people," [1] or like the ephemeral fraternity of journeymen tailors of 1415–17, to " a race at once youthful and unstable," [2] from whose inexperienced ranks it would be hard to draw a supply of good Trade Union leaders. We are therefore able to understand how it is that, whilst industrial oppression belongs to all ages, it is not until the changing conditions of industry had reduced to an infinitesimal chance the journeyman's prospect of becoming himself a master, that we find the passage of ephemeral combinations into permanent trade societies. This inference is supported by

[1] Dugdale's *Antiquities of Warwickshire* (1656), p. 125.
[2] Riley's *Memorials*, p. 653 ; Clode, *Early History of Merchant Taylors' Company*, vol. i. p. 63.

the experience of an analogous case in the Lancashire of to-day. The "piecers," who assist at the "mules," are employed and paid by the operative cotton-spinners under whom they work. The "big piecer" is often an adult man, quite as skilled as the spinner himself, from whom, however, he receives very inferior wages. But although the cotton operatives display a remarkable aptitude for Trade Unionism, attempts to form an independent organisation among the piecers have invariably failed. The energetic and competent piecer is always looking forward to becoming a spinner, interested rather in reducing than in raising piecers' wages. The leaders of any incipient movement among the piecers have necessarily fallen away from it on becoming themselves employers of the class from which they have been promoted. But though the Lancashire piecers have always failed to form an independent Trade Union, they are not without their associations, in the constitution of which we may find some hint of the relation between the gild of the master craftsmen and the Bachelors' Company or other subordinate association in which journeymen may possibly have been included. The spinners have, for their own purposes, brigaded the piecers into piecers' associations. These associations, membership of which is usually compulsory, form a subordinate part of the spinners' Trade Union, the officers of which fix and collect the contributions, draw up the rules, dispense the funds, and in every way manage the affairs, without in the slightest degree consulting the piecers themselves. It is not difficult to understand that the master craftsmen who formed the court of a mediæval gild might, in a similar way, have found it convenient to brigade the journeymen or other inferior members of the trade into a subordinate fraternity, for which they fixed the quarterly dues, appointed the "wardens" or "wardens' substitutes," administered the funds, and in every way controlled the affairs, without admitting the journeymen to any voice in the proceedings.[1]

---

[1] Compare Fagniez, *Études sur l'industrie et la classe industrielle à Paris* (Paris, 1877), p. 123.

If further proof were needed that it was the prospect of economic advancement that hindered the formation of permanent combinations among the hired journeymen of the Middle Ages, we might adduce the fact that certain classes of skilled manual workers, who had no chance of becoming employers, do appear to have succeeded in establishing long-lived combinations which had to be put down by law. The masons, for instance, had long had their " yearly congregations and confederacies made in their general chapiters assembled," which were expressly prohibited by Act of Parliament in 1425.[1] And the tilers of Worcester are ordered by the Corporation in 1467 to " sett no parliament amonge them." [2] It appears probable, indeed, that the masons, wandering over the country from one job to another, were united, not in any local gild, but in a trade fraternity of national extent. Such an association may, if further researches throw light upon its constitution and working, not improbably be found to possess some points of resemblance to the Friendly Society of Operative Stonemasons of the present day, which was established in 1832. But, unlike the operative in the modern building trades, the mason of the Middle Ages served, not a master *entrepreneur*, but the customer himself, who provided the materials, supervised the work, and engaged, at specified daily rates, both the skilled mechanics and their labourers or apprentices.[3] In contrast with the handicraftsmen of the towns, the masons, tilers, etc., remained, from the completion of their apprenticeship to the end of their working lives, in one and the same economic position, a position which appears to have been intermediate between those of the master craftsman and the journeyman of the other trades. Like the jobbing carpenter of the country village of to-day, they were independent producers, each controlling the processes of his

[1] 3 Henry VI. c. 1 ; see also 34 Edward III. c. 9.
[2] " Ordinances of Worcester," Art. lvii. in Toulmin Smith's *English Gilds*, p. 399.
[3] Compare the analogous instances given by Fagniez, *Études sur l'industrie et la classe industrielle à Paris*, p. 203 (Paris, 1877).

own craft, and dealing directly with the customer. But unlike the typical master craftsman of the handicraft trades they sold nothing but labour, and their own labour only, at regulated customary rates, and were unconcerned, therefore, with the making of profit, whether upon the purchase and sale of materials or upon the hiring of subordinate workers.[1] The stability of their combinations was accordingly not prevented by those influences which, as we have suggested, proved fatal in England to the corresponding attempts of the hired journeymen of the handicrafts.

But if the example of the building trades in the Middle Ages supports our inference as to the cause of the tardy growth of combination among the journeymen in other trades, the " yearly congregations and confederacies " of the masons might themselves demand our attention as instances of early Trade Unionism. Of the constitution, function, or ultimate development of these mediæval associations in the building trades we know unfortunately next to nothing.[2] It is remarkable that there is, so far as we are aware, no trace of their existence in Great Britain later than the fifteenth century. During the eighteenth century there is, as we shall see, no lack of information as to combinations of workmen in nearly every other skilled trade. The employers appear to have been perpetually running to Parliament to complain of the misdeeds of their workmen. But of combinations in the building trades we have found scarcely a trace until the very end of that century. If, therefore, adhering strictly to the letter of our definition, we accepted the masons' confederacy as a Trade Union, we should be compelled to regard the building trades as presenting the unique instance of an industry which had

[1] Dr. Brentano has noticed (p. 81) that the great majority of the legal regulations of wages in the Middle Ages relate (if not to agriculture) to the building trades ; and it may be that these were, like modern cabfare regulations, intended more for the protection of the customer than for that of the capitalist.

[2] See " Notes on the Organisation of the Mason's Craft in England," by Dr. William Cunningham (*British Academy Proceedings*).   B 2

a period of Trade Unionism in the fifteenth century, then passed for several centuries into a condition in which Trade Unionism was impossible, and finally changed once. more to a state in which Trade Unions flourished. Our own impression is however that the " congregations and confederacies " of the masons are more justly to be considered the embryonic stage of a gild of master craftsmen than of a Trade Union. There appears to us to be a subtle distinction between the economic position of workers who hire themselves out to the individual consumer direct, and those who, like the typical Trade Unionist of to-day, serve an employer who stands between them and the actual consumers, and who hires their labour in order to make out of it such a profit as will provide him with his interest on capital and " wages of management." We suggest that, with the growing elaboration of domestic architecture, the superior craftsmen tended more and more to become employers, and any organisations of such craftsmen to pass insensibly into the ordinary type of masters' gild.[1] Under such a system of industry the journeymen would possess the same prospects of economic advancement that hindered the growth of stable combinations in the ordinary handicrafts, and in this fact may lie the explanation of the striking absence of evidence of any Trade Unionism in the building trades right down to the eighteenth century.[2] When, how-

---

[1] Such a master craftsmen's society we see in the Masons' " Lodge of Atchison's Haven," which, on December 27, 1735, passed the following resolution : " The Company of Atchison's Haven being mett together, have found Andrew Kinghorn guilty of a most atrocious crime against the whole Trade of Masonry, and he not submitting himself to the Company for taking his work so cheap that no man could have his bread of it. Therefore in not submitting himself he has excluded himself from the said Company ; and therefore the Company doth hereby enact that no man, neither fellow craft nor enter'd prentice after this shall work as journeyman under the said Andrew Kinghorn, under the penalty of being cut off as well as he. Likewise if any man shall follow the example of the said Andrew Kinghorn in taking work at eight pounds Scots per rood the walls being twenty feet high, and rebates at eighteen pennies Scots per foot, that they shall be cut off in the same manner " (*Sketch of the Incorporation of Masons*, by James Cruikshank, Glasgow, 1879, pp. 131, 132).

[2] Thorold Rogers points out that the Merton College bell-tower was

ever, the capitalist builder or contractor began to supersede the master mason, master plasterer, etc., and this class of small *entrepreneurs* had again to give place to a hierarchy of hired workers, Trade Unions, in the modern sense, began, as we shall see, to arise. " Just as we found the small master in the sixteenth century struggling to adapt and appropriate the traditions of the superseded handicraft organisation, so we shall find the journeyman at the close of the seventeenth century [in some trades and at the close of the eighteenth century in others] endeavouring to build up a new status out of the ruins of the small master." [1]

We have dwelt at some length upon these ephemeral associations of wage-earners and on the journeymen fraternities of the Middle Ages, because it might plausibly be argued that they were in some sense the predecessors of the Trade Union. But strangely enough it is not in these institutions that the origin of Trade Unionism has usually been sought. For the predecessor of the modern Trade

---

built in 1448-50 by direct employment at wages. The new quadrangle, early in the seventeenth century, was put out to contract with a master mason and a master carpenter respectively, but the college still supplied all the material (*History of Agriculture and Prices*, vol. i. pp. 258-60; iii. pp. 720-37; v. pp. 478, 503, 629).

[1] *Industrial Organisation in the Sixteenth and Seventeenth Centuries*, by George Unwin, 1904, p. 201. In this connection may be mentioned the London watermen, who have always dealt directly with their customers, and who possess a tradition of having been continuously organised since 1350. Power to regulate the trade of watermen was, in 1555, conferred by Act of Parliament upon the then incorporated Thames Watermen and Lightermen's Company, the administration of which appears to have been, from the first, entirely in the hands of the master lightermen. The watermen, who had no masters, were compelled to take out the freedom of this Company, and the existing Trade Union, the Amalgamated Society of Watermen and Lightermen, was established in 1872 for the express purpose of obtaining some representation of the working watermen and the journeymen lightermen on the Court of the Company. Previous associations of working watermen for trade purposes seem to have been in existence in 1789 (a Rotherhithe Society of Watermen) and in 1799 (Friendly Society of Watermen usually plying at the Hermitage Stairs, in the parish of St. John, Wapping); and Mayhew describes, in 1850, local " turnway societies," regulating the sharing of custom, and a Watermen's Protective Society, to resist non-freemen (*London Labour and the London Poor*, 1851).

Union, men have turned, not to the mediæval associations of the wage-earners, but to those of their employers—that is to say, the Craft Gilds.[1]   The outward resemblance of the Trade Union to the Craft Gild had long attracted the attention, both of the friends and the enemies of Trade Unionism ; but it was the publication in 1870 of Professor Brentano's brilliant study on the " Origin of Trades Unions " that gave form to the popular idea.[2]   Without in the least implying that any connection could be traced between the mediæval gild and the modern Trade Union, Dr. Brentano suggested that the one was in so far the successor of the other, that both institutions had arisen " under the breaking up of an old system, and among the men suffering from this disorganisation, in order that they might maintain independence and order." [3]   And when George Howell

[1] Schanz, however, in his *Zur Geschichte der deutschen Gesellenver-bände* (Leipzig, 1877), suggests that the associations of journeymen which flourished in Germany side by side with the Craft Gilds prior to the Thirty Years' War (1618) were, in fact, virtually Trade Unions.   Compare Schmoller's *Strassburger Tucher- und Weberzunft* (Strassburg, 1879).   Pro-fessor G. Des Marez, the learned archivist of Brussels, supplies evidence of the persistence of journeymen's organisations in Belgium, resembling those of Germany, down to the beginning of the sixteenth century ; and of the rise of new ones towards the end of the seventeenth century, without trace of continuity (in *Le Compagnonnage des chapeliers bruxellois*, Brussels, 1909.   See Professor Unwin's article in *English Historical Review* (October 1910) ;   and compare *Les Compagnonnages des arts et métiers à Dijon aux xviie et xviiie siècles*, by H. House, 1909, and *Enquêtes sur les associations professionnelles d'artisans et ouvriers en Belgique*, by E. Vandervelde, 1891.

[2] Dr. Brentano's essay was originally prefixed to Toulmin Smith's *English Gilds*, published by the Early English Text Society in 1870.   It was republished separately as *The History and Development of Gilds and the Origin of Trades Unions* (135 pp., 1870), and it is to this edition that we refer.   Dr. Brentano's larger work, *Die Arbeitergilden der Gegenwart* (Leipzig, 2 vols., 1871–72), includes this essay, and also his article in the *North British Review* for October 1870 on " The Growth of a Trades Union."   It is only fair to say that in this, the ablest study of English Trade Union history down to that time, Dr. Brentano lent no support to the popular idea of any actual descent of the Trade Unions from the gilds. The *Cobden Club Essays* (1872) contain a good article on Trade Unions, by Joseph Gostick, in which it is argued that these associations were, in England, unknown before the eighteenth century, and had no connection with the gilds.

[3] Page 102.

prefixed to his history of Trade Unionism a paraphrase of Dr. Brentano's account of the gilds, it became commonly accepted that the Trade Union had, in some undefined way, really originated from the Craft Gild.[1] We are therefore under the obligation of digressing to examine the relation between the mediæval gild and the modern Trade Union. If it could be shown that the Trade Unions were, in any way, the descendants of the old gilds, it would clearly be the origin of the latter that we should have to trace.

The supposed descent in this country of the Trade Unions from the mediæval Craft Gilds rests, as far as we have been able to discover, upon no evidence whatsoever. The historical proof is all the other way. In London, for instance, more than one Trade Union has preserved an unbroken existence from the eighteenth century. The Craft Gilds still exist in the City Companies, and at no point in their history do we find the slightest evidence of the branching off from them of independent journeymen's societies. By the eighteenth century the London journeymen had in nearly all cases lost whatever participation they may possibly once have possessed in the Companies,

---

[1] The first hundred pages of George Howell's *Conflicts of Capital and Labour* (first edition, 1877 ; second edition, 1890) are a close paraphrase of Dr. Brentano's essay, practically the whole of which appears, often in the same words, as Howell's own. But already in 1871 Dr. Brentano, in his *Arbeitergilden der Gegenwart* (vol. i. ch. iii. p. 83), expressly connected the Trade Unions, like Schanz, not with the gilds, but with the Journeymen Fraternities, which he suggests may have "awaked under changed circumstances to new strength and life, and to a new policy." We gather that Sir William Ashley inclines to this view. "My own impression," he says, "is that we shall by and by find that, like the usages of the German journeymen in the eighteenth century that centred into Herbergen, the trade clubs of eighteenth century England were broken-down survivals from an earlier period, undergoing, with the advent of the married journeyman and other causes, the slow transformation from which they emerged in the nineteenth century as the nuclei of the modern Trade Union." Sir William Ashley does not assert that any continuity of organisation can be proved. "What is suggested is only that the habit of acting together in certain ways, which we find to characterise the journeymen of the eighteenth century, had been formed in a much earlier period" (*Surveys: Historic and Economic*, by Sir William Ashley, 1900).

which had for the most part already ceased to have any
connection with the trades of which they bore the names.[1]
It is sometimes suggested that the London Companies have
had an exceptional history, and that in towns in which
the gilds underwent a more normal development they may
have given rise to the modern trade society. So far as
Great Britain is concerned we have satisfied ourselves that
this suggestion rests on no better foundation than the other.
Neither in Bristol nor in Preston, neither in Newcastle nor
in Glasgow, have we been able to trace the slightest connection between the slowly dying gilds and the upstarting
Trade Unions. At Sheffield J. M. Ludlow, basing himself
on an account by Frank Hill, once expressly declared [2]
that direct affiliation could be proved. Diligent inquiry
into the character and history of the still flourishing Cutlers'
Company demonstrates that this exclusively masters'
association at no time originated or engendered any of the
numerous Trade Unions with which Sheffield abounds.
There remains the case of Dublin, where some of the older
unions themselves claim descent from the gilds. Here,
too, careful search reveals, not only the absence of any
affiliation or direct descent, but also the impossibility of
any organic connection between the exclusively Protestant
gilds which were not abolished until 1842, and the mainly
Roman Catholic Trade Unions which attained their greatest
influence many years before.[3] We assert, indeed, with
some confidence, that in no case did any Trade Union in
the United Kingdom arise, either directly or indirectly,
by descent, from a Craft Gild.

[1] So long as the Companies continued to exercise any jurisdiction
over their trades, we find them (as in the cases of the London Framework-knitters and the Dublin Silkweavers) supported by any workmen's
combinations that existed. In exceptional instances, such as the London
Brushmakers, Basketmakers, and Watermen, we find this alliance for the
exclusion of " illegal men " continuing into the nineteenth century, and
(as regards the Watermen) down to the present time.

[2] *Macmillan's Magazine* (February 1861), relying on the Social Science
Report on Trade Societies and Strikes (1860), p. 521.

[3] See Appendix *On the Assumed Connection between the Trade Unions
and the Gilds in Dublin.*

It is often taken for granted that the Trade Union whatever may have been its origin, represents the same elements, and plays the same part in the industrial system of the nineteenth century, as the Craft Gild did in that of the Middle Ages. A brief analysis of what is known of the gilds will be sufficient to show that these organisations were even in their purest days essentially different, both in structure and function, from the modern trade society.

For the purpose of this comparison it will be unnecessary for us to discuss the rival theories of historians as to the nature and origin of the Craft Gilds. We may agree, on the one hand, with Dr. Brentano [1] in maintaining that the free craftsmen associated in order to stop the deterioration of their condition and encroachments on their earnings, and to protect themselves against " the abuse of power on the part of the lords of the town, who tried to reduce the free to the dependence of the unfree." On the other hand, we may believe with Dr. Cunningham [2] that the Craft Gilds were " called into being, not out of antagonism to existing authorities, but as new institutions, to which special parts of their own duties were delegated by the burgh officers or the local Gild Merchant," as a kind of " police system," in fact, by which the community controlled the local industries in the interest of the consumer. Or again, we may accept the middle view advanced by Sir William Ashley,[3] that the gilds were self-governing bodies of craftsmen, initiating their own trade regulations, the magistrates or town council having a real, if somewhat vague, authority to sanction or veto these ordinances for the good of the citizens. Each of these three views is supported by numerous instances, and to determine which theory represents the rule and which the exception would involve a statistical knowledge of Craft Gilds for which

[1] *Gilds and Trade Unions* (1870), p. 54.

[2] *History of Industry and Commerce*, vol. i. p. 310. Dr. Gross, in his *Gild Merchant*, apparently takes a similar view.

[3] See his *Introduction to Economic History and Theory*, vol. i. (1891); vol. ii. (1893) ; see also his *Surveys : Historic and Economic* (1900).

the material has not yet been collected. It will be evident that, if Dr. Cunningham's theory of the Craft Gild is the correct one, there can be no essential resemblance between these semi-municipal bodies and the Trade Unions of to-day. Dr. Brentano, however, produces ample evidence that, in some cases at any rate, the gilds acted, not with any view to the protection of the consumer, but, like the Trade Unions, for the furtherance of the interests of their own members—that is, of one class of producers. Accepting for the moment the view that the Craft Gild, like the Trade Union, or the Employers' Association, belonged to the genus of " associations of producers," let us examine briefly how far the gild was similar to modern combinations of wage-earners.

Now, the central figure of the gild organisation, in all instances, and at all periods of its development, was the master craftsman, owning the instruments of production, and selling the product. Opinions may differ as to the position of the journeymen in the gild or to the extent of the prevalence of subordinate or semi-servile labour outside it. Different views may be entertained as to the reality of that regard for the interests of the consumer which forms the ostensible object of many gild ordinances. But through-out the whole range of gild history the master craftsman, controlling the processes and selling the products of the labour of his little industrial group, was the practical administrator of, and the dominant influence in, the gild system.[1] In short, the typical gild member was not wholly, or even chiefly, a manual worker. From the first he supplied not only whatever capital was needed in his industry, but also that knowledge of the markets for both raw material and

---

[1] Dr. Brentano himself makes this clear. " We must not forget that these gilds were not unions of labourers in the present sense of the word, but of persons who, with the help of some stock, carried on their craft on their own account. The gild contests were, consequently, not contests for acquiring political equality for labour and property, but for the recognition of political equality of trade stock and real property in the towns " (*Gilds and Trade Unions*, p. 73).

product, and that direction and control which are the special functions of the *entrepreneur*. The economic functions and political authority of the gild rested, not upon its assumed inclusion of practically the whole body of manual workers, but upon the presence within it of the real directors of industry of the time. In the modern Trade Union, on the contrary, we find, not an association of *entrepreneurs*, themselves controlling the processes of their industry, and selling its products, but a combination of hired wage-workers, serving under the direction of industrial captains who are outside the organisation. The separation into distinct social classes of the capitalist and the brainworker on the one hand, and the manual workers on the other—the sub-stitution, in fact, of a horizontal for a vertical cleavage of society—vitiates any treatment of the Trade Union as the analogue of the Craft Gild.

On the other hand, to regard the typical Craft Gild as the predecessor of the modern Employers' Association or capitalist syndicate would, in our opinion, be as great a mistake as to believe, with George Howell, that it was the "early prototype" of the Trade Union. Dr. Brentano himself laid stress on the fact, afterwards brought into special prominence by Dr. Cunningham, that the Craft Gild was looked upon as the representative of the interests, not of any one class alone, but of the three distinct and somewhat antagonistic elements of modern society, the capitalist *entrepreneur*, the manual worker, and the con-sumer at large. We do not need to discuss the soundness of the mediæval lack of faith in unfettered competition as a guarantee of the genuineness and good quality of wares. Nor are we concerned with their assumption of the identity of interest between all classes of the community. It seemed a matter of course to the statesman, no less than to the public, that the leading master craftsmen of the town should be entrusted with the power and the duty of seeing that neither themselves nor their competitors were per-mitted to lower the standard of production. "The

Fundamental Ground," says the petition of the Carpenters' Company in 1681, " of Incorporating Handicraft Trades and Manual Occupations into distinct Companies was to the end that all Persons using such Trades should be brought into one Uniform Government and Corrected and Regulated by Expert and Skilful Governors, under certain Rules and Ordinances appointed to that purpose." [1] The leading men of the gild became, in effect, officers of the municipality, charged with the protection of the public from adulteration and fraud. When, therefore, we remember that the Craft Gild was assumed to represent, not only all the grades of producers in a particular industry, but also the consumers of the product, and the community at large, the impossibility of finding, in modern society, any single inheritor of its multifarious functions will become apparent. The powers and duties of the mediæval gild have, in fact, been broken up and dispersed. The friendly society and

[1] Jupp's *History of the Carpenters' Company*, p. 313, second edition, 1848. In certain cases we see the workmen seeking incorporation as a gild or company, in order that they might themselves lawfully regulate their trades. Thus, in 1670 the wage-earning woodsawyers of the City of London, who were employed by the members of the Carpenters', Joiners' and Shipwrights' Companies, formally applied to the Corporation to be made a Company. Their employers strongly objected, alleging that they had already by combination raised their wages during the past quarter of a century from 5s. to nearly 10s. per load ; that they were only day labourers who worked on material provided by their employers, and consequently not entitled to rank as masters ; and that if their combination were recognised by incorporation they would be able to bring the whole building trade to a standstill, as experience had already demonstrated even without incorporation. Moreover, their main object, it was alleged, was to exclude from employment " all that sort of labourers who daily resort to the City of London and parts adjacent, and by that means keep the wages and prices of these sorts of labourers at an equal and indifferent rate ; and then success would be an evil precedent, all other labourers, the masons, bricklayers, plasterers, etc., having the same reason to allege for incorporation " (*Ibid.* p. 307). The London coalporters in 1699 unsuccessfully petitioned the House of Commons that a Bill might be passed to establish them as " a Fellowship in such government and rules as shall be thought meet " (House of Commons Journals, vol. xiii. p. 69). Professor Unwin suggests that it was "by its failure along these traditional lines " that " the wage-earning class was driven into secret combinations, from the obscurity of which the Trade Union did not emerge till the 19th century " (*Industrial Organisation in the 16th and 17th Centuries*, 1904).

the Trade Union, the capitalist syndicate and the employers
association, the factory inspector and the Poor Law relieving
officer, the School Attendance officer, and the municipal
officers who look after adulteration and inspect our weights
and measures—all these persons and institutions might,
with equal justice, be put forward as the successors of the
Craft Gild.[1]

Although there is an essential difference in the composition of the two organisations, the popular theory of
their resemblance is easily accounted for. First, there are
the picturesque likenesses which Dr. Brentano discovered
—the regulations for admission, the box with its three
locks, the common meal, the titles of the officers, and so
forth. But these are to be found in all kinds of association in England. The Trade Union organisations share
them with the local friendly societies, or sick clubs, which
have existed all over England for the last two centuries.
Whether these features were originally derived from the
Craft Gilds or not, it is practically certain that the early
Trade Unions took them, in the vast majority of cases,
not from the traditions of any fifteenth-century organisation, but from the existing little friendly societies around
them. In some cases the parentage of these forms and
ceremonies might be ascribed with as much justice to the
mystic rites of the Freemasons as to the ordinances of the
Craft Gilds. The fantastic ritual peculiar to the Trade
Unionism of 1829–34, which we shall describe in a subsequent chapter, was, as we shall see, taken from the ceremonies of the Friendly Society of Oddfellows. But we
are informed that it bears traces of being an illiterate
copy of a masonic ritual. In our own times the " Free

[1] " The Trade Union of to-day is often spoken of as the lineal de-
scendant of the ancient Craft Gilds. There is, however, no direct or
indirect connection between the ancient and modern forms of trade
combination. Beyond the fact that they each had for their objects the
establishment of certain trade regulations, and the provision of certain
similar benefits, they had nothing in common." " Trade Unions as a
Means of Improving the Conditions of Labour," by John Burnett; published in *The Claims of Labour* (Edinburgh, 1886).

Colliers of Scotland," an early attempt at a national miners
union, were organised into " Lodges " under a " Grand
Master," with much of the terminology and some of the
characteristic forms of Freemasonry. No one would,
however, assert any essential resemblance between the
village sick club and the trade society, still less between
Freemasonry and Trade Unionism. The only common
feature between all these is the spirit of association, clothing
itself in more or less similar picturesque forms.

But other resemblances between the gild and the union
brought out by Dr. Brentano are more to the point. The
fundamental purpose of the Trade Union is the protection
of the Standard of Life—that is to say, the organised
resistance to any innovation likely to tend to the degradation of the wage-earners as a class. That some social
organisation for the protection of the Standard of Life
was necessary was a leading principle of the Craft Gild,
as it was, in fact, of the whole mediæval order. " Our
forefathers," wrote the Emperor Sigismund in 1434, " have
not been fools. The crafts have been devised for this
purpose : that everybody by them should earn his daily
bread, and nobody shall interfere with the craft of another.
By this the world gets rid of its misery, and every one may
find his livelihood." [1]   But in this respect the Trade Union
does not so much resemble the Craft Gild, as reassert what
was once the accepted principle of mediæval society, of
which the gild policy was only one manifestation. We do
not wish, in our historical survey of the Trade Union Movement, to enter into the far-reaching controversy as to the
political validity either of the mediæval theory of the com-

" To attempt to find an immediate connection between the Gild and
the Trade Union is like attempting to derive the English House of Commons
from the Saxon Witanagemot. In the one case as in the other the two
institutions were separated by centuries of development, and the earlier
one was dead before the later one was born " (*Industrial Organisation
in the 16th and 17th Centuries*, by Professor George Unwin, 1904, p. 8).

[1] Goldasti's *Constitutiones Imperiales*, tom. iv. p. 189, quoted by
Dr. Brentano, p. 60.

pulsory maintenance of the Standard of Life, or of such analogous modern expedients as Collective Bargaining on the one hand, or Factory Legislation on the other. Nor do we wish to imply that the mediæval theory was at any time so effectively and so sincerely carried out as really to secure to every manual worker a comfortable maintenance. We are concerned only with the historical fact that, as we shall see, the artisans of the seventeenth and eighteenth centuries sought to perpetuate those legal or customary regulations of their trade which, as they believed, protected their own interests. When these regulations fell into disuse the workers combined to secure their enforcement. When legal redress was denied, the operatives, in many instances, took the matter into their own hands, and endeavoured to maintain, by Trade Union regulations, what had once been prescribed by law. In this respect, and practically in this respect only, do we find any trace of the gild in the Trade Union.

Let us now turn from the hypothetical origin of Trade Unionism to the recorded facts. We have failed to discover in the manuscript records of companies or municipal corporations, in the innumerable trade pamphlets and broadsheets of the time, or in the Journals of the House of Commons, any evidence of the existence, prior to the latter half of the seventeenth century,[1] or indeed much before

---

[1] A pamphlet of 1669 contains what appears at first sight to be a mention of Trade Unionism. " The general conspiracy amongst artificers and labourers is so apparent that within these twenty-five years the wages of joiners, bricklayers, carpenters, etc., are increased, I mean within 40 miles of London (against all reason and good government), from eighteen and twenty pence a day, to 2/6 and 3/-, and mere labourers from 10 and 12 pence a day unto 16 and 20 pence, and this not since the dreadful fire of London only, but some time before. A journeyman shoemaker has now in London (and proportionately in the country) 14 pence for making that pair of shoes, which within these 12 years he made for 10 pence. . . . Nor has the increase of wages amongst us been occasioned by quickness of trade and want of hands (as some do suppose) which are indeed justifiable reasons, but through an exacting humour and evil disposition in our people (like our Gravesend watermen, who by some temporary and mean pretences of the late Dutch war, have raised their ferry double to what it was, and finding the sweet thereof, keep it up still), that so they may live the better above their station, and work so much the fewer days by how much the more they exact in their wages "

the very close of that century, of continuous associations of wage-earners for maintaining or improving the conditions of their working lives.   And when we remember that during the latter decades of the seventeenth century the employers of labour, and especially the industrial " companies " or corporations, memorialised the House of Commons on every conceivable grievance which affected their particular trade, the absence of all complaints of workmen's combinations suggests to us that few, if any, such combinations existed.[1] We do, however, discover in the latter half of the seventeenth century various traces of sporadic combinations and associations, some of which appear to have maintained in obscurity a continuous existence.   In the early years of the eighteenth century we find isolated complaints of combinations " lately entered into " by the skilled workers in certain trades.   As the century progresses we watch the gradual multiplication of these complaints, met by counter-accusations presented by organised bodies of workmen.   From the middle of the century the Journals of the House of Commons abound in petitions and counter-petitions revealing the existence of journeymen's associations in most of the skilled trades. And finally, we may infer the wide extension of the movement from the steady multiplication of the Acts against combinations in particular industries, and their culmination in the comprehensive statute of 1799 forbidding all combinations whatsoever.

If we examine the evidence of the rise of combinations in particular trades, we see the Trade Union springing,

(*Usury at Six Per Cent. Examined*, by Thomas Manley, London, 1669). But we cannot infer from this unique and ambiguous passage anything more than the possibility of ephemeral combinations.   It is significant that Defoe, with all his detailed description of English industry in 1724, does not mention any combinations of workmen.

[1] In an able pamphlet dated 1681, entitled *The Trade of England Revived*, it is stated that " we cannot make our English cloth so cheap as they do in other countries, because of the strange idleness and stubbornness of our poor," who insist on excessive wages.   But the author attributes this state of things, not to the existence of combinations, of which he seems never to have heard, but to the Poor Law and the prevalence of almsgiving.

not from any particular institution, but from every opportunity for the meeting together of wage-earners of the
same occupation. Adam Smith remarked that " people of
the same trade seldom meet together, even for merriment
and diversion, but the conversation ends in a conspiracy
against the public, or in some contrivance to raise prices." [1]
And there is actual evidence of the rise of one of the oldest
of the existing Trade Unions out of a gathering of the
journeymen " to take a social pint of porter together." [2]
More often it is a tumultuous strike, out of which grows
a permanent organisation. Elsewhere, as we shall see,
the workers meet to petition the House of Commons, and
reassemble from time to time to carry on their agitation
for the enactment of some new regulation, or the enforcement of an existing law. In other instances we shall find
the journeymen of a particular trade frequenting certain
public-houses, at which they hear of situations vacant, and
the " house of call " becomes thus the nucleus of an organisation. Or we watch the journeymen in a particular trade
declaring that " it has been an ancient custom in the kingdom
of Great Britain for divers Artists to meet together and

[1] *Wealth of Nations*, bk. i. ch. x. p. 59 of McCulloch's edition, 1863.
In an operative's description, dated 1809, of the gatherings of the Paisley
weavers, we see the Trade Union in the making. " The Paisley operatives
are of a free, communicative disposition. They are fond to inform one
another in anything respecting trade, and in order to receive information
in a collective capacity they have, for a long course of years, associated in
a friendly manner in societies denominated clubs. . . . When met the
first hour is devoted to reading the daily newspapers out aloud. . . . At
nine o'clock the chairman calls silence ; then the report of trade is heard.
The chairman reports first what he knows or what he has heard of such
a manufacturing house or houses, as wishing to engage operatives for
such fabric or fabrics ; likewise the price, the number of the yarn, etc.
Then each reports as he is seated ; so in the period of an hour not only
the state of the trade is known, but any difference that has taken place
between manufacturers and operatives " (*An Answer to Mr. Carlile's
Sketches of Paisley*, by William Taylor, Paisley, 1809, pp. 15-17).
[2] See Dunning's account of the origin of the Consolidated Society of
Bookbinders in 1779–80, in the Social Science Association's *Report on
Trade Societies*, 1860, p. 93 ; also *Workers on their Industries*, edited by
F. W. Galton, 1895 ; *Women in the Printing Trades*, edited by J. R.
MacDonald, 1904, p. 30.

unite themselves in societies to promote Amity and true Christian Charity," and establishing a sick and funeral club, which invariably proceeds to discuss the rates of wages offered by the employers, and insensibly passes into a Trade Union with friendly benefits.[1]   And if the trade is one in which the journeymen frequently travel in search of work, we note the slow elaboration of systematic arrangements for the relief of these " tramps " by their fellow-workers in each town through which they pass, and the

---

[1] *Articles of Agreement made and confirmed by a Society of Taylors, begun March* 25, 1760 (London, 1812). In 1790 Francis Place joined the Breeches Makers' Benefit Society " for the support of the members when sick and their burial when dead "—its real object being to support the members "in a strike for wages " (*Life of Francis Place*, by Professor Graham Wallas, new edition, 1918). Local friendly societies giving sick pay and providing for funeral expenses had sprung up all over England during the eighteenth century. Towards its close their number seems to have rapidly increased until, in some parts at any rate, every village ale-house became a centre for one or more of these humble and spontaneous organisations. The rules of upwards of a hundred of these societies, dating between 1750 and 1820, and all centred round Newcastle-on-Tyne, are preserved in the British Museum. At Nottingham, in 1794, fifty-six of these clubs joined in the annual procession (*Nottingham Journal*, June 14, 1794). So long as they were composed indiscriminately of men of all trades, it is probable that no distinctively Trade Union action could arise from their meetings. But in some cases, for various reasons, such as high contributions, migratory habits, or the danger of the calling, the sick and burial club was confined to men of a particular trade. This kind of friendly society frequently became a Trade Union. Some societies of this type can trace their existence for nearly a century and a half. The Glasgow coopers, for instance, have had a local trade friendly society, confined to journeymen coopers, ever since 1752. The London Sailmakers Burial Society dates from 1740. The Newcastle shoemakers established a similar society as early as 1719 (*Observations upon the Report from the Select Committee of the House of Commons on the laws respecting Friendly Societies*, by the Rev. J. T. Becher, Prebendary of Southwell, 1826). On the occurrence of any dispute with the employers their funds, as this contemporary observer in another pamphlet deplores, " have also too frequently been converted into engines of abuse by paying weekly sums to artisans out of work, and have thereby encouraged combinations among workmen not less injurious to the misguided members than to the Public Weal" (*Observations on the Rise and Progress of Friendly Societies*, 1824, p. 55). Similar friendly societies among workmen of particular trades appear to have existed in the Netherlands in the seventeenth and eighteenth centuries, where they perhaps bridged the gap between the mediæval fraternities and the modern Trade Unions (see review in the *English Historical Review*, October 1918, of P. J. Blok's *Geschiedenes einer Hollandischen Stad*).

inevitable passage of this far-extending tramping society into a national Trade Union.[1]

All these, however, are but opportunities for the meeting of journeymen of the same trade. They do not explain the establishment of continuous organisations of the wage-earners in the seventeenth and eighteenth rather than in the fifteenth or sixteenth centuries. The essential cause of the growth of durable associations of wage-earners must lie in something peculiar to the later centuries. This fundamental condition of Trade Unionism we discover in the economic revolution through which certain industries were passing. In all cases in which Trade Unions arose,

---

[1] Schanz (*Gesellenverbände*, p. 25) follows Brentano (p. 94) in attributing the formation of journeymen's fraternities in the Middle Ages mainly to a desire to provide for the wandering craftsmen. The connection between the " Herbergen " or " Schenken," designed to find lodging and employment, with the journeymen's associations was certainly close. (See Dr. Bruno Schoenlank's article in 1894, quoted in Sir William Ashley's *Surveys: Historic and Economic*, 1900.) It may be suggested that the contrast between the absence or scanty existence of such fraternities in England and their spread in Germany is, perhaps, to be ascribed in some measure to the fact that English journeymen seem never to have adopted the German custom of " Wanderjahre," or regular habit of spending, on completing their apprenticeship, a few years in travelling about the country to complete their training. When the local privileges of the old gilds had fallen somewhat into abeyance, the restrictions of the successive Settlement Acts must in England, to some extent, have checked the mobility of labour. But, from the beginning of the eighteenth century at any rate, we find it customary for journeymen of certain trades—it is to be noticed that these are relatively new trades in England—to " tramp " from town to town in search of work, and the description, subsequently quoted, of the organisations of the wool-combers and worsted weavers in 1741, shows that the relief of these travelling journeymen was a prominent object of the early unions. The hatters in the middle of the eighteenth century had a regular arrangement for such relief. The compositors at the very beginning of the nineteenth century had already covered the country with a network of local clubs, the chief function of which appears to have been the facilitation of this wandering in search of work. And the calico-printers had a systematic way of issuing a ticket which entitled the tramp to collect from each journeyman, in any " print-field " that he visited, at first a voluntary contribution, and latterly a fixed relief of a halfpenny per head in England, and a penny per head in Scotland (*Minutes of evidence taken before the Committee to whom the petition of the several journeymen Calico printers and others working in that trade, etc., was referred*, July 4, 1804, and the *Report* from that Committee, July 17, 1806).

the great bulk of the workers had ceased to be independent producers, themselves controlling the processes, and owning the materials and the product of their labour, and had passed into the condition of lifelong wage-earners, possessing neither the instruments of production nor the commodity in its finished state. "From the moment that to establish a given business more capital is required than a journeyman can easily accumulate within a few years, gild mastership—the mastership of the masterpiece—becomes little more than a name. . . . Skill alone is valueless, and is soon compelled to hire itself out to capital. . . . Now begins the opposition of interest between employers and employed, now the latter begin to group themselves together ; now rises the trade society." [1] Or, to express this Industrial Revolution in more abstract terms, we may say, in the words of Dr. Ingram, that "the whole modern organisation of labour in its advanced forms rests on a fundamental fact which has spontaneously and increasingly developed itself—namely, the definite separation between the functions of the capitalist and the workman, or, in other words, between the direction of industrial operations and their execution in detail." [2]

It is often assumed that the divorce of the manual worker from the ownership of the means of production resulted from the introduction of machinery, the use of power, and the factory system. Had this been the case we should not, upon our hypothesis, have expected to find Trade Unions at an earlier date than factories, or in industries untransformed by machinery. The fact that the earliest durable combinations of wage-earners in England precede the factory system by a whole century, and occur in trades carried on exclusively by hand labour, reminds us that the creation of a class of lifelong wage-servants came about in more than one way.

---

[1] J. M. Ludlow, in article in *Macmillan's Magazine*, February 1861.
[2] *Work and the Workman*, by Dr. J. K. Ingram (Address to the Trades Union Congress at Dublin, 1880).

We may note, to begin with, the very old institution of the printers' " chapel," with its " father " and " clerk," an informal association among the compositors of a particular establishment for the discussion and regulation, not only of their own workshop conditions, but also of their relations with the employer, who must, in early days, have been a man of superior education, with an outlook much wider than that of his journeymen.

The " chapel " may possibly be nearly as old as the introduction of printing into this country.[1] We have no evidence as to the date at which the " chapels " of different printing offices entered into communication with each other in London, so as to form a Trade Union. But already in 1666 we have *The Case and Proposals of the Free Journeymen Printers in and about London*, in which they complain of the multiplication of apprentices and the prevalence of " turnovers "—grievances which vexed every compositors' Trade Union throughout the nineteenth century.[2] Whether the " Free Journeymen Printers " managed to continue in existence as a Trade Union is uncertain. We have found no actual evidence of any other combination among com-

[1] Benjamin Franklin mentions the " chapel " and its regulations in 1725. A copy, dated 1734, of the *Rules and Orders to be observed by the Members of this Chapel : by Compositors, by Pressmen, by Both*, is preserved in the Place MSS. 27799—88.

[2] This petition (in the British Museum) is printed in Brentano's *Gilds and Trade Unions*, p. 97. Benjamin Franklin, who worked in London printing offices in 1725, makes no mention of Trade Unionism. The Stationers' Company continued, so far as the City of London was concerned, to regulate apprenticeship ; and we see it, in 1775, taking steps to prevent employers having an undue number. Regulations agreed to by the employers and the compositors, as to the rates of pay for different kinds of work, can be traced back to 1785, at least. A copy of the rules of " The Phœnix, or Society of Compositors " meeting at " The Hole in the Wall " tavern, Fleet Street, shows that this organisation was " instituted March 12th, 1792." In 1798 five members of the " Pressmen's Friendly Society " were indicted for conspiracy in meeting for the purpose of restricting the number of apprentices (they sought to limit them to three for seven presses). Although the secretary to the " Society of Master Printers " had requested these men to attend the meeting, in order to get settled the pending dispute, they were convicted and sentenced to two years' imprisonment (*Conflicts of Capital and Labour*, by George Howell, 1890, p. 92).

positors than the " chapel " earlier than the eighteenth century.

One of the earliest proven cases of continuous association among journeymen is that of the hatters (or feltmakers), whose combination—now the Journeymen Hatters' Trade Union of Great Britain and Ireland—may perhaps claim to trace its ancestry from 1667, the very year in which the Feltmakers' Company, consisting of their employers, obtained a charter from Charles II. Within a few months the journeymen in the various London workshops—each of which had apparently a workshop organisation somewhat resembling the printers' " chapel "—had combined to present a petition to the Court of Aldermen against the Master, Wardens and Assistants of the Company. The Court of Aldermen decided that, in order " that the journeymen may not by combination or otherwise excessively at their pleasure raise their wages," a piecework list is to be annually settled and presented for enactment by the Court of Aldermen. The journeymen seem to have co-operated with the employers in presenting this list, and in preventing the employment of non-freemen. The rates fixed did not, however, always satisfy the journeymen, especially when the employers were successful in getting them lowered ; and in 1696 we read of a deputation appearing before the Court to declare that they had resolved among themselves not to accept any less wages than they had formerly received, and to ask for a revision of the order. They had, according to the masters' statement, not confined themselves to peaceful resolutions, but had made an example of a journeyman who had remained at work at the reduced rates. " They stirred up the apprentices to seize upon him as he was working, to tie him in a wheelbarrow, and in a tumultuous and riotous manner to drive him through all the considerable places in London and Southwark." It was alleged that the men were organised in " clubs," which " raised several sums of money for the abetting and supporting such of them who should desert their masters' service." In 1697 the employers introduced the " character note " or " leaving certificate," the Company enacting that no master should employ a journeyman who did not bring with him a certificate from his previous employer. Successive prosecutions of journeymen took place for refusing to work at the lawful rates, but the workmen seem to have had good legal advice, and to have defended themselves with skill. On one occasion they pleaded guilty, and promised amendment and the abandonment of their combination, whereupon the prosecution was withdrawn. On another occasion they got the case removed by writ of *certiorari* from the Lord Mayor's session to the Assizes, where Lord Chief Justice Holt referred the dispute to arbitration. The award of June 1699 was a virtual victory for the journeymen, after a three years' struggle, as it gave them an increase of rates, with a stoppage of all legal proceedings.[1] That the London Trade Clubs of the journeymen hatters, or at any rate their several workshop organisations, maintained a continuous existence we need not doubt ; though we do not hear of them again until 1771, when they seem to have established a national federation of the local trade clubs existing in more than a dozen provincial towns with those of Southwark and the West End of London, very largely for the purpose of maintaining and enforcing the statutory limitation of apprentices. In 1775 this federation appears to have been strong enough, not only to obtain increased rates of wages, but also the exclusive employment of " clubmen." There were " congresses " of the hatters in 1772, 1775, and 1777, held in London for the adoption of " byelaws " for the whole trade ; but we believe that these " congresses " were attended by delegates from the workshops in and near London only.

---

[1] For this interesting case we are indebted to Professor George Unwin's researches in the records of the Feltmakers' Company, whose " Court Book " contains the record. See *Industrial Organisation in the 16th and 17th Centuries*, by George Unwin, 1904 ; " A Seventeenth-Century Trade Union," by the same, in *Economic Journal*, 1910, pp. 394-403 ; the chapter " Mediæval Journeymen's Clubs " in Sir William Ashley's *Surveys. Historic and Economic*, 1900.

It is clear that similar organisations existed in the other towns in which the trade was carried on. The members who were unemployed " tramped " from town to town, and regulations for their relief were framed. A weekly contribution of 2d. appears to have been paid by each member. The employers successfully petitioned Parliament in 1777 for a repeal of the old limitation of apprentices and a renewed prohibition of combination.[1]

More definite evidence is afforded by the development of the tailoring trade. In tailoring for rich customers the master craftsmen appear at the very beginning of the eighteenth century to have been recruited from the comparatively small number of journeymen who acquired the specially skilled part of the business—namely, the cutting-out.[2] " The tailor," says an eighteenth-century manual for the young tradesman, " ought to have a quick eye to steal the cut of a sleeve, the pattern of a flap, or the shape of a good trimming at a glance, . . in the passing of a chariot, or in the space between the door and a coach." There grew up accordingly a class of mere sewers, " not one in ten " knowing " how to cut out a pair of breeches : they are employed only to sew the seam, to cast the buttonholes, and prepare the work for the finisher. . . . Generally as poor as rats, the House of Call runs away with all their earnings, and keeps them constantly in debt and want." [3]

---

[1] House of Commons Journals, vol. xxxvi. ; 8 Eliz. c. 11 ; 1 James I. c. 14 ; and 17 George III. c.55 ; Place MSS. 27799—68 ; Committee on Artisans and Machinery, 1824 ; *Industrial Democracy*, p. 11 ; " A Seventeenth Century Trade Union," by Professor George Unwin, in *Economic Journal*, 1910, pp. 394-403 ; *Conflicts of Capital and Labour*, by G. Howell, 1890, p. 83. The organisation evidently continued in existence, at least in its local form ; but the existing national " Journeymen Hatters' Trade Union of Great Britain and Ireland " claims to date only from 1798. In 1806 the Macclesfield hatters were indicted for conspiracy in striking for higher wages, and sentenced to twelve months' imprisonment. Particulars of this organisation will be found in *The Trial of W. Davenport . . . Hatters of Macclesfield for a Conspiracy against their Masters . . .* by Thomas Mulineaux, 1806.

[2] For the whole history of this industry, see *The Tailoring Trade*, by F. W. Galton, 1896.

[3] *The London Tradesman*, by Campbell, 1747, p. 192.

This differentiation was promoted by the increasing need of capital for successfully beginning business in the better quarters of the metropolis. Already in 1681 the " shop-keeping tailor " was deplored as a new and objectionable feature, " for many remember when there were no new garments sold in London (in shops) as now there are." [1] The " accustomed tailor," or working craftsman, making up the customer's own cloth, objected to " taylers being sales-men," paying high rents for shops in fashionable neigh-bourhoods, giving long credit to their aristocratic clients, and each employing, in his own workshops, dozens or even scores of journeymen, who were recruited from the houses of call in times of pressure, and ruthlessly turned adrift when the season was over And although it remained pos-sible in the reign of King William the Third, as it still is in that of King George the Fifth, to start business in a back street as an independent master tailor with no more capital or skill than the average journeyman could command, yet the making of the fine clothes worn by the Court and the gentry demanded, then as now, a capital and a skill which put this extensive and lucrative trade altogether out of the reach of the thousands of journeymen whom it employed. Thus we find that at the very beginning of the eighteenth century the typical journeyman tailor in London and West-minster had become a lifelong wage-earner. It is not sur-prising, therefore, that one of the earliest instances of permanent Trade Unionism that we have been able to dis-cover occurs in this trade. The master tailors in 1720 complain to Parliament that " the Journeymen Taylors in and about the Cities of London and Westminster, to the number of seven thousand and upwards, have lately entered into a combination to raise their wages and leave off working an hour sooner than they used to do ; and for the better carrying on their design have subscribed their respective names in books prepared for that purpose, at the several houses of call or resort (being publick-houses in and about

[1] *The Trade of England Revived*, 1681, p. 36.

London and Westminster) which they use ; and collect
several considerable sums of money to defend any prosecutions against them." [1] Parliament listened to the masters'
complaint, and passed the Act 7, Geo. I. st. 1, c. 13,
restraining both the giving and the taking of wages in excess
of a stated maximum, all combinations being prohibited.
From that time forth the journeymen tailors of London and
Westminster have remained in effective though sometimes
informal combination, the organisation centring round the
fifteen or twenty " houses of call," being the public-houses
to which it was customary for the workmen to resort, and
at which the employers sought any additional men whom
they wished to engage. In 1744 the Privy Council was
set in motion against their refusal to obey the Act of
1720.[2] In 1750–51 they invoked the assistance of the
Middlesex Justices, and obtained an order requiring the
masters to pay certain rates. In 1767 further legislation
was, in spite of their eloquent protests, obtained against
them.[3] In 1810 a master declared before a Select Committee that their combination had existed for over a
century.[4]

An equally early instance of permanent trade combination is the woollen manufacture of the West of England.

---

[1] House of Commons Journals, vol. xix. pp. 416, 424, 481 ; *The Case
of the Master Taylors residing within the Cities of London and Westminster,
in relation to the great abuses committed by their journeymen ; An Abstract of
the Master Taylors' Bill before the Honourable House of Commons, with the
Journeymen's Observation on each clause of the said Bill ; The Case of the
Journeymen Taylors residing in the Cities of London and Westminster* (all
1720). These and other documents relating to combinations in this trade
have now been published in a useful volume (*The Tailoring Trade*, by F. W.
Galton, 1896), with an elaborate bibliography.

[2] *London*, by David Hughson (1821), pp. 392-3 ; House of Commons
Journals, vol. xxiv. Place MSS. 27799, pp. 4, 5. *The Case of the Journeymen
Taylors in and about the Cities of London and Westminster* (January 7, 1745).

[3] *Gentlemen's Magazine*, 1750, 1768.

[4] Place MSS. 27799—10 ; see *The Life of Francis Place, 1771–1854*, by
Professor Graham Wallas, 1898 ; second edition, 1918. There is evidence
of very similar organisation in other towns. At Birmingham, for instance,
there was a systematically organised strike in 1777 against a reduction of
wages, which lasted for some months (Langford's *Century of Birmingham
Life*, pp. 225, etc. : *The Tailoring Trade*, by F. W. Galton, 1896).

Here the rise of a class of lifelong wage-earners took a form altogether different from that in the London tailoring trade, but it produced the same result of combinations among the workers. The " wealthy clothiers " of Somerset, Gloucestershire, and Devon, who during the sixteenth century had " mightily increased in fame and riches, their houses frequented like kings' courts," [1] provided and owned the material of the industry throughout the whole manufacturing process, but employed a separate class of operatives at each stage. Buying the wool at one of the market towns, the capitalist clothier gave this to one set of hand-workers to be carded and spun into yarn in the village households. The yarn was passed on to another set—the hand-loom weavers—to be made into cloth in their cottages. The cloth was then " fulled " at the capitalist's own mill (usually a water-mill) and again given out to be " dressed " by a new set of hand-workers, after which it was ready to be packed in the warehouse, and dispatched to Bristol or London for shipment or sale. In this case, as in that of the tailors, the operatives still retained the ownership of the tools of their particular processes, but it was practically impossible for them to acquire either the capital or the commercial knowledge necessary for the success of so highly organised an industry, and we accordingly find them entering into extensive combinations from the closing years of the seventeenth century. Already in 1675 the journeymen clothworkers of London combined to petition the Court of the Clothworkers' Company against the engagement of workmen from the country. In 1682 we hear of them taking advantage of an extensive shipping order to refuse,

[1] *A Declaration of the Estate of Clothing now used within this Realme of England*, by John May, Deputy Alnager (1613, 51 pp., in B.M. 712, g. 16), a volume which contains many interesting pamphlets on the woollen manufacture between 1613 and 1753. Already in 1622, a year of depression of trade, we hear of numerous riots and tumults among the weavers of the West of England, notably those of certain Devonshire towns, who paraded the streets demanding work or food (*Quarter Sessions from Elizabeth to Anne*, by A. H. A. Hamilton, 1878, pp. 95-6). But there is as yet no evidence of durable combinations at so early a date.

C

in concert, to work under 12s. per week.   But it is not
clear whether any lasting association then resulted.[1]   In the
West of England the ephemeral revolts of the early part of
the seventeenth century seem to have developed into lasting
combinations by the end of that century.   We hear of
them at Tiverton as early as 1700.[2]   In 1717 the Journals
of the House of Commons contain evidence of the existence
of a widespread combination of the woollen-workers in
Devonshire and Somerset.   The Mayor and Corporation of
Bradninch complain " that for some years past the woolcombers and weavers in those parts have been confederat-
ing how to incorporate themselves into a club : and have
to the number of some thousands in this county, in a very
riotous and tumultuous manner, exacted tribute from
many." [3]   The House of Commons apparently thought the
evil could be met by Royal Authority and requested the
King to issue a Proclamation.   Accordingly on February 4,
1718, a Royal Proclamation was issued against these " lawless clubs and societies which had illegally presumed to use
a common seal, and to act as Bodies Corporate, by making
and unlawfully conspiring to execute certain By-laws or
Orders, whereby they pretend to determine who had a right
to the Trade, what and how many Apprentices and Journeymen each man should keep at once, together with the prices
of all their manufactures, and the manner and materials of
which they should be wrought." [4]   This kingly fulmination,
which was read at the Royal Exchange, failed to effect its
purpose, for the Journals of the House of Commons for
1723 and 1725 contain frequent complaints of the continuance of the combinations,[5] which are constantly heard

---

[1] MS. Minutes, Court Book of the Clothworkers' Company, December 10,
1675 ;   August 16, 1682 ;   *Industrial Organisation of the Sixteenth and
Seventeenth Centuries*, by George Unwin, 1904, p. 199.

[2] *History of Tiverton*, by Martin Dunsford (Exeter, 1790).

[3] House of Commons Journals, vol. xviii. p. 715, February 5, 1717.
Tiverton and Exeter petition to the same effect.

[4] Hughson's *London*, p. 337.   The proclamation was reprinted in *Notes
and Queries*, September 21, 1867, from a copy preserved by the Sun Fire Office.

[5] See the petitions from Exeter and Dartmouth, February 24, 1723,

of throughout the whole of the eighteenth century, dying away only on the supersession of the male by the female weaver at the beginning of the nineteenth century, not to be effectively revived until the beginning of the twentieth.

This early development of trade combinations in the West of England stands in striking contrast with their absence in the same industry where pursued, as in Yorkshire, on the so-called " Domestic System." The Yorkshire weaver was a small master craftsman of the old type, himself buying and owning the raw material, and once or twice a week selling his cloth in the markets of Leeds or Wakefield, to which, we are told by Defoe in 1724, " few clothiers bring more than one piece." " Almost at every house," he writes of the country near Halifax, " there was a Tenter, and almost on every Tenter a piece of cloth, or kersey, or shalloon, . . . at every considerable house was a manufactory ; . . . then, as every clothier must keep a horse, perhaps two, to fetch and carry for the use of his manufacture, viz., to fetch home his wool and his provisions from the market, to carry his yarn to the spinners, his manufacture to the fulling mill, and when finished, to the market to be sold, and the like ; so every manufacturer generally keeps a cow or two or more, for his family, and this employs the two or three or four pieces of enclosed land about his house, for they scarce sow corn enough for their cocks and hens." [1] Not until the Yorkshire cloth

---

vol. xx. pp. 268-9 ; and those from Taunton, Tiverton, Exeter, and Bristol, March 3 and 7, 1725, vol. xx. pp. 598, 602, 648. In 1729 the Bristol weavers, " while the corporation was at church," riotously attacked the house of an obnoxious employer, and had to be repulsed by the troops (*History of Bristol*, p. 261, by J. Evans ; Bristol, 1824). In 1738 they forced the clothiers to sign a bond that they would " for ever forward " give fifteen pence a yard for weaving, under penalty of £1000 (*Gentlemen's Magazine*, 1738, p. 658 ; see also " An Essay on Riots, their Causes and Cure," published in the *Gloucester Journal*, and reprinted in the *Gentlemen's Magazine*, 1739, pp. 7-10). In 1756 there was an extensive and serious uprising (see *A State of the Case and Narrative of Facts relating to the late Commotion and Rising of the Weavers in the County of Gloucester*. in the Gough Collection, Bodleian Library).

[1] Defoe's *Tour*, vol. iii. pp. 97-101, 116 (1724). John Bright mentions

dealers began, about 1794, to establish factories on a large scale do we find any Trade Unions, and then journeymen and small masters struggled with one accord to resist the new form of capitalist industry which was beginning to deprive them of their control over the product of their labour.

The worsted industry appears everywhere to have been carried on rather like the woollen manufactures of the West of England than the same industry in Yorkshire. The woolcomber frequently owned the inexpensive hand-combs and pots with which he worked. But the wool-combers, like the weavers of the West of England, formed but one of several classes of workers for whose employment both capital and commercial knowledge was indispensable. We hear, already in 1674, of an attempt by the Leicester woolcombers to " form a company," [1] though with what success we know not. In 1741 it was remarked that the woolcombers had " for a number of years past erected themselves into a sort of corporation (though without a charter) ; their first pretence was to take care of their poor brethren that should fall sick, or be out of work ; and this was done by meeting once or twice a week, and each of them contributing 2d. or 3d. towards the box to make a bank, and when they became a little formidable they gave laws to their masters, as also to themselves— viz., That no man should comb wool under 2s. per dozen ; that no master should employ any comber that was not of their club : if he did they agreed one and all not to work for him ; and if he had employed twenty they all of them turned out, and oftentimes were not satisfied with that, but would abuse the honest man that would labour, and in

---

his father's apprenticeship, about 1789, to " a most worthy man who had a few acres of ground, a very small farm, and three or four looms in his house " (speech reported in *Beehive*, February 2, 1867). For a less optimistic account of the Yorkshire clothiers, who were, even in the seventeenth century, often mere wage-earners, see Cartwright's *Chapters of Yorkshire History*.

[1] *History of Leicester*, by James Thompson, 1849, pp. 431-2.

a riotous manner beat him, break his comb-pots, and destroy his working tools ; they further support one another in so much that they are become one society throughout the kingdom. And that they may keep up their price to encourage idleness rather than labour, if any one of their club is out of work, they give him a ticket and money to seek for work at the next town where a box club is, where he is also subsisted, suffered to live a certain time with them, and then used as before ; by which means he can travel the kingdom round, be caressed at each club, and not spend a farthing of his own or strike one stroke of work. This hath been imitated by the weavers also, though not carried through the kingdom, but confined to the places where they work." [1] The surviving members of the Old Amicable Society of Woolstaplers retain a tradition of local trade clubs dating from the very beginning of the eighteenth century, and of their forming a federal union in 1785. Old members of the United Journeymen Curriers' Society have seen circulars and tramping cards, showing that a similar tramping federation existed in their trade from the middle of the century. [2]

In other cases the expensive nature of the raw material or the tools aided the creation of a separate class. The Spitalfields silk-weavers, whom we find forming a permanent organisation in 1773, could never have owned the costly silks they wove. [3] The gold-beaters, whose union dates at any rate from 1777, were similarly debarred from owning the material.

---

[1] *A Short Essay upon Trade in General*, by " A Lover of his Country," 1741, quoted in James' *History of the Worsted Manufacture in England*, p. 232.

[2] See, in corroboration, *Leicester Herald*, August 24, 1793 ; *Morning Chronicle*, October 13, 1824 ; Place MSS., 27801—246, 247.

[3] The Dublin silk-weavers, owing perhaps to their having been largely Huguenot refugees in a Roman Catholic town, appear to have been associated from the early part of the eighteenth century ; see, for instance, *The Case of the Silk and Worsted Weavers in a Letter to a Member of Parliament* (Dublin, 1749, 8 pp.). Compare *A Short Historical Account of the Silk Manufacture in England*, by Samuel Sholl, 1811, and *Industrial Dublin since 1698 and the Silk Industry in Dublin*, by J. J. Webb, 1913.

Another remarkable instance of combination prior to the introduction of mechanical power and the factory system is that of the " stockingers," the hosiery workers, or framework knitters, described by Dr. Brentano. From the very beginning of the use of the stocking-frame, in the early part of the seventeenth century, servants appear to have been set to work upon frames owned by capitalists, though the bulk of the trade was in the hands of men who worked upon their own frames as independent producers. The competition of these embryo factories was severely felt by the domestic framework knitter, and on the final breakdown, in 1753, of the legal limitation of apprentices, it became disastrous. There grew up a " ruinous practice of parishes giving premiums to manufacturers for employing their poor," and this flooding of the labour market with subsidised child labour reduced the typical framework knitter to a state of destitution. Though he continued to work in his cottage, he rapidly lost the ownership of his frame, and a system arose under which the frames were hired at a rent, either from a small capitalist frame-owner, or from the manufacturer by whom the work was given out. The operative was thus deprived, not only of the ownership of the product, but also of the instruments of his labour. Hence, although from the very beginning of the eighteenth century there were ephemeral combinations among the framework knitters, in which masters and men often joined, it was not until 1780, when the renting of frames had become general, that a durable Trade Union of wage-earners arose.[1]

The development of the industrial organisation of the

---

[1] The condition of the framework knitters may be gathered from the elaborate Parliamentary Inquiry, the proceedings of which fill fifteen pages of the Journals of the House of Commons, vol. xxvi., April 19, 1753. See also vols. xxxvi. and xxxvii., and the Report from the Committee on Framework Knitters' Petitions, 1812 ; and *Conflicts of Capital and Labour,* by G. Howell, 1890. Felkin's *History of the Machine-wrought Hosiery and Lace Manufactures,* 1867, contains an exhaustive account of the trade, founded on Gravener Henson's *History of the Framework Knitters,* 1831, now a scarce work, of which only one volume was published.

cutlery trades affords another example of this evolution. At the date of the establishment in Sheffield of the Cutlers' Company (1624) the typical craftsman was himself the owner of his " wheel " and other instruments, and a strict limitation of apprentices was maintained. By 1791, when the masters obtained from Parliament a formal ratification of the prevalent relaxation in the customary restrictions as to apprentices, we find this system largely replaced by something very like the present order of things, in which the typical Sheffield operative works with material given out by the manufacturer, upon wheels rented either from the latter or from a landlord supplying power. It is no mere coincidence that in the year 1790 the Sheffield employers found themselves obliged to take concerted action against the " scissorgrinders and other workmen who have entered into unlawful combinations to raise the price of labour." [1]

The shipwrights of Liverpool, and probably those of other shipbuilding ports, were combined in trade benefit clubs early in the eighteenth century. At Liverpool, where this society had very successfully maintained the customary limitation of apprentices, the members were all freemen of the municipal corporation, and as such entitled to the Parliamentary franchise. As a result the shipwrights' organisation became intensely political, by which was meant chiefly the negotiation of the sale of its members' votes. At the election of 1790, when Whigs and Tories compromised in order to avoid the expense of a contest, it was the Shipwrights' Society, then at the zenith of its power, which insisted on forcing a contest by nominating its own candidate, and, in the end, actually put him at the head of the poll. The society, which had a contribution in 1824 of fifteen pence per month, and had built almshouses for its old members, is reputed to have been at one

---

[1] *Sheffield Iris*, August 7 and September 9, 1790. The Scissorsmiths' Friendly Society, cited by Dr. Brentano, was established in April 1791. Other trade friendly societies in Sheffield appear to date from a much earlier period.

time so powerful that any employer who refused to obey
its rules found his business absolutely brought to a standstill.[1]

But the cardinal example of the conception of Trade
Unionism with the divorce of the worker from the instruments of production is seen in the rapid rise of trade combinations on the introduction of the factory system. We
have already noticed that Trade Unions in Yorkshire began
with the erection of factories and the use of power. When,
in 1794, the clothiers of the West Riding failed to prevent
the Leeds merchants from establishing large factories,
" wherein it is intended to employ a great number of persons
now working at their own homes," the journeymen took
the matter into their own hands, and founded " the Clothiers'
Community," or " Brief Institution," professedly to gather
" briefs " or levies for the relief of the sick, and to carry on
a Parliamentary agitation for hampering the factory owners
by a legal limitation of apprentices. " It appears," reports
the Parliamentary Committee of 1806, " that there has
existed for some time an institution or society among the
woollen manufacturers, consisting chiefly of clothworkers.
In each of the principal manufacturing towns there appears
to be a society, composed of deputies chosen from the
several shops of workmen, from each of which town societies
one or more deputies are chosen to form what is called the
central committee, which meets, as occasion requires, at
some place suitable to the local convenience of all parties.
The powers of the central committee appear to pervade
the whole institution ; and any determination or measure
which it may adopt may be communicated with ease throughout the whole body of manufacturers. Every workman,
on his becoming a member of the society, receives a certain
card or ticket, on which is an emblematical engraving—the

---

[1] Sir J. A. Picton's *Memorials of Liverpool,* 1875; *A Digest of the
Evidence before the Committee on Artizans and Machinery,* by George
White, 1824, p. 233; *Conflicts of Labour and Capital,* by G. Howell,
1890, pp. 82-3.

same, the Committee are assured, both in the North and the West of England—that by producing his ticket he may at once show he belongs to the society. The same rules and regulations appear to be in force throughout the whole district, and there is the utmost reason to believe that no clothworker would be suffered to carry on his trade, otherwise than in solitude, who should refuse to submit to the obligations and rules of the society."[1] The transformation of cotton-spinning into a factory industry, which may be said to have taken place round about the year 1780, was equally accompanied by the growth of Trade Unionism. The so-called benefit clubs of the Oldham operatives, which we know to have existed from 1792, and those of Stockport, of which we hear in 1796, were the forerunners of that network of spinners' societies throughout the northern counties and Scotland which rose into notoriety in the great strikes of the next thirty years.[2]

It is easy to understand how the massing together in factories of regiments of men all engaged in the same trade facilitated and promoted the formation of journeymen's trade societies. But with the cotton-spinners, as with the tailors, the rise of permanent trade combinations is to be ascribed, in a final analysis, to the definite separation between the functions of the capitalist *entrepreneur* and the manual worker—between, that is to say, the direction of industrial operations and their execution. It has, indeed, become a commonplace of modern Trade Unionism that only in those industries in which the worker has ceased to be concerned in the profits of buying and selling—that inseparable characteristic of the ownership and management of the means of production—can effective and stable trade organisations be established.

The positive proofs of this historical dependence of Trade Unionism upon the divorce of the worker from the

---

[1] *Report of Committee on the Woollen Manufacture*, 1806, p. 16 ; see also *Conflicts of Labour and Capital*, by G. Howell, 1890.
[2] See Chapter III.

C 2

ownership of the means of production are complemented by the absence of any permanent trade combinations in industries in which the divorce had not taken place. The degradation of the Standard of Life of the skilled manual worker on the break-up of the mediæval system occurred in all sorts of trades, whether the operative retained his ownership of the means of production or not, but Trade Unionism followed only where the change took the form of a divorce between capital and labour. The Corporation of Pinmakers of London are found petitioning Parliament towards the end of the seventeenth century or beginning of the eighteenth, as follows :

" This company consists for the most part of poor and indigent people, who have neither credit nor mony to purchase wyre of the merchant at the best hand, but are forced for want thereof to buy only small parcels of the second or third buyer as they have occasion to use it, and to sell off the pins they make of the same from week to week, as soon as they are made, for ready money to feed themselves, their wives and children, whom they are constrained to imploy to go up and down every Saturday night from shop to shop to offer their pins to sale, otherwise cannot have money to buy bread. And these are daily so exceedingly multiplyed and encreased by reason of the unlimited number of apprentices that some few covetous-minded members of the company (who have considerable stocks) do constantly imploy and keep. . . . The persons that buy the pins from the maker to sell again to other retailing shopkeepers, taking advantage of this necessity of the poor workmen (who are always forced to sell for ready mony, or otherwise cannot subsist), have by degrees so beaten down the price of pins that the workman is not able to live of his work, . . . and betake themselves to be porters, tankard bearers, and other day labourers, . . . and many of their children do daily become parish charges." [1]

---

[1] In volume entitled *Tracts Relating to Trade*, in British Museum, 816, m. 13.   Tankard-bearers were water carriers.

And the glovers complain at the same period that " they are generally so poor that they are supplied with leather upon credit, not being able to pay for that or their work-folk's wages till they have sold the gloves." [1]

Now, although these pinmakers and glovers, and other trades in like condition, fully recognised the need for some protection of their Standard of Life, we do not find any trace of Trade Unionism among them. Selling as they did, not their labour alone, but also its product, their only resource was legislative protection of the price of their wares. [2] In short, in those industries in which the cleavage between capitalist and artisan, manager and manual labourer, was not yet complete, the old gild policy of commercial monopoly was resorted to as the only expedient for protecting the Standard of Life of the producer.

We do not contend that the divorce supplies, in itself, a complete explanation of the origin of Trade Unions. At all times in the history of English industry there have existed large classes of workers as much debarred from becoming the directors of their own industry as the eighteenth-century tailor or woolcomber, or as the modern cotton-spinner or miner. Besides the semi-servile workers on the land or in the mines, it is certain that there were in the towns a considerable class of unskilled labourers, excluded, through lack of apprenticeship, from any participation in the gild. [3] By the eighteenth century, at any rate,

---

[1] *Reasons against the designed leather impositions on gloves*, B.M. 816, m. 13.

[2] We shall have occasion later to refer to the absence of effective Trade Unionism in those trades which are still carried on by small working masters.

[3] The assumption frequently made that the Craft Gilds, at their best period, included practically the whole working population, appears to us unfounded. The gild system at no time extended to any but the skilled handicraftsmen, alongside of whom must always have worked a large number of unapprenticed labourers, who received less than half the wages of the craftsmen. We venture to suggest that it is doubtful whether the Craft Gilds at any time numbered as large a proportion of the working population as the Trade Unions of the present day. See *Industrial Democracy*, p. 480.

the numbers of this class must have been largely swollen, by the increased demand for common labour involved in the growth of the transport trade, the extensive building operations, etc. But it is not among the farm servants, miners, or general labourers, ill-paid and ill-treated as these often were, that the early Trade Unions arose. We do not even hear of ephemeral combinations among them, and only very occasionally of transient strikes.[1] The formation of independent associations to resist the will of employers requires the possession of a certain degree of personal independence and strength of character. Thus we find the earliest Trade Unions arising among journeymen whose skill and Standard of Life had been for centuries encouraged and protected by legal or customary regulations as to apprenticeship, and by the limitation of their numbers which the high premiums and other conditions must have involved. It is often assumed that Trade Unionism arose as a protest against intolerable industrial oppression. This was not so. The first half of the eighteenth century was certainly not a period of exceptional distress. For fifty years from 1710 there was an almost constant succession of good harvests, the price of wheat remaining unusually low. The tailors of London and Westminster united, at the very beginning of the eighteenth century, not to resist any reduction of their customary earnings, but to wring from their employers better wages and shorter hours of labour. The few survivors of the hand woolcombers still cherish the tradition of the eighteenth century, when they styled themselves " gentlemen woolcombers," refused to

---

[1] " Tumults," or strikes, among the coal-miners are occasionally mentioned during the eighteenth century, but no lasting combinations. See, for those in Somerset, Carmarthenshire, etc., in 1757, *Gentlemen's Magazine*, 1757, pp. 90, 185, 285, etc. In 1765 there was a prolonged strike against the " yearly bond " by the Durham miners (*Calendar of Home Office Papers*, 1765 ; Sykes' *Local Records*, vol. i, p. 254). The Keelmen, who loaded coals on the Tyne, "mutinied" in 1654 and 1671 "for the increase of wages " ; and there were fierce strikes in 1710, 1744, 1750, 1771, and 1794. We have, however, no particulars as to their associations, which were probably ephemeral (Sykes' *Local Records* ; Richardson's *Local Historian's Table Book* ; *Gentlemen's Magazine*, 1750).

drink with other operatives, and were strong enough, as we have seen, to give " laws to their masters." [1] The very superior millwrights, whose exclusive trade clubs preceded any general organisation of the engineering trade, had for " their everyday garb " a " long frock coat and tall hat." [2] And the curriers, hatters, woolstaplers, shipwrights, brush-makers, basketmakers, and calico-printers, who furnish prominent instances of eighteenth-century Trade Unionism, all earned relatively high wages, and long maintained a very effectual resistance to the encroachments of their employers.

It appears to us from these facts that Trade Unionism would have been a feature of English industry, even without the steam-engine and the factory system. Whether the association of superior workmen which arose in the early part of the century would, in such an event, ever have developed into a Trade Union Movement is another matter. The typical " trade club " of the town artisan of this time was an isolated " ring " of highly skilled journeymen, who were even more decisively marked off from the mass of the manual workers than from the small class of capitalist employers. The customary enforcement of the apprenticeship prescribed by the Elizabethan statutes, and the high premiums often exacted from parents not belonging to the trade, long maintained a virtual monopoly of the better-paid handicrafts in the hands of an almost hereditary caste of " tradesmen " in whose ranks the employers themselves had for the most part served their apprenticeship. Enjoying, as they did, this legal or customary protection, they found their trade clubs of use mainly for the provision of friendly benefits, and for " higgling " with their masters for better terms. We find little trace among such trade clubs of that sense of solidarity between the manual workers

---

[1] Many instances of insolence and aggression by the woolcombers are on record ; the employers' advertisements in the *Nottingham Journal*, August 31, 1795, and the *Leicester Herald* of June 1792, are only two out of many similar recitals.

[2] *Jubilee Souvenir History of the Amalgamated Society of Engineers*, 1901, p. 12.

of different trades which afterwards became so marked a feature of the Trade Union Movement. Their occasional disputes with their employers resembled rather family differences than conflicts between distinct social classes. They exhibit more tendency to " stand in " with their masters against the community, or to back them against rivals or interlopers, than to join their fellow-workers of other trades in an attack upon the capitalist class. In short, we have industrial society still divided vertically trade by trade, instead of horizontally between employers and wage-earners. This latter cleavage it is which has transformed the Trade Unionism of petty groups of skilled workmen into the modern Trade Union Movement.[1]

The pioneers of the Trade Union Movement were not the trade clubs of the town artisans, but the extensive combinations of the West of England woollen-workers and the Midland framework knitters. It was these associations that initiated what afterwards became the common purpose of nearly all eighteenth-century combinations—the appeal to the Government and the House of Commons to save the wage-earners from the new policy of buying labour, like the raw material of manufacture, in the cheapest

---

[1] That such clubs were common in the handicraft trades in London as early as 1720 appears from the following extract from *The Case of the Master Taylors residing within the Cities of London and Westminster*, a petition which led to the Act of 1720 : " This combination of the Journeymen Taylors . . . is of very ill example to Journeymen in all other trades ; as is sufficiently seen in the Journeymen Curriers, Smiths, Farriers, Sailmakers, Coachmakers, and artificers of divers other arts and mysteries, who have actually entered into Confederacies of the like nature ; and the Journeymen Carpenters, Bricklayers, and Joyners have taken some steps for that purpose, and only wait to see the event of others." And the Journeymen Tailors in their petition of 1745 allude to the large number of " Monthly Clubs " among the London handicraftsmen. With regard to the curriers at this date, see Place MSS, 27801—246, 247.

It may be conveniently noticed here that, although strikes are, as we have seen, as old as the fourteenth century at least, the word " strike " was not commonly used in this sense until the latter part of the eighteenth century. The Oxford Dictionary gives the first instance of its use as in 1768, when the *Annual Register* refers to the hatters having " struck " for a rise in wages. The derivation appears to be from the sailors' term of " striking " the mast, thus bringing the movement to a stop.

market. The rapidly changing processes and widening markets of English industry seemed to demand the sweeping away of all restrictions on the supply and employment of labour, a process which involved the levelling of all classes of wage-earners to their " natural wages." The first to feel the encroachment on their customary earnings were the woollen-workers employed by the capitalist clothiers of the Western counties. As the century advances we find trade after trade taking up the agitation against the new conditions, and such old-established clubs as the hatters and the woolcombers joining the general movement as soon as their own industries are menaced. To the skilled craftsman in the towns the new policy was brought home by the repeal of the regulations which protected his trade against an influx of pauper labour. His defence was to ask for the enforcement of the law relating to apprenticeship.[1] This would not have helped the operative in the staple textile industries. To him the new order took the form of constantly declining piecework rates. What he demanded, therefore, was the fixing of the " convenient proportion of wages " contemplated by Elizabethan legislation. But, whether craftsmen or factory operatives, the wage-earners turned, for the maintenance of their Standard of Life, to that protection by the law upon which they had been taught to rely. So long as each section of workers believed in the intention of the governing class to protect their trade from the results of unrestricted competition no community of interest arose. It was a change of industrial policy on the part of the Government that brought all trades into line, and for the first time produced what can properly be called a Trade Union Movement. In order, therefore, to make this movement fully intelligible, we must now retrace our steps, and follow the political history of industry in the eighteenth century.

[1] So much is this the case that Dr. Brentano asserts that " Trade Unions originated with the non-observance of " the Elizabethan Statute of Apprentices (p. 104), and that their primary object was, in all cases, the enforcement of the law on the subject.

The dominant industrial policy of the sixteenth century was the establishment of some regulating authority to perform, for the trade of the time, the services formerly rendered by the Craft Gilds. When, for instance, in the middle of the century the weavers found their customary earnings dwindling, they managed so far to combine as to make their voice heard at Westminster. In 1555 we find them complaining " that the rich and wealthy clothiers do many ways oppress them " by putting unapprenticed men to work on the capitalists' own looms, by letting out looms at rents, and " some also by giving much less wages and hire for the weaving and workmanship of clothes than in times past they did." [1]   To the Parliament of these days it seemed right and natural that the oppressed wage-earners should turn to the legislature to protect them against the cutting down of their earnings by the competing capitalists. The statutes of 1552 and 1555 forbid the use of the gig-mill, restrict the number of looms that one person may own to two in towns and one in the country, and absolutely prohibit the letting-out of looms for hire or rent. In 1563, indeed, Parliament expressly charged itself with securing to all wage-earners a " convenient " livelihood. The old laws fixing a maximum wage could not, in face of the enormous rise of prices, be put in force " without the great grief and burden of the poor labourer and hired man." Circumstances were changing too fast for any rigid rule. But by the celebrated " Statute of Apprentices " the statesmen of the time contrived arrangements which would, as they hoped, " yield unto the hired person, both in the time of scarcity and in the time of plenty, a convenient proportion of wages." Every year the justices of each locality were to meet, " and calling unto them such discreet and grave persons . . . as they shall think meet, and conferring together respecting the plenty or scarcity of the

---

[1] Preamble to " An Act touching Weavers " (2 and 3 Philip and Mary, c. xi.) ; see Froude's *History of England*, vol. i. pp. 57-9 ; and W. C. Taylor's *Modern Factory System*, pp. 53-5.

time," were to fix the wages of practically every kind of labour,[1] their decisions being enforceable by heavy penalties. Stringent regulations as to the necessity of apprenticeship, the length of its term, and the number of apprentices to be taken by each employer, received the confirmation of law. The typical ordinances of the mediæval gild were, in fact, enacted in minute detail in a comprehensive general statute applying to the greater part of the industry of the period.

We need not discuss the very debatable question whether this celebrated law was or was not advantageous to the labouring folk of the time, or whether and to what extent its provisions were actually put in force.[2] But codifying and enacting as it did the fundamental principles of the mediæval social order, we can scarcely be surprised that its adoption by Parliament confirmed the working man in the once universal belief in the essential justice and good policy securing by appropriate legislation " the getting of a competent livelihood " by all those concerned in industry.[3] Exactly the same view prevailed at the beginning of the eighteenth century. We again find the newly established associations of the operatives appealing to the King, to the House of Commons, or to Quarter Sessions against the beating down of their wages by their employers. For the first half of the century the governing classes continued to act on the assumption that the industrious mechanic had a right to the customary earnings of his trade. Thus in 1726 the weavers of Wilts and Somerset combine to petition

---

[1] As expanded by 1 James I. c. 6 and 16 Car. I. c. 4 ; see R. v. Justices of Kent, 14 East, 395.

[2] See on these points, Dr. Cunningham's *History of English Industry and Commerce*, Mr. Hewins' *English Trade and Finance chiefly in the 17th Century*, and Thorold Rogers' *History of Agriculture and Prices*, vol. v. pp. 625-6, etc. Adam Smith observes that the fixing of wages had, in 1776, " gone entirely into disuse " (*Wealth of Nations*, bk. i. ch. x. p. 65), a statement broadly true, although formal determinations of wages are found in the MS. Minutes of Quarter Sessions for another half century.

[3] This forms the constant refrain of the numerous broadsheets or *Tracts relating to Trade* of 1688-1750, which are preserved in the British Museum, the Guildhall Library, and in the Goldsmith Company's Library at the University of London.

the King against the harshness and fraud of their employers the clothiers, with the result that a Committee of the Privy Council investigates their grievances, and draws up " Articles of Agreement " for the settlement of the matters in dispute,[1] admonishing the weavers " for the future " not to attempt to help themselves by unlawful combinations, but always " to lay their grievances in a regular way before His Majesty, who would be always ready to grant them relief suitable to the justice of their case." [2] More often the operatives appealed to the House of Commons. In 1719 the " broad and narrow weavers " of Stroud and places round, petitioned Parliament to put down the tyrannical capitalist clothiers by enforcing the " Act touching Weavers " of 1555.[3] In 1728 the Gloucestershire operatives appealed to the local justices of the peace, and induced them, in spite of protests from the master clothiers, and apparently for the first time, to fix a liberal scale of wages for the weavers of the country.[4] Twenty years later the operatives obtained from Parliament a special prohibition of truck.[5] Finally, in 1756 they persuaded the House of Commons to pass an Act [6] providing for the fixing of piecework prices by the justices, in order that the practice of cutting down rates and underselling might be stopped. " A Table or Scheme for Rates of Wages " was accordingly settled at Quarter Sessions, November 6, 1756, with which the operatives were fairly contented.[7]

The next few years saw a revolutionary change in the industrial policy of the legislature which must have utterly

----

[1] Privy Council Minutes of 1726, p. 310 (unpublished) ; see also House of Commons Journals, vol. xx. p. 745 (February 20, 1726).

[2] Privy Council Minutes, February 4, 1726.

[3] House of Commons Journals, vol. xix. p. 181 (December 5, 1719).

[4] Petition of " Several weavers of Woollen Broadcloth on behalf of themselves and several thousands of the Fraternity of Woollen Broadcloth Weavers " (House of Commons Journals, vol. xxvii. p. 503 ; see also pp. 730-2).

[5] 22 Geo. II. c. 27.

[6] 29 Geo. II. c. 33.

[7] *Report of Committee on Petitions of West of England Clothiers*, House of Commons Journals, vol. xxvii. pp. 730-2.

bewildered the operatives. Within a generation the House of Commons exchanged its policy of mediæval protection for one of " Administrative Nihilism." The Woollen Cloth Weavers' Act of 1756 had not been one year in force when Parliament was assailed by numerous petitions and counter petitions. The employers declared that the rates fixed by the justices were, in face of the growing competition of Yorkshire, absolutely impracticable. The operatives, on the other hand, asked that the Act might be strengthened in their favour. The clothiers asserted the advantages of freedom of contract and unrestrained competition. The weavers received the support of the landowners and gentry in claiming the maintenance by law of their customary earnings. The perplexed House of Commons wavered between the two. At first a Bill was ordered to be drawn strengthening the existing law ; but ultimately the clothiers were held to have proved their case.[1] The Act of 1756 was, in 1757, unconditionally repealed ; and Parliament was now heading straight for *laisser-faire.*

The struggle over this Woollen Cloth Weavers' Act of 1756 marks the passage from the old ideas to the new. When, in 1776, the weavers, spinners, scribblers, and other woollen operatives of Somerset petitioned against the evil that was being done to their accustomed livelihood by the introduction of the spinning-jenny into Shepton Mallet, the House of Commons, which had two centuries before absolutely prohibited the gig-mill, refused even to allow the petition to be received.[2]

The change of policy had already affected another trade. The London Framework Knitters' Company, which had been incorporated in 1663 for the express purpose of regulating the trade, found itself during the first half of the eighteenth century in continual conflict with recalcitrant masters who set its bye-laws at defiance. This long struggle, in which the journeymen took vigorous action in support of

[1] For all these proceedings, see House of Commons Journals, vol. xxvii.
[2] House of Commons Journals, vol. xxxvi. p. 7 (November 1, 1776).

the Company, was brought to an end in 1753 by an exhaustive Parliamentary inquiry.   The bye-laws of the Company, upon the enforcement of which the journeymen had rested all their hopes, were solemnly declared to be " injurious and vexatious to the manufacturers," whilst the Company's authority was pronounced to be " hurtful to the trade." [1]   The total abandonment of all legal regulation of the trade led, after numerous transitory revolts, to the establishment in 1778 of " The Stocking Makers' Association for the Mutual Protection in the Midland Counties of England," having for its objects the limitation of apprentices, and the enactment of a fixed rate of wages.   Dr. Brentano has summarised the various attempts made by the operatives during the next two years to secure the protection of the legislature. [2]   Through the influence of their Union a sympathetic member was returned for the borough of Nottingham.   Investigation by a committee brought to light a degree of " sweating " scarcely paralleled even by the worst modern instances.   A Bill for the fixing of wages had actually passed its second reading when the employers, whipping up all their friends in the House, defeated it on the third reading—a rebuff to the workmen which led to serious riots at Nottingham, and thrust the unfortunate framework knitters back into despairing poverty. [3]

By this time the town craftsmen were also beginning to be menaced by the revolutionary proposals of their employers.   The hatters, for example, whose early combination we have already mentioned, had hitherto been protected by the strict limitation of the number of apprentices prescribed by the Acts of 1566 and 1603, and enforced by the Feltmakers' Company.   We gather from the employers' complaints that the journeymen's organisation, which by

[1] House of Commons Journals, April 13 and 19, 1753, vol. xxvi. pp. 764, 779 ; Felkin's *History of the Machine-wrought Hosiery and Lace Manufacture*, p. 80 ; Cunningham, *Growth of English Industry and Commerce in Modern Times*, 1903, vol. i. p. 663.
[2] *Gilds and Trade Unions*, pp. 115-21.
[3] House of Commons Journals, vols. xxxvi. and xxxvii.

this time extended to most of the provincial towns in which hats were made, was aiming at a strict enforcement of the law limiting the number of apprentices which each master might take. This caused the leading master hatters to promote, in 1777, a Bill to remove the limitation. Against them was marshalled the whole strength of the journeymen's organisation. Petitions poured in from London, Burton, Bristol, Chester, Liverpool, Hexham, Derby, and other places, the " piecemaster hat or feltmakers and finishers " usually joining with the journeymen against the demand of the capitalist employers. The men asserted that, even with the limitation, " except at brisk times many hundreds are obliged to go travelling up and down the kingdom in search of employ." But the House was impressed with the evidence and arguments of the large employers, and their Bill passed into law.[1]

The action of the House of Commons on occasions like these was not as yet influenced by any conscious theory of freedom of contract. What happened was that, as each trade in turn felt the effect of the new capitalist competition, the journeymen, and often also the smaller employers, would petition for redress, usually demanding the prohibition of the new machines, the enforcement of a seven years' apprenticeship, or the maintenance of the old limitation of the number of boys to be taught by each employer. The House would as a rule appoint a Committee to investigate the complaint, with the full intention of redressing the alleged grievance. But the large employers would produce before that Committee an overwhelming array of evidence proving that without the new machinery the growing export trade must be arrested ; that the new processes could be learnt in a few months instead of seven years ; and that the restriction of the old master-craftsmen to two or three apprentices apiece was out of the question with the new buyers of labour on a large scale. Confronted with such a

---

[1] House of Commons Journals, vol. xxxvi. pp. 192, 240, 268, 287, 1777; Act 17 Geo. III. c. 55, repealing 8 Eliz. c. 11, and 1 Jac. 1.

case as this for the masters even the most sympathetic committee seldom found it possible to endorse the proposals of the artisans.   In fact, these proposals were impossible. The artisans had a grievance—perhaps the worst that any class can have—the degradation of their standard of liveli- hood by circumstances which enormously increased the pro- ductivity of their labour.   But they mistook the remedy ; and Parliament, though it saw the mistake, could devise nothing better.   Common sense forced the Government to take the easy and obvious step of abolishing the mediæval regulations which industry had outgrown.   But the problem of protecting the workers' Standard of Life under the new conditions was neither easy nor obvious, and it remained unsolved until the nineteenth century discovered the ex- pedients of Collective Bargaining and Factory Legislation, developing, in the twentieth century, into the fixing by law of a Minimum Wage.   In the meantime the workers were left to shift for themselves, the attitude of Parliament to- wards them being for the first years one of pure perplexity, quite untouched by the doctrine of freedom of contract.

That the House of Commons remained innocent of any general theory against legislative interference long after it had begun the work of sweeping away the mediæval regula- tions is proved by the famous case of the Spitalfields silk- weavers, in which the old policy of industrial regulation was reverted to.   In 1765 the Spitalfields weavers protested that they were without employment, owing to the importa- tion of foreign silk.   Assembling in crowds, they marched in processions to Westminster, headed by bands and banners, and demanded the prohibition of the import of the foreign product.   Riots occurred sufficiently serious to induce Par- liament to pass an Act in the terms desired ; [1] but this experiment in Protection failed to maintain wages, and the riots were renewed in 1769.   Finally Sir John Fielding, the well-known London police magistrate, suggested to the

---

[1] 5 Geo. III. c. 48 ; see *Annual Register*, 1765, p. 41 ; Cunningham, *Growth of English Industry and Commerce in Modern Times*, 1903, pp. 519, 796.

London silkweavers that they should secure their earnings by an Act.[1] Under the pressure of another outbreak of rioting in 1773, Parliament adopted this proposal, and empowered the justices to fix the rates of wages and to enforce their maintenance. The effect of this enactment upon the men's combination is significant. " A great man " had told the weavers, as one of them relates, that the governing class " made laws, and we, the people, must make legs to them." [2] The ephemeral combination to obtain the Act became accordingly a permanent union to enforce it. From this time forth we hear no more of strikes or riots among the Spitalfields weavers. Instead, we see arising a permanent machinery, designated the " Union," for the representation, before the justices, of both masters and men, upon whose evidence the complicated lists of piecework rates are periodically settled. Clearly the Parliaments which passed the Spitalfields Acts of 1765 and 1773 had no conception of the political philosophy of Adam Smith, whose *Wealth of Nations*, afterwards to be accepted as the English gospel of freedom of contract and " natural liberty," was published in 1776. At the same time, so exceptional had such acts become, that when Adam Smith's masterpiece came into the hands of the statesmen of the time, it must have seemed not so much a novel view of industrial economics as the explicit generalisation of practical conclusions to which experience had already repeatedly driven them.

Towards the end of the century the governing classes, who had found in the new industrial policy a source of enormous pecuniary profit, eagerly seized on the new economic theory as an intellectual and moral justification of that policy. The abandonment of the operatives by the law, previously resorted to under pressure of circumstances, and, as we gather, not without some remorse, was now carried out on principle, with unflinching determination.

[1] Act 13 Geo. III. c. 68 ; see *A Short Historical Account of the Silk Manufacture in England*, by Samuel Sholl, 1811
[2] *Ibid.* p. 4.

When the handloom-weavers, earning little more than a
third of the livelihood they had gained ten years before,
and unable to realise that the factory system would be
deliberately allowed to ruin them, made themselves heard
in the House of Commons in 1808, a Committee reported
against their proposal to fix a minimum rate of wages on
the ground that it was " wholly inadmissible in principle,
incapable of being reduced to practice by any means which
can possibly be devised, and, if practicable, would be productive of the most fatal consequences " ; and " that the
proposition relative to the limiting the number of apprentices
is also entirely inadmissible, and would, if adopted by the
House, be attended with the greatest injustice to the manufacturer as well as to the labourer." [1]   Here we have *laisser-
faire* fully established in Parliament as an authoritative
industrial doctrine of political economy, able to overcome
the great bulk of the evidence given before this Committee,
which was decidedly in favour of the minimum wage.   The
House of Commons had no lack of opportunities for educat-
ing itself on the question.   The special misery caused by
bad harvests and the prolonged war between 1793 and
1815 [2] brought a rush of appeals, especially from the newly
established associations of cotton operatives.   In the early
years of the present century petition after petition poured
in from Lancashire and Glasgow, showing that the rates for
weaving had steadily declined, and reiterating the old
demands for a legally fixed scale of piecework rates and the
limitation of apprentices.   In 1795, and again in 1800, and
once more in 1808, Bills fixing a minimum rate were introduced into the House of Commons, sometimes meeting with
considerable favour.   The report of the Committee of 1808,
which took voluminous evidence on the subject, has already
been quoted.   Petitions from the calico-printers for a legal

---

[1] *Reports on Petitions of Cotton Weavers, 1809 and 1811.*
[2] " The period between 1795 and 1815 was characterised by dearths
which on several occasions became well-nigh famines " (Thorold Rogers,
History of Agriculture and Prices, vol. i. p. 692).

limitation of the number of apprentices, although warmly supported by the Select Committee to which they were referred, met with the same fate. Sheridan, indeed, was not convinced, and brought in a Bill proposing, among other things, to limit the number of apprentices. But Sir Robert Peel (the elder), whose own factories swarmed with boys, opposed it in the name of industrial freedom, and carried the House of Commons with him.[1]

Meanwhile the despairing operatives, baffled in their attempts to procure fresh legislation, turned for aid to the existing law. Unrepealed statutes still enabled the justices in some trades to fix the rate of wages, limited in others the number of apprentices ; in others, again, prohibited certain kinds of machinery, and forbade any but apprenticed men to exercise the trade. So completely had these statutes fallen into disuse that their very existence was in many instances unknown to the artisans. The West of England weavers, however, combined with those of Yorkshire in 1802 to employ an attorney, who took proceedings against employers for infringing the old laws. The result was that Parliament hastily passed an Act suspending these statutes, in order to put a stop to the prosecutions.[2] " At a numerous meeting of the cordwainers of the City of New Sarum in 1784," says an old circular that we have seen, " it was unanimously resolved . . . that a subscription be entered into for putting the law in force against infringements on the Trade," but apparently without result.[3] The Edinburgh

---

[1] *Minutes of Evidence and Report of the Committee on the Petition of the Journeymen Calico-printers,* July 4, 1804, July 17, 1806. See also Sheridan's speech reported in Hansard's Parliamentary Debates, vol. ix. pp. 534-8.

[2] 43 Geo. III. c. 136, continued in successive years until the definite repeal, in 1809, of most of the laws regulating the woollen manufacture by 49 Geo. III. c. 109 ; see Cunningham, 1903, vol. ii. p. 659.

[3] It was reprinted in the 121st Quarterly Report of the Amalgamated Society of Boot and Shoemakers. The proceedings were taken by the Friendly Society of Cordwainers of England, " instituted the 15th of November 1784." Particulars of the London Bootmakers' Society, which was in correspondence with seventy or eighty provincial societies, are given in *A Digest of the Evidence before the Committee on Artizans and Machinery.* by George White, 1824, p. 97.

compositors were more successful ; on being refused an advance of wages, to correspond with the rise in the cost of living, they presented, February 28, 1804, a memorial to the Court of Session, and obtained the celebrated " Interlocutor " of 1805, which fixed a scale of piecework prices for the Edinburgh printing trade.[1] But the chief event of this campaign for the enforcement of the old laws began in Glasgow. The cotton-weavers of that city, after four or five years of Parliamentary agitation for additional legislation, resorted to the law empowering the justices to fix the rates of wages. After an unsuccessful attempt to fix a standard rate by agreement with a committee of employers, the men's association which now extended throughout the whole of the cotton-weaving districts in the United Kingdom commenced legal proceedings at the Lanarkshire Quarter Sessions. The employers in 1812 disputed the competence of the magistrates, and appealed to the Court of Sessions at Edinburgh. The Court held that the magistrates were competent to fix a scale of wages, and a table of piecework rates was accordingly drawn up. The employers immediately withdrew from the proceedings ; but the operatives were nevertheless compelled, at great expense, to produce witnesses to testify to every one of the numerous rates proposed. After one hundred and thirty witnesses had been heard, the magistrates at length declared the rates to be reasonable, but made no actual order enforcing them. The employers, with few exceptions, refused to accept the table, which it had cost the operatives £3000 to obtain. The result was the most extensive strike the trade has ever known. From Carlisle to Aberdeen every loom stopped, forty thousand weavers ceasing work almost simultaneously. After three weeks' strike the employers

---

[1] Professor Foxwell kindly placed at our disposal a unique series of pamphlets relating to these proceedings, which are now in the Goldsmiths Company's Library at the University of London, including the *Memorials* of the journeymen and the employers, the *Report in the Process* by Robert Bell, and the *Scale of Prices* as settled by the Court. A full account of the proceedings is given in the *Scottish Typographical Circular*, June 1858.

were preparing to meet the operatives, when the whole
Strike Committee was suddenly arrested by the police, and
held to bail under the common law for the crime of combination, of which the authorities, in that revolutionary
period, were very jealous on purely political grounds. The
five leaders were sentenced to terms of imprisonment varying from four to eighteen months ; and this blow broke up
the combination, defeated the strike, and put an end to
the struggles of the operatives against the progressive
degradation of their wages.[1]

The London artisans, though they were not put down
by prosecution and imprisonment, met with no greater
success than their Glasgow brethren. Between 1810 and
1812 a number of trade societies combined to engage the
services of a solicitor, who prosecuted masters for employing
" illegal men," that is to say, men who had not by apprenticeship gained a right to follow the trade. The original " case "
which the journeymen curriers submitted to counsel in
1810 (fee two guineas), with a view to putting in force the
Statute of Apprentices, was in our possession, together
with the somewhat hesitating opinion of the legal adviser.[2]
In a few cases proceedings were even taken against employers
for having set up in trades to which they had not themselves
served their time. Convictions were obtained in some
instances ; but no costs were allowed to the prosecutors,
who were, on the other hand, condemned to pay heavy
costs when they failed. Lord Ellenborough, moreover, held
on appeal that new trades, such as those of engineer and
lockmaker, were not included within the Elizabethan Act.
In 1811 certain journeymen millers of Kent petitioned the
justices to fix a rate of wages under the Elizabethan Act.
When the justices refused to hear the petition a writ of

---

[1] See, for these proceedings, the two *Reports of the Committee on the
Petitions of the Cotton Weavers*, April 12, 1808, and March 29, 1809 ; and
Richmond's evidence before the Committee on Artisans and Machinery,
1824, Second Report, pp. 59-64.
[2] It is now in the British Library of Political Science at the London
School of Economics.

mandamus was applied for.   Lord Ellenborough granted
the writ to compel them to hear the petition, but said they
were to exercise their own discretion as to whether they
would fix any rate.   The justices, on this hint, declined to
fix the wages.[1]   It soon became apparent that legal proceedings under these obsolete statutes were, in face of the
adverse bias of the courts, as futile as they were costly.
There was nothing for it then but either to abandon the
line of attack or to petition Parliament to make effective
the still unrepealed laws.   This they accordingly did, with
the unexpected result that the " pernicious " law empowering
justices to fix wages was in 1813 peremptorily repealed.[2]

The law thus swept away was but one section of the
great Elizabethan statute, and its repeal left the other
clauses untouched.   A Select Committee had already,
in 1811, reported that " no interference of the legislature
with the freedom of trade, or with the perfect liberty of
every individual to dispose of his time and of his labour
in the way and on the terms which he may judge most
conducive to his own interest, can take place without
violating general principles of the first importance to the
prosperity and happiness of the community ;   without
establishing the most pernicious precedent, or even without
aggravating, after a very short time, the pressure of the
general distress, and imposing obstacles against that distress
being ever removed."   The repeal of the wages clauses
of the statute made this emphatic declaration of the new
doctrine law as far as the fixing of wages was concerned ;
but there remained the apprenticeship clauses.   Petitions
for the enforcement of these, and their extension to the new
trades, kept pouring in.   They were finally referred to a
large and influential committee which included Canning,
Huskisson, Sir Robert Peel, and Sir James Graham among
its members.   The witnesses examined were strongly in

[1] R. *v.* Justices of Kent, 14 East, 395 ;   see F. D. Longe's *Inquiry into
the Law of Strikes*, 1860, pp. 10, 11.
[2] 53 Geo. III. c. 40 (1813).

favour of the retention of the laws, with amendments bringing them up to date. The chairman (George Rose) was apparently converted to the view of the operatives by the evidence. The committee, which had undoubtedly been appointed to formulate the complete abolition of the apprenticeship clauses, found itself unable to fulfil its virtual mandate. Not venturing, in the teeth of the manufacturers and economists, to recommend the House to comply with the operatives' demands, it got out of the difficulty by making no recommendation at all. Hundreds of petitions in favour of the laws continued to pour in from all parts of the country, 300,000 signatures being for retention against 2000 for repeal, masters often joining in the journeymen's prayer. A public meeting of the " Master Manufacturers and Tradesmen of the Cities of London and Westminster," at the Freemasons' Tavern, passed resolutions strongly supporting the amendment and enforcement of the existing law. On the other hand, a committee on which the master engineers Maudsley and Galloway were prominent members, argued forcibly in favour of freedom and against " the monstrous and alarming but misguided association." In 1814 Mr. Serjeant Onslow, who had not served on the committee of the previous session, introduced a Bill to repeal the whole apprenticeship law. The " Masters and Journeymen of Westminster " were heard by counsel against this measure, but the House had made up its mind in favour of the manufacturers, and by the Act of 54 Geo. III. c. 96 swept away the apprenticeship clauses of the statute, and with them practically the last remnant of that legislative protection of the Standard of Life which survived from the Middle Ages.[1] The triumphant manufacturers presented Serjeant Onslow with several pieces of plate for his championship of commercial liberty.[2]

[1] The Spitalfields Acts, relating to the silkweavers, were, however, not repealed until 1824 ; and the last sections of 5 Eliz. c. 4 were not formally repealed until 1875.

[2] White's *Digest of all the laws at present in existence respecting Masters and Workpeople*, 1824, p. 59. Place wrote to Wakefield, January 2, 1814.

So thoroughly had the new doctrine by this time driven out the very recollection of the old ideals from the mind of the governing class that it was now the operatives who were regarded as innovators, and we are hardly surprised to find another committee gravely declaring that " the right of every man to employ the capital he inherits, or has acquired, according to his own discretion, without molestation or obstruction, so long as he does not infringe on the rights or property of others, is one of those privileges which the free and happy constitution of this country has long accustomed every Briton to consider as his birthright." [1] But it must be added that the governing class was by no means impartial in the application of its new doctrine. Mediæval regulation acted not only in restriction of free competition in the labour market to the pecuniary loss of the employers, but also in restriction of free contract to the loss of the employees, who could only obtain the best terms for their labour by collective instead of individual bargaining. Consequently the operatives, if they had clearly understood the situation, would have been as anxious

---

" The affair of Serjeant Onslow partly originated with me, but I had no suspicion it would be taken up and pushed as vigorously as it has been and is likely to be " (*Life of Francis Place*, by Prof. Graham Wallas, p. 159).

The proceedings in this matter can be best traced in the House of Commons Journals for 1813 and 1814, vols. lxviii. and lxix.; and in Hansard's Parliamentary Debates, vols. xxv. and xxvii. The master's case is given in a pamphlet, *The Origin, Object, and Operation of the Apprentice Laws*, 1814, 26 pp., preserved in the *Pamphleteer*, vol. iii. The *Resolutions of the Master Manufacturers and Tradesmen of the Cities of London and Westminster on the Statute 5 Eliz. c. 4*, 1814, 4 pp., gives the contrary view (B.M. 1882, d. 2). The contemporary argument for freedom is expressed in *An Estimate of the Comparative Strength of Great Britain*, by G. Chalmers, 1810; see *Cunningham*, 1903, vol. ii. p. 660. The Nottingham Library possesses a unique copy of the *Articles and General Regulations of a Society for obtaining Parliamentary Relief, and the Encouragement of Mechanics in the Improvement of Mechanism*, printed at Nottingham in 1813. This appears to have been a federation of framework knitters' societies, and possibly others, for Parliamentary action, as well as trade protection; and its establishment in 1813 was perhaps connected with the movement for the revival of the Apprenticeship Laws.

[1] *Report of the Committee on the State of the Woollen Manufacture in England*, July 4, 1806, p. 12.

to abolish the laws against combination as to maintain those fixing wages and limiting apprenticeship ; just as the capitalists, better informed, were no less resolute in maintaining the anti-combination laws than in repealing the others. We shall presently see how slow the workers were to realise this, in spite of the fact that the laws against combinations of workmen were maintained in force, and even increased in severity. Strikes, and any organised resistance to the employers' demands, were put down with a high hand. The first twenty years of the nineteenth century witnessed a legal persecution of Trade Unionists as rebels and revolutionists. This persecution, thwarting the healthy growth of the Unions, and driving their members into violence and sedition, but finally leading to the repeal of the Combination Laws and the birth of the modern Trade Union Movement, will be the subject of the next chapter.

CHAPTER II

[1799–1825]

THE traditional history of the Trade Union Movement represents the period prior to 1824 as one of unmitigated persecution and continuous repression. Every Union that can nowadays claim an existence of over a century possesses a romantic legend of its early years. The midnight meeting of patriots in the corner of a field, the buried box of records, the secret oath, the terms of imprisonment of the leading officials—all these are in the sagas of the older Unions, and form material out of which, in an age untroubled by historical criticism, a semi-mythical origin might easily have been created. That the legend is not without a basis of fact, we shall see in tracing the actual effect upon the Trade Union Movement of the legal prohibitions of combinations of wage-earners which prevailed throughout the United Kingdom up to 1824. But we shall find that some combinations of journeymen were at all times recognised by the law, that many others were only spasmodically interfered with, and that the utmost rigour of the Combination Laws was not felt until the far-reaching change of policy marked by the severe Acts of 1799–1800, which applied to all industries whatsoever. This will lead us naturally to the story of the repeal of the whole series of Combination Laws in 1824–5, the most impressive event in the early history of the movement.

There is a clear distinction—at any rate, as regards England—between the various statutes which forbade combination prior to the end of the eighteenth century, and the general Combination Acts of 1799–1800. In the numerous earlier Acts recited and repealed in 1824 the prohibition of combination was in all cases incidental to the regulation of the industry. It was assumed to be the business of Parliament and the law courts to regulate the conditions of labour ; and combinations could, no more than individuals, be permitted to interfere in disputes for which a legal remedy was provided. The object primarily aimed at by the statutes was not the prohibition of combinations, but the fixing of wages, /the prevention of embezzlement or damage, the enforcement of the contract of service or the proper arrange-/ ments for apprenticeship. And although combinations to interfere with these statutory aims were obviously illegal, and were usually expressly prohibited, it was an incidental result that combinations formed to promote the objects of the legislation, however objectionable they might be to employers, were apparently not regarded as unlawful.[1]

Thus one of the earliest types of combination among journeymen—the society to enforce the law—seems always to have been tacitly accepted as permissible. Although it is probable that such associations came technically within the definitions of combination and conspiracy, whether under the common law or the early statutes, we know of no case in which they were indicted as illegal. We have already described, for instance, how, in 1726, the woollen weavers of Wiltshire and Somersetshire openly combined to present a petition to the King in Council against their masters, the broad clothiers. The Privy Council, far from deeming the action of the weavers illegal, considered and dealt with their complaint. And when the employers persisted in disobeying the law, we have seen how, in 1756, the

---

[1] An elaborate account of this legislation will be found in *Labour Legislation, Labour Movements, and Labour Leaders*, by G. Howell, 1902, pp. 21-42.

D

Fraternity of Woollen Clothweavers petitioned the House
of Commons to make more effectual the power of the justices
to fix wages, and obtained a new Act of Parliament in accordance with their desires. The almost perpetual combinations
of the framework knitters between 1710 and 1800 were
never made the subject of legal proceedings. The combinations of the London silkweavers obtained a virtual
sanction by the Spitalfields Acts, under which the delegates
of the workmen's organisations regularly appeared before
the justices, who fixed and revised the piecework prices.
Even in 1808, after the stringency of the law against combinations had been greatly increased, the Glasgow and Lancashire cottonweavers were permitted openly to combine for
the purpose of seeking a legal fixing of wages, with the
results already described. Nor was it only the combination to obtain a legally fixed rate of wages that was left
unmolested by the law. Combinations to put in force the
sections of the Statute of Apprentices (5 Eliz. c. 4), or
other prohibitions of the employment of " illegal workmen,"
occurred at intervals down to 1813. In 1749 a club of
journeymen painters of the City of London proceeded against
a master painter for employing a non-freeman ; and the
proceedings led, in 1750, to a conference of thirty journeymen and thirty masters with the City Corporation, at which
the regulations were altered.[1]   No one seems to have questioned the legality of the 1811–13 outburst of combinations
to prosecute masters who had not served an apprenticeship,
or who were employing unapprenticed workmen. One
reason, doubtless, for the immunity of combinations to
enforce the law was that they included employers and
sympathisers of all ranks. For instance, the combinations
in 1811–13 to enforce the apprenticeship laws comprised
both masters and journeymen, who were equally aggrieved

---

[1] Act of Common Council, November 22, 1750 : Hughson's *London*,
p. 422.   There is evidence of at least one other club of painters in London
dating back to the eighteenth century. the " Original Society of Painters
and Glaziers " existing in 1779, which afterwards became the St. Martin's
Society of Painters and Glaziers (*Beehive*, October 24, 1863).

by the competition of the new capitalist and his " hire-
lings." [1] The Yorkshire Clothiers' Community, or " Brief
Institution," to which reference has already been made,
included, in some of its ramifications, the " domestic "
master manufacturers, who fought side by side with the
journeymen against the new factory system.

On the other hand, combinations of journeymen to
regulate for themselves their wages and conditions of
employment stood, from the first, on a different footing.
The common law doctrine of the illegality of proceedings
" in restraint of trade," as subsequently interpreted by the
judges, of itself made illegal all combinations whatsoever
of journeymen to regulate the conditions of their work.
Moreover, with the regulation by law of wages and the
conditions of employment, any combination to resist the
order of the justices on these matters was obviously of the
nature of rebellion, and was, in fact, put down like any
individual disobedience of the law. Nor was express statute
law against combinations wanting. The statute of 1305,
entitled, " Who be Conspirators and who be Champertors "
(33 Edw. I. st. 2), was in 1818 held to apply to a combination to raise wages among cotton-spinners, whose leaders
were sentenced to two years' imprisonment under this
Act. The " Bill of Conspiracies of Victuallers and Craftsmen " of 1549 (2 and 3 Edw. VI. c. 15), though aimed
primarily at combinations to keep up the prices charged to
consumers, clearly includes within its prohibitions any combinations of journeymen craftsmen to keep up wages or
reduce hours.

It is some proof of the novelty of the workmen's combinations in the early part of the eighteenth century, that
neither the employers nor the authorities thought at first
of resorting to the very sufficient powers of the existing law
against them. When, in 1720, the master tailors of London

---

[1] This term was used to denote men who had not served a legal apprenticeship. See " Rules and Regulations of the Journeymen Weavers,"
reprinted in Appendix No. 10 to Report on Combination Laws, 1825.

found themselves confronted with an organised body of
journeymen claiming to make a collective bargain, seriously
" in restraint of trade," they turned, not to the law courts,
but to Parliament for protection, and obtained, as we have
seen, the Act " for regulating the Journeymen Tailors within
the bills of mortality " (7 Geo. I. st. 1, c. 13, amended by
8 Geo. III. c. 17).[1] Similarly, when the clothiers of the
West of England began between 1717 and 1725 to be inconvenienced by the " riotous and tumultuous clubs and
societies " of woolcombers and weavers, who made bye-laws
and maintained a Standard Rate,[2] they did not put in force
the existing law, but successfully petitioned Parliament for
the Act " to prevent unlawful combinations of workmen
employed in the Woollen Manufactures " (12 Geo. I. c. 34).
Indeed, prior to the general Acts of 1799 and 1800 against
all combinations of journeymen, Parliament was, from the
beginning of the eighteenth century, perpetually enacting
statutes forbidding combinations in particular trades.[3]

In the English statutes this prohibition of combination
was, as we have seen, only a secondary feature, incidental
to the main purpose of the law.   The case is different with
regard to the early Irish Acts, the terms of which point to
a much sharper cleavage between masters and men, due,
perhaps, to difference of religion and race.   The very first
statute against combinations which was passed by the Irish
Parliament, the Act of 1729 (3 Geo. II. c. 14), contained no
provisions protecting the wage-earner, and prohibited com-

---

[1] The case of R. *v.* the Journeymen Tailors of Cambridge in 1721
(8 Mod. 10) is obscurely reported ; and it is uncertain under what law the
men were convicted.   See Wright's *Law of Criminal Conspiracies and
Agreements*, p. 53.

[2] See the petitions from Devonshire towns, House of Commons Journals,
1717, vol. xviii. p. 715, which, with others in subsequent years, led to a
Select Committee in 1726 (Journals, vol. xx. p. 648, March 31, 1726).

[3] See, for instance, the Acts regulating the woollen industry, 12 Geo. I.
c. 34 (1725) ; against embezzlement or fraud by shoemakers, 9 Geo. I.
c. 27 (1729) ; relating to hatters, 22 Geo. II. c. 27 (1749) ; to silkweavers,
17 Geo. III. c. 55 (1777) ; and to papermaking, 36 Geo. III. c. 111 (1795).
Whitbread declared in the House of Commons that there were in 1800 no
fewer than forty such statutes.

binations in all trades whatsoever. The Act of 1743 (17 Geo. II. c. 8), called forth by the failure of the previous prohibition, equally confined itself to drastic penal measures, including the punishment of the keepers of the public-houses which were used for meetings. But in later years the English practice seems to have been followed ; for the laws of 1758 (31 Geo. II. c. 17), 1763 (3 Geo. III. 34, sec. 23), 1771 (11 and 12 Geo. III. c. 18, sec. 40, and c. 33), and 1779 (19 and 20 Geo. III. c. 19, c. 24, and c. 36) provide for the fixing of wages, and contain other regulations of industry, amongst which the prohibition of combinations comes as a matter of course.

By the end of the century, at any rate, the common law, both in England and in Ireland, had been brought to the aid of the special statutes, and the judges were ruling that any conspiracy to do an act which they considered unlawful in a combination, even if not criminal in an individual, was against the common law. Soon the legislature followed suit. In 1799 the Act 39 Geo. III. c. 81 expressly penalised all combinations whatsoever.

The grounds for this drastic measure appear to have been found in the marked increase of Trade Unionism among workers of various kinds. The operatives' combinations were regarded as being in the nature of mutiny against their employers and masters; destructive of the " discipline " necessary to the expansion of trade ; and interfering with the right of the employer to " do what he liked with his own." The immediate occasion was a petition from London engineering employers, complaining of an alarming strike of the millwrights. This led to a Bill suppressing combination in the engineering trade, which was passed by the House of Commons, in spite of the protests of Sir Francis Burdett and Benjamin Hobhouse. The measure was, however, dropped in the House of Lords in favour of a more comprehensive Bill, applicable to all trades, which Wilberforce had suggested. This was introduced on June 17, 1799, by William Pitt himself, then Chancellor of the Exchequer, who referred to the alarming growth of combination, not merely in the Metropolis but also in the north of England. Subsequent stages of the Bill were moved by George Rose, another member of the Administration ; and the measure was hurried through all its stages in both Houses with great rapidity, receiving the Royal Assent only twenty-four days after its introduction into the House of Commons. There was therefore little opportunity for any effective demonstration against its provisions, but the Journeymen Calicoprinters' Society of London petitioned against the measure, and instructed counsel to put forward their objections. They represented that, although the Bill professed merely "to prevent unlawful combinations," it created "new crimes of so indefinite a nature that no one journeyman or workman will be safe in holding any conversation with another on the subject of his trade or employment." Only a few other petitions were presented, and, though Benjamin Hobhouse opposed it in the Commons and Lord Holland in the Lords, the Bill passed unaltered into law.[1]

But the struggle was not yet over. The employers were not satisfied with the 1799 Act ; and *The Times* announced in January 1800 that "one of the first Acts of the Imperial Parliament [of the United Kingdom] will be for the preven-

---

[1] *A Full and Accurate Report of the Proceedings of the Petitioners, etc.* By One of the Petitioners (London, January 1800, 19 pp.). A rare pamphlet in the Goldsmiths' Library at the University of London. "It is remarkable," says Mr. Justice Stephen, "that in the parliamentary history for 1799 and 1800 there is no account of any debate on these Acts, nor are they referred to in the Annual Register for those years" (*History of the Criminal Law*, vol. iii. p. 208). That the measure excited some interest in the textile districts may be inferred from the publication at Leeds of a pamphlet entitled an *Abstract of an Act to prevent Unlawful Combinations among Journeymen to raise Wages, etc.* (Leeds, 1799), which is in the Manchester Public Library (P. 1735). Lord Holland's speeches against it are said to have been reprinted for distribution in Manchester and Liverpool (Lady Holland's *Journal*, vol. ii. p. 102).

Mr. and Mrs. Hammond have now traced fairly full accounts of the proceedings, elucidating the scanty references in the Journals of the House of Commons and House of Lords for 1799–1800 by quotations from the *Parliamentary Register*, the *Senator*, *The Times*, *London Chronicle*, *True Briton*, and *Morning Post*. See *The Town Labourer*, 1917, ch. vii. pp 111-42 ; also Cunningham, *Growth, etc.*, 1903, pp. 732-7.

tion of conspiracies among journeymen tradesmen to raise their wages. All benefit clubs and societies are to be immediately suppressed."[1] On the other hand, the trade clubs in all parts of the country poured in petitions of protest; and the Whig and Tory members for Liverpool, General Tarleton and Colonel Gascoyne, among whose constituents were the strongly combined shipwrights, who were freemen and Parliamentary electors, united to bring in an amending Bill. This was supported in a series of brilliant speeches by Sheridan, whose attempts to reduce to a minimum the mischief of the 1799 Act were strenuously resisted by Pitt and the Law Officers of the Crown. The petitions were considered by a Committee, which recommended certain amendments. Two justices were substituted for one as the tribunal; no justice engaged in the same trade as the defendant could act; the qualifying words " wilfully and maliciously " were introduced in the description of the offences. A clause protecting trade friendly societies was proposed but eventually rejected. A particularly odious feature of the 1799 Act, under which defendants were required to give evidence against themselves under severe penalties for refusal, was left unaltered. A series of interesting clauses providing for the reference of wage disputes to arbitration—copied from the contemporary Act relating to the cotton trade [2]—aroused great opposition, as tending " to fix wages " and as involving the recognition of the Trade Union representative, but they were finally adopted; without, so far as we are aware, ever being put in force.[3]

The general Combination Act of 1800 was not merely the codification of existing laws, or their extension from

---

[1] *Times*, January 7, 1800; *Labour Legislation, Labour Movements, and Labour Leaders*, by George Howell, 1902, p. 23.

[2] 39 and 40 George III. c. 90; see *Cunningham*, 1903, p. 634.

[3] 39 and 40 George III. c. 60; see, for all this, *The Town Labourer*, *1760–1832*, by J. L. and B. Hammond, 1917, ch. vii. A case in which an attempt to put the arbitration clauses in force was baulked by the employers was mentioned to the Committee on Artisans and Machinery, 1824, p. 603.

particular trades to the whole field of industry. It represented a new and momentous departure. Hitherto the
central or local authority had acted as a court of appeal
on all questions affecting the work and wages of the citizen.
If the master and journeyman failed to agree as to what
constituted a fair day's wage for a fair day's work, the
higgling of the market was peremptorily superseded by the
authoritative determination, presumably on grounds of
social expediency, of the standard of remuneration.   Probably the actual fixing of wages by justices of the peace fell
very rapidly into disuse as regards the majority of industries,
although formal orders are found in the minutes of Quarter
Sessions during the first quarter of the nineteenth century,
and deep traces of the practice long survived in the customary rates of hiring.   Towards the end of the eighteenth
century, at any rate, free bargaining between the capitalist
and his workmen became practically the sole method of
fixing wages.   Then it was that the gross injustice of prohibiting combinations of journeymen became apparent.
" A single master," said Lord Jeffrey, " was at liberty at
any time to turn off the whole of his workmen at once—
100 or 1000 in number—if they would not accept of the
wages he chose to offer.   But it was made an offence for
the whole of the workmen to leave that master at once if
he refused to give the wages they chose to require." [1]   What
was even more oppressive in practice was the employers'
use of the threat of prosecution to prevent even the beginnings of resistance among the workmen to any reduction
of wages or worsening of conditions.

It is true that the law forbade combinations of employers
as well as combinations of journeymen.   Even if it had
been impartially carried out, there would still have remained
the inequality due to the fact that, in the new system of
industry, a single employer was himself equivalent to a

---

[1] *Combinations of Workmen : Substance of the Speech of Francis Jeffrey
at the Dinner to Joseph Hume, M.P., at Edinburgh, November 18, 1825*
(Edinburgh, 1825).

very numerous combination. But the hand of justice was not impartial. The " tacit, but constant " combination of employers to depress wages, to which Adam Smith refers, could not be reached by the law. Nor was there any disposition on the part of the magistrates or the judges to find the masters guilty, even in cases of flagrant or avowed combination. No one prosecuted the master cutlers who, in 1814, openly formed the Sheffield Mercantile and Manufacturing Union, having for its main rule that no merchant or manufacturer should pay higher prices for any article of Sheffield make than were current in the preceding year, with a penalty of £100 for each contravention of this illegal agreement.[1] During the whole epoch of repression, whilst thousands of journeymen suffered for the crime of combination, there is no case on record in which an employer was punished for the same offence.

To the ordinary politician a combination of employers and a combination of workmen seemed in no way comparable. The former was, at most, an industrial misdemeanour : the latter was in all cases a political crime. Under the shadow of the French Revolution, the English governing classes regarded all associations of the common people with the utmost alarm. In this general terror lest insubordination should develop into rebellion were merged both the capitalist's objection to high wages and the politician's dislike of Democratic institutions. The Combination Laws, as Francis Place tells us, " were considered as absolutely necessary to prevent ruinous extortions of workmen, which, if not thus restrained, would destroy the whole of the Trade, Manufactures, Commerce, and Agriculture of the nation. . . . This led to the conclusion that the workmen were the most unprincipled of mankind. Hence the continued ill-will, suspicion, and in almost every possible way the bad conduct of workmen and their employers towards one another. So thoroughly was this false notion entertained that whenever men were prosecuted to con-

[1] *Sheffield Iris*, March 23, 1814.

viction for having combined to regulate their wages or the hours of working, however heavy the sentence passed on them was, and however rigorously it was inflicted, not the slightest feeling of compassion was manifested by anybody for the unfortunate sufferers. Justice was entirely out of the question : they could seldom obtain a hearing before a magistrate, never without impatience or insult ; and never could they calculate on even an approximation to a rational conclusion. . . . Could an accurate account be given of proceedings, of hearings before magistrates, trials at sessions and in the Court of King's Bench, the gross injustice, the foul invective, and terrible punishments inflicted would not, after a few years have passed away, be credited on any but the best evidence." [1]

It must not, however, be supposed that every combination was made the subject of prosecution, or that the Trade Union leader of the period passed his whole life in gaol. Owing to the extremely inefficient organisation of the English police, and the absence of any public prosecutor, a combination was usually let alone until some employer was sufficiently inconvenienced by its operations to be willing himself to set the law in motion. In many cases we find employers apparently accepting or conniving at their men's combinations.[2] The master printers in London not only recognised the very ancient institution of the " chapel," but evidently found it convenient, at any rate from 1785 onwards, to receive and consider proposals from the journeymen as an organised body. In 1804 we even hear of a joint committee consisting of an equal number of masters and journeymen, authorised by their respective bodies to frame regulations for the future payment of labour, and resulting in the elaborate " scale " of 1805, signed by both masters and men.[3] The London coopers had a recognised organisa-

---

[1] Place MSS. 27798—7. The Act of 1800 was scathingly denounced by Cobbett in the *Political Register*, August 30, 1823.

[2] This is a constant subject of complaint by other employers.

[3] Introduction to the London Scale of Prices (in London Society of Compositors' volume).

tion in 1813, in which year a list of prices was agreed upon by representatives of the masters and men. This list was revised in 1816 and 1819, without any one thinking of a prosecution.[1] The Trade Union was openly reformed in 1821 as the Philanthropic Society of Coopers. The London brushmakers in 1805 had " A List of Prices agreed upon between the Masters and Journeymen," which is still extant. The framework knitters, and also the tailors of the various villages in Nottinghamshire, were, from 1794 to 1810, in the habit of freely meeting together, both masters and men, " to consider of matters relative to the trade," the conferences being convened by public advertisement.[2] The minute books of the local Trade Union of the carpenters of Preston for the years 1807 to 1824 chronicle an apparently unconcealed and unmolested existence, in correspondence with other carpenters' societies throughout Lancashire. The accounts contain no items for the expense of defending their officers against prosecutions, whereas there are several payments for advertisements and public meetings, and, be it added, a very large expenditure in beer. And there is a lively tradition among the aged block printers of Glasgow that, in their fathers' time, when their very active Trade Union exacted a fee of seven guineas from each new apprentice, this money was always straightway drunk by the men of the print-field, the employer taking his seat at the head of the table, and no work being done by any one until the fund was exhausted. The calico-printers' organisation appears, at the early part of the nineteenth century, to have been one of the strongest and most complete of the Unions. In an impressive pamphlet of 1815 the men are thus appealed to by the employers : " We have by turns conceded what we ought all manfully to have resisted, and you, elated with success, have been led on from one extravagant demand to another, till the burden is become too intolerable to be borne. You fix the number of our

---

[1] House of Commons Return, No. 135, of 1834.
[2] Advertisements in *Nottingham Journal*, 1794–1810.

apprentices, and oftentimes even the number of our journeymen.   You dismiss certain proportions of our hands, and
will not allow others to come in their stead.   You stop all
Surface Machines, and go the length even to destroy the
rollers before our face.   You restrict the Cylinder Machine,
and even dictate the kind of pattern it is to print.   You
refuse, on urgent occasions, to work by candlelight, and
even compel our apprentices to do the same.   You dismiss
our overlookers when they don't suit you ;   and force
obnoxious servants into our employ.   Lastly, you set all
subordination and good order at defiance, and instead of
showing deference and respect to your employers, treat
them with personal insult and contempt." [1]   Notwithstanding all this, no systematic attempt appears to have
been made to put down the calico-printers' combination,
and only one or two isolated prosecutions can be traced.
In Dublin, too, the cabinetmakers in the early part of the
present century were combined in a strong union called
the Samaritan Society, exclusively for trade purposes ;
" but though illegal, the employers do not seem to have
looked upon it with any great aversion ; and when on one
occasion the chief constable had the men attending a meeting
arrested, the employers came forward to bail them.   Indeed,
they professed that their object, though primarily to defend
their own interests against the masters, was also to defend
the interests of the masters against unprincipled journeymen.   Many of the masters on receiving the bill of a
journeyman were in the habit of sending it to the trades'
society committee to be taxed, after which the word Committee was stamped upon it.   One case was mentioned,
when between two and three pounds were knocked off
a bill of about eight pounds by the trade committee." [2]

[1] *Considerations addressed to the Journeymen Calico-Printers by one of
their Masters* (Manchester, 1815) ; see also the Report of House of
Commons Committee on the Case of the Calico-Printers, 1806.
[2] Evidence before Committee on Artisans and Machinery, 1824, as
summarised in the *Report on Trade Societies* (1860) of the Social Science
Association : see also *A Digest of the Evidence before the Committee on
Artizans and Machinery*, by George White, 1824.

And both in London and Edinburgh the journeymen openly published, without fear of prosecution, elaborate printed lists of piecework prices, compiled sometimes by a committee of the men's Trade Union, sometimes by a joint committee of employers and employed.[1] " The London Cabinet-makers' Union Book of Prices," of which editions were published in 1811 and 1824, was a costly and elaborate work, with many plates, published " by a Committee of Masters and Journeymen . . . to prevent those litigations which have too frequently existed in the trade." Various supplements and " index keys " to this work were published ; and other similar lists exist. So lax was the administration of the law that George White, 'the energetic clerk to Hume's Committee, asserted that the Act of 1800 had " been in general a dead letter upon those artisans upon whom it was intended to have an effect—namely, the shoemakers, printers, papermakers, shipbuilders, tailors, etc., who have had their regular societies and houses of call, as though no such Act was in existence ; and in fact it would be almost impossible for many of those trades to be carried on without such societies, who are in general sick and travelling relief societies ; and the roads and parishes would be much pestered with these travelling trades, who travel from want of employ-ment, were it not for their societies who relieve what they call tramps." [2]

But although clubs of journeymen might be allowed to take, like the London bookbinders, " a social pint of porter together," and even, in times of industrial peace, to provide for their tramps and perform all the functions of a Trade Union, the employers had always the power of

---

[1] *The Edinburgh Book of Prices for Manufacturing Cabinet Work* (Edinburgh, 1805, 126 pp.), " as mutually agreed upon by the Masters and Journeymen." In 1825 the journeymen prepared a *Supplement*, which, after the masters had concurred in it, was published by the men (Edinburgh, 1825). Both these are in the Goldsmiths' Library at the University of London.

[2] *A Few Remarks on the State of the Laws at present in Existence for regu-lating Masters and Workpeople*, 1823 (142 pp.), p. 84. Anonymous, but evidently by George White and Gravener Henson.

meeting any demands by a prosecution.   Even those trades
in which we have discovered evidence of the unmolested
existence of combinations furnish examples of the rigorous
application of the law.   In 1819 we read of numerous
prosecutions of cabinetmakers, hatters, ironfounders, and
other journeymen, nominally for leaving their work unfinished, but really for the crime of combination.[1]   In
1798 five journeymen printers were indicted at the Old
Bailey for conspiracy.   The employers had sent for the
men's leaders to discuss their proposals, when, as it was
complained, " the five defendants came, clothed as delegates,
representing themselves as the head of a Parliament as we
may call it."   The men were in fact members of a trade
friendly society of pressmen " held at the Crown, near St.
Dunstan's Church, Fleet Street," which, as the prosecuting
counsel declared, " from its appearance certainly bore no
reproachable mark upon it.   It was called a friendly society,
but by means of some wicked men among them this society
degenerated into a most abominable meeting for the purpose
of a conspiracy ; those of the trade who did not join their
society were summoned, and even the apprentices, and were
told unless they conformed to the practices of these journeymen, when they came out of their times they should not
be employed."   Notwithstanding the fact that the employers
had themselves recognised and negotiated with the society,
the Recorder sentenced all the defendants to two years'
imprisonment.[2]

Twelve years later it was the brutality of another prosecution of the compositors that impressed Francis Place with
the necessity of an alteration in the law.   " The cruel
persecutions," he writes, " of the Journeymen Printers
employed in *The Times* newspaper in 1810 were carried to
an almost incredible extent.   The judge who tried and

[1] See, for instance, *The Times* from 17th to 25th of June 1819.
[2] *An Account of the Rise and Progress of the Dispute between the Masters
and Journeymen Printers exemplified in the Trial at large, with Remarks
Thereon*, 1799, a rare pamphlet, in the Goldsmiths' Library at the University of London.

sentenced some of them was the Common Sergeant of
London, Sir John Sylvester, commonly known by the cogno-
men of ' Bloody Black Jack.' . . . No judge took more
pains than did this judge on the unfortunate printers, to
make it appear that their offence was one of great enormity,
to beat down and alarm the really respectable men who
had fallen into his clutches, and on whom he inflicted
scandalously severe sentences." [1] Nor did prosecution
always depend on the caprice of an employer. In December 1817 the Bolton constables, accidentally getting to
know that ten delegates of the calico-printers from the
various districts of the kingdom were to meet on New
Year's Day, arranged to arrest the whole body and seize
all their papers. The ten delegates suffered three months'
imprisonment, although no dispute with their employers
was in progress. [2] But the main use of the law to the
employers was to checkmate strikes, and ward off demands
for better conditions of labour. Already, in 1786, the law
of conspiracy had been strained to convict, and punish with
two years' imprisonment, the five London bookbinders
who were leading a strike to reduce hours from twelve to
eleven. [3] When, at the Aberdeen Master Tailors' Gild, in
1797, " it was represented to the trade that their journeymen
had entered into an illegal combination for the purpose of
raising their wages," the masters unanimously " agreed
not to give any additional wages to their servants," and
backed up this resolution of their own combination by
getting twelve journeymen prosecuted and fined for the
crime of combining. [4] In 1799 the success of the London
shoemakers in picketing obnoxious employers led to the
prosecution of two of them, which was made the means of
inducing the men to consent to dissolve their society, then

[1] Place MSS. 27798—8 ; *Times*, November 9, 1810.
[2] Report in *Manchester Exchange Herald*, preserved in Place MSS.
27799—156.
[3] *Bookfinishers' Friendly Circular*, 1845-51, pp. 5, 21.
[4] Bain's *Merchant and Craft Gilds of Aberdeen*, p. 261. An earlier
combination of 1768 is also mentioned.

seven years old, and return to work at once.[1] Two other shoemakers of York were convicted in the same year for the crime of " combining to raise the price of their labour in making shoes, and refusing to make shoes under a certain price," and counsel said that " in every great town in the North combinations of this sort existed." [2] The coachmakers' strike of 1819 was similarly stopped, and the " Benevolent Society of Coachmakers " broken up by the conviction of the general secretary and twenty other members, who were, upon this condition, released on their own recognisances.[3] In 1819 some calico-engravers in the service of a Manchester firm protested against the undue multiplication of apprentices by their employers, and enforced their protest by declining to work. For this " conspiracy " they were fined and imprisoned.[4] And though the master cutlers were allowed, with impunity, to subscribe to the Sheffield Mercantile and Manufacturing Union, which fixed the rates of wages, and brought pressure to bear on recalcitrant employers, the numerous trade clubs of the operatives were not left unmolested. In 1816 seven scissor-grinders were sentenced to three months' imprisonment for belonging to what they called the " Misfortune Club," which paid out-of-work benefit, and sought to maintain the customary rates.[5]

[1] R. v. Hammond and Webb, 2 Esp. 719 ; see the *Morning Chronicle* report, preserved in Place MSS. 27799—29.

[2] *Star*, November 26, 1799.

[3] R. v. Connell and others, *Times*, July 10, 1819.

[4] R. v. Ferguson and Edge, 2 St. 489.

[5] *Sheffield Iris*, December 17, 1816. The men's clubs often existed under the cloak of friendly societies. In the overseers' return of sick clubs, made to Parliament in 1815, the following trade friendly societies are included, many of these, at any rate, being essentially Trade Unions :

Tailors,	with 360 members, and £740
Braziers,	,, 664 ,, ,, 1768
Masons,	,, 693 ,, ,, 1852
Scissorsmiths,	,, 550 ,, ,, 1309
Filesmiths,	,, 260 ,, ,, 600
United Silversmiths,	,, 240 ,, ,, 299
Cutlers,	,, 65 ,, ,, 450
Grinders,	,, 283 ,,

Sheffield Iris, 1857.

But it was in the new textile industries that the weight of the Combination Laws was chiefly felt. White and Henson describe the Act of 1800 as being in these trades "a tremendous millstone round the neck of the local artisan, which has depressed and debased him to the earth : every act which he has attempted, every measure that he has devised to keep up or raise his wages, he has been told was illegal : the whole force of the civil power and influence of the district has been exerted against him because he was acting illegally : the magistrates, acting, as they believed, in unison with the views of the legislature, to check and keep down wages and combination, regarded, in almost every instance, every attempt on the part of the artisan to ameliorate his situation or support his station in society as a species of sedition and resistance of the Government : every committee or active man among them was regarded as a turbulent, dangerous instigator, whom it was necessary to watch and crush if possible."[1]   To cite one only of the instances, it was given in evidence before Hume's Committee that in 1818 certain Bolton millowners suggested to the operative weavers that they should concert together to leave the employment of those who paid below the current rate.   Acting on this hint a meeting of forty delegates took place, at which it was resolved to ask for the advance agreed to by the good employers.   A fortnight later the president and the two secretaries were arrested, convicted of conspiracy, and imprisoned for one and two years respectively, although their employers gave evidence on the prisoners' behalf to the effect that they had themselves requested the men to attend the meeting, and had approved the resolutions passed.[2]   In the following year fifteen cotton-spinners of Manchester, who had met "to receive contributions to bury their dead," under "Articles" sanctioned by Quarter Sessions in 1795, were seized in the committee-room by the police, and committed to trial for conspiracy, bail being

---

[1] *A Few Remarks, etc.,* p. 86.
[2] Committee on Artisans and Machinery, 1824, p. 395.

refused. After three or four months' imprisonment they were brought to trial, the whole local bar—seven in number—being briefed against them. Collections were made in London and elsewhere (including the town of Lynn in Norfolk) for their defence. The enrolment of their club as a friendly society availed little. It was urged in court that "all societies, whether benefit societies or otherwise, were only cloaks for the people of England to conspire against the State," and most of the defendants were sentenced to varying terms of imprisonment.[1]

But the Scottish Weavers' Strike of 1812, described in the preceding chapter, is the most striking case of all. In the previous year certain cotton-spinners had been convicted of combination and imprisoned, the judge observing that there was a clear remedy in law, as the magistrates had full power and authority to fix rates of wages or settle disputes. In 1812 many of the employers refused to accept the rates which the justices had declared as fair for weaving ; and all the weavers at the forty thousand looms between Aberdeen and Carlisle struck to enforce the justices' rates. The employers had already made overtures through the sheriff of the county for a satisfactory settlement when the Government arrested the central committee of five, who were directing the proceedings. These men were sentenced to periods of imprisonment varying from four to eighteen months ; the strike failed, and the association broke up.[2] The student of the newspapers between 1800 and 1824 will find abundant record of judicial barbarities, of which the cases cited above may be taken as samples. No statistics exist as to the frequency of the prosecutions or the severity of the sentences ; but it is easy to understand, from such reports as are available, the sullen resentment which the working class suffered under these laws. Their repeal was

---

[1] See the *Gorgon* for January and February 1819.
[2] Second Report of Committee on Artisans and Machinery, 1824, p. 62. For other cases, see *The Town Labourer*, by J. L. and B. Hammond, 1917, pp. 130-33

a necessary preliminary to the growth among the most oppressed sections of the workers of any real power of protecting themselves, by Trade Union effort, against the degradation of their Standard of Life.

The failure of the Combination Laws to suppress the somewhat dictatorial Trade Unionism of the skilled handicraftsmen, and their efficacy in preventing the growth of permanent Unions among other sections of the workers, is explained by class distinctions, now passed away or greatly modified, which prevailed at the beginning of the present century. To-day, when we speak of " the aristocracy of labour" we include under that heading the organised miners and factory operatives of the North on the same superior footing as the skilled handicraftsman. In 1800 they were at opposite extremes of the social scale in the wage-earning class, the weaver and the miner being then further removed from the handicraftsman than the docker or general labourer is from the Lancashire cotton-spinner or Northumberland hewer of to-day. The skilled artisans formed, at any rate in London, an intermediate class between the shopkeeper and the great mass of unorganised labourers or operatives in the new machine industries. The substantial fees demanded all through the eighteenth century for apprenticeship to the " crafts " had secured to the members and their eldest sons a virtual monopoly.[1] Even after the repeal of the laws requiring a formal apprenticeship some time had to elapse before the supply of this class of handicraftsmen overtook the growing demand. Thus we gather from the surviving records that these trades have never been more completely organised in London than between 1800 and 1820.[2] We find the London hatters,

[1] Throughout the century it seems to have been customary in most handicrafts for the artisan to be allowed the privilege of apprenticing one son, usually the eldest, free of charge. For other boys, especially for the sons of parents not belonging to the trade, a fee of £5 to £20 was exacted by the employer. The secretary of the Old Amicable Society of Wool-staplers thirty years ago informed us that, as his brother had already entered the trade, his father had to pay £100 for his indentures.

[2] To take, for instance, the cabinetmakers and millwrights. When

coopers, curriers, compositors, millwrights, and shipwrights maintaining earnings which, upon their own showing, amounted to the comparatively large sum of thirty to fifty shillings per week. At the same period the Lancashire weaver or the Leicester hosier, in full competition with steam-power and its accompaniment of female and child labour, could, even when fully employed, earn barely ten shillings. We see this difference in the Standard of Life reflected in the characters of the combinations formed by the two classes.

In the skilled handicrafts, long accustomed to corporate government, we find, even under repressive laws, no unlawful oaths, seditious emblems, or other common paraphernalia of secret societies. The London Brushmakers, whose Union apparently dates from the early part of the eighteenth century, expressly insisted " that no person shall be admitted a member who is not well affected to his present Majesty and the Protestant Succession, and in good health and of a respectable character." But this loyalty was not inconsistent with their subscribing to the funds of the 1831 agitation for the Reform Bill.[1] The prevailing tone of the superior workmen down to 1848 was, in fact, strongly Radical ; and their leaders took a prominent part in all the working class politics of the time. From their ranks came such organisers as Place, Lovett, and Gast.[2] But wherever

---

Lovett came to London in 1819 he found that he could not get employment without joining the Union (*Life of William Lovett*, by himself). The millwrights at the beginning of the century were so strongly organised— this probably led to the engineering employers' petition in 1799 out of which the Combination Acts sprang—that when Fairbairn (after being actually engaged at Rennie's works) was refused admission into their society, he was driven to tramp out of London in search of work in a non-union district (*Life of Sir William Fairbairn*, by himself, 1877, pp. 89, 92). For the last three-quarters of the century a considerable proportion of the cabinetmakers and engineers employed in London have been outside the Trade Union ranks.

[1] *Articles of the Society of Journeymen Brushmakers, held at the sign of the Craven Head, Drury Lane*, 1806 ; Minutes, April 27, 1831.

[2] John Gast, a shipwright of Deptford, was evidently one of the ablest Trade Unionists of his time. We first hear of him in 1802, when there was a serious strike in London that attracted the attention of the Government

we have been able to gain any idea of their proceedings, their trade clubs were free from anything that could now be conceived as political sedition. It was these clubs of handicraftsmen that formed the backbone of the various " central committees " which dealt with the main topics of Trade Unionism during the next thirty years. They it was who furnished such assistance as was given by working men to the movement for the repeal of the Combination Laws. And their influence gave a certain dignity and stability to the Trade Union Movement, without which, under hostile governments, it could never have emerged from the petulant rebellions of hunger-strikes and machine-breaking.

The principal effect of the Combination Laws on these well-organised handicrafts in London, Liverpool, Dublin, and perhaps other towns, was to make the internal discipline more rigid and the treatment of non-unionists more arbitrary. Place describes how " in these societies there are some few individuals who possess the confidence of their fellows, and when any matter relating to the trade has

---

(Home Office Papers in Record Office, 65—1, July and August 1802), as the author of a striking pamphlet entitled *A Vindication of the Conduct of the Shipwrights during the late disputes with their Employers* (1802, 38 pp.). In 1818 he is found advocating the first recorded proposal for a general workmen's organisation, as distinguished from separate trade clubs—to be described in our next chapter ; and his *Articles of the Philanthropic Hercules for the Mutual Support of the Labouring Mechanics,* which were printed in the *Gorgon,* attracted the attention of Francis Place, who described him (Place MSS, 27819—23) as having " long been secretary to the Shipwrights' Club : he was a steady, respectable man. He had formed several associations of working men, but had been unable to keep up any one of them." He became one of Place's most useful allies in the agitation for a repeal of the Combination Laws, and when, in 1825, their re-enactment was threatened, his " committee of trades delegates " was Place's strongest support. Gast was the leading spirit in the establishment of the *Trades Newspaper* in July 1825, and became chairman of the committee of management, as well as a frequent contributor. In the same year he was actively engaged in the shipwrights' struggle for a " Book of Rates," or definite list of piecework prices, and the energy with which he counteracted the design of the Board of Admiralty, of allowing the London shipbuilders to borrow men from the Portsmouth Navy Yard, contributed mainly to the success of the fight.

been talked over, either at the club or in a separate room, or in a workshop or a yard, and the matter has become notorious, these men are expected to direct what shall be done, and they do direct—simply by a hint. On this the men act ; and one and all support those who may be thrown out of work or otherwise inconvenienced. If matters were to be discussed as gentlemen seem to suppose they must be, no resolution would ever be come to. The influence of the men alluded to would soon cease if the law were repealed. It is the law and the law alone which causes the confidence of the men to be given to their leaders. Those who direct are not known to the body, and not one man in twenty, perhaps, knows the person of any one who directs. It is a rule among them to ask no questions, and another rule among them who know most, either to give no answer if questioned, or an answer to mislead." [1]

In the new machine industries, on the other hand, the repeated reductions of wages, the rapid alterations of processes, and the substitution of women and children for adult male workers, had gradually reduced the workers to a condition of miserable poverty. The reports of Parliamentary committees, from 1800 onward, contain a dreary record of the steady degradation of the Standard of Life in the textile industries. " The sufferings of persons employed in the cotton manufacture," Place writes of this period, " were beyond credibility : they were drawn into combinations, betrayed, prosecuted, convicted, sentenced, and monstrously severe punishments inflicted on them : they were reduced to and kept in the most wretched state of existence." [2] Their employers, instead of being, as in the older handicrafts, little more than master workmen, recog-

---

[1] Place MSS. 27800—195.

[2] Place MSS. 27798—11 ; and *The Town Labourer, 1760-1832*, by J. L. and B. Hammond, 1917. Between 1798-1803 and 1804-16 the piecework wages for handloom cotton weaving were reduced in some cases by 80 per cent at a time of war prices (*Geschichte der englischen Lohnarbeit*, by Gustav Steffen, Stuttgart, 1900, vol. ii. pp. 19-20). See *History of Wages in the Cotton Trade during the Past Hundred Years*, by G. H. Wood, 1910 ; and Cunningham. *Growth, etc.*, 1903, p. 634.

nising the customary Standard of Life of their journeymen, were often capitalist *entrepreneurs*, devoting their whole energies to the commercial side of the business, and leaving their managers to buy labour in the market at the cheapest possible rate. This labour was recruited from all localities and many different occupations. It was brigaded and controlled by despotic laws, enforced by numerous fines and disciplinary deductions. Cases of gross tyranny and heartless cruelty are not wanting. Without a common standard, a common tradition, or mutual confidence, the workers in the new mills were helpless against their masters. Their ephemeral combinations and frequent strikes were, as a rule, only passionate struggles to maintain a bare subsistence wage. In place of the steady organised resistance to encroachments maintained by the handicraftsmen, we watch, in the machine industries, the alternation of outbursts of machine-breaking and outrages, with intervals of abject submission and reckless competition with each other for employment. In the conduct of such organisation as there was, repressive laws had, with the operatives as with the London artisans, the effect of throwing great power into the hands of a few men. These leaders were implicitly obeyed in times of industrial conflict, but the repeated defeats which they were unable to avert prevented that growth of confidence which is indispensable for permanent organisation.[1] Both leaders and rank and file, too, were largely implicated in political seditions, and were the victims of spies and Ministerial emissaries of all sorts. All these circumstances led to the prevalence among them of fearful oaths, mystic initiation rites, and other manifestations of a sensationalism which was sometimes puerile and sometimes criminal.

The most notorious of these " seditions," about which little is really known, was the " Luddite " upheaval of 1811–12, when riotous mobs of manual workers, acting

---

[1] See on all these points the evidence given before the Committee on Artisans and Machinery, 1824 ; especially that of Richmond.

under some sort of organisation, went about destroying textile machinery and sometimes wrecking factories. To what extent this had any direct connection with the Trade Union Movement seems to us, pending more penetrating investigation of the unpublished evidence, somewhat uncertain. That the operatives very generally sympathised with the most violent protest against the displacement of hand labour by machinery, and the extreme distress which it was causing, is clear. The Luddite movement apparently began among the Framework-knitters, who had long been organised in local clubs, with some rudimentary federal bond ; and the whole direction of the Luddites was often ascribed, as by the Mayor of Leicester in 1812, to " the Committee of Framework-knitters, who have as complete an organisation of the whole body as you could have of a regiment." [1]   But money was collected from men of other trades, notably bricklayers, masons, spinners, weavers, and colliers, as well as from the soldiers in some of the regiments stationed at provincial centres ; and such evidence as we have found points rather to a widespread secret oath-bound conspiracy, not of the men of any one trade, but of wage-earners of all kinds. We find an informer stating (June 22, 1812), with what truth we know not, " that the Union extends from London to Nottingham, and from thence to Manchester and Carlisle. Small towns lying between the principal places are not yet organised, such as Garstang and Burton. Only some of the trades have taken the first oath. He says there is a second oath taken by suspicious persons." [2]   On the other hand, it looks as if the various local Trade Clubs were made use of, in some cases informally, as agents or branches of the conspiracy.

General Maitland, writing from Buxton (June 22, 1812) to the Home Secretary, says that, in his opinion, " the whole of this business . . . originated in those constant efforts

---

[1] Letter to the local Major-General, June 15, 1812, in Home Office Papers, 40—1.   [2] *Ibid.*

made by these associations for many years past to keep up the price of the manufacturers' wages ; that finding their efforts for this unavailing, both from the circumstances of the trade and the high price of provisions, they in a moment of irritation, for which it is but just to say they had considerable ground from the real state of distress in which they were placed . . . began to think of effecting that by force which they had ever been trying to do by other means ; and that in this state the oath was introduced. . . . I believe the whole to be, certainly a most mischievous, but undefined and indistinct attempt to be in a state of preparation to do that by force which they had not succeeded in carrying into effect as they usually did by other means." The whole episode has been too much ignored, even by social historians ; and " Byron's famous speech and Charlotte Brontë's more famous novel give to most people their idea of the misery of the time, and of its cause, the displacement of hand labour by machinery." [1]

The coal-miners were in many respects even worse off than the hosiery workers and the cotton weavers. In Scotland they had been but lately freed from actual serfdom, the final act of emancipation not having been passed until 1799. In Monmouthshire and South Wales the oppression of the " tommy shops " of the small employers was extreme. In the North of England the " yearly bond," the truck

---

[1] *The Town Labourer, 1760-1832*, by J. L. and B. Hammond, 1917, p. 15. Whether Gravener Henson, the bobbin-net maker of Nottingham, subsequently author of a *History of the Framework-Knitters* (1831), who had long been a leader of the Framework-knitters, was the " King Lud " under whose orders the machine-breakers often purported to act, is yet unproven (*Life of Francis Place*, by Prof. Graham Wallas, revised edition, 1918). The Report of the House of Commons Committee on the Framework-knitters' petitions (1812) affords evidence of the all-pervading misery of the time. For other glimpses of the Luddite organisation, see *An Appeal to the Public, containing an account of services rendered during the disturbances in the North of England in the year 1812*, by Francis Raynes, 1817 (in Home Office Papers, 40) ; *Report of Proceedings under Commission of Oyer and Terminer, January 2 to 12, 1813, at York*, by J. and W. B. Gurney, 1813 ; *Digest of Evidence of Committee on Artizans and Machinery*, by George White, 1824 (see p. 36, Richmond's evidence as to the appeals of the Luddites to the Glasgow cotton-spinners) ; and *Annual Register, 1812*.

system, and the arbitrary fines kept the underground workers in complete subjection. The result is seen in the turbulence of their frequent " sticks " or strikes, during which troops were often required to quell their violence. The great strike of 1810 was carried on by an oath-bound confederacy recruited by the practice of " brothering," " so named because the members of the union bound themselves by a most solemn oath to obey the orders of the brotherhood, under the penalty of being stabbed through the heart or of having their bowels ripped up." [1]

Notwithstanding these differences between various classes of workers, the growing sense of solidarity among the whole body of wage-earners rises into special prominence during this period of tyranny and repression. The trades in which it was usual for men to tramp from place to place in search of employment had long possessed, as we have seen, some kind of loose federal organisation extending throughout the country. In spite of the law of 1797 forbidding the existence of " corresponding societies," the various federal organisations of Curriers, Hatters, Calicoprinters, Woolcombers, Woolstaplers, and other handicraftsmen kept up constant correspondence on trade matters, and raised money for common trade purposes. In some cases there existed an elaborate national organisation, with geographical districts and annual delegate meetings, like that of the Calico-printers who were arrested by the Bolton constables in 1818. The rules of the Papermakers,[2] which certainly date from 1803, provide for the division of England into five districts, with detailed arrangements for

---

[1] Evidence of a colliery engineer in the Newcastle district before Committee on Combination Laws, 1825 ; summarised in *Report on Trade Societies*, 1860, by Social Science Association. See also *A Voice from the Coalmines*, 1825 ; *A Candid Appeal to the Coalowners and Viewers of Collieries on the Tyne and Wear, including a copy of the Collier's Bond, with Animadversions thereon and a series of proposed Amendments, from the Committee of the Colliers' United Association*, 1826 (in Home Office Papers, H.O. 40 (19), with Lord Londonderry's letter of February 28, 1826) ; *The Miners of Northumberland and Durham*, by Richard Fynes, pp. 12–16 (1873) ; *An Earnest Address . . . on behalf of the Pitmen*, by W. Scott, 1831.

[2] See Appendix to Report of Select Committee on Combinations, 1825.

representation and collective action. This national organisation was, notwithstanding repressive laws, occasionally very effective. We need cite only one instance, furnished by the Liverpool Ropemakers in 1823. When a certain firm attempted to put labourers to the work, the local society of ropespinners informed it that this was " contrary to the regulations of the trade," and withdrew all their members. The employers, failing to get men in Liverpool, sent to Hull and Newcastle, but found that the Ropespinners' Society had already apprised the local trade clubs at those towns. The firm then imported " blacklegs " from Glasgow, who were met on arrival by the local unionists, inveigled to a " trade club-house," and alternately threatened and cajoled out of their engagements. Finally the head of the firm went to London to purchase yarn ; but the London workmen, finding that the yarn was for a " struck shop," refused to complete the order. The last resource of the employers was an indictment at the Sessions for combination, but a Liverpool jury, in the teeth of the evidence and the judge's summing up, gave a verdict of acquittal.[1]

This solidarity was not confined to the members of a particular trade. The masters are always complaining that one trade supports another, and old account books of Trade Unions for this period abound with entries of sums contributed in aid of disputes in other trades, either in the same town or elsewhere. Thus the small society of London Goldbeaters, during the three years 1810–12, lent or gave substantial sums, amounting in all to £200, to fourteen other trades.[2] The Home Secretary was informed in 1823 that

---

[1] R. v. Yates and Others, Liverpool Sessions, August 10, 1823. See newspaper report preserved in Place MSS. 27804—154.

[2] The entries in this old cash-book are of some interest :

May 29, 1810	Paid ye Brushmakers .	.	.	.	£15	0	0
	Lent ye Brushmakers .	.	.	.	10	0	0
	Paid ye Friziers .	.	.	.	20	0	0
June 26, 1810	Paid ye Silversmiths .	.	.	.	10	0	0
	Expenses to Pipemakers .	.	.	0	4	10
July 24, 1810	Paid ye Braziers .	.	.	.	10	10	0
	Paid ye Bookbinders .	.	.	.	10	0	0
	Paid ye Curriers .	.	.	.	10	0	0

a combination of cotton-spinners at Bolton, whose books had been seized, had received donations, not only from twenty-eight cotton-spinners' committees in as many Lancashire towns, but also from fourteen other trades, from coal-miners to butchers.[1] A picturesque illustration of this brotherly help in need occurs in the account of an appeal to the Pontefract Quarter Sessions by certain Sheffield cutlers against their conviction for combination : " The appellants were in court, but hour after hour passed, and no counsel moved the case. The reason was a want of funds for the purpose. At last, whilst in court, a remittance from the clubs in Manchester, to the amount of one hundred pounds, arrived, and then the counsel was fee'd, and the case, which, but for the arrival of the money from this town, must have dropped in that stage, was proceeded with." [2] And although the day of Trades Councils had not yet come, it was a common thing for the various trade societies of a particular town to unite in sending witnesses to Parliamentary Committees, preparing petitions to the House of Commons and paying counsel to support their case, engaging solicitors to prosecute offending employers, and collecting subscriptions for strikes.[3] This tendency to form joint

---

Aug. 21, 1810	Lent ye Bit and Spurmakers	.	£5	0	0
	Lent ye Scalemakers .	. .	5	0	0
	Paid ye Leathergrounders .	.	5	0	0
Oct. 26, 1810	Paid ye Tinplate Workers	. .	30	0	0
Dec. 11, 1810	Lent ye Ropemakers .	. .	10	0	0
May 30, 1811	Received of Scale Beam-makers	.	5	0	0
June 25, 1811	Expenses with Papermakers	.	0	12	6
July 20, 1812	Lent ye Sadlers .	. .	10	0	0
Oct. 12, 1812	Paid to Millwrights .	. .	50	0	0
Dec. 7, 1812	Borrowed from the Musical Instrument-makers	. .	2	0	0

[1] Home Office Papers, 40—18, March 31, 1823.

[2] See report in the *Manchester Exchange Herald*, about 1818, preserved in Place MSS. 27799—156.

[3] See, for instance, the witnesses delegated by the Glasgow and Manchester trades to the Select Committee on Petitions of Artisans, etc., report of June 13, 1811 ; or the joint action of the Yorkshire and West of England Woollen-workers given in evidence before the Select Committee of 1806. These cases are typical of many others.

committees of local trades was, as we shall see, greatly strengthened in the agitation against the Combination Laws from 1823–25. With the final abandonment of all legislative protection of the Standard of Life, and the complete divorce of the worker from the instruments of production, the wage-earners in the various industrial centres became indeed ever more conscious of the widening of the old separate trade disputes into " the class war " which has characterised the past century.

It is difficult to-day to realise the naïve surprise with which the employers of that time regarded the practical development of working - class solidarity. The master witnesses before Parliamentary Committees, and the judges in sentencing workmen for combination, are constantly found reciting instances of mutual help to prove the existence of a widespread " conspiracy " against the dominant classes. That the London Tailors should send money to the Glasgow Weavers, or the Goldbeaters to the Ropespinners, seemed to the middle and upper classes little short of a crime.

The movement for a repeal of the Combination Laws began in a period of industrial dislocation and severe political repression. The economic results of the long war, culminating in the comparatively low prices of the peace for most manufactured products, though not for wheat, led in 1816 to an almost universal reduction of wages throughout the country. In open defiance of the law the masters, in many instances, deliberately combined in agreements to pay lower rates. This agreement was not confined to the employers in a particular trade, who may have been confronted by organised bodies of journeymen, but extended, in some cases, to all employers of labour in a particular locality. The landowners and farmers of Tiverton, for instance, at a " numerous and respectable meeting at the Town Hall " in 1816, resolved " that, in consequence of the low price of provisions," not more than certain specified wages should be given to smiths, carpenters,

masons, thatchers, or masons' labourers.[1]   The Compositors,
Coopers, Shoemakers, Carpenters, and many other trades
record serious reductions of wages at this period.   In these
cases the masters justified their action on the ground that,
owing to the fall of prices, the Standard of Life of the
journeymen would not be depressed.   But in the great
staple industries there ensued a cutting competition between
employers to secure orders in a falling market, their method
being to undersell each other by beating down wages below
subsistence level—an operation often aided by the practice,
then common, of supplementing insufficient earnings out of
the Poor Rate.   This produced such ruinous results that
local protests were soon made.   At Leicester the authorities
decided to maintain the men's " Statement Price " by
agreeing to wholly support out of a voluntary fund those
who could not get work at the full rates.   This was bitterly
resented by the neighbouring employers, who seriously
contemplated indicting the lord-lieutenant, mayor, aldermen, clergy, and other subscribers for criminal conspiracy
to keep up wages.[2]   And in 1820 a public meeting of the
ratepayers of Sheffield protested against the " evil of parish
pay to supplement earnings," and recommended employers
to revert to the uniform price list which the men had gained
in 1810.[3]   Finally we have the employers themselves
publicly denouncing the ruinous extent to which the cutting
of wages had been carried.   A declaration dated June 16,
1819, and signed by fourteen Lancashire manufacturers,

---

[1] Printed handbill signed by thirty-two persons, issued in the summer
of 1816, preserved in Place MSS. 27799—141.   Place has also preserved
the rejoinder of the workmen, which is unsigned, as he notes, for fear of
prosecution.

[2] *The Stocking Makers' Monitor*, January 1818 ; *A few Remarks on the
State of the Law, etc.*, by White and Henson, p. 88 ; *An Appeal to the Public
on the subject of the Framework-Knitters' Fund*, by the Rev. Robert Hall
(Leicester, 1819) ; Cobbett's *Weekly Register*, vol. xxxix.; *A Reply to the
Principal Objections advanced by Cobbett and Others*, by the Rev. Robert
Hall (Leicester, 1821): *Digest of Evidence before the Committee on Artizans
and Machinery*, by George White, 1824.

[3] *Proceedings at a public Meeting of the Inhabitants of the Township of
Sheffield, held at the Town Hall, March 15, 1820* (Sheffield, 1820, 16 pp.).

regrets that they have been compelled by the action of a few competitors to lower wages to the present rates, and strongly condemns any further reduction ; whilst twenty-five of the most eminent calico-printing firms append an emphatic approval of the protest, and state " that the system of paying such extremely low wages for manufacturing labour is injurious to the trade at large." [1] At Coventry the ribbon manufacturers combined with the Weavers' Provident Union to maintain a general adherence to the agreed list of prices, and in 1819 subscribed together no less than £16,000 to cover the cost of proceedings with this object. This combination formed the subject of an indictment at Warwick Assizes, which put an end to the association, the remaining funds being handed over to the local " Streets Commissioners " for paving the city. These protests and struggles of the better employers were in vain. Rates were reduced and strikes occurred all over the country, and were met, not by redress or sympathy, but by an outburst of prosecutions and sentences of more than the usual ferocity. The common law and ancient statutes were ruthlessly used to supplement the Combination Acts, often by strained constructions. The Scotch judges in particular, as an eminent Scotch jurist declared to the Parliamentary Committee in 1824, applied the criminal procedure of Scotland to cases of simple combination, from 1813–19, in a way that he, on becoming Lord Advocate, refused to countenance.[2] The workers, on attempting some spasmodic preparations for organised political agitation, were further coerced, in 1819, by the infamous " Six Acts," which at one blow suppressed practically all public meetings, enabled the magistrate to search for arms, subjected all working-class publications to the crushing stamp duty, and rendered more stringent the law relating to seditious libels. The whole system of repression which had characterised the

---

[1] *Times*, August 5, 1819.
[2] Evidence of Sir William Rae, Bart., before Select Committee on Artisans and Machinery, 1824, p. 486.

statesmanship of the Regency culminated at this period in a tyranny not exceeded by any of the monarchs of the " Holy Alliance." The effect of this tyranny was actually to shield the Combination Laws by turning the more energetic and enlightened working-class leaders away from all specific reforms to a thorough revolution of the whole system of Parliamentary representation. Hence there was no popular movement whatever for the repeal of the Combination Laws. If we were writing the history of the English working class instead of that of the Trade Union Movement, we should find in William Cobbett or " Orator " Hunt, in Samuel Bamford or William Lovett, a truer representative of the current aspirations of the English artisan at this time than in the man who now came unexpectedly on the scene to devise and carry into effect the Trade Union Emancipation of 1824.

Francis Place was a master tailor who had created a successful business in a shop at Charing Cross. Before setting up for himself he had worked as a journeyman breeches-maker, and had organised combinations in his own and other trades. After 1818 he left the conduct of the business to his son, and devoted his keenly practical intellect and extraordinary persistency first to the repeal of the Combination Laws, and next to the Reform Movement. In social theory he was a pupil of Bentham and James Mill, and his ideal may be summed up as political Democracy with industrial liberty, or, as we should now say, thoroughgoing Radical Individualism. No one who has closely studied his life and work will doubt that, within the narrow sphere to which his unswerving practicality confined him, he was the most remarkable politician of his age. His chief merit lay in his thorough understanding of the art of getting things done. In agitation, permeation, wire-pulling, Parliamentary lobbying, the drafting of resolutions, petitions, and bills—in short, of all those artifices by which a popular movement is first created and then made effective on the Parliamentary system—he was an inventor and tactician of the first order. Above all, he possessed in perfection the rare quality of permitting other people to carry off the credit of his work, and thus secured for his proposals willing promoters and supporters, some of the leading Parliamentary figures of the time owing all their knowledge on his questions to the briefs with which he supplied them. The invaluable collection of manuscript records left by him, now in the British Museum, prove that modesty had nothing to do with his contemptuous readiness to leave the trophies of victory to his pawns provided his end was attained. He was thoroughly appreciative of the fact that in every progressive movement his shop at Charing Cross was the real centre of power when the Parliamentary stage of a progressive movement was reached. It remained, from 1807 down to about 1834, the recognised meeting-place of all the agitators of the time.[1]

It was in watching the effect of the Combination Laws in his own trade that Place became converted to their repeal. The special laws of 1720 and 1767, fixing the wages of journeymen tailors, as well as the general law of 1800 against all combinations, had failed to regulate wages, to prevent strikes, or to hinder those masters who wished in times of pressure to engage skilled men, from offering the bribe of high piecework rates, or even time wages in excess of the legal limit. Place gave evidence as a master tailor before the Select Committee of the House of Commons which inquired into the subject in 1810 ; and it was chiefly his weighty testimony in favour of freedom of contract that averted the fresh legal restrictions which a combination of employers was then openly promoting.[2] This experience of the practical freedom of employers to combine intensified Place's sense of the injustice of denying a like freedom to the journeymen, whilst the brutal prose-

[1] An admirable biography has now been written, *The Life of Francis Place, 1771–1854,* by Prof. Graham Wallas; first edition, 1898; revised edition, 1918.

[2] Place MSS. 27798—8, 12, etc. ; *Times,* November 9, 1810; *The Tailoring Trade,* by F. W. Galton, 1896, pp. 110-11.

E

cution of the compositors of the *Times* in the same year brought home to his mind the severity of the law. Four years later (1814), as he himself tells us, he " began to work seriously to procure a repeal of the laws against combinations of workmen, but for a long time made no visible progress." The employers were firmly convinced that combinations of wage-earners would succeed in securing a great rise of wages, to the serious detriment of profits. Far from contemplating a repeal of the Act of 1800, they were in 1814 and 1816 pestering the Home Secretary for legislation of greater stringency as the only safeguard for their " freedom of enterprise." [1] The politicians were equally certain that Trade Union action would raise prices, and thus undermine the foreign trade upon which the prosperity and international influence of England depended. The working men themselves afforded in the first instance no assistance. Those who had suffered legal prosecution were hopeless of redress from an unreformed Parliament, and offered no support. One trade, the Spitalfields silk-weavers, supported the Government because they enjoyed what they deemed to be the advantage of legal protection from the lowering of wages by competition.[2] Others were suspicious of the intervention of one who was himself an employer, and who had not yet gained recognition as a friend to labour. But Place was undismayed by hostility and indifference. Knowing that with an English public the strength of his cause would lie, not in any abstract

---

[1] See the petitions of the Master Manufacturers of Glasgow, Lancashire, and Nottinghamshire, in the Home Office Papers (42—141, 149, 150, 195, etc.).

[2] When Place in 1824 urged the " Committee of Engine Silk-weavers " of Spitalfields to petition for a repeal of the Combination Laws, the meeting " Resolved, that protected as we have been for years under the salutary laws and wisdom of the Legislature, and being completely unapprehensive of any sort of combination on our part, we cannot therefore take any sort of notice of the invitation held out by Mr. Place." When this resolution was put by the chairman, " an unanimous burst of applause followed, with a multitude of voices exclaiming, ' The law, cling to the law, it will protect us ! ' " Place MSS. 27800—52 ; *Morning Chronicle*, February 9, 1824.

reasoning or appeal to natural rights, but in an enumeration of actual cases of injustice, he made a point of obtaining the particulars of every trade dispute.   He intervened, as he says, in every strike, sometimes as a mediator, sometimes as an ally of the journeymen.   He opened up a voluminous correspondence with Trade Unions throughout the kingdom, and wrote innumerable letters to the newspapers.   In 1818 he secured a useful medium in the *Gorgon*,[1] a little working-class political newspaper, started by one Wade, a wool-comber, and subsidised by Bentham and Place himself. This gained him his two most important disciples, event-ually the chief instruments of his work, J. R. McCulloch and Joseph Hume.   McCulloch, afterwards to gain fame as an economist, was at that time the editor of the *Scotsman*, perhaps the most important of the provincial newspapers. A powerful article based on Place's facts which he con-tributed to the *Edinburgh Review* in 1823 secured many converts ;   and his constant advocacy gave Place's idea a weight and notoriety which it had hitherto lacked.   Joseph Hume was an even more important ally.   His acknow-ledged position in the House of Commons as one of the leaders of the growing party of Philosophic Radicalism gained for the repeal movement a steadily increasing support with advanced members of Parliament.   Among a certain section in the House the desirability of freedom of com-bination began to be discussed ; presently it was considered practicable ;   and soon many came to regard it as an inevit-able outcome of their political creed.   In 1822 Place thought the time ripe for action ;   and Hume accordingly gave notice of his intention to bring in a Bill to repeal all the laws against combinations.

Place's manuscripts and letters contain a graphic account of the wire-pullings and manipulations of the next two years.[2]   In these contemporary pictures of the inner

---

[1] The volumes for 1818–19 are in the British Museum.
[2] The story has now been well told in *The Life of Francis Place*, by Prof. Graham Wallas, revised edition, 1918, ch. viii. ; and in *The Town*

workings of the Parliamentary system we watch Hume cajoling Huskisson and Peel into granting him a Select Committee, staving off the less tactful proposals of a rival M.P.,[1] and finally, in February 1824, packing the Committee of Inquiry at length appointed. Hume, with some art, had included in his motion three distinct subjects— the emigration of artisans, the exportation of machinery, and combinations of workmen, all of which were forbidden by law. To Place and Hume the repeal of the Combination Laws was the main object ; but Huskisson and his colleagues regarded the Committee as primarily charged with an inquiry into the possibility of encouraging the rising manufacture of machinery, which was seriously hampered by the prohibition of sales to foreign countries. Huskisson tried to induce Hume to omit from the Committee's reference all mention of the Combination Laws, evidently regarding them as only a minor and unimportant part of the inquiry. But Place and Hume were now masters of the situation ; and for the next few months they devoted their whole time to the management of the Committee. At first no one seems to have had any idea that its proceedings were going

---

Labourer, by J. L. and B. Hammond, 1917, ch. vii. A few other details will be found in *Digest of Evidence before the Committee on Artisans and Machinery*, by George White, 1824, and in *Labour Legislation, Labour Movements, and Labour Leaders*, by G. Howell, 1902, pp. 43-57.

[1] In 1823 George White, a "clerk of committees" of the House of Commons, had formed an alliance with Gravener Henson, the bobbin-net maker of Nottingham, who had long been a leader of the framework-knitters' combinations, to whom reference has been made in preceding pages. Together they prepared an elaborate Bill repealing all the Combination Acts, and substituting a complicated machinery for regulating piecework and settling industrial disputes. Some of these proposals were meritorious anticipations of subsequent factory legislation ; but the time was not ripe for such measures. This Bill, promptly introduced by Peter Moore, the member for Coventry, had the effect of scaring some timid legislators, and especially alarming the Front Bench. Hume was at a loss to know how to act; but Place, in a letter displaying great political sagacity, advised him to baulk the rival Bill by putting its author on the Committee of Inquiry, explaining that "Moore is not a man to be put aside. The only way to put him down is to let him talk his nonsense in the Committee, where, being outvoted, he will be less of an annoyance in the House." See Place MSS. 27798—12.

to be of any moment ; and no trouble was taken by the Ministry with regard to its composition. " It was with difficulty," writes Place, " that Mr. Hume could obtain the names of twenty-one members to compose the Committee ; but when it had sat three days, and had become both popular and amusing, members contrived to be put upon it ; and at length it consisted of forty-eight members." [1] Hume, who was appointed chairman, appears to have taken into his own hands the entire management of the proceedings. A circular explaining the objects of the inquiry was sent to the mayor or other public officer of forty provincial towns, and appeared in the principal local newspapers. Public meetings were held at Stockport and other towns to depute witnesses to attend the Committee. [2] Meanwhile Place, who had by this time acquired the confidence of the chief leaders of the working class, secured the attendance of artisan witnesses from all parts of the kingdom. Read in the light of Place's private records and daily correspondence with Hume, the proceedings of this " Committee on Artisans and Machinery " reveal an almost perfect example of political manipulation. Although no hostile witness was denied a hearing, it was evidently arranged that the employers who were favourable to repeal should be examined first, and that the preponderance of evidence should be on their side. And whilst those interests which would have been antagonistic to the repeal were neither professionally represented nor deliberately organised, the men's case was marshalled with admirable skill by Place, and fully brought out by Hume's examination. Thus the one acted as the Trade Unionists' Parliamentary solicitor, and the other as their unpaid counsel. [3]

[1] Place MSS. 27798—30.
[2] This attracted the attention of the Home Secretary (Home Office Papers, 40—18).
[3] Place offered to act as Hume's " assistant " ; but the members of the Committee, whose suspicions had been aroused, refused to permit him to remain in the room, on the double ground that he was not a member of the House, nor even a gentleman !

Place himself tells us how he proceeded : " The delegates from the working people had reference to me, and I opened my house to them.   Thus I had all the town and country delegates under my care.   I heard the story which every one of these men had to tell, I examined and cross-examined them, took down the leading particulars of each case, and then arranged the matter as briefs for Mr. Hume, and as a rule, for the guidance of the witnesses, a copy was given to each. . . . Each brief contained the principal questions and answers. . . . That for Mr. Hume was generally accompanied by an appendix of documents arranged in order, with a short account of such proceedings as were necessary to put Mr. Hume in possession of the whole case.   Thus he was enabled to go on with considerable ease, and to anticipate or rebut objections." [1]

The Committee sat in private ; but Hume's numerous letters to Place show how carefully the latter was kept posted up in all the proceedings : " As the proceedings of the Committee were printed from day to day for the use of the members, I had a copy sent to me by Mr. Hume, which I indexed on paper ruled in many columns, each column having an appropriate head or number.   I also wrote remarks on the margins of the printed evidence ; this was copied daily by Mr. Hume's secretary, and then returned to me.   This consumed much time, but enabled Mr. Hume to have the whole mass constantly under his view ; and I am very certain that less pains and care would not have been sufficient to have carried the business through." [2]

From Westminster Hall we are transported, by these private notes for Hume's use, all now preserved in the British Museum, into the back parlour of the Charing Cross shop, where the London and provincial artisan witnesses came for their instructions.   " The workmen," as Place tells us, " were not easily managed.   It required great care and pains not to shock their prejudices so as

---

[1] Place MSS. 27798—22.   [2] *Ibid.* 27798—23.

to prevent them doing their duty before the Committee. They were filled with false notions, all attributing their distresses to wrong causes, which I, in this state of the business, dared not attempt to remove. Taxes, machinery, laws against combinations, the will of the masters, the conduct of magistrates—these were the fundamental causes of all their sorrows and privations. . . . I had to discuss everything with them most carefully, to arrange and prepare everything, and so completely did these things occupy my time that for more than three months I had hardly any rest." [1]

The result of the inquiry was as Hume and Place had ordained. A series of resolutions in favour of complete freedom of combination and liberty of emigration was adopted by the Committee, apparently without dissent. A Bill to repeal all the Combination Laws and to legalise trade societies was passed through both Houses, within less than a week, at the close of the session, without either debate or division. Place and Hume contrived privately to talk over and to silence the few members who were alive to the situation ; and the measure passed, as Place remarks, "almost without the notice of members within or newspapers without." [2] So quietly was the Bill smuggled through Parliament that the magistrates at a Lancashire town unwittingly sentenced certain cotton-weavers to imprisonment for combination some weeks after the laws against that crime had been repealed.[3]

Place and Hume had, however, been rather too clever. Whilst the governing classes were quite unconscious that any important alteration of law or policy had taken place, the unlooked-for success of Place's agitation produced, as Nassau Senior describes, "a great moral effect" in all the industrial centres. "It confirmed in the minds of the

---

[1] Place MS. 27798—22.

[2] The Act was 5 George IV. c. 95. The question of the exportation of machinery was deferred until the next session.

[3] Letter in the *Manchester Gazette*, preserved in the Place MSS. 27801—214.

operatives the conviction of the justice of their cause, tardily and reluctantly, but at last fully, conceded by the Legislature. That which was morally right in 1824 must have been so, they would reason, for fifty years before. . . . They conceived that they had extorted from the Legislature an admission that their masters must always be their rivals, and had hitherto been their oppressors, and that combinations to raise wages, and shorten the time or diminish the severity of labour, were not only innocent, but meritorious." [1] Trade Societies accordingly sprang into existence or emerged into aggressive publicity on all sides. A period of trade inflation, together with a rapid rise in the price of provisions, favoured a general increase of wages. For the next six months the newspapers are full of strikes and rumours of strikes. Serious disturbances occurred at Glasgow, where the employers had been exceptionally oppressive, where the cotton operatives committed several outrages, and where a general lock-out took place. The cotton-spinners were once more striking in the Manchester district. The shipping trade of the North-East Coast was temporarily paralysed by a strong combination of the seamen on the Tyne and Wear, who refused to sail except with Unionist seamen and Unionist officers. The Dublin trades, then the best organised in the kingdom, ruthlessly enforced their byelaws for the regulation of their respective industries, and formed a joint committee, the so-called " Board of Green Cloth," whose dictates became the terror of the employers. The Sheffield operatives have to be warned that, if they persist in demanding double the former wages for only three days a week work, the whole industry of the town will be ruined.[2] The London shipwrights insisted on what their employers considered the preposterous demand for a " book of rates " for piecework The London coopers demanded a revision of their wages, which led to a long-

---

[1] MS. Report of Nassau Senior to Lord Melbourne on Trade Combinations (1831; unpublished; in Home Office Library).
[2] *Sheffield Iris*, April 2, 1825.

sustained conflict. In fact, as a provincial newspaper remarked a little later, " it is no longer a particular class of journeymen at some single point that have been induced to commence a strike for an advance of wages, but almost the whole body of the mechanics in the kingdom are combined in the general resolution to impose terms on their employers." [1]

The opening of the session of 1825 found the employers throughout the country thoroughly aroused. Hume and Place had in vain preached moderation, and warned the Unions of the danger of a reaction. The great shipowning and shipbuilding interest, which had throughout the century preserved intact its reputation for unswerving hostility to Trade Unionism, had possession of the ear of Huskisson, then President of the Board of Trade and member for Liverpool. Early in the session he moved for a committee of inquiry into the conduct of the workmen and the effect of the recent Act, which, he complained, had been smuggled through the House without his attention having been called to the fact that it went far beyond the mere repeal of the special statutes against combinations. [2] This time the composition of the committee was not left to chance, or to Hume's manipulation. The members were, as Place complains, selected almost exclusively from the Ministerial benches, twelve out of the thirty being placemen, and many being representatives of rotten boroughs. Huskisson, [3]

---

[1] *Sheffield Mercury* October 8, 1825 ; see the *Manchester Guardian* for August 1824 to a similar effect.

[2] Later in the year Lord Liverpool, the Prime Minister, and Lord Eldon, the Lord Chancellor, protested in debate that they had been quite unaware of the passing of the Act, and that they would never have assented to it.

[3] The *Annual Register* for 1825 gives a fuller report of Huskisson's speech than Hansard's Parliamentary Debates. Further particulars are supplied in George White's *Abstract of the Act repealing the Laws against Combinations of Workmen* (1824) ; in Place's *Observations on Mr. Huskisson's Speech on the Law relating to Combinations of Workmen*, by F. P. (1825, 32 pp.) ; in Wallas's *Life of Francis Place*, revised edition, 1918, ch. viii. ; in Hammond's *The Town Labourer*, ch. vii. ; and in Howell's *Labour Legislation, Labour Movements, and Labour Leaders*, pp. 51-7.

Peel, and the Attorney-General themselves took part in its proceedings ; Wallace, the Master of the Mint, was made chairman, and Hume alone represented the workmen. Huskisson regarded the Committee as merely a formal preliminary to the introduction of the Bill which the shipping interest had drafted,[1] under which Trade Unions, and even Friendly Societies, would have been impossible. For the inner history of this Committee we have to rely on Place's voluminous memoranda, and Hume's brief notes to him. According to these, the original intention was to call only a few employers as witnesses, to exclude all testimony on the other side, and promptly to report in favour of the repressive measure already prepared. Place, himself an expert in such tactics, met them by again supplying Hume daily with detailed information which enabled him to cross-examine the masters and expose their exaggerations. And, if Place's account of the animus of the Committee and the Ministers against himself be somewhat highly coloured, we have ample evidence of the success with which he guided the alarmed Trade Unions to take effectual action in their own defence. His friend John Gast, secretary to the London Shipwrights, called for two delegates from each trade in the metropolis, and formed a committee which kept up a persistent agitation against any re-enactment of the Combination Laws. Similar committees were formed at Manchester and Glasgow by the cotton operatives, at Sheffield by the cutlers, and at Newcastle by the seamen and shipwrights. Petitions, the draft of which appears in Place's manuscripts, poured in to the Select Committee and to both Houses. If we are to believe Place, the passages leading to the committee-room were carefully kept thronged by crowds of workmen insisting on being examined to rebut the accusations of the employers, and waylaying individual members to whom they explained their grievances. All this

---

[1] This included a provision to forbid the subscription of any funds to a trade or other association, unless some magistrate approved its objects and became its treasurer.

energy on the part of the Unions was, as Place observes, in marked contrast with their apathy the year before. The workmen, though they had done nothing to gain their freedom of association, were determined to maintain it. Doherty, the leader of the Lancashire Cotton-spinners, writing to Place in the heat of the agitation, declared that any attempt at a re-enactment of the Combination Laws would result in a widespread revolutionary movement.[1] The nett result of the inquiry was, on the whole, satisfactory. The Select Committee found themselves compelled to hear a certain number of workmen witnesses, who testified to the good results of the Act of the previous year. The ship-owners' Bill was abandoned, and the House of Commons was recommended to pass a measure which nominally re-established the general common-law prohibition of combinations, but specifically excepted from prosecution associations for the purpose of regulating wages or hours of labour. The master shipbuilders were furious at this virtual defeat. The handbill is still extant which they distributed at the doors of the House of Commons on the day of the second reading of the emasculated Bill.[2] They declared that its provisions were quite insufficient to save their industry from destruction. If Trade Unions were to be allowed to exist at all, they demanded that these bodies should be compelled to render full accounts of their expenditure to the justices in Quarter Sessions, and that any diversion of monies raised for friendly society purposes should be severely punished. They pleaded, moreover, that at any rate all federal or combined action among trade clubs should be prohibited. Place and Hume, on the other hand, were afraid, and subsequent events proved with what good grounds, that the narrow limits of the trade combinations allowed by the Bill, and still more the vague terms " molest " and " obstruct," which it contained, would be used as weapons against Trade Unionism. The Government, however, held to the draft of the Committee

---

[1] Place MSS. 27803—299.   [2] *Ibid.* 27803—212.

The shipbuilders secured nothing.   Hume induced Ministers to give way on some verbal points, and took three divisions in vain protest against the measure.   Place carried on the agitation to the House of Lords, where Lord Rosslyn extracted the concession of a right of appeal to Quarter Sessions, which was afterwards to prove of some practical value.

The Act of 1825 (6 Geo. IV. c. 129)[1]—which became known among the manufacturers as " Peel's Act "—though it fell short of the measure which Place and Hume had so skilfully piloted through Parliament the year before, effected a real emancipation.   The right of collective bargaining, involving the power to withhold labour from the market by concerted action, was for the first time expressly established. And although many struggles remained to be fought before the legal freedom of Trade Unionism was fully secured, no overt attempt has since been made to render illegal this first condition of Trade Union action.[2]

It is a suggestive feature of this, as of other great re-forms, that the men whose faith in its principle, and whose indefatigable industry and resolution carried it through, were the only ones who proved altogether mistaken as to its practical consequences.   If we read the lesson of the century aright, the manufacturer was not wholly wrong when he protested that liberty of combination must make the workers the ultimate authority in industry, although his narrow fear as to the driving away of capital and commercial skill and the reduction of the nation to a dead level of anarchic pauperism were entirely contradicted by subse-quent developments.   And the workman, to whom liberty to combine opened up vistas of indefinite advancement of

---

[1] Home Office Papers, letter of January 3, 1832 (H.O. 40—30).

[2] It is pleasant to record that some of the workmen expressed their gratitude for Francis Place's indefatigable services.   " Soon after the proceedings in 1825 were closed," he writes, " the seamen of the Tyne and Wear sent me a handsome silver vase, paid for by a penny-a-week sub-scription ;   and the cutlers of Sheffield sent me an incomparable set of knives and forks in a case " (Place MSS. 27798—66).

his class at the expense of his oppressors, was, we now see, looking rightly forward, though he, too, greatly miscalculated the distance before him, and overlooked many arduous stages of the journey. But what is to be said of the forecasts of Place and the Philosophic Radicals ? " Combinations," writes Place to Sir Francis Burdett in 1825, " will soon cease to exist. Men have been kept together for long periods only by the oppressions of the laws ; these being repealed, combinations will lose the matter which cements them into masses, and they will fall to pieces. All will be as orderly as even a Quaker could desire. . . . He knows nothing of the working people who can suppose that, when left at liberty to act for themselves without being driven into permanent associations by the oppression of the laws, they will continue to contribute money for distant and doubtful experiments, for uncertain and precarious benefits. If let alone, combinations—excepting now and then, and for particular purposes under peculiar circumstances—will cease to exist." [1]

It is pleasant to feel that Place was right in regarding the repeal as beneficial and worthy of his best efforts in its support ; but in every less general respect he and his allies were as wrong as it was possible for them to be. The first disappointment, however, came to the workmen. Over and over again they had found their demands for higher wages parried only by the employers' resort to the law, and they now saw the way clear before them for an organised attack upon their masters' profits. Trades which had not yet enjoyed permanent combinations began to organise in the expectation of raising their wages to the level of those of their more fortunate brethren. The Sheffield shop-assistants combined to petition for early closing.[2] The cotton-weavers of Lancashire met in delegate meeting at Manchester in August 1824 to establish a permanent organisation to prevent reductions in prices and to secure

[1] June 25, 1825. *Ibid.* 27798—57.
[2] *Sheffield Iris*, September 27, 1825.

a uniform wage, the notice stating that it was by their secret combinations that the tailors, joiners, and spinners had succeeded in keeping up wages.[1]   In the same month the Manchester dyers turned out for an advance, and paraded the streets, which they had placarded with their proposals.[2] The Glasgow calender-men struck for a regular twelve hours' day, and carried their point.   The success of the ship-wrights on the north-east coast [3] induced the London ship-wrights to convert their " Committee for conducting the Business in the North " into the " Shipwrights' Provident Union of the Port of London," which existed continuously until its absorption in the twentieth century by the national society dominating the trade.

" Such is the rage for union societies," reports the *Sheffield Iris* of July 12, 1825, " that the sea apprentices in Sunderland have actually had regular meetings every day last week on the moor, and have resolved not to go on board their ships unless the owners will allow them tea and sugar." Local trade clubs expanded, like the Manchester Steam-Engine Makers' Society, into national organisations.   In other cases corresponding clubs developed into federal bodies.   The object in all these cases was the same.   The preamble to the first rules of the Friendly Society of Opera-tive House Carpenters and Joiners of Great Britain, which was established by a delegate meeting in London in 1827, states that, " for the amelioration of the evils attendant on our trade, and the advancement of the rights and privileges of labour," it was considered " absolutely necessary that a firm compact of interests should exist between the whole of the operative carpenters and joiners throughout the United Kingdom of Great Britain." [4]

---

[1] Handbill preserved in Place MSS. 27803—255.

[2] *Manchester Guardian*, August 7, 1824 ; see also *On Combinations of Trades* (1830).

[3] This is expressly stated in the preamble to the rules adopted at the meeting on August 16, 1824, and recorded in the first minute-book.

[4] This society afterwards developed into the existing General Union of Carpenters and Joiners of Great Britain.

Nor was it only in the multiplication of trade societies that the expansion showed itself. A committee of delegates from the London trades meeting during the summer of 1825 set on foot the *Trades Newspaper and Mechanics' Weekly Journal*, a sevenpenny stamped paper, with the motto, " They helped every one his neighbour, and every one said to his brother, ' Be of good cheer.' "[1] A vigorous attempt was made to promote Trade Union organisation in all industries, and to bring to bear a body of instructed working-class opinion upon the political situation of the day.[2]

The high hopes of which all this exultant activity was the symptom were soon rudely dashed. The year 1825 closed with a financial panic and widespread commercial disaster. The four years that followed were years of contraction and distress. Hundreds of thousands of workmen in all trades lost their employment, and wages were reduced all round. In many manufacturing districts the operatives were kept from starvation only by public subscriptions.[3] Strikes under these circumstances ended invariably in disaster. A notable stand made by the Bradford woolcombers and weavers in 1825 resulted in complete defeat and the break-up of the Union.[4]

During the greater part of the following year all Lancashire was convulsed by incessant strikes of coal-miners and textile workers against the repeated reductions of wages to

[1] Two rival journals, *The Journeyman's and Artisan's London and Provincial Chronicle*, and *The Mechanic's Newspaper and Trade Journal*, were also started, but soon expired.

[2] The *Trades Newspaper* was managed by a committee of eleven delegates from different trades, of which John Gast was chairman, and was edited, at first by Mr. Baines, son of the proprietor of the *Leeds Mercury*, and afterwards by a Mr. Anderson. *The Laws and Regulations of the Trades Newspaper* (1825, 12 pp.) are preserved in the Place MSS. 27803—414. The issues from July 17, 1825, to its amalgamation with *The Trades Free Press* in 1828, are in the British Museum.

[3] £232,000 was raised by one committee alone between 1826 and 1829. See *Report of the Committee appointed at a Public Meeting at the City of London Tavern, May 2, 1826, to relieve the Manufacturers*, by W. H. Hyett, 1829.

[4] *Wool and Wool-combing*, by Burnley, p. 169.

which the employers resorted—strikes which were marred by
serious disorder, the destruction of many hundreds of looms,
and severe repression by the troops.[1]

At Kidderminster, three years later, practically the whole
trade of the town was brought to a standstill by the carpet-
weavers' six months' resistance to a reduction of 17 per
cent in their wages [2]—a resistance in which the operatives
received the sympathy and support of many who did not
belong to their class. In the same year the silk-weavers of
London and other towns maintained an embittered resistance to a further cut at wages.[3] The emancipated combinations were no more able to resist reductions than the
secret ones had been, and in some instances the workmen
again resorted to violence and machine-breaking.

For a moment the repeal seemed, after all, to have done
nothing but prove the futility of mere sectional combination, and the working men turned back again from Trade
Union action to the larger aims and wider character of the
Radical and Socialistic agitations of the time, with which,
from 1829 to 1842, the Trade Union Movement became
inextricably entangled. This is the phase which furnishes
the theme of the following chapter.

[1] Home Office Papers, 40—20, 21, etc. ; *Annual Register*, 1826, pp. 63,
70, 111, 128 ; Walpole's *History of England*, vol. ii. p. 141.

[2] *A Letter to the Carpet Manufacturers of Kidderminster*, by the Rev.
H. Price (1828, 16 pp.) ; *A Letter to the Rev. H. Price, upon the Tendency of
Certain Publications of his*, by Oppidanus, 1828 ; and *A Verbatim Report
of the Trial of the Rev. Humphrey Price upon a Criminal Information by the
Kidderminster Carpet Manufacturers for Alleged Inflammatory Publications
during the Turn-out of the Weavers*, 1829.

[3] *Resolutions of the Meeting of Journeymen Broad Silk Weavers at
Spitalfields, April 16, 1829* ; in Home Office Papers, 40—23, 24.   See, for
this period, Cunningham's *Growth of English Industry and Commerce in
Modern Times*, 1903, pp. 759-762 ; and also *The Skilled Labourer*, by
J. L. and B. Hammond, 1919, published too late for us to make use of its
interesting descriptions of the principal trades.

mittee and the other trades, and promised the support
of all, both in approved trade movements and in case of
legal prosecution or oppression. A committee of eleven
was to be chosen by ballot, one-third retiring monthly by
rotation ; and was to be assisted by a similar local organisation in each town.[1] How far the " General Union," as
the " Philanthropic Society " seems also to have been called,
got under way in Lancashire or Staffordshire remains
uncertain ; but in London the idea was taken up by one
of the ablest Trade Unionists of the time—the shipwright
John Gast, whom we have already mentioned as an ally of
Francis Place, who became president and called upon " the
general body of mechanics " to subscribe a penny per
week to a central fund for the defence of their common
interests.[2]

Whether anything came of the attempts at a General
Union in 1818–19 we have not discovered, but in all probability the project immediately failed. Seven years later
a similar effort met with no greater success. " In 1826,"
as we incidentally learn from a subsequent Labour journal,[3]
" a Trades Union was formed in Manchester, which extended
slightly to some of the surrounding districts, and embraced
several trades in each ; but it expired before it was so much
as known to a large majority of the operatives in the neighbourhood."

What was aimed at is clear enough. It was being
recommended to the workmen by some of their intellectual
advisers. An able pamphlet of 1827 tells them that
" Against the competition of the underpaid of surrounding
trades, the ready remedy is a central union of all the general

---

[1] See the reports to the Home Secretary (Home Office Papers, 42—179,
180, 181, 182) ; *The Town Labourer* (by J. L. and B. Hammond, 1917),
pp. 306-11.

[2] See the " Articles of the Philanthropic Hercules, for the Mutual
Support of the Labouring Mechanics," dated December 24, 1818, which
Gast contributed to the *Gorgon*. Gast's preliminary address appears in
the issue for December 5, 1818, and in that of January 29, 1819, the
society is described as established (Place MSS. 27899—143).

[3] *The Herald of the Rights of Industry* (Manchester, April 5, 1834).

unions of all the trades of the country. The remuneration of all the different branches of artisans and mechanics in the country might then be fixed at those rates which would leave such an equalised remuneration to all as would take away any temptation from those in one branch to transfer their skill in order to undersell the labour of the well-remunerated in another branch : the Central Union fund being always ready to assist the unemployed in any particular branch, when their own local and general funds were exhausted ; provided always their claims to support were by the Central Union deemed to be just." [1]

Experience seems to show that national organisation of particular trades must precede the formation of any General Trades Union ; and it was in this way that the project now took form. In 1829 we see renewed attempts at national organisation, in which the Lancashire and Yorkshire textile and building operatives were pioneers. The year 1829, closing the long depression of trade which began in the autumn of 1825, after the repeal of the Combination Laws, witnessed the establishment of important national Unions in both industries, but that of the Cotton-spinners claims precedence in respect of its more rapid development.

The Cotton-spinners' trade clubs of Lancashire date apparently from 1792, and they spread, within a generation, to thirty or forty towns, remaining always strictly local organisations. In the early years of the nineteenth century attempts had been made by the Glasgow spinners to unite the Lancashire and Scottish organisations in a national association ; but these attempts had not resulted in more than temporary alliances in particular emergencies. The rapid improvement of spinning machinery, and the enterprise of the Lancashire millowners, were, at the date of the repeal of the Combination Laws, shifting the centre

---

[1] *Labour Rewarded : The Claims of Labour and Capital : How to secure to Labour the Whole Product of its Exertions*, by One of the Idle Classes [William Thompson], 1827 ; see *The Irish Labour Movement*, by W. P. Ryan, 1919.

of the trade from Glasgow to Manchester ; and it was the Lancashire Cotton-spinners who now took the lead in trade matters. The failure of a disastrous six months' strike in 1829 at Hyde, near Manchester, led to the conviction that no local Union could succeed against a combination of employers ; and the spinners' societies of England, Scotland, and Ireland were therefore invited to send delegates to a conference to be held at Ramsay, in the Isle of Man, in the month of December 1829.

This delegate meeting, of which there is an excellent report,[1] lasted for nearly a week. The proceedings were of a remarkably temperate character, the discussions turning chiefly on the relative advantages of one supreme executive to be established at Manchester, and three co-equal national executives for England, Scotland, and Ireland. No secrecy was attempted. John Doherty,[2] secretary and leader of

---

[1] *A Report of the Proceedings of the Meeting of Cotton-spinners at Ramsay,* etc. (Manchester, 1829, 56 pages) ; *Copy of Resolutions of the Delegates from the Operative Cotton-spinners who met at the Isle of Man* (Manchester, 1830), in Home Office Papers, 40—27.

[2] John Doherty, described by Place as a somewhat hot-headed Roman Catholic—really one of the acutest thinkers and stoutest leaders among the workmen of his time—was born in Ireland in 1799, and went to work in a cotton-mill at Larne, Co. Antrim, at the age of ten. In 1816 he migrated to Manchester, where he quickly became one of the leading Trade Unionists, and secretary to the local Cotton-spinners' Society. We find him, for instance, taking a prominent part in the agitation against the proposed re-enactment of the Combination Laws in 1825. Whether he was concerned in the Philanthropic Society or General Union of 1818 or 1826 we do not know. In 1829 he organised the great strike of the Hyde spinners against a reduction of rates, and became, as described in the text, successively General Secretary to the Federation of Spinners' Societies, and to the National Association for the Protection of Labour, in which office he is reported, probably inaccurately, to have received the then enormous salary of £600 a year. We naturally find him the object of great suspicion by the Government, but no charge seems ever to have been brought against him (Home Office Papers, 40—26, 27). The articles in the *Voice of the People* and the *Poor Man's Advocate*, which are evidently from his pen, show him to have been a man of wide information, great natural shrewdness, and far-reaching aims. His idea was that all the local and district Unions were to be federated in a national organisation for the sole purpose of dealing with trade matters, and that they should also be federated in a National Association for obtaining political reforms. In 1832, during the Reform crisis, Place describes him as advising the working classes to use the occasion for a social revolution. He sub-

the Manchester Cotton-spinners, advocated a central executive ; while Thomas Foster (a man of independent means who attended the conference at his own expense) favoured a scheme of home rule. Eventually a " Grand General Union of the United Kingdom " was established, subject to an annual delegate meeting and three national committees. The union was to include all male spinners and piecers, the women and girls being urged to form separate organisations, which were to receive all the aid of the whole confederation in supporting them to obtain " men's prices." The union was to promote local action for a further legislative restriction of the hours of labour, to apply to all persons under 21 years of age. Its income consisted of a contribution of a penny per week per member, to be levied in addition to the contribution to the local society. Doherty was general secretary, and Foster and a certain Patrick McGowan were appointed to organise the spinners throughout the United Kingdom.

The Boroughreeve and Constables of Manchester, on May 26, 1830, wrote in alarm to Sir Robert Peel : " The combination of workmen, long acknowledged a great evil, and one most difficult to counteract, has recently assumed so formidable and systematic a shape in this district that we feel it our duty to lay before you some of its most alarming features. . . . A committee of delegates from the operative spinners of the three Kingdoms have established an annual assembly in the Isle of Man to direct the proceedings of the general body towards their employers, the orders for which they promulgate to their respective districts and sub-committees. To these orders the most implicit deference

---

sequently acted as secretary to an association of operatives and masters established to enforce the Factory Acts, and was one of Lord Shaftesbury's most strenuous supporters. In 1838, when he had become a printer and bookseller in Manchester, he gave evidence before the Select Committee on Combinations of Workmen, in which he described the spinners' organisations and strikes. There is a pamphlet by him in the Goldsmiths' Library at the University of London, entitled *A Letter to the Members of the National Association for the Protection of Labour* (Manchester, 1831).

is shown ; and a weekly levy or rent of one penny per head on each operative is cheerfully paid. This produces a large sum, and is a powerful engine, and principally to support those who have turned out against their employers, agreeable to the orders of the committee, at the rate of ten shillings per week for each person. The plan of a general turnout having been found to be impolitic, they have employed it in detail, against particular individuals or districts, who, attacked thus singly, are frequently compelled to submit to their terms rather than to the ruin which would ensue to many by allowing their machinery (in which their whole capital is invested) to stand idle." [1]

Whether this Cotton-spinners' Federation, as we should call it, became really representative of the three kingdoms does not appear. A second general delegate meeting was held at Manchester in December 1830, which intervened in the great spinners' strike then in progress at Ashton-under-Lyne. At this conference the constitution of 1829 was re-enacted with some alterations. The three national executives were apparently replaced by an executive council of three members elected by the Manchester Society, to be reinforced at its monthly meetings by two delegates chosen in turn by each of the neighbouring districts. A general delegate meeting seems also to have been held, attended by one delegate from each of the couple of scores of towns in which there were local clubs. [2] Foster was appointed general secretary ; and a committee was ordered to draw up a general list of prices, for which purpose one member in each mill was directed to send up a copy of the list by which he was paid. Although another delegate meeting of this " Grand General Union " was fixed for Whit Monday 1831 at Liverpool, no further record of its existence can be traced. It is probable that the attempt to include Scotland and Ireland proved a failure, and that the union had dwindled

[1] Home Office Papers, 40—27.
[2] *Ibid.*, December 3, 1830, 40—26.

into a federation of Lancashire societies, mainly preoccupied in securing a legislative restriction of the hours of labour.[1]

But the National Union of Cotton-spinners prepared the way for the more ambitious project of the Trades Union. Doherty, who seems to have resigned his official connection with the Cotton-spinners' Union, conceived the idea of a National Association, not of one trade alone, but of all classes of wage-earners. Already in May 1829 we find him, as Secretary of the Manchester Cotton-spinners, writing to acknowledge a gift of ten pounds from the Liverpool Sailmakers, and expressing " a hope that our joint efforts may eventually lead to a Grand General Union of all trades throughout the United Kingdom." [2] At his instigation a meeting of delegates from twenty organised trades was held at Manchester in February 1830, which ended in the establishment, five months later, of the National Association for the Protection of Labour. The express object of this society was to resist reductions, but not to strike for advances. In an eloquent address to working men of all trades, the new Association appealed to them to unite for their own protection and in order to maintain " the harmony of society " which is destroyed by their subjection. How is it, the Association asks, that whilst everything else increases—knowledge, wealth, civil and religious liberty, churches, madhouses, and prisons—the circumstances of the working man become ever worse ? " He, the sole producer of food and raiment, is, it appears, destined to sink whilst others rise." To prevent this evil

[1] Foster died in 1831, and McGowan settled at Glasgow. " Almost every spinning district," writes the *Poor Man's Advocate* of June 23, 1832, " of any consequence, was enrolled in the Union. The power of the Union, of course, increased with its members, and a number of the worst-paying employers were compelled to advance the wages of the spinners to something like the standard rate. . . . The Union, however, which Mr. McGowan had mainly contributed to mature, has since, from distrust or weariness, sunk into comparative insignificance."

[2] The letter is preserved in the MS. " Contribution Book " of the Liverpool Sailmakers' Friendly Association, established 1817.

the Association is formed.[1] Its constitution appears to
have been largely borrowed from that of the contemporary
Cotton-spinners, which it resembled in being a combination,
not of directly enlisted individuals, but of existing separate
societies, each of which paid an entrance fee of a pound,
together with a shilling for each of its members, and contributed at the rate of a penny per week per head of its
membership. Doherty was the first secretary, and the
Association appears very soon to have enrolled about 150
separate Unions, mostly in Lancashire, Cheshire, Derby,
Nottingham, and Leicester. The trades which joined were
mainly connected with the various textile industries—the
cotton-spinners, hosiery-workers, calico-printers, and silk-
weavers taking a leading part. The Association also
included numerous societies of mechanics, moulders, blacksmiths, and many miscellaneous trades. The building
trades were scarcely represented—a fact to be accounted
for by the contemporary existence of the Builders' Union
hereafter described. The list [2] of the receipts of the Association for the first nine months of its existence includes payments amounting to £1866, a sum which indicates a membership of between 10,000 and 20,000, spread over the five
counties already mentioned. A vigorous propaganda was
carried on throughout the northern and midland counties
by its officials, who succeeded in establishing a weekly
paper, the *United Trades Co-operative Journal*, which was
presently brought to an end by the intervention of the
Commissioners of Stamps, who insisted on each number
bearing a fourpenny stamp.[3] Undeterred by this failure,
the committee undertook the more serious task of starting
a sevenpenny stamped weekly, and requested Francis Place

[1] *Address of the National Association for the Protection of Labour to
the Workmen of the United Kingdom* (4 pp. 1830), in Home Office Papers,
40—27.

[2] Given as Appendix to the pamphlet *On Combination of Trades*
(1830). Compare Wade's *History of the Middle and Working Classes*
(1834), p. 277.

[3] Thirty-one numbers, extending from March 6 to October 2, 1830,
are in the Manchester Public Library (620 B).

to become the treasurer of an accumulated fund. " The subscription," writes Place to John Cam Hobhouse, December 5, 1830, " extends from Birmingham to the Clyde ; the committee sits at Manchester ; and the money collected amounts to about £3000, and will, they tell me, shortly be as much as £5000, with which sum, when raised, they propose to commence a weekly newspaper to be called the *Voice of the People*." Accordingly in January 1831 appeared the first number of what proved to be an excellent weekly journal, the object of which was declared to be " to unite the productive classes of the community in one common bond of union." Besides full weekly reports of the committee meetings of the National Association at Manchester and Nottingham, this newspaper, ably edited by John Doherty, gave great attention to Radical politics, including the Repeal of the Union with Ireland, and the progress of revolution on the Continent.[1]

From the reports published in the *Voice of the People* we gather that the first important action of the Association was in connection with the almost continuous strikes of the cotton-spinners at Ashton-under-Lyne, which flamed up into a sustained conflict on a large scale, during which Ashton, a young millowner, was murdered by some unknown person in the winter of 1830–31, in resistance to a new list of prices arbitrarily imposed by the Association of Master Spinners in Ashton, Dukinfield, and Stalybridge.[2] Considerable sums were raised by way of levy for the support of the strike, the Nottingham trades subscribing liberally. But the Association soon experienced a check. In February 1831 a new secretary decamped with £100. This led a delegate meeting at Nottingham, in April 1831, to decree that each Union should retain in hand the money contributed by its own members. But the usual failings of unions of various trades quickly showed themselves.

---

[1] The numbers from January to September 1831 are in the British Museum. See Place's letter in *Westminster Review* (1831), p. 243.
[2] Home Office Papers, 40—26, 27.

The refusal of the Lancashire branches to support the great Nottingham strike which immediately ensued led to the defection of the Nottingham members. Nevertheless the Association was spreading over new ground. We hear of delegates from Lancashire inducing thousands of colliers in Derbyshire to join, whilst other trades, and even the agricultural labourers, were talking about it.[1] At the end of April a delegate meeting at Bolton, representing nine thousand coalminers of Staffordshire, Yorkshire, Cheshire, and Wales, resolved to join. The Belfast trades applied for affiliation. In Leeds nine thousand members were enrolled, chiefly among the woollen-workers. Missionaries were sent to organise the Staffordshire potters ; and a National Potters' Union, extending throughout the country, was established and affiliated. All this activity lends a certain credibility to the assertion, made in various quarters, that the Association numbered one hundred thousand members, and that the *Voice of the People*, published at 7d. weekly, enjoyed the then enormous circulation of thirty thousand.

Here at last we have substance given to the formidable idea of " the Trades Union." It was soon worked up by the newspapers to a pitch at which it alarmed the employers, dismally excited the imaginations of the middle class, and compelled the attention of the Government. But there was no cause for apprehension. Lack of funds made the Association little more than a name. Practically no trade action is reported in such numbers of its organ as are still extant. The business of the Manchester Committee seems to have been confined to the promotion of the " Short Time Bill." On April 23, 1831, at the general meeting of the Association, then designated the Lancashire Trades Unions, it was resolved to prepare petitions in favour of extending this measure to all trades and all classes of workers. Active support was given in the meantime to Mr. Sadler's Factory Bill. Towards the end of the year we suddenly lose all

---

[1] Home Office Papers, April 8, 1831, 44—25.

trace of the National Association for the Protection of Labour, as far as Manchester is concerned. " After it had extended about a hundred miles round this town," writes a working-class newspaper of 1832, " a fatality came upon it that almost threatened its extinction. . . . But though it declined in Manchester it spread and flourished in other places ; and we rejoice to say that the resolute example set by Yorkshire and other places is likely once more to revive the drooping energies of those trades who had the honour of originating and establishing the Association." [1]

What the fatality was that extinguished the Association in Manchester is not stated ; but Doherty, to whose organising ability its initial success had been due, evidently quarrelled with the executive committee, and the *Voice of the People* ceased to appear.   In its place we find Doherty issuing, from January 1832, the *Poor Man's Advocate*, and vainly striving, in face of the " spirit " of " jealousy and faction," to build up the Yorkshire branches of the Association into a national organisation, with its headquarters in London. After the middle of 1832 we hear no more, either of the Association itself or of Doherty's more ambitious projects concerning it. [2]

The place of the National Association was soon filled by other contemporary general trade societies, of which the first and most important was the Builders' Union, or

---

[1] *Union Pilot and Co-operative Intelligencer*, March 24, 1832 (Manchester Public Library, 640 E).

[2] Meanwhile the coalminers of Northumberland and Durham, under the leadership of " Tommy Hepburn," an organiser of remarkable ability, had formed their first strong Union in 1830, which for two years kept the two counties in a state of excitement.   Strikes and riotings in 1831 and 1832 caused the troops to be called out : marines were sent from Portsmouth, and squadrons of cavalry scoured the country.   After six months' struggle in 1832 the Union collapsed, and the men submitted. See Home Office Papers for these years, 40—31, 32, &c. ; Sykes' *Local Records of Northumberland*, &c., vol. ii. pp. 293, 353 ; Fynes' *Miners of Northumberland and Durham* (Blyth, 1873), chaps. iv. v. vi. ; *An Earnest Address and Urgent Appeal to the People of England in behalf of the Oppressed and Suffering Pitmen of the Counties of Northumberland and Durham* (by W. Scott, Newcastle, 1831) ; *History and Description of Fossil Fuel*, etc. (by John Holland, 1835), pp. 298-304.

the General Trades Union, as it was sometimes termed. It consisted of the separate organisations of the seven building trades, viz. joiners, masons, bricklayers, plasterers, plumbers, painters, and builders' labourers, and is, so far as we know, the solitary example, prior to the present century, in the history of those trades of a federal union embracing all classes of building operatives, and purporting to extend over the whole country.[1]

The Grand Rules of the Builders' Union set forth an elaborate constitution in which it was attempted to combine a local and trade autonomy of separate lodges with a centralised authority for defensive and aggressive purposes. The rules inform us that " the object of this society shall be to advance and equalise the price of labour in every branch of the trade we admit into this society." Each lodge shall be " governed by its own password and sign, masons to themselves, and joiners to themselves, and so on ; " and it is ordered that " no lodge be opened by any

---

[1] It is not clear whether this scheme was initiated by carpenters or masons. The carpenters and joiners are distinguished among the building trades for the antiquity of their local trade clubs, which are known to have existed in London as far back as 1799. A national organisation was established in London in July 1827, called the Friendly Society of Operative Carpenters and Joiners, which still survives under the title of the " General Union." MS. records in the office of the latter show that this federation had 938 members in 1832, rising to 3691 in 1833, and to 6774 in 1834, a total not paralleled until 1865. This rapid increase marks the general upheaval of these years. But this Society did not throw in its lot with the Builders' Union until 1833. On the other hand, the existing Operative Stonemasons' Friendly Society, which dates its separate existence from 1834, but which certainly existed in some form from 1832, has among its archives what appear to be the original MS. rules and initiation rites of its predecessor, the Builders' Union ; and in these documents the masons figure as the foremost members. Moreover, these rules and rites closely resemble those of contemporary unions among the Yorkshire woollen-workers ; and an independent tradition fixes the parent lodge of the Masons' Society at the great woollen centre of Huddersfield, whereas the Friendly Society of Carpenters and Joiners, founded in London, had its headquarters at Leicester. But however this may be, the constitution and ceremonies described in these documents owe their significance to the fact that they are nearly identical with those adopted by many of the national Unions of the period, and were largely adopted by the Grand National Consolidated Trades Union of 1834.

other lodge that is not the same trade of that lodge that opens them, that masons open masons, and joiners open joiners, and so on ; " moreover, " no other member [is] to visit a lodge that is not the same trade unless he is particularly requested." Each trade had its own bye-laws ; but these were subject to the general rules adopted at an annual delegate meeting. This annual conference of the " Grand Lodge Delegates," better known as the " Builders' Parliament," consisted of one representative of each lodge, and was the supreme legislative authority, altering rules, deciding on general questions of policy, and electing the president and other officials. The local lodges, though directly represented at the annual meetings, had had apparently little connection in the interim with the seat of government. The society was divided into geographical districts, the lodges in each district sending delegates to quarterly district meetings, which elected a grand master, deputy grand master, and corresponding secretary for the district, and decided which should be the " divisional lodge," or district executive centre. These divisional lodges or provincial centres were, according to the rules, to serve in turn as the grand lodge or executive centre for the whole society. Whether the members of the general committee were chosen by the general lodge or by the whole society is not clear ; but they formed, with the president and general corresponding secretary, the national executive. The expenses of this executive and of the annual delegate meeting were levied on the whole society, each lodge sending monthly returns of its members and a summary of its finances to the general secretary. The main business of the national executive was to determine the trade policy of the Associations, and to grant or withhold permission to strike. As no mention is made of friendly benefits, we may conclude that the Builders' Union, like most of the national or general Unions of this militant time, confined itself exclusively to defending its members against their employers.

The operative builders did not rest content with an elaborate constitution and code. There was also a ritual. The Stonemasons' Society has preserved among its records a MS. copy of a " Making Parts Book," ordered to be used by all lodges of the Builders' Union on the admission of members. Under the Combination Laws oaths of secrecy and obedience were customary in the more secret and turbulent Trade Unions, notably that of the Glasgow Cotton-spinners and the Northumberland Miners. The custom survived the repeal ; and admission to the Builders' Union involved a lengthy ceremony conducted by the officers of the lodge—the " outside and inside tylers," the " warden," the " president," " secretary," and " principal conductor "—and taken part in by the candidates and the members of the lodge. Besides the opening prayer, and religious hymns sung at intervals, these " initiation parts " consisted of questions and responses by the *dramatis personæ* in quaint doggerel, and were brought to a close by the new members taking a solemn oath of loyalty and secrecy. Officers clothed in surplices, inner chambers into which the candidates were admitted blindfolded, a skeleton, drawn sword, battle-axes, and other mystic " properties " enhanced the sensational solemnity of this fantastic performance.[1] Ceremonies of this kind, including

[1] A similar ritual is printed in *Character, Objects, and Effects of Trades Unions* (1834), as used by the Woolcombers' Union. Probably the Builders' Union copied their ritual from some union of woollen-workers. The Stonemasons' MS. contains, like the copy printed in this pamphlet, a solemn reference to " King Edward the Third," who was regarded as the great benefactor of the English wool trade, but whose connection with the building trade is not obvious. In a later printed edition of *The Initiating Parts of the Friendly Society of Operative Masons*, dated Birmingham, 1834, his name is omitted, and that of Solomon substituted, apparently in memory of the Freemasons' assumed origin at the building of the Temple at Jerusalem.

The actual origin of this initiation ceremony is not certainly known John Tester, who had been a leader of the Bradford Woolcombers in 1825, afterwards turned against the Unions, and published, in the *Leeds Mercury* of June and July 1834, a series of letters denouncing the Leeds Clothiers' Union. In these he states that " the mode of initiation was the same as practised for years before by the flannel-weavers of Rochdale, with a party of whom the thing, in the shape it then wore, had at first

what were described to the Home Office as " oaths of a most execrable nature," [1] were adopted by all the national and general Unions of the time : thus we find items for " washing surplices " appearing in the accounts of various lodges of contemporary societies. Although in the majority of cases the ritual was no doubt as harmless as that of the Freemasons or the Oddfellows, yet the excitement and sensation of the proceedings may have predisposed light-headed fanatical members, in times of industrial conflict, to violent acts in the interest of the Association. At all events, the references to its mock terrors in the capitalist press seem to have effectually scared the governing classes.

The first years of the Builders' Union, apparently, were devoted to organisation. During 1832 it rapidly spread through the Lancashire and Midland towns ; and at the beginning of the following year a combined attack was made upon the Liverpool employers. The ostensible grievance of the men was the interference of the " contractor," who, supplanting the master mason, master carpenter, etc., undertook the management of all building operations. A placard issued by the Liverpool Painters announces that they have joined " the General Union of the Artisans employed in the process of building," in order to put down " that baneful, unjust, and ruinous system

---

originated. . . . A great part of the ceremony, . . . particularly the death scene, was taken from the ceremonial of one division of the Oddfellows, . . . who were flannel-weavers at Rochdale, in Lancashire ; and all that could be well turned from the rules and lectures of one society into the regulations of the others was so turned, with some trifling verbal alterations." In another letter he says that the writer of the " lecture book " was one Mark Warde. Tester is not implicitly to be believed, but it seems probable that the regalia, doggerel rhymes, and mystic rites of the unions of this time were copied from those of an Oddfellows' Lodge, with some recollections of Freemasonry. In his *Mutual Thrift* (1891), the Rev. J. Frome Wilkinson describes (p. 14) the initiation ceremony of the " Patriotic Oddfellows," a society which merged in the present " Grand United Order of Oddfellows " before the close of the century. The ceremony so described corresponds in many characteristic details with that of the Trades Unions. All the older friendly society " Orders " imposed an oath, and were consequently unlawful.

[1] Home Office Papers, December 29, 1832, 40—31.

of monopolising the hard-earned profits of another man's business, called 'contracting.'" Naturally, the little masters were not friendly to the contracting system; and most of them agreed with the men's demand that its introduction should be resisted. Encouraged by this support, the several branches of the building trade in Liverpool simultaneously sent in identical claims for a uniform rate of wages for each class of operatives, a limitation of apprentices, the prohibition of machinery and piecework, and other requirements special to each branch of the trade. These demands were communicated to the employers in letters couched in dictatorial and even insulting terms, and were coupled with a claim to be paid wages for any time they might lose by striking to enforce their orders. "We consider," said one of these letters, "that as you have not treated our rules with that deference you ought to have done, we consider you highly culpable and deserving of being severely chastised." And "further," says another, "that each and every one in such strike shall be paid by you the sum of four shillings per day for every day you refuse to comply." [1]

[1] At Birmingham, when the builders' strike presently extended to that town, the following was the manifesto drawn up for adoption by the Builders' Union, for presentation to the leading building contractor who had just undertaken to erect the new grammar-school. (No record of its adoption and presentation has been found.) "We, the delegates of the several Lodges of the Building Trades, elected for the purpose of correcting the abuses which have crept into the modes of undertaking and transacting business, do hereby give you notice that you will receive no assistance from the workingmen in any of our bodies to enable you to fulfil an engagement which we understand you have entered into with the Governors of the Free Grammar School to erect a new school in New Street, unless you comply with the following conditions:

"Aware that it is our labour alone that can carry into effect what you have undertaken, we cannot but view ourselves as parties to your engagement, if that engagement is ever fulfilled; and as you had no authority from us to make such an engagement, nor had you any legitimate right to barter our labour at prices fixed by yourself, we call upon you to exhibit to our several bodies your detailed estimates of quantities and prices at which you have taken the work; and we call upon you to arrange with us a fixed percentage of profit for your own services in conducting the building, and in finding the material on which our labour is to be applied.

"Should we find upon examination that you have fixed equitable

F

This sort of language brought the employers of all classes into line. At a meeting held in June 1833 they decided not only to refuse all the men's demands, but to make a deliberate attempt to extinguish the Union. For this purpose they publicly declared that henceforth no man need apply for work unless he was prepared to sign a formal renunciation of the Trades Union and all its works. The insistence on this formal renunciation, henceforth to be famous in Trade Union records as the " presentation of the document," exasperated the Builders' Union. The Liverpool demands were repeated in Manchester, where the employers adopted the same tactics as at Liverpool.[1]

In the very heat of the battle (September 1833) the Builders' Union held its annual delegate meeting at Manchester. It lasted six days ; cost, it is said, over £3000 ; and was attended by two hundred and seventy delegates, representing thirty thousand operatives. This session of the " Builders' Parliament " attracted universal attention. Robert Owen addressed the Conference at great length, confiding to it his " great secret " " that labour is the source of all wealth," and that wealth can be retained in the hands of the producers by a universal compact among the productive classes. It was decided, perhaps under his influence, to build central offices at Birmingham, which should also serve as an educational establishment. The design for this " Builders' Gild Hall," as it was termed, was made by Hansom, an architect who, as an enthusiastic disciple of Owen, threw himself heartily into the strike

---

prices which will not only remunerate you for your superintendence but us for our toil, we have no objections upon a clear understanding to become partners to the contract, and will see you through it, after your having entered yourself a member of our body, and after your having been duly elected to occupy the office you have assumed " (*Robert Owen: A Biography*, by Frank Podmore, 1906 vol. ii. p. 442-4).

[1] *An Impartial Statement of the Proceedings of the Members of the Trades Union Societies, and of the Steps taken in consequence by the Master Traders of Liverpool* (Liverpool, 1833) ; *Remarks on the Nature and Probable Termination of the Struggle now existing between the Master and Journeyman Builders* (Manchester, 1833) ; *Times*, June 27, 1833.

that was proceeding also in this town. It included, on paper, a lecture-hall and various schoolrooms for the children of members. The foundation-stone was laid with great ceremony on December 5, 1833, when the Birmingham trades marched in procession to the site, and enthusiastic speeches were made.[1]

We learn from the *Pioneer, or Trades Union Magazine* (an unstamped penny weekly newspaper published at first at Birmingham, at that time the organ of the Builders' Union [2]), the ardent faith and the vast pretensions of these New Unionists. " A union founded on right and just principles," wrote the editor in the first number, " is all that is now required to put poverty and the fear of it for ever out of society." " The vaunted power of capital will now be put to the test : we shall soon discover its worthlessness when deprived of your labour. Labour prolific of wealth will readily command the purchase of the soil ; and at a very early period we shall find the idle possessor compelled to ask of you to release him from his worthless holding." Elaborate plans were propounded for the undertaking of all the building of the country by a Grand National Gild of Builders : each lodge to elect a foreman ; and the foremen to elect a general superintendent. The disappointment of these high hopes was rude and rapid. The Lancashire societies demurred to the centralisation which had been voted by the delegate meeting in September at the instigation of the Midland societies. Two great strikes at Liverpool and Manchester ended towards the close of the year in total failure. The Builders' Gild Hall was abandoned ;[3] and the *Pioneer* moved to London, where it became the organ of another body, the Grand National Consolidated

[1] *Pioneer*, December 7, 1833 ; *History of Birmingham*, by W. Hutton (Birmingham, 1835), p. 87.

[2] It was edited by James Morrison, an enthusiastic Owenite, who died, worn out, in 1835 (*Beer's History of British Socialism*, 1919, p. 328).

[3] It was eventually finished by the landlord, and still exists as a metal warehouse in Shadwell Street.

Trades Union, with which the south country and metropolitan branches of the building trade had already preferred to affiliate themselves. Nevertheless the Builders' Union retained its hold upon the northern counties during the early months of 1834, and held another " parliament " at Birmingham in April, at which Scotch and Irish representatives were present.[1]

The aggressive activity and rapid growth of the Builders' Union during 1832–33 had been only a part of a general upheaval in labour organisation. The Cotton-spinners had recovered from the failure of the Ashton strike (1830–31) by the autumn of 1833, when we find Doherty prosecuting with his usual vigour the agitation for an eight hours day which had been set on foot by his Society for National Regeneration. " The plan is," writes J. Fielden (M.P. for Oldham) to William Cobbett, " that about the 1st March next, the day the said Bill (now Act) limits the time of work for children under eleven years of age to eight hours a day, those above that age, both grown persons and adults, should insist on eight hours a day being the maximum of time for them to labour ; and their present weekly wages for sixty-nine hours a week to be the minimum weekly wages for forty-eight hours a week after that time " ; and he proceeds to explain that the Cotton-spinners had adopted this idea of securing shorter hours by a strike rather than by legislation on Lord Althorpe's suggestion that they should " make a short-time bill for themselves." [2] Fielden and Robert Owen served, with Doherty, on the committee of this society, which included a few employers. The Lancashire textile trades followed the lead of the Cotton-spinners, and prepared for a " uni-

[1] In May 1834 an informer offered to supply the Home Secretary with full particulars of its organisation, leading members and their activities, for two sums of £50 each (Home Office Papers, 40—32).

[2] Letters to Cobbett's *Weekly Register*, reprinted in the *Pioneer*, December 21, 1833. See also Home Office Papers, 40—32 ; and the *Crisis* for November and December 1833. *The Voice of the West Riding*, an unstamped weekly, June and July 1833, was devoted to this agitation in the Yorkshire textile industry (see Home Office Papers, 40—31).

versal " strike. Meanwhile their Yorkshire brethren were already engaged in an embittered struggle with their employers. The Leeds Clothiers' Union, established about 1831, and apparently one of the constituent societies of the National Association for the Protection of Labour, bore a striking resemblance to the Builders' Union, not only in ceremonial and constitution, but also in its policy and history.[1] In the spring of 1833 it made a series of attacks on particular establishments with the double aim of forcing all the workers to join the Union and of obtaining a uniform scale of prices. These demands were met with the usual weapon. The employers entered into what was called " the Manufacturers' Bond," by which they bound themselves under penalty to refuse employment to all members of the Union. The men indignantly refused to abandon the society ; and a lock-out ensued which lasted some months, and was the occasion of repeated leading articles in the *Times*.[2]

The Potters' Union (also established by Doherty in 1830) numbered, in the autumn of 1833, eight thousand members, of whom six thousand belonged to Staffordshire and the remainder to the lodges at Newcastle-on-Tyne, Derby, Bristol, and Swinton [3]—another instance of the extraordinary growth of Trade Unions during these years.

How far these and other societies were joined together in any federal body is not clear. The panic-stricken references in the capitalist press to " the Trades Union," and the vague mention in working-class newspapers of the affiliation of particular societies to larger organisations,

---

[1] For an unfavourable account of this Union, see the extremely biassed statement given in the pamphlet *Character, Objects, and Effects of Trades Unions* (1834). The employers seem to have regarded all the demands of the men as equally unreasonable, even the request for a list of piecework prices. See *Times*, October 2, 1833. A printed address *To the Flax and Hemp Trade of Great Britain*, issued by the flaxworkers of Leeds, November 30, 1832, refers with admiration to the effectiveness of this Union (Home Office Papers, 40—31 ; see also 41—11).

[2] *Times*, October 28, 1833.

[3] *Crisis*, October 19, 1833.

lead us to believe that during the year 1833 there was
more than one attempt to form a " General Union of All
Trades." The Owenite newspapers, towards the end of
1833, are full of references to the formation of a " General
Union of the Productive Classes." What manner of
association Owen himself contemplated may be learnt
from his speech to the Congress of Owenite Societies in
London on the 6th of October. " I will now give you,"
said he, " a short outline of the great changes which are
in contemplation, and which shall come suddenly upon
society like a thief in the night. . . It is intended that
national arrangements shall be formed to include all the
working classes in the great organisation, and that each
department shall become acquainted with what is going
on in other departments ; that all individual competition
is to cease ; that all manufactures are to be carried on by
National Companies. . . . All trades shall first form Associations of lodges to consist of a convenient number for carrying on the business : . . . all individuals of the specific
craft shall become members." [1] Immediately after this we
find in existence a " Grand National Consolidated Trades
Union," in the establishment and extraordinary growth of
which the project of " the Trades Union " may be said
to have culminated. This organisation seems to have
actually started in January 1834. Owen was its chief
recruiter and propagandist. During the next few months
his activity was incessant ; and lodges were affiliated all
over the country. Innumerable local trade clubs were

---

[1] *Crisis*, October 12, 1833. The history of the General Trades Unions
from 1832 to 1834 is mainly to be gathered from the files of the Owenite
press, the *Crisis*, the *Pioneer*, and the *Herald of the Rights of Industry*,
with frequent ambiguous references in the Home Office Papers for these
years. The *Poor Man's Guardian* and the *Man* also contain occasional
references. The *Official Gazette*, issued by the Grand National Consolidated Trades Union itself in June 1834, has unfortunately not been
preserved. We have also been unable to discover any copy of the
Glasgow Owenite journals, the *Tradesman*, *Trades Advocate*, *Liberator*,
etc., mostly edited or written by Owen's disciple, Alexander Campbell,
the secretary of the local joiners' Trade Union.

absorbed. Early in February 1834 a special delegate meeting was held at Owen's London Institute in Charlotte Street, Fitzroy Square, at which it was resolved that the new body should take the form of a federation of separate trade lodges, each lodge to be composed usually of members of one trade, but with provision for " miscellaneous lodges " in places where the numbers were small, and even for " female miscellaneous lodges." Each lodge retained its own funds, levies being made throughout the whole order for strike purposes. The Conference urged each lodge to provide sick, funeral, and superannuation benefits for its own members ; and proposals were adopted to lease land on which to employ " turn-outs," and to set up co-operative workshops. The initiation rites and solemn oath, common to all the Unions of the period, were apparently adopted.

Nothing in the annals of Unionism in this country at all approached the rapidity of the growth which ensued.[1] Within a few weeks the Union appears to have been joined by at least half a million members, including tens of thousands of farm labourers and women. This must have been in great measure due to the fact that, as no discoverable regular contribution was exacted for central expenses, the affiliation or absorption of existing organisations was very easy. Still, the extension of new lodges in previously unorganised trades and districts was enormous. Numerous missionary delegates, duly equipped with all the paraphernalia required for the mystic initiation rites, perambulated the country; and a positive mania for Trade Unionism set in. In December 1833 we are told that " scarcely a branch of trade exists in the West of

---

[1] It is interesting to notice how closely this organisation resembles, in its Trade Union features, the well-known " Knights of Labour " of the United States, established in 1869, and for some years one of the most powerful labour organisations in the world (" Historical Sketch of the Knights of Labour," by Carroll D. Wright, *Quarterly Journal of Economics*, January, 1887). Its place was taken by the American Federation of Labour, with exclusively Trade Union objects.

Scotland that is not now in a state of Union." [1] The *Times* reports that two delegates who went to Hull enrolled in one evening a thousand men of various trades.[2] At Exeter the two delegates were seized by the police, and found to be furnished with " two wooden axes, two large cutlasses, two masks, and two white garments or robes, a large figure of Death with the dart and hourglass, a Bible and Testament." [3] Shop-assistants on the one hand, and journeymen chimney-sweeps on the other, were swept into the vortex. The cabinetmakers of Belfast insisted on joining " the Trades Union, or Friendly Society, which had for its object the unity of all cabinetmakers in the three kingdoms." [4] We hear of " Ploughmen's Unions " as far off as Perthshire,[5] and of a " Shearman's Union " at Dundee. And the then rural character of the Metropolitan suburbs is quaintly brought home to us by the announcement of a union of the " agricultural and other labourers " of Kensington, Walham Green, Fulham, and Hammersmith. Nor were the women neglected. The " Grand Lodge of Operative Bonnet Makers " vies in activity with the miscellaneous " Grand Lodge of the Women of Great Britain and Ireland " ; and the " Lodge of Female Tailors " asks indignantly whether the " Tailors' Order " is really going to prohibit women from making waistcoats. Whether the Grand National Consolidated Trades Union was responsible for the lodges of " Female Gardeners " and " Ancient Virgins," who afterwards distinguished themselves in the riotous demand for an eight hours day at Oldham,[6] is not clear.

How the business of this colossal federation was actually

---

[1] *Glasgow Argus*, quoted in *People's Conservative*, December 28, 1833.
[2] May 5, 1834.
[3] *Times*, January 23 and 30, 1834.
[4] *Kerr's Exposition of Legislative Tyranny and Defence of the Trades Union* (Belfast, 1834), vol. 1611 of the Halliday Tracts in the Royal Irish Academy, Dublin ; see *The Irish Labour Movement*, by W. P. Ryan, 1919.
[5] *Poor Man's Guardian*, July 26, 1834.
[6] *Times*, April 19, 1834.

managed we do not know.[1] Some kind of executive committee sat in London, with four paid officers. The need
for statesmanlike administration was certainly great. The
avowed policy of the federation was to inaugurate a general
expropriatory strike of all wage-earners throughout the
country, not "to condition with the master-producers of
wealth and knowledge for some paltry advance in the arti-
ficial money price in exchange for their labour, health,
liberty, natural enjoyment, and life ; but to ensure to
every one the best cultivation of all their faculties and the
most advantageous exercise of all their powers." But
from the very beginning of its career it found itself incessantly involved in sectional disputes for small advances
of wages and reduction of hours. The mere joining of
" the Trades Union " was often made the occasion of the
dismissal by the employers of all those who would not
sign the " document " abjuring all combinations. Thus
the accession of the Leicester Hosiers in November 1833
led to a disastrous dispute, in which over 1300 men had
to be supported. In Glasgow a serious strike broke out
among the building trades at a time when the Calico-
printers, Engineers, and Cabinetmakers were already
struggling with their employers. The most costly conflict,
however, which the Grand National found on its hands
during the winter was that which raged at Derby, where
fifteen hundred men, women, and children had been locked
out by their employers for refusing to abandon the Union.
The " Derby turn-outs " were at first supported, like their
fellow-victims elsewhere, by contributions sent from the
trade organisations in various parts of the kingdom ; but
it soon became evident that without systematic aid they

---

[1] The only record of this organisation known to us is a copy of the
Rules in the Goldsmiths' Library at the University of London, which
we print in the Appendix. A "Memorial from the Grand National
Consolidated Trades Union of Great Britain and Ireland to the Producers
and Non-Producers of Wealth and Knowledge " is printed in the *Crisis*,
May 17, 1834 ; another, "to the Shopmen, Clerks, Porters and other
industrious non-producers," in the issue for April 26, 1834.

would be compelled to give way. A levy of a shilling per member was accordingly decreed by the Grand National Executive in February 1834. Arrangements were made for obtaining premises and machinery upon which to set a few of the strikers to work on their own account. The struggle ended, after four months, in the complete triumph of the employers, and the return of the operatives to work.

The "Derby turn-out" was widely advertised by the newspapers, and brought much odium on the Grand National. But the denunciation of "the Trades Union" greatly increased when part of London was laid in darkness by a strike of the gas-stokers. The men employed by the different gas companies in the metropolis had been quietly organising during the winter, with the intention of simultaneously withdrawing from work if their demands were not acceded to. The plot was discovered, and the companies succeeded in replacing their Union workmen by others. But weeks elapsed before the new hands were able completely to perform their work,[1] and early in March 1834 Westminster was for some days in partial darkness. Amid the storm of obloquy caused by these disputes the Grand National suddenly found itself in conflict with the law. The conviction of six Dorchester labourers in March 1834 for the mere act of administering an oath, and their sentence to seven years' transportation, came like a thunderbolt on the Trade Union world.

To understand such a barbarous sentence we must picture to ourselves the effect on the minds of the Government and the propertied classes of the menacing ideal of "the Trades Union," brought home by the aggressive policy of the Unions during the last four years. Already in 1830 the formation of national and General Unions had excited the attention of the Government. "When we first came into office in November last," writes Lord Melbourne, the Whig Home Secretary, to Sir Herbert Taylor, " the

---

[1] See the London newspapers for March 1834; a good summary is given in the *Companion to the Newspaper* for that month (p. 71).

Unions of trades in the North of England and in other parts of the country for the purpose of raising wages, etc., and the General Union for the same purpose, were pointed out to me by Sir Robert Peel [the outgoing Tory Home Secretary] in a conversation I had with him upon the then state of the country, as the most formidable difficulty and danger with which we had to contend ; and it struck me as well as the rest of His Majesty's servants in the same light." [1]

To advise the Cabinet in this difficulty Lord Melbourne called in Nassau Senior, who had just completed his first term of five years as Professor of Political Economy at Oxford, and directed him to prepare, in conjunction with a legal expert named Tomlinson, a report on the situation and a plan of remedial legislation. This document throws light both on the state of mind and on the practical judgement of the trusted economist. The two commissioners appear to have made no inquiries among workmen, and to have accepted implicitly every statement, including hearsay gossip, offered by employers. The evidence thus collected naturally led to a very unfavourable conclusion. It produced, as the commissioners recite, " upon our minds the conviction that if the innocent and laborious workman and his family are to be left without protection against the cowardly ferocity by which he is now assailed ; if the manufacturer is to employ his capital and the mechanist or chemist his ingenuity, only under the dictation of his short-sighted and rapacious workmen, or his equally ignorant and avaricious rivals ; if a few agitators are to be allowed to command a strike which first paralyses the industry of the peculiar class of workpeople over whom they tyrannise,

[1] September 26, 1831 : *Lord Melbourne's Papers* (1889), ch. v. p. 130. The note he left on leaving the Home Office was as follows : " I take the liberty of recommending the whole of this correspondence *re* the Union to the immediate and serious consideration of my successor at the Home Department " (Home Office Papers, 40—27). See also the statements in the House of Lords debate, *Times*, April 29, 1834 ; and the comments in *Labour Legislation, Labour Movements, and Labour Leaders*, by George Howell, 1902, p. 23.

and then extends itself in an increasing circle over the many thousands and tens of thousands to whose labour the assistance of that peculiar class of workpeople is essen- tial ;—that if all this is to be unpunished, and to be almost sanctioned by the repeal of the laws by which it was formerly punishable ;—it is in vain to hope that we shall long retain the industry, the skill, or the capital on which our manu- facturing superiority, and with that superiority our power and almost our existence as a nation, depends." They accordingly conclude with a series of astounding proposals for the amendment of the law. The Act of 1825 could not conveniently be openly repealed ; but its mischievous results were to be counteracted by drastic legislation. They recommend that a law should be passed clearly reciting the common law prohibitions of conspiracy and restraint of trade. The law should go on to forbid, under severe penalties, " all attempts or solicitations, combinations, subscriptions, and solicitations to combinations " to threaten masters, to persuade blacklegs, or even simply to ask work- men to join the Union.[1] Picketing, however peaceful, was to be comprehensively forbidden and ruthlessly punished. Employers or their assistants were to be authorised them- selves to arrest men without summons or warrant, and hale them before any justice of the peace. The encouragement of combinations by masters was to be punished by heavy pecuniary penalties, to be recovered by any common informer. " This," say the commissioners, " is as much as we should recommend in the first instance. But if it should be proved that the evil of the combination system cannot be subdued at a less price, . . . *we must recommend the experiment of confiscation*,"—confiscation, that is, of the " funds sub- scribed for purposes of combination and deposited in Savings Banks or otherwise." [2]

---

[1] " We recommend that the soliciting of any person to join in com- binations, or to subscribe to the like purposes, should be punishable on summary conviction by imprisonment for a shorter period, say not ex- ceeding two months."

[2] The report was never published, and lies in MS. in the Home

The Whig Government dared not submit either the report or the proposals to a House of Commons pledged to the doctrines of Philosophic Radicalism. " We considered much ourselves," writes Lord Melbourne,[1] " and we consulted much with others as to whether the arrangements of these unions, their meetings, their communica-

Office library. Ten years later, when Nassau Senior was acting as Commissioner to report on the condition of the handloom weavers, he revived a good deal of his 1830 Report, but not the astonishing proposals quoted in the text. The portion thus revived appears in his *Historical and Philosophical Essays* (1865), vol. ii. We had placed in our hands, through the kindness of Mrs. Simpson, daughter of Nassau Senior, the original answers and letters upon which his report was based. This correspondence shows that the leading Manchester manufacturers were not agreed upon the desirability of re-enacting the Combination Laws, though they, with one accord, advocated stringent repression of picketing. Nor were they clear that combinations had, on the whole, hindered the introduction of new machinery, one employer even maintaining that the Unions indirectly promoted its adoption. But the most interesting feature of the correspondence is the extent to which the employers complained of the manner in which their rivals incited, and even subsidised, strikes against attempted reductions of rates. The millowner, whose improved processes gave him an advantage in the market, found any corresponding reduction of piecework rates resisted, not only by his own operatives, but by all the other manufacturers in the district, who sometimes went so far as to publish a joint declaration that any such reduction was ' highly inexpedient.' The evidence, in fact, from Nassau Senior's point of view, justified his somewhat remarkable proposal to punish employers for conniving at combinations.

[1] Lord Melbourne to Sir Herbert Taylor, September 26, 1831 (*Papers*, chap. v. p. 131). The workmen's combinations began at this time to attract more serious attention from capable students than they had hitherto received. Two able pamphlets, published anonymously—there is reason to believe at the instance and at the cost of the Whig Government—*On Combinations of Trades* (1830), and *Character, Objects, and Effects of Trades Unions* (1834), set forth the constitution and proceedings of the new unions, and criticise their pretensions in a manner which has not since been surpassed. The second of these was by Edward Carlton Tufnell, one of the factory commissioners, and remains perhaps the best statement of the case against Trades Unionism. Tufnell also wrote a pamphlet, entitled *Trades Unionism and Strikes* (1834 ; 12mo) ; and Harriet Martineau one *On the Tendency of Strikes and Sticks to produce Low Wages* (Durham, 1834 ; 12mo), neither of which we have seen. A well-informed but hostile article, founded on these materials, appeared in the *Edinburgh Review* for July 1834. Charles Knight published in the same year a sixpenny pamphlet, *Trades Unions and Strikes* (1834, 99 pp.), which took the form of a bitter denunciation of the whole movement.

tions, or their pecuniary funds could be reached or in any way prevented by any new legal provisions ; but it appeared upon the whole impossible to do anything effectual unless we proposed such measures as would have been a serious infringement upon the constitutional liberties of the country, and to which it would have been impossible to have obtained the consent of Parliament."

The King, however, had been greatly alarmed at the meeting of the " Builders' Parliament," and pressed the Cabinet to take strong measures.[1] Rotch, the member for Knaresborough, gave notice in April 1834 of his intention to bring in a Bill designed to make combinations of trades impossible—a measure which would have obtained a large amount of support from the manufacturers.[2] The coal-owners and ship-owners, the ironmasters, had all been pressing the Home Secretary for legislation of this kind.

But although Lord Melbourne's prudent caution saved the Unions from drastic prohibitory laws, the Government lost no opportunity of showing its hostility to the workmen's combinations. When in August 1833 the Yorkshire manufacturers presented a memorial on the subject of " the Trades Union," Lord Melbourne directed the answer to be returned that " he considers it unnecessary to repeat the strong opinion entertained by His Majesty's Ministers of the criminal character and the evil effects of the unions described in the Memorial," adding that " no doubt can be entertained that combinations for the purposes enumerated are illegal conspiracies, and liable to be prosecuted as such at common law."[3] The employers scarcely needed this hint. Although combination for the sole purpose of fixing hours or wages had ceased to be illegal, it was possible

[1] See his letter of March 30, 1834, in *Lord Melbourne's Papers*, chap. v.

[2] *Leeds Mercury*, April 26, 1834. Joseph Hume said he had had the " greatest difficulty in prevailing upon the Ministers not to bring in a bill for putting down the Trades Unions " (*Poor Man's Guardian*, March 29, 1834).

[3] Letter dated September 3, 1833, in *Times*, September 9, 1833.

to prosecute the workmen upon various other pretexts. Sometimes, as in the case of some Lancashire miners in 1832, the Trade Unionists were indicted for illegal combination for merely writing to their employers that a strike would take place.[1] Sometimes the " molestation or obstruction " prohibited in the Act of 1825 was made to include the mere intimation of the men's intention to strike against the employment of non-unionists. In a remarkable case at Wolverhampton in August 1835, four potters were imprisoned for intimidation, solely upon evidence by the employers that they had " advanced their prices in consequence of the interference of the defendants, who acted as plenipotentiaries for the men," without, as was admitted, the use of even the mildest threat.[2] Picketing, even of the most peaceful kind, was frequently severely punished under this head, as four Southwark shoemakers found in 1832 to their cost.[3] More generally the men on strike were proceeded against under the laws relating to masters and servants, as in the case of seventeen tanners at Bermondsey in February 1834, who were sentenced to imprisonment for the offence of leaving their work unfinished.[4]

With the authorities in this temper, their alarm at the growth of the Grand National Consolidated Trades Union may be imagined. A new legal weapon was soon discovered. At the time of the mutiny at the Nore in 1797 an Act had been passed (37 Geo. III. c. 123) severely penalising the administering of an oath by an unlawful society. In 1819, when political sedition was rife, a measure prohibiting unlawful oaths had formed one of the notorious " Six Acts." In neither case were trade combinations aimed at, though

[1] R. *v.* Bykerdike, 1 Moo. and Rob. 179, Lancaster Assizes, 1832. A letter was written to certain coal-owners, " by order of the Board of Directors for the body of coal-miners," stating that unless certain men were discharged the miners would strike. Held to be an illegal combination. See *Leeds Mercury*, May 24, 1834.
[2] *Times*, August 22, 1835.
[3] *Poor Man's Guardian*, September 29, 1832.
[4] *Times*, February 27, 1834.

Lord Ellenborough, in an isolated prosecution in 1802,[1] had held that an oath administered by a committee of journeymen shearmen in Wiltshire came within the terms of the earlier statute. It does not seem to have occurred to any one to put the law in force against Trade Unions until the oath-bound confederacy of the Grand National Consolidated Trades Union began to make headway even in the rural villages of the South of England.

The story of the trial and transportation of the Dorchester labourers is the best-known episode of early Trade Union history.[2] The agricultural labourers of the southern counties, oppressed by the tacit combinations of the farmers and by the operation of the Corn Laws, as well as exceptionally demoralised by the Old Poor Law, had long been in a state of sullen despair. The specially hard times of 1829 had resulted in outbursts of machine-breaking, rick-burning, and hunger riots, which had been put down in 1830 by the movement of troops through the disturbed districts, and the appointment of a Special Commission of Assize to try over 1000 prisoners, several of whom were hung and hundreds transported. The whole wage-earning population of these rural districts was effectually cowed.[3] With the improvement of trade a general movement for higher

---

[1] R. *v.* Marks and others, 3 East Rep. 157.

[2] Lengthy accounts appeared in the newspapers for March and April 1834. The indictment is given in full in the House of Commons Return, No. 250, of 1835 (June 1st). The legal report is in 6 C. and P. 596 (R. *v.* Loveless and others). The *Times* reported the judge's charge at some length, March 18, 1834, and the case itself March 20, 1834, giving the rules of the projected union. An able article in the *Law Magazine*, vol xi pp. 460-72, discusses the law of the case. The defendants subsequently published two statements for popular circulation, viz. *Victims of Whiggery, a statement of the persecution experienced by the Dorchester Labourers*, by George Loveless (1837), and *A narrative of the sufferings of James Loveless, etc.* (1838), which are in the British Museum. See also *Labour Legislation, Labour Movements, and Labour Leaders*, by G. Howell, 1902, pp. 62-75; Spencer Walpole's *History of England*, vol. iii. chap. xiii. pp. 229-31; and *Hansard's Parliamentary Debates*, vols. xxii. and xxiii.

[3] The student is referred to the admirable account of these proceedings in *The Village Labourer*, by J. L. and B. Hammond, 1912. See, for a contemporary account, *Swing Unmasked, or the Cause of Rural Incendiarism*, by G. C. Wakefield, M.P., 1831.

wages seems to have been set on foot. In 1832 we find the Duke of Wellington, as Lord-Lieutenant of Hampshire, reporting to Lord Melbourne that more than half the labourers in his county were contributing a penny per week to a network of local societies affiliated, as he thought, to some National Union. " The labourers said that they had received directions from the Union not to take less than ten shillings, and that the Union would stand by them."[1] These societies, whatever may have been their constitution, had apparently the effect of raising wages not only in Hampshire, but also in the neighbouring counties. In the village of Tolpuddle, in Dorsetshire, as George Loveless tells us, an agreement was made between the farmers and the men, in the presence of the village parson, that the wages should be those paid in other districts. This involved a rise to ten shillings a week. In the following year the farmers repented of their decision, and successively reduced wages shilling by shilling until they were paying only seven shillings a week. In this strait the men made inquiries about " the Trades Union," and two delegates from the Grand National visited the village. Upon their information the Lovelesses established " the Friendly Society of Agricultural Labourers," having its " Grand Lodge " at Tolpuddle. For this village club the elaborate ritual and code of rules of one of the national orders of the Grand National Consolidated Trades Union were adopted. No secrecy seems to have been observed, for John Loveless openly ordered of the village painter a figure of " Death painted six feet high for a society of his own,"[2] with which to perform the initiation rites. The farmers took alarm, and induced the local magistrates, on February 21, 1834, to issue placards warning the labourers that any one joining

---

[1] *Lord Melbourne's Papers*, pp. 147-150, letters dated November 3 and 7, 1832. Lord Melbourne seems to have thought, probably quite incorrectly, that these rural organisations were in connection with the political organisation called the National Union of the Working Classes, founded by William Lovett in 1831, to support the Reform Bill.

[2] *Times*, March 20, 1834.

the Union would be sentenced to seven years' transportation. This was no idle threat. Within three days of the publication of the notice the Lovelesses and four other members were arrested and lodged in gaol.

The trial of these unfortunate labourers was a scandalous perversion of the law. The Lovelesses and their friends seem to have been simple-minded Methodists, two of them being itinerant preachers. No accusation was made, and no evidence preferred against them, of anything worse than the playing with oaths, which, as we have seen, formed a part of the initiation ceremony of the Grand National and other Unions of the time, with evidently no consciousness of their statutory illegality. Not only were they guiltless of any intimidation or outrage, but they had not even struck or presented any application for higher wages. Yet the judge (John Williams), who had only recently been raised to the bench, charged the grand jury on the case at portentous length, as if the prisoners had committed murder or treason, and inflicted on them, after the briefest of trials, the monstrous sentence of seven years' transportation.

The action of the Government shows how eagerly the Home Secretary accepted the blunder of an inexperienced judge as part of his policy of repression. Lord Melbourne expressed his opinion that " the law has in this case been most properly applied " ;[1] and the sentence, far from exciting criticism in the Whig Cabinet, was carried out with special celerity. The case was tried on March 18, 1834 ; before the 30th the prisoners were in the hulks ; and by the 15th of the next month Lord Howick was able to say in the House of Commons that their ship had already sailed for Botany Bay.[2]

The Grand National Consolidated Trades Union proved to have a wider influence than the Government expected.

---

[1] *Lord Melbourne's Papers*, p. 158.
[2] *Times*, March 18, 20, 31 ; April 1, 16, 19, 1834; *Leeds Mercury*, April 26, 1834.

The whole machinery of the organisation was turned to the preparation of petitions and the holding of public meetings, and a wave of sympathy rallied, for a few weeks, the drooping energies of the members. Cordial relations were established with the five great Unions which remained outside the ranks, for the northern counties were mainly organised by the Builders' Union, the Leeds, Huddersfield and Bradford District Union, the Clothiers' Union, the Cotton-spinners' Union, and the Potters' Union, which on this occasion sent delegates to London to assist the executive of the Grand National. The agitation culminated in a monster procession of Trade Unionists to the Home Office to present a petition to Lord Melbourne—the first of the great " demonstrations " which have since become a regular part of the machinery of London politics. The proposal to hold this procession had excited the utmost alarm, both in friends and to foes. The *Times*, with the Parisian events of 1830 still in its memory, wrote leader after leader condemning the project, and Lord Melbourne let it be known that he would refuse to receive any deputation or petition from a procession. Special constables were sworn in, and troops brought into London to prevent a rising. At length the great day arrived (April 21, 1834). Owen and his friends managed the occasion with much skill. In order to avoid interference by the new police, the vacant ground at Copenhagen Fields, on which the processionists assembled, was formally hired from the owner. The trades were regularly marshalled behind thirty-three banners, each man decorated by a red ribbon. At the head of the procession rode, in full canonicals and the scarlet hood of a Doctor of Divinity, the corpulent " chaplain to the Metropolitan Trades Unions," Dr. Arthur S. Wade.[1] The demonstration, in point of numbers, was undoubtedly a success. We learn, for instance, that the tailors alone paraded from 5000 to 7000 strong, and the master builders

[1] A prominent Owenite agitator of the time, incumbent of St. Nicholas, Warwick, who is said to have been inhibited from preaching by his bishop.

subsequently complained that their works had been entirely suspended through their men's participation. Over a quarter of a million signatures had been obtained to the petition, and, even on the admission of the *Times*, 30,000 persons took part in the procession, representing a proportion of the London of that time equivalent to 100,000 to-day.[1]

Meanwhile Radicals of all shades hastened to the rescue. A public meeting was held at the Crown and Anchor Tavern at which Roebuck, Colonel Perronet Thompson, and Daniel O'Connell spoke ; and a debate took place in the House of Commons in which the ferocious sentence was strongly attacked by Joseph Hume.[2] But the Government, far from remitting the punishment, refused even to recognise that it was excessive ; and the unfortunate labourers were allowed to proceed to their penal exile.[3]

The Dorchester conviction had the effect of causing the oath to be ostensibly dropped out of Trade Union ceremonies, although in particular trades and districts

---

[1] *Times*, April 22 ; *Companion to the Newspaper*, May and June 1834. Trade Union accounts declare that 100,000 to 200,000 persons were present. A detailed description of the day is given in Somerville's *Autobiography of a Working Man* (1848), not usually a trustworthy work.

[2] *Times*, April 19, 1834.

[3] The agitation for their release was kept up, both in and out of Parliament, by the " London Dorchester Committee " ; and in 1836 the remainder of the sentence was remitted. Through official blundering it was two years later (April 1838) before five out of the six prisoners returned home. The sixth, as we learn from a circular of the Committee, dated August 20, 1838, had even then not arrived. " Great and lasting honour," writes a well-informed contemporary, " is due to this body of workmen (the London Dorchester Committee), about sixteen in number, by whose indefatigable exertions, extending over a period of five years, and the valuable assistance of Thomas Wakley, M.P. for Finsbury, the same Government who banished the men were compelled to pardon them and bring them home free of expense. From the subscriptions raised by the working classes during this period, amounting to about £1300, the Committee, on the return of the men, were enabled to place five of them, with their families, in small farms in Essex, the sixth preferring (with his share of the fund) to return to his native place." (Article in the *British Statesman*, April 9, 1842, preserved in Place MSS. 27820—320.) See also House of Commons Return, No. 191 of 1837 (April 12) ; and *Hansard's Parliamentary Debates*, vol. xxxii. p. 253.

it lingered a few years longer.[1] At their "parliament" in April 1834 the Builders' Union formally abolished the oath. The Grand National quickly adopted the same course; and the Leeds and other Unions followed suit. But the judge's sentence was of no avail to check the aggressive policy of the Unions. Immediately after the excitement of the procession had subsided, one of the most important branches of the Grand National precipitated a serious conflict with its employers. The London tailors, hitherto divided among themselves, formed in December 1833 the "First Grand Lodge of Operative Tailors," and resolved to demand a shortening of the hours of labour. The state of mind of the men is significantly shown by the language of their peremptory notice to the masters. "In order," they write, "to stay the ruinous effects which a destructive commercial competition has so long been inflicting on the trade, they have resolved to introduce certain new regulations of labour into the trade, which regulations they intend shall come into force on Monday next." A general strike ensued, in which 20,000 persons are said to have been thrown out of work, the whole burden of their maintenance being cast on the Grand National funds. A levy of eighteenpence per member throughout the country was made in May 1834, which caused some dissatisfaction; and the proceeds were insufficient to prevent the tailors' strike pay falling to four shillings a week. The result was

[1] The series of "Initiation Parts," or forms to be observed on admission of new members, which are preserved in the archives of the Stonemasons' Society, reveal the steady tendency to simplification of ritual. We have first the old MS. doggerel already described, dating probably from 1832. The first print of 1834, whilst retaining a good deal of the ceremonial, turns the liturgy into prose and the oath into an almost identical "declaration," invoking the "dire displeasure" of the Society in case of treachery. The second print, which bears no date, is much shorter; and the declaration becomes a mere affirmation of adhesion. The Society's circulars of 1838 record the abolition, by vote of the members, of all initiation ceremonies, in view of the Parliamentary Inquiry about to be held into Trade Unionism. But even the simplified form of 1838 retains, in its reference to the workmen as "the real producers of *all* wealth," an unmistakable trace of the Owenite spirit of the Builders' Union of 1832.

that the men gradually returned to work on the employers'
terms.[1]

These disasters, together with innumerable smaller
strikes in various parts, all of which were unsuccessful,
shook the credit of the Grand National. The executive
attempted in vain to stem the torrent of strikes by publishing a " Declaration of the Views and Objects of Trades
Unions," in which they deprecated disputes and advocated
what would now be called Co-operative Production by
Associations of Producers.[2] They gave effect to this
declaration by refusing to sanction the London shoemakers'
demand for increased wages, on the ground that a conflict
so soon after the tailors' defeat was inopportune. The
result was merely that a general meeting of the London
shoemakers voted, by 782 to 506, for secession from the
federation, and struck on their own account.[3]

An even more serious blow was the lock-out of the
London building trades in July 1834. These trades in
London had joined the Grand Consolidated rather than
the Builders' Union ; and in the summer of 1834 an act of
petty tyranny on the part of a single firm brought about
a general conflict. The workmen employed by Messrs.
Cubitt had resolved not to drink any beer supplied by
Combe, Delafield & Co., in retaliation for the refusal of
that firm to employ Trade Unionists. Messrs. Cubitt
thereupon refused to allow any other beer to be drunk
on their premises, and locked out their workmen. The
employers throughout London, angered by the Union's
resistance to sub-contract and piecework, embraced this
opportunity to insist that all their employees should sign
the hated " document." The heads of the Government

---

[1] *Times*, April 30 to June 10 ; House of Lords debate, April 28 ;
Globe, May 21, 1834 ; Home Office Papers, May 10, 1834, 40—32 ; *The
Tailoring Trade*, by F. W. Galton, 1896.

[2] *Leeds Mercury*, May 3, 1834.

[3] See the address of the " Grand Master " to the " Operative Cordwainers of the Grand National Consolidated Trades Union," *Crisis*,
June 28, 1834 ; also *Times*, May 2, 1834 ; Home Office Papers, 40—32.

departments in which building operatives were employed placed themselves in line with private employers by making the same demands.[1] The struggle dragged on until November 1834, when the document seems to have been tacitly withdrawn, and the men returned to work, accepting the employers' terms on the other points at issue.[2] We learn from the correspondence of the Stonemasons' Society that this defeat—for such it virtually was—completely broke up the organisation in the London building trade. What was happening to the Builders' Union during these months is not clear. The federal organisation apparently broke up at about this time ; and the several trades fell back upon their local clubs and national societies.

Whilst the London builders were thus engaged, similar struggles were going on in the other leading industries At Leeds, for instance, in May 1834 the masters were again presenting the "document" ; and the men, after much resistance and angry denunciation, were compelled to abandon the Clothiers' Union. The Cotton-spinners, whom we left preparing to carry out Fielden's idea of a general strike for an eight hours day with undiminished wages for all cotton operatives, resolved to demand the reduction of hours from the 1st of March 1834, the day appointed for the operation of the new Factory Act of 1833 limiting the hours of children to eight per day. The operatives in many mills sent in notices, which were simply ignored by the employers. In this they seem to have estimated the weakness of the men correctly ; for the expected general strike was deferred by a delegate meeting until the 2nd of June. That date found the men still unprepared for action, and the strike was further postponed until the 1st of September. After that we hear no more of it.

The Oldham operatives did indeed in April 1834 make

---

[1] *Times*, August 21, 1834.

[2] *Statement of the Master Builders of the Metropolis in explanation of the differences between them and the workmen respecting the Trades Unions,* 1834. See also *Times*, July 27 to November 29, 1834.

an unpremeditated attempt to secure eight hours. It happened that the local constables broke up a Trade Union
meeting. A rescue took place, followed by an attack on
an obnoxious mill, and the shooting of one of the rioters
by a " Knobstick." The affray provoked the Oldham
working class into a spasm of insurrection. The workers
in all trades, both male and female, ceased work, and held
huge meetings on the Moor, where they were addressed by
Doherty and others from Manchester, and demanded the
eight hours day. Within a week the excitement subsided,
and work was resumed.[1]

By the end of the summer it was obvious that the
ambitious projects of the Grand National Consolidated
and other " Trades Unions " had ended in invariable and
complete failure. In spite of the rising prosperity of trade,
the strikes for better conditions of labour had been uniformly unsuccessful. In July 1834 the federal organisations all over the country were breaking up. The great
association of half a million members had been completely
routed by the employers' vigorous presentation of the
" document." Of the actual dissolution of the organisation
we have no contemporary record, but the impression which
it made on the more sober Trade Unionists may be gathered
from the following description, which appeared in a working-
class journal seven years afterwards. "We were present,"
says the editor of the *Trades Journal*, " at many of the
meetings of the Grand National Consolidated Trades Union,
and have a distinct recollection of the excitement that prevailed in them—of the apparent determination to carry
out its principles in opposition to every obstacle—of the
enthusiasm exhibited by some of the speakers—of the
noisy approbation of the meeting—the loud cries of ' hear
hear,' ' bravo,' ' hurra,' ' union for ever,' etc. It was the

[1] The *Times* honoured these events by long descriptive reports from
its " own correspondent," then an unusual practice ; see the issues from
April 17 to 25, 1834. A good account is also to be found in the *Leeds
Mercury*, April 19 and 26, 1834; see also the *History of the Marcroft
Family* (1889), pp. 1036.

opinion of many at that time that little real benefit would be effected by this union, as their proceedings were indicative, not of a calm and dispassionate investigation of the causes of existing evils, but of an over-excited state of mind which would speedily evaporate, and leave them in the same condition as before. The event proved that this opinion was not ill-founded. A little mole-hill obstructed their onward progress ; and rather than commence the labour of removing so puny an obstacle, they chose to turn back, each taking his own path, regardless of the safety or the interests of his neighbour. It was painful to see the deep mortification of the generals and leaders of this quickly inflated army, when left deserted and alone upon the field." [1]

A period of general apathy in the Trade Union world ensued. The " London Dorchester Committee " continued with indomitable perseverance to collect subscriptions and present petitions for the return of the six exiled labourers ; but " the Trades Union," together with the ideal from which it sprang, vanished in discredit. The hundreds of thousands of recruits from the new industries or unskilled occupations rapidly reverted to a state of disorganisation. The national " orders " of Tailors and Shoemakers, the extended organisations of Cotton-spinners and Woollen-workers, split up into fragmentary societies. Throughout the country the organised constituents of the Grand National fell back upon their local trade clubs.

The records of the rise and fall of the " New Unionism " of 1830–4 leave us conscious of a vast enlargement in the ideas of the workers, without any corresponding alteration in their tactics in the field. In council they are idealists, dreaming of a new heaven and a new earth; humanitarians, educationalists, socialists, moralists : in battle they are still the struggling, half-emancipated serfs of 1825, armed only with the rude weapons of the strike and boycott ; some-

---

[1] *Trades Journal*, March 1, 1841; probably written by Alexander Hutchinson, general secretary of the Friendly United Smiths of Great Britain and Ireland.

times feared and hated by the propertied classes ; sometimes merely despised ; always oppressed, and miserably poor. We find, too, that they are actually less successful with the old weapons now that they wield them with new and wider ideas. They get beaten in a rising market instead of, as hitherto, only in a falling one. And we shall soon see that they did not recover their lost advantage until they again concentrated their efforts on narrower and more manageable aims. But we have first to inquire how they came by the new ideas.

In the bad times which followed the peace of 1815 the writings of Cobbett had attained an extraordinary influence and authority over the whole of that generation of working men. His trenchant denunciation of the governing classes, and his incessant appeals to the wage-earners to assert their right to the whole administration of affairs, were inspired by the political tyranny of the anti-Jacobin reaction, the high prices and heavy taxes, and the apparent creation by " the Funding System " of an upstart class of non-producers living on the interest of the huge debt contracted by the nation during the war—evils the least of which was enough to stimulate an eager politician like Cobbett to the utmost exercise of his unrivalled power of invective. But the working classes were suffering, in addition, from a calamity which no mere politician of that time grasped, in the effects of the new machine and factory industry, which was blindly crushing out the old methods by the mere brute force of competition instead of replacing it with due order and adjustment to the human interests involved. This phenomenon was beyond the comprehension of its victims. Each of them knew what was happening to himself as an individual ; but only one man—a manufacturer—seems to have understood what was happening to the entire industry of the country. This man was Robert Owen. To him, therefore, political Democracy, which was all-in-all to Cobbett and his readers, appeared quite secondary to industrial Democracy, or the co-operative ownership and control of industry answerable to the economic co-operation in all industrial processes which had been brought about by machinery and factory organisation, and which had removed manufacture irrevocably from the separate firesides of independent individual producers. With Cobbett and his followers the first thing to be done was to pass a great Reform Bill, behind which, in their minds, lay only a vague conception of social change. Owen and his more enthusiastic disciples, on the other hand, were persuaded that a universal voluntary association of workers for productive purposes on his principles would render the political organisation of society of comparatively trivial account.

The disillusionment of the newly emancipated Trade Clubs in the collapse of 1825 left the working-class organisations prepared for these wider gospels. Social reform was in the air. " Concerning the misery and degradation of the bulk of the people of England," writes a contemporary observer, " men of every order, as well as every party, unite and speak continually ; farmers, parish officers, clergymen, magistrates, judges on the bench, members on either side of both Houses of Parliament, the King in his addresses to the nation, moralists, statesmen, philosophers ; and finally the poor creatures themselves, whose complaints are loud and incessant." [1] Cobbett and the Reformers had the first turn. The chief political organisation of the working classes during the Reform Bill agitation began as a trade club. In 1831 a few carpenters met at their house of call in Argyle Street, Oxford Street, to form a " Metropolitan Trades Union," which was to include all trades, and to undertake, besides its Trade Union functions, a vague scheme of co-operative production and a political agitation for the franchise.[2] But under the influence of

---

[1] *England and America : a Comparison of the Social and Political State of both Nations,* 1833, 2 vols.

[2] *Poor Man's Guardian,* March 12, 1831 ; Place MSS. 27791—246, 272. " There were seven Co-operative Congresses in the years 1830-5 in which the Trade Union and Labour Exchange elements were prominent" (Prof. Foxwell's Introduction to *The Right to the Full Produce of Labour,* by Anton Menger, 1899).

William Lovett the last object soon thrust aside all the rest. The purely Trade Union aims were dropped ; the Owenite aspirations sank into the background ; and under the title of the " National Union of the Working Classes " the humble carpenters' society expanded into a national organisation for obtaining Manhood Suffrage. As such it occupies, during the political turmoil of 1831–2, by far the largest place in the history of working-class organisation, and was largely implicated in the agitation and disturbances connected with the Reform Bill.[1]

The Reform Bill came and passed, but no Manhood Suffrage. The effect of this disappointment at the hands of the most advanced political party in the country is thus described by Francis Place, now become an outside observer of the Trade Union Movement. " The year (1833) ended leaving the (National) Union (of the Working Classes) in a state of much depression. The nonsensical doctrines preached by Robert Owen and others respecting communities and goods in common ; abundance of everything man ought to desire, and all for four hours' labour out of every twenty-four ; the right of every man to his share of the earth in common, and his right to whatever his hands had been employed upon ; the power of masters under the present system to give just what wages they pleased ; the right of the labourer to such wages as would maintain him and his in comfort for eight or ten hours' labour ; the right of every man who was unemployed to employment and to such an amount of wages as have been indicated—and other matters of a similar kind which were continually inculcated by the working men's political unions, by many small knots of persons, printed in small pamphlets and handbills which were sold twelve for a penny and distributed to a great extent—had pushed politics aside . . . among the working people. These pamphlets were written almost wholly by men of talent and of some standing in the world,

---

[1] See the volumes of the *Poor Man's Guardian*, preserved in the British Museum.

professional men, gentlemen, manufacturers, tradesmen, and men called literary. The consequence was that a very large proportion of the working people in England and Scotland became persuaded that they had only to combine, as it was concluded they might easily do, to compel not only a considerable advance in wages all round, but employment for every one, man and woman, who needed it, at short hours. This notion induced them to form themselves into Trades Unions in a manner and to an extent never before known." [1]

This jumble of ordinary Trade Union aims and communist aspirations, described from the hostile point of view of a fanatical Malthusian and staunch believer in the " Wage Fund," probably fairly represents the character of the Owenite propaganda. It made an ineradicable impression on the working-class leaders of that generation, and inspired the great surge of solidarity which rendered possible the gigantic enlistments of the Grand National, with its unprecedented regiments of agricultural labourers and women. Its enlargement of consciousness of the working class was no doubt a good in itself which no mistakes in practical policy could wholly cancel.[2] But Owen did

[1] Place MSS. 27797—290 ; see a similar account in the *Life of William Lovett*, by himself, p. 86. James Mill writes to Lord Brougham on September 3, 1832, as follows : " Nothing can be conceived more mischievous than the doctrines which have been preached to the common people. . . . The nonsense to which your lordship alludes about the right of the labourer to the whole produce of the country, wages, profits, and rent all included, is the mad nonsense of our friend Hodgskin, which he has published as a system, and propagates with the zeal of perfect fanaticism. . . . The illicit cheap publications, in which the doctrine of the right of the labouring people, who they say are the only producers, to all that is produced, is very generally preached, . . . are superseding the Sunday newspapers and every other channel through which the people might get better information " (Bain's *James Mill*, p. 363, 1882). The series of Socialist authors of these years, usually ignored, have been well described by Prof. Foxwell in his Introduction to the English translation of Menger's *Right to the Whole Produce of Labour*, 1899 ; and more fully and philosophically in M. Beer's *History of British Socialism*, 1919, vol. i.

[2] "Owen's chief merit was that he filled the working classes with renewed hope at a time when the pessimism, both of orthodox economists and of their unorthodox opponents, had condemned labour to be an appendage of machinery, a mere commodity whose value, like that of all commodities, was determined by the bare cost of keeping up the

mischief as well as good ; and as both the evil and the good live after him—for nothing that Owen did can yet be said to be interred with his bones—it is necessary to examine his Trade Union doctrine in some detail. He was at his best when, as the experienced captain of industry, he denounced with fervent emphasis that lowering of the Standard of Life which was the result of the creed of universal competition. It was to combat this that he advocated Factory Legislation, and promoted combinations " to fix a maximum time and a minimum wages " ; and it was by thus attempting to secure the workers' Standard of Life by legislation and Trade Union action that he gained the influential support, not only of philanthropists, but also of certain high-minded manufacturers, with whose aid he formed in December 1833 the " Society for National Regeneration," [1] to which we have already referred. The most definite proposal of this society, the shortening of the hours of labour to eight per day, was what led to that suggestion of Fielden's on which the Lancashire cotton operatives acted in their abortive general strike for an eight hours day. It also produced the long series of " Short Time Committees " in the textile towns whose persistent agitation eventually secured the passing of the Ten Hours Bill, itself only an instalment of our great Factory Code. History has emphatically justified Owen on this side of his labour policy.

But there was a Utopian side to it which acted more

---

necessary supply. Owen laid stress upon the human side of economics. The object of industry was to produce happier and more contented men and women " (*The Chartist Movement*, by Mark Hovell, 1918, p. 45).

[1] The prospectus of this Society is in the British Library of Political Science at the London School of Economics. A copy is given in the *Morning Chronicle*, December 7, 1833. Its Manchester meetings are reported in the *Crisis* for November and December 1833. It seems to have had for its organ a penny weekly called *The Herald of the Rights of Industry*, some numbers of which are in the British Museum. Professor Foxwell has kindly drawn our attention to a further reference to it in the *Life of James Deacon Hume*, p. 55. It excited the curiosity of the Home Secretary. See Home Office Papers, 40—31.

questionably. The working-class world became, under his influence, inflated with a premature conception and committed to an impracticable working scheme of social organisation. He proved himself an able thinker and seer when he pointed out that the horrible poverty of the time was a new economic phenomenon, the inevitable result of unfettered competition and irresponsible individual ownership of the means of production now that those means had become enormously expensive and yet compact enough to employ hundreds of men under the orders of a few, besides being so prodigiously efficient as to drive the older methods quite out of the market. But from the point of view of the practical statesman, it must be confessed that he also showed himself something of a simpleton in supposing, or at least assuming, that competition could be abolished and ownership socialised by organising voluntary associations to supersede both the millowners and the State. He had tried the experiment in America with the famous community of New Harmony, and its failure had for the time thoroughly disgusted him with communities. But his disgust was not disillusion, for its only practical effect was to set him to repeat the experiment with the Trade Unions. Under his teaching the Trade Unionists came to believe that it was possible, by a universal non-political compact of the wage-earners, apparently through a universal expropriatory strike, to raise wages and shorten the hours of labour " to an extent," as Place puts it, " which, at no very distant time, would give them the whole proceeds of their labour." The function of the brain-worker as the director of industry was disregarded, possibly because in the cotton industry (in which Owen had made a fortune) it plays but an insignificant part in the actual productive processes, and is mainly concerned with that pursuit of cheap markets to buy in and dear markets to sell in which formed no part of the Utopian commonwealth at which " the Trades Union " aimed. The existing capitalists and managers were therefore considered as usurpers to be as soon as possible superseded by the elected representatives of voluntary and sectional associations of producers, in which it seems to have been assumed all the brain-working technicians would be included. The modern Socialist proposal to substitute the officials of the Municipality or State was unthinkable at a period when all local governing bodies were notoriously inefficient and corrupt and Parliament practically an oligarchy. Under the system proposed by Owen the instruments of production were to become the property, not of the whole community, but of the particular set of workers who used them. " There is no other alternative," he said, " than National Companies for each trade. . . . Thus all those trades which relate to clothing shall form a company—such as tailors, shoemakers, hatters, milliners, and mantua-makers ; and all the different manufacturers [*i.e.* operatives] shall be arranged in a similar way ; communications shall pass from the various departments to the Grand National establishment in London." In fact, the Trade Unions were to be transformed into " national companies " to carry on all the manufactures.[1] The Agricultural Union was to take possession of the land, the Miners' Union of the mines, the Textile Unions of the factories. Each trade was to be carried on by its particular Trade Union, centralised in one " Grand Lodge."

Of all Owen's attempts to reduce his Socialism to practice this was certainly the very worst. For his short-lived communities there was at least this excuse : that within their own area they were to be perfectly homogeneous little Communist States. There were to be no conflicting sections ; and profit-making and competition were to be effectually eliminated. But in " the Trades Union," as he conceived it, the mere combination of all the workmen in a trade as co-operative producers no more abolished commercial competition than a combination of

---

[1] See Owen's elaborate speech, reported in the *Crisis*, October 12, 1833 ; *Robert Owen : a Biography*, by Frank Podmore, 1906 ; and *Trade Unionism*, by C. M. Lloyd, 1915.

all the employers in it as a Joint Stock Company. In effect
his Grand Lodges would have been simply the head offices
of huge Joint Stock Companies owning the entire means of
production in their industry, and subject to no control by
the community as a whole. They would therefore have
been in a position at any moment to close their ranks and
admit fresh generations of workers only as employees at
competitive wages instead of as shareholders, thus creating
at one stroke a new capitalist class and a new proletariat.
Further, the improvident shareholders would soon have
begun to sell their shares in order to spend their capital,
and thus to drop with their children into the new proletariat ;
whilst the enterprising and capable shareholders would
equally have sold their shares to buy into other and momen-
tarily more profitable trades. Thus there would have been
not only a capitalist class and proletariat, but a speculative
stock market. Finally there would have come a competitive struggle between the Joint Stock Unions to supplant
one another in the various departments of industry. Thus
the shipwrights, making wooden ships, would have found the
boilermakers competing for their business by making iron
ships, and would have had either to succumb or to transform their wooden ship capital into iron ship capital and
enter into competition with the boilermakers as commercial
rivals in the same trade. This difficulty was staring Owen
in the face when he entered the Trade Union Movement ;
for the trades, then as now, were in continual perplexity
as to the exact boundaries between them ; for example,
the minute-books of the newly formed Joiners' Society in
Glasgow (whose secretary was a leading Owenite) show
that its great difficulty was the demarcation of its trade
against the cabinetmaker and the engineer-patternmaker,
each of whom claimed certain technical operations as proper
to himself alone. In short, the Socialism of Owen led him
to propose a practical scheme which was not even socialistic,
and which, if it could possibly have been carried out, would
have simply arbitrarily redistributed the capital of the

G

country without altering or superseding the capitalist system in the least.

All this will be so obvious to those who comprehend our capitalist system that they will have some difficulty in believing that it could have escaped so clever a man and so experienced and successful a capitalist as Owen. How far he made it a rule to deliberately shut his eyes to the difficulties that met him, from a burning conviction that any change was better than leaving matters entirely alone, cannot even be guessed ; but it is quite certain that he acted in perfect good faith, simply not knowing thoroughly what he was about.   He had a boundless belief in the power of education to form character ; and if any scheme promised just sufficient respite from poverty and degradation to enable him and his disciples to educate one generation of the country's children, he was ready to leave all economic consequences to be dealt with by " the New Moral World " which that generation's Owenite schooling would have created.   Doubtless he thought that " the Trades Union " promised him this much ; and besides, he did not foresee its economic consequences.   He was disabled by that confident sciolism and prejudice which has led generations of Socialists to borrow from Adam Smith and the " classic " economists the erroneous theory that labour is by itself the creator of value, without going on to master that impregnable and more difficult law of economic rent which is the very corner-stone of collectivist economy.   He took his economics from his friend William Thompson,[1] who, like Hodgskin and Hodgskin's illustrious disciple, Karl Marx, ignored the law of rent in his calculations, and taught that all exchange values could be measured in terms of " labour

[1] *Inquiry into the Principles of the Distribution of Wealth most conducive to Human Happiness*, by William Thompson, 1824 ; also his *Labour Rewarded, the Claims of Labour and Capital ; How to secure to Labour the whole Product of its Exertions*, by One of the Idle Classes, 1827 ; see Professor Foxwell's Introduction to *The Right to the whole Produce of Labour*, by Anton Menger, 1899; *History of British Socialism*, by M. Beer, 1919, vol. i. ; and *The Irish Labour Movement*, by W. P. Ryan, 1919, ch. iii.

time " alone. Part of the Owenite activity of the time actually resulted in the opening of labour bazaars, in which the prices were fixed in minutes. The fact that it is the consumer's demand which gives to the product of labour any exchange-value at all, and that the extent and elasticity of this demand determines how much has to be produced ; and the other governing consideration, namely, that the expenditure of labour required to bring articles of the same desirability to market varies enormously according to natural differences in fertility of soil, distance to be traversed, proximity to good highways, waterways, or ports, accessibility of water-power or steam fuel, and a hundred other circumstances, including the organising ability and executive dexterity of the producer, found themselves left entirely out of account. Owen assumed that the labour of the miner and that of the agricultural labourer, whatever the amount and nature of the product of each of them, would spontaneously and continuously exchange with each other equitably at par of hours and minutes when the miners had received a monopoly of the bowels of the country, and the agricultural labourers of its skin. He did not even foresee that the Miners' Union might be inclined to close its ranks against newcomers from the farm labourers, or that the Agricultural Union might refuse to cede sites for the Builders' Union to work upon. In short, the difficult economic problem of the equitable sharing of the advantages of superior sites and opportunities never so much as occurred to the enthusiastic Owenite economists of this period.

One question, and that the most immediately important of all, was never seriously faced : How was the transfer of the industries from the capitalists to the Unions to be effected in the teeth of a hostile and well-armed Government ? The answer must have been that the overwhelming numbers of " the Trades Union " would render conflict impossible. His enthusiastic disciple, William Benbow, successively a shoemaker, bookseller, and coffee-house keeper, invented the instrument of the General Strike—a sacred

" holiday month " prepared for and participated in by the entire wage-earning class, the mere " passive resistance " of which would, without violence or conflict, bring down all existing institutions.   Whether this was in Owen's mind in 1834, as it was, in 1839, avowedly in those of the Chartists, is uncertain.[1]   At all events, Owen, like the early Christians, habitually spoke as if the Day of Judgment of the existing order of society was at hand.   The next six months, in his view, were always going to see the " New Moral World " really established.   The change from the capitalist system to a complete organisation of industry under voluntary associations of producers was to " come suddenly upon society like a thief in the night."   " One year," comments his disciple, " may disorganise the whole fabric of the old world, and transfer, by a sudden spring, the whole political government of the country from the master to the servant." [2]   It is impossible not to regret that the first introduction of the English Trade Unionist to Socialism should have been effected by a foredoomed scheme which violated every economic principle of Collectivism, and left the indispensable political preliminaries to pure chance.

It was under the influence of these large plans and confident hopes that the Trade Unions were emboldened to adopt the haughty attitude and contemptuous language towards the masters which provoked Manchester and Liverpool employers to meet the challenge of the Builders' Union by " the Document."   The " intolerable tyranny " of the Unions, so much harped on by contemporary writers, represents, to a large extent, nothing more than the rather

---

[1] The pamphlet, entitled *The Grand National Holiday and Congress of the Productive Classes*, by William Benbow, 1831, had an extensive circulation.   Mark Hovell (*The Chartist Movement*, 1918, p. 91) thinks he was the same William Benbow whom Bamford mentions as a delegate from Manchester in 1817 (*Life of a Radical*, p. 8), and whom Henry Hunt describes as of the Manchester Hampden Club, and as having been reported by a Government spy to be manufacturing pikes in 1816 (*The Green Bag Plot*, 1918).

[2] Leading article in the *Crisis*, October 12, 1833.

bumptious expression of the Trade Unionists' feeling that they were the rightful directors of industry, entitled to choose the processes, and select their fellow-workers, and even their managers and foremen. And it must be remembered that this occurred at a period when class prejudice was so strong that any attempt at a parley made by the workers, however respectfully, was regarded as presumptuous and unbecoming. Hence the working class had always too much reason to believe that civility on their part would be thrown away. It is certain that during the Owenite intoxication the impracticable expectations of national dominion on the part of the wage-earners were met with an equally unreasonable determination by the governing classes to keep the working men in a state not merely of subjection, but of abject submission. The continued exclusion of the workmen from the franchise made constitutional action on their side impossible. The employers, on the other hand, used their political and magisterial power against the men without scruple, inciting a willing Government to attack the workmen's combinations by every possible perversion of the law, and partiality in its administration. Regarding absolute control over the conduct of their workpeople as a *sine qua non* of industrial organisation, even the genuine philanthropists among them insisted on despotic authority in the factory or workshop. Against the abuse of this authority there was practically no guarantee. On the other side it can be shown that large sections of the wage-earners were not only moderate in their demands, but submissive in their behaviour. As a rule, wherever we find exceptional aggression and violence on the part of the operatives, we discover exceptional tyranny on the side of the employers. To give an example or two, the continual outrages which disgrace the annals of Glasgow Trade Unionism for the first forty years of this century are accounted for by the reports of the various Parliamentary Inquiries which mark out the Glasgow millowners as extraordinarily autocratic in their views and tyrannous in their conduct.

Again, the aggressive conduct of certain sections of the building trades is frequently complained of in the capitalist press between 1830–40. But the agreements which the large contractors of that time required " all those to sign who enter into their employ," printed copies of which are still extant, show that the demands of the employers were intolerably arbitrary.[1] Then there is the case of the miners of Great Britain, who were in very ill repute for riotous proceedings from 1837–44. The provocation they received may be judged from a manifesto issued by Lord Londonderry in his dual capacity as mine-owner and Lord-Lieutenant of Durham County during the great strike of the miners in 1844 for fairer terms of hiring. He not only superintends, as Lord-Lieutenant, the wholesale eviction of the strikers from their homes, and their supersession by Irishmen specially imported from his Irish estates, but he peremptorily orders the resident traders in " his town of Seaham," on pain of forfeiting his custom and protection, to refuse to supply provisions to the workmen engaged in what he deems " an unjust and senseless warfare *against their proprietors and masters.*"[2] The same intolerance

---

[1] A specimen dated 1837 is preserved by the Stonemasons' Society, according to which a Liverpool contractor bound all his employees to serve him at a fixed wage for a long term of years, any time lost by sickness or otherwise not to be paid for and to be added to the term ; all " lawful commands " to be obeyed ; and no present or future club or other society to be joined without the employer's consent.

[2] See his manifestoes reprinted in *Northern Star*, July 6 and July 27, 1844. " Lord Londonderry again warns all the shopkeepers and tradesmen in his town of Seaham that if they still give credit to pitmen who hold off work, and continue in the Union, such men will be marked by his agents and overmen, and will never be employed in his collieries again, and the shopkeepers may be assured that they will never have any custom or dealings with them from Lord Londonderry's large concerns that he can in any manner prevent.

" Lord Londonderry further informs the traders and shopkeepers, that having by his measures increased very largely the last year's trade to Seaham, and if credit is so improperly and so fatally given to his unreasonable pitmen, thereby prolonging the injurious strike, it is his firm determination to carry back all the outlay of his concerns even to Newcastle.

" Because it is neither fair, just, or equitable that the resident traders in his own town should combine and assist the infatuated workmen and

marks the magazines and journals of the dominant classes of the period. It seems to have been habitually taken for granted that the workman had not merely to fulfil his contract of service, but to yield implicit obedience in the details of his working life to the will of his master. Combinations and strikes on the part of the " lower orders " were regarded as futile and disorderly attempts to escape from their natural position of social subservience. In short, the majority of employers, even in this time of negro emancipation, seem to have been unconsciously acting upon the dictum subsequently attributed to J. C. Calhoun, the defender of American slavery, that " the true solution of the contest of all time between labour and capital is that capital should own the labourer whether white or black."

The closing scene of Owen's first and last attempt at " the Trades Union " shows how ephemeral had been his participation in the real life of the Trade Union Movement. In August 1834 he called together one of his usual miscellaneous congresses, consisting of delegates from all kinds of Owenite societies, with a few from the Grand National and other Trade Unions. At this congress the " Grand National Consolidated Trades Union," which was to have brought to its feet Government, landlords, and employers, was formally converted into the " British and Foreign Consolidated Association of Industry, Humanity, and Knowledge," having for its aim the establishment of a " New Moral World " by the reconciliation of all classes. Beyond one or two small and futile experiments in co-operative production, it had attempted nothing to realise Owen's Utopia. Its whole powers had been spent, seemingly with his own consent, in a series of aggressive strikes. For all that, Owen's meteoric appearance in the Trade Union World left a deep impression on the movement. The minute-books and other contemporary records of the Trade Unions of the next decade abound in Owenite

---

pitmen in prolonging their own miseries by continuing an insane strike, and an unjust and senseless warfare against their proprietors and masters."

phraseology, such as the classification of Society into the " idle " and the " industrious " classes, the latter apparently meaning—and being certainly understood to mean—only the manual workers.   More important is the persistence of the idea that the Trade Unions, as Associations of Producers, should recover control of the instruments of production. From this time forth innumerable attempts were made, by one Trade Union or another, to employ its own members in Productive Co-operation.   A long series of industrial disasters, culminating in the great losses of 1874, has, even now, scarcely eradicated the last remnant of this Joint Stock Individualism from the idealists of the Trade Union Movement ; or taught them to distinguish accurately between it and the demonstrably successful Co-operative Production of the Associations of Consumers which constitute the Co-operative Movement of to-day.   Outside the organised ranks his effect upon general working-class opinion was, as Place remarks, enormous, as we could abundantly show were we here concerned with the " Union Shops," " Equitable Labour Exchanges," and industrial communities which may be considered the most direct result of the Owenite propaganda, or with the fortunes of the innumerable co-operative associations of producers, whose delegates formed the backbone of the Owenite congresses of these years.[1]

The Trade Union Movement was not absolutely left for dead when Owen quitted the field.   The skilled mechanics of the printing and engineering trades had, as we shall presently see, held aloof from the general movement, and their trade clubs were unaffected either by the Owenite boom or its subsequent collapse.   In some other trades the inflation of 1830–4 spread itself over a few more years.   The Potters' Union went on increasing in strength, and in 1835 gained a notable victory over the employers, when a " Green Book of Prices " was agreed to, which long remained famous

---

[1] Some account of these developments will be found in *The Co-operative Movement in Great Britain*, by Beatrice Potter (Mrs. Sidney Webb).

in the trade. Renewed demands led to the formation by the employers of a Chamber of Commerce to resist the men's aggression. The " yearly bond " was rigidly insisted upon, and a great strike ensued, which ended in 1837 in the complete collapse of the Union.[1] In 1836 the Scottish compositors formed the General Typographical Association of Scotland, which for a few years exercised an effective control over the trade. The same year saw a notable strike by the Preston Cotton-spinners, from which is dated the general adoption of the self-acting mule.[2] But the most permanent effect is seen in the building trades. The national Unions of Plumbers and Carpenters have preserved an unbroken existence down to the present day,[3] whilst the Friendly Society of Operative Stonemasons remained for nearly another half century one of the most powerful of English Unions. The fortnightly circulars of the English Stonemasons reveal, for a few years, not only a vigorous life and quick growth, but also many successful short strikes to secure Working Rules and to maintain Time Wages. The Scottish Stonemasons are referred to as being even more active and influential in trade regulation, and as having included practically all the Scottish masons. There is evidence, too, of informal federal action between the National Unions of Stonemasons, Carpenters, and Bricklayers. Unfortunately the absence of such modern machinery of organisation as Trades Councils, Trade Union Congresses,

[1] The collapse was duly reported to the Home Secretary (Home Office Papers, 40—33, 34, 35).

[2] See Ashworth's paper before British Association, 1837 ; *Remarks upon the Importance of an Inquiry into the Amount and Appropriation of Wages by the Working Classes,* by W. Felkin, 1837 ; *Appeal to the Public from the United Trades of Preston,* February 14, 1837 (in Home Office Papers, 40—35).

[3] The United Society of Operative Plumbers (reorganised 1848) still dominates its branch of the trade, and retains traces of the federal constitution of the Builders' Union. The sister organisation of carpenters (now styled the General Union of Carpenters and Joiners) has been overtaken and overshadowed by the newer Amalgamated Society of Carpenters and Joiners ; whilst the Operative Bricklayers' Society has absorbed practically all the older societies in its own branch of the trade.

and standing joint committees prevented the scattered sectional organisations from forming any general movement. This state of things was broken into during the year 1837 by the sensational strikes in Glasgow, the prolonged legal prosecution and severe punishment of their leaders, and the appointment of a Parliamentary Committee of Inquiry into the results of the repeal of the Combination Laws.

We do not propose to enter here into the details of the famous trial of the five Glasgow cotton-spinners for conspiracy, violent intimidation, and for the murder of fellow-workers. But it is one of the " leading cases " of Trade Union history, and the manifestations of feeling which it provoked show to the depths the state of mind of the working classes.[1]   The evidence given in court, and repeated before the Select Committee of 1838, leaves no reasonable doubt that the Cotton-Spinners' Union in its corporate capacity had initiated a reign of terror extending over twenty years, and that some of the incriminated members had been personally guilty not of instigation alone, but of actual violence, if not of murder.   In spite of this, the whole body of working-class opinion was on their side, and the

[1] Glasgow was still the principal centre of the cotton industry, especially in weaving.   In 1838 there were in the Glasgow area about 36,000 handlooms devoted mainly to cotton, with two persons to a loom, whilst in all Lancashire there were only 25,000 (Parliamentary Papers, xlii. of 1849 and xxiv. of 1840 ; *The Chartist Movement*, by Mark Hovell, 1918, p. 14).   Combination among the cotton operatives of Glasgow was of old standing.   After the strike of 1812, already referred to, trouble broke out again in 1820 and 1822, when outrages were committed (*Arts and Artisans*, by J. G. Symons, 1839, p. 137).

Besides securing full reports in the newspapers, the Trade Union committee conducting the case published at a low price an account of the trial in parts, which has not been preserved.   Two other exhaustive reports were issued, and may still be consulted, viz. *Report of the trial of Thomas Hunter and other operative cotton-spinners in Glasgow in* 1838, by Archibald Swinton (Edinburgh, 1838), and *The trial of Thomas Hunter, etc., the Glasgow Cotton-spinners*, by James Marshall (Glasgow, 1838).   See also the *Autobiography of Sir Archibald Alison*, 1883; the *Northern Star* for 1837–8 ; the *Annual Register* for 1838, pp. 206-7 ; and the evidence before the Select Committee on Combinations, 1838.   A summary will be found in Howell's *Labour Legislation, Labour Movements and Labour Leaders*, 1902, pp. 83-4.

sentence of seven years' transportation was received with as much indignation as that upon the Dorchester labourers four years before. This was one of the natural effects of the class despotism and scarcely veiled rebellion which we have already described. The use of violence by working men, either against obnoxious employers or against traitors in their own ranks, was regarded in much the same way as the political offences of a subject race under foreign dominion. Such deeds did not, in fact, necessarily indicate any moral turpitude on the part of the perpetrators. No one accused the five Glasgow cotton-spinners of bad private character or conduct, and at least four out of the five were men of acknowledged integrity and devotedness.[1] Their unjust treatment whilst awaiting trial, and still more their sentence to transportation, enlisted the sympathy of the Parliamentary Radicals, and Wakley, the member for Finsbury, did not hesitate to bring their case before the House of Commons as one of legal persecution and injustice.

At this time the trade societies of Dublin and Cork had caused serious complaint by attempting to establish, and not without violence, an effective monopoly in certain skilled industries. Their action had been reproved by Daniel O'Connell, whom they, in their turn, had repudiated and denounced. O'Connell defeated Wakley's friendly motion for an inquiry into the cotton-spinners' case by a serious indictment of Trade Unionism. By a clever analysis of the rules of the Irish societies, which he made out to be purely obstructive and selfish, he condemned, in a speech of great power, all attempts on the part of trade combinations to regulate the conditions of labour. The well-established methods of modern Trade Unionism, such as the maintenance of a minimum rate, received from him the same condemnation as the unsocial and oppressive

[1] The five prisoners were pardoned in 1840, in consequence of their exemplary conduct. There is a joint letter by them in the *Trades Journal* for August, 1840, relating to the subscriptions raised for them by a London committee.

monopolies for which the Irish trades had long been notorious. The Government met this speech by granting a Select Committee under Sir Henry Parnell to inquire into the whole question ; and Trade Unionism accordingly found itself once more on its defence as a permanent element in social organisation. The case of the Glasgow cotton-spinners and the appointment of this Parliamentary Committee for the moment revived the sentiment of solidarity in the Trade Union world. A joint committee of the Glasgow trades was formed to collect subscriptions for the defence of the prisoners ; and communications for this purpose were made to all the known Trade Unions. Considerable funds were subscribed, as the trial was repeatedly postponed at great expense to the prisoners ; and when at last, in January, 1838, they were convicted and sentenced, a combined agitation for some mitigation of their punishment was begun. By this time it had become known that some kind of inquiry into Trade Unionism was in contemplation. The Unions at once set their house in order. The Stonemasons, who had already given up the administration of oaths, resolved, for greater security against illegal practices, " that all forms of regalia, initiation, and passwords be dispensed with and entirely abolished." [1] The Dublin Plasterers formally suspended their exclusive rules, and deferred the issue of a new edition until after the inquiry.[2] In Glasgow, the chief seat of the disorder, many societies—among others, the local Carpenters—deliberately burned their minute-books and archives for the past year. The London societies appointed a committee, " The London Trades Combination Committee," to conduct the Unionist case in the Parliamentary inquiry. Lovett, then well known as a Radical politician, became secretary, and issued a stirring address to the Trade Unions throughout the country, asking for subscriptions and evi-

---

[1] *Stonemasons' Fortnightly Circular*, January 19, 1838.
[2] Evidence of W. Darcy, the secretary, second report of 1838 Committee, p. 130.

dence.[1] But the Parliamentary Committee proved both perfunctory and inconclusive. The Government, which had conceded it merely to rid itself of the importunity of Wakley on the one hand and O'Connell on the other, had evidently no intention of taking any action on the subject ; and the Committee, always thinly attended, made no attempt at a general inquiry, and confined itself practically to Dublin and Glasgow. O'Connell got the opportunity he desired of demonstrating, through selected witnesses, the violent and exclusive spirit which animated the Irish Unions. With regard to Glasgow, the chief witness was Sheriff, afterwards Sir Archibald, Alison, whose vigorous action had quelled the cotton-spinners in that city. It was scarcely necessary to call witnesses on behalf of the Unions ; but John Doherty, then become a master-printer and bookseller, was allowed to describe the Manchester spinners' organisation and the ill-fated associations of 1829–31. The inquiry resulted in nothing but the presentation to the House of two volumes of evidence, without even so much as a report. It seems to have been expected that the Committee would be reappointed to complete its task ; but when the next session came the matter was quietly dropped.[2]

The temporary fillip given by the cotton-spinners' trial and the Parliamentary Committee did not stop the steady decline of Trade Unionism throughout the country. Trade, which had been on the wane since 1836, grew suddenly worse. The decade closed with three of the leanest years ever known ; and widespread distress prevailed. The membership of the surviving Trade Unions rapidly decreased. The English Stonemasons, perhaps the strongest

[1] Circular dated March 1, 1838, in Stonemasons' archives ; and *An Address from the London Trades Committee appointed to watch the Parliamentary Inquiry into Combinations,* 1838.

[2] George Howell suggests, we are not sure with what authority, that Nassau Senior, whose report on Trade Unionism to the Home Secretary in 1830 we have already described, tendered this to Sir Henry Parnell as the basis of a report by the Committee of 1838, but the proposal was not accepted (*Labour Legislation, Labour Movements and Labour Leaders,* 1902, pp. 83-4). See also *The Irish Labour Movement,* by W. P. Ryan, 1919.

of the contemporary societies, reduced themselves, in 1841, temporarily, to absolute bankruptcy by their disastrous strike against an obnoxious foreman on the rebuilding of the Houses of Parliament. The Scottish Stonemasons' Society, of equal or greater strength, collapsed at about the same time, from causes not known to us. The Glasgow trades had been completely disorganised by the disasters of 1837. The Lancashire textile operatives showed no sign of life ; whilst such growing societies as the Ironfounders, the Journeymen Steam-Engine Makers and Millwrights, and the Boilermakers were crippled by the heavy drafts made upon their funds by unemployed members. The state of mind of the working classes was no more propitious than the state of trade. Fierce discontent and sullen anger are the characteristics of this period Hatred of the New Poor Law, of the iniquitous taxes on food, of the general oppression by the dominant classes, blazes out in the Trade Union records of the time. The agitation for the " Six Points," set on foot by Lovett and others in the Working Men's Association of 1836, became the centre of working-class aspiration. The *Northern Star*, started at the end of 1837, rapidly distanced all other provincial journals in circulation. The lecturers of the Anti-Corn Law League increased the popular discontent, even when their own particular panacea failed to find acceptance. A general despair of constitutional reform led to the growing supremacy of the " Physical Force " section of the Chartists, and to the insurrectionism of 1839–42.

The political developments of these years are outside the scope of this work. The Chartist Movement plays the most important part in working-class annals from 1837 to 1842, and does not quit the stage until 1848. Made respectable by sincerity, devotion, and even heroism in the rank and file, it was disgraced by the fustian of many of its orators and the political and economic quackery of its pretentious and incompetent leaders whose jealousies and intrigues, by successively excluding all the nobler

elements, finally brought it to nought.   An adequate history
of it would be of extreme value to our young Democracy.[1]
Here it is only necessary to say that whilst the Chartist
Movement commanded the support of the vast majority
of the manual-working wage-earners, outside the ranks of
those who were deeply religious, there is no reason to believe
that the Trade Unions at any time became part and parcel
of the Movement, as they had, during 1833–4, of the Owenite
agitation, though some of their members furnished the most
ardent supporters of the Charter.   Individual trades, such
as the shoemakers, seem to have been thoroughly permeated
with Chartism, and were always attempting to rally other
trade societies to the cause.   The angry strikes of 1842 in
Lancashire and the Midlands, fostered, as some said, by
the Anti-Corn Law League, were " captured " by the
Chartists, and almost converted into political rebellions.
The delegate meeting of the Lancashire and Yorkshire trade
clubs, which was conducting the " general strike " then in
progress " for the wages of 1840," resolved in August 1842
to recommend all wage-earners " to cease work until the
Charter becomes the law of the land." [2]   For a few weeks,
indeed, it looked as if the Trade Union Movement, such as
it was, would become merged in the political current.   But
the manifest absurdity of persuading starving men to
remain on strike until the whole political machinery of the
country had been altered, must have quickly become
apparent to the shrewder Trade Unionists.   When Chartist

---

[1] A series of subsequent publications has now gone far to fill this gap.
The Chartist Movement, by R. G. Gammage (republished 1894), may
now be supplemented by *The Life of Francis Place*, by Professor Graham
Wallas (revised edition, 1918) ;   *Le Chartisme, 1830–48*, by E. Dolléans,
2 vols. (Paris, 1912–13) ; *The Chartist Movement*, by Mark Hovell, 1918;
The Social and Economic Aspects of the Chartist Movement, by F. F.
Rosenblatt (New York, 1916) ;   *The Decline of the Chartist Movement*, by
P. W. Slosson (New York, 1916) ;   *Chartism and the Churches*, by H. V.
Faulkner (New York, 1916) ; *Die Entstehung und die ökonomischen Grund-
sätze der Chartistenbewegung*, by John Tildsley (Jena, 1898) ; and especially by the two separate volumes on the *History of British Socialism*,
by M. Beer, 1919 and 1920.

[2] *Northern Star*, August 20, 1842.

meetings at Sheffield were calling for a " general strike " to obtain the Charter, the secretaries of seven local Unions wrote to the newspapers explaining that their trades had nothing to do with the meetings or the resolutions.[1] It must be remembered in this connection that the number of Trade Unionists was, in these years, relatively small — probably not so great as a hundred thousand in the whole kingdom — so that they could not have formed any appreciable proportion of the two, three or four million adherents that the Chartist leaders were in the habit of claiming. And it may be doubted whether in any case a Trade Union itself, as distinguished from particular members who happened to be delegates, made any formal profession of adherence to Chartism. In the contemporary Trade Union records that are still extant, such as those of the Bookbinders, Compositors, Ironfounders, Cotton-spinners, Steam-engine makers, and Stonemasons, there are no traces of Chartist resolutions ; although denunciations of the " Notorious New Poor Law oppression " abound in the *Fortnightly Circular* of the Stonemasons ;[2] whilst the Ironfounders, Compositors, and Cotton-spinners pass resolutions in favour of Free Trade. A partial explanation of this reticence on the more exciting topic of the Charter is doubtless to be found in the frequently adopted rule excluding politics and religion from Trade Union discussions—a rule which was, in 1842, protested against by an enthusiastic Chartist delegate from the Bookbinders at the Manchester Conference.[3] There must, however, have been something more than mere obedience to the rule in the unwillingness of the trade societies to be mixed up with the Chartist agitation. The rule had not prevented the organised trades of 1831-2

---

[1] *Sheffield Iris*, August 1842.

[2] See, for instance, that for October 1839.

[3] *Northern Star*, August 20, 1842. " It is clear that the trade societies as a whole stood outside the Chartist Movement, though many Trade Unionists were no doubt Chartists too. The societies could not be induced to imperil their funds and existence at the orders of the Chartist Convention " (*The Chartist Movement*, by Mark Hovell, 1918, p. 169).

from taking a prominent part in the Reform Bill Movement. The banners of the Edinburgh trade clubs were conspicuous in the public demonstration on the rejection of the Bill of 1831. When the House of Lords gave way, the Birmingham Trade Unions themselves organised a triumphal procession, which was discountenanced by the middle class.[1] The records of the London Brushmakers show that they even subscribed from the Union funds to Reform associations. But we never find the trade societies of 1839–42 contributing to Chartist funds, or even collecting money for Chartist victims. The cases of Frost, Williams, and Jones, the Newport rebels of 1839, were at least as deserving of the working-class sympathy as those of the Glasgow cotton-spinners. But the Trade Unions showed no inclination to subscribe money or get up petitions in aid of them. " Never," writes Fergus O'Connor, in 1846, " was there more criminal apathy than that manifested by the trades of Great Britain to the sufferings of those men ; " and he adds, " that if one half that was done for the Dorchester labourers or the Glasgow cotton-spinners had been done for Frost, Williams, and Jones, they would long since have been restored." [2]

Insurrectionism, whether Owenite or Chartist, was, in fact, losing its attraction for the working-class mind. Robert Owen's economic axioms of the extinction of profit and the elimination of the profit-maker were, during these very years, passing into the new Co-operative Movement, inaugurated in 1844 by the Rochdale Pioneers. The believers in a " new system of society," to be brought about by universal agreement, were henceforth to be found in the ranks of the commercial-minded Co-operators rather than in those of the militant Trade Unionists. Chartism, meanwhile, had degenerated from Lovett's high ideal of a complete political democracy to an ignoble scramble for the

---

[1] *History of Birmingham*, by W. Hutton (Birmingham, edition of 1835), p. 149.
[2] *Northern Star*, August 24, 1846.

ownership of small plots of land. The example of the French Revolution of 1848 fanned the dying embers for a few weeks into a new flame ; and many of the London trades swung into the somewhat theatrical fête of April 10, 1848, swelling the procession against which the Duke of Wellington had marshalled the London middle class. But the danger of revolution had passed away. A new generation of workmen was growing up, to whom the worst of the old oppression was unknown, and who had imbibed the economic and political philosophy of the middle-class reformers. Bentham, Ricardo, and Grote were read only by a few ; but the activity of such popular educationalists as Lord Brougham and Charles Knight propagated " useful knowledge " to all the members of the Mechanics' Institutes and the readers of the *Penny Magazine*. The middle-class ideas of " free enterprise " and " unrestricted competition " which were thus diffused received a great impetus from the extraordinary propaganda of the Anti-Corn Law League, and the general progress of Free Trade. Fergus O'Connor and Bronterre O'Brien struggled in vain against the growing dominance of Cobden and Bright as leaders of working-class opinion. And so we find in the Trade Union records of 1847–8, that vigorous resistance begins to be made to any movement in support of the old ideals. The Steam-Engine Makers' Society suspended some of their branches for depositing the branch funds in Fergus O'Connor's Land Bank. When two branches of the Stonemasons' Society propose the same investment, the others indignantly protest against it as an absurd political speculation. And it is significant that these protests came, not from the cautious elders whose enthusiasm had outlived many failures, but from those who had never shared the old faith. When in 1848 the Yorkshire Woolstaplers proposed to take a farm upon which to set to work their unemployed men, it was the younger members, as we are expressly told, who strenuously but vainly resisted this action, which resulted ruinously for the society.

All this makes the close of the " revolutionary " period of the Trade Union Movement. For the next quarter of a century we shall watch the development of the new ideas and the gradual building up of the great " amalga- mated " societies of skilled artisans, with their centralised administration, friendly society benefits, and the substitu- tion, wherever possible, of Industrial Diplomacy for the ruder methods of the Class War.

CHAPTER IV

THE NEW SPIRIT AND THE NEW MODEL

[1843–1860]

WE have seen the magnificent hopes of 1829–42 ending in bitter disillusionment : we shall now see the Trade Unionists of the next generation largely successful in reaching their more limited aims. Laying aside all projects of Social Revolution, they set themselves resolutely to resist the worst of the legal and industrial oppressions from which they suffered, and slowly built up for this purpose organisations which have become integral parts of the structure of a modern industrial state. This success we attribute mainly to the spread of education among the rank and file, and the more practical counsels which began, after 1842, to influence the Trade Union world. But we must not overlook the effect of economic changes. The period between 1825 and 1848 was remarkable for the frequency and acuteness of its commercial depressions. From 1850 industrial expansion was for many years both greater and steadier than in any previous period.[1] It is no mere coincidence

---

[1] Between 1850 and 1874 there was (except, perhaps, during the American Civil War) no falling off in the value of our export trade comparable to the serious declines of 1826, 1829, 1837, 1842, and 1848. We do not pretend to account for this difference, but may remind the reader of the coincident increase in the production of gold, the influence of Free Trade and railways, and, as the bimetallists would tell us, the currency arrangements which were brought to an end in 1873.

that these years of prosperity saw the adoption by the Trade Union world of a " New Model " of organisation, under which Trade Unionism obtained a financial strength, a trained staff of salaried officers, and a permanence of membership hitherto unknown.

The predominance of Chartism over Trade Unionism was confined to the bad times of 1837–42. Under the influence of the rapid improvement and comparative prosperity which followed, the Chartist agitation dwindled away; and a marked revival in Trade Unionism took effect in the re-establishment, about 1843, of the Potters' Union, and of an active Cotton-spinners' Association, and, in 1845, by the amalgamation of the metropolitan and provincial societies of compositors into the National Typographical Society.[1] The powerful United Flint Glass Makers' Society (reorganised in 1849 as the Flint Glass Makers' Friendly Society of Great Britain and Ireland) dates from the same year. Delegate meetings of other trades were held; and national societies of tailors and shoemakers were set on foot. A national conference of curriers in 1845 established a federal union of all the local clubs in the trade. But the most important of the new bodies was the Miners' Association of Great Britain and Ireland, formed at Wakefield in 1841.[2] Up to this period the miners, held in virtual serfage by the truck system and the custom of yearly hirings, had not got beyond ephemeral strike organisations. Strong county Unions now grew up in

---

[1] This was an elaborate national organisation with 60 branches, grouped under five District Boards. But it enrolled only 4320 members, and broke up in 1847, after numerous local strikes. In June 1849 most of the provincial branches joined in the Typographical Association, from which for some time the strong Manchester and Birmingham societies stood aloof; whilst the London men formed the London Society of Compositors.

[2] *The Colliers' Guide, showing the Necessity of the Colliers Uniting to Protect their Labour from the Iron Hand of Oppression*, etc., by J. B. Thompson (Bishop Wearmouth, 1843); and see many reports in the *Northern Star*, from 1843 to 1848; *The Miners of Northumberland and Durham*, by Richard Fynes, 1873; *A Great Labour Leader* [Thomas Burt], by Aaron Watson, 1908, pp. 19-23.

Northumberland and Durham on the one hand, and Lancashire and Yorkshire on the other ; and the new body was
a federation of these.   Under the leadership of Martin
Jude, it developed an extraordinary propagandist activity,
at one time paying no fewer than fifty-three missionary
organisers, who visited every coalpit in the kingdom.   The
delegate meetings at Manchester and Glasgow in the year
1844 soon came to represent practically the whole of the
mining districts of Great Britain ;   and the membership
rose, it is said, to at least 100,000.[1]

A leading feature of this Trade Unionist revival was a
dogged resistance to legal oppression.   Although the more
sensational prosecutions of Trade Union leaders had ceased
with the abandonment of unlawful oaths, there was still
going on, up and down the kingdom, an almost continuous
persecution of the rank and file, by the magistrates' interpretation of the law relating to masters and servants.   The
miners, in particular, were hampered by lengthy hirings,
during which they were compelled to serve if required,
but were not guaranteed employment.   Unskilled in legal
subtleties, and not yet served by an experienced class of
Trade Union secretaries, they were made the victims of
a thousand and one quibbles and technicalities.   The
Northumberland and Durham Miners' Union grappled with
the difficulty in a thoroughly practical spirit.   They engaged
W. P. Roberts,[2] an able and energetic solicitor, with strong

[1] *Northern Star* for 1843–4 ; Fynes' *Miners of Northumberland and
Durham*, 1873, chap. viii. ; *Condition of the Working Class in England in
1844*, by Friedrich Engels, 1892, pp. 253-9.

[2] William Prowting Roberts, the youngest son of the Rev. Thomas
Roberts, of Chelmsford, was born in 1806, and became a solicitor at
Manchester.   He was an enthusiastic Chartist, and friend of Fergus
O'Connor, to whose Land Bank he acted as legal adviser.   From 1843
onwards his name appears in nearly all the legal business of the Trade
Unions.   The collapse of 1848 somewhat damaged his reputation, but he
continued to be frequently retained for many years.   In 1867 he organised
the defence of Allen, Larking, and O'Brien, the Irish " Manchester
Martyrs," who were hanged for the rescue of Fenian prisoners and the
murder of a policeman.   In later years Roberts retired to a country
house in the neighbourhood of " O'Connorville," near Rickmansworth, the
scene of one of O'Connor's colonies, where he died on September 7, 1871.

labour sympathies, to fight every case in the local courts. In 1844 the Miners' Association of Great Britain and Ireland followed this excellent example by appointing Roberts their standing legal adviser at a salary of £1000 a year. When the Durham miners had to relinquish his services at the end of 1844, he was taken over by the newly formed Lancashire Miners' Union. The "miners' attorney-general," as he was called, showed an indefatigable activity in the defence of his clients, and was soon retained in all Trade Union cases. The magistrates throughout the country found themselves for the first time confronted by a pertinacious legal expert, who, far more ingenious than the employers, was not less unscrupulous in taking advantage of every technicality of the law.

In a letter written to the Flint Glass Makers' Friendly Society in 1851, Roberts himself gives a vivid picture of the difficulties against which the Unions had to contend. After explaining the law, as he understood it, he proceeds as follows : " But it is exceedingly difficult to induce those of the class opposed to you to take this view of things. I do not say this sarcastically, but as a fact learnt by long and observant experience. There are indeed men on the bench who are honest enough, and desirous of doing their duty. But all their tendencies and circumstances are against you. They listen to your opponents, not only often, but cheerfully—so they know more fully the case against you than in your favour. To you they listen too— but in a sort of temper of ' Prisoner at the Bar, you are entitled to make any statement you think fit, and the Court is bound to hear you ; but mind, whatever you say,' etc. In the one case you observe the hearty smile of good-will ; in the other the derisive sneer, though sometimes with a ghastly sort of kindliness in it. Then there is the knowledge of your overwhelming power when acting unitedly,

---

A pamphlet on the Trade Union Bill of 1871 is the only publication of his that we have discovered, but he appears also to have edited a report of the engineers' trial in 1847, and reports of some other legal proceedings

and this begets naturally a corresponding desire to resist you at all hazards.   And there are hundreds of other considerations all acting the same way—meetings, political councils, intermarriages, hopes from wills, etc.   I do not say that all occupants of the bench are thus influenced, nor to the same extent ; but it certainly is at the best an uphill game to contend in favour of a working man in a question which admits of any doubt against him.   It never happened to me to meet a magistrate who considered that an agreement among masters not to employ any particular ' troublesome fellow ' was an unlawful act ; reverse the case, however, and it immediately becomes a formidable conspiracy, which must be put down by the strong arm of the law, etc. . . . When I was acting for the Colliers' Union in the North we resisted every individual act of oppression, even in cases where we were sure of losing ; and the result was that in a short time there was no oppression to resist.   For it is to be observed that oppression like that we are speaking of— which after all is merely a more genteel and cowardly mode of thieving—shrinks at once from a determined and decided opposition.   In the North we should have tried this case, first in the County Court, then at the Assizes, and then perhaps in the Queen's Bench." [1]

---

[1] *Flint Glass Makers' Magazine*, October 1851.   The years 1847–8 had witnessed many strikingly vindictive prosecutions of Trade Unionists. Besides the case of the engineers, to which we shall refer hereafter, twenty-one stonemasons of London were indicted in 1848 for conspiracy, but, after repeated postponements, the prosecuting employer failed to proceed with the case.   The Sheffield razor-grinders stood in greater jeopardy.   John Drury, and three other members of their society, were tried and sentenced to ten years' transportation at the instance of the Sheffield Manufacturers' Protection Association on the random accusations of two dissolute convicts that they had incited them to destroy machinery.   This monstrous perversion of justice aroused the greatest indignation.   Public meetings were held by the National Association of United Trades.   The indictment was quashed on a technical point, but a new one was immediately preferred against the defendants.   The local feeling was, however, so great that they were finally, after a year's suspense, released on their own recognisances (July 12, 1849).   A Sheffield Trade Unionist declared that " the tyranny of the employers had been so great," in perverting the local administration of the law, " that the men laid

One result of Roberts' successful advocacy is perhaps to be seen in the introduction, during the Parliamentary session of 1844, of a Bill " for enlarging the powers of justices in determining complaints between masters, servants, and artificers," which the Government got referred to a committee, by which various extraordinary interpolations were made in what was at first a harmless measure.[1] Not only was any J.P to be authorised to issue a warrant for the summary arrest of any workman complained of by his employer, but " any misbehaviour concerning such service or employment " was to be punished by two months' imprisonment, at the discretion of a single justice. It is easy to see what a wide interpretation would have been given by many a justice of the peace to this vague phrase ; and Roberts was not slow to point out the danger to his clients. Upon his incitement the delegate meeting of coal-miners at Sheffield set on foot a vigorous agitation against the Bill, which had already slipped through second reading and committee without a division. The Potters' Union took the matter up with special vigour, and circulated draft petitions throughout the Midlands.[2] A friendly member, Thomas Slingsby Duncombe, obstructed its further progress, and got it postponed until after the Easter recess. Meanwhile petitions poured in upon the astonished House, amounting, it was said, to a total of two hundred, and representing two millions of workmen. When the Bill came on again all the Radicals and the " Young England " Tories were marshalled against it. Sir James Graham in vain protested that the Government meant nothing more than a consolidation of the existing law, and led into the lobby all his colleagues who were present, including Mr.

---

their grievances before the Government. Sir George Grey ordered an inquiry. . . . Twenty cases of parties who had been convicted by the magistrates were brought before a Board of Inquiry, seventeen of which were quashed " (*Stonemasons' Fortnightly Circular*, November 23, 1848).

[1] Bill No. 58 of 1844, introduced by William Miles, M.P. (Hansard, vols. 73 and 74.)

[2] *Potters' Examiner*, April 13, 1844.

Gladstone. But the combination on the other side of Duncombe, Wakley, Hume, and Ferrand, with Tories like Lord John Manners, and a few enlightened Whigs such as C. P. Villiers, settled the fate of this attempt on the part of the employers to sharpen the blunted weapon of the law against the hated Trade Unions.[1]

The miners were less successful in their strikes than in their legal and political business. In 1844 their National Conference at Glasgow, representing 70,000 men, voted, by 28,042 to 23,357, in favour of striking against their grievances, and the Durham men, numbering some 30,000, engaged in that prolonged struggle with Lord Londonderry and their other employers for more equitable terms of hiring and payment, to which we have already alluded.[2] After many months' embittered strife the strike failed disastrously; and the great Miners' Association, whose proceedings form so important a feature of the *Northern Star* for 1844 and 1845, gradually disappears from its pages, and in the general collapse of the coal trade in 1847–8 it came completely to an end.

But the culminating point in this revival of Trade Union activity was the formation, at Easter, 1845, of the National Association of United Trades for the Protection of Labour, an organisation which resuscitated and combined some of the ideas both of Owen and of Doherty. This Association was explicitly based, as its rules inform us, " upon two great facts : first, that the industrious classes do not receive a fair day's wage for a fair day's labour ; and, secondly, that for some years past their endeavours to obtain this have, with few exceptions, been unsuccessful. The main causes of this state of things are to be found in the isolation of the different sections of working men, and

---

[1] Hansard, vols. 73 and 74. The Bill was lost by 54 to 97 (May 1, 1844) ; see *Condition of the Working Class in England in 1844*, by Friedrich Engels, 1892, pp. 283-4.

[2] *The Miners of Northumberland and Durham*, by Richard Fynes, 1873, chap. ix.; *The British Coal Trade*, by H. Stanley Jevons, 1915, pp. 448-51.

the absence of a generally recognised and admitted authority from the trades themselves." But, unlike the Owenite movement of 1833-4, the National Association of United Trades was from the first distinguished by the moderation of its aims and the prudence of its administration—qualities to which we may attribute its comparatively lengthy survival for fifteen years. No attempt was made to supersede existing organisations of particular trades by a " General Trades Union." " The peculiar local internal and technical circumstances of each trade," say the rules, " render it necessary that for all purposes of efficient internal government its affairs should be administered by persons possessing a practical knowledge of them. For this reason it is not intended to interfere with the organisation of existing Trade Unions." Moreover, the promoters evidently intended the Association to become more of a Parliamentary Committee than a federation for trade purposes. Its purpose and duty was declared to be " to protect the interests and promote the well-being of the associated trades " by mediation, arbitration, and legal proceedings, and by promoting " all measures, political and social and educational, which are intended to improve the condition of the labouring classes." [1]

This new attempt to form a National Federation originated in a suggestion from the " United Trades " of Sheffield, embodied in an able letter written to Duncombe [2] by their secretary, John Drury. Duncombe had become widely

---

[1] *Rules and Regulations of the Association of United Trades for the Protection of Industry* (London, August 2, 1845). There is, as far as we know, only one copy of these rules in existence, but full particulars of its establishment and working are to be found in the *Northern Star*, which it used for a time as its official organ.

[2] Thomas Slingsby Duncombe was the aristocratic demagogue of the period. An accomplished man of the world, with the habits of a dandy, he nevertheless devoted himself with remarkable assiduity not only to the Parliamentary business of the Chartists and Trade Unionists, but also to the dry details of the committee work of the association of which he became president. The *Life and Correspondence* of Duncombe, which his son published in 1868, describes him almost exclusively as a fashionable man of the world and House of Commons politician, and entirely ignores his more solid work for Trade Unionism during the years 1845-8.

known to the Trade Unionists, not only through his friendship with Fergus O'Connor, and his outspoken support of
Chartism in the House of Commons, but also by his successful obstruction and defeat of the Masters and Servants
Bill of the previous Session. He appears to have laid
Drury's proposals before the leading men in the London
Unions, who agreed to form a committee to report on the
scheme, and to summon a conference of Trade Union
delegates from all parts of the country. At Easter, 1845,
110 delegates, representing not only the London trades, but
also the Lancashire miners and textile operatives, the
hosiery and woollen-workers of Yorkshire and the Midlands,
and the " United Trades " of Manchester, Sheffield, Norwich,
Hull, Bristol, Rochdale, and Yarmouth, met together in
London.

The preliminary report made to the Conference by the
London Committee of Trade Delegates is practically the
first manifestation of that spirit of cautious if somewhat
limited statesmanship which characterised the Trade Union
leaders of the next thirty years.[1] The Committee, whilst
recommending the immediate formation of a national
organisation, " to vindicate the rights of labour," and " to
oppose the tyranny of any legislative enactments to coerce

[1] In this document we may perhaps trace the hand of T. J. Dunning,
one of the ablest Trade Unionists of his time. Born in 1799, he became
Secretary of the Consolidated Society of Bookbinders in 1843. In 1845
he joined the National Association of United Trades, but left that body
after a few years. The *Bookbinders' Circular*, which he started in 1850,
was, during the rest of his life, largely written by himself, and contains
many well-reasoned articles on Trade Union matters. In 1858 Dunning
joined the celebrated Committee of Inquiry into Trade Societies which
was appointed by the Social Science Association. He contributed a
history of his own society to the Report, and frequently took part in the
subsequent annual congresses. His chief literary production is the essay
entitled, *Trades Unions and Strikes ; their philosophy and intention* (1860,
50 pp.), which he wrote for the prize instituted by his own Union for the
best defence of the workmen's organisation. This essay, which no pub-
lisher would accept, and which was printed by his society, remains, perhaps—apart from George Howell's historical researches in *Conflicts of
Capital and Labour*, and *Labour Legislation, Labour Movements and Labour
Leaders*—the best presentation of the Trade Union case which any manual
worker has produced. He died in harness on the 23rd of December 1873.

trade societies, or of a similar character to the Masters and
Servants Bill of last session, were deeply impressed with the
importance of, and beneficial tendency arising from, a good
understanding between the employer and the employed;
seeing that their interests are mutual, and that neither can
injure the other without the wrong perpetrated recoiling
upon the party who inflicts it. They would therefore
suggest it to be one of the principal objects of this Conference to cultivate a good understanding with the employer,
and thereby remove those prejudices which exist against
trade combinations, by showing upon all occasions that
they only seek by combination to place themselves upon
equal terms as disposers of their labour with those who
purchase it; to secure themselves from injury, but by no
means to inflict it upon others. Although the Committee
are anxious that this desirable and important organisation
should be carried out to the fullest possible extent, they
feel that great caution must be observed in the formation
of its laws and regulations, in order that the evils which
existed and eventually destroyed the Consolidated Union
of 1833 shall be carefully avoided. The Committee conceive it necessary to call the attention of those trades who
are comparatively disunited, and whose men are consequently working for different rates of wages, to the great
necessity that exists, that those who are receiving the highest
wages should use every effort within their power to secure
to their fellow-workmen a fair remuneration for their labour;
and that every inducement should be held out by the several
trade societies to their separated brethren to join them, in
order that they may be the better enabled to make common
cause in cases of aggression, which would be the certain
result if each trade were to form itself into one well-regu-
lated society for their mutual interests. . . . And, finally,
the Committee would earnestly recommend to this Conference, in order that these important points may be considered and dispassionately argued, that no proposition of
a political nature, beyond what has been already alluded

to, should be introduced, or occupy its attention ; convinced as they are that the only way to carry out these desirable objects satisfactorily, and with a due consideration to the best interests of all those who are concerned, is to consider and dispose of but one question at a time : and, moreover, to keep trade matters and politics as separate and distinct as circumstances will justify." [1]

The proceedings of this Conference show that the change of front on the part of the Trade Union leaders was reflected in the attitude of the rank and file. The surviving influence of Owenism is to be traced in the frequent recurrence of the idea of co-operative production, the desire to establish agricultural communities, and the proposal for a legislative shortening of the hours of labour. But of the aggressive policy and ambitious aims of 1830–34 scarcely a vestige remains. Strikes were deprecated, and the idea of a general cessation of work was entirely abandoned. The projects of co-operative production were on an altogether different plane from Owen's grand schemes. The Trade Unionists of the National Conference of 1845 had apparently no vision of a general transfer of the instruments of production from the capitalists to the Trade Unions ; co-operative production was regarded simply as an auxiliary to Trade Union action, the union workshop furnishing a cheap alternative to unproductive strike pay. Besides thus formally abandoning the methods and pretensions of 1834, the Conference declared its allegiance to a new method of Trade Union activity—the policy of conciliation and arbitration. In the demand for " local Boards of Trade," a phrase borrowed apparently from the silk-weavers, we see the beginning of that system of authoritative mutual negotiation between the representatives of capital and labour which became a very distinctive feature of British Trade Unionism in the last half of the nineteenth century.

[1] Report of London Committee of Trades Delegates to the National Conference of Trades Delegates, Easter, 1845 ; preserved in the archives of the Friendly Society of Operative Stonemasons.

But the shadow of the failure of 1834 still hung over projects of universal Trade Unions. Although nearly all trades had been represented at the first conference, most of the larger organisations decided, on consideration, to hold aloof from the new body. We find, for instance, the Manchester Lodge of the Stonemasons' Society promptly protesting against the adherence of the society's delegate, and expressing their emphatic opinion " that past experience has taught us that we have had general union enough." This view was endorsed by the Central Committee, which, in submitting the matter to the votes of the members, observes that " there are several trade societies in England as perfectly organised as ourselves, although their machinery may be somewhat various ; but we can hear of none of these societies being desirous to join this national movement. . . It may be very well for trades who are divided into sections and have no national organisation amongst themselves to join such an association—they have nothing to lose ; but it is a question for serious reflection whether a general union of each trade separately would not be far more effective than the heterogeneous association in question." [1] A similar view seems to have been taken by the Coal-miners, whose national federation was still in existence. A delegate meeting of the newly formed National Typographical Association decided by a large majority to remain outside. The Lancashire Cotton-spinners sent a delegate to the adjourned conference, and even proposed to have perambulating lecturers to explain the advantages of the new organisation, but never actually decided to join. [2]

The adjourned conference on July 28, 1845, was therefore composed, in the main, of the delegates of the smaller or less organised trades. About fifty delegates took part in the proceedings, which extended over six days. It was

[1] *Stonemasons' Fortnightly Circular*, May 14, 1846.
[2] Minutes of delegate meetings of the " Operative Cotton-spinners, Self-acting Minders, Twiners, and Rovers," held every other Sunday. See July 20, August 3, and December 14, 1845.

eventually decided to separate the Trade Union from the co-operative aims, and to form two distinct but mutually helpful associations. The " National Association of United Trades for the Protection of Labour " undertook to deal with disputes between masters and men, and look after the interests of labour in the House of Commons. The "National United Trades Association for the Employment of Labour " proposed to raise capital with which to employ men who were on strike under circumstances approved by its twin brother. At the second conference, held at Manchester in June 1846, when 126 delegates, representing, it was said, 40,000 members, were present, the contribution to the Trade Association was fixed at twopence in the pound of weekly earnings; and it was decided that the strike allowance should vary from nine shillings up to fourteen shillings per week, the latter sum being the wages agreed on for men employed in the association's own workshops. Up to this date no strike had been supported, as it was desired to avoid the premature action which had, it was held, destroyed the Grand National Consolidated Union. A number of paid organisers were engaged. The Association, which hitherto had consisted of woollen and hosiery-workers and of the Midland hardware trades, spread in various new directions. The executive of the Friendly Society of Operative Carpenters and Joiners—the association that had played so important a part in the movement of 1830—issued a manifesto to its members in favour of joining, and the general secretary became an active member of the Executive of the National Association. The Manchester Section of the National Cordwainers' Society urged all its members and all societies of boot and shoemakers to join. The Potters of Staffordshire, the Miners of Scotland, the new-born National Association of Tailors, as well as the Metropolitan branches of the Boilermakers' and Masons' Societies came in. The Association, in fact, became reputed a power in the land, and drew down upon itself the abusive censure of the *Times*.[1]

[1] *Times*, November 16, 1846.

But in spite of the wise intentions of its founders, it soon began to suffer from the characteristic complaints of general unions. The depression of trade which began in 1845 brought about during the next two years reductions of wages, followed by strikes and turn-outs in almost every branch of industry. The local committees of the National Association, frequently composed of the officials of the trades concerned, promised their members the support of the national funds, and took umbrage when the Executive sitting in London reversed their decisions. Each constituent trade felt that its interests were misunderstood, or its grievances neglected. A prolonged strike of the Manchester building trades in 1846, begun without sanction, failed miserably, the local committee of the National Association declaring that the collapse was due to lack of the financial support which had been promised on behalf of the central body. The coal and iron miners at Holytown in Lanarkshire engaged in a struggle against their employers which excited the sympathy of the Trade Union world, but which ended in failure. An equally severe conflict by the calico-printers at Crayford in Kent met with no better success. The Scottish miners complained that they had been inadequately supported by the association; and the Lancashire miners made this the pretext for continued abstention.

Though Duncombe's association had discouraged strikes, and acted principally as a mediating body, the employers throughout the country showed themselves uniformly hostile. The " document " which had figured so prominently in 1833–4 reappeared in a slightly altered form. The employers signified their toleration if not their approval of local trade clubs, but condemned with equal acrimony national unions of particular trades, or general unions of all trades. Affecting a sudden concern for the independence of character of their workmen, they insisted that the existence of any kind of central committee, however representative it might be, prevented the men from being free agents,

H

and exposed them to the arbitrary commands of an irresponsible body. In face of this attitude, the efforts of the National Association to bring about peaceful settlements met with only qualified success. The London Executive, unable to cope with the applications for assistance that poured in daily from all parts of the country, issued strong admonitions against unauthorised strikes, but had eventually to give or withhold support without sufficient knowledge of the local circumstances. Duncombe was principally occupied in drawing up and presenting petitions in favour of the legislative shortening of the hours of labour, and in this direction he rendered valuable assistance to the Lancashire cotton-spinners' "Short Time Committee," which secured the Ten Hours Act of 1847. The Central Executive was, indeed, during these years, more a Parliamentary Committee for the whole movement than a federation of Trade Unions. The plan of co-operative workshops, from which so much had been expected, proved entirely futile in the prolonged contests of the staple trades. One flourishing boot workshop was started ; and the 1847 conference found, in all, one hundred and twenty-three men at work, the enterprises being confined to those trades carried on by hand labour in a small way. In 1848 it was decided to merge the two associations in one, and to set about raising £50,000 in order to start on a larger scale. But before this could be attempted the association suffered a double reverse from which it never recovered. Duncombe was compelled, by failing health, to withdraw during 1848 from active participation in its work. And at the end of the following year a strike of the Wolverhampton tinplate-workers involved the National Association in a struggle with employers and with the law which drained its funds and destroyed its credit.[1]

[1] The tinplate-workers of Wolverhampton had been endeavouring, ever since they joined the Association in 1845, to obtain a uniform list of piecework rates. By the influence of the National Association, such a list was agreed to during 1849 by all the employers except two. One of these treated the men with exceptional duplicity. Having, as he

The later history of the association is obscure.[1] It lingered on for many years in a small way, its paid officers serving as advisers and representatives to a number of minor Trade Unions. Its principal work in later years was the promotion and support of bills for the establishment of councils of conciliation, and its persistent efforts certainly paved the way for the Joint Boards subsequently set on foot. But it ceases after 1851 to exercise any influence or play any important part in the Trade Union Movement.

The National Association of United Trades stands, in constitution and objects, half-way between the revolutionary voluntaryism of 1830–4 and the Parliamentary action of 1863–75. It may, in fact, be regarded either as a belated " General Trades Union " of an improved type, or as a premature and imperfect Parliamentary Committee of the Trade Union world. And although the great national Unions of the time took no part in its

thought, adequately prepared himself, he threw off the mask in July 1850, and flatly refused to continue the negotiations. The fierce industrial and legal conflict which ensued attracted general attention. Many of the strikers were imprisoned for breach of contract ; and the struggle culminated in the prosecution of three members of the committee of the National Association, together with several of the local Unionists, for conspiracy to molest and intimidate the employer by inducing men to leave his employment. Owing to legal quibbles, raised first on behalf of the Crown, and then on behalf of the defendants, the case was tried no fewer than three times, the final judgment not being delivered until November 1851, when five of the prisoners were sentenced to three months', and one to one month's imprisonment. See R. *v.* Rowlands, 5 Cox C. C. p. 436 ; also Appendix A to *The Law relating to Trade Unions*, by Sir William Erle, 1869.

[1] Duncombe formally resigned the presidency in 1852. In 1856 its secretary, Thomas Winters, gave evidence in favour of conciliation before the Select Committee on Masters and Operatives (Equitable Councils, etc.). He stated that the membership then numbered between 5,000 and 6,000, and that the central committee consisted of three salaried members, who gave up their whole time to the work. A subsequent secretary (E. Humphries) appeared before a similar committee four years later, his evidence showing that the association, though it was still in existence, had taken no part in any of the important labour struggles of the past seven or eight years. Mr. George Howell incidentally puts the date of its dissolution at 1860 or 1861 (see his article " Trades Union Congresses and Social Legislation " in *Contemporary Review* for September 1889).

proceedings, its moderate and unaggressive policy was only one manifestation of the new spirit which now prevailed in Trade Union councils. We see rising up in the Unions of the better-paid artisans a keen desire to get at the facts of their industrial and social condition. This new feeling for exact knowledge may to some extent be attributed to the increasing share which the printing trades were now beginning to take in the Trade Union Movement. The student of the reports of the larger compositors' societies, from the very beginning of the century, will be struck, not only by the moderation, but also by the elaborate Parliamentary formality—one might almost say the stateliness of their proceedings. Instead of rhetorical abuse of all employers as " the unproductive classes," and total abstinence from investigation of the details of disputes, we find the compositors dealing only with concrete instances of hardship, and referring every important question to a " Select Committee " for inquiry and report. In 1848 the London Consolidated Society of Bookbinders, established in 1786, used part of its funds to form a library for the benefit of its members. By 1851 a reading-room furnished with daily and weekly newspapers had been opened Four years later a similar library was established by the London Society of Compositors. In 1842, the Journeymen Steam-Engine and Machine Makers' Friendly Society started a Mutual Improvement Class at Manchester. Even the Stonemasons, at that time a rough and somewhat turbulent body, were reached by the new desire for self-improvement. The Glasgow branch of the Scottish United Operative Masons report with pride, in 1845, that they have " formed a class for mutual instruction . . . an association for moral, physical, and intellectual improvement " which was setting itself to investigate the question—" Is the present improved condition of machinery beneficial to the working classes, or is it hurtful ? " [1] But the most effective outcome of this desire for information was the starting by the Unions

---

[1] *English Stonemasons' Fortnightly Circular*, December 25, 1845.

of special trade journals. The United Branches of the Operative Potters set on foot in 1843 the *Potters' Examiner*, a weekly newspaper which dealt with the trade interests and technical processes of their industry.[1] The Journeymen Steam-Engine and Machine Makers' Friendly Society issued the *Mechanics' Magazine* between 1841 and 1847. In November 1850 Dunning persuaded the London Consolidated Society of Bookbinders to publish the *Bookbinders' Trade Circular*, in the pages of which he promulgated a theory of Trade Unionism, from which McCulloch himself would scarcely have dissented,[2] and made that humble organ of his society into a monthly magazine of useful information on all matters connected with books and their manufacture. But the best of these trade publications, and the only one which has enjoyed a continuous existence down to the present day, was the *Flint Glass Makers' Magazine*, an octavo monthly of ninety-six pages, established at Birmingham in 1850 by the Flint Glass Makers' Friendly Society,[3] which advocated " the education of every man in our trade, beginning at the oldest and coming down to the youngest. . . . If you do not wish to stand as you are and suffer more oppression," it enjoined its readers, " we say to you get knowledge, and in getting knowledge you get

[1] The *Potters' Examiner*, started December 1843, was converted, in July 1848, into the *Potters' Examiner and Emigrants' Advocate*, published at Liverpool and concerned chiefly with emigration. It ceased to appear soon after 1851.

[2] See especially the articles on " Wages of Labour and Trade Societies " in the second, third, and fourth numbers (December 1850 to February 1851), in which he assumes that the general level of wages is irresistibly determined by Supply and Demand, but that Trade Unionism, in providing out-of-work pay, enables the individual workman to resist exceptional tyranny or exaction.

[3] This journal contains a mass of useful information relating to the trade, special reports of the Trades Union Congresses, and well-written articles on industrial and economic problems. It is marked throughout by moderation of tone and fairness of argument. Unfortunately, so far as we know, it is not preserved in any public library, and we were indebted to Mr. Haddleton, Secretary to the Birmingham Trades Council, who, in 1893, possessed a complete set, for our acquaintance with its contents.

power. . . . Let us earnestly advise you to educate ; get intelligence instead of alcohol—it is sweeter and more lasting." [1]

With increased acquaintance with industrial conditions came a reaction against the policy of reckless aggression which marked the Owenite inflation. Here again we find the printing trades taking the lead. Already in 1835, when the London Compositors were reorganising their society, the committee went out of their way to denounce the great general Unions. " Unfortunately almost all Trades Unions hitherto formed," they report to their members, " have relied for success upon extorted oaths and physical force. . . . The fault and the destruction of all Trades Unions has hitherto been that they have copied the vices which they professed to condemn. While disunited and powerless they have stigmatised their employers as grasping taskmasters ; but as soon as they (the workmen) were united and powerful, then they became tyrants in their turn, and unreasonably endeavoured to exact more than the nature of their employment demanded, or than their employers could afford to give. Hence their failure was inevitable. . . . Let the Compositors of London show the Artisans of England a brighter and better example ; and casting away the aid to be derived from cunning and brute strength, let us, when we contend with our opponents, employ only the irresistible weapons of truth and reason." [2] The disasters of 1837–42 caused this spirit to spread to other trades. From this time forth the minutes and circulars of the larger Unions abound in impressive warnings against aggressive action. " Strikes are prolific," say the delegates of the Ironmoulders in council assembled ; " in certain cases they beget others. . . . How often have disputes been averted by a few timely words with employers ! It

[1] Opening Address to the Glass Makers of England, Ireland, and Scotland, No. 1.
[2] Report of London Compositors' Committee on Amalgamation, 1834 ; Annual Report, February 2. 1835.

is surely no dishonour to explain to your employer the nature and extent of your grievance." [1] The Stonemasons' Central Committee repeatedly caution their members " against the dangerous practice of striking. . . . Keep from it," they urge, " as you would from a ferocious animal that you know would destroy you. . . . Remember what it was that made us so insignificant in 1842. . . . We implore you, brethren, as you value your own existence, to avoid, in every way possible, those useless strikes. Let us have another year of earnest and attentive organisation ; and, if that does not perfect us, we must have another ; for it is a knowledge of the disorganised state of working men generally that stimulates the tyrant and the taskmaster to oppress them." [2] A few years later the Liverpool lodge invites the support of all the members for the proposition " that our society no longer recognise strikes, either as a means to be adopted for improving our condition, or as a scheme to be resorted to in resisting infringements," [3] and suggests, as an alternative, the formation of an Emigration Fund. The Portsmouth lodge caps this proposal by insisting not only that strikes should cease, but also that the word " strike " be abolished ! The *Flint Glass Makers' Magazine*, between 1850 and 1855, is full of similar denunciations. " We believe," writes the editor, " that strikes have been the bane of Trades Unions." [4] In 1854 the Flint Glass Makers, on the proposition of the Central Committee, abolished the allowance of " strike-money " by a vote of the whole of the members. As an alternative it was often suggested that a bad employer should be defeated by quietly withdrawing the men one by one, as situations could be found for them elsewhere. " As man after man leaves, and no one [comes] to supply their place, then it is that the proud and haughty spirit of the

[1] *Address of Delegate Meeting to the Members of the Friendly Society of Ironmoulders of England, Ireland, and Wales*, September 26, 1846.
[2] *Fortnightly Circular*, December 25, 1845.
[3] *Ibid.*, June 1849.
[4] January 1855.

oppressor is brought down, and he feels the power he cannot see." [1]

It was part of the same policy of restricting the use of the weapon of the strike that the power of declaring war on the employers was, during these years, taken away from the local branches. In the two great societies of which we have complete records—the Ironmoulders and the Stonemasons—we see a gradual tightening up of the control of the central executive. The Delegate Meeting of the Ironmoulders in 1846 vested the entire authority in the Executive Committee. " The system," they report, " of allowing disputes to be sanctioned by meetings of our members, generally labouring under some excitement or other, or misled by a plausible letter from the scene of the dispute, is decidedly bad. Our members do not feel that responsibility on these occasions which they ought. They are liable to be misled. A clever speech, party feeling, a misrepresentation, or a specious letter—all or any of these may involve a shop, or a whole branch, in a dispute, unjustly and possibly without the least chance of obtaining their object. . . . Impressed with the truth of these opinions, we have handed over for the future the power of sanctioning disputes to the Executive Committee alone." [2] The Stonemasons' Central Committee, after 1843, peremptorily forbid lodges to strike shops, even if they do not mean to charge the society's funds with strike-pay. And though in this Union, unlike the Ironmoulders, the decision to strike or not to strike was not vested in the Executive, any lodge had to submit its demand, through the *Fortnightly Circular*, to the vote of the whole body of members throughout the kingdom—a procedure which involved delay and gave the Central Committee an opportunity of using its influence in favour of peace.

[1] Letter on " The Evil Consequences of Strikes," in *Flint Glass Makers' Magazine*, July 1850. The suggested alternative—the Strike in Detail—is discussed in our *Industrial Democracy*.

[2] *Address of the Delegate Meeting to the Members of the Friendly Society of Ironmoulders*, 1846.

The fact that most of the Executive Committees were, from 1845 onward, setting their face against strikes, did not imply the abandonment of an energetic trade policy. The leaders of the better educated trades had accepted the economic axiom that wages must inevitably depend upon the relation of Supply and Demand in each particular class of labour. It seemed an obvious inference that the only means in their power to maintain or improve their condition was to diminish the supply. " All men of experience agree," affirms the Delegate Meeting of the Ironmoulders in 1847, " that wages are to be best raised by the demand for labour." Hence we find the denunciations of strikes accompanied by an insistence on the limitation of apprentices, the abolition of overtime, and the provision of an Emigration Fund. The Flint Glass Makers declare that " the scarcity of labour was one of the fundamental principles laid down at our first conference held in Manchester in 1849." " It is simply a question of supply and demand, and we all know that if we supply a greater quantity of an article than what is actually demanded that the cheapening of that article, whether it be labour or any other commodity, is a natural result." [1] In this application of the doctrine of Supply and Demand the Flint Glass Makers were joined by the Compositors, Bookbinders, Ironmoulders, Potters, and, as we shall presently see, the Engineers. [2] For the next ten years an Emigration Fund becomes a constant feature of many of the large societies, to be abandoned only when it was discovered that the few thousands of pounds which could be afforded for this purpose produced no visible

[1] " Emigration as a Means to an End," *Flint Glass Makers' Magazine,* August 1854 ; address of Executive, September 1857.

[2] " Thus if in a depression you have fifty men out of work they will receive £1,015 in a year, and at the same time be used as a whip by the employers to bring your wages down ; by sending them to Australia at £20 per head you save £15, and send them to plenty instead of starvation at home ; you keep your own wages good by the simple act of clearing the surplus labour out of the market " (Farewell Address of the Secretary, *Flint Glass Makers' Magazine,* August, 1854). " Remove the surplus labour and oppression itself will soon be a thing of the past " (*Ibid.*).

H 2

effect in diminishing the surplus labour.   Moreover, it was
the vigorous and energetic member who applied for his
passage-money, whilst the chronically unemployed, if he
could be persuaded to go at all, frequently reappeared at
the clubhouse after a brief trip at the society's expense.[1]

The harmless but ineffective expedient of emigration
was accompanied by the more equivocal plan of closing
the trade to new-comers.   The Flint Glass Makers, like
the other sections of the glass trade, have always been
notorious for their strict limitation of the number of apprentices.   The constant refrain of their trade organ is " Look
to the rule and keep boys back ; for this is the foundation
of the evil, the secret of our progress, the dial on which our
society works, and the hope of future generations." [2]   The
printing trades were equally active.   Select Committees
of the London Society of Compositors were constantly
inquiring into the most effective way of checking boy-
labour and regulating " turnover " apprentices.   And the
engineering trades, at this time entering the Trade Union
world, were basing their whole policy on the assumption
that the duly apprenticed mechanic, like the doctor or the
solicitor, had a right to exclude " illegal men " from his
occupation.

Such was the " New Spirit " which, by 1850, was

[1] Emigration Funds begin to appear in Trade Union Reports about
1843 (see the *Potters' Examiner*).   For thirty years the accounts of the
larger societies include, off and on, considerable appropriations for the
emigration of members.   The tabular statement of expenditure published
in the Ironmoulders' Annual Report shows, for instance, that £4,712 was
spent in this way between 1855 and 1874.   In the Amalgamated Carpenters
an Emigration Benefit lingered until 1886, when it was finally abolished
by the General Council ; the members resident in the United States and
Colonies strongly objecting to this use of the funds.   But it was between
1850 and 1860 that emigration found most favour as an integral part of
Trade Union policy.   The Trade Unions of the United States and the
Australian Colonies addressed vigorous protests to the officials of the
English societies (see, for example, the *Stonemasons' Fortnightly Circular*,
June 1856), a fact which co-operated with the dying away of the "gold
rush," and the change of Trade Union opinion, to cause the abandonment of the policy, until it was revived in 1872 for a decade or so, by
the Agricultural Labourers' Unions.

[2] *Flint Glass Makers' Magazine*, September 1857.

dominating the Trade Union world. Meanwhile the steady growth of national Unions, each with three to five thousand members, ever-increasing friendly benefits, and a weekly contribution per member which sometimes exceeded a shilling, involved a considerable development of Trade Union structure. The little clubs and local societies had been managed, in the main, by men working at their trades, and attending to their secretarial duties in the evening. With the growth of such national organisations as the Stonemasons, the Ironmoulders, and the Steam-Engine Makers, the mere volume of business necessitated the appointment of one of the members to devote his whole time to the correspondence and accounts. But the new official, however industrious and well-meaning, found upon his hands a task for which neither his education nor his temperament had fitted him. The archives of these societies reveal the pathetic struggles of inexperienced workmen to cope with the difficulties presented by the combination of branch management and centralised finance. The disbursement of friendly benefits by branch meetings, the custody and remittance of the funds, the charges for local expenses (including " committee liquor "),[1] the mysteries

---

[1] During these years the Executive Committees of the larger societies were waging war on the " liquor allowance." In the reports and financial statements of the Unions for the first half of the century, drink was one of the largest items of expenditure, express provision being made by the rules for the refreshment of the officers and members at all meetings. The rules of the London Society of Woolstaplers (1813) state that " the President shall be accommodated with his own choice of liquors, wine only excepted." The Friendly Society of Ironmoulders (1809) ordains that the Marshal shall distribute the beer round the meeting impartially, members being forbidden to drink out of turn " except the officers at the table or a member on his first coming to the town." Even as late as 1837 the rules of the Steam-Engine Makers' Society direct one-third of the weekly contribution to be spent in the refreshment of the members, a provision which drops out in the revision of 1846. In that year the Delegate Meeting of the Ironmoulders prohibited drinking and smoking at its own sittings, and followed up this self-denying ordinance by altering the rules of the society so as to change the allowance of beer at branch meetings to its equivalent in money. " We believe," they remark in their address to the members, " the business of the society would be much better done were there no liquor allowance. Interruption, con-

of bookkeeping, and the intricacies of audit all demanded a new body of officers specially selected for and exclusively engaged in this work.   During these years we watch a shifting of leadership in the Trade Union world from the casual enthusiast and irresponsible agitator to a class of permanent salaried officers expressly chosen from out of the rank and file of Trade Unionists for their superior business capacity.   But besides the daily work of administration, the expansion of local societies into organisations of national extent, and the transformation of loose federations into consolidated unions, involved the difficult process of constitution-making.   The records of the Ironmoulders and the Stonemasons show with what anxious solicitude successive Delegate Meetings were groping after a set of rules that would work smoothly and efficiently.   One Union, however, the Journeymen Steam-Engine and Machine Makers and Millwrights' Friendly Society, tackled the problems of internal organisation with peculiar ability, and eventually produced, in the Amalgamated Society of Engineers, a " New Model " of the utmost importance to Trade Union history.

To understand the rise of this remarkable society, we must revert to the earlier history of combinations which have hitherto scarcely claimed attention in our account of the general movement.   The origin of Trade Unionism in the engineering trades is obscure.   We learn that at the close of the last century the then dominant class of mill-

---

fusion, and scenes of violence and disorder are often the characteristic of meetings where order, calmness, and impartiality should prevail." By 1860 most of the larger societies had abolished all allowance for liquor, and some had even prohibited its consumption during business meetings. It is to be remembered that the Unions had, at first, no other meeting place than the club-room freely placed at their disposal by the publican, and that their payment for drink was of the nature of rent.   Meanwhile the Compositors and Bookbinders were removing their headquarters from public-houses to offices of their own, and the Steam-Engine Makers were allowing branches to hire rooms for meetings so as to avoid temptation. In 1850 the Ironmoulders report that some publicans were refusing to lend rooms for meetings, owing to the growth of Temperance.

wrights possessed strong, exclusive, and even tyrannical trade societies, the chief of them being the " London Fellowship," meeting at the Bell Inn, Old Bailey.[1] The millwrights, who were originally constructors of mill-work of every kind, both wood and iron, were, on the introduction of the steam-engine, gradually superseded by specialised workers in particular sections of their trade. The introduction of what was termed " the engineer's economy," that is to say, the parcelling out of the trade of the millwright among distinct classes of workmen, and the substitution of " payment according to merit " for the millwrights' Standard Rate, completely disorganised the skilled mechanics of the engineering trade. This condition was not materially improved by the establishment, from 1822 onward, of numerous competing Trade Friendly Societies. The Ironmoulders alone concentrated their efforts upon maintaining one national society. The millwrights, smiths, pattern-makers, and other skilled mechanics engaged in engine and machine making had societies in London, Manchester, Newcastle, Bradford, Derby, and other engineering centres. Of these the Steam-Engine Makers (established 1824) ; the Journeymen Steam-Engine and Machine Makers and Millwrights (established 1826) ; the Associated Fraternity of Iron Forgers, usually called the " Old Smiths " (established 1830) ; and the Boilermakers (established 1832) are known to have been organisations of national extent, with branches in all parts of the country, competing, not only with each other, but with the Metropolitan and other local societies of Millwrights, Smiths, Pattern-makers,

---

[1] It was the strength of their organisation in London in 1799, as we have seen, that led to the employers' petition to the House of Commons, out of which sprang the Combination Acts of 1799 and 1800. See also the evidence given by Galloway and other employers before the 1824 Select Committee on Artisans and Machinery ; also incidental references in the *Life of Sir William Fairbairn*, 1877, and other works. We have been unable to discover any documents of engineering societies prior to 1822. Sir William Fairbairn, in the preface to his *Mills and Mill-work*, 1861, attributes the supersession of the millwright to the changes consequent on the introduction of the steam-engine.

and General Engineers. This anarchic rivalry prevented any effectual trade action, and tempted employers to give the work to the lowest bidder, and to introduce the worst features of competitive piecework and sub-contract.

We are, therefore, not surprised to find that the engineers' societies took little part in the great upheaval of 1830–4. But the wave of solidarity which then swept over the labour world seems to have had considerable, though tardy, effect even in this trade. The chief districts affected were London and Lancashire. In 1836 a London joint committee of several of the sectional societies successfully conducted an eight months' strike for a shortening of the hours of labour to sixty per week, and for extra payment for overtime. Again, in 1844 a joint committee obtained from the London employers a further reduction of hours. Encouraged by these successes, the members of the Metropolitan societies and branches began to discuss the possibility of a national amalgamation. The most prominent personality in this movement was that of William Newton,[1]

[1] William Newton was born at Congleton in 1822, his father, who had once occupied a superior position, being then a journeyman machinist. The boy went to work in engine shops at the age of fourteen, joined the Hanley Branch of the Journeymen Steam-Engine Makers' Society in 1842, soon afterwards moving to London (where he worked in the same shop as Henry James, afterwards Lord James of Hereford, then an engineer pupil, and later noted for his knowledge of Trade Unionism), and rose to be foreman. After his dismissal in 1848 for his Trade Union activity he took a public-house at Ratcliffe, and devoted himself largely to the promotion of the amalgamation of the engineering societies. In 1852 he became, for a short period, secretary to a small insurance company. At the General Election of 1852 he became a candidate for the Tower Hamlets. He was opposed by both the great political parties, but the show of hands at the hustings was in his favour. At the poll he was unsuccessful, receiving, however, 1,095 votes. In 1860 he was presented with a testimonial (including a sum of £300) from his A.S.E. fellow-members. In later years he became the proprietor of a prosperous local newspaper and was elected by the Stepney Vestry as its chairman and also as its representative on the Metropolitan Board of Works. He became one of the leading members of that body, on which he served from 1862 to 1876, filling the important office of deputy chairman to the Parliamentary, Fire Brigade, and other influential committees. In 1868 he again contested the Tower Hamlets against both Liberals and Conservatives, receiving

a leading member of the Journeymen Steam-Engine and Machine Makers and Millwrights' Friendly Society, the association which afterwards became, as we shall see, the parent of the amalgamation.

William Newton had exactly the qualities needed for his task. Gifted with remarkable eloquence, astute and conciliatory in his methods, he was equally successful in inspiring masses of men with a large idea, and in persuading the representatives and officials of rival societies to agree with the details of his scheme. His influence was augmented by his tried devotion to the cause of Trade Unionism. In 1848 he was dismissed from a first-rate position as foreman in a large establishment owing to his activity in trade matters, and in the following years his business as a publican was seriously damaged by his constant absence on society business. But though from the first he had been an active member of his Union, and was for many years a Branch Secretary, he was, so far as we know, at no time its full-time salaried official. He stands, therefore, midway between the casual and amateur leaders of the old Trade Unionism and the new class of permanent officials, sticking closely to office work, and acquiring a detailed experience in Trade Union organisation.

Whilst Newton was bringing the London societies into line, the Lancashire engineers were moving in the same direction. Already in 1839 a " committee of the engineering trades " at Bolton urged upon their comrades the establishment of " one concentrated union "; and in the following year, through the energy of Alexander Hutchinson, the secretary of the Friendly United Smiths of Great Britain and Ireland, a United Trades Association was set on foot in Lancashire, to comprise the " Five Trades of Mechanism, viz. Mechanics, Smiths, Moulders, Engineers, and Millwrights." The objects of this association were ably repre-

---

2,890 votes; and in 1875 he unsuccessfully fought a bye-election at Ipswich. He died March 9, 1876, when his funeral, in which the Metropolitan Board of Works took part, assumed a public character.

sented and promoted by its organ, the *Trades Journal*, established to extend and " improve Trades Unions generally in Great Britain and Ireland." [1]   The attempt proved, however, premature, and it was not until the year 1844 that the Bolton men, under the leadership of John Rowlinson, succeeded in establishing a permanent " Protection Society," composed of delegates from the Societies of Smiths, Millwrights, Ironmoulders, Engineers, and Boilermakers.   Inspirited by the success of the Bolton society, which successfully maintained a nine months' strike (costing it £9,000) against the " Quittance Paper " (character note, or leaving certificate) which the employers eventually agreed to abandon, joint committees of engineering operatives were formed between 1844 and 1850 in all the principal Lancashire centres.   These were repeatedly addressed by Rowlinson and Hutchinson, and the ground was prepared for a systematic attempt at national amalgamation.

The leading part in the amalgamation was taken by the society to which Newton belonged.   The Journeymen Steam - Engine and Machine Makers and Millwrights' Friendly Society, with its headquarters at Manchester, at this time far exceeded any other trade society in membership and wealth.   Established in 1826 as the Friendly Union of Mechanics, it had absorbed in 1837 a strong Yorkshire society dating from 1822 (the Mechanics' Friendly Union Institution), and by 1848 it numbered seven thousand members organised in branches all over the kingdom, and possessed an accumulated reserve fund of £25,000.   The silent growth of this Union, the slow perfecting of its constitution by repeated delegate meetings held at intervals during the preceding twenty years, stand in marked contrast with the dramatic advent of the ephemeral organisations of 1830–34.   But this task of internal organisation, with its

---

[1] This journal is preserved in the Manchester Public Library (341, P. 37).   It was a well-written 16 pp. 8vo, issued, at first fortnightly and afterwards monthly, at 2d.   No. 1 is dated July 4, 1840.

gradual working out of the elaborate financial and administrative system which afterwards became celebrated in the constitution of the Amalgamated Engineers, seems to have absorbed, during the first fifteen years of its existence, all the energy of its members. In none of the working-class movements of this period did the society play any part, nor do we find that it, as a whole, engaged in any important conflicts with its members' employers. At last, in 1843, a delegate meeting urged the members to oppose systematic overtime, and in 1844 the society, as we have seen, took part in the London movement for the shortening of the hours of labour. By 1845 it seems to have felt itself strong enough to undertake aggressive trade action by itself, and a delegate meeting in that year attacked the employment of labourers on machines, " the piece master system," and systematic overtime, by stringent resolutions upon which the Executive Committee sitting at Manchester were directed to take early action.[1] During the following year accordingly a simultaneous attempt appears to have been made by many of the branches to enforce these rules. This action led, at Belfast, Rochdale, and Newton-le-Willows, to legal proceedings by the employers, and the officers of the society, together with over a score of its members, found themselves in the dock indicted for conspiracy and illegal combination.[2] The trial

[1] Minutes of delegate meeting at Manchester, May 12, 1845. An admirable account of this society, founded on documents no longer extant, is given in an article by Professor Brentano in the *North British Review*, October 1870, entitled " The Growth of a Trades Union." For some other particulars see the *Jubilee Souvenir History of the Amalgamated Society of Engineers*, 1901.

[2] Executive Circular, 1846, cited in proceedings in *R*. v. *Selsby*. Two full accounts of the trial were published, viz. a *Verbatim Report of the Trial for Conspiracy in R*. v. *Selsby and others* (Liverpool, 1847, 66 pp.), published under the " authority of the Executive of the Steam-Engine Makers' Society," and a *Narrative, etc., of the Trial, R*. v. *Selsby* (London, 1847, 68 pp.). Both are preserved in the Manchester Public Library, P. 2198. The legal report is in Cox's *Crown Cases*, vol. v. p. 496, etc. Contemporary Trade Union reports contain many references to the proceedings. It was noticed as an instance of the animus of the prosecution that the indictment contained 4914 counts, and measured fifty-

of the twenty-six engineers of Newton-le-Willows, and the conviction of nine of them, including Selsby, the General Secretary of the great mechanics' Union, caused a sensation in the Trade Union world, and tended to draw closer together the rival societies in the engineering trade.

The progressive trade policy of the Journeymen Steam-Engine and Machine Makers' Society greatly increased the ascendency which its superiority in wealth and numbers gave it over the numerous other trade friendly societies in the engineering trades. William Allan, a young Scotchman, succeeded Selsby in the salaried post of general secretary when the latter obtained a commercial post in 1848. A close friend and ardent disciple of William Newton, he quickly manifested, in the administration of his own society, the capacity and energy which enabled him in future years to play so important a part in the general history of the Labour Movement. The cause of amalgamation was well served by the indefatigable missionary efforts of these two men. The anniversary dinners and friendly social meetings of the joint committees of the societies in the Lancashire iron trades were, as we know from contemporary records, made the occasion of propagandist speeches, and were doubtless used also by these astute organisers to talk over the leading men to agreement with their proposals. The natural jealousy felt by the great provincial centre of Trade Unionism of the interference of the Metropolis in its concerns was allayed by Allan's suggestion that the Lancashire societies should call a conference of delegates at Warrington in March 1850, for the purpose of consultation and discussion only. At this meeting, which was attended only by the representatives of three of the larger societies (including the Steam-Engine Makers established at Liverpool in 1824, and the Smiths' Benevolent, Friendly, Sick and

---

seven yards in length. W. P. Roberts organised the defence, which cost the Union £1800. The firm in whose works the dispute arose became bankrupt within a few years. See the *Jubilee Souvenir History of the Amalgamated Society of Engineers*, 1901.

Burial Society, established in 1830), Newton and Allan succeeded in getting through the outlines of their scheme of amalgamation. During the next six months these proposals were the subject of exhaustive discussion at every joint committee and branch meeting. Meanwhile the leaders had established in Manchester a weekly journal for the express purpose of promoting amalgamation, engaging as editor, under a written contract, Dr. John Watts, afterwards well known as one of the ablest advocates of co-operation. This journal, the *Trades Advocate and Herald of Progress*, stated to be " established by the Iron Trades," discussed the advantages of union, and incidentally taught the doctrines of Free Trade and Co-operative Production.[1]

Lancashire converted and conciliated, London could now go ahead. Under Newton's influence the London joint committee summoned a second delegate meeting at Birmingham in September 1850, which was attended by representatives of seven engineering societies. At this conference the scheme of amalgamation was definitely adopted ; and the Metropolitan " Central Committee " was charged, as a " Provisional Committee," to complete the details of the transfer of the old organisation to the new body. The tact and skill with which Allan and Newton carried out their project are conspicuously shown by the way in which the act of union was regarded by all concerned. There is no trace of suspicion on the part of the minor societies that they were taking part in anything but an amalgamation on equal terms. The whole Trade Union world, including the Amalgamated Society of Engineers itself, has retained the tradition that this great organisation was the outcome of a genuine amalgamation of societies of fairly equivalent standing. What happened,

[1] *The Trades Advocate and Herald of Progress* was an 8 pp. quarto weekly, price 1d., No. 1 being dated June 1850. The volume from June to December 1850 is preserved in the Manchester Public Library (401 E, 18). An able article by John Burnett in the *Newcastle Weekly Chronicle*, July 3, 1875, gives a vivid picture of the struggle for amalgamation.

as a matter of fact, was that the society led by Allan and Newton absorbed its rivals.[1] The new body took over, in its entirety, the elaborate constitution, the scheme of benefits (with the addition of Sick Benefit and the adoption of the innovation of an Emigration Benefit of £6), the trade policy, and even the official staff of the Journeymen Steam-Engine and Machine Makers and Millwrights' Society, which contributed more than three-fourths of the membership with which the amalgamation started, and found itself continued, down to the minutest details, in the rules and regulations of the new association. An important addition was, however, the adoption of a definite trade policy of restricting overtime and preventing piecework ; the institution of District Committees charged to carry out that policy ; and the establishment of a new Strike Pay of 15s. per week.

The conclusions of the Birmingham delegates were not accepted without demur. Many of the branches in Lancashire and elsewhere objected to the position obtained by the London Committee, and stood aloof from the amalgamation. The Manchester Committee showed signs of jealousy at the transfer of the seat of government to the Metropolis. But the most important defection was that of the rank and file of the members of the Steam-Engine Makers' Society, an association which stood in membership and funds second only to the Journeymen Steam-Engine Makers and Machine Makers' Society. Newton and Allan had succeeded in persuading the whole of the Executive to throw in their lot with the amalgamation, but the bulk of the members revolted, and the society maintained a separate existence down to the end of 1919, when it joined the other societies in the creation of the Amalgamated Engineering Union. Even in Newton's own society, in which the main principles of the amalgamation had been carried by large majorities, a considerable number of the

[1] This was pointed out in Professor Brentano's article in the *North British Review*, already quoted.

provincial branches remained hostile. On January 6, 1851, when the Provisional Committee formally assumed office as the Executive Committee of the " Amalgamated Society of Engineers, Machinists, Smiths, Millwrights and Pattern-makers," scarcely 5000 members out of the 10,500 represented at the Birmingham Conference were paying to the amalgamated funds.[1] For some months, indeed, the success of Newton's ambitious scheme looked doubtful. Though London had rallied to his help, only one small society standing aloof, the provincial branches came in very slowly. It took three months' persuasion to raise the membership of the amalgamation up to the level of the parent society. Delegate meetings of the Steam-Engine Makers and the Smiths' Societies decided against amalgamation, though many of their branches broke away and joined the new society. But towards the end of May the tide turned. The remaining branches of the Journeymen Steam-Engine and Machine Makers and Millwrights' Society held a delegate meeting, at which it was decided no longer to oppose the amalgamation ; the Smiths' Society of London and several other small societies came in ; and by October Newton and Allan were at the head of a united society of 11,000 members paying 1s. per week each, the largest and most powerful Union that had ever existed in the engineering trades, and far exceeding in membership, and still more in annual income, any other trade society of the time.[2]

[1] The organ of the Executive Council was the *Operative*, a well-written weekly journal, which was set on foot by Newton in January 1851. The price was at first 1½d., and afterwards 1d. per number. The issues from the beginning down to July 1852, probably all that were published, are preserved in the British Museum (P. P. 1424, a.m.). Newton acted as editor, and contributed nearly all the articles relating to the engineers and Trade Unions generally.

[2] The largest and most powerful of the other Unions in 1851 were those of the Ironfounders and the Stonemasons, which numbered between four and five thousand members each. It must be remembered that the previous ephemeral associations of the cotton-spinners and miners, which often for a time counted their tens of thousands of members, were exclusively strike organisations, with contributions of 1d. or 2d. per week only. The huge associations of 1830–34 had usually no regular subscrip-

The successful accomplishment of the amalgamation was followed by a conflict with the employers, which riveted the attention of the whole Trade Union world upon the new body. The aggressive trade policy initiated by Selsby and Allan in Lancashire and Newton in London had been repeatedly confirmed by the delegate meetings of their society, and was formally incorporated in the basis of the larger organisation.[1] The more energetic branches were not slow in acting upon it. In 1851 the men at Messrs. Hibbert & Platt's extensive works at Oldham made a series of demands, not only for the abolition of overtime, but also for the exclusion of " labourers and other ' illegal ' men " from the machines. With these demands Messrs. Hibbert & Platt and other employers had to comply. The private minutes of the London Executive prove conclusively that the strike to oust labourers from machines was not authorised by the central body ;[2] but as William Newton, now a member of the Executive, acted as the representative of the Oldham men in submitting these demands to Messrs. Hibbert & Platt, the employers, naturally inferring that his action was the direct outcome of the amalgamation, formed in December 1851 the Central Association of Employers of Operative Engineers to resist the, men's Union.

Meanwhile the London Executive had been consulting the whole of the members on the proposal to abolish systematic overtime and piecework, and had obtained an almost unanimous vote in favour of immediate action. A

---

tion at all, and depended on irregularly paid levies. A trade society which, like the Amalgamated Engineers, could count on a regular income of £500 a week was without precedent.

[1] See the resolutions of the Birmingham Delegate Meeting of the Iron Trades, September 28, 1850, in the *Trades Union Advocate*, November 1850.

[2] It was resolved : " That we are prepared to assist the workmen at Messrs. Platt to the utmost of our power, but cannot consent to the men leaving their situations, because they may not at present be able to obtain the working of the machines." The best account of the struggle is to be found in the *Jubilee Souvenir History of the A.S.E.* (1901), pp. 34-41.

manifesto was issued to the employers, in which the Executive announced the intention of the society to put an end to piecework and systematic overtime after December 31, 1851. The employers replied by an imperious declaration in the *Times* that a strike at any one establishment would be met seven days later by a general lock-out of the whole engineering trade. The men thereupon offered to submit the question to arbitration, a proposal which the employers ignored. On January 1, 1852, the members of the Amalgamated Society refused to work overtime, and on the 10th the masters closed, as they had threatened, every important engineering establishment in Lancashire and the Metropolis.

The three months' struggle that followed interested the general public more than any previous conflict. The details were described, and the action of the employers and the policy of the Union was discussed in every newspaper. The men found unexpected friends in the little group of " Christian Socialists," who threw themselves heartily into the fray, and rendered excellent service, not only by liberal subscriptions,[1] but also by letters to the newspapers, public lectures, and other explanations of the men's position. The masters remained obdurate, insisting not only upon the unconditional withdrawal of the men's demands, but also upon their signing the well-known " document " forswearing Trade Union membership. The capitalists, in fact, took up the old line of absolute supremacy in their establishments, and expressly denied the men's right to take any collective action whatsoever.

Notwithstanding the subscription of £4000 by the public and £5000 by other trade societies, the funds at the disposal of the Union soon began to run short. The Executive had undertaken to support not only the 3500 of its own members and the 1500 mechanics who were out,

---

[1] Lord Goderich, afterwards the Marquis of Ripon, gave the Executive a cheque for £500 to enable the strike pay to be kept up on a temporary emergency ; one of many generous efforts, during a long lifetime, to assist the wage-earning class.

but also the 10,000 labourers who had been made idle. Altogether over £43,000 was dispensed during the six months in out-of-work pay. Early in February the masters opened their workshops. By the middle of March the issue of the struggle was plain, and during April the men resumed work on the employers' terms. Almost all the masters insisted on the actual signature of the " document " by their men, and most of these, under pressure of imminent destitution, reluctantly submitted, without, however, carrying out their promise by abandoning the Union. Judge Hughes, writing in 1860, describes this act of bad faith by the men as " inexcusable," but there is much to be said for the view taken by the Amalgamation Executive, who declared that they held themselves " and every man who unwillingly puts his hand to that detestable document which is forced upon us to be as much destitute of that power of choice which should precede a contract as if a pistol were at his head and he had to choose between death and degradation." [1] A promise extorted under " duress " carries with it little legal and still less moral obligation, and whatever discredit attaches to the transaction must be ascribed at least as much to the masters who made the demand as to the unfortunate victims of the labour war who unwillingly complied with it. [2]

It was the dramatic events of 1852 which made the

[1] Executive Circular of April 26, 1852, in *Operative*, May 1, 1852. A number of the men refused to sign, and many emigrated. E. Vansittart Neale advanced £1030 to members for this purpose, the whole of which was repaid by the borrowers.

[2] Among the abundant literature on this great struggle may be mentioned the *Account*, by Thomas (afterwards Judge) Hughes, in the *Report on Trade Societies*, by the Social Science Association, 1860 ; J. M. Ludlow's lectures, entitled *The Master Engineers and their Workmen*, 1852 ; a pamphlet, *May I not do what I will with my own ?* by E. Vansittart Neale ; *Jubilee Souvenir History of the A.S.E.*, 1901 ; and the evidence given by William Newton (for the men) and Sidney Smith (for the employers) before the Select Committee on Masters and Operatives (Equitable Councils, etc.) in 1856. The employers' manifestoes will be found in the *Times* from December 1851 to April 1852 ; the men's documents and reports of their meetings in the *Operative* (edited by Newton), and in the *Northern Star*, then at its last gasp.

establishment of the Amalgamated Society of Engineers a turning-point in the history of the Trade Union Movement. The complete victory gained by the employers did not, as they had hoped, destroy the Engineers' Union. The membership of the society was, in fact, never seriously shaken.[1] On the other hand, the publicity which it gained in the conflict gave it a position of unrivalled prominence in the Trade Union world. From 1852 to 1889 the elaborate constitution of the Amalgamated Society of Engineers served as the model for all new national trade societies, whilst old organisations found themselves gradually incorporating its leading features. The place occupied in 1830–34 by the cotton-spinners and the builders was, in fact, now taken by the iron trades.

The " New Model " thus introduced differed, both for good and evil, from the typical Trade Unionism of the preceding generation. The engineering societies had to some extent inherited the exclusive policy of the organisations of the skilled handicraftsmen of the beginning of the century. Unlike the General Trades Unions of 1830–34 they restricted their membership to legally apprenticed workmen. Their records bear traces of the old idea of the legal incorporation of separate trades, rather than of any general union of " the productive classes." The generous but impracticable " universalism " of the Owenite and Chartist organisations was replaced by the principle of the protection of the vested interests of the craftsman in his occupation. The preface to the rules of the parent society expresses this dominant idea by a forcible analogy :

---

[1] It ended the struggle with £700 in hand. Its membership at the end of 1852 had fallen from 11,829 to 9737, but even then it had a balance in hand of £5382, and within three years the members had increased to 12,553, and the accumulated funds to the unprecedented total of £35,695. And unlike all previous trade societies, its record from 1852 down to the present time has been one of continued growth and prosperity, the membership at the end of 1919 being 320,000, with accumulated funds not far short of three million pounds, being greater in aggregate amount than the possessions of any other Trade Union organisation of this or any other country.

"The youth who has the good fortune and inclination for preparing himself as a useful member of society by the study of physic, and who studies that profession with success so as to obtain his diploma from the Surgeons' Hall or College of Surgeons, naturally expects, in some measure, that he is entitled to privileges to which the pretending quack can lay no claim ; and if in the practice of that useful profession he finds himself injured by such a pretender, he has the power of instituting a course of law against him. Such are the benefits connected with the learned professions. But the mechanic, though he may expend nearly an equal fortune and sacrifice an equal proportion of his life in becoming acquainted with the different branches of useful mechanism, has no law to protect his privileges." [1] He is therefore urged to join the society, which aims at securing the same protection of his trade against interlopers as is enjoyed by the learned professions.

This spirit of exclusiveness has had, as we shall hereafter discern, an equivocal effect, not only on the history of the society itself, but on that of the Trade Union Movement. But the contemporary trade movements either did not observe or failed to realise the tendency of this attempt to retain or reconstruct an aristocracy of skilled workmen. What impressed the working men was not the trade policy which had brought about the defeat of 1852, but the admirably thought-out financial and administrative system, which enabled the Union to combine the functions of a trade protection society with those of a permanent insurance company, and thus attain a financial stability hitherto undreamt of.   Time proved that this constitution had its peculiar defects.   But for over twenty years no Trade Unionist questioned its excellence, and the minute criticism and heated abuse which it evoked from employers and their advocates seemed only another testimony to its effectiveness. We think it worth while, therefore, at the risk of introducing

[1] Preface to Rules of the Journeymen Steam-Engine, Machine Makers, and Millwrights' Friendly Society, edition of 1845.

tedious detail, to describe the main features of this " New Model."

In striking contrast with the Cotton-spinners' and Builders' Unions of 1830-34, with their exclusively trade purposes, the societies in the engineering trades had, like the trade organisations of the handicraftsmen of the last century, originated as local benefit clubs. The Journeymen Steam-Engine Makers' Society, for instance, had from the first provided its members with out-of-work pay, a travelling allowance, a funeral benefit, and a lump sum in case of accidental disablement. In 1846 it added to these benefits a small sick allowance, and shortly afterwards an old age pension to superannuated members. The administration of these friendly benefits was from the outset the primary object of the organisation. As the local benefit club expanded into a national society by the migration of its members from town to town, the extreme difficulty of combining local autonomy with a just and economical administration of extensive benefits became apparent. For the society, it must be remembered, was not a federation of independent bodies, each having its own exchequer and contributing to the central fund its determinate quota of the expenses of the central office : it was from the first a single association with a common purse, into which all contributions were paid, and out of which all expenditure, down to the stationery and ink used by a branch secretary, was defrayed. This concentration of funds carried with it the practical advantage of forming a considerable reserve at the disposal of the Executive. But so long as it was combined with local autonomy, it was open to the obvious objection that a branch might dispense benefits to its own members with undue liberality, and thus absorb an unfair amount of the moneys of the whole society. And hence we find that in 1838 an attempt was made to centralise the administration, by transforming the local officials from the servants of the branches into agents of the central authority. The inherent love of self-government of the British artisan defeated this proposal, which would inevitably have led to local apathy and suspicion, if not to grosser evils. Some other method of harmonising local autonomy with centralised finance had therefore to be invented.

Under the constitution which the Amalgamated Society took over from the Journeymen Steam-Engine and Machine Makers and Millwrights, we find this problem solved with considerable astuteness. The branch elects and controls its own local officers, but acts in all cases within rules which provide explicitly for every detail. Each branch retains its own funds and administers the friendly benefits payable to its own members, including the allowance to men out of work. The financial autonomy of the branch is, however, more apparent than real. No penny must be expended except in accordance with precise rules. The branch retains its own funds, but these are the property of the whole society, and at the end of each year the balances are " equalised " by a complicated system of remittances from branch to branch, ordered by the Central Executive in such a way that each branch starts the year with the same amount of capital per member. The cumbrous plan of annual equalisation is a device adopted in order to maintain the feeling of local self-government under a strictly centralised financial system.[1] From the decision of the branch any member may appeal to the Central Executive Council. The decisions of this Council on all questions of friendly benefits are, however, strictly limited to the interpretation of the existing laws of the society. These rules, which

[1] This plan of " equalisation " is, so far as we know, peculiar to Trade Unions, though we understand from Dr. Baernreither's *English Associations of Working Men*, pp. 283-84, that a few branches of some of the Friendly Societies adopted a somewhat similar system. Its origin is unknown to us, but the device is traditionally ascribed to the Journeymen Steam-Engine and Machine Makers and Millwrights' Society, established in 1826. It was also in early use by the Steam-Engine Makers' Society, established in 1824. Until the Trade Union Act of 1871 it had a positive use. Depending, as Trade Unions were obliged to do, upon the integrity of their officers, there were great advantages in the wide distribution of the funds and the local responsibility of each branch for the safe keeping of its share.

include in equal detail both the constitutional and the financial code, cannot be altered or modified except by a specially convened meeting of delegates from every district. Careful provision is, moreover, made against the danger of hasty or ill-considered legislation even by this supreme authority. No amendment may be so much as considered without having been circulated to all the branches six weeks prior to the delegate meeting, and having thereupon been discussed and re-discussed by the members at two successive general meetings convened for the purpose. Thus every delegate comes to his legislative duties charged with a direct and even detailed mandate from his constituents. Moreover, it is expressly provided that no friendly benefit shall be abrogated unless the decision of the delegate meeting to that effect is ratified by a majority of two-thirds on a vote of the members of the whole society. As a friendly society, therefore, the Association consists of a number of self-governing branches acting according to the provisions of a detailed code, and amenable, in respect of its interpretation, to a Central Executive.

As a Trade Union, on the contrary, the Association has been from the first a highly centralised body. The great object of the amalgamation was to secure uniformity in trade policy, and to promote the equalisation of what the economists call "real wages"[1] throughout the whole country. With this view the Central Executive has always retained the absolute power of granting or withholding strike pay. No individual can receive strike allowance from his branch except upon an express order of the Executive. Local knowledge, however, is clearly needed for the decision in matters of trade policy, and on the amalgamation "district" committees were established, consisting of the representatives of neighbouring branches. These committees have no concern with the administration of friendly benefits, which, as we have seen, is the business of

---

[1] That is to say, local differences in the cost of living have always been taken into account.

each branch. Their function is to guard the local interests of the trade, to watch for encroachments, and to advise the Executive Council in the administration of strike pay. Unlike the branches, they possess no independent authority, and are required to act strictly under the orders of head-quarters, to which the minutes of their proceedings are regularly sent for confirmation.

Not less impressive than this elaborate constitution, with its system of checks and counter-checks, was the magnitude of the financial transactions of the new society. The high contribution of a shilling a week, paid with unexampled regularity by a constantly increasing body of members, provided an income which surpassed the wildest dreams of previous Trade Union organisations, and enabled the society to meet any local emergency without serious effort. A large portion of this income was absorbed by the expensive friendly benefits, which were on a scale at that time unfamiliar to the societies in other trades. And when it was found that the contribution of a shilling a week not only met all these requirements, but also provided an accumulating balance, which could be drawn upon for strike pay, the indignation of the employers knew no bounds. For many years the union of friendly benefits with trade protection funds, now considered as the guarantee of a peaceful Trade Union policy, was denounced as a dishonest attempt to subsidise strikes at the expense of the innocent subscriber to a friendly society insurance against sickness, accident, and old age.[1]

In scarcely less marked contrast with the current tradition of Trade Unionism was the publicity which the Amalgamated Engineers from the first courted. Powerful societies, such as the existing Union of Stonemasons, had

---

[1] Such protests were frequent in the evidence before the Royal Commission of 1867–68, and form the staple of the innumerable criticisms on Trade Unionism between 1852 and 1879. A good vindication of the Trade Union position is contained in Professor Beesly's article in the *Fortnightly Review*, 1867, which was republished as a pamphlet, *The Amalgamated Society of Carpenters and Joiners*, 1867, 20 pp.

between 1834 and 1850 elaborated a constitution which proved as durable as that of the Amalgamated Engineers, though of a slightly different type. But the old feeling of secretiveness still dominated both the leaders and the rank and file. The *Stonemasons' Fortnightly Circular*, which, regularly appearing as it has done since 1834, constitutes perhaps the most valuable single record of the Trade Union Movement, was never seen outside the branch meeting-place.[1] At the Royal Commission of 1867–8 the employers' witnesses bitterly complained of their inability to get copies of this publication and of a similar periodical circular of the Bricklayers' Society.[2] As late as 1871 we find the liability to publicity adduced by some Unions as an argument against seeking recognition by the law.

The leaders of the Engineers believed, on the contrary, in the power of advertisement. We have already noticed the two short-lived newspapers which Newton and Allan published in 1850 and 1851–2, for the express purpose of making known the society and its objects. For many years after the amalgamation it was a regular practice to forward to the press, for publication or review, all the monthly, quarterly, and annual reports, as well as the more important of the circulars issued to the members. Representatives were sent to the Conference on Capital and Labour held by the Society of Arts in 1854, and to the congresses of the Social Science Association from 1859 onward. Newton and Allan appear, indeed, to have eagerly seized every opportunity of writing letters to the newspapers, reading papers, and delivering lectures about the organisation which they had established.

It is easy to understand the great influence which, during

---

[1] The unique collection of these circulars, containing not only statistical and other information of the society, but also frequent references to the building trades and the general movement, was generously placed at our disposal for the purpose of this work, and we have found it of the utmost value.

[2] See, for instance, the evidence of Mault, Questions 3980 in Second Report and 4086 in Third Report.

the next twenty years, this " New Model " exercised upon the Trade Union world. Its most important imitator was the Amalgamated Society of Carpenters, which, as we shall see, arose out of the great London strike of 1859–60. The tailors in 1866 drew together into an amalgamated society, which adopted, almost without alteration, the whole code of the engineers, and in 1869 the London Society of Compositors appointed a special committee to report upon " the constitution and working of the Amalgamated Trades," with a view to their imitation in the printing industry— an intention which, in spite of the favourable character of the report, was not carried out.[1] Scarcely a trade exists which did not, between 1852 and 1875, either attempt to imitate the whole constitution of the Amalgamated Engineers, or incorporate one or other of its characteristic features.

The five or six years following the collapse of the great lock-out of 1852, though constituting a period of quiet progress in particular societies, are, for the historian of the general Trade Union Movement, almost a blank. The severe commercial depression of 1846–49 was succeeded by seven years of steadily expanding trade, which furnished no occasion for general reduction of wages. The reaction against the ambitious projects of the Trade Union of 1834 continued to discourage even federal action;[2] whilst the complete failure of the struggle of the engineers, followed as it was in 1853 by the disastrous strike of the Preston cotton-spinners for a ten per cent advance, by an equally unsuccessful struggle of the Kidderminster carpet-weavers, and by a fierce and futile conflict by the Dowlais iron-workers,[3] increased the disinclination of the Unions to aggressive trade action on a large scale. The disrepute

[1] Report of Special Committee, 1869.

[2] The National Association of United Trades continued, as we have already seen, in nominal existence until 1860 or 1861, but after 1852 it sank to a membership of a few thousands, and played practically no part in the Trade Union world.

[3] *Times*, June to December 1853.

into which strikes had fallen was intensified by the spread among the more thoughtful working men of the principles of Industrial Co-operation. This new development of Owen's teaching took two forms, both, it need hardly be said, differing fundamentally from the Owenism of 1834. In Lancashire the success of the " Rochdale Pioneers," established in 1844, had led to the rapid extension of the Co-operative Store, the association of consumers for the supply of their own wants. To some extent the stalwart leaders of the Lancashire and Yorkshire working men were diverted from the organisation of trade combinations to the establishment of co-operative shops and corn-mills. Meanwhile the " Christian Socialists " of London had caught up the idea of Buchez and the Parisian projects of 1848, and were advocating with an almost apostolic fervour the formation of associations of producers, in which groups of working men were to become their own employers.[1]

The generous enthusiasm with which the " Christian Socialists " had thrown themselves into the Engineers' struggle, and their obvious devotion to the interests of Labour, gave their schemes of " Self-governing Workshops " a great vogue. Numberless small undertakings were started by operative engineers, cabinetmakers, tailors, bootmakers, and hatters in the Metropolis and in other large industrial centres, and for a few years the Executives and Committees of the various Unions vied with each other in recommending co-operative production to their members. But it soon became apparent that this new form of co-operation was intended, not as an adjunct or a development of the Trade Union, but as an alternative form of industrial organisation. For, unlike the Owenites of 1834, the Christian Socialists had no conception of the substitution of profit-making

---

[1] A more detailed account of these developments will be found in *The Co-operative Movement in Great Britain* (1891 ; second edition, 1893), by Beatrice Potter (Mrs. Sidney Webb); *Co-operative Production*, by Benjamin Jones, 1894; and in the Report of the Fabian Research Department on Co-operative Production, published as a supplement to *The New Statesman*, February 14, 1914.

I

enterprise by the whole body of wage-earners, organised either in a self-contained community or in a complete Trades Union. They sought only to replace the individual capitalist by self-governing bodies of profit-making workmen. A certain number of the ardent spirits among the London and north country workmen became the managers and secretaries of these undertakings, and ceased to be energetic members of their respective Unions. "We have found," say the Engineers' Executive in their annual report of 1855, "that when a few of our own members have commenced business hitherto they have abandoned the society, and conducted the workshops even worse than other employers." Fortunately for the Trade Union Movement the uniform commercial failure of these experiments, so long, at any rate, as they retained their original form of the self-governing workshop, soon became obvious to those concerned. The idea of "Co-operative Production" constantly reappears in contemporary Trade Union records, but after the failure of the co-operative establishments of 1848–52 it ceases, for nearly twenty years, to be a question of "practical politics" in the Trade Union world.

In spite of this intellectual diversion the work of Trade Union consolidation was being steadily carried on. The Amalgamated Engineers doubled their numbers in the ten years that followed their strike, and by 1861 their Union had accumulated the unprecedented balance of £73,398. The National Societies of Ironfounders and Stonemasons grew in a similar proportion. A revival of Trade Unionism took place among the textile operatives. The present association of Lancashire cotton-spinners began its career in 1853, whilst the cotton-weavers secured in the same year what has been fitly termed their Magna Charta, the "Blackburn List" of piecework rates. But with the exception of the building trades, Trade Unionism assumed, during these years, a peaceful attitude. The leaders no longer declaimed against "the idle classes," but sought to justify the Trade Union position with arguments based on middle-class economics. The contributions of the Amalgamated Engineers are described " as a general voluntary rate in aid of the Poor's Rate."[1] The Executive Council cannot doubt that employers will not " regard a society like ours with disfavour. They will begin to understand that it is not intended, nor adapted, to damage their interests, but rather to advance them, by elevating the character of their workmen, and proportionately lessening their own responsibilities." The project of substituting " Councils of Conciliation " for strikes and lock-outs grew in favour with Trade Union leaders. Hundreds of petitions in favour of their establishment were got up by the National Association of United Trades, then on its last legs. The House of Commons Committees in 1856 and 1860 found the operatives in all trades disposed to support the principle of voluntary submission to arbitration. For a brief period it seemed as if peace was henceforth to prevail over the industrial world.

The era of strikes which set in with the contraction of trade in 1857 proved how fallacious had been these hopes. The building trades, in particular, had remained less affected than the Engineers or the Cotton Operatives by the change of tone. The local branches of the Stonemasons, Bricklayers, and other building trade operatives, often against the wish of their Central Committees, were engaged between 1853 and 1859 in an almost constant succession of little strikes against separate firms, in which the men were generally successful in gaining advances of wages.[2]

---

[1] *Address of the Executive Council of the Amalgamated Society of Engineers to their Fellow-Workmen*, 1855.

[2] See *The Strikes, their Extent, Evils, and Remedy, being a Description of the General Movement of the Mass of the Building Operatives throughout the United Kingdom*, by Vindex (1853), 56 pp. One consequence of this renewed outburst of strikes was the appointment in 1858 by the newly formed National Association for the Promotion of Social Science of a Committee to inquire into trade societies and disputes. This inquiry, conducted by able and zealous investigators, resulted in 1860 in the publication of a volume which contains the best collection of Trade Union material and the most impartial account of Trade Union action that has ever been issued. As a source of history and economic illustra-

These years were, moreover, notable for the recognition in the provincial building trades of " working rules," or signed agreements between employers and workmen (usually between the local Masters' Associations and the Trade Unions), specifying in minute detail the conditions of the collective bargain. Without doubt the adoption of these rules was a step forward in the direction of industrial peace ; but, like international treaties, they were frequently preceded by desperate conflicts in which both sides exhausted their resources, and learnt to respect the strength of the other party. With the depression of trade more important disputes occurred. During 1858 fierce conflicts arose between masters and men in the flint glass industry and in the West Yorkshire coalfield. The introduction of the sewing-machine into the boot and shoemaking villages of Northamptonshire led to a series of angry struggles. But of the great disputes of 1858 to 1861, the builders' strike in the Metropolis in 1859–60 was by far the most important in its effect upon the Trade Union Movement.

The dispute of 1859 originated in the growing movement for a shortening of the hours of labour.[1] The demand for a Nine Hours Day in the Building Trades was first made by the Liverpool Stonemasons in 1846, and renewed by the London Stonemasons in 1853. In neither case, however, was the claim persisted in. Four years later the movement was revived by the London Carpenters, whose memorial to their employers was met, after a joint

---

tion this *Report on Trade Societies and Strikes* (1860, 651 pp.) is far superior to the Parliamentary Blue Books of 1824, 1825, 1838, and 1867–68. Among the contributors were Godfrey Lushington (afterwards Under-Secretary of State for the Home Department), J. M. Ludlow (afterwards Registrar of Friendly Societies), Thomas (afterwards Judge) Hughes, Q.C., Mr. G. Shaw-Lefevre (afterwards Lord Eversley), F. D. Longe, and Frank Hill. The Committee was presided over by the late Sir James Kay-Shuttleworth, and amongst its other members may be mentioned W. E. Forster, Henry Fawcett, R. H. Hutton, Rev. F. D. Maurice, Dr. William Farr, and one Trade Union secretary, T. J. Dunning, of the London Bookbinders.

[1] See the account of it in *Labour Legislation, Labour Movements, and Labour Leaders*, by G. Howell, 1902.

conference, by a decisive refusal. Meanwhile the Stone-masons were seeking to obtain the Saturday half-holiday, which the employers equally refused. This led, in the autumn of 1858, to the formation of a Joint Committee of Carpenters, Masons, and Bricklayers, which, on November 18, 1858, addressed a dignified memorial to the master builders, urging that the hours of labour should be shortened by one per day, and that future building contracts should be accepted on this basis. At first ignored by the employers, this request was eventually refused as decidedly as it had been in 1853 and 1857. The Joint Committee thereupon made a renewed attempt by petitioning four firms selected by ballot. Among these was that of Messrs. Trollope, who promptly dismissed one of the men who had presented the memorial. This action led to an immediate strike against Messrs. Trollope. Within a fortnight every master builder in London employing over fifty men had closed his establishment, and twenty-four thousand men were peremptorily deprived of their employment. The contro-versy which raged in the columns of contemporary news-papers during this pitched battle between Capital and Labour brought out in strong relief the state of mind of the Metropolitan employers. Uninfluenced by the progress of public opinion, or by the new tone of respect and modera-tion adopted by Trade Union leaders, the London employers took up the position of their predecessors of 1834. They absolutely refused to recognise the claim of the representa-tives of the men even to discuss with them the conditions of employment. This attitude was combined with a deter-mined attempt to destroy all combination, the instru-ment adopted being the well-worn Document. The Central Association of Master Builders resolved, in terms almost identical with its predecessor of 1834, that " no member of this Association shall engage or continue in his employ-ment any contributor to the funds of any Trades Union or Trades Society which practises interference with the regulation of any establishment, the hours or terms of labour, the contracts or agreements of employers or employed, or the qualification or terms of service."

This declaration of war on Trade Unionism gained for the men on strike the support of the whole Trade Union world. The Central Committee of the great society of Stonemasons, which had hitherto discouraged the Metropolitan Nine Hours Movement as premature, took up the struggle against the Document as one of vital importance. Meetings of delegates from the organised Metropolitan trades were held in order to rally the forces of Trade Unionism to the cause of the builders. The subscriptions which poured in from all parts of the kingdom demonstrated the possession, in the hands of trade societies, of heavy and hitherto unsuspected reserves of financial strength. The London Pianoforte Makers contributed £300. The Flint Glass Makers, who had just emerged from a prolonged struggle on their own account, sent a similar sum. " Trades Committees " were formed in all the industrial centres, and remitted large amounts. Glasgow and Manchester sent over £800 each, and Liverpool over £500. The newly formed Yorkshire Miners' Association forwarded £230. The Boilermakers, Coopers, and Coachmakers' Societies were especially liberal in their gifts. But the sensation of the subscription list was the grant by the Amalgamated Engineers of three successive weekly donations of £1000 each—an event long recalled with emotion by the survivors of the struggle. Altogether some £23,000 were subscribed (exclusive of the payments by the societies directly concerned), an amount far in excess of any previous strike subsidy.

Such abundant support enabled the men to defeat the employers' aims, though not to secure their own demands. The Central Association of Master Builders clung desperately to the Document, but failed to obtain an adequate number of men willing to subscribe to its terms. In December 1859 a suggestion was made by Lord St. Leonards that the Document be withdrawn, a lengthy statement of the law relating to trade combinations being hung up in all the establishments as a substitute. The employers' obstinacy held out for two months longer, but finally succumbed in February 1860, when the Platonic suggestion of Lord St. Leonards was adopted, and the embittered dispute was brought to an end.

This drawn battle between the forces of Capital and Labour ranks as a leading event in Trade Union history, not only because it revived the feeling of solidarity between different trades, but also on account of the importance of two consolidating organisations to which it gave birth. Out of the Building Trades Strike of 1859–60 arose the London Trades Council (to be described in the following chapter) and the Amalgamated Society of Carpenters, the most notable adoption by another trade of the " New Model " introduced by Newton and Allan.

The strike had revealed to the London carpenters the complete state of disorganisation into which their industry had fallen. It was they, it is true, who had initiated the Nine Hours Movement in the Metropolis, but the committee which memorialised the employers had represented no body of organised workmen. George Potter, who was the leader of this movement, could draw around him only a group of delegates elected by the men in each shop. There were, indeed, not more than about a thousand carpenters in London who were members of any trade society whatsoever, and these were scattered among numerous tiny benefit clubs. The Friendly Society of Operative Carpenters, which, as we have seen, was a militant branch of the Builders' Union of 1830–34, had, like the Stonemasons' Society, maintained a continuous existence. Unlike that society, however, it had kept the old character of a loose federation for trade purposes only, depending for its finances upon occasional levies. Perhaps for this reason it had lost its exclusive hold upon the provinces, and had gained no footing in London. As a competent observer remarks : " At the time of the 1859–60 strikes the masons alone of the building trades were organised into a single society extending throughout England, and providing not only for trade purposes, but for the ordinary benefits. . . . The London masons locked out were supported regularly and punctually by their society, and could have continued the struggle for an indefinite time ; but the other trades, split up into numerous local societies, were soon reduced to extremities." [1] The Carpenters' Committee saw with envy the capacity of the Stonemasons' Society to provide long-continued strike pay for its members, and were profoundly impressed by the successive donations of £1000 each made by the Amalgamated Engineers. Directly the strike was over, the leading members of the little benefit clubs met together to discuss the formation of a national organisation on the Engineers' model. William Allan lent them every assistance in adapting the rules of his own society to the carpenters' trade, and watched over the preliminary proceedings. The new society started on June 4, 1860, with a few hundred members. For the first two years its progress was slow ; but in October 1862 it had the good fortune to elect as its general secretary a man whose ability and cautious sagacity promptly raised it to a position of influence in the Trade Union world. Robert Applegarth, secretary of a local Carpenters' Union at Sheffield, had been quick to perceive the advantages of amalgamation, and had brought his society over with him. Under his administration the new Union advanced by leaps and bounds, and in a few years it stood, in magnitude of financial transactions and accumulated funds, second only to the Amalgamated Society of Engineers itself. Moreover, Applegarth's capacity brought him at once into that little circle of Trade Union leaders whose activity forms during the next ten years the central point of Trade Union history.

[1] Prof. E. S. Beesly, *Fortnightly Review*, 1867.

CHAPTER V

THE JUNTA AND THEIR ALLIES

MANY influences had during the preceding years been co-operating to form what may almost be described as a cabinet of the Trade Union Movement. The establishment of such great trade friendly societies as the Amalgamated Engineers had created, in some sense, a new school of Trade Union officials, face to face with intricate problems of administration and finance. The presence in London of the headquarters of these societies brought their salaried officers into close personal intimacy with each other. And it so happened that during these years the little circle of secretaries included men of marked character and ability, who were, both by experience and by temperament, admirably fitted to guide the movement through the acute crisis which we shall presently describe.

Foremost in this little group—which we shall hereafter call the Junta—were the general secretaries of the two amalgamated societies of Engineers and Carpenters, William Allan and Robert Applegarth, whose success in building up these powerful organisations had given them great influence in Trade Union councils. Bound to these in close personal friendship were Daniel Guile, the general secretary of the old and important national society of Ironfounders, Edwin Coulson, general secretary of the " London Order " of Bricklayers, and George Odger, a prominent member of a small union of highly skilled makers of ladies' shoes, and an influential leader of London working-class Radicalism.

William Allan was the originator of the " New Unionism "
of his time.[1] We have already described how, with the aid
of William Newton, he had gathered up the scattered fragments of organisation in the engineering trade, and had
adapted the elaborate constitution and financial system of
an old-established society to the needs of a great national
amalgamation. In long hours of patient labour in the office
he had built up an extremely methodical, if somewhat
cumbrous, system of financial checks and trade reports, by
which the exact position of each of his tens of thousands
of members was at all times recorded in his official pigeon-
holes. The permanence of his system is the best testimony
to its worth. Even to-day the Engineers' head office retains
throughout the impress of Allan's tireless and methodical
industry. Excessive caution, red-tape precision, an almost
miserly solicitude for the increase of the society's funds,
were among Allan's defects. But at a time when working
men " agitators " were universally credited with looseness
in money matters and incapacity for strenuous and regular
mental effort, these defects, however equivocal may have
been their ultimate effect on the policy and development
of the Amalgamated Society of Engineers, produced a
favourable impression on the public. Allan, moreover,
though not a brilliant speaker, or a man of wide general
interests, was a keen working-class politician, whose temper
and judgement could always be depended on. And he has

[1] William Allan was born of Scotch parents at Carrickfergus, Ulster,
in 1813. His father, who was manager of a cotton-spinning mill, removed to a mill near Glasgow, and William became in 1825 a piecer in
a cotton factory at Gateside. Three years later he left the mill to be
bound apprentice to Messrs. Holdsworth, a large engineering firm at
Anderston, Glasgow. At the age of nineteen, before his apprenticeship
was completed, he married the niece of one of the partners. In 1835 he
went to work as a journeyman engineer at Liverpool, moving thence,
with the railway works, to their new centre at Crewe, where he joined
his Union. On the imprisonment of Selsby, in 1847, he became its general
secretary, retaining this office when, in 1851, the society became merged
in the Amalgamated Society of Engineers. For over twenty years he
was annually re-elected secretary of this vast organisation, dying at last
in office in 1874.

left behind him the tradition, not only of absolute integrity and abnormal industry, but also of a singular freedom from personal vanity or ambition.

Whilst Allan aimed at transforming the " paid agitator " into the trusted officer of a great financial corporation, Robert Applegarth sought to win for the Trade Union organisation a recognised social and political status. Astute and lawyer-like in temperament, he instinctively made use of those arguments which were best fitted to overcome the prejudices and disarm the criticisms of middle-class opponents. Nor did he limit himself to justifying the ways of Trade Unionists to the world at large. He made persistent attempts to enlarge the mental horizon of the rank and file of his own movement, opening out to those whose vision had hitherto been limited to the strike and the tap-room, whole vistas of social and political problems in which they as working men were primarily concerned. Hence we find him, during his career as general secretary, a leading member of the famous " International," [1]

[1] The celebrated " International Association of Working Men," which loomed so large in the eyes of Governments and the governing classes about 1869–70, had arisen out of the visit of two French delegates to London in 1863, to concert joint action on behalf of Poland. It was formally established at a meeting in London on September 28, 1864, at which an address prepared by Karl Marx was read. Its fundamental aim was the union of working men of all countries for the emancipation of labour ; and its principles went on to declare that " the subjection of the man of labour to the man of capital lies at the bottom of all servitude, all social misery, and all political dependence." Between 1864 and 1870, branches were established in nearly all European countries, as well as in the United States, the majority of trade societies in some European countries joining in a body. The central administration was entrusted to a General Council of fifty-five members sitting in London, which was composed of London residents of various nationalities, elected by the branches in the countries to which they belonged. The General Council had, however, no legislative or other control over the branches, and in practice served as little more than a means of communication between them, each country managing its own affairs in its own way. The principles and programme of the Association underwent a steady development in the succession of annual international congresses attended by delegates from the various branches. The extent to which English working men really participated in its fundamental objects is not clear. In 1870 Odger was president and Applegarth chairman of the General Council, which included Benjamin Lucraft, afterwards a member of the London

and an energetic promoter of the Labour Representation League, the National Education League, and various philanthropic and political associations. Political reformers became eager to secure his adhesion to their projects : he was, for instance, specially invited to attend the important conferences of the National Education League at Birmingham as the special representative of the working classes ; and it was owing to his reputation as a social reformer that he was in 1870 selected to sit on the Royal Commission upon the Contagious Diseases Acts, thus becoming the first working man to be styled by his Sovereign " Our Trusty and Well-beloved." Open-minded, alert, and conciliatory, he formed an ideal representative of the English Labour Movement in the political world.[1]

School Board, and other well-known working-men politicians. But few English Trade Unions (among them being the Bootmakers and Curriers) joined in their corporate capacity ; and when, in October 1866, the General Council invited the London Trades Council to join, or, that failing, to give permission for a representative of the International to attend its meetings, with a view of promptly reporting all Continental strikes, the Council's minutes show that both requests were refused. The London Trades Council declined indeed to recognise the International even as the authorised medium of communication with trade societies abroad, and decided to communicate with these directly. Applegarth attended several of the Continental congresses as a delegate from England, and elaborately explained the aims and principles of the Association in an interview published in the *New York World* of May 21 1870. After the suppression of the Commune the branches in France were crushed out of existence ; and the membership in England and other countries fell away. The annual Congress held in 1872 at The Hague decided to transfer the General Council to New York, and the " International" ceased to play any part in the English Labour Movement. An interesting account of its Trade Unionist action appeared in the *Fortnightly Review* for November 1870, by Professor E. S. Beesly.

[1] Robert Applegarth, the son of a quartermaster in the Royal Navy, was born at Hull on January 23, 1833. At the age of eleven he went to work as errand boy, eventually drifting into the shop of a joiner and cabinetmaker, where, unapprenticed, he picked up the trade as best he could. In 1852 he moved to Sheffield ; but in 1855, on the death of his parents, he emigrated to the United States, returning to Sheffield in the following year, as the health of his wife did not allow her to follow him to the land of promise. Joining the local Carpenters' Union, he quickly became its most prominent member, and brought it over in a body when the formation in 1861 of the Amalgamated Society of Carpenters and Joiners offered a prospect of more efficient trade action.

The permanent officials of the Ironfounders and the London Bricklayers were men of less originality than Allan or Applegarth. Guile was a man of attractive personality and winning manner, gifted with a certain rugged eloquence. Coulson is described by an opponent as being " stolid and obstinate," and again as " bricky and stodgy " ; but the expansion, under his influence, of the little London Society of Bricklayers into a powerful Union of national scope, proves him to have possessed administrative ability of no mean order. The special distinction of all four alike was their business capacity, shown by the persistency and success with which they pursued, each in his own trade, the policy originated by Newton and Allan, of basing Trade Union organisation upon an insurance company of national extent. George Odger brought to the Junta quite other qualities than the cautious industry of Allan or the lawyer-like capacity of Applegarth. Of the five men we have mentioned he was the only one who continued to work at his trade, and who retained to the last the full flavour of a working-class leader. An orator of remarkable power, he swayed popular meetings at his will, and was the idol of Metropolitan Radicalism. But he was no mere demagogue. Beneath his brilliant rhetoric and emotional fervour there

---

Elected general secretary in 1862, he retained the office until 1871, when, in consequence of various personal disputes in the society, he voluntarily resigned. In 1870, on the formation of the London School Board, he stood as a candidate for the Lambeth division, but was unsuccessful, though he received 7600 votes. In the same year he was invited to become a candidate for Parliament for the borough of Maidstone, but he retired in favour of Sir John Lubbock. In 1871 he was appointed a member of the Royal Commission on the Contagious Diseases Act. On resigning his secretaryship he turned for a time to journalism, and acted as war correspondent in France for an American newspaper. Shortly afterwards he became foreman to a firm of manufacturers of engineering and diving apparatus, eventually becoming the proprietor of this flourishing business and retiring with a small competence. Mr. Applegarth, who is (1920) the sole survivor of the " Junta " of 1867–71, still retains his membership of the Amalgamated Society of Carpenters and his interest in Trade Unionism, about which he has given us valuable documents and reminiscences. See *The Life of Robert Applegarth*, by A. W. Humphrey, 1915.

lay a large measure of political shrewdness, and he shared with his colleagues the capacity for deliberately concerted action and personal subordination. His dilatory and un-businesslike habits made him incapable of building up a great organisation. Had he stood alone, he would have added little to the strength of Trade Unionism ; as the loyal adherent of the great officials and their popular mouth-piece to the working-class world, Unionist and non-Unionist alike, he gave the movement a wider basis, and attracted into its ranks every ardent reformer belonging to the artisan class.[1]

It is difficult to-day to convey any adequate idea of the extraordinary personal influence exercised by these five men, not only on their immediate associates, but also as interpreters of the Trade Union Movement, upon the public and the governing classes. For the first time in the century

[1] Daniel Guile was born at Liverpool, October 21, 1814, the son of a shoemaker. Bound apprentice to an ironfounder in 1827, he joined the Union in June 1834. In 1863 he became its corresponding secretary, a position he retained until his retirement at the end of 1881. He was a member of the Parliamentary Committee, 1871-5, and died December 7, 1883.

George Odger, the son of a Cornish miner, was born in 1820, at Rouborough, near Tavistock, South Devon, and became a shoemaker at an early age. Tramping about the country, as was then customary, he eventually settled in London, becoming a prominent member of the Ladies' Shoemakers' Society. His first important public action was in connection with the meetings of delegates of London trades on the build-ing trades lock-out in 1859. On the formation of the London Trades Council in 1860 he became one of its leading members, and from 1862 until the reconstruction of the Council in 1872 he acted as its secretary. As one of the leaders of London working-class Radicalism he made five attempts to get into Parliament, but was each time baulked by the opposi-tion of the official Liberal party. At Chelsea in 1868, at Stratford in 1869, and at Bristol in 1870 he retired rather than split the vote, but at Southwark in 1870 he went to the poll, and failed of success only by 304 votes, the official Liberal, Sir Sidney Waterlow, being at the bottom with 2966 votes as against 4382 given for Odger. At the General Election of 1874 he again stood, to be once more opposed by both Liberals and Conservatives with the same result as before. He died in 1877, his funeral, which was attended by Professor E. Beesly, Professor Fawcett, and Sir Charles Dilke, being made the occasion of a remarkable demonstra-tion by the London working men. An eulogy of him by Professor Beesly appeared in the *Weekly Despatch*, March 11, 1877. A brief biographical sketch was published under the title of *The Life and Labour of George Odger*, 1877.

the working-class movement came under the direction, not of middle and upper class sympathisers like Place, Owen, Roberts, O'Connor, or Duncombe, but of genuine workmen specially trained for the position. For the first time, moreover, the leaders of working-class politics stood together in a compact group, united by a close personal friendship, and absolutely free from any trace of that suspiciousness or disloyalty which have so often marred popular movements. They brought to their task, it is true, no consistent economic theory or political philosophy. They subscribed with equal satisfaction to the crude Collectivism of the "International," and the dogmatic industrial Individualism of the English Radicals. This absence of a definite basis to their political activity accounts, we think, for the drying up of Trade Union politics after their withdrawal. We shall have occasion hereafter to notice other " defects of their qualities," and the way in which these subsequently stunted the further development of their own movement. But it was largely their very limitations which made them, at this particular crisis, such valuable representatives of the Trade Union Movement. They accepted, with perfect good faith, the economic Individualism of their middle-class opponents, and claimed only that freedom to combine which the more enlightened members of that class were willing to concede to them. Their genuine if somewhat restrained enthusiasm for political and industrial freedom gave them a persistency and determination which no check could discourage. Their understanding of the middle-class point of view, and their appreciation of the practical difficulties of the situation, saved them from being mere demagogues. For the next ten years, when it was all-important to obtain a legal status for trade societies and to obliterate the unfortunate impression created by the Sheffield outrages, their qualities exactly suited the emergency. The possession of good manners, though it may seem a trivial detail, was not the least of their advantages. To perfect self-respect and integrity they added correctness of expression, habits of personal propriety, and a remarkable freedom from all that savoured of the tap-room. In Allan and Applegarth, Guile, Coulson, and Odger, the traducers of Trade Unionism found themselves confronted with a combination of high personal character, exceptional business capacity, and a large share of that official decorum which the English middle class find so impressive.

Round these central personalities grouped themselves in London a number of men of like temperament and aims. We have already had occasion to mention T. J. Dunning, of the Bookbinders, grown old in the service of Trade Unionism. The building trades contributed a younger generation, John Prior, George Howell, Henry Broadhurst, and George Shipton. The whole group were in touch with certain provincial leaders, who adhered to the new views, and acted in close concert with the Junta. Of these, the most noteworthy were Alexander Macdonald, then busily organising the Miners' National Union, John Kane,[1] of the North of England Ironworkers, William Dronfield, the Sheffield compositor, and Alexander Campbell, the leading spirit of the Glasgow Trades Council.

The distinctive policy of the Junta was the combination of extreme caution in trade matters and energetic agitation for political reforms. It is indeed somewhat doubtful how far Allan and Applegarth, Coulson and Guile shared the popular belief that trade combinations could effect a general rise of wages or resist a general reduction in a falling market. They had more faith in the moral force of great reserve funds, by the aid of which, dispensed in liberal out-of-work donations, one capitalist, or even a

---

[1] John Kane was born at Alnwick, Northumberland, in 1819. Sent to work at seven, he served in various capacities until the age of fifteen, when he moved to Newcastle-on-Tyne, and entered the ironworks of Messrs. Hawke at Gateshead. Here he took part in the Chartist and other progressive movements, making a vain attempt in 1842 to form a Union in his trade. Not until 1863 was a durable society established, and when in 1868 the Amalgamated Ironworkers' Association was formed on a national basis, John Kane became general secretary, a position he retained until his death in March 1876.

whole group of capitalists, might be effectually prevented from obtaining labour at anything but the standard conditions. Their trade policy was, in fact, restricted to securing for every workman those terms which the best employers were willing voluntarily to grant. For this reason they were constantly accused of apathy by those hotter spirits whose idea of successful Trade Unionism was a series of general strikes for advances or against reductions. The Junta were really looking in another direction for the emancipation of the worker. They believed that a levelling down of all political privileges, and the opening out of educational and social opportunities to all classes of the community, would bring in its train a large measure of economic equality. Under the influence of these leaders the London Unions, and eventually those of the provinces, were drawn into a whole series of political agitations, for the Franchise, for amendment of the Master and Servant law, for new Mines Regulation Acts, for National Education, and finally for the full legalisation of Trade Unions themselves.

Practical difficulties hampered the complete execution of the Junta's policy. The use of the Trade Union organisation for Parliamentary agitation, on which Macdonald, Applegarth, and Odger based all their expectations of progress, came as a new idea to the Trade Union world. The rank and file of Trade Unionists, still excluded from the franchise, took practically no interest in any social or political reform, and regarded their trade combinations exclusively as means of extorting a rise of wages or of compelling their fellow-workmen to join their clubs. This was especially the case with the provincial organisations, where the officials usually shared the obscurantism of their members. The " Manchester Order " of Bricklayers and the General Union of Carpenters (headquarters, Manchester) were, like the Midland Brickmakers and the Sheffield Cutlers, still wedded to the old ideas of secrecy and coercion, whilst the powerful society of Masons, then centred at Leeds, held aloof from the general movement. But this resistance was not confined to the older societies, nor to those of any particular locality. All the Unions of that time, even those of the Metropolis, retained a strong traditional repugnance to political action. In many cases the rules expressly forbade all mention of politics in their meetings. And although the societies could be occasionally induced to take joint action of a political character in defence of Trade Unionism itself, not even the great influence of the Junta upon their own Unions sufficed to persuade the members to turn their organisations to account for legislative reform. The Junta turned, therefore, to the newly established Trades Councils and made these the political organs of the Trade Union world.

The formation between 1858 and 1867 of permanent Trades Councils in the leading industrial centres was an important step in the consolidation of the Trade Union Movement. Local delegate meetings, summoned to deal with particular emergencies, had been a feature of Trade Union organisation, at any rate since the beginning of the nineteenth century. In early times every important strike had its committee of sympathisers from other trade societies, who collected subscriptions and rendered what personal aid they could. But the most notable of these committees were those which started up in all the centres of Trade Unionism when the movement was threatened by some particular legal or Parliamentary danger. Such joint committees had in 1825 contributed powerfully to defeat the re-enactment of the Combination Laws, in 1834 to arouse public feeling in the case of the Dorchester labourers, and in 1838 to conduct the Trade Union case before the Parliamentary Committee of that year. But these earlier committees were formed only for particular emergencies, and had, so far as we know, no continuous existence. By 1860 permanent councils were in existence in Glasgow, Sheffield, Liverpool, and Edinburgh, and their example was, in 1861, followed by the London trades.[1]

[1] The first permanent committee of the nature of a Trades Council

Like many provincial organisations, the London Trades Council originated in a " Strike Committee." During the

appears to have been, according to our information, the Liverpool " Trades Guardian Association," which was established in 1848 with the object of protecting Trade Unions from suppression by the employers' use of the criminal law. From its printed report and balance sheet for 1848, and the references in the *Fortnightly Circular* of the Stonemasons' Society for November 23, 1848, we gather that it took vigorous action to protect the Sheffield razor-grinders from malicious prosecution, and to help the Liverpool masons who had been indicted for conspiracy. Of its activity from 1850 to 1857 we possess no records, but in August 1857 it subscribed £400 in aid of the Liverpool cabinetmakers, and in 1861 it was assisting the London bricklayers' strike. In July of that year it was merged in a " United Trades Protection Association," formed upon the model of the newly established London Trades Council. In Glasgow there appears to have been, since 1825, an almost continuous series of joint committees of delegates for particular purposes. An attempt was made in 1851 to place these on a permanent footing, but the trades soon ceased to send delegates. A renewed attempt in 1858, made at the instance of Alexander Campbell, met with greater success ; and the Council then established, composed principally of the building trades, was in 1860 enjoying a vigorous life. Sheffield, too, had long had ephemeral federations of the local trades, which came near having a continuous existence. One of these, the " Association of Organised Trades," established in 1857 with the special object of assisting the Sheffield Typographical Society in defending a libel action, became the permanent Trades Council. Other towns, such as Dublin and Bristol, had almost constantly some kind of Council of the local trades. An appeal of the Trade Defence Association of Manchester, signed by representatives of nine thousand operatives on behalf of the dyers' strike, occurs in the *Stonemasons' Fortnightly Circular* for 1854. In London, as may be gathered from George Odger's evidence before the Master and Servant Law Committee in 1867, the meetings of " Metropolitan Trades Delegates " had been particularly frequent since 1848. In 1852, for instance, as we discover from the *Bookbinders' Trade Circular* (November 1853), a committee of the London trades took the case of the Wolverhampton tinplate workers out of the hands of the somewhat decrepit National Association of United Trades, and bore the whole cost of these expensive legal proceedings. No sooner had the task of this committee been completed, when another committee was formed to assist the strike of the Preston cotton operatives. It was to this committee, sitting at the Bell Inn, Old Bailey, the historic meeting-place of London Trade Unionism, that Lloyd Jones, in March 1855, communicated his fears that a certain Friendly Societies' Bill, then before the House of Commons, would make the legal position of trade societies even more equivocal than it then was. A " Metropolitan Trades Committee on the Friendly Societies' Bill " was accordingly formed, the printed report of which is reviewed by Dunning in his *Circular* for December 1855. From this we learn that it was presided over by William Allan, and that it included his old friend William Newton, as well as the general secretaries of the Stonemasons' and Bricklayers' Societies, and representatives of the

winter of 1859-60 weekly meetings of delegates from the Metropolitan trades had been held to support the Building Operatives in their resistance to the " document." " At the termination of that memorable struggle," states the Second Annual Report of the London Trades Council," it was felt that something should be done to establish a general trades committee so as to be able on emergency to call the trades together with despatch for the purpose of rendering each other advice or assistance as the circumstances required."[1] In March 1860 the provisional committee formed with this object issued an " Address " to the trades, which resulted, on July 10, 1860, in the first meeting of the present London Trades Council.

It is interesting to notice that the Council, at the outset, was composed mainly of the representatives of the smaller societies. The Executive Committee elected at its first meeting included no delegates from the engineers, compositors, masons, bricklayers, or ironfounders, who were then the most influential of the London Trade Societies. The first action of the young Council affords a significant indication of the feeling of isolation which led to its formation. In order to facilitate communications with other trade societies throughout the kingdom it resolved to compile a *General Trades Union Directory*, containing the names and addresses of all Trade Union secretaries. This

---

Compositors and Bookbinders. It was supported by eighty-seven different Trade Unions with forty-eight thousand members, who contributed a halfpenny per member to cover the expenses. Its Parliamentary action seems to have been vigorous and effective. The objectionable clauses were, by skilful Parliamentary lobbying, dropped out of the Bill, and what seemed at the time to be an important step towards the legislation of trade societies was, through the help of Thomas Hughes and Lord Goderich, secured. Between 1858 and 1867 Trades Councils were established in about a dozen of the largest towns. The Trade Union expansion of 1870–73 saw their number doubled. But their great increase was one of the effects of the great wave of Trade Union organisation which swept over the country in 1889–91, when over sixty new councils were established, and those already in existence were reorganised and greatly increased in membership.

[1] Second Annual Report of London Trades Council, March 31, 1862.

praiseworthy enterprise took up all the attention of the new body for the first year, and the printing of two thousand copies of the result of its work crippled its finances for long afterwards. For, unfortunately, the *General Trades Union Directory*, published at one shilling per copy, did not sell and was, we fear, soon consigned to the pulping mill, as we have, after exhaustive search, been able to discover only two copies in existence.[1]

But the direction of the Council was falling into abler hands. In 1861 George Howell became secretary, to be succeeded in the following year by George Odger, who for the next ten years remained its most prominent member. The Amalgamated Society of Engineers joined in 1861, and the veteran Dunning brought over the old-established Union of Bookbinders. By 1864, at any rate, the new organisation was entirely dominated by the Junta. The two " amalgamated " societies of Engineers and Carpenters supplied, in some years, half its income. The great trade friendly society of Ironfounders and the growing " London Order " of Bricklayers sent their general secretaries to its meetings. The Council became, in effect, a joint committee of the officers of the large national societies. In the meetings at the old Bell Inn, under the shadow of Newgate, we have the beginnings of an informal cabinet of the Trade Union world.

Meanwhile war had again broken out between the master builders and their operatives, caused partly by a renewed agitation for the Nine Hours Day, and partly by the employers' desire to substitute payment by the hour for the previous custom of payment by the day.[2] For the

---

[1] No copy is preserved in the British Museum nor among the archives of the Trades Council itself. Mr. Robert Applegarth kindly presented us with a copy, which is now in the British Library of Political Science at the London School of Economics. The only other one known to us is in the Goldsmiths' Library at the University of London.

[2] On receipt of a memorial from the operatives asking for the introduction of the Nine Hours Day, three of the principal London builders gave notice that henceforth they would engage their workmen, not by the day, but by the hour. " This arrangement," they added, " of payment

historian of the general movement the dispute is chiefly important as furnishing the occasion of the first intervention of the talented group of young barristers and literary men who, from this time forth, became the trusted legal experts and political advisers of the leaders of the Trade Union Movement. The workmen had totally failed to make clear their objection to the Hour System, or even to obtain a hearing of their case. Their position was, for the first time, intelligibly explained in two brilliant letters addressed to the newspapers by eight Positivists and Christian Socialists, which did much to bring about the tacit compromise in which the struggle ended.[1]

Of more immediate interest to us is the action taken by the newly formed London Trades Council. Among the building operations suspended by the dispute was the

---

by the hour will enable any workman employed by us to work any number of hours he may think proper." This specious proposal involved a total abandonment of the principle of Collective Bargaining. What the master builders proposed was, in effect, to do away with the very conception of a normal day, and to revert, as far as the hours were concerned, to separate contracts with each individual workman. The workmen realised, what they failed clearly to explain, that the proffered freedom was illusory. In the modern organisation of industry on a large scale there can be no freedom for the individual workman to drop his tools at whatever moment he chooses. Without a concerted normal day, each workman must inevitably find his task continue as long as the engines are going or the works are open. The real question at issue was how the common hours of labour should be fixed. The master builders of 1861 rightly calculated that if each man was really free to earn as many hours' wages in the day as they chose to offer him, the hours during which the whole body would work would, in effect, be governed, not by the general convenience, but by the desire and capacity of those willing to work the longest day. On this, the essential issue, the men maintained their position. The normal day in the London building trades was tacitly fixed according to the prevailing custom, and has since been repeatedly regulated and reduced by formal collective agreement until the average working week throughout the year consists of less than 48 hours. The minor point of the unit of remuneration was gradually conceded by the men, and the Hour System, guarded by strict limitation of the working day, has come to be preferred by both parties.

[1] The letters were drawn up by Frederic Harrison and Godfrey Lushington, after personal investigation and inquiry, and were signed also by T. Hughes, J. M. Ludlow, E. S. Beesly, R. H. Hutton, R. B. Litchfield, and T. R. Bennett. They appeared in July 1861.

construction, by a large contractor, of the new Chelsea barracks. The War Department saw no harm in permitting him to engage the sappers of the Royal Engineers to take the place of the men on strike. A similar course had been taken by the Government in strikes of 1825 and 1834. But the Trade Unions were now too powerful to allow of any such interference in their battles. A delegate meeting of the London trades, comprising representatives of fifty industries and fifty thousand operatives, sent a deputation to the War Office. Sir George Cornwall Lewis returned at first an equivocal answer, but the new Trades Council proved the efficacy of Parliamentary agitation by getting questions put to the Minister in the House of Commons, and stirring up enough feeling to compel him to withdraw the troops.

The minute-books of the London Trades Council from 1860 to 1867 present a mirror of the Trade Union history of this period. Odger had the rare gift of making his minutes interesting, and he describes, in his terse but graphic English, all the varied events of the Labour Movement as they were brought before the Council. In 1861-62, for instance, we see the Council trying vainly to settle the difficult problem of " overlap " between the trades of the shipwrights and the iron-shipbuilders ; we notice the shadow cast by the Lancashire cotton famine, and we read indignant resolutions condemning the Sheffield outrages of those years. But the special interest of these minutes lies in their unconscious revelation of the way in which the Council became the instrument of the new policy of participation in general politics. Under Odger's influence the Council took a prominent part in organising the popular welcome to Garibaldi, and in 1862 it held a great meeting in St. James's Hall in support of the struggle of the Northern States against negro slavery, at which John Bright was the principal speaker. In 1864 the Junta placed itself definitely in opposition to the " Old Unionists," who objected to all connection between the Government and the

concerns of working men. W. E. Gladstone, who was then
Chancellor of the Exchequer, had introduced a Bill enabling
the Post Office to sell Government Annuities for small
amounts. Against this harmless project George Potter, the
leading opponent of the Junta, summoned great public
meetings of the London trades, enlisted on his side the
Operative Stonemasons and other provincial organisations,
and vehemently denounced the Bill as an insidious attempt
to divert the savings of working men from their Trade
Unions and benefit societies into an exchequer controlled
by the governing classes. The London Trades Council sent
an influential deputation to Gladstone publicly to disavow
the action of Potter, and to welcome the proposal of the
Government to utilise the administrative organisation for
the advantage of the working class. Of more significance
was the alteration of the Council's policy with regard to
political reform. The early members had set themselves
against the introduction of politics in any guise whatsoever, and during the years 1861-62 Howell and Odger strove
in vain to enlist the Council in the agitation for a new
Reform Bill. But in 1866, under the influence of Odger
and Applegarth, Allan and Coulson, the Council enthusiastically threw itself into the demonstration in favour of
the Reform Bill brought in by the Liberal Government,
and took a leading part in the agitation which resulted in
the enfranchisement of the town artisan.[1] In the same
year the Council agreed to co-operate with the " International " in demanding Democratic Reform from all
European Governments.

The widely advertised public action of the London
Trades Council excited considerable interest in provincial
centres of Trade Unionism. We see the Council in frequent

---

[1] Many of the local Birmingham Trade Unions became directly affiliated
to the National Reform League. But with the exception of two small
clubs at Wolverhampton, and the West End Cabinetmakers (London),
no other Trade Union appears to have joined the League in a corporate
capacity, though its Council included Allan, Applegarth, Coulson, Cremer,
Odger Potter, and Conolly.

correspondence with similar bodies at Glasgow, Nottingham, Sheffield, and other provincial towns, and often exercising a kind of informal leadership in general movements. But it would be unfair to ascribe the whole initiative in legislative reform to the London officials. Under the brilliant leadership of Alexander Macdonald, whose work we shall hereafter describe, the force of the coal-miners was being marshalled for Parliamentary agitation; and Macdonald's friend, Alexander Campbell, was bringing the Glasgow Trades Council round to the new policy. And it was Campbell and Macdonald, working through these organisations, who carried through the most important Trade Union achievement of the next few years, the amendment of the law relating to master and servant.

It is difficult in these days, when equality of treatment before the law has become an axiom, to understand how the flagrant injustice of the old Master and Servant Acts seemed justifiable even to a middle-class Parliament. If an employer broke a contract of service, even wilfully and without excuse, he was liable only to be sued for damages, or, in the case of wages under £10, to be summoned before a court of summary jurisdiction, which could order payment of the amount due. The workman, on the other hand, who wilfully broke his contract of service, either by absenting himself from his employment, or by leaving his work, was liable to be proceeded against for a criminal offence, and punished by three months' imprisonment. This inequality of treatment was, moreover, aggravated by various other anomalies. It followed by the general law of evidence that, whilst a master sued by a servant could be witness in his own favour, the servant prosecuted by his employer could not give evidence on his own behalf; and it frequently happened that no other evidence than the employer's could be produced. It was in the power of a single justice of the peace, on an information on oath, to issue a warrant for the summary arrest of the workman, who thus found himself, when a dispute occurred, suddenly seized, even in his bed,[1] and haled to prison at the discretion of a magistrate, who was in many cases himself an employer of labour. The case was heard before a single justice of the peace, and the hearing might take place at his private house. The only punishment that could be inflicted was imprisonment, the law not allowing the alternative of a fine or the payment of damages. From the decision of the justice, however arbitrary, there was no appeal. Finally, it must be added, the sentence of imprisonment was no discharge for a debt, so that a workman was liable to be imprisoned over and over again for the same breach of contract.[2]

[1] The obligation to proceed by warrant was at first universal, as the Act of 1824, 4 Geo. IV. c. 34, gave the magistrate no discretion. By that act the master was to be served with a summons at the instance of the workman, whilst the workman was to be arrested on a warrant on the complaint upon oath of the master. But, in 1848, Jervis's Act, 11 & 12 Vic. c. 43, gave justices power in all cases to issue a summons in the first instance. The practice was accordingly gradually introduced in England of summoning the workman ; and the issue of a warrant was in general confined to cases in which the workman had gone away, or had failed to appear to a summons. Jervis's Act, however, did not apply to Scotland, so that summary arrests of workmen on warrants continued until 1867 ; and this was one of the principal grievances adduced by the Glasgow representatives. Even in England warrants were occasionally granted by vindictive magistrates. In 1863 a dispute took place at a Durham colliery, and the employer proceeded against the miners under the Master and Servant Law. "In the middle of the next night twelve of them were taken out of their beds by the police and lodged in Durham lock-up, on the charge of deserting their work without notice" (Letter by Professor E. S. Beesly in *Spectator*, December 12, 1863).

[2] See Question 864, Master and Servant Law Select Committee, 1866 ; Unwin *v.* Clarke, 1 Law Reports, Queen's Bench, p. 417 ; and Second Report of Labour Laws Commission, c. 1157 (1875), p. 7.

The enactments rendering the workman liable to imprisonment for simple breach of a contract of service are historically to be traced to the period when the law denied to the labourer the right to withhold his service or to bargain as to his wages. Any neglect or abandonment of his work was, therefore, like a simple refusal to work at all, a breach, not so much of contract, as of a duty arising out of status and enforced by statute. The law on the subject dates, indeed, back to the celebrated Statute of Labourers of 1349 (23 Ed. III.), the primary object of which was to enforce service at the rates of hiring that existed prior to the Black Death. The second section of this law enacts that if a workman or servant depart from service before the time agreed upon he shall be imprisoned. The same principle was asserted in the Statute of Appren-

Early in 1863 Alexander Campbell [1] brought the Master

___

tices in 1563 (5 Eliz. c. 4), which consolidated the law relating to all artificers and labourers, and expressly applied it to workers by the piece, who were rendered liable to imprisonment if they left before completing their job. During the eighteenth century, which abounded, as we have seen, in enactments dealing with particular trades, a long series of statutes made the provisions of law more definite and stringent in the industries in question. The principal English Acts were 7 Geo. I. st. 1, c. 13 (tailors) ; 9 Geo. I. c. 27 (shoemakers) ; 13 Geo. II. c. 8 (all leather trades) ; 20 Geo. II c. 19 ; 27 Geo. II. c. 6 ; 31 Geo. II. c. 11 (various trades); 6 Geo. III. c. 25 (agreements for a term) ; 17 Geo. III. c. 56 (textiles, etc.) ; 39 & 40 Geo. III. c. 77 (coal and iron) ; 4 Geo. IV. c. 34 (all trades); 10 Geo. IV. c. 52 (general) ; 6 & 7 Vic. c. 40 (textiles).

The intolerable oppression which these laws enabled unscrupulous employers to commit was, at the beginning of the century, scarcely inferior to that brought about by the Combination Laws. This was strongly urged by the authors of *A few Remarks on the State of the Laws at present in existence for regulating Masters and Workpeople* (preserved among the Place MSS. 27804), which George White, the prompter of Peter Moore, M.P., published in 1823. The pieceworker clause of the Statute of Apprentices was particularly oppressive. "This clause," says White, " has been much abused, as in many businesses they never finish their work, as the nature of the employment is such that they are compelled to begin one before they finish another, as wheelwrights, japanners, and an infinite number of trades ; therefore if any dispute ariseth respecting the amount of wages, and a strike or turn-out commences, or men leave their work, having words, the master prosecutes them for leaving their work unfinished. Very few prosecutions have been made to effect under the Combination Acts, but hundreds have been made under this law, and the labourer or workman can never be free, unless this law is modified. The Combination Act is nothing : it is the law which regards the finishing of work which masters employ to harass and keep down the wages of their workpeople ; unless this is modified nothing is done, and by repealing the Combination Acts you leave the workman in ninety-nine cases out of a hundred in the same state you found him—at the mercy of his master " (p. 51). But, in spite of this somewhat exaggerated protest, neither Place nor Hume took up the amendment of the law relating to contracts of service. Their paramount concern was to secure for the workman freedom to enter into a contract, and oppressive punishment for its breach attracted, for the moment, little attention.

Besides White's Manual, the following may be referred to for the history of the law, and of its amendment : *Report of Conference on the Law of Master and Workman under the Contract of Service* (Glasgow, 1864) ; the Reports of the Select Committee on the Law of Master and Servant, 1866, and of the Royal Commission on the Labour Laws, 1875 ; *The Labour Laws*, by James Edward Davis (1875); and Stephen's *History of the Criminal Law*, vol. iii.

[1] Alexander Campbell, who had been a prominent disciple of Robert Owen, and whom we have already seen as secretary to the little Glasgow Carpenters' Union of 1834, was, in 1863, editing the *Glasgow Sentinel*,

and Servant Law under the notice of the Glasgow Trades
Council. A Parliamentary Return was obtained showing
that the enormous number of 10,339 cases of breach of
contract of service came before the courts in a single year.
A committee was formed to agitate for the amendment of
the law, and communication was opened up, not only with
the London leaders, but also with sympathisers in other
provincial towns. The Trades Councils of London, Bristol,
Sheffield, Nottingham, Newcastle, and Edinburgh were
formally invited to unite in a combined movement. In
Leeds and elsewhere local Trades Councils were established
for the express purpose of forwarding the agitation ; and
15,000 copies of a " Memorial of Information intended for
the use of such workmen as fall under the provisions of the
Statute 4 Geo. IV. c. 34 " [1] were circulated to all the leading
workmen throughout the country. At the instance of
Campbell and Macdonald, the Glasgow Trades Council convened a conference of Trade Union representatives to consider how the object of the agitation could best be secured.
This Conference, which was held in London during four
days of May 1864, marks an epoch in Trade Union history.
For the first time a national meeting of Trade Union
delegates was spontaneously convened by a Trade Union
organisation to discuss a purely workman's question, in
the presence of working men alone. The number of delegates did not exceed twenty, but these included the leading
officials of all the great national and amalgamated Unions.[2]

---

which became the chief organ of Macdonald and his National Association
of Miners. Campbell is described as having been, in 1858, the virtual
founder of the Glasgow Trades Council.

[1] The Memorial, which contains an exact statement of the law and
suggestions for its amendment, is preserved in the *Flint Glass Makers'
Magazine*, December 1863.

[2] Among those present were Robert Applegarth, George Odger,
Daniel Guile, T. J. Dunning, Alexander Macdonald, William Dronfield,
Alexander Campbell, Edwin Coulson, and George Potter. The societies
represented included the London Trades Council, Glasgow Trades Com-
mittee, Sheffield Association of Organised Trades, Liverpool United Trades
Protection Society, Nottingham Association of Organised Trades, and the
Northumberland and Durham United Trades and Labourers ; the Amal-

The transactions of the Conference were thoroughly businesslike. Three members of the Government were asked to receive deputations ; a large number of members of Parliament were " lobbied " on the subject of an immediate amending Bill ; and finally a successful meeting of legislators was held in the " tea-room " of the House of Commons itself, at which the delegates impressed their desires upon all the friendly members. The terms of the draft Bill were settled ; Cobbett agreed to introduce it in the House of Commons, and the Glasgow Trades' Committee was authorised to support it by an agitation on behalf of all the Trade Unions of the kingdom.

The Bill introduced by Cobbett never became law ; but a vigorous agitation kept the matter under the notice of Parliament, and in 1866 a Select Committee was appointed to inquire into the subject. Upon its report Lord Elcho [1] succeeded, in 1867, in carrying through Parliament a Bill which remedied the grossest injustice of the law. The Master and Servant Act of 1867 (30 & 31 Vic. c. 141), the first positive success of the Trade Unions in the legislative field, did much to increase their confidence in Parliamentary agitation.

But whilst the Junta and their allies were, by the capture of the Trades Councils, using the Trade Union organisation for an active political campaign, their steady discouragement of aggressive strikes was bringing down upon them the wrath of the " Old Unionists " of the time. It was one of the principal functions of the London Trades Council to grant " credentials " to trade societies having disputes on hand, recommending them for the support of workmen in other trades. As these credentials were not confined to London disputes, the custom placed the Council under the invidious necessity of either giving its sanction

---

gamated Societies of Engineers and Carpenters, the National Societies of Bricklayers, Masons, Ironfounders, Miners, and Bookbinders, the London Society of Compositors, the Scottish Bakers, Sheffield Sawmakers, etc.

[1] Afterwards Earl of Wemyss.

to, or withholding approval from, practically every important strike in the kingdom—an arrangement which quickly
brought the Council into conflict with the more aggressive
societies.   In two cases especially the divergence of policy
raised serious and heated discussions.   A building trades
strike had broken out in the Midlands at the beginning of
1864, initiated by the old Friendly Society (now styled the
General Union) of Operative Carpenters.   The men's action
was strongly disapproved by Applegarth and the Executive
of the Amalgamated Society of Carpenters.   The London
Trades Council unhesitatingly took Applegarth's view,
thereby alienating whole sections of the building trades,
whose local trade clubs and provincial societies had retained
much of the spirit of the Builders' Union of 1834.   But the
internal dissension arising from the carpenters' dispute fell
far short of that brought about by the strike of the Staffordshire puddlers.   It is unnecessary to go into the details of
this angry struggle against a 10 per cent reduction.   The
conduct of the men in refusing the arbitration offered by
the Earl of Lichfield met with the disapproval of the London
Trades Council.   The hotter spirits were greatly incensed
at the Council's moderation.   George Potter, in particular,
distinguished himself by addressing excited meetings of the
men on strike, advising them to stand firm.

Potter, who figures largely in the newspapers of this
time, was in fact endeavouring to work up a formidable
opposition to the policy of the Junta.   After the building
trades disputes of 1859–60, in which he had taken a leading
part, he had started the *Beehive*, a weekly organ of the Trade
Union world.   Himself a member of a tiny trade club of
London carpenters, he was bitterly opposed to Applegarth
and the Amalgamated Society, and from 1864 onward we
find him at the head of every outbreak of disaffection.   An
expert in the arts of agitation and of advertisement, Potter
occasionally cut a remarkable figure, so that the unwary
reader, not of the *Beehive* only, but also of the *Times*,
might easily believe him to have been the most influential

leader of the working-class movement. As a matter of fact, he at no time represented any genuine trade organisation, the " Working Men's Association," of which he was president, being an unimportant society of nondescript persons. However, from 1864 to 1867 we find him calling frequent meetings of delegates of the London trades to denounce the Junta, and their instrument, the London Trades Council. The minutes of the latter body contain abundant evidence of the bitter feelings caused by these attacks, and make clear the essential difference between the two policies. At a special meeting called to condemn Potter's action, Howell, Allan, Coulson, and Applegarth enlarged upon the evil consequences of irresponsible agitation in trade disputes ; and Danter, the outspoken president of the Amalgamated Engineers, emphatically declared that Potter " had become the aider and abettor of strikes. He thought of nothing else ; he followed no other business ; strikes were his bread-and-cheese ; in short, he was a strike-jobber, and he made the *Beehive* newspaper his instrument for pushing his nose into every unfortunate dispute that sprang up." [1]

Responsible and cautious leadership of the Trade Union Movement was becoming increasingly necessary. The growth of the great national Unions, alike in wealth and in membership, and the manner in which they subscribed in aid of each other's battles, had aroused the active enmity of the employers. To counteract the men's renewed strength, the employers once more banded themselves into powerful associations, and made use of a new weapon. The old expedient of the " document " had, since its failure to break down the Amalgamated Engineers in 1852, and to subdue the building operatives in 1859, fallen somewhat into discredit. It was now reinforced by the general " lock-out " of all the men in a particular industry, even those who accepted the employer's terms, in order to reduce to subjection the recalcitrant employees of one or

[1] Minutes of meeting of London Trades Council, March 1864.

two firms only.[1] The South Yorkshire coal-owners especially distinguished themselves during those years by their frequent use of the "lock-out." One Yorkshire miner complained in 1866 that he had been "locked out about twenty-four months in six years."[2] During the year 1865 it seemed as if the lock-outs were about to become a feature of every large industry, the most notable instances being those of the Staffordshire ironworkers, to which we have already alluded, and the shipbuilding operatives on the Clyde. In both these cases large sections of the men were willing to work at the employers' terms, but were either known to belong to a Union or suspected of contributing to the men on strike. But though this practice of "locking out" created great excitement among working men, it did not achieve the employers' aim of breaking up the Unions. Nothing but absolute suppression by law appeared open to those who regarded trade combinations as "a poisonous plant" and an "anomalous anachronism," and who were vainly looking to "the happy period," both for masters and men, when the questions, "What is the price of a quarter of wheat?" and "What is the price of a workman's day wage?" shall be settled on the same principles.[3]

Nor were the employers the only people who began to talk once more of putting down Trade Unions by law. The industrial dislocation which the lock-outs, far more than the strikes, produced occasioned widespread loss and public inconvenience. The quarrels of employer and employed came to be vaguely regarded as matters of more than private concern. Unfortunately a handle was given to the enemies of Trade Unionism by the continuance of outrages, committed in the interest of Trade Unions, which began to be widely advertised by the press. Isolated cases of violence

---

[1] It must not be supposed that the lock-out was a new invention. Place describes its use by the master breeches-makers at the end of the last century : *Life of Francis Place*, by Professor Graham Wallas (1918).

[2] *Report of Conference of Trade Delegates at Sheffield* (June 1866), p. 22.

[3] "An Ironmaster's View of Strikes," by W. R. Hopper, *Fortnightly Review* (August 1, 1865).

and intimidation, restricted, as we shall hereafter see, to certain trades and localities, were magnified by press rumours into a systematic attempt on the part of the Trade Unions generally to obtain their ends by deliberate physical violence. In the general fear and disapproval the public failed to discriminate between the petty trade clubs of Sheffield and such great associations as the Amalgamated Engineers and Carpenters. The commercial objection to industrial disputes became confused with the feeling of abhorrence created by the idea of vast combinations of men sticking at neither violence nor murder to achieve their ends. The " terrorism of Trade Unions " became a nightmare. " On one side," says a writer who represents the public feeling of the time, " is arrayed the great mass of the talent, knowledge, virtue, and wealth of the country, and, on the other, a number of unscrupulous men, leading a half-idle life, and feeding on the contributions of their dupes, and on a tax levied on such of the intelligent artisans as are forced into their ranks, but who would be only too happy to throw off their thraldom and join the supporters of law and justice, did these but offer them adequate protection." [1]

The Trade Unions world seems to have been quite unconscious of the gathering storm. In June 1866 138 delegates, representing all the great Unions, and a total membership of about 200,000, met at Sheffield to devise some defence against the constant use of the lock-out. The student of the proceedings of this conference will contrast with wonder the actual conduct of the Trade Union leaders with the denunciations to which these " few unscrupulous men " were at this time exposed. Nothing could be more worthy, even from the middle-class point of view, than the discussions of these representative workmen, who denounced

[1] " Measures for Putting an End to the Abuses of Trades Unions," by Frederic Hill, Barrister-at-Law : Paper in Sessional Proceedings of the National Association for the Promotion of Social Science, 1867–68, p. 24. The popular middle-class sentiment is reflected in Charles Reade's novel, *Put Yourself in his Place* (1871).

K

with equal energy the readiness with which their impetuous
followers came out on strike and the arbitrary lock-out of
the masters, and whose resolutions express their desire for
the establishment of Councils of Conciliation and the general
resort to arbitration in industrial disputes.[1]   Meanwhile, in
order to meet the great federations of employers, they
formed " The United Kingdom Alliance of Organised
Trades," to support the members of any trade who should
find themselves " locked out " by their employers.[2]   Unfortunately the conference utterly failed to decide what
constituted a " lock-out," as distinguished from a strike ;
and the " Judicial Council " of the Alliance, consisting of
one delegate from each of the nine districts into which the
kingdom was divided, found itself continually at issue with
its constituents as to the disputes to be supported.   This
friction co-operated with the increasing depression of trade
in causing the calls for funds to be very unwillingly responded
to ; and the Executive Committee, sitting at Sheffield, had
seldom any cash at its command.   The Alliance lingered on
until about the end of 1870, when the defection of its last
important Unions brought it absolutely to an end.[3]   In

---

[1] See, for instance, the speech of George Newton, the secretary of the
Glasgow Trades Committee : " A great many strikes, and perhaps lock-
outs, too, have arisen from a stubborn refusal on the part of both sides
to look the question honestly and fairly in the face. . . . Let us examine
ourselves and see if there be any wicked way in us that contributes to
this unsatisfactory state of things, and if we discover that we are not
blameless, then we ought, first of all, to set our own house in order. . . .
Then let us examine the opposite side of the camp and see how they
stand, and if we find that they have not done all that they ought to have
done with a view to prevent these serious evils, let us undisguisedly and
in plain language point out where we consider they have erred, and by
increasing public opinion in a healthy way against tyranny—some people
call it, but perhaps a milder word would be better—against the unwise
policy used, it will do much to repress it in future " (*Conference Report*,
Sheffield, 1866).

[2] Rules adopted at Manchester Conference, 1867 (Sheffield, 1867,
12 pp.).

[3] The Alliance was always administered by an executive elected by
the Sheffield trades, the leading men amongst which had been active in
its formation.   The veteran secretary of the Typographical Society,
William Dronfield, was the first general secretary.   Among the trades
represented were the South Yorkshire and Nottingham Miners, the Amal-

1866, however, the Alliance was young and hopeful. It received its first blow in October of this year, when it and the Trade Union Conference were forgotten in the sensation produced by the explosion of a can of gunpowder in a workman's house in New Hereford Street, Sheffield.

This outrage was only one of a class of crimes for which Sheffield was already notorious. But in the state of public irritation against Trade Unionism, which had been growing during the past few years of lock-outs and strikes, the news served to precipitate events. On all sides there arose a cry for a searching investigation into Trade Unionism. The Trade Unions themselves joined in the demand. As no clue to the perpetrators of the last crime could be discovered by the local police, the leaders of the Sheffield trade clubs united with the Town Council and the local Employers' Association in pressing for a Government inquiry. The London Trades Council and the Executive of the Amalgamated Engineers sent a joint deputation to Sheffield to investigate the case. The deputation discovered no more than the local police had done about the perpetrators of the crime, and therefore innocently reported that there was no evidence of Trade Union complicity ; but they accompanied this report by a strong condemnation of " the abominable practice of rattening, which is calculated

gamated Tailors, Boilermakers, Cotton-spinners, Scottish Associated Carpenters, Yorkshire Glass-bottle Makers, North of England Iron-workers, and the trades of Wolverhampton. The minute books from 1867 to 1870, and its printed *Monthly Statement*, show that the Alliance at first supported the men in numerous lock-outs, especially among the tailors, miners, and ironworkers, but that there were constant complaints of unpaid levies. Dronfield informed us that the Judicial Committee and the Executive experienced great difficulties from the absence of any control over the constituent Unions, and the impossibility of accurately defining a lock-out. The first conference of the Alliance was held at Manchester from the 1st to the 4th of January 1867, when fifty-three trades had been enrolled, numbering 59,750 members. The " Rules " adopted at this conference contain an interesting address by Dronfield upon the principles and objects of the federation. The next conference was at Preston in September 1867, when the membership had fallen to 23,580, in forty-seven trades, the Boilermakers, among others, formally withdrawing (*Minutes of Conference at Preston*, Sheffield, 1867, 16 pp.).

to demoralise those who are concerned in it, and to bring disgrace on all trade combinations." [1] Public meetings of Trade Unionists were held throughout the country, at which the leaders expressed their indignation both at the outrage itself and at the common assumption that it was a usual and necessary incident of Trade Unionism. These meetings invariably concluded with a demand on behalf of the Trade Unionists to be allowed an opportunity of refuting the accusations of the enemies of the movement. Robert Applegarth saw the Home Secretary on the subject, and suggested a Commission of Inquiry. The appointment of a Royal Commission of Inquiry was officially announced in the Queen's Speech of February 1867. That the Government meant business was proved by the prompt introduction of a Bill empowering the Commission to pursue its investigations by exceptional means. The inquiry was to extend to all outrages during the past ten years, whether in Sheffield or elsewhere. Not only were accomplices in criminal acts promised an indemnity, provided that they

---

[1] The town of Sheffield had long been noted for the custom of "rattening," that is, the temporary abstraction of the wheelbands or tools of a workman whose subscription to his club was in arrear. This had become the recognised method of enforcing, not merely the payment of contributions, but also compliance with the trade regulations of the club. The lawless summary jurisdiction thus usurped by the Sheffield clubs easily passed into more serious acts of lynch law if mere rattening proved ineffectual. Recalcitrant workmen were terrorised by explosions of cans of gunpowder in the troughs of their grinding wheels, or thrown down their chimneys ; and in some cases these explosions caused serious injury. The various Grinders' Unions (saw, file, sickle, fork, and fender) enjoyed an unhappy notoriety for outrages of this natu1e, which had, from time to time, aroused the spasmodic indignation of the local press, notably in :843–4. An attempt, in 1861, to blow up a small warehouse in Acorn Street provoked a special outburst of public disapproval; and the minutes of the London Trades Council record that already on this occasion the Council publicly expressed its abhorrence of such criminal violence. After this date there was for three or four years a diminution in the number of serious acts of violence committed ; but the years 1865–6 saw a renewal of the evil practices, especially in connection with the Saw-Grinders' Union. The explosion in New Hereford Street in October 1866 was afterwards proved to have been instigated by this Union in order to terrorise a certain Thomas Fernehough, who had twice deserted the society, and was at the time working for a firm against whom the saw-handle makers, as well as the saw-grinders, had struck.

gave evidence, but the same privilege was extended to the actual perpetrators of the crimes. The investigation, moreover, was not restricted to the supposed criminal practices of particular trade clubs, but was to embrace the whole subject of Trade Unionism and its effects.

The Trade Union movement thus found itself for the third time at the bar of a Parliamentary inquiry at a moment when public opinion, as well as the enmity of employers, had been strongly excited against it. At the very height of this crisis, which had been brought about by the violence of some of the old-fashioned Unions, the new Amalgamated Societies themselves received a serious check from a decision of the Court of Queen's Bench.

The formation of the Amalgamated Society of Engineers, with its large accumulated funds, had renewed the anxiety of the Trade Union officials as to the extent to which a trade society enjoyed the protection of the law. Although the Act of 1825 had made trade societies, as such, no longer unlawful, nothing had been done to give them any legal status, or to enable them to take proceedings as corporate entities. But in 1855 a " Metropolitan Trades Committee " succeeded in getting a clause intended to relate to Trade Unions inserted in the Friendly Societies Act of that year. By the 44th section of this Act it was provided that a society established for any purpose not illegal might, by depositing its rules with the Registrar of Friendly Societies, enjoy the privilege of having disputes among its own members summarily dealt with by the magistrates. Under this provision several of the larger societies had deposited their rules, believing, with the concurrence of the Registrar, that this secured to them the power to proceed summarily against any member who should, in his capacity of secretary or treasurer, detain or make away with the society's funds.[1] So thoroughly has the legality of their position been accepted

---

[1] Among other societies, the Amalgamated Engineers and Carpenters and the national Unions of Boilermakers and Ironfounders appear to have deposited their rules.

by all concerned, that on the establishment by Gladstone
of the Post Office Savings Banks in 1861, he had, at the
request of the Trade Union leaders, expressly conceded to
the Unions, equally with the Friendly Societies, the privilege
of making use of the new banks.

This feeling of security was, in 1867, completely shattered.
The Boilermakers' Society had occasion to proceed against
the treasurer of their Bradford branch for wrongfully withholding the sum of £24 ; but the magistrates, to the general
surprise of all concerned, held that the society could not
proceed under the Friendly Societies Act, being, as a Trade
Union, outside the scope of that measure. The case was
thereupon carried to the Court of Queen's Bench, where
four judges, headed by the Lord Chief Justice, confirmed
the decision, giving the additional reason that the objects
of the Union, if not, since 1825, actually criminal, were yet
so far in restraint of trade as to render the society an illegal
association. Thus the officers of the great national Trade
Unions found their societies deprived of the legal status
which they imagined they had acquired, and saw themselves once more destitute of any legal protection for their
accumulated funds.

The grounds of the decision went a great deal further
than the decision itself. As was pointed out to the workmen by Frederic Harrison, " the judgement lays down not
merely that certain societies have failed to bring themselves
within the letter of a certain Act, but that Trade Unions,
of whatever sort, are in their nature contrary to public
policy, and that their object in itself will vitiate every
association and every transaction into which it enters. . . .
In a word, Unionism becomes (if not according to the
suggestion of the learned judge—criminal) at any rate
something like betting and gambling, public nuisances and
immoral considerations—things condemned and suppressed
by the law." [1]

Trade Unionism was now at bay, assailed on both sides.

[1] *Beehive*, January 26, 1867.

It was easy to foresee that the employers and their allies would make a determined attempt to use the Royal Commission and the Sheffield outrages to suppress Trade Unionism by the criminal law. On the other hand, the hard-earned accumulations of the larger societies, by this time amounting to an aggregate of over a quarter of a million sterling, were at the mercy of their whole army of branch secretaries and treasurers, any one of whom might embezzle the funds with impunity.

The crisis was too serious to be dealt with by the excited delegate meetings of the London Trades Council. For over four years we hear of only occasional and purely formal meetings of this body. Immediately on the publication of the decision of the judges in January 1867 Applegarth convened what was called a " Conference of Amalgamated Trades," but what consisted in reality of weekly private meetings of the five leaders and a few other friends. From 1867 to 1871 this " conference " acted as the effective cabinet of the Trade Union Movement. Its private minute-book, kept by Applegarth, reveals to the student the whole political life of the Trade Union world.

The first action of the Junta was to call to their councils those middle-class allies upon whose assistance and advice they had learned to rely. We have already noticed the adhesion of the " Christian Socialists " to the Amalgamated Engineers in 1852, and the intervention of the Positivists in the Building Trades disputes of 1859–61. Frederic Harrison and E. S. Beesly were now rendering specially valuable services as the apologists for Trade Unionism in the public press. " Tom Hughes " was in Parliament, almost the only spokesman of the men's whole claim. Henry Crompton was bringing his acute judgement and his detailed experience of the actual working of the law to bear upon the dangers which beset the Unions in the Courts of Justice. Applegarth's minutes show how frequently all four were ready to spend hours in private conference at the Engineers' office in Stamford Street, and how unreservedly they, in this crisis, placed their professional skill at the disposal of the Trade Union leaders. It would be difficult to exaggerate the zeal and patient devotion of these friends of Trade Unionism, or the service which they rendered to the cause in its hour of trial.[1]

It is obvious from the private transactions of the conference that the main object of the Junta was to gain for Trade Unionism that legal status which was necessary alike to the security of the funds and to the recognition of the Trade Union organisation as a constituent part of the State. But the first thing to be done was to defeat the employers in their endeavour to use the Royal Commission as an instrument for suppressing Trade Unionism by direct penal enactment. The Junta had therefore not only to dissociate themselves from the ignorant turbulence of the old-fashioned Unions, but also to prove that the bulk of their own members were enlightened and respectable. It was, moreover, of the utmost importance to persuade the public that the Junta and their friends, not the strike-jobbers or the outrage-mongers, were the authorised and typical representatives of the Trade Union Movement. All this it was necessary to bring out in the inquiry by the Royal Commission before which Trade Unionism was presently to stand on its defence. The composition of the Commission was accordingly a matter of the greatest concern for the Junta. The Government had resolved to select, as Commissioners, not representatives of each view, but persons presumably impartial, with Sir William Erle, who had lately retired from the Lord Chief Justiceship of the Common Pleas, as their chairman. In this arrangement representatives of the employers were to be excluded ; and the appointment of working men was not dreamed of. The Commission was to be made up

---

[1] Along with these, in helping and advising the Trade Unions at this time, were Vernon Lushington, Godfrey Lushington (afterwards Permanent Under-Secretary of State for the Home Department), J. M. Ludlow (afterwards Registrar of Friendly Societies), Neate (formerly Professor of Political Economy and then M.P. for Oxford), Sir T. Fowell Buxton, M.P., and A. J. Mundella.

chiefly from the ranks of high officials, with four members from the two Houses of Parliament, and the chairman of a great industrial undertaking. The active part which Thomas Hughes had taken in the debates secured him a seat on the Commission, though he felt that single-handed he could do little for his friends. All possible pressure was accordingly brought to bear on the Government with a view to the appointment of a Trade Unionist member ; but the idea of a working-man Royal Commissioner was inconsistent with official traditions. The utmost that could be obtained was that the workmen and the employers should each suggest a special representative to be added. For the workmen a wise and extremely fortunate choice was made in the person of Frederic Harrison, the Junta obtaining also permission for representative Trade Unionists to be present during the examination of the witnesses.[1]

The actual conduct of the Trade Unionist case was undertaken by Harrison and Hughes, in consultation with Applegarth, whom the Junta deputed to attend the sittings on their behalf. The ground of defence was chosen with considerable shrewdness. The policy of the Junta and their allies was to focus the attention of the Commissioners upon the great trade friendly societies in contradistinction to the innumerable little local trade clubs of the old type. The evidence of Applegarth, who was the first witness examined, did much to dispel the grosser prejudices against the Unions. The General Secretary of the Amalgamated Society of Carpenters was able to show that his society, then standing third in financial magnitude in the Trade Union world, far

[1] The Junta did not, however, confine its efforts to action before the Commission. One of the taunts constantly thrown by the press at the Trade Union leaders was that they did not themselves know what they wanted. Partly as a reply to this, but also as a manifesto to consolidate the Unionist forces, in the autumn of 1867 a Bill was prepared by Henry Crompton and laid before the Junta, and after considerable discussion adopted by them and by a delegate meeting of Trades held at the Bell Inn. It was introduced into the House of Commons early in the following session, and served as basis of the Trade Union demand at some of the elections in 1868, notably that of Sheffield when A. J. Mundella first was candidate.

from fomenting strikes, was mainly occupied in the work
of an insurance company. He was in a position to lay
effective stress on the total absence of secrecy or coercion
in its proceedings. He disclaimed, on behalf of its members, all objection to machinery, foreign imports, piecework,
overtime, or the free employment of apprentices. The
fundamental position upon which he entrenched his Trade
Unionism was the maintenance, at all hazards, of the
Standard Rate of Wages and the Standard Hours of Labour,
to be secured by the accumulation of such a fund as would
enable every member of the Union effectually to set a reserve-
price on his labour. William Allan, who came up on the
third day, followed Applegarth's lead, though with some
reservations ; and the evidence of these two officers of what
were primarily national friendly societies made a marked
impression on the Commission.

The employers were not as well served as the men. It
is true that they succeeded, in spite of Applegarth's dis-
claimers, in persuading the Commission that some of the
most powerful Unions strenuously objected to piecework
and sub-contract in any form whatsoever, and in some
instances even to machinery. In other cases it was proved
that attempts were made to enforce a rigid limitation of
apprentices. Owing to the energy of the Central Association of Master Builders, the restrictive policy of the older
Unions in the building trades was brought well to the
front ; and this fact accounts, even to-day, for most of the
current impression of Trade Unionism among the middle
and upper classes. But the employers did not discriminate
in their attack. Almost with one accord they objected to
the whole principle of Trade Unionism. They reiterated
with a curious impenetrability the old argument of the
" individual bargain," and protested against any kind of
industrial organisation on the part of their employees. All
attempts by the men to claim collectively any share in
regulating the conditions of labour were denounced as " un-
warrantable encroachments on their rights as employers."

The number of apprentices, like indeed the whole administration of industry, was claimed as of private concern, the settlement of which " exclusively belongs to the employer himself ; a matter in which no other party, much less the operatives, have got anything to do." And they objected even more to the centrally administered national society with extensive reserve funds than to the isolated local clubs whose spasmodic outbursts they could afford to disregard. But the confusion between the small local bodies with their narrow policy of outrage and violence, and the amalgamated societies with their far-reaching power and accumulated wealth, effective as it had been in alarming the public, proved disastrous to the employers when their case was subjected to the acute cross-examination of Frederic Harrison. The masters, by directing their attack mainly on the great Amalgamated Societies and the newly-formed local Trades Councils, played, in fact, directly into the hands of the Junta. It was easy for Allan and Applegarth to show that the influence of central Executive Councils and the formation of a public opinion among trade societies tended to restrain the more aggressive action of men embittered by a local quarrel. The combination of friendly benefits with trade objects was destined to be hotly attacked twenty years later by the more ardent spirits in the Trade Union world, as leading to inertia and supineness in respect of wages, hours, and conditions of labour. The evidence adduced in 1867–8, read in the light of later events, reveals that this tendency had already begun ; and it was impossible for the Commissioners to resist the conclusion that they had, in the Amalgamated Engineers and Carpenters, types of a far less aggressive Trade Unionism than such survivals as the purely trade societies of the brickmakers or the Sheffield industries.

Foiled in this attempt the employers fell back upon an indictment of the Amalgamated Unions considered as friendly societies. The leading actuaries were called to prove that neither the Amalgamated Engineers nor the

Amalgamated Carpenters could possibly meet their accumulating liabilities, and that these must, in a few years, inevitably bring both societies to bankruptcy.   The whole of
this evidence is a striking instance of the untrustworthiness
of expert witnesses off their own ground.   Neither Finlaison
nor Tucker, who were called as actuaries on behalf of the
employers, ever realised that a Trade Union, unlike a
Friendly Society, possesses and constantly exercises an unlimited power to raise funds by special levies, or by increased contributions, whenever it may seem good to the
majority of the members.   But even had the actuarial indictment been completely warranted, it was a mistake in
tactics on the part of the employers.   The Commissioners
found themselves shunted into an inquiry, not into the
results of Trade Unionism upon the common weal, but into
the arithmetical soundness of the financial arrangements
which particular groups of workmen chose to make among
themselves.

Meanwhile the primary business of the Commission, the
investigation into the Sheffield outrages, had been remitted
to special " examiners," whose local inquiry attracted far
less attention than the proceedings of the main body.   At
first the investigation elicited little that was new ; but in
June 1867 the country was startled by dramatic confessions
on the part of Broadhead and other members of the grinders'
trade clubs, unravelling a series of savage crimes instigated
by them, and paid for out of Club funds.   For a short time
it looked as if all the vague accusations hurled at Trade
Unionism at large were about to be justified ; but the
examiners reported that four-fifths of the societies even of
the Sheffield trades were free from outrages, and that these
had been most prevalent from 1839 to 1861, and had since
declined.   The only other place in which the Commissioners
thought it necessary to make inquiry into outrages was
Manchester, where the Brickmakers' Union had committed
many crimes, but where no complicity on the part of other
trades was shown.   It was made evident to all candid

students that these criminal acts were not chargeable to Trade Unionism as a whole. They represented, in fact, the survival among such rough and isolated trades as the brickmakers and grinders of the barbarous usages of a time when working men felt themselves outside the law, and oppressed by tyranny.[1]

The success with which the case of the Trade Unionists had been presented to the Commission was reflected in a changed attitude on the part of the governing class, a change expressly attributed to the " greater knowledge and wider experience " of Trade Unions which had been gained through the Royal Commission. " True statesmanship," declared the *Times*, " will seek neither to augment nor to reduce their influence, but, accepting it as a fact, will give it free scope for legitimate development." [2] Thus the official report of the Commission, from which the enemies of Trade Unionism had hoped so much, contained no recommendation which would have made the position of any single Union worse than it was before. An inconclusive and somewhat inconsistent document, it argued that trade combination could be of no real economic advantage to the workman, but nevertheless recommended the legalisation of the Unions under certain conditions. Whereas the Act of 1825 had excepted from the common illegality only combinations in respect of wages or hours of labour, the

---

[1] The Broadhead disclosures created a great stir, and Professor Beesly, who had ventured to point out " that a trades union murder was neither better nor worse than any other murder," was denounced as an apologist for crime, and nearly lost his professorship at University College, London, for his sturdy defence of the principle of Trade Unionism. See his pamphlet, *The Sheffield Outrages and the Meeting at Exeter Hall*, 1867, 16 pp. ; and that by Richard Congreve, *Mr. Broadhead and the Anonymous Press*, 1867, 16 pp.

[2] *Times* leader, July 8, 1869. The occasion was the epoch-marking speech of Mr. (afterwards Lord) Brassey, in which, speaking as the son of a great contractor, he declared himself on the side of the Trade Unions, and asserted that, by exercising a beneficial influence on the character of the workmen, they tended to lower rather than to raise the cost of labour (Hansard's Parliamentary Debates, July 7, 1869). The speech was afterwards republished, with some additions, under the title of *Trade Unions and the Cost of Labour*, by T. Brassey, 1870, 64 pp.

Commissioners recommended that no combination should henceforth be liable to prosecution for restraint of trade, except those formed " to do acts which involved breach of contract," and to refuse to work with any particular person. But the privilege of registration, carrying with it the power to obtain legal protection for the society's funds, was to be conferred only on Unions whose rules were free from certain restrictive clauses, such as the limitation of apprentices or of the use of machinery, and the prohibition of piecework and sub-contract. The employers' influence on the Commission was further shown in a special refusal of the privilege of registration to societies whose rules authorised the support of the disputes of other trades.

So far the result of the Commission was purely negative. No hostile legislation was even suggested. On the other hand, it was obvious that no Trade Union would accept " legalisation " on the proposed conditions. But Harrison and Hughes had not restricted themselves to casting out all dangerous proposals from the majority report. Their minority report, which was signed also by the Earl of Lichfield, exposed in terse paragraphs the futility of the suggestions made by the majority, and laid down in general terms the principles upon which all future legislation should proceed. It advocated the removal of all special legislation relating to labour contracts, on the principle, first, that no act should be illegal if committed by a workman unless it was equally illegal if committed by any other person ; and secondly, that no act by a combination of men should be regarded as criminal if it would not have been criminal in a single person. To this was appended a detailed statement, drafted by Frederic Harrison, in which the character and objects of Trade Unionism, as revealed in the voluminous evidence taken by the Commission, were explained and defended with consummate skill. What was perhaps of even greater service to the Trade Union world was a precise and detailed exposition of the various amendments required to bring the law into accordance with the general principles referred to. We have here a striking instance of the advantage to a Labour Movement of expert professional advice. The Junta had been demanding the complete legalisation of their Unions in the same manner as ordinary Friendly Societies. They had failed to realise that such a legalisation would have exposed the Amalgamated Society of Engineers to be sued by one of its members who might be excluded for " blacklegging," or otherwise working contrary to the interests of the trade. The whole efficacy, from a Trade Union point of view, of the amalgamation of trade and friendly benefits would have been destroyed. The bare légalisation would have brought the Trades Unions under the general law, and subjected them to constant and harassing interference by Courts of Justice. They had grown up in despite of the law and the lawyers ; which as regards the spirit of the one and the prejudices of the other were, and still are, alien and hostile to the purposes and collective action of the Trades Societies. The danger of any member having power to take legal proceedings, to worry them by litigation and cripple them by legal expenses, or to bring a society within the scope of the insolvency and bankruptcy law, became very apparent. The Junta easily realised, when their advisers explained the position, that mere legalisation would place the most formidable weapon in the hands of unscrupulous employers. To avoid this difficulty Harrison proposed the ingenious plan of bringing the Trade Union under the Friendly Societies Acts, so far as regards the protection of its funds against theft or fraud, whilst retaining to the full the exceptional legal privilege of being incapable of being sued or otherwise proceeded against as a corporate entity. Had a Trade Union official been selected as the sole representative of the Unions on the Commission, such detailed and ingenious amendments of the law would not have been devised and made part of an authoritative official report. The complete charter of Trade Union liberty, which Harrison and his friends had elaborated, became for seven years the political programme of the Trade Unionists.

And it is a part of the curious irony of English party politics that whilst the formation of this programme, and the agitation by which it was pressed on successive Parliaments, were both of them exclusively the work of a group of Radicals it was, as we shall see, a Conservative Cabinet which eventually passed it into law.[1]

The effective though informal leadership of the movement which the Junta had assumed during the sittings of the Royal Commission had not gone entirely unquestioned. Those who are interested in the cross-currents of personal intrigues and jealousies which detract from the force of popular movements can read in the pages of the *Beehive* full accounts of the machinations of George Potter. The *Beehive* summoned a Trade Union Conference at St. Martin's Hall in March 1867, which was attended by over one hundred delegates from provincial societies, Trades Councils, and the minor London clubs.[2] The Junta, perhaps rather unwisely, refused to have anything to do with a meeting held under Potter's auspices. But many of their provincial allies came up without any suspicion of the sectional character of the conference, and found themselves in the anomalous position of countenancing what was really an attempt to seduce the London Trades from their allegiance

---

[1] The Sheffield Outrages and the Royal Commission produced a large crop of literature, most of which is of little value. The Commission itself presented no fewer than eleven reports, with voluminous evidence and appendices. The Examiners appointed to investigate the outrages at Sheffield and Manchester presented separate reports, which were laid before Parliament. The mass of detailed information about strikes and other proceedings of Trade Societies contained in these reports has been the main source of all subsequent writings on the subject. *The Trade Unions of England*, by the Comte de Paris, 1869, 246 pp., and *The Trade Unions*, by Robert Somers (Edinburgh, 1876, 232 pp.), are, for instance, little better than summaries, the former friendly, the latter unfriendly, of the evidence before the Commission. The chapters relating to Trade Unionism in W. T. Thornton's work *On Labour*, 1870, which made so permanent an impression on the economic world, are entirely based upon the same testimony. Among other publications may be mentioned *Trades Unions Defended*, by W. R. Callender (Manchester, 1870, 16 pp.) ; and *Measures for Putting an End to the Abuses of Trades Unions*, by Frederic Hill, 1868, 16 pp.

[2] *Report of the Trades Conference*, 1867, 32 pp.

to the Junta and the London Trades Council. The Conference sat for four days, and made, owing to Potter's energy, no little stir. A committee was appointed to conduct the Trade Union case before the Commission, and Conolly, the President of the Operative Stonemasons, was deputed to attend the sittings. But although special prominence was given by the *Beehive* to all the proceedings of this committee, we have failed to discover with what it actually concerned itself. An indiscreet speech by Conolly quickly led to his exclusion from the sittings of the Commission ; and the management of the Trade Union case remained in the hands of Applegarth and the Junta.

Apart, however, from jealousy and personal intrigue, there was some genuine opposition to the policy of the Junta. The great mass of Trade Unionists were not yet converted to the necessity of obtaining for their societies a recognised legal status. There were even many experienced officials, especially in the provincial organisations of the older type, who deprecated the action that was being taken by the London leaders, on the express ground that they objected to legalisation. " The less working men have to do with the law in any shape the better," was the constant note of the old Unionists. This view found abundant expression at the Congresses convened in 1868 by the Manchester Trades Council, and in 1869 by that of Birmingham. But in spite of the absence of the Junta from the Manchester Congress, their friend, John Kane, of the North of England Ironworkers' Association, succeeded in inducing the delegates to pass a resolution expressing full confidence in the policy and action of the Conference of Amalgamated Trades.[1] And at the Congress of 1869, Odger and Howell, as representatives of the Junta, managed to get adopted a series of resolutions embodying Frederic Harrison's proposals.[2]

Meanwhile a change had come over the political situation. At the outset of the crisis Frederic Harrison had urged upon the Trade Union world the necessity of turning

[1] *Beehive*, June 13, 1868.   [2] *Ibid.*, August 28, 1869.

to the polling booth for redress. " Nothing," he writes in January, 1867, " will force the governing classes to recognise [the workmen's] claims and judge them fairly, until they find them wresting into their own hands real political power. Unionists who, till now, have been content with their Unions, and have shrunk from political action, may see the pass to which this abstinence from political movements has brought them." [1] Within a few months of this advice the Reform Bill of 1867 had enfranchised the working man in the boroughs. The Trade Union leaders were not slow to use the advantage thus given to them. The Junta, under the convenient cloak of the Conference of Amalgamated Trades, issued, in July, 1868, a circular urging upon Trade Unionists the importance of registering their names as electors, and of pressing on every candidate the question in which they were primarily interested. The Trades Councils throughout the country followed suit ; and we find the Junta's electoral tactics adopted even by societies which were traditionally opposed to all political action. The Central Committee of the Stonemasons, for instance, strongly urged their members to vote at the ensuing election only for candidates who would support Trade Union demands. [2]

By the beginning of 1869 Frederic Harrison had drafted a comprehensive Bill, embodying all the legislative proposals of his minority report. This was introduced by Mundella and Hughes, and although its provisions were received with denunciations by the employers, [3] it gained some support among the newly elected members, and was strongly backed up outside the House. The Liberal Government of that day, and nearly all the members of the House of Commons, were still covertly hostile to the very principles

---

[1] *Beehive*, January 26, 1867.

[2] *Fortnightly Circular*, June 1868.

[3] See, for instance, *Some opinions on Trade Unions and the Bill of 1869*, by Edmund Potter, M.P., 1869, 45 pp. ; also the *Observations upon the Law of Combinations and Trades Unions, and upon the Trades Unions Bill*, by a Barrister, 1869, 64 pp.

of Trade Unionism, and every attempt was made to burke the measure.[1] But the Junta were determined to make felt their new political power. From every part of the country pressure was put upon members of Parliament. A great demonstration of workmen was held at Exeter Hall, at which Mundella and Hughes declared their intention of forcing the House and the Ministry to vote upon the hated measure. Finding evasion no longer possible, the Government abandoned its attitude of hostility and agreed to a formal second reading, upon the understanding that the Cabinet would next year bring in a Bill of its own. A provisional measure giving temporary protection to Trade Union funds was accordingly hurried through Parliament at the end of the session pending the introduction of a complete Bill.[2] The Junta had gained the first victory of their political campaign.

[1] In his *Letters to the Working Classes,* 1870, Professor Beesly gives a graphic account of the shuffling of the Government, and advises political action. The annual report of the General Union of House Painters (the "Manchester Alliance") for 1871 shows how eagerly the advice was received : " Away with the cry of no politics in our Unions ; this foolish neutrality has left us without power or influence." See also, for the whole episode, *Robert Applegarth,* by A. W. Humphrey, 1912, pp. 138-170 ; *Labour Legislation, Labour Movements and Labour Leaders,* by G. Howell, 1902, pp. 156-172.

[2] 32 and 33 Vic. c. 61 (1869). This provisional measure was bitterly opposed in the House of Lords by Earl Cairns, who argued that its universal protection of the funds of all Unions alike, without requiring the abandonment of their objectionable rules, was in direct opposition to the majority report of the Royal Commission. No such surrender to the Trade Unions was, in his opinion, necessary, as their funds had, in the previous year, been incidentally protected by an " Act to amend the law relating to larceny and embezzlement " (31 and 32 Vic. c. 116), passed at the instance of Russell Gurney, the Recorder of London. This act had no reference to Trade Unions as such, but it enabled members of a co-partnership to be convicted for stealing or embezzling the funds of their co-partnership. Its possible application to defaulting Trade Union officials was perceived by Messrs. Shaen, Roscoe & Co., who have for three generations acted as solicitors of the leading Unions. At their instance a case was submitted to the Attorney-General of the time (Sir John Karslake), who advised that a Trade Union could now prosecute in its character of a partnership. Criminal proceedings were accordingly taken by the Operative Bricklayers' Society against a defaulting officer who had set the Executive at defiance, with the result that the prisoner was, in December 1868, sentenced to six months' hard labour. This successful

The next session found the Government reluctant to fulfil its promise in the matter. But the Trade Unionists were not disposed to let the question sleep, and after much pressure Henry Bruce (afterwards Lord Aberdare), who was then Home Secretary, produced, in 1871, a Bill which was eagerly scanned by the Trade Union world. The Government proposed to concede all the points on which it had been specially pressed by the Junta. No Trade Union, however wide its objects, was henceforth to be illegal merely because it was " in restraint of trade." Every Union was to be entitled to be registered, if its rules were not expressly in contravention of the criminal law. And, finally, the registration which gave the Unions complete protection for their funds was so devised as to leave untouched their internal organisation and arrangements, and to prevent their being sued or proceeded against in a court of law.

The employers vehemently attacked the Government for conceding, as they said, practically all the Trade Union demands.[1] But from the men's point of view this " complete charter legalising Unions " had a serious drawback. The Bill, as was complained, " while repealing the Combination Laws, substituted another penal law against workmen " as such. A lengthy clause provided that any violent threat or molestation for the purpose of coercing either employers or employed should be severely punished. All the terms of the old Combination Laws, " molest," " obstruct," " threaten," " intimidate," and so forth, were used

---

prosecution was widely advertised throughout the Trade Union world, and was frequently quoted as showing that no further legislation was needed. But, as was forcibly pointed out by Frederic Harrison and other advisers of the Junta, Russell Gurney's Act, though it enabled Trade Unions to put defaulting officials in prison, gave them no power to recover the sums due, or to take any civil proceedings whatever, and did not remove the illegality of any combinations of workmen " in restraint of trade." See Harrison's article, " The Trades Union Bill," in *Fortnightly Review*, July 1, 1869, and the leaflet published by the Amalgamated Society of Engineers, on Russell Gurney's Act, December, 1868.

[1] See, for instance, the report of the Leeds meeting of the Master Builders' Association to object to the Bill, *Beehive*, March 11, 1871.

without any definition or limitation, and picketing, moreover, was expressly included in molestation or obstruction
by a comprehensive prohibition of " persistently following "
any person, or " watching or besetting " the premises in
which he was, or the approach to such premises. The Act
of 1859, which had expressly legalised peaceful persuasion
to join legal combinations, was repealed.[1] It seemed only
too probable that the Government measure would make it
a criminal offence for two Trade Unionists to stand quietly
in the street opposite the works of an employer against
whom they had struck, in order to communicate peacefully
the fact of the strike to any workmen who might be ignorant
of it.

It does not appear that Bruce's fiercely resented " Third

[1] A short Act had been passed in 1859 (22 Vic. c. 34) which excluded
from the definition of " molestation " or " obstruction " the mere agreement to obtain an alteration of wages or hours, and also the peaceful
persuasion of others without threat or intimidation to cease or abstain
from work in order to obtain the wages or hours aimed at. The Act
was passed without discussion or comment, probably with reference to
some recent judicial decisions, but its actual origin is not clear. The
Stonemasons' Society refused to have anything to do with it, and referred sneeringly to its promoters as busybodies. Alexander Macdonald
alluded to it in his speech on the Employers and Workmen Bill on June 28,
1875 (Hansard, vol. 225, pp. 66-7), as having been enacted at the instance
of himself and others in order to permit men to persuade others to join
combinations, and that it had had a most beneficial effect. An obscure
pamphlet, entitled *Letters to the Trades Unionists and the Working Classes*,
by Charles Sturgeon, 1868, 8 pp., gives the only account of its origin that
we have seen. " Some of the judges had decided that the liberty to
combine was only during the period he was not in the employ of any
master (*i.e.* while on tramp). So obvious a misreading, under which the
working men were getting imprisoned, while their masters combined at
their pleasure, created numerous petitions for relief, which lay as usual on
the table ; however, the Executive of the National Association of United
Trades assembled in my rooms in Abingdon Street, and we drew a little
Bill of nine lines in length to explain to the judges how they had failed
to explain the views of the legislator. . . . I introduced our friends to
the late Henry Drummond, Thomas Duncombe, and Joseph Hume, two
Radicals and an honest Tory, and, strange to say, they worked well
together when in pursuit of justice. After fighting hard against the
great Liberal Party for four or five years, we passed our little Bill (22
Vic. c. 34), to the great joy of the working classes and chagrin of the
Manchester Radicals." But the decision of the R. *v.* Druitt and
R. *v.* Bailey in 1867 showed that it did not serve to protect pickets from
prosecution.

Clause " was intended to effect any alteration in the law
Its comprehensive prohibition of violence, threats, intimidation, molestation, and obstruction did no more than sum
up and codify the various judicial decisions of past years
under which the Trade Unionists had suffered. But the
law had hitherto been obscure and conflicting ; both the
statutes and the judicial decisions had proceeded largely
from a presumption against the very existence of Trade
Unionism which was now passing away ; and the workmen
and their advisers not unreasonably feared the consequences
of an explicit re-enactment of provisions which practically
made criminal all the usual methods of trade combination.
A recent decision had brought the danger home to the minds
of the Trade Union leaders and their legal friends. In
July 1867 a great strike had broken out among the London
tailors, in which the masters' shops had been carefully
" picketed." [1]   Druitt, Shorrocks, and other officers of the

---

[1] Henry Crompton gives the following account of the practice of
picketing :—" Picketing is generally much misunderstood. It occurs in
a strike when war has begun. The struggle, of course, consists in the
employer trying to get fresh men, and the men on strike trying to prevent
this. They naturally do their best to induce all others to join them.
Very often the country is scoured by the employers, and men brought
long distances who never would have come if they had known there was
a strike. Men do not wish to undersell their fellows. A man is posted
as a picket, to give information of the grievances complained of, and to
urge the fresh comers not to defeat the strike that is going on.

" Not only is this justifiable, but it is far better that this should be
legal and practised in full publicity than that it should be illegal and done
secretly, for, if done secretly, then bad practices are sure to arise. No
doubt it is done with a view to coerce the employers, just as the lock-out
is with a view to coerce the employed.

" Picketing has other uses and effects. It enables those on strike to
know whether the employers are getting men, and what probability there
is of the strike being successful, to check any fraudulent claims for strike
pay. Besides this, the publicity which the system of picketing gives
does, doubtless, exercise a considerable influence upon men's conduct.
Those on strike naturally regard any one acting contrary to the general
interests of the trade with disfavour, just as an unpatriotic man is condemned by those imbued with a higher sense of national duty. Picketing
is justified on these grounds by the workmen, but all physical molestation or intimidation is condemned. The workmen have never urged that
such proceedings should not be repressed by penal law." (See *The Labour
Law Commission*, by Henry Crompton, adopted and published by the
Parliamentary Committee of the Trades Union Congress.)

Union were thereupon indicted, not for personal violence or actual molestation, but for the vague crime of conspiracy. The Judge (Baron, afterwards Lord, Bramwell) held that pickets, if acting in combination, were guilty of " molestation " if they gave annoyance only by black looks, or even by their presence in large numbers, without any acts or gestures of violence, and that if two or more persons combined to do anything unpleasant and annoying to another person they were guilty of a common law offence. The Tailors' officers and committeemen were found guilty merely of organising peaceful picketing, and it became evident that, if the elastic law of conspiracy could thus be brought to bear on Trade Union disputes, practically every incident of strike management might become a crime.[1] Nor did Druitt's case stand alone. Within the memory of the Junta men had been sent to prison for the simple act of striking, or even for a simple agreement to strike.[2] Indeed, merely giving notice of a projected strike, even in the most courteous and peaceful manner, had frequently been held to be an act of intimidation punishable as a crime.[3] In 1851 the posting up of placards announcing a strike was held to be intimidation of the employers.[4] The Government Bill, far from accepting Frederic Harrison's proposed repeal of all criminal legislation specially applying to workmen, left these judicial decisions untouched, and, by re-enacting them in

---

[1] Baron Bramwell's view of the law excited much animadversion even among lawyers. See Stephen's *History of the Criminal Law*, vol. iii. pp. 221-2. R. *v*. Druitt is reported in 10 Cox, 600.

[2] R. *v*. Hewitt, 5 Cox, 162 (1851). Compare also the observations of Mr. Justice Hannam as to the mere act of striking being in itself sometimes criminal, in Farrer *v*. Close, 4 L.R.Q.B. 612 (1869).

[3] R. *v*. Hewitt, 5 Cox, C.C. 163 (1851).

[4] See Walsby *v*. Anley, 30 L.J.M.C. 121 (1861) ; Skinner *v*. Kitch, 10 Cox, 493 (1867) ; O'Neil *v*. Kruger, 4 Best and Smith, 389 (1863) ; Wood *v*. Bowron, 2 Law Report, Q.B. 21 (1866) ; R. *v*. Rowlands, 5 Cox, C.C. 493 (1851).

Compare on the whole subject the Appendix to our *Industrial Democracy*, 1897; *The Law of Criminal Conspiracies and Agreements*, by R. S. (afterwards Mr. Justice) Wright (1873); Sir William Erle's *Law Relating to Trade Unions* (1873) ; and Stephen's *History of the Criminal Law*, vol. iii. chap. xxx.

a codified form, proposed even to make their operation more uniform and effectual.

There was, accordingly, some ground for the assertion of the Trade Unionists that the Government was withdrawing with one hand what it was giving with the other. It seemed of little use to declare the existence of trade societies to be legal if the criminal law was so stretched as to include the ordinary peaceful methods by which these societies attained their ends. Above all, the Trade Unionists angrily resented the idea that any act should be made criminal if done by them, or in furtherance of their Unions, that was not equally a crime if committed by any other person, or in pursuance of the objects of any other kind of association.

A storm of indignation arose in the Trade Union world. The Junta sat in anxious consultation with their legal advisers, who all counselled the utmost resistance to this most dangerous re-enactment of the law. A delegate meeting of the London trades was summoned to protest against the criminal clauses of Bruce's Bill. But it was necessary to attack the House of Commons from a wider area than the Metropolis. With this view the Junta determined to follow the example set by the Manchester and Birmingham Trades Councils in 1868 and 1869 by calling together a national Trade Union Congress.[1]

---

[1] Whilst the constant meetings of the Junta, the informal cabinet of the movement, grew out of the great Amalgamated Societies, the Trades Union Congress, or " Parliament of Labour," took its rise in the Trades Councils. We have already described the special Conference held in London in 1864, on the Master and Servant Law, which was convened by the Glasgow Trades Council, and its successor, summoned by the Sheffield Trades Council in 1867 to concert measures of defence against lock-outs. But the credit of initiating the idea of an Annual Conference to deal with all subjects of interest to the Trade Union world belongs to the Manchester and Salford Trades Council, who issued in April 1868 a circular (fortunately preserved in the *Ironworkers' Journal* for May 1868, and printed at the end of this volume) convening a Congress to be held in Manchester during Whit-week, 1868. This Congress was attended by thirty-four delegates, who claimed to represent about 118,000 Trade Unionists. The place of meeting of the next Congress was fixed at Birmingham, and the delegates were in due course convened by the Birmingham Trades Council.

The meeting of the Congress was fixed for March 1871, by which time it was rightly calculated that the obnoxious Bill would be actually under discussion in the House of Commons. The delegates spent most of their time in denouncing the criminal clauses of the Bill, and came very near to opposing the whole measure. But it was ultimately agreed to accept the legalising part of the Bill, whilst using every effort to throw out the Third Section. A deputation was sent to the Home Secretary. Protest after protest was despatched to the legislators, and the Congress adjourned at half-past four each day, in order, as it was expressly declared, that delegates might " devote the evening to waiting upon Members of Parliament." But neither the Government nor the House of Commons was disposed to show any favour to Trade Union action in restraint of that " free competition " and individual bargaining which had so long been the creed of the employers. The utmost concession that could be obtained was that the

---

This second Congress, which met in August 1869, included forty-eight delegates from forty separate societies, having, it was said, 250,000 members. But although these general congresses were attended by some of the most prominent of the provincial Trade Unionists, they were rather frowned on by the London Junta. The thirty-four delegates at the Manchester Congress included indeed hardly any Metropolitan delegates other than George Potter. Half a dozen representatives from London societies went to the Birmingham Congress, including Odger and George Howell, but when a Parliamentary Committee was appointed Odger refused to serve upon it, regarding it apparently as an unnecessary rival of the Conference of Amalgamated Trades. The next Congress was appointed for London in 1870, but the London leaders took no steps to convene it, until it became necessary, as we have seen, to call up all forces to oppose the projected legislation of 1871. The London Congress of March 1871 was, in fact, the first in which the real leaders of the movement took part, and the Parliamentary Committee which it appointed, acting at first in conjunction with Applegarth's Conference, naturally took the place of this on its dissolution. The 1872 Congress at Nottingham was attended by seventy-seven delegates, representing 375,000 members. Reports of the earliest four congresses must be sought in the *Beehive* and (as regards those of Manchester, Birmingham, and Nottingham) in the contemporary local newspapers. From 1873 onward the Congress has issued an authorised report of its proceedings. A useful chronological record has now been published by W. J. Davis, entitled *A History of the British Trades Union Congress*, vol. i. 1910; vol. ii. 1916.

Bill should be divided into two, so that the law legalising the existence of trade societies might stand by itself, whilst the criminal clauses restraining their action were embodied in a separate " Criminal Law Amendment Bill." This illusory concession sufficed to detach from the opposition many of those who had at the General Election professed friendship to the Unions. In the main debate Thomas Hughes and A. J. Mundella stood almost alone in pressing the Trade Unionists' full demands ; and though a few other members were inclined to help to some extent, the second reading was agreed to without a division. The other stages were rapidly run through without serious opposition. In the House of Lords the provisions against picketing were made even more stringent, " watching and besetting " by a single individual being made as criminal as " watching and besetting " by a multitude. In this unsatisfactory shape the two Bills passed into law.[1] Trade Societies became, for the first time, legally recognised and fully protected associations ; whilst, on the other hand, the legislative prohibition of Trade Union action was expressly reaffirmed, and even increased in stringency.

In the eyes of the Trade Unions this result amounted to a defeat ; and the conduct of the Government caused the bitterest resentment.[2] The Secretaries of the Amalgamated Societies, especially Allan and Applegarth, had, indeed, attained the object which they personally had most at heart. The great organisations for mutual succour, which had been built up by their patient sagacity, were now, for the first time, assured of complete legal protection. A number of the larger societies promptly availed themselves of the Trade Union Act, by registering their rules in accordance with its provisions ;[3] and in September

---

[1] 34 and 35 Vic. c. 31 (Trade Union Act), and 34 and 35 Vic. c. 32 (Criminal Law Amendment Act).

[2] See, for instance, the article by Henry Crompton in the *Beehive*, September 2, 1871.

[3] The Operative Bricklayers' Society (London), of which Coulson was general secretary, stands No. 1 on the Register.

1871 the Conference of Amalgamated Trades "having," as its final minutes declared, "discharged the duties for which it was organised," formally dissolved itself.

The wider issue which remained to be fought required a more representative organisation. In struggling for legal recognition the Junta had, as we have seen, represented the more enlightened of the Trade Unionists rather than the whole movement. But, by the Criminal Law Amendment Act, the Government had deliberately struck a blow against the methods of all trade societies at all periods. The growing strength of the organisations of the coal-miners and cotton-spinners, and the rapid expansion of Trade Unionism which marked this period of commercial prosperity, had for some time been tending towards the development of the informal meetings of the Junta into a more representative executive. The dissolution of the Conference of Amalgamated Trades left the field open ; and the leadership of the Trade Union Movement was assumed by the Parliamentary Committee which had been appointed at the Trades Union Congress in the previous March, and which included all the principal leaders of the chief metropolitan and provincial societies of the time.

The agitation which was immediately begun to secure the repeal of the Criminal Law Amendment Act became during the next four years the most significant feature of the Trade Union world. Throughout all the various struggles of these years the Trade Union leaders kept steadily in view the definite aim of getting rid of a law which they regarded, not only as hampering their efforts for better conditions of employment, but also as an indignity and an insult to the hundreds of thousands of intelligent artisans whom they represented. The whole history of this agitation proves how completely the governing classes were out of touch with the recently enfranchised artisans. The legislation of 1871 was regarded by the Government and the House of Commons as the full and final solution of a long-standing problem. " The judges, however, declared," as Henry Crompton points out, " that the only effect of the legislation of 1871 was to make the trade object of the strike not illegal. A strike was perfectly legal ; but if the means employed were calculated to coerce the employer they were illegal means, and a combination to do a legal act by illegal means was a criminal conspiracy. In other words, a strike was lawful, but anything done in pursuance of a strike was criminal. Thus the judges tore up the remedial statute, and each fresh decision went further and developed new dangers." [1] But Gladstone's Cabinet steadfastly refused, right down to its fall in 1874, even to consider the possibility of altering the Criminal Law Amendment Act. It was in vain that deputation after deputation pointed out that men were being sent to prison under this law for such acts as peacefully accosting a workman in the street. In 1871 seven women were imprisoned in South Wales merely for saying " Bah " to one blackleg. Innumerable convictions took place for the use of bad language. Almost any action taken by Trade Unionists to induce a man not to accept employment at a struck shop resulted, under the new Act, in imprisonment with hard labour. The intolerable injustice of this state of things was made more glaring by the freedom allowed to the employers to make all possible use of " black-lists " and " character notes," by which obnoxious men were prevented from getting work. No prosecution ever took place for this form of molestation or obstruction. No employer was ever placed in the dock under the law which professedly applied to both parties. In short, boycotting by the employers was freely permitted ; boycotting by the men was put down by the police.

The irritation caused by these petty prosecutions was, in December 1872, deepened into anger by the sentence of twelve months' imprisonment passed upon the London gas-stokers. These men were found guilty of "conspiracy"

---

[1] *Digest of the Labour Laws*, signed by F. Harrison and H. Crompton, and issued by the Trades Union Congress Parliamentary Committees, September 1875.

to coerce or molest their employers by merely preparing for a simultaneous withdrawal of their labour. The vindictive sentence inflicted by Lord Justice Brett was justified by the governing classes on the ground of the danger to the community which a strike of gas-stokers might involve; and the Home Secretary refused to listen to any appeal on behalf of the men.[1] The Trade Union leaders did not fail to perceive that no legal distinction could, under the law as it then stood, be drawn between a gas-stoker and any other workmen. If preparing for a strike was punishable, under " the elastic and inexplicable law of conspiracy," by twelve months' imprisonment, it was obvious that the whole fabric of Trade Unionism might be overthrown by any band of employers who chose to put the law in force. The London Trades Council accordingly summoned a delegate meeting " to consider the critical legal position of all trade societies and their officers consequent upon the recent conviction of the London gas-stokers." Representation after representation was made to the Government and to members of Parliament ; and the movement for the repeal of the Criminal Law Amendment Act of 1871 was widened into a determined attempt to get rid of all penal legislation bearing on trade disputes.[2]

Rarely has political agitation been begun in such apparently unpromising circumstances, and carried so rapidly to a triumphant issue. The Liberal administration of these years, like the majority of both parties in the House of Commons, was entirely dominated by the antagonism felt by the manufacturers to any effective collective bargaining on the part of the men. The representations of the Parliamentary Committee found no sympathy either with Henry Bruce or with Robert Lowe, who succeeded him as Home Secretary. Gladstone, as Prime Minister,

---

[1] They were, however, eventually released after a few months' imprisonment ; see *Henry Broadhurst, the Story of His Life*, by himself, 1901, pp. 59-64 ; *Labour Legislation, Labour Movements and Labour Leaders*, by G. Howell, 1902, pp. 237-53.

[2] See letter to *Beehive*, January 11, 1873.

refused in 1872 to admit that there was any necessity for further legislation, and utterly declined to take the matter up ; [1] and during that session the Parliamentary Committee were unable to find any member willing to introduce a Bill for the repeal of the Criminal Law Amendment Act.

The Trade Union leaders, however, did not relax their efforts. Allan, Guile, Odger, and Howell were strongly reinforced by the representatives of the miners, cotton-spinners, and ironworkers. Alexander Macdonald and John Kane, themselves men of remarkable ability, had behind them thousands of sturdy politicians in all the industrial centres. The agitation was fanned by the publication of details of the prosecutions under the new Act. Effective *Tracts for Trade Unionists* were written by Henry Crompton and Frederic Harrison　Congresses at Nottingham in 1872, at Leeds in 1873, at Sheffield in 1874 kept up the fire, and passed judgment on those members of Parliament who treated the Parliamentary Committee with contumely. As the time of the General Election drew near, the pressure on the two great political parties was increased. Lists of questions to candidates were prepared embodying the legislative claims of labour ; and it was made clear that no candidate would receive Trade Union support unless his answers were satisfactory.

It will be a question for the historian of English politics whether the unexpected rout of the Liberal party at the election of 1874 was not due more to the active hostility of the Trade Unionists than to the sullen abstention of the Nonconformists. The time happened to be a high-water mark of Trade Unionism. In these years of good trade every society had been rapidly increasing its membership. The miners, the agricultural labourers, and the textile operatives in particular had swarmed into organisation in a manner which recalls the rush of 1834. The Trades Union Congress at Sheffield, held just before the General Election of 1874, claimed to represent over 1,100,000

[1] Hansard, vol. 212, p. 1132, July 15, 1872.

organised workmen, including a quarter of a million of coal-miners, as many cotton operatives, and a hundred thousand agricultural labourers. The proceedings of this Congress reveal the feeling of bitter anger which had been created by the obtuseness to the claims of labour of the Liberal leaders of that day. Not content with turning a deaf ear to all the representatives of the workmen, they had, with blundering ignorance, retained as Secretary of the Liberal Association of the City of London the Sidney Smith who had, since 1851, been the principal officer of the various associations of employers in the engineering and iron trades.[1] As such he had proved himself a bitter and implacable enemy of Trade Unionism. We may imagine what would be the result to-day if either political party were to face a General Election with Mr. Laws, the organiser of the Shipping Federation, as its chief of the staff. And whilst the Liberal party was treating the new electorate with contumely, the Conservative candidates were listening blandly to the workmen's claims, and pledging themselves to repeal the obnoxious law.

Under these circumstances it is not surprising that the old idea of Trade Union abstention from politics gave way to a determined attempt at organised political action. Nor were the Trade Unionists content with merely pressing the organised political parties in the House of Commons. The running of independent Labour candidates against both parties alike was a most significant symptom of the new feeling in Labour politics. The Labour Representation League, composed mainly of prominent Trade Unionists, had for some years been endeavouring to secure the election of working men to the House of Commons; and the independent candidatures of George Odger during 1869 and 1870 had provoked considerable feeling.[2] At a bye-election

---

[1] This formed the subject of bitter comment in the *Beehive*, January 1874, just before the General Election.

[2] The following letter, addressed to Odger by John Stuart Mill, will be of interest in connection with the perennial question of the expediency of

at Greenwich in 1873, a third candidate was run with working-class support against both the great parties, with the result that Boord, the Conservative, gained the seat. In what spirit this was regarded by the organised workmen and their trusted advisers may be judged from the following leading article which Professor E. S. Beesly wrote for the *Beehive*, then at the height of its influence : " The result of the Greenwich election is highly satisfactory. . . . The workman has at length come to the conclusion that the difference between Liberal and Tory is pretty much that between upper and nether millstone. The quality of the two is essentially the same. They are sections of the wealth-possessing class, and on all Parliamentary questions affecting the interests of labour they play into one another's hands so systematically and imperturbably that one would suppose they thought workmen never read a newspaper or hear a speech. . . . The last hours of the Session were marked by the failure of two Bills about which workmen cared infinitely more than about all the measures put together for which Mr. Gladstone takes credit since his accession to office—I mean Mr. Harcourt's Conspiracy Bill and Mr. Mundella's Nine Hours Bill. As for Mr. Mundella's Bill for repealing the Criminal Law Amendment Act, it has never

---

"independent" candidatures. It will be found in the *Beehive* for February 13, 1875 :—

" AVIGNON, *February* 19, 1871.

" DEAR MR. ODGER,—Although you have not been successful, I congratulate you on the result of the polling in Southwark, as it proves that you have the majority of the Liberal party with you, and that you have called out an increased amount of political feeling in the borough. It is plain that the Whigs intend to monopolise political power as long as they can without coalescing in any degree with the Radicals. The working men are quite right in allowing Tories to get into the House to defeat this exclusive feeling of the Whigs, and may do it without sacrificing any principle. The working men's policy is to insist upon their own representation, and in default of success to permit Tories to be sent into the House until the Whig majority is seriously threatened, when, of course, the Whigs will be happy to compromise, and allow a few working men representatives in the House. JOHN STUART MILL."

LIVERPOOL
JOHN MOORES UNIVERSITY
TRUEMAN STREET LIBRARY
TEL. 051 231 4022/4023

had a chance. For the failure of all these Bills the Ministry must be held responsible. . . .

"This being the case, it is simply silly for Liberal newspapers to mourn over the Greenwich Election as an unfortunate mistake. . . . There was no mistake at all at Greenwich. There was a 'third party' in the field knowing perfectly well what it wanted, and regarding Mr. Boord and Mr. Angerstein with impartial hostility. I trust that such a third party will appear in every large town in England at the next General Election, even though the result should be a Parliament of six hundred and fifty Boords. Everything must have a beginning, and workmen have waited so long for justice that seven years of Tory government will seem a trifling addition to the sum total of their endurance if it is a necessary preliminary to an enforcement of their claims." [1]

The movement for direct electoral action remained without official support from Trade Unions as such until at the 1874 Congress Broadhurst was able to report that the miners, ironworkers, and some other societies had actually voted money for Parliamentary candidatures. At the General Election which ensued no fewer than thirteen "Labour candidates" went to the poll. In most cases both Liberal and Conservative candidates were run against them, with the result that the Conservatives gained the seats.[2] But at Stafford and Morpeth the official Liberals accepted what they were powerless to prevent ; and Alexander Macdonald and Thomas Burt, the two leading

---

[1] *Beehive*, August 9, 1873 ; see also that of August 30.

[2] Halliday, the Secretary of the Amalgamated Association of Miners offered himself as Labour candidate for Merthyr Tydvil. A fortnight before the polling day he was indicted at Burnley for conspiracy in connection with a local miners' strike, but nevertheless went to the poll, receiving the large total of 4912 votes (*Beehive*, January 31, 1874). Among the other "third candidates" were Broadhurst (Wycombe), Howell (Aylesbury), Cremer (Warwick), Lucraft (Finsbury), Potter (Peterborough), Bradlaugh (Northampton), Kane (Middlesborough), Odger (Southwark), Mottershead (Preston), and Walton (Stoke). See *History of Labour Representation*, by A. W. Humphrey, 1912.

L

LIVERPOOL
JOHN MOORES UNIVERSITY
TRUEMAN STREET LIBRARY
TEL. 051 231 4022/4023

officials of the National Union of Miners, became the first
" Labour members " of the House of Commons.

It is significant of the electioneering attitude of the
Conservative leaders that, with the advent of the new
Conservative Government, the Trade Unionists appear to
have assumed that the Criminal Law Amendment Act would
be instantly repealed. Great was the disappointment when it
was announced that a Royal Commission was to be appointed
to inquire into the operation of the whole of the so-called
" Labour Laws." This was regarded as nothing more than
a device for shelving the question, and the Trade Union
leaders refused either to become members of the Commission
or to give evidence before it. Thomas Burt absolutely refused a seat on the Commission. It needed the most specific
assurances by the Home Secretary that the Government
really intended the earliest possible legislation to induce
any working man to have anything to do with the Commission. Ultimately Alexander Macdonald, M.P., allowed
himself to be persuaded to serve, together with Tom Hughes;
and George Shipton, the Secretary of the London Trades
Council, Andrew Boa, the Secretary of the Glasgow Trades
Council, and a prominent Birmingham Trade Unionist
gave evidence. The investigation of the Commission was
perfunctory, and the report inconclusive But the Government were too fully alive to the new-found political power
of the Unions to attempt to play with the question. At
the beginning of 1875 the imprisonment of five cabinetmakers employed at Messrs. Jackson & Graham, a well-
known London firm, roused considerable public feeling,
and led to many questions in Parliament.[1] In June the
Home Secretary, in an appreciative and conciliatory speech,
introduced two Bills for altering respectively the civil and
criminal law. As amended in Committee by the efforts
of Mundella and others, these measures resulted in Acts
which completely satisfied the Trade Union demands. The

---

[1] See House of Commons Returns. No. 237 of the 2nd, and No. 273
of the 23rd of June 1875.

LIVERPOOL
JOHN MOORES UNIVERSITY
TRUEMAN STREET LIBRARY
TEL. 051 231 4022/4023

Criminal Law Amendment Act of 1871 was formally and unconditionally repealed. By the Conspiracy and Protection of Property Act (38 and 39 Vic. c. 86), definite and reasonable limits were set to the application of the law of conspiracy to trade disputes. The Master and Servant Act of 1867 was replaced by an Employers and Workmen Act (38 and 39 Vic. c. 90), a change of nomenclature which expressed a fundamental revolution in the law. Henceforth master and servant became, as employer and employee, two equal parties to a civil contract. Imprisonment for breach of engagement was abolished. The legalisation of Trade Unions was completed by the legal recognition of their methods. Peaceful picketing was expressly permitted. The old words " coerce " and " molest," which had, in the hands of prejudiced magistrates, proved such instruments of oppression, were omitted from the new law, and violence and intimidation were dealt with as part of the general criminal code. No act committed by a group of workmen was henceforth to be punishable unless the same act by an individual was itself a criminal offence. Collective bargaining, in short, with all its necessary accompaniments, was, after fifty years of legislative struggle, finally recognised by the law of the land.[1]

[1] It is not surprising that this sweeping Parliamentary triumph evoked great enthusiasm in the Trade Union ranks. At the Trade Union Congress in October 1875, such ardent Radicals as Odger, Guile, and George Howell joined in the warmest eulogies of J. K. (afterwards Viscount) Cross, whose sympathetic attitude had surpassed their utmost hopes. " The best friends they had in Parliament," said Howell, " with one or two exceptions, never declared for the repeal of the Criminal Law Amendment Act. He, with some friends, was under the gallery of the House of Commons when the measure was under discussion, and they could scarcely believe their ears when they heard Mr. Cross declare for the total repeal of the Act." And Odger paid testimony to the " immense singleness of purpose " with which the Home Secretary " had attended to every proposition that had been placed before him," and accorded them " the greatest boon ever given to the sons of toil." An amendment deprecating such " fulsome recognition of the action of the Conservative party " received only four votes (Report of Glasgow Congress, 1875). Some minor amendments of the law relating to the registration and friendly benefits of Trade Unions were embodied in the Trade Union Act Amendment Act of 1876 (39 and 40 Vic. c. 22). See the *Handybook of the Labour Laws*, by George Howell, 1876, and his *Labour Legislation, Labour Movements and Labour Leaders*, 1902, pp. 156-72.

The paramount importance of the legal and Parliamentary struggle from 1867 to 1875 has compelled us to relegate to the next chapter all mention of striking contemporary events in Trade Union history. The sustained efforts of this decade, too often ignored by a younger generation of Trade Unionists, are even now referred to by the survivors as constituting the finest period of Trade Union activity. For over eight years the Unions had been subjected to the strain of a prolonged and acute crisis, during which their very existence was at stake. Out of this crisis they emerged, as we have seen, triumphantly successful, " liberated," to use George Howell's words, " from the last vestige of the criminal laws specially appertaining to labour." [1]

This tangible victory was not the only result of the struggle. In order to gain their immediate end the Trade Union leaders had adopted the arguments of their opponents, and had been led to take up a position which, whilst it departed from the Trade Union traditions of the past, proved in the future a serious impediment to their further theoretic progress. To understand the intellectual attitude of the Junta and their friends, we must consider in some detail the position which they had to attack. From the very beginning of the century the employers had persistently asserted their right to make any kind of bargain with the individual workman, irrespective of its effect on the Standard of Life. They had, accordingly, adopted the principle, as against both the Trade Unionists and the Factory Act philanthropists, of perfect freedom of contract and complete competition between both workers and employers. In order to secure absolute freedom of competition between individuals it was necessary to penalise any attempt on the part of the workmen to regulate, by combination, the conditions of the bargain. But this involved, in reality, a departure from the principle of legal freedom of contract. One form of contract, that of the collective bargain, was, in effect, made

[1] Speech at Trades Union Congress, Glasgow, October 1875.

a criminal offence, on the plea that, however beneficial it might seem to the workmen, it cut at the root of national prosperity. It will be obvious that in urging this contention the employers were taking up an inconsistent position. Their pecuniary interest in complete competition outweighed, in fact, their faith in freedom of contract.

Meanwhile the astute workmen who led the movement were gradually concentrating their forces upon the only position from which they could hope to be victorious. They had, it must be remembered, no means of imposing their own view upon the community. Even after 1867 their followers formed but a small minority of the electorate, whilst the whole machinery of politics was in the hands of the middle class. Powerless to coerce or even to intimidate the governing classes, they could win only by persuasion. It was, however, hopeless to dream of converting the middle class to the essential principle of Trade Unionism, the compulsory maintenance of the Standard of Life. In the then state of Political Economy the Trade Unionists saw against them, on this point, the whole mass of educated opinion in the country. John Bright, for instance, did but express the common view of the progressive party of that time when he solemnly assured the working man that " combinations, in the long run, must be as injurious to himself as to the employer against whom he is contending." [1] Lord Shaftesbury, the lifelong advocate of factory legislation, was praying that " the working people may be emancipated from the tightest thraldom they have ever yet endured. All the single despots, and all the aristocracies that ever were or ever will be, are as puffs of wind compared with these tornadoes, the Trade Unions." [2] The Sheffield and other outrages, the rumours of constant persecution of non-Unionists, the hand-workers' perpetual objection to

---

[1] In his letter to a Blackburn mill-owner, November 3, 1860. *Public Letters of John Bright*, collected and edited by H. J. Leech, 1885, p. 80.

[2] Letter to Colonel Maude, quoted by Professor Beesly in his address to the London Trades Council, 1869, reported in *Bricklayers' Circular*, March 1870.

machinery, the restrictions on piecework and apprentice-ship—all these real and fancied crimes had created a mass of prejudice against which it was hopeless for the Trade Unionists to struggle.

The Union leaders, therefore, wisely left this part of their case in the background. They avoided arguing whether Trade Unionism was, in principle, useful or detri-mental, right or wrong. They insisted only on the right of every Englishman to bargain for the sale of his labour in the manner he thought most conducive to his own interests. What they demanded was perfect freedom for a workman to substitute collective for individual bargaining, if he imagined such a course to be for his own advantage. Freedom of association in matters of contract became, therefore, their rejoinder to the employers' cry of freedom of competition.

It is clear that the Trade Unionists had the best of the argument. It was manifestly unreasonable for the em-ployers to insist on the principle of non-interference of the State in industry whenever they were pushed by the advo-cates of factory legislation, and at the same time to clamour for the assistance of the police to put down peaceful and voluntary combinations of their workmen. The capitalists were, in short, committed to the principle of *laissez-faire* in every phase of industrial life, from " Free Trade in Corn " to the unlimited use of labour of either sex at any age and under any conditions ; and what the workmen demanded was only the application of this principle to the wage con-tract. " The Trade Union question," writes, in 1869, their chosen representative and most powerful advocate, " is another and the latest example of the truth, that the sphere of legislation is strictly and curiously limited. After legis-lating about labour for centuries, each change producing its own evils, we have slowly come to see the truth, that we must cease to legislate for it at all. The public mind has been of late conscious of serious embarrassment, and eagerly expecting some legislative solution, some heaven-born discoverer to arise, with a new Parliamentary nostrum. As usual in such cases, it now turns out that there is no legislative solution at all ; and that the true solution requires, as its condition, the removal of the mischievous meddling of the past." [1] This doctrine " that all men may lawfully agree to work or not to work, to employ or not to employ, on any terms that they think fit," forms the whole burden of the speeches and petitions of the Trade Union leaders throughout this controversy. " We do not," say the official representatives of Trade Unionism in their memorial to the Home Secretary in April 1875, " seek to interfere with the free competition of the individual in the exercise of his craft in his own way ; but we reserve to ourselves the right either to work for, or to refuse to work for, an employer according to the circumstances of the case, just as the master has the right to discharge a workman, or workmen ; and we deny that the individual right is in any way interfered with when it is done in concert."

The working men had, in fact, picked up the weapon of their opponents and left these without defence. But in so doing the leading Trade Unionists of the time drifted into a position no less inconsistent than that of the employers. When they contended that the Union should be as free to bargain as the individual, they had not the slightest intention of permitting the individual to bargain freely if they could prevent him. Though Allan and Applegarth were able conscientiously to inform the Royal Commission that the members of their societies did not refuse to work with non-society men, they must have been perfectly aware that this convenient fact was only true in those places and at those periods in which society men were not in a sufficiently large majority to do otherwise. The trades to which Henry Broadhurst and George Howell belonged were notorious for the success with which the Unions had maintained their practice of excluding non-society men from their jobs.

[1] *Fortnightly Review*, July 1, 1869. " The Trades Union Bill," by Frederic Harrison.

The coal-miners of Northumberland and Durham habitually refused to descend the shaft in company with a non-Unionist.[1]

We have shown, in our *Industrial Democracy*, that this universal aspiration of Trade Unionism—the enforcement of membership—stands, in our opinion, on the same footing as the enforcement of citizenship. But, however this may be, it is evident that the refusal of the Northumberland miners to " ride " with non-society men is, in effect, as coercive on the dissentient minority as the Mines Regulation Act or an Eight Hours Bill. The insistence upon the Englishman's right to freedom of contract was, in fact, in the mouths of staunch Trade Unionists, perilously near cant ; and we find Frederic Harrison himself, when dealing with other legislation, warning them that it would be suicidal for working men to adopt as their own the capitalist cry of " non-interference." [2] The force of this caution must have

[1] William Crawford, the trusted leader of the Durham miners, and a steadfast opponent of the Eight Hours Bill, in a well-known letter of later date (of which we have had a copy), emphatically urges the complete ostracism of non-society men. " You should at least be consistent. In numberless cases you refuse to descend and ascend with non-Unionists. The right or wrong of such action I will not now discuss ; but what is the actual state of things found in many parts of the country ? While you refuse to descend and ascend with these men, you walk to and from the pit, walk in and out bye with them—nay, sometimes work with them. You mingle with them at home over your glass of beer, in your chapels, and side by side you pray with them in your prayer meeting. The time has come when there must be plain speaking on this matter. It is no use playing at shuttlecock in this important portion of our social life. Either mingle with these men in the shaft, as you do in every other place, or let them be ostracised at all times and in every place. Regard them as unfit companions for yourselves and your sons, and unfit husbands for your daughters. Let them be branded, as it were, with the curse of Cain, as unfit to mingle in ordinary, honest, and respectable society. Until you make up your minds to thus completely and absolutely ostracise these goats of mankind, cease to complain as to any results that may arise from their action." Compare *A Great Labour Leader* [Thomas Burt], by Aaron Watson, 1908.

[2] See his letter on the Government Annuities Bill, 1864 : " Lastly, we are told of Government dictation and interference. I cannot believe men of sense will say this twice seriously. . . . Leave it to the political economists to complain. . . . Let working men remember that whenever a measure in their interest is proposed to Parliament, or suggested in the country—whether it be to limit excessive hours of labour, to protect

been evident to the Junta, who had had too much experience of the workings of modern industry not to realise the need for a compulsory maintenance of the Standard of Life. No Trade Unionist can deny that, without some method of enforcing the decision of the majority, effective trade combination is impossible.

It must not be inferred from the above criticism of the theoretic position taken by the men who steered the Trade Union Movement through its great crisis that they were conscious of their inconsistency with regard to State intervention, or that they deliberately set to work to win their case upon false premises. No one can study the history of their leadership without being impressed by their devotion, sagacity, and high personal worth. We must regard their inconsistency as a striking instance of the danger which besets a party formed without any clear idea of the social state at which it is aiming. In the struggle of these years we watch the English Trade Unionists driven from their Utopian aspirations into an inconsistent opportunism, from which they drifted during the next generation into the crude " self-help " of an " aristocracy of labour." During the whole of this process there was no moment at which the incompatibility of their Individualist and Collectivist views was perceived. Applegarth and Odger, for instance, saw no inconsistency in becoming leading officials of the " International " on a programme drafted by Karl Marx, and at the same time supporting the current Radical demand for a widespread peasant proprietorship. But it was inevitable

---

women and children, to regulate unhealthy labour, to provide them with the means of health, cleanliness, or recreation, to save them from the exactions of unscrupulous employers—it is universally met with opposition from one quarter, that of unrestricted competition ; and opposed on one ground, that of absolute freedom of private enterprise. We all know —at least, we all explain—how selfish and shallow this cry is in the mouth of unscrupulous capitalists who resist the Truck System Bill or the Ten Hours Bill. Is it not suicidal in working men to raise a cry which has ever been, and still will be, the great resource of those who strive to set obstacles to their welfare ? The next time working men promote a Short Time Bill of any kind they will be told to stick to their principle of non-interference with private capital " (*Beehive*, March 19, 1864).

L 2

that the exclusive insistence upon the Individualist arguments, through which alone the victory of 1875 could be
won, should impress the Individualist ideal upon the minds
of those who stood round the leaders.   Other influences,
moreover, promoted the acceptance by the Trade Unionists
of the economic shibboleths of the middle class.   The failure
of the crude experiments of Owen and O'Connor, the striking
success of the policy of Free Trade, the growing participation of working men in the Liberal politics of the time, and,
above all, the close intimacy which many of them enjoyed
with able and fertile thinkers of the middle class, all tended
to create a new school of Trade Unionists.   In a subsequent
chapter we shall describe the results of this intellectual
conversion upon the Trade Union Movement.   First, however, we must turn to the internal development of these
years, which our description of the Parliamentary struggles
of 1867–75 has forced us temporarily to ignore.[1]

[1] From 1861 to 1877 the principal working-class organ was the *Beehive*,
established by a group of Trade Unionists who formed a company in
which over a hundred Unions are said to have taken shares.   The editor
and virtual proprietor during its whole life appears to have been George
Potter, who was assisted by a Consulting Committee, on which appeared,
at some time or another, the names of all the leading London Trade
Unionists.   Potter, as we have already mentioned, was a man of equivocal
character and conduct, who at no time held any important position in
the Trade Union world, though his London Working Men's Association
made a useful start of the movement for Trade Union representation in
the House of Commons.   Under his editorship the *Beehive* became the
best Labour newspaper which has yet appeared.   This was due to the
persistent support of Frederic Harrison, Henry Crompton, E. S. Beesly,
Lloyd Jones, and other friends of Trade Unionism who, for fifteen years,
contributed innumerable articles, whilst such Trade Union leaders as
Applegarth, Howell, and Shipton frequently appeared in its columns.
These contributions make it of the greatest possible value to the student
of Trade Union history. . Unfortunately, the most complete file in any
public library—that in the British Museum—begins only in 1869. Mr.
John Burns possesses a unique set beginning in 1863, which he kindly
placed at our disposal.   In 1877 it was converted into the *Industrial
Review*, which came to an end in 1879.

    The place of the *Beehive* was, in 1881, to some extent taken by the
Labour Standard, a penny weekly established by George Shipton, the
Secretary of the London Trades Council.   It ran from May 7, 1881, to
April 29, 1882, and contained articles by Henry Crompton and Professor
E. S. Beesly, together with much Trade Union information.

CHAPTER VI

[1863–1885]

FROM 1851 to 1863 all the effective forces in the Trade Union Movement were centred in London. Between 1863 and 1867, as we described in the course of the last chapter, provincial organisations, such as the Glasgow and Sheffield Trades Councils, and provincial leaders such as Alexander Macdonald and John Kane, began to play an important part in the general movement. The dramatic crisis of 1867, and the subsequent political struggle, compelled us to break off our description of the growth of the movement in order to follow the Parliamentary action of the London leaders. But whilst the Junta and their allies were winning their great victories at Westminster, the centre of gravity of the Trade Union world was being insensibly shifted from London to the industrial districts north of the Humber. This was primarily due to the rapid growth of two great provincial organisations, the federations of Coal-miners and Cotton Operatives.

The Miners, now one of the most powerful contingents of the Trade Union forces, were, until 1863, without any effective organisation. The Miners' Association of Great Britain, which, as we have seen, sprang in 1841–43 into a vigorous existence, collapsed in 1848. An energetic attempt made by Martin Jude to re-establish a National Association in 1850, when a conference was held at Newcastle, was, in consequence of the continued depression in the coal trade, entirely unsuccessful. For the next few years " the fragments of union that existed got less by degrees and more minute till, at the close of 1855, it might be said that union among the miners in the whole country had almost died out." [1] The revival which took place between 1858 and 1863 was due, in the main, to the persistent work of the able man who became for fifteen years their trusted leader.

Alexander Macdonald, to whose lifelong devotion the miners owe their present position in the Trade Union world, stands, like William Newton, midway between the casual and amateur leaders of the old Trade Unionism and the paid officials of the new type. Himself originally a miner and the son of a miner, the education and independent

---

[1] Address of Alexander Macdonald to the Leeds Conference, 1873. Alexander Macdonald, the son of a sailor, who became a miner in Lanarkshire, was born at Airdrie in 1821, and went to work in the pit at the age of eight. Having an ardent desire for education he prepared himself as best he could for Glasgow University, which he entered in 1846, supporting himself from his savings, and from his work as a miner in the summer. Whilst still at the University he became known as a leader of the miners all over Scotland. In 1850 he became a mine manager, and in 1851 he opened a school at Airdrie, an occupation which he abandoned in 1855 to devote his whole time to agitation on behalf of the miners. On the formation, in 1863, of the National Union of Miners, he was elected president, a position which he retained until his death. Meanwhile he was, by a series of successful commercial speculations, acquiring a modest fortune, which enabled him to devote his whole energies to the promotion of the Parliamentary programme which he had impressed upon the miners. He gave important evidence before the Select Committee of 1865 on the Master and Servant Law. In 1868 he offered himself as a candidate for the Kilmarnock Burghs, but retired to avoid a split. At the General Election of 1874 he was more successful, being returned for Stafford, and thus becoming (with Thomas Burt) the first " Labour Member." He was shortly afterwards appointed a member of the Royal Commission on the Labour Laws, and eventually presented a minority report of his own on the subject. He died in 1881. A history of the coal-miners which he projected was apparently never written, and, with the exception of numerous presidential addresses and other speeches, and a pamphlet entitled *Notes and Annotations on the Coal Mines Regulation Act, 1872* (Glasgow, 1872, 50 pp.), we have found nothing from his pen. A eulogistic notice of his life by Lloyd Jones appeared in the *Newcastle Chronicle*, November 17, 1883, most of which is reprinted in Dr. Baernreither's *English Associations of Working Men*, p. 408.

means which he had acquired enabled him, from 1857 onwards, to apply himself continuously to the miners' cause. A florid style, and somewhat flashy personality, did him no harm with the rough and uneducated workmen whom he had to marshal. The main source of his effectiveness lay, however, neither in his oratory nor in his powers of organisation, but in his exact appreciation of the particular changes that would remedy the miners' grievances, and in the tactical skill with which he embodied these changes in legislative form. Like his friends, Allan and Applegarth, he relied almost exclusively on Parliamentary agitation as a means for securing his ends. But whilst the Junta were contenting themselves with securing political freedom for Trade Unionists, Macdonald from the first persistently pressed for the legislative regulation of the conditions of labour. And though, like his London allies, he consorted largely with the middle-class friends of Trade Unionism, and freely utilised their help in the House of Commons, he proved his superior originality and tenacity of mind by never in the slightest degree abandoning the fundamental principle of Trade Unionism—the compulsory maintenance of the workman's Standard of Life.

" It was in 1856," said Macdonald on a later occasion, " that I crossed the Border first to advocate a better Mines Act, true weighing, the education of the young, the restriction of the age till twelve years, the reduction of the working hours to eight in every twenty-four, the training of managers, the payment of wages weekly in the current coin of the realm, no truck, and many other useful things too numerous to mention here. Shortly after that, bone began to come to bone, and by 1858 we were in full action for better laws." [1] The pit clubs and informal committees that pressed these demands upon the legislature became centres of local organisation, with which Macdonald kept up an incessant correspondence. An arbitrary lock-out of several thousand men by the South Yorkshire coal-owners in 1858 welded

[1] Address to the Miners' National Conference at Leeds, 1873.

the miners of that coal-field into a compact district association, and enabled Macdonald, in the same year, to get together a national conference at Ashton-under-Lyne, at which, however, the delegates could claim to represent only four thousand men in union. In 1860, when the Mines Regulation Act was being passed into law, Macdonald was able to score a success in the " checkweigher " clause, to which we shall again refer. Not until the end of 1863, however, can the Miners' National Union be said to have been effectively established ; and the proceedings of the Leeds Conference of that year strike the note of the policy which Macdonald, to the day of his death, never ceased to press upon the miners, and to which the great majority of them have now, after a temporary digression, once more returned.

The Miners' Conference at Leeds was in many respects a notable gathering. Instead of the formless interchange of talk which had marked the previous conference, Macdonald induced the fifty-one delegates who sat from the 9th to the 14th of November 1863 at the People's Co-operative Hall to organise their meeting on the model of the National Association for the Promotion of Social Science, and divide themselves into three sections, on Law, on Grievances, and on Social Organisation, each of which reported to the whole conference.[1] The proceedings of the day were opened with prayer by the " Chaplain to the Conference," the Rev. Joseph Rayner Stephens, celebrated as the opponent of the New Poor Law and the advocate of factory legislation and Chartism.[2] In the reports of the sections and the

---

[1] The Conference appointed a sub-committee to compile and publish its proceedings, " a thing," as the preface explains, " altogether unparalleled in the records of labour." And indeed the elaborate volume, regularly published by the eminent firm of Longmans in 1864, entitled *Transactions and Results of the National Association of Coal, Lime, and Ironstone Miners of Great Britain, held at Leeds, November 9, 10, 11, 12, 13, and 14, 1863*, with its 174 pages, its frontispiece representing the pit-brow women, and its motto on the title-page extracted from the writings of W. E. Gladstone, formed a creditable and impressive appeal to the reading public.

[2] For this militant Chartist (1805–79), see *Life of Joseph Rayner Stephens*, by G. J. Holyoake, 1881.

numerous resolutions of the conference we find all the points of Macdonald's programme. The paramount importance of securing the Standard of Life by means of legislative regulation of the conditions of work is embodied in a lengthy series of proposals which have nearly all since been inserted in the detailed code of mining law. In contradistinction to the view which would make wages depend upon prices, the principle of controlling industry in such a way as to prevent encroachments on the workman's standard maintenance is clearly foreshadowed. "Overtoil," says the report, "produces over-supply; low prices and low wages follow; bad habits and bad health follow, of course; and then diminished production and profits are inevitable. Reduction of toil, and consequent improved bodily health, increases production in the sense of profit; and limits it so as to avoid overstocking; better wages induce better habits, and economy of working follows. . . . The evil of overtoil and over-supply upon wages, and upon the labourer, is therefore a fair subject of complaint; and, we submit, as far as these are human by conventional arrangements, are a fair and proper subject of regulation. Regulations must, of course, be twofold. Part can be legislated for by compulsory laws; but the principle (*sic*) must be the subject of voluntary agreement." [1] The restriction of labour in mines to a maximum of eight hours per day was strongly urged; but at Macdonald's instance it was astutely resolved not to ask for a legal regulation of the hours of adult men, but to confine the Parliamentary proposal to a Bill for boys. And it is interesting to observe already at this time the beginning of the deep cleavage between the miners of Northumberland and Durham and their fellow-workers elsewhere. The close connection between the legal regulation of the hours of boys and the fixing of the men's day is brought out by William Crawford, the future leader

---

[1] *Transactions and Results of the National Association of Coal, Lime, and Ironstone Miners of Great Britain, held at Leeds, November 9, 10, 11, 12, 13, and 14, 1863,* p. 14.

of the Durham men. The general feeling of the conference was in favour of a drastic legal prohibition of boys being kept in the mine for more than eight hours, but Crawford declared that " an eight hours bill could not be carried out in his district. He wanted the boys to work ten hours a day, and the men six hours." [1] He therefore proposed a legal Ten Hours Day for the boys. The conference, however, declined to depart from the principle of Eight Hours ; and the Bill drafted in this sense was eventually adopted without dissent.

Another reform advocated by Macdonald has had far-reaching though unforeseen effect upon the miners' organisation. The arbitrary confiscation of the miners' pay for any tubs or hutches which were declared to be improperly filled had long been a source of extreme irritation. It had become a regular practice of unscrupulous coal-owners to condemn a considerable percentage of the men's hutches, and thus escape payment for part of the coal hewn. The grievance was aggravated by the absolute dependence of the miner, working underground, upon the honesty and accuracy of the agent of the employer on the surface, who recorded the amount of his work. A demand was accordingly made by the men for permission to have their own representative at the pit-bank, who should check the weight to be paid for. During the year 1859 great contests took place in South Yorkshire, in which, after embittered resistance, the employers in several collieries conceded this boon. A determined attempt was then made by the South Yorkshire Miners' Union, aided by Macdonald, to insert a clause in the Mines Regulation Bill, making it compulsory to weigh the coal, and to allow a representative of the men to check the weight. A great Parliamentary fight took place on the men's amendment, with the result that the Act of 1860 empowered the miners of each pit to appoint a checkweigher, but confined their choice to persons actually in employment

[1] *Transactions and Results of the National Association of Coal, Lime, and Ironstone Miners of Great Britain, held at Leeds, November 9, 10, 11, 12, 13, and 14, 1863*, p. 17. In Northumberland and Durham the hewers very largely work in two shifts, whilst there used to be only one shift of boys.

at the particular mine.[1] This important victory was long
rendered nugatory by the evasions of the coal-owners. At
Barnsley, for instance, Normansell, appointed checkweigher,
was promptly dismissed from employment and refused
access to the pit's mouth. When the employer was fined
for this breach of the law he appealed to the Queen's Bench ;
and it cost the Union two years of costly litigation to
enforce the reinstatement of the men's agent.[2] The next
twenty years are full of attempts by coal-owners to avoid
compliance with this law. Where the men could not be
persuaded or terrified into forgoing their right to appoint
a checkweigher, every device was used to hamper his work.
Sometimes he was excluded from close access to the weighing-
machine. In other pits the weights were fenced up so that
he could not clearly see them. His calculations were hotly
disputed, and his interference bitterly resented. The
Miners' Unions, however, steadily fought their way to perfect independence for the checkweigher. The Mines Regulation Act of 1872 slightly strengthened his position. Finally
the Act of 1887, confirmed by that of 1911, made clear the
right of the men, by a decision of the majority of those

[1] Section 29 of Mines Regulation Act of 1860.
[2] Normansell *v.* Platt. John Normansell, the agent of the South
Yorkshire Miners' Association, stands second only to Macdonald as a
leader of the miners between 1863 and 1875. The son of a banksman,
he was born at Torkington, Cheshire, in 1830, and left an orphan at an
early age. At seven he entered the pit, and when, at the age of nineteen, he married, he was unable to write his own name. Migrating to
South Yorkshire, he became a leader in the agitation to secure a checkweigher, which the local coal-owners conceded in 1859. Normansell was
elected to the post for his own pit, and rapidly became the leading spirit
in the district. After the lock-out of 1864 he was elected secretary to
the Union, then counting only two thousand members. Within eight
years he had raised its membership to twenty thousand, and built up an
elaborate system of friendly benefits. Normansell was the first working-
man Town Councillor, having been triumphantly elected at Barnsley, his
Union subscribing £1000 to lodge in the bank in his name, in order to
enable him to declare himself possessed of the pecuniary qualification at
that time required. On his death the amount was voted to his widow.
Normansell gave evidence in 1867 before the Select Committee on Coal-
mining, and before that on the Master and Servant Law, in 1868 before
the Royal Commission on Trade Unions, and in 1873 before that on the
Coal Supply.

employed in any pit, to have, at the expense of the whole pit, a checkweigher with full power to keep an accurate and independent record of each man's work.

It would be interesting to trace to what extent the special characteristics of the miners' organisations are due to the influence of this one legislative reform. Its recognition and promotion of collective action by the men has been a direct incitement to combination. The compulsory levy, upon the whole pit, of the cost of maintaining the agent whom a bare majority could decide to appoint has practically found, for each colliery, a branch secretary free of expense to the Union. But the result upon the character of the officials has been even more important. The checkweigher has to be a man of character insensible to the bullying or blandishments of manager or employers. He must be of strictly regular habits, accurate and business-like in mind, and quick at figures. The ranks of the check-weighers serve thus as an admirable recruiting ground from which a practically inexhaustible supply of efficient Trade Union secretaries or labour representatives can be drawn.

The Leeds Conference of 1863 was the first of a series of yearly or half-yearly gatherings of miners' delegates which did much to consolidate their organisation. The powerful aid brought by Macdonald to the movement for the Master and Servant Act of 1867 has already been described. But between 1864 and 1869 the almost uninterrupted succession of strikes and lock-outs, in one county or another, prevented the National Association from taking a firm hold on the men in the less organised districts. In 1869 a rival federation, called the Amalgamated Association of Miners, was formed by the men of some Lancashire pits, to secure more systematic support of local strikes. This split only increased the number of miners in union, which in a few years reached the unprecedented total of two hundred thousand.

It is easy to understand how much this army of miners, marshalled by an expert Parliamentary tactician, added to the political weight of the Trade Union leaders. Though only partially enfranchised, their influence at the General Election of 1868 was marked ; and when, in 1871, the Trades Union Congress appointed a Parliamentary Committee Macdonald became its chairman. Next year he succeeded in getting embodied in the new Mines Regulation Act many of the minor amendments of the law for which he had been pressing ; and in 1874 he and his colleague, Thomas Burt, became, as we have seen, the first working-men members of the House of Commons.

Not less important than the somewhat scattered hosts of the Coal-miners was the compact body of the Lancashire Cotton Operatives, who, from 1869 onward, began to be reckoned as an integral part of the Trade Union world. The Lancashire textile workers, who had, in the early part of the century, played such a prominent part in the Trade Union Movement, and whose energetic " Short Time Committees " had, in 1847, obtained the Ten Hours Act, appear to have fallen, during the subsequent years, into a state of disorganisation and disunion. In 1853, it is true, the present Amalgamated Association of Cotton-spinners was established ; but this federal Union was weakened, until 1869, by the abstention or lukewarmness of the local organisations of such important districts as Oldham and Bolton. The cotton-weavers were in a somewhat similar condition. The Blackburn Association, established in 1853, was gradually overshadowed by the North-East Lancashire Association, a federation of the local weavers' societies in the smaller towns, established in 1858. This association, growing out of a secession from the Blackburn organisation, had for its special object the combined support of a skilled calculator of prices, able to defend the operatives' interests in the constant discussions which arose upon the complicated lists of piecework rates which characterise the English cotton industry.[1]

[1] The best and indeed the only exact account of these cotton lists is that prepared for the Economic Section of the British Association by a

It is difficult to convey to the general reader any adequate idea of the important effect which these elaborate " Lists " have had upon the Trade Union Movement in Lancashire. The universal satisfaction with, and even preference for, the piecework system among the Lancashire cotton operatives is entirely due to the existence of these definitely fixed and published statements. An even more important result has been the creation of a peculiar type of Trade Union official. For although the lists are elaborately worked out in detail—the Bolton Spinning List, for instance, comprising eighty-five pages closely filled with figures [1]—the intricacy of the calculations is such as to be beyond the comprehension not only of the ordinary operative or manufacturer, but even of the investigating mathematician without a very minute knowledge of the technical detail. Yet the week's earnings of every one of the tens of thousands of operatives are computed by an exact and often a separate calculation under these lists. And when an alteration of the list is in question, the standard wage of a whole district may depend upon the quickness and accuracy with which the operatives' negotiator apprehends the precise effect of each projected change in any of the numerous factors in the calculation. It will be obvious that for work of this nature

committee consisting of Professor Sidgwick, Professor Foxwell, A. H. D. (now Sir Arthur) Acland, Dr. W. Cunningham, and Professor J. E. C. Munro, the report being drawn up by the latter. (*On the Regulation of Wages by means of Lists in the Cotton Industry*, Manchester, 1887 ; in two parts—Spinning and Weaving.) See *History of Wages in the Cotton Trade during the Past Hundred Years*, by G. H. Wood, 1910 ; *A Century of Fine Cotton Spinning*, by McConnel & Co., 1906 ; and *Standard Piece Lists and Sliding Scales*, by the Labour Department of the Board of Trade, Cd. 144, 1900.

The principles upon which the lists are framed are so complicated that we confess, after prolonged study, to be still perplexed on certain points ; and though Professor Munro clears up many difficulties, we are disposed to believe that even he, in some particulars, has not in all cases correctly stated the matter. We have discussed the whole subject in our *Industrial Democracy*.

[1] *Bolton and District Net List of Prices for Spinning Twist, Reeled Yarn or Bastard Twist, and Weft, on Self-actor Mules* (Bolton, 1887; 85 pp.).

the successful organiser or " born orator " was frequently quite unfit. There grew up, therefore, both among the weavers and the spinners, a system of selection of new secretaries by competitive examination, which has gradually been perfected as the examiners—that is, the existing officials—have themselves become more skilled. The first secretary to undergo this ordeal was Thomas Birtwistle,[1] who in 1861 began his thirty years' honourable and successful service of the Lancashire Weavers. Within a few years he was reinforced by other officials selected for the same characteristics. From 1871 onwards the counsels of the Trade Union Movement were strengthened by the introduction of " the cotton men," a body of keen, astute, and alert-minded officials—a combination, in the Trade Union world, of the accountant and the lawyer.

Under such guidance the Lancashire cotton operatives achieved extraordinary success. Their first task was in all districts to obtain and perfect the lists. The rate and method of remuneration being in this way secured, their energy was devoted to improving the other conditions of their labour by means of appropriate legislation. Ever since 1830 the Lancashire operatives, especially the spinners, have strongly supported the legislative regulation of the hours and other conditions of their industry. In 1867 a delegate meeting of the Lancashire textile operatives, under the presidency of the Rev. J. R. Stephens, had resolved " to agitate for such a measure of legislative restriction as shall secure a uniform Eight Hours Bill in factories, exclusive of meal-times, for adults, females, and young persons, and that such Eight Hours Bill have for its foundation a restriction on the moving power." [2]   On the improvement of trade

[1] Birtwistle was, in 1892, at an advanced age, appointed by the Home Secretary an Inspector in the Factory Department, under the " particulars clause " (sec. 24 of the Factory and Workshops Act, 1891), as the only person who could be found competent to understand and interpret the intricacies of the method of remuneration in the weaving trade.

[2] *Beehive*, February 23, 1867. The circular announcing the resolution is signed by the leading officers of the Cotton-spinners' and Cotton-weavers' Unions of the time.

and the revival of Trade Union strength in 1871–72 this policy was again resorted to. The Oldham spinners tried, indeed, in 1871, to secure a " Twelve-o'clock Saturday " by means of a strike. But on the failure of this attempt the delegates of the various local societies, both of spinners and weavers—usually the officials of the trade—met together and established, on the 7th of January 1872, the Factory Acts Reform Association, for the purpose of obtaining such an amendment of the law as would reduce the hours of labour from sixty to fifty-four per week.

The Parliamentary policy of these shrewd tacticians is only another instance of the practical opportunism of the English Trade Unionist. The cotton officials demurred in 1872 to an overt alliance with the Parliamentary Committee of the Trades Union Congress, just then engaged in its heated agitation for a repeal of the Criminal Law Amendment Act. " Some members of the Short Time Committee," states, without resentment, the Congress report, " thought that even co-operation with the Congress Committee would be disastrous rather than useful, . . . as Lord Shaftesbury and others declared they would not undertake a measure proposed in the interest of the Trades Unions." [1] So far as the public and the House of Commons were concerned, the Bill was accordingly, as we are told, " based upon quite other grounds." Its provisions were ostensibly restricted, like those of the Ten Hours Act, to women and children ; and to the support of Trade Union champions such as Thomas Hughes and A. J. Mundella was added that of such philanthropists as Lord Shaftesbury and Samuel Morley. But it is scarcely necessary to say that it was not entirely, or even exclusively, for the sake of the women and children that the skilled leaders of the Lancashire cotton operatives had diverted their " Short Time Movement " from aggressive strikes to Parliamentary agitation. The private minutes of the Factory Acts Reform Association contain no mention

---

[1] Report of the Parliamentary Committee to the Trades Union Congress, January 1873.

of the woes of the women and the children, but reflect throughout the demand of the adult male spinners for a shorter day. And in the circular " to the factory operatives," calling the original meeting of the association, we find the spinners' secretary combating the fallacy that " any legislative interference with male adult labour is an economic error," and demanding " a legislative enactment largely curtailing the hours of factory labour," in order that his constituents, who were exclusively adult males, might enjoy " the nine hours per day, or fifty-four hours per week, so liberally conceded to other branches of workmen." [1] It was, however, neither necessary nor expedient to take this line in public. The experience of a generation had taught the Lancashire operatives that any effective limitation of the factory day for women and children could not fail to bring with it an equivalent shortening of the hours of the men who worked with them. And in the state of mind, in 1872, of the House of Commons, and even of the workmen in other trades, it would have proved as impossible as it did in 1847 to secure an avowed restriction of the hours of male adults.

The Short Time Bill was therefore so drafted as to apply in express terms only to women and children, whose sufferings under a ten hours day were made much of on the platform and in the press. The battle, in fact, was, as one of the leading combatants has declared,[2] " fought from behind the women's petticoats." But it was a part of the irony of the situation that, as Broadhurst subsequently pointed out,[3] the Bill " encountered great opposition from

[1] Circular of December 11, 1871, signed on behalf of the preliminary meeting by Thomas Mawdsley—not to be mistaken for James Mawdsley, J.P., a subsequent secretary.

[2] Thomas Ashton, J.P. (died 1919), then secretary of the Oldham Spinners, often made this statement. On the 26th of May 1893 the *Cotton Factory Times*, the men's accredited organ, declared, with reference to the Eight Hours Movement, that " now the veil must be lifted, and the agitation carried on under its true colours. Women and children must no longer be made the pretext for securing a reduction of working hours for men."

[3] Speech at Trades Union Congress, Bristol, 1878.

the female organisations " ; and it was, in fact, expressly in the interests of working women that Professor Fawcett, in the session of 1873, moved the rejection of the measure.[1] Even as limited to women and children the proposal encountered a fierce resistance from the factory owners and the capitalists of all industries. The opinion of the House of Commons was averse from any further restriction upon the employers' freedom. The Ministry of the day lent it no assistance. The Bill, introduced in 1872, and again in 1873, made no progress. At length, in 1873, the Government shelved the question by appointing a Royal Commission to inquire into the working of the Factory Acts. But a General Election was now drawing near ; and " a Factory Nine Hours Bill for Women and Children " was incorporated in the Parliamentary programme pressed upon candidates by the whole Trade Union world.[2]

We have already pointed out what an attentive ear the Conservative party was at this time giving to the Trade Union demands. It is therefore not surprising that when Mundella, in the new Parliament, once more introduced his Bill, the Home Secretary, Mr. (afterwards Viscount) Cross, announced that the Government would bring forward a measure of their own. The fact that the Government draft was euphemistically entitled the " Factories (Health of Women, etc.) Bill " did not conciliate the opponents of the shorter factory day which it ensured ; but, to the great satisfaction of the spinners, this opposition was unsuccessful ; and, if not a nine hours day, at any rate a 56½ hours week became law. This short and successful Parliamentary campaign brought the cotton operatives into closer contact with the London leaders ; and from 1875 the Lancashire representatives exercised an important influence in the Trades Union Congress and its Parliamentary Committee.

[1] " From what I have heard," writes Professor Beesly in the *Beehive*, May 16, 1874, " I am inclined to think that no single fact had more to do with the defeat of the Liberal Party in Lancashire at the last election than Mr. Fawcett's speech on the Nine Hours Bill in the late Parliament."

[2] Report of Trades Union Congress, Sheffield, January 1874.

Henceforth detailed amendments of the Factory Acts, and increased efficiency in their administration, become almost standing items in the official Trade Union programme.

An interesting parallelism might be traced between the cotton operatives on the one hand and the coal-miners on the other. To outward seeming no two occupations could be more unlike. Yet without community of interest, without official intercourse, and without any traceable imitation, the organisations of the two trades show striking resemblances to each other in history, in structural development, and in characteristics of policy, method, and aims. Many of these similarities may arise from the remarkable local aggregation in particular districts, which is common to both industries. From this local aggregation spring, perhaps, the possibilities of a strong federation existing without centralised funds, and of a permanent trade society enduring without friendly benefits. A further similarity may be seen in the creation, in each case, of a special class of Trade Union officials, far more numerous in proportion to membership than is usual in the engineering or building trades. But the most noticeable, and perhaps the most important, of these resemblances is the constancy with which both the miners and the cotton operatives have adhered to the legislative protection of the Standard of Life as a leading principle of their Trade Unionism.

Whilst these important divisions of the Trade Union army were aiming at legislative protection, victories in another field were bringing whole sections of Trade Unionists to a different conclusion. The successful Nine Hours Movement of 1871–72—the reduction, by collective bargaining, of the hours of labour in the engineering and building trades —rivalled the legislative triumphs of the miners and the cotton operatives.

Since the great strikes in the London building trades in 1859–61, the movement in favour of a reduction of the hours of labour had been dragging on in various parts of the country. The masons, carpenters, and other building

operatives had in many towns, and after more or less conflict, secured what was termed the Nine Hours Day. In
1866 an agitation arose among the engineers of Tyneside for
a similar concession ; but the sudden depression of trade
put an end to the project. In 1870, when the subject was
discussed at the Newcastle " Central District Committee "
of the Amalgamated Society of Engineers, the spirit of
caution prevailed, and no action was taken. Suddenly, at
the beginning of 1871, the Sunderland men took the matter
up, and came out on strike on the 1st of April. After
four weeks' struggle, almost before the engineers elsewhere
had realised that there was any chance of success, the local
employers gave way, and the Nine Hours Day was won.

It was evident that the Sunderland movement was
destined to spread to the other engineering centres in the
neighbourhood ; and the master engineers of the entire
North-Eastern District promptly assembled at Newcastle
on April 8 to concert a united resistance to the men's
demands. The operatives had first to form their organisation. Though Newcastle has since become one of the
best centres of Trade Unionism, the Amalgamated Society
of Engineers could, in 1871, count only five or six hundred
members in the town ; the Boilermakers, Steam-Engine
Makers, and Ironfounders were also weak, and probably
two out of three of the men in the engineering trade belonged to no Union whatsoever. A " Nine Hours League,"
embracing Unionists and non-Unionists alike, was accordingly formed for the special purpose of the agitation ; and
this body was fortunate enough to elect as its President
John Burnett,[1] a leading member of the local branch of

---

[1] John Burnett, who was born at Alnwick, Northumberland, in 1842,
became, after the Nine Hours Strike, a lecturer for the National Education League, and joined the staff of the *Newcastle Chronicle*. In 1875, on
Allan's death, he was elected to the General Secretaryship of the Amalgamated Society of Engineers. He was a member of the Parliamentary
Committee of the Trades Union Congress from 1876 to 1885. In 1886
he was appointed to the newly-created post of Labour Correspondent of
the Board of Trade, in which capacity he prepared and issued a series
of reports on Trade Unions and Strikes. On the establishment of the

the Amalgamated Society, afterwards to become widely known as the General Secretary of that great organisation. The " Nine Hours League " became, in fact though not in name, a temporary Trade Union, its committee conducting all the negotiations on the men's behalf, appealing to the Trade Union world for funds for their support, and managing all the details of the conflict that ensued.[1]

The five months' strike which led up to a signal victory for the men was, in more than one respect, a notable event in Trade Union annals. The success with which several thousands of unorganised workmen, unprovided with any accumulated funds, were marshalled and disciplined, and the ability displayed in the whole management of the dispute, made the name of their leader celebrated throughout the world of labour. The tactical skill and literary force with which the men's case was presented achieved the unprecedented result of securing for their demands the support of the *Times*[2] and the *Spectator*. Money was

Labour Department in 1893 he became Chief Labour Correspondent under the Commissioner for Labour, and was selected to visit the United States to prepare a report on the effects of Jewish immigration. He retired in 1907 and died 1914.

[1] A full account of this conflict is given by John Burnett in his *History of the Engineers' Strike in Newcastle and Gateshead* (Newcastle, 1872 ; 77 pp.). A description by the Executive of the Amalgamated Society of Engineers is given in their " Abstract Report " up to December 31, 1872. The *Newcastle Daily Chronicle*, from April to October 1871, furnishes a detailed contemporary record. The leading articles and correspondence in the *Times* of September 1871 are important.

[2] See the *Times* leader of September 11, 1871. This leader, which pronounced " the conduct of the employers throughout this dispute as imprudent and impolitic," called forth the bewildered remonstrance of Sir William (afterwards Lord) Armstrong, writing on behalf of " the Associated Employers." " We were amazed," writes the great captain of industry, " to see ourselves described in your article as being in a condition of hopeless difficulty ; and we really felt that, if the League themselves had possessed the power of inspiring that article, they could scarcely have used words more calculated to serve their purposes than those in which it is expressed. The concurrent appearance in the *Spectator* of an article exhibiting the same bias adds to our surprise. We had imagined that a determined effort to wrest concessions from employers by sheer force of combination was not a thing which found favour with the more educated and intelligent classes, whose opinions generally find expression in the columns of the *Times*" (*Times* September 14, 1871).

subscribed slowly at first, but after three months poured in from all sides. Joseph Cowen, of the *Newcastle Daily Chronicle*, was from the first an ardent supporter of the men, and assisted them in many ways. The employers in all parts of the kingdom took alarm ; and a kind of levy of a shilling for each man employed was made upon the engineering firms in aid of the heavy expenses of the Newcastle masters. In spite of the active exertions of the " International," several hundred foreign workmen were imported ; but many of these were subsequently induced to desert.[1] Finally the employers conceded the principal of the men's demands ; and fifty-four hours became the locally recognised week's time in all the engineering trades.

This widely advertised success, coming at a time of expanding trade, greatly promoted the movement for the Nine Hours Day. From one end of the kingdom to the other, every little Trade Union branch discussed the expediency of sending in notices to the employers. The engineering trades in London, Manchester, and other great centres induced their employers to grant their demands without a strike. The great army of workmen engaged in the shipbuilding yards on the Clyde even bettered this example, securing a fifty-one hours week. The building operatives quickly followed suit. Demands for a diminution of the working day, with an increased rate of pay per hour, were handed in by local officials of the Carpenters, Masons, Bricklayers, Plumbers, and other organisations. In many cases non-society men took the lead in the movement ; but it was soon found that the immediate success of the applications depended on the estimate formed by the employers of the men's financial resources, and their capacity to withhold their labour for a time sufficient to cause embarrassment to business. Wherever the employers were

---

[1] Here the " International " was of use. At Burnett's instigation, Cohn, the Danish secretary in London, proceeded to the Continent to check this immigration, his expenses being paid by the Amalgamated Society of Engineers.

assured of this fact, they usually gave way without a conflict. The successes accordingly did much to create, in the industries in question, a preference for combination and collective bargaining as a means of improving the conditions of labour. The prevalence of systematic overtime, which has since proved so formidable a deduction from the advantages gained by the Nine Hours Movement, was either overlooked by sanguine officials, or covertly welcomed by individual workmen as affording opportunities for working at a higher rate of remuneration.[1] On the other hand, it was a patent fact that the mechanic employed in attending to the machinery of a textile mill was the only member of his trade who was excluded from participation in the shortening of hours enjoyed by his fellow-tradesmen ; and that his failure to secure a shorter day was an incidental consequence of the existence of legislative restrictions. Thus, at the very time that the textile operatives and coal-miners were, as we have seen, exhibiting a marked tendency to look more and more to Parliamentary action for the protection of the Standard of Life, the facts, as they presented themselves to the Amalgamated Engineer or Carpenter, were leading the members of these trades to a diametrically opposite conclusion.

But though faith in trade combinations and collective bargaining was strengthened by the success of the Nine Hours Movement, the victories of the men did not increase the prestige of the two great Amalgamated Societies. The growing adhesion of the Junta to the economic views of their middle-class friends was marked by the silent abandonment by Allan, Applegarth, and Guile of all leadership in trade matters. Already in 1865 we find the Executive Council of the Amalgamated Engineers explaining that, although they sympathised with advance movements, they felt unable to either support them by grants or to advise

---

[1] With regard to overtime, Burnett informed us that " it was found impossible to carry a Nine Hours Day pure and simple at the time of the strike of 1871, and that overtime should still be worked as required was insisted upon as a first condition of settlement by the employers."

their members to vote a special levy.[1] The " backwardness of the Council of the Engineers " constantly provoked angry criticism. The chief obstacles to advancement were declared to be Danter, the President of the Council, and the General Secretary, whose minds had been narrowed " by the routine of years of service within certain limits. . . . Never, since it effected amalgamation, has the Society solved one social problem ; nor has it now an idea of future progress. Its money is unprofitably and injudiciously invested—even with a miser's care—while its councils are marked with all the chilly apathy of a worn-out mission." [2] What proved to be the greatest trade movement since 1852 was undertaken in spite of the official disapproval of the governing body, and was carried to a successful issue without the provision from headquarters of any leadership or control. Though the Nine Hours Strike actually began in Sunderland on April 1, 1871, the London Executive remained silent on the subject until July. Towards the end of that month, when the Newcastle men had been out for seven weeks, a circular was issued inviting the branches to collect voluntary subscriptions for their struggling brethren. Ultimately, in September, the " Contingent Fund," out of which strike pay is given, was re-established by vote of the branches ; and the strike allowance of 5s. per week, over and above the ordinary out-of-work pay, was issued, after fourteen weeks' struggle, to the small minority of the men on strike who were members of the Society. An emissary was sent to the Continent, at the Society's expense, to defeat the employers' attempt to bring over foreign engineers ; but with this exception all the expenses of the struggle were defrayed from the subscriptions collected by the Nine Hours League.[3] And if we turn

---

[1] Meeting of London pattern-makers to seek advance of wages, *Beehive*, October 21, 1865.

[2] Letter from " Amalgamator," *Beehive*, January 19, 1867.

[3] The rank and file were more sympathetic than the Executive. The machinery for making the collections was mostly furnished by the branches and committees of the Society.

for a moment from the Amalgamated Society of Engineers to the other great trade and friendly societies of the time, it is easy, in the minutes of their Executive Councils and the proceedings of their branches, to watch the same tendency at work. Whether it is the Masons or the Tailors, the Ironfounders or the Carpenters, we see the same abandonment by the Central Executive of any dominant principle of trade policy, the same absence of initiative in trade movements, and the same more or less persistent struggle to check the trade activity of its branches. In the Amalgamated Society of Carpenters, for example, we find, during these years, no attempt by headquarters to " level up " the wages of low-paid districts, or to grapple with the problems of overtime or piecework. We watch, on the contrary, the branches defending themselves before the Executive for their little spurts of local activity, and pleading, in order to wring from a reluctant treasury the concession of strike pay, that they have been dragged into the " Advance Movement " by the more aggressive policy of the " General Union " (the rival trade society of the old type), or by irresponsible " strike-committees " of non-society men.

Time and growth were, in fact, revealing the drawbacks of the constitution with which Newton and Allan had endowed their cherished amalgamation, and which had been so extensively copied by other trades. The difficulties arising from the attempt to unite, in one organisation, men working in the numerous distinct branches of the engineering trade, demanded constant thought and attention. The rapid changes in the industry, especially in connection with the growing use of new machinery, needed to be met by a well-considered flexibility, dictated by full knowledge of the facts, and some largeness of view. To maintain a harmonious yet progressive trade policy in all the hundreds of branches would, of itself, have taxed the skill of a body of experts free from other preoccupations. All these duties were, however, cast upon a single salaried officer,[1] working under a committee of artisans who met in the evening after an exhausting day of physical toil.

The result might have been foreseen. The rapid growth of the society brought with it a huge volume of detailed business. Every grant of accident benefit or superannuation allowance was made by the Executive Council. Every week this body had to decide on scores of separate applications for gifts from the Benevolent Fund. Every time any of the tens of thousands of members failed to get what he wanted from his branch, he appealed to the Executive Council. Every month an extensive trade report had to be issued. Every quarter the branch accounts had to be examined, dissected, and embodied in an elaborate summary, itself absorbing no small amount of labour and thought. The hundreds of branch secretaries and treasurers had to be constantly supervised, checked by special audits, and perpetually admonished for negligent or accidental breaches of the complicated code by which the Society was governed. The Executive Council became, in fact, absorbed in purely " treasury " work, and spent a large part of its time in protecting the funds of the Society from extravagance, laxity of administration, or misappropriation. The quantity of routine soon became enormous ; and the whole attention of the General Secretary was given to coping with the mass of details which poured in upon him by every post.

This huge friendly society business brought with it, too, its special bias. Allan grew more and more devoted to the accumulating fund, which was alike the guarantee and the symbol of the success of his organisation. Nothing

---

[1] An " Assistant Secretary " was subsequently added, and eventually another. But these assistants were, like the General Secretary himself, recruited from the ranks of the workmen, and however experienced they may have been in trade matters, were necessarily less adapted to the clerical labour demanded of them. The great Trade Friendly Societies of the Stonemasons, Bricklayers, and Ironfounders long continued to have only one assistant secretary, and no clerical staff whatever.

was important enough to warrant any inroad on this sacred balance. The Engineers' Central Executive, indeed, practically laid aside the weapon of the strike. "We believe," said Allan before the Royal Commission in 1867, "that all strikes are a complete waste of money, not only in relation to the workmen, but also to the employers." [1] The "Contingent Fund," out of which alone strike pay could be given, was between 1860 and 1872 repeatedly abolished by vote of the members, re-established for a short time, and again abolished. Trade Unionists who remembered the old conflicts viewed with surprise and alarm the spirit which had come over the once active organisation. Even the experienced Dunning, whose moderation had, as we have suggested, dictated the first manifesto in which the new spirit can be traced, was moved to denunciation of Allan's apathy. "As a Trade Union," he writes in 1866, "the once powerful Amalgamated Society of Engineers is now as incapable to engage in a strike as the Hearts of Oak, the Foresters, or any other extensive benefit society. . . . It formerly combined both functions, but now it possesses only one, that of a benefit society, with relief for members when out of work or travelling for employment superadded. . . . The Amalgamated Engineers, as a trade society, has ceased to exist." [2]

It would be a mistake to assume that the inertia and supineness of the "Amalgamated" Societies was a necessary result of their accumulated funds or their friendly benefits. The remarkable energy and success of the United Society of Boilermakers and Iron-shipbuilders, established in 1832, and between 1865 and 1875 rapidly increasing in membership and funds, shows that elaborate friendly benefits are not inconsistent with a strong and consistent trade policy. This quite exceptional success is, we believe, due to the fact that the Boilermakers provided an adequate salaried staff to attend to their trade affairs. The "district delegates" who were, between 1873 and 1889, appointed

---

[1] Question 827 in Report of Trade Union Commission (March 26, 1867).
[2] *Bookbinders' Trade Circular*, January 1866.

M

for every important district, are absolutely unconcerned with the administration of friendly benefits, and devote themselves exclusively to the work of Collective Bargaining. Unlike the General Secretaries of the Engineers, Carpenters, Stonemasons, or Ironfounders, who had but one salaried assistant, Robert Knight, the able secretary of the Boilermakers had under his orders an expert professional staff, and was accordingly able, not only to keep both employers and unruly members in check, but also successfully to adapt the Union policy to the changing conditions of the industry. In short, it was not the presence of friendly benefits, but the absence of any such class of professional organisers as exists in the organisations of the Coal-miners, Cotton Operatives, and Boilermakers, that created the deadlock in the administration of the great trade friendly societies.[1]

The direct result of this abnegation of trade leadership was a complete arrest of the tendency to amalgamation, and, in some cases, even a breaking away of sections already within the organisation. The various independent societies, such as the Boilermakers, Steam-Engine Makers, and the Co-operative Smiths, gave up all idea of joining their larger rival. In 1872 the Patternmakers, who had long been discontented at the neglect of their special trade interests, formed an organisation of their own, which has since competed with the Amalgamated for the allegiance of this exceptionally skilled class of engineers. Nor was Allan at all eager to make his organisation co-extensive with the whole engineering industry. The dominant idea of the early years of the amalgamation—the protection of those who had, by regular apprenticeship, acquired " a right to the trade "—excluded many men actually working at one branch or another, whilst the friendly society bias against unprofitable recruits co-operated to restrict the membership to such sections of

---

[1] In 1892 the Amalgamated Engineers provided themselves, not only with district delegates, like those of the Boilermakers, but also with a salaried Executive Council. The Amalgamated Society of Carpenters has since started district delegates, and the other national societies gradually followed suit.

the engineering industry, and such members of each section, as could earn a minimum time wage fixed for each locality by the District Committee.

This exclusiveness necessarily led to the development of other societies, which accepted those workmen who were not eligible for the larger organisation. The little local clubs of Machine-workers and Metal-planers expanded between 1867 and 1872 into national organisations, and began to claim consideration at the hands of the better paid engineers, on whose heels they were treading. New societies, such as those of the National Society of Amalgamated Brass-workers, the Independent Order of Engineers and Machinists, and the Amalgamated Society of Kitchen Range, Stove Grate, Gas Stoves, Hot Water, Art Metal, and other Smiths and Fitters, sprang into existence during 1872, in avowed protest against the " aristocratic " rule of excluding all workmen who were not receiving a high standard rate. The Associated Blacksmiths of Scotland, which had been formed in 1857 out of a class of smiths which was, at the time, unrecognised in the rules of the Amalgamated, now began steadily to increase in membership. Finally, during the decade various local societies were refused the privilege of amalgamation on the ground that either they included sections of the trade not recognised by the rules, or that the average age of their constituents was such as to make them unprofitable members of a society giving heavy super-annuation benefit. To the tendency to create an " aristo-cracy of labour " was added, therefore, the fastidiousness of an insurance company.

Many causes were thus co-operating to shift the centre of Trade Union influence from London to the provinces. The great trade friendly societies of Engineers, Carpenters, and Ironfounders were losing that lead in Trade Union matters which the political activity of the Junta had acquired for them. The Junta itself was breaking up. Applegarth, in many respects the leader of the group, resigned his secretaryship in 1871, and left the Trade Union Movement.

Odger, who lived until 1877, was from 1870 onwards devoting himself more and more to general politics. Allan, long suffering from an incurable disease, died in 1874. Meanwhile provincial Trade Unionism was growing apace. The Amalgamated Society of Engineers, so long pre-eminent in numbers, began to be overshadowed by the federations of Coal-miners and Cotton Operatives. Even in the iron trades it found rivals in the rapidly growing organisations of Boilermakers (Iron-shipbuilders), whose headquarters were at Newcastle, and the Ironworkers centred at Darlington, whilst minor engineering societies were cropping up in all directions in the northern counties. The tendency to abandon London was further shown by the decision of the Amalgamated Society of Carpenters in 1871 to remove their head office to Manchester, a change which had the incidental effect of depriving the London leaders of the counsels of Applegarth's successor, J. D. Prior, one of the ablest disciples of the Junta.

But although London was losing its hold on the Trade Union Movement, no other town inherited the leadership. Manchester, it is true, attracted to itself the headquarters of many national societies, and contained in these years perhaps the strongest group of Trade Union officials.[1] But there was no such concentration of all the effective forces as had formerly resulted in the Junta. Though Manchester might have furnished the nucleus of a Trade Union Cabinet, Alexander Macdonald was to be found either in Glasgow or London, Robert Knight at Liverpool and afterwards in Newcastle, John Kane at Darlington, the miners' agents all

---

[1] Mention should here be made of the Manchester and District Association of Trade Union Officials, an organisation which grew out of a joint committee formed to assist the South Wales miners in their strike of 1875. The frequent meetings, half serious, half social, of this grandly named association, known to the initiated as " the Peculiar People," served for many years as opportunities for important consultations on Trade Union policy between the leaders of the numerous societies having offices in Manchester. It also had as an object the protection of Trade Union officials against unjust treatment by their own societies (see *History of the British Trades Union Congress*, by W. J. Davis, vol. i., 1910, p. 89).

over the country, whilst Henry Broadhurst (who in 1875 succeeded George Howell as the Secretary of the Parliamentary Committee), John Burnett, the General Secretary of the Amalgamated Society of Engineers, and George Shipton, the Secretary of the London Trades Council, naturally remained in the Metropolis. The result of the shifting from London was, accordingly, not the establishment elsewhere of any new executive centre of the Trade Union Movement, but the rise of a sectional spirit, the promotion of sectional interests, and the elaboration of sectional policies on the part of the different trades.

We have attempted in some detail to describe the internal growth of the Trade Union Movement between 1867 and 1875, in order to enable the reader to understand the disheartening collapse which ensued in 1878-79, and the subsequent splitting up of the Trade Union world into the hostile camps once more designated the Old Unionists and the New. But all the unsatisfactory features of 1871–75 were, during these years, submerged by a wave of extraordinary commercial prosperity and Trade Union expansion. The series of Parliamentary successes of 1871–75 produced, as we have seen, a feeling of triumphant elation among the Trade Union leaders. To the little knot of working men who had conducted the struggle for emancipation and recognition, the progress of these years seemed almost beyond belief. In 1867 the officials of the Unions were regarded as pothouse agitators, " unscrupulous men, leading a half idle life, fattening on the contributions of their dupes," and maintaining, by violence and murder, a system of terrorism which was destructive, not only of the industry of the nation, but also of the prosperity and independence of character of the unfortunate working men who were their victims. The Unionist workman, tramping with his card in search of employment, was regarded by the constable and the magistrate as something between a criminal vagrant and a revolutionist. In 1875 the officials of the great societies found themselves elected to the local School Boards.

and even to the House of Commons, pressed by the Government to accept seats on Royal Commissions, and respectfully listened to in the lobby. And these political results were but the signs of an extraordinary expansion of the Trade Union Movement itself. " The year just closed," says the report of the Parliamentary Committee in January 1874, " has been unparalleled for the rapid growth and development of Trade Unionism. In almost every trade this appears to have been the same ; but it is especially remarkable in those branches of industry which have hitherto been but badly organised." Exact numerical details cannot now be ascertained ; but the Trades Union Congress of 1872 claimed to represent only 375,000 organised workmen, whilst that of 1874 included delegates from nearly three times as many societies, representing a nominal total of 1,191,922 members.[1] It is possible that between 1871 and 1875 the number of Trade Unionists was more than doubled.

We see this progress reflected in the minds of the employers. At the end of 1873 we find the newly established National Federation of Associated Employers of Labour declaring that " the voluntary and intermittent efforts of individual employers," or even employers' associations confined to a single trade or locality, are helpless against " the extraordinary development—far-reaching, but openly-avowed designs—and elaborate organisation of the Trade Unions." " Few are aware," continues this manifesto, " of the extent, compactness of organisation, large resources, and great influence of the Trade Unions. . . . They have the control of enormous funds, which they expend freely in furtherance of their objects ; and the proportion of their earnings which the operatives devote to the service of their leaders is startling. . . . They have a well-paid and ample staff of leaders, most of them experienced in the conduct of strikes, many of them skilful as organisers, all forming a class

[1] Report of the Trades Union Congress, Sheffield, 1874. A table printed in the Appendix to the present volume gives such comparative statistics of Trade Union membership as we have been able to compile.

apart, a profession, with interests distinct from, though not necessarily antagonistic to, those of the workpeople they lead, but from their very *raison d'être* hostile to those of the employers and the rest of the community. . . . They have, through their command of money, the imposing aspect of their organisation, and partly, also, from the mistaken humanitarian aspirations of a certain number of literary men of good standing, a large army of literary talent which is *prompt* in their service on all occasions of controversy. They have their own press as a field for these exertions. Their writers have free access to some of the leading London journals. They organise frequent public meetings, at which paid speakers inoculate the working classes with their ideas, and urge them to dictate terms to candidates for Parliament. Thus they exercise a pressure upon members of Parliament, and those aspirant to that honour, out of all proportion to their real power, and beyond belief except to those who have had the opportunity of witnessing its effects. They have a standing Parliamentary Committee, and a programme ; and active members of Parliament are energetic in their service. They have the attentive ear of the Ministry of the day ; and their communications are received with instant and respectful attention. They have a large representation of their own body in London whenever Parliament is likely to be engaged in the discussion of the proposals they have caused to be brought before it. Thus, untrammelled by pecuniary considerations, and specially set apart for this peculiar work, without other clashing occupations, they resemble the staff of a well-organised, well-provisioned army, for which everything that foresight and preoccupation in a given purpose could provide, is at command." [1] It is

[1] " Statement as to Formation and Objects of the National Federation of Associated Employers of Labour," December 11, 1873, reprinted by the Parliamentary Committee of the Trades Union Congress. This Federation comprised in its ranks a large proportion of the great " captains of industry " of the time, including such shipbuilders as Laird and Harland & Wolff ; such textile manufacturers as Crossley, Brinton, Marshall, Titus Salt, Akroyd, and Brocklehurst ; such engineers as Mawdsley, Son & Field, Combe, Barbour & Combe, and Beyer & Peacock ; such ironmasters

not surprising that the Parliamentary Committee of the Trades Union Congress, composed, as it was, of the " staff of leaders " referred to, should have had this involuntary tribute to their efficiency reprinted and widely circulated among their constituents.

The student will form a more qualified estimate of the position in 1873–75 than either the elated Trade Unionists or the alarmed employers. In the first place, great as was the numerical expansion of these years, the reader of the preceding chapters will know that it was not without parallel. The outburst of Trade Unionism between 1830 and 1834 was, so far as we can estimate, even greater than that between 1871 and 1875, whilst it was far more rapid in its development. There were, during the nineteenth century, three high tides in the Trade Union history of our country, 1833–34, 1872–74, and 1889–90. In the absence of complete and trustworthy statistics it is difficult to say at which of these dates the sweeping in of members was greatest. But it is easy to discern that the expansion of 1873–74 was marked by features which were both like and unlike those of its predecessor.

Like the outburst of 1833–34, the marked extension of Trade Unionism in 1872 reached even the agricultural labourers. For more than thirty years since the transportation of the Dorchester labourers good times and bad had passed over their heads without resulting in any combined effort to improve their condition. There seems to have been a short-lived combination in Scotland in 1865. We hear of an impulsive strike of some Buckinghamshire labourers in 1867, which spread into Hertfordshire. A more effective Union was formed in Herefordshire in 1871, which pursued a quiet policy of emigration, and enrolled 30,000 subscribers in half a dozen counties. But a more

---

as David Dale and John Menelaus ; such builders as Trollope of London and Neill of Manchester, and such representatives of the great industrial peers as Sir James Ramsden, who spoke for the Duke of Devonshire, and Fisher Smith, the agent of the Earl of Dudley.

energetic movement now arose. On February 7, 1872, the labourers of certain parishes of Warwickshire met at Wellesbourne to discuss their grievances. At a second meeting, a little later, Joseph Arch, a labourer of Barford, who owned a freehold cottage, and had become known as a Primitive Methodist preacher, made a speech which bore fruit. On the 11th of March two hundred men resolved to strike for higher wages, namely, 16s. per week for a working day from 6 A.M. to 5 P.M. Unlike most strikes this one attracted from the first the favourable notice of the press.[1] Publicity brought immediate funds and sympathisers. On the 29th of March the inaugural meeting of the Warwickshire Agricultural Labourers' Union was held at Leamington, under the presidency of the Hon. Auberon Herbert, M.P., a donation of one hundred pounds being handed in by a rich friend. Through the eloquence, the revivalist fervour, and the untiring energy of Joseph Arch, the movement spread like wildfire among the rural labourers of the central and eastern counties.

[1] The immediate publicity given to the agitation was due, in the first place, to the sympathy of J. E. Matthew Vincent, the editor of the *Leamington Chronicle*, and secondly, to the instinct of the *Daily News*, which promptly sent Archibald Forbes, its war correspondent, to Warwickshire, and " boomed " the movement in a series of special articles. A contemporary account of the previous career of Joseph Arch is given by the Rev. F. S. Attenborough in his *Life of Joseph Arch* (Leamington, 1872; 37 pp.). See also *The Revolt of the Field*, by A. W. Clayden (1874), 234 pp. ; and "Zur Geschichte der englischen Arbeiterbewegung im Jahre 1872–1873," by Dr. Friedrich Kleinwächter in *Jahrbücher für Nationalökonomie und Statistik*, 1875, and Supplement I. of 1878 ; "Die jüngste Landarbeiter-bewegung in England," by Lloyd Jones, in Nathusius-Thiel's *Landwirthschaftliche Jahrbücher*, 1875 ; *The Romance of Peasant Life*, 1872, and *The English Peasantry*, 1872, by F. G. Heath ; *The Agricultural Labourer*, by F. E. Kettel, 1887 ; *Joseph Arch, the Story of his Life, told by Himself*, 1898 ; *A History of the English Agricultural Labourer*, by Dr. W. Hasbach, 1908 ; "The Labourers in Council," a valuable article in *The Congregationalist*, 1872 ; "The Agricultural Labourers' Union," in *Quarterly Review*, 1873 ; "The Agricultural Labourers' Union," by Canon Girdlestone, in *Macmillan's Magazine*, vol. xxviii. ; "The Agricultural Labourer," by F. Verinder, in *The Church Reformer*, 1892 ; and others in this magazine during 1891–93 ; *Conflicts of Capital and Labour*, by G. Howell, 1878 and 1890 editions ; *Labour Legislation, Labour Movements and Labour Leaders*, by the same, 1902 ; and *Village Trade Unions in Two Centuries*, by Ernest Selley, 1919.

M 2

The mania for combination which came over the country population during the next few months recalls, indeed, the mushroom growth of the Grand National Consolidated Trades Union of forty years before. Within two months delegates from twenty-six counties met to transform the local society into a National Agricultural Labourers' Union, organised in district Unions all over the country, with a central committee at Leamington, which, by the end of the year, boasted of a membership of nearly a hundred thousand.[1]

The organised Trade Unions rallied promptly to the support of the labourers, and contributed largely to their funds. The farmers met the men's demand by a widespread lock-out of Unionist labourers, which called forth the support of Trades Councils and individual societies all over the country.[2] George Howell, then Secretary of the

[1] Other Labourers' Unions sprang up which refused to be absorbed in the National; and the London Trades Council summoned a conference in March 1873 to promote unity of action. Considerable jealousy was shown of any centralising policy, and eventually a Federal Union of Agricultural and General Labourers was formed by half a dozen of the smaller societies, with an aggregate membership of 50,000.

[2] The Birmingham Trades Council, for instance, issued the following poster :

" Great Lock-out of Agricultural Labourers !

" An Appeal. Is the Labourer worthy of his Hire ?

" This question is to all lovers of freedom and peaceful progress, and it is left for them to say whether that spark of life and hope which has been kindled in the breasts of our toiling brothers in the agricultural districts shall be extinguished by the pressure of the present lock-out. The answer is No ! and the echo resounds from ten thousand lips. But let us be practical ; a little help is of more value than much sympathy ; we must not stand to pity, but strive to send relief. The cause of the agricultural labourer is our own ; the interests of labour in all its forms are very closely bound up together, and the simple question for each one is, How much can I help, and how soon can I do it ? If we stay thinking too long, action may come too late ; these men, our brethren, now deeply in adversity, may have fallen victims when our active efforts might have saved them. The strain upon the funds of their Union must be considerable with such a number thrown into unwilling idleness, and that for simply asking that their wages, in these times of dear food, might be increased from 13s. to 14s. per week. Money is no doubt wanted, and it is by that alone the victory can be won. Let us therefore hope that Birmingham

Parliamentary Committee, George Shipton, the Secretary of the newly revived London Trades Council, and many other leaders, gave up their nights and days to perfecting the labourers' organisations. The skilled trades, indeed, furnished many of the officials of the new Union. Joseph Arch found for his headquarters an able general secretary in Henry Taylor, a carpenter, whilst the Kentish labourers, organised in the separate Kent Union, enjoyed the services of a compositor. This help, together with the funds and countenance of influential philanthropists, made the outburst less transient than that of 1833–34. In many villages the mere formation of a branch led to an instantaneous rise of wages. But, as in 1833–34, the audacity of the field labourer in imitating the combinations of the town artisan provoked an almost indescribable bitterness of feeling on the part of the squirearchy and their connections. The

---

will once again come to the rescue, determined to assist these men to a successful resistance of the oppression that is attempted in this lock-out.

" The great high priest and deliverer of this people now seeks our aid. We must not let him appeal to us in vain ; his efforts have been too noble in the past, the cause for which he pleads is too full of righteousness, and the issues too great to be passed by in heedless silence. Let us all to work at once. We can all give a little, and each one may encourage his neighbour to follow his example. The conflict may be a severe one. It is for freedom and liberty to unite as we have done. We have reaped some of the advantages of our Unions ; we must assist them to establish theirs, and not allow the ray of hope that now shines across the path of our patient but determined fellow-toilers to be darkened by the blind folly of their employers, who, being in a measure slaves to the powers above them, would, if they could, even at their own loss, consign all below them to perpetual bondage. This must not be. We must not allow these men to be robbed of their right to unite, or their future may be less hopeful than their past. Let some one in every manufactory and workshop collect from those disposed to give, and so help to furnish the means to assist these men to withstand the powers brought against them, showing to their would-be oppressors that we have almost learned the need and duty of standing side by side until all our righteous efforts shall be crowned by victory.

" All members of the Birmingham Trades Council are authorised to collect and receive contributions to the fund, and will be pleased to receive assistance from others.

" By order of the Birmingham Trades Council,

" W. GILLIVER, Secretary."

farmers, wherever they dared, ruthlessly " victimised " any man who joined the Union.   It is needless to say that they received the cordial support of the rural magistracy.   In aid of a lock-out near Chipping Norton, two justices, who happened both to be clergymen, sent sixteen labourers' wives, some with infants at the breast, to prison with hard labour, for " intimidating " certain non-Union men.   An attempt to punish the leaders of a meeting at Farringdon, on the ground of " obstruction of the highway," was only defeated by bringing down an eminent Queen's Counsel from London to overawe the local bench.   The " dukes "— notably those of Marlborough and Rutland—denounced the " agitators and declaimers " who had " too easily succeeded in disturbing the friendly feeling which used to unite the labourer and his employer in mutual feelings of generosity and confidence."   Innumerable acts of petty tyranny and oppression proved how far the landed interest had lagged behind the capitalist employers in the matter of Freedom of Combination.   Nor was the Established Church more sympathetic.   At the great meeting held at Exeter Hall on behalf of the labourers, when the chair was taken by Samuel Morley, M.P., the only ecclesiastic who appeared on the platform was Archbishop (afterwards Cardinal) Manning. In fact, the spirit in which the rural clergy viewed this social upheaval is not unfairly typified by the public utterance of a learned bishop.   On September 2, 1872, Dr. Ellicott, the Bishop of Gloucester, speaking at a meeting of the Gloucester Agricultural Society, significantly suggested the village horsepond as a fit destination for the " agitators," or dele- gates sent by the Union to open new branches.   And the farmers, the squires, and the Church were supported by the army.   When the labourers in August 1872 struck for an increase of wages, the officers, in Oxfordshire and Berk- shire, placed the soldiers at the disposal of the farmers for the purpose of getting in the harvest and so defeating the Union.

This insurrection of the village and the autocratic spirit

which it aroused in the owners of land and tithe had, we believe, a far-reaching political effect. With its results upon the agitation for Church disestablishment and the growing Radicalism of the counties we are not here concerned. We trace, however, from these months, the appearance in the Trade Union programme of the proposals relating to the Land Law Reform and the Summary Jurisdiction of the Magistrates, which seem, at first sight, unconnected with the grievances of the town artisan. But though the agricultural labourer had his effect upon the Trade Union Movement, Trade Unionism was not, at this time, able to do much for him. Funds and personal help were freely placed at his service by his brother Unionists. The minute-books and balance-sheets of the great Unions and the Trade Councils show how warm and generous was the response made to his appeal by the engineers, carpenters, miners, and other trades. The London Trades Council successfully exerted itself to stop the lending of troops to the farmers, and procured a fresh regulation explicitly prohibiting for the future such assistance " in cases where strikes or disputes between farmers and their labourers exist." [1] The public disapproval of the sentence in the Chipping Norton case was used by the Trade Union leaders as a powerful argument for the repeal of the Criminal Law Amendment Act.

But all this availed the agricultural labourer little. The feverish faith in combination as a panacea for all social ills gradually subsided. The farmers, after their first surprise, during which the labourers, in many counties, secured advances of from eighteenpence to as much as four shillings per week, met the Union demands and successes by a stolid resistance, and took every opportunity to regain their ground. In 1874 the Agricultural Unions sustained their first severe defeat. Some of those in Suffolk asked for an advance of

---

[1] *Queen's Regulations for the Army for 1873*, Article 180 ; the whole correspondence is given in the Report of the London Trades Council, June 1873.

wages from 13s. to 14s. for a 54-hours week. The farmers' answer was an immediate lock-out, which was rapidly taken up throughout the Eastern and Midland counties, no fewer than 10,000 members of the Union being thus " victimised." The struggle had to be closed in July 1874, after an expenditure by the National Union of £21,365 in strike pay. After this the membership rapidly declined. Every winter saw the lock-out used as a means for smashing particular branches of the Union. And in this work of destruction the farmers were aided by their personal intimacy with the labourer. It was easy to drop into the suspicious mind of the uneducated villager a fatal doubt as to the real destination of the pennies which he was sending away to the far-off central treasury. Nor was the Union organisation perfect. Difficulties and delays occurred in rendering aid to threatened branches or victimised men. The clergyman, the doctor, and the village publican were always at hand to encourage distrust of the " paid agitator." Within a very few years most of the independent Unions had ceased to exist, whilst Arch's great national society had dwindled away to a steadily diminishing membership, scattered up and down the midland counties, in what were virtually village sick and funeral clubs. With the decline of prosperity of British farming, which set in about 1876–77, men were everywhere dismissed, grass replaced grain over hundreds of thousands of acres, and the demand for agricultural labour fell off ; and even Joseph Arch had repeatedly to advise the local branches to acquiesce in lower wages. By 1881 the National Union could claim only 15,000 members, and in 1889 only 4254.[1]

We have, therefore, in the sudden growth and quick collapse of this revolt " of the field " a marked likeness to the meteoric career of the general Trades Unions of 1833–34.

[1] The rival Kent Union, which had become the Kent and Sussex Agricultural and General Labourers' Union, enrolling all sorts of labourers, claimed in 1889 still to have 10,000 members, with an annual income of £10,000 a year, mostly disbursed in sick and funeral benefits.

But the expansion of the Trade Union Movement in 1871–75 had another point of resemblance to previous periods of inflation. In 1871–75, as in 1833–34 and in 1852, the project of recovering possession of the instruments of production seizes hold of the imagination of great bodies of Trade Unionists. Again we see attempts by trade organisations to establish workshops of their own. The schemes of Co-operative Production of 1871–75 bore more resemblance to those of 1852 than to Owen's crude communism. In the Trade Unionism of 1833–34 the fundamental Trade Union principle of the maintenance of the Standard of Life was overshadowed and absorbed by the Owenite idea of carrying on the whole industry of the country by national associations of producers, in which all the workmen would be included. But in the more practical times of 1852 and 1871–75 the project of " self-employment " remained strictly subordinate to the main functions of the organisation.[1] Whatever visions may have been indulged in by individual philanthropists, the Trade Union committees of both these periods treated the co-operative workshop either as merely a convenient adjunct to the Union, or as a means of affording to a certain number of its members a chance of escape from the conditions of wage-labour.[2] The failure of all

[1] See *Die Strikes, die Co-operation, die Industrial Partnerships*, by Dr. Robert Jannasch (Berlin, 1868; 66 pp.).

[2] Amid the great outburst of feeling in favour of Co-operative Production it is difficult to distinguish in every case between the investments of the funds of the Trade Unions in their corporate capacity, and the subscriptions of individual members under the auspices, and sometimes through the agency, of their trade society. The South Yorkshire Miners' Association used £30,000 of its funds in the purchase of the Shirland Colliery in 1875, and worked it on account of the Association. In a very short time, however, the constant loss on the working led to the colliery being disposed of, with the total loss of the investment. The Northumberland and Durham Miners in 1873 formed a " Co-operative Mining Company " to buy a colliery, a venture in which the Unions took shares, but which quickly ended in the loss of all the capital. Some of the Newcastle engineers on strike for Nine Hours in 1871 were assisted by sympathisers to start the Ouseburn Engine Works, which came to a disastrous end in 1876. In 1875 the Leicester Hosiery Operatives' Union, having 2000 members, began manufacturing on its own account, and bought up a small business. In the following year a vote of the members decided

these attempts belongs, therefore, rather to the history of Co-operation than to that of Trade Unionism. For our present purpose it suffices to note that the loss in these experiments of tens of thousands of pounds finally convinced the officials of the old-established Unions of the impracticability of using Trade Union organisations and Trade Union funds for Co-operative Production. The management of industry by associations of producers still remains the ideal of one school of co-operators, and still periodically captures the imagination of individual Trade Unionists. But other ideals of collective ownership of the means of production have displaced the Owenism of 1833–34 and the " Christian Socialism " of 1852. Of co-operative experiments by Trade Societies, in their corporate capacity, we hear practically no more.[1]

---

against such an investment of the funds, and the Union sold out to a group of individuals under the style of the Leicester Hosiery Society. It became fairly successful, but scarcely a tenth of the shareholders were workers in the concern, and it was eventually merged in the Co-operative Wholesale Society. Innumerable smaller experiments were set on foot during these years by groups of Trade Unionists with more or less assistance from their societies, but the great majority were quickly abandoned as unsuccessful. In a few cases the business established still exists, but in every one of these any connection with Trade Unionism has long since ceased. In later years renewed attempts have been made by a few Unions. Several local branches of the National Union of Boot and Shoe Operatives, for instance, have taken shares in the Leicester Co-operative Boot and Shoe Manufacturing Society. The London Bassdressers, the Staffordshire Potters, the Birmingham Tinplate Workers, and a few other societies have also taken shares in co-operative concerns started in their respective trades. Full particulars will be found in the exhaustive work of Benjamin Jones on *Co-operative Production*, 1894.

[1] In one other respect the Trade Union expansion of 1872–74 resembled that of 1833–34. Both periods were marked by an attempt to enrol the women wage-earners in the Trade Union ranks. Ephemeral Unions of women workers had been established from time to time, only to collapse after a brief existence. The year 1872 saw the establishment of the oldest durable Union for women only—the Edinburgh Upholsterers' Sewers' Society. Two years later Mrs. Paterson, the real pioneer of modern women's Trade Unions, began her work in this field, and in 1875 several small Unions among London Women Bookbinders, Upholsteresses, Shirt and Collar Makers, and Dressmakers were established, to be followed, in subsequent years, by others among Tailoresses, Laundresses, etc. Mrs. Emma Ann Paterson (*née* Smith), who was born in 1848, the daughter of a London schoolmaster, served from 1867 to 1873 successively as an

On the whole the contrast between the Trade Union expansion of 1873–74 and that of 1833–34 is more significant than any likeness that may be traced between the two periods. The Trade Unionists of 1833–34 aimed at nothing less than the supersession of the capitalist employer ; and they were met by his absolute refusal to tolerate, or even to recognise, their organisation. The new feature of the expansion of 1873–74 was the moderation with which the workmen claimed merely to receive some share of the enormous profits of these good times. The employers, on the other hand, for the most part abandoned their objection to recognise the Unions, and even conceded, after repeated refusals, the principle of the regulation of industry by Joint Boards of Conciliation or impartial umpires chosen from outside the trade. From 1867 to 1875 innumerable Boards of Conciliation and Arbitration were established, at which representatives of the masters met representatives of the Trade Unions on equal terms. In fact, it must have been difficult for the workmen at this period to realise with what stubborn obstinacy the employers, between 1850 and 1870, had resisted any kind of intervention in what they had then regarded as essentially a matter of private concern. When the Amalgamated Society of Engineers offered, in 1851, to refer the then pending dispute to arbitration, the master

---

Assistant Secretary of the Working Men's Club and Institute Union and the Women's Suffrage Association, and married, in 1873, Thomas Paterson, a cabinetmaker. On a visit to the United States she became acquainted with the " Female Umbrella Makers' Union of New York," and strove, on her return in 1874, to promulgate the idea of Trade Unionism among women workers in the South of England. After some newspaper articles, she set on foot the Women's Protective and Provident League (now the Women's Trade Union League), for the express purpose of promoting Trade Unionism, and established in the same year the National Union of Working Women at Bristol. From 1875 to 1886 she was a constant attendant at the Trades Union Congress, and was several times nominated for a seat on the Parliamentary Committee, at the Hull Congress heading the list of unsuccessful candidates. An appreciative notice of her life and work appeared in the *Women's Union Journal* on her death in December 1886 ; see also *Dictionary of National Biography*, and *Women in the Printing Trades* edited by J. R. MacDonald (1904), pp. 36, 37.

engineers simply ignored the proposal. The Select Committees of the House of Commons in 1856 and 1860 found the workmen's witnesses strongly in favour of arbitration, but the employers sceptical as to its possibility. Nor did the establishment of A. J. Mundella's Hosiery Board at Nottingham in 1860, and Sir Rupert Kettle's Joint Committees in the Wolverhampton building trades in 1864, succeed in converting the employers elsewhere. But between 1869 and 1875 opinion among the captains of industry, to the great satisfaction of the Trade Union leaders, gradually veered round. " Twenty-five years ago," said Alexander Macdonald in 1875, " when we proposed the adoption of the principle of arbitration, we were then laughed to scorn by the employing interests. But no movement has ever spread so rapidly or taken a deeper root than that which we then set on foot. Look at the glorious state of things in England and Wales. In Northumberland the men now meet with their employers around the common board. . . . In Durhamshire a Board of Arbitration and Conciliation has also been formed ; and 75,000 men repose with perfect confidence on the decisions of the Board. There are 40,000 men in Yorkshire in the same position." [1]

But though the establishment, from 1869 onwards, of Joint Boards and Joint Committees represented a notable advance for the Trade Unions, and marked their complete recognition by the great employers, yet this victory brought results which largely neutralised its advantages.[2] As in the

[1] Speech quoted in *Capital and Labour*, June 16, 1875.

[2] It must be remembered that the words "arbitration" and "conciliation" were at this time very loosely used, often meaning no more than a meeting of employers and Trade Union representatives for argument and discussion. The classic work upon the whole subject is Henry Crompton's *Industrial Conciliation*, 1876. It receives detailed examination in the various contributions of Mr. L. L. Price, notably his *Industrial Peace* (1887) and the supplementary papers entitled " The Relations between Industrial Conciliation and Social Reform," and " The Position and Prospects of Industrial Conciliation," published in the *Statistical Society's Journal* for June and September 1890 (vol. liii. pp. 290 and 420). For an American summary may be consulted Joseph D. Weeks' *Report on the Practical Working of Arbitration and Conciliation in the Settlement of Differences*

case of the political triumphs, the men gained their point at the cost of adopting the intellectual position of their opponents. When the representatives of the employers and the delegates of the men began to meet to discuss the future scale of wages, we see the sturdy leaders of many Trade Union battles gradually and insensibly accepting the capitalists' axiom that wages must necessarily fluctuate according to the capitalists' profits, and even with every variation of market prices.[1] At Darlington, for instance, we watch the shrewd leader of the employers, David Dale, succeeding in completely impressing John Kane and a whole subsequent generation of ironworkers with a firm

between Employers and Employees in England (Harrisburg, 1879), and his paper on *Labour Differences* (New York, 1886). The working of arbitration is well set forth in *Strikes and Arbitration*, by Sir Rupert Kettle, 1866 ; in A. J. Mundella's evidence before the Trade Union Commission, 1868 ; in his address, *Arbitration as a Means of Preventing Strikes* (Bradford, 1868 ; 24 pp.) ; and in the lecture by Dr. R. Spence Watson entitled "Boards of Arbitration and Conciliation and Sliding Scales," reported in the *Barnsley Chronicle*, March 20, 1886. An early account of the Nottingham experience is contained in the paper by E. Renals, "On Arbitration in the Hosiery Trades of the Midland Counties" (*Statistical Society's Journal*, December 1867, vol. xxx. p. 548). See also the volume edited by Dr. Brentano, *Arbeitseinstellungen und Fortbildung des Arbeitvertrags* (Leipzig, 1890), and *Zum socialen Frieden*, by Dr. von Schulze Gaevernitz (Leipzig, 2 vols., 1892). The whole subject of the relation between Trade Unions and employers is fully dealt with in our *Industrial Democracy*. For the latest British Official reports on the subject see Cd. 6603, 6952, and 9099.

[1] The course of prices after 1870 demonstrates how disastrously this principle would have operated for the wage-earners had it been universally adopted. Between 1870 and 1894 the Index Number compiled by the *Economist*, representing the average level of market prices, fell steadily from 2996 to 2082, irrespective of the goodness of trade or the amount of the employers' profits. Any exact correspondence between wages and the price of the product would exclude the wage-earners, as such, from all share in the advantages of improvements in production, cheapening of carriage, and the fall in the rate of interest, which might otherwise be turned to account in an advance in the workman's Standard of Life. On the other hand, in an era of rising prices, when these influences are being more than counteracted by currency inflation, increasing difficulty of production, or a world-shortage of supply, an automatic correspondence between money wages and the cost of living would be useful, if it did not lead to the implication that the only ground for an advance in wages was an increase in the cost of living. The workmen have still to contend for a progressive improvement of their Standard of Life whatever happens to profits.

belief in the principle of regulating wages according to the market price of the product. The high prices of 1870–73 removed the last scruples of the workmen as to the new doctrine. In 1874 a delegate meeting of the Northumberland Miners decided to use the formal expression of the Executive Committee,[1] " that prices should rule wages "— a decision expressly repeated by delegate meetings in 1877 and 1878. In 1879, when prices had come tumbling down, we find the Executive still maintaining that " as an Association we have always contended that wages should be based on the selling price of coal." [2] In an interesting letter dated February 1, 1878, Burt, Nixon, and Young (then the salaried officers of the Northumberland Miners), in describing the negotiations for a Sliding Scale, take occasion to mention that they had agreed with the employers that there should be no Minimum Wage.[3] And though the practical difficulties involved in the establishment of automatic wage-adjustments hindered the spread of Sliding Scales to other industries, the principle became tacitly accepted among whole sections of Trade Unionists. The compulsory maintenance, in good times and bad, of the workman's Standard of Life was thus gradually replaced by faith in a scale of wages sliding up and down according to the commercial speculations of the controllers of the market.

The new doctrine was not accepted without vigorous protests from the more thoughtful working-men leaders. Lloyd Jones, writing in 1874, warns " working men of the danger there is in a principle that wages should be regulated by market prices, accepted and acted on, and therefore presumably approved of by Trades Unions. These bodies, it is to be regretted, permit it in arbitration, accept it in negotiations with their employers, and thus give the highest

---

[1] Executive Circular, October 12, 1874.

[2] *Ibid.*, October 21, 1879 ; as to the Sliding Scales actually adopted, see Appendix II.

[3] *Miners' Watchman and Labour Sentinel*, February 9, 1878—a quasi-official organ of the Northern Miners, which was published in London from January to May 1878.

sanction they can to a mode of action most detrimental to the cause of labour. . . . The first thing, therefore, those who manage trade societies should settle is a minimum, which they should regard as a point below which they should never go. . . . Such a one as will secure sufficiency of food and some degree of personal and home comfort to the worker; not a miserable allowance to starve on, but living wages. . . . The present agreements they are going into on fluctuating market prices is a practical placing of their fate in the hands of others. It is throwing the bread of their children into a scramble of competition where everything is decided by the blind and selfish struggles of their employers." [1] " I entirely agree," writes Professor Beesly, " with an admirable article by Mr. Lloyd Jones [2] in a recent number of the *Beehive*, in which he maintained that colliers should aim at establishing a minimum price for their labour, and compelling their employers to take that into account as the one constant and stable element in all their speculations. All workmen should keep their eyes fixed on this ultimate ideal." [3]

Nor was this view confined to friendly allies of the Trade

[1] " Should Wages be Regulated by Market Prices ? " by Lloyd Jones, *Beehive*, July 18, 1874 ; see also his article in the issue for March 14, 1874.

[2] Lloyd Jones, one of the ablest and most loyal friends of Trade Unionism, was born at Bandon, in Ireland, in 1811, the son of a small working master in the trade of fustian-cutting. Himself originally a working fustian-cutter, Lloyd Jones became, like his father, a small master, but eventually abandoned that occupation for journalism. He became an enthusiastic advocate of Co-operation, and in 1850 he joined Thomas Hughes and E. Vansittart Neale in a memorable lecturing tour through Lancashire. A few years later we find him in London, in close touch with the Trade Union leaders, with whom he was on terms of intimate friendship. From the establishment of the *Beehive* in 1861 he was for eighteen years a frequent contributor, his articles being uniformly distinguished by literary ability, exact knowledge of industrial facts, and shrewd foresight. From 1870 until his death in 1886 he was frequently selected by the various Unions to present their case in Arbitration proceedings. At the General Election of 1885 he stood as candidate for the Chester-le-Street Division of Durham, where he was opposed by both the official Liberals and the Conservatives, and was unsuccessful. In conjunction with J. M. Ludlow, he wrote *The Progress of the Working Classes*, 1867, and afterwards published *The Life, Times, and Labours of Robert Owen*, to which a memoir by his son, Mr. W. C. Jones, has since been prefixed.

[3] *Beehive*, May 16, 1874.

Union Movement. We shall have occasion to notice how forcibly both the Cotton Operatives and the Boilermakers protested against the dependence of wages on the fluctuations of the market. Alexander Macdonald himself, though he approved of Joint Committees, instinctively maintained an attitude of hostility to the innovating principle of a sliding scale.[1] And, as we shall hereafter see, the conflict between Macdonald's teaching with regard to both wages and the hours of labour, and the economic views of the Northumberland and Durham leaders, presently divided the organised miners into two hostile camps.

The Trade Union world of 1871–75 was therefore more complicated, and presented many more difficult internal problems than was imagined, either by the alarmed employers or the triumphant Trade Unionists. It needed only the stress of hard times to reveal to the Trade Unionists themselves that they were not the compact and well-organised army described by the National Federation of Associated Employers, but a congeries of distinct sections, pursuing separate and sometimes antagonistic policies.

The expansion of trade, under the influence of which Trade Unionism, as we have seen, reached in 1873–74 one of its high-water marks, came suddenly to an end. The contraction became visible first in the coal and iron industries, those in which the inflation had perhaps been greatest.[2] The first break occurred in February 1874, when the coal-miners of the East of Scotland submitted to a reduction of a shilling a day. During the rest of the year prices and wages came tumbling down in both these staple trades. In

---

[1] This information we owe to personal friends and colleagues of Macdonald, Thomas Burt, M.P., and Ralph Young, who, as we have seen, differed from him on this point, and also on the allied question of regulation of output according to demand, to be preached by the coal-miners as well as by the colliery companies, which Macdonald, throughout his whole career, persistently advocated. See, for instance, his speech at the local conference on the Depression of Trade, *Bristol Mercury*, February 13, 1878.

[2] A useful summary of these events is given in Dr. Kleinwächter's pamphlet, *Zur Geschichte der englischen Arbeiterbewegung in den Jahren 1871 und 1874* (Jena, 1878; 150 pp.).

January 1875 a furious conflict broke out in South Wales, where many thousand miners and ironworkers refused to submit to a third reduction of ten per cent. The struggle dragged on until the end of May, when work was resumed at a reduction, not of ten, but of twelve and a half per cent, with an understanding that " any change in the wage rates . . . shall depend on a sliding scale of wages to be regulated by the selling price of coal." [1] In the following year the depression spread to the textile industries, and gradually affected all trades throughout the country. The building trades were, however, still prosperous ; and the Manchester Carpenters chose this moment for an aggressive advance movement. The disastrous strike that followed early in 1877, and lasted throughout the year, resulted in the virtual collapse of the General Union of Carpenters and Joiners, at that time the third in magnitude among the societies in the building trades, and left the Manchester building operatives in a state of disorganisation from which they never fully recovered. In April 1877 the Clyde ship-wrights demanded an increase of wages, to which the employers replied by a general lock-out of all the operatives engaged in the shipbuilding yards, in the expectation that this would cause pressure on the shipwrights to withdraw their claim. For more than three months the main industry of the Clyde was at a standstill, the dispute being eventually ended, in September 1877, by submission to the arbitration of Lord Moncreiff, in which the men were completely worsted. In July 1877 a conflict broke out between the stonemasons and their employers, in which Bull & Co., the contractors for the new law courts in London, caused the bitterest resentment by importing German workmen as blacklegs. The demand had originally been for an increase of wages and reduction of hours for the London men ; but as the obstinate struggle progressed it became, in effect, a battle between the Stonemasons' Union and the federated master builders throughout the country. Large levies were

[1] *Beehive*, June 5, 1875.

raised, and over £2000 collected from other trade societies ; but in March 1878, after eight months' conflict, the remnant of the strikers returned to work on the employers' terms. The cotton trade, too, was made the scene of one of the greatest industrial struggles on record. After several minor reductions of wages during 1877, which resulted in local strikes, in March 1878, as the *Times* reports, " all the way through a centre of 70 miles, where 250,000 cotton operatives are employed, notices have been posted giving a month's notice of ten per cent. reduction in wages."   A colossal strike ensued, which brought into prominence the rival theories of the cotton operatives and their employers. It was conceded by the men that the mill-owners were losing money, and that some change had to be made.   But as the employers admitted that their losses arose from the glutted state of the market, the operatives contended that the proper remedy was the cessation of the over-production ; and they therefore offered to accept the 10 per cent reduction on condition that the mills should only work four days a week.   A heated controversy ensued, but the mill-owners persisted in their demand for the unconditional surrender of the men, and refused all proposals for arbitration.   The cause of the men was unfortunately prejudiced by serious riots at Blackburn, at which the house of Colonel Raynsford Jackson, the leader of the associated employers, was looted and burnt.   After ten weeks' struggle the men went in on the employers' terms.[1]

[1] The operatives' case is well put in the Weavers' Manifesto of June 1878 :
" Fellow-workers—We are and have been engaged during the past nine weeks in the most memorable struggle between Capital and Labour in the history of the world. One hundred thousand factory workers are waging war with their employers as to the best possible way to remove the glut from an overstocked cloth market, and at the same time reduce the difficulties arising from an insufficient supply of raw cotton. To remedy this state of things the employers propose a reduction of wages to the extent of ten per cent below the rate of wages agreed upon twenty-five years ago. On the other hand, we have contended that a reduction in the rate of wages cannot either remove the glut in the cloth market or assist to tide us over the difficulty arising from the limited supply of raw

The great struggles of 1875–78 were only the precursors of a general rout of the Trade Union forces. The increasing depression of trade culminated during 1878–79 in a stagnation which must rank as one of the most serious which has ever overtaken British industry. The paralysis of business was intensified, especially in Scotland, by the widespread ruin caused by the failure of the City of Glasgow Bank. From one end of the kingdom to the other great firms became bankrupt, mines and ironworks were stopped, ships lay idle in the ports, and a universal feeling of despondency and distrust spread like a blight into every corner of the industrial world. Every industry had its crowds of unemployed workmen, the proportion of men on the books of the Trade Unions rising, in some cases, to as much as 25 per cent. The capitalists, as might have been expected, chose the moment of trial for attempting to take back the rest of the concessions extorted from them in the previous years. " It has appeared to employers of labour," stated the private circular issued by the Iron Trade Employers' Association in December 1878, " that the time has arrived when the superfluous wages

---

material. However, this has been the employers' theory, and at various periods throughout the struggle we have made the following propositions as a basis of settlement of this most calamitous struggle :

" 1. A reduction of ten per cent, with four days' working, or five per cent with five days' working, until the glut in the cloth market and the difficulties arising from the dearth of cotton had been removed.

" 2. To submit the whole question of short time or reduction, or both, to the arbitrement of any one or more impartial gentlemen.

" 3. To submit the entire question to two Manchester merchants or agents, two shippers conversant with the Manchester trade, and two bankers, one of each to be selected by the employers and the other by the operatives, with two employers and two operatives, with Lord Derby, the Bishop of Manchester, or any other impartial gentleman, as chairman, or, if necessary, referee.

" 4. To split the difference between us, and go to work unconditionally at a reduction of five per cent.

" 5. Through the Mayor of Burnley, to go to work three months at a reduction of five per cent, and if trade had not sufficiently improved at that time, to submit to a further reduction.

" 6. And lastly, to an unconditional reduction of seven and a half per cent."

which have been dissipated in unproductive consumption must be retrenched, and when the idle hours which have been unprofitably thrown away must be reclaimed to industry and profit by being redirected to reproductive work." The result is reflected in the Trade Union reports. " All over the United Kingdom," states the Monthly Report of the Amalgamated Carpenters for January 1879, " notices of reductions in wages and extended hours of labour come pouring in from employers with an eagerness and audacity which contrast strangely with the lessons of forbearance and moderation so incessantly dinned into the ears of the British workman in happier times." " At no time in our history," reports the Executive Council of the Amalgamated Society of Engineers, " have we had such a number of industrial disturbances throughout the country. Bad trade has prevailed; and our employers, now better organised than ever before, seem to have made it their aim to raise as many points of contention with us as ever possible. In one place sweeping reductions of wages would be carried out or attempted ; and in others the rates paid for overtime were sought to be reduced, while in many cases the hours of labour have been attacked, and in the Clyde district successfully, three hours being, as a result, added to the week's work all over Scotland. . . . Another notable feature of the depression has been the continued oppression by the employers of the men in the most submissive districts, where conciliatory measures were adopted, and where little objection was made to any innovation. The Clyde district has been a notable example of this fact, passing in the first instance through two considerable reductions of wages almost passively, only to be almost immediately after the victims of desultory attacks upon the hours question. Irregular attack appears almost to have been the system adopted by the employers in preference to the development of any general movement by their Associations." [1] The

[1] Amalgamated Society of Engineers, etc., Abstract Report of the Council's Proceedings, 1878–79, p. 18.

years 1878–1880 witnessed, accordingly, a great increase in the number of strikes in nearly all trades,[1] most of which terminated disastrously for the workmen. Sweeping reductions of wages occurred in all industries. The Northumberland miners, whose normal day's earnings had been 9s. 1½d. in March 1873, found themselves reduced, in November 1878, to 4s. 9d. per day, and in January 1880 to 4s. 4d. Scotch mechanics suffered an even more sudden reduction. The Glasgow stonemasons, for instance, who had been earning 9d. and 10d. per hour during 1877, dropped by the end of 1878 to 6d. per hour, and found it difficult to find employment even at that figure. A still more dangerous encroachment was made in connection with the hours of labour. Employers on all sides sought to lengthen the working day. The mechanics on the Clyde lost the fifty-one hours week which they had won. The Iron Trades Employers' Association, whose circular we have quoted, resolved upon a general attack on the Nine Hours Day. " It has been resolved," writes the secretary, " by a large majority of the Iron Trades Employers' Association, supported by a general agreement among other employers, to give notice in their workshops that the hours of labour shall be increased to the number prevailing before the adoption of the nine hours limit." [2] The concerted action of the associated employers was, however, baulked by the energy of John Burnett, then General Secretary of the Amalgamated Society of Engineers. Placed in possession of the Circular for a couple of hours,

---

[1] See *The Strikes of the Past Ten Years*, by G. Phillips Bevan (March 1880, *Stat. Soc. Journal*, vol. xliii. pp. 35-54). We have ascertained that the strikes mentioned in the *Times* between 1876 and 1889 show the following variations :

1876	.	.	. 17	1881	.	. 20	1886 . . . 24
1877	.	. . 23	1882	.	. 14	1887 . . . 27
1878	.	. . 38	1883	.	. 26	1888 . . . 37
1879	.	. . 72	1884	.	. 31	1889 . . . 111
1880	.	. . 46	1885	.	. 20	

[2] Secret circular from the London Secretary (Sidney Smith) of the Iron Trades Employers' Association, December 1878 ; republished in Circular of Amalgamated Society of Engineers, January 3, 1879, and in Report of Executive Council for 1878–79, p. 31.

he promptly reproduced it in an ably reasoned appeal to his own members, which was sent broadcast·to the press. Publicity proved fatal to the employers' plans, and no uniform or systematic action was taken. Isolated attempts were, however, made in all directions by the master engineers to revert to fifty-seven or fifty-nine hours per week ; and only by the most strenuous action was the normal fifty-four-hours week retained in " society shops."

Other trades were not equally successful in maintaining even their nominal day. In many towns the carpenters had two or three hours per week added to their working time.[1] More serious was the fact that in numerous minor trades the very conception of a definitely fixed normal day was practically lost. Even among such well-organised trades as the Engineers, Carpenters, and Stonemasons the practice of systematic overtime, coupled with the prevalence of piecework, reduced the normal day to a nullity.[2] In the abundant Trade Union records of these years we watch the progress and results of these economic disasters. The number of men drawing the out-of-work benefit steadily rises, until the societies of Ironfounders and Boilermakers, which in 1872-73 had scarcely 1 per cent unemployed, had in 1879 over 20 per cent on their funds. The Amalgamated Society of Engineers paid away, under this one head, during the three years 1878-80, a sum of no less than £287,596. The Operative Plumbers had to exclude, in the

[1] At Manchester, Bolton, Ramsbottom, Wrexham, Falmouth, Aldershot, etc., the hours were thus lengthened.

[2] To the ordinary reader it may be desirable to explain that the Unions have, in most trades, succeeded in establishing the principle of the payment of higher rates for overtime. But in most cases this is limited to workers paid by time, no extra allowance being given to the man working by the piece.

It will be obvious that if a workman, ostensibly enjoying a Nine Hours Day, is habitually required to work overtime, and is paid only at the normal piecework rate for his work, he obtains no advantage whatever from the nominal fixing of his hours of labour. To many thousands of men in the engineering and building trades the nominal maintenance of the Nine Hours Day meant, in 1878 and succeeding years, no more than this. See for the whole subject of " the Normal Day," *Industrial Democracy,* by S. and B. Webb.

two years 1880–82, nearly a third of their members for non-payment of contributions. The Ironfounders, who in 1876 had accumulated a fund of over £5 per member, paid away every penny of it by the end of 1879, and were only saved from actual stoppage by the numerous loans made to the society by its more prosperous members. The Stonemasons' Society drained itself equally dry, and resorted to the same expedient to avoid default. The Scottish societies had to meet the crisis in an even more aggravated form. The total collapse which followed the City of Glasgow Bank failure absolutely ruined all but half a dozen of the Scotch Trade Unions, a blow from which Trade Unionism in Scotland did not recover for the rest of the century.

The year 1879, indeed, was as distinctly a low-water mark of the Trade Union Movement as 1873–74 registered a full tide of prosperity. The economic trials through which Trade Unionism passed in 1879 are only to be paralleled by those through which it had gone in 1839–42. But the solid growth which we have described prevented any such total collapse as marked the previous periods. The depression of 1879 swept, it is true, many hundreds of trade societies into oblivion. The Unions of agricultural labourers, which had sprung up with such mushroom rapidity, either collapsed altogether or dwindled into insignificant benefit clubs. Up and down the country the hundreds of little societies in miscellaneous trades which had flourished during the good years, went down before the tide of adversity. Widespread national organisations shrank up practically into societies of local influence, concentrated upon the strongholds of their industries. The great National Union of Miners, established, as we have seen, in 1862–63, survived, after 1879, only in Northumberland, Durham, and Yorkshire. Its younger rival, the Amalgamated Association of Miners, which had, up to 1875, dominated South Wales and the Midlands, broke up and disappeared. The National Amalgamated Association of Ironworkers, also established in 1862, which in 1873 numbered 35,000 members in all parts of the country, was reduced in 1879 to 1400 members, confined to a few centres in the North of England.[1] In some districts, such as South Wales, Trade Unionism practically ceased to exist.[2] The total membership of the Trade Union Movement returned, it is probable, to the level of 1871. But despite all these contractions the backbone of the movement remained intact. In the engineering and building trades the great national societies, though they were denuded of their reserve funds, retained their membership. Nor was it only the trade friendly societies that weathered the storm. The essentially trade organisations of the cotton operatives, and of the Northumberland and Durham miners, maintained their position with only a temporary contraction of membership. The political organisation of the movement was, moreover, unaffected. The local Trades Councils went on undisturbed. The annual Trades Union Congress continued to meet, and to appoint its standing Parliamentary Committee. In short, though many individual Unions disappeared, and many others saw their balances absorbed and their membership reduced, the trials of 1879 proved that the Trade Union Movement was at last beyond all danger of destruction or collapse, and that the Trade Union organisation had become a permanent element in our social structure.

We see, therefore, that the work which Allan and Applegarth had done towards consolidating the Trade Union Movement had not been fruitless. But along with increasing consolidation and definiteness of purpose had come an increasing differentiation of policy and interest. Each trade

[1] The lowest point reached in the statistics of the annual Trades Union Congresses was in 1881, when the delegates claimed to represent little more than a third of the numbers of 1874. These statistics of membership are, however, in many respects misleading. The Congress of 1879 was attended by a much smaller number of delegates than any Congress since 1872, and the number of Unions represented was also the smallest since that date.

[2] " Four years ago," writes the President of the Bristol Coopers' Society in 1878, " upwards of 40,000 workmen were in combination in these valleys [South Wales], and to-day not a single Union is in existence throughout the entire district " (Paper at Local Conference on the Depression of Trade, *Bristol Mercury*, February 13, 1878).

was working out its own industrial problems in its way. Whilst the miners and the cotton operatives, for instance, were elaborating their own codes of legislative regulation of the conditions of labour, the engineering and building trades were becoming pledged to the legislative *laissez-faire* of their leaders. Under the influence of the able spokesmen of the northern counties the coal-miners and iron-workers were accepting the principle that wages must follow prices ; whilst the cotton operatives, and to some extent the boilermakers,[1] were making a notable stand for the contrary view that the Standard Rate of Wages should be a first charge on industry. And while the miners and cotton operatives regarded their organisations primarily as societies for trade protection, there was growing up among the successors of the Junta in the iron and building trades a fixed belief that the really " Scientific Trade Unionism " consisted in elaborate friendly benefits and judiciously invested superannuation funds. So long as trade was expanding, and each policy was pursued with success, no antagonism arose between the different sections. The cotton operatives cordially approved the Nine Hours Movement of the engineers, whilst these, in their turn, supported the Factory Bill desired by the Lancashire spinners. The miners applauded the gallant stand made by the cotton operatives against the reductions of 1877–79, whilst the cotton operatives saw no objection to the acquiescence of the miners in the dependence of wages on prices. And though all Trade Unions regarded with respect the high contributions and accumulated funds of the Amalgamated Engineers, they were equally respectful of the success with which the Northumberland coal-miners, through bad times and good, had for half a generation maintained a strong Union with exclusively trade objects. Thus the divergences of policy, which were

---

[1] See the injunctions of the General Secretary, Monthly Report, March 1862 ; Annual Reports, 1882 and 1888. Robert Knight consistently opposed " violent fluctuations of wages, at one time a starvation pittance, at another exorbitantly high."

destined from 1885 onward to form the battle-ground between what has been once more termed the " Old " Unionism
and the " New," did not at first prevent cordial co-operation in the common purposes of the Trade Union Movement.
It was in the dark days after 1878–79, when every Union
suffered reverses, that internal discontent as to Trade Union
policy became acute, and a new spirit of criticism arose.
Not until the purely trade society, on the one hand, had
been found lacking in stability, and the trade friendly
society, on the other, had been convicted of apathy in trade
matters ; not until the Lancashire and Yorkshire coal-
miners had been driven to protest against the constant
reductions brought about by the sliding scales, and some of
the leaders of the Lancashire cotton operatives hesitated
in their advocacy of the legal day ; finally, not until a
powerful section of the miners opposed any further extension of the Mines Regulation Acts, and a section of the
engineers and building operatives began to advocate the
legal fixing of their own labour day—do we find it declared
that " the two systems cannot co-exist ; they are contradictory and opposed." [1]

In more than one direction, therefore, the depression
of trade was bringing into prominence wide divergences
of opinion upon Trade Union policy. But the adverse
industrial circumstances of the time were revealing, in
certain industries, a more invidious cleavage. As manufacturing processes develop and change with the progress of
invention and the substitution of one material for another
—iron for wood in shipbuilding, for instance—the skilled
members of one trade find themselves superseded for certain work by the members of another. A modern Atlantic
liner, practically a luxuriously-fitted, electric-lighted float-
ing hotel, built of rolled steel plates, would obviously not
fall within the work of a shipwright like Peter the Great.
But the old-fashioned shipwright naturally refused to relinquish without a struggle the right to build ships of every

[1] *Trade Unionism, New and Old*, by George Howell, M.P. (1891), p. 235.

kind. The depression of 1879 was severely felt in the ship-building and engineering trades, every one of which had a large percentage of its members unemployed. The societies found, as we have seen, the out-of-work donation a serious drain on their funds, and were inclined to look more narrowly into cases of " encroachment " upon the work which each regarded as the legitimate sphere of its own members. Disputes between Union and Union as to overlap and apportionment of work become, in these years, of frequent occurrence ; and to the standing conflict with the employers was added embittered internecine warfare between the men of one branch of trade and those of another. The Engineers complained of the monopoly which the Boilermakers main-tained of all work connected with angle-iron. The Pattern-makers protested vigorously against the Carpenters presum-ing to make any engineering patterns. At Glasgow the Brassfounders objected to the Ironmoulders continuing to make the large brass castings which the workers in brass had at first been unable to undertake. The line of de-marcation in iron shipbuilding between the work of a ship-wright and that of a boilermaker was a constant source of friction. The disregard of the ordinary classification of trades by the authorities of the Royal Dockyards created great discontent among the Engineers, who saw shipwrights put to do fitters' work, and Broadhurst brought the matter in 1882 before the House of Commons.[1] Nor were the disputes confined to the puzzling question of the lines of demarcation between particular trades. In 1877 the re-cently formed Union of " Platers' Helpers " complained bitterly to the Trades Union Congress that the whole force of the Boilermakers' Society had been used to destroy their

[1] House of Commons Journals, Motion of March 14, 1882 : " That in the opinion of this House it is detrimental to the public service, fatal to the efficiency of our war ships, and unjust to the fitters in Her Majesty's Dockyards, that superintending leading men should be placed in authority over workmen with whose trades they have no practical acquaintance, or that men should be put to execute work for which they are unsuited either by training or experience." See *Henry Broadhurst, the Story of his Life from a Stonemason's Bench to the Treasury Bench,* by himself, 1901.

N

organisation. The Platers' Helpers, it may be explained, constitute a large class of labourers in shipbuilding yards, who are usually employed and paid, not by the owners of the yards, but by members of the Boilermakers' Society. In the building trades numerous cases of friction were occurring between bricklayers and masons on the one hand, and the builders' labourers on the other. The introduction of terra cotta led to a whole series of disputes between the bricklayers and the plasterers as to the trade to which the new work properly belonged. Disputes of this kind were, of course, no new thing. What gave the matter its new importance was the dominance of the great trade friendly societies in the skilled occupations. The loss of employment by individual members became in bad times a serious financial drain on Unions giving out-of-work pay. In place of the bickerings of individual workmen we have the conflicts of powerful societies, each supporting the claim of its own members to do the work in dispute. " When men are not organised in a Trade Union," says the general secretary of a large society, " these little things are not taken much notice of, but the moment the two trades become well organised, each trade is looking after its own particular members' interests. . . ." [1]

We have in our *Industrial Democracy* analysed the history, character, and extent of this rivalry among competing branches of the same trade. Here we need do no more than record its result in weakening the bond of union between powerful sections of the Trade Union world. The local Trades Councils, which might have attained a position of political influence, were always being disintegrated by the disputes of competing trades. The powerful Shipping Trades Council of Liverpool, for instance, which played an important part in Samuel Plimsoll's agitation for a new Merchant Shipping Act, was broken up in 1880 by the

---

[1] Evidence of Mr. Chandler, then general secretary of Amalgamated Society of Carpenters and Joiners (Labour Commission, 1892, vol. iii. Q. 22,014).

quarrel between the separate societies of Shipwrights, Ship-joiners, and House Carpenters over ship work. The minutes of every Trades Council, especially those in seaports, relate innumerable well-intentioned attempts to settle similar disputes, almost invariably ending in the secession of one or other of the contending Unions. These quarrels prevented, moreover, the formation of any effective general federation. An attempt was made in 1875 by the officers of the Amalgamated Engineers', Boilermakers', Ironfounders', and Steam-Engine Makers' Societies to establish a federation for mutual defence against attacks upon the Nine Hours System. After a few months, the disputes between the Engineers and Boilermakers on the one hand, and between the members of the Amalgamated Society and the Steam-Engine Makers' Society on the other, led to the abandonment of the attempt.[1] A similar movement initiated by the Boilermakers in 1881 equally failed to get established.[2]

Wider federations met with no better success than those confined to the engineering and shipbuilding trades. The Trades Union Congress repeatedly declared itself in favour of universal brotherhood among Trade Unionists, and the formation of a federal bond between the different societies. But the inherent differences between trade and trade, the numerous distinct types into which societies were divided, the wide divergences as to Trade Union policy which we have been describing, and, above all, the rivalry for members and employment between competing societies in the same industry, rendered any universal federation impossible. After the Sheffield Congress in 1874, representatives of the leading Unions in the iron and building trades set on foot

---

[1] Abstract Report of Amalgamated Engineers, June 30, 1876.

[2] In 1890, however, Robert Knight, who had been throughout the foremost worker for federation, succeeded in establishing a Federation of the Engineering and Shipbuilding Trades of the United Kingdom, described in our *Industrial Democracy*, from which the Amalgamated Society of Engineers has held aloof. A large part of the work of the Federal Executive consisted, for many years, of adjusting disputes between Union and Union with regard to overlap and apportionment of work. For the whole subject, see our *Industrial Democracy*, 1897.

a " Federation of Organised Trade Societies," which all
Unions were invited to join for mutual defence.   But the
Cotton-spinners, with their preference for legislative regulation, refused to have anything to do with a federation
which contemplated nothing but strike benefits.   The whole
scheme was, indeed, more a project of certain Trade Union
officials than a manifestation of any general feeling in
favour of common action.   Each trade was, as we have
said, working out its own policy, and attending almost
exclusively to its own interests.   Under such circumstances
any attempt at effective federation must necessarily have
been still-born.   Nevertheless the Edinburgh Congress of
1879 called for a renewed attempt ; and the Parliamentary
Committee circulated to every Trade Union in the kingdom
their proposed rules for another " Federation of Organised
Trade Societies."   To this invitation not half a dozen replies
were received.[1]   At the Congress of 1882, when the resolution in favour of a universal federation was again proposed,
it found little support.   The representatives of the local
Trades Councils urged that these bodies furnished all that
was practicable in the way of federation.   Thomas Ashton,
the outspoken representative of the cotton-spinners, was
more emphatic.   " For years," he said, " the Parliamentary
Committee and others had been trying to bring about such
an organisation as that mentioned in the resolution, but it
had been found utterly impossible. . . . It was all nonsense
to pass such a resolution.   It was impossible for the trades of
the country to amalgamate, their interests were so varied and
they were so jealous with regard to each other's disputes." [2]

The foregoing examination of the internal relations of
the Trade Union world between 1875 and 1879, though in-
complete, demonstrates the extent to which the movement
during these years was dominated by a somewhat narrow
" particularism."   From 1880 to 1885 the various societies

[1] When, in 1890, the project of universal federation was revived, the
draft rules of 1879 were simply reprinted.

[2] Report of Manchester Congress, 1882 ; see also *History of the British
Trades Union Congress,* by W. J. Davis, vol. i., 1910.

were absorbed in building up again their membership and balances, which had so seriously suffered during the continued depression. The annual Trades Union Congress, the Parliamentary Committee, and the political proceedings of these years constitute practically the only common bond between the isolated and often hostile sections. In all industrial matters the Trade Union world was broken up into struggling groups, destitute of any common purpose, each, indeed, mainly preoccupied with its separate concerns, and frequently running counter to the policy or aims of the rest. The cleavages of interest and opinion among working men proved to be deeper and more numerous than any one suspected. In the following chapter we shall see how an imperfect appreciation of each other's position led to that conflict between the " Old Unionists " and the " New " which for some years bade fair to disintegrate the whole Labour Movement.

CHAPTER VII

THE OLD UNIONISM AND THE NEW

[1875-1890]

SINCE 1875 the Trades Union Congress has loomed before the general public with ever-increasing impressiveness as the representative Parliament of the Trade Union world. To the historical student, on the other hand, it has, during the last fifty years, been wanting in significance as an index to the real factors of the Trade Union Movement. Between 1871 and 1875, the period of the struggle for complete legalisation, the Congress concentrated the efforts of the different sections upon the common object they had all at heart. On the accomplishment of that object it became for ten years little more than an annual gathering of Trade Union officials, in which they delivered, with placid unanimity, their views on labour legislation and labour politics.[1]

---

[1] See the *History of the British Trades Union Congress*, by W. J. Davis, of which two volumes have been issued by the Parliamentary Committee (1910 and 1916). William John Davis, one of the most successful Trade Union administrators, was born in 1848, at Birmingham. In 1872, when the National Society of Amalgamated Brassworkers was established in a trade hitherto entirely unorganised, he became General Secretary, a post which, except for one short interval, he has ever since retained. Within six months he obtained from the employers the 15 per cent increase which they had refused to the unorganised men, and established branches throughout the kingdom ; and presently he completed the difficult and laborious task of constructing a list of prices for all brasswork, for which he obtained the employers' recognition. He was elected to the Birmingham School Board in 1876, and to the Town Council in 1880. In 1883 he accepted appointment as Factory Inspector, but six years later returned to his former

From 1885 to 1890 we shall watch the Congress losing its decorous calm, and gradually becoming the battle-field of contending principles and rival leaders. But throughout its whole career it has, to speak strictly, been representative less of the development of Trade Unionism as such, than of the social and political aspirations of its leading members.

The reader of the Congress proceedings between 1875 and 1885 would, for instance, fail to recognise our description of the characteristics of the movement in these years. The predominant feature of the Trade Union world between 1875 and 1885 was, as we have seen, an extreme and complicated sectionalism. It might therefore have been expected that the annual meeting of delegates from different trades would have been made the debating ground for all the moot points and vexed questions of Trade Unionism, not to say the battle-field of opposing interests. But though the Trades Union Congress, like all popular assemblies, had its stormy scenes and hot discussions, from 1875 to 1885 these episodes arose only on personal questions, such as the conduct of individual members of the committee or the *bona fides* of particular delegates. On all questions of policy or principle before the Congress the delegates were generally unanimous. This was brought about by the deliberate exclusion of all Trade Union problems from the agenda. The relative merits of collective bargaining and legislative regulation were, during these years, never so much as discussed. The alternative types of benefit club and trade society were not compared. The difficulties of overlap and apportionment of work were not even referred

post at the urgent request of the workmen, whose Union had in his absence sunk almost to nothing, a condition from which he was able quickly to restore it to far more than its highest previous strength ; and to take on, in addition, the secretaryship of the Amalgamated Metal Wire and Tube Makers' Society. He was made a J.P. in 1906. Since 1881 he has been elected twenty-six times to the Parliamentary Committee of the Trades Union Congress. He is the author, in addition to the *History of the British Trades Union Congress*, of *The Token Coinage of Warwickshire* and *Nineteenth-Century Token Coinage* (*The Life Story of W. J. Davis*, by W B. Dalley, 1914).

to. No mention was made of Sliding Scales, Wage-Boards, Piecework Lists, or other expedients for avoiding disputes. Piecework itself, when introduced by a delegate in 1876, was dropped as a dangerous topic. The disputes between Union and Union were regarded by the Committee as outside the proper scope of Congress.[1] In short, the knotty problems of Trade Union organisation, the divergent views as to Trade Union policy, the effect on Trade Unionism of different methods of remuneration—all the critical issues of industrial strife were expressly excluded from the agenda of the Congress.

For the narrow limits thus set to the functions of the Congress there was an historical reason. Arising as it did between 1868 and 1871, when the one absorbing topic was the relation of Trade Unionism to the law, it had retained the character then impressed upon it of an exclusively political body. For many years its chief use was to give weight to the Parliamentary action of the standing committee, whose influence in the lobby of the House of Commons was directly proportionate to the numbers they were believed to represent. Publicity and advertisement, the first requisites of a successful Congress, were worse than useless without unanimity of opinion. The deliberate refusal of the Trade Union leaders to discuss internal problems in public Congress under such circumstances was not surprising. Most men in their position would have hesitated to let the world know that the apparent solidarity of Trade Unionism covered jealous disputes on technical questions, and fundamental differences as to policy. They easily persuaded themselves that a yearly meeting of shifting delegates was fitted neither to debate technical questions nor to serve as a tribunal of appeal. But these difficulties could have been overcome. The quinquennial delegate meeting of the Amalgamated Society of Engineers

---

[1] In 1878, for instance, the Parliamentary Committee resolved that Congress ought not to interfere either between the English and Scottish Tailors' Societies or between the Boilermakers and the Platers' Helpers.

secures absolute frankness of discussion by the exclusion of reporters ; and the frequent national conferences of miners achieve the same end by supplying the press with their own abstract of the proceedings. The Miners' Conference of 1863, which we have already described, had shown, too, how successfully a large conference of workmen could resolve itself, for special questions, into private committees, the reports being laid before the whole conference at its public sittings—a device not yet adopted by the Trades Union Congress. And the London Society of Compositors, which is governed practically by mass meetings, had, for over half a century, known how to combine detailed investigation of complicated questions with Democratic decisions on principles of policy, by appointing special committees to report to the next subsequent members' meeting. The fact that no such expedients were suggested shows that in these years the jealousy of most workmen of outside interference and their apathy about questions unconnected with their immediate trade interests, made their leaders unwilling to trust them with real opportunities for full Democratic discussion.

We shall therefore not attempt to reconstruct the Trade Union Movement from the proceedings of its annual congresses. The following brief analysis of their programmes and the achievements of the Parliamentary Committee is meant to show, not the facts as to Trade Union organisation throughout the country, with which we have already dealt, but the political and social ideals that filled the minds of the more thoughtful and better educated working men, and the rapid transformation of these ideals in the course of the last decade.[1]

[1] The Congress, from 1871, annually elected a Parliamentary Committee of ten members and a secretary. The members of the Committee were always chosen from the officials of the more important Unions, with a strong tendency to re-elect the same men year after year. Between 1875 and 1889 the composition of the Committee was, in fact, scarcely changed, except through death or the promotion of members to Government appointments. George Potter was secretary from 1869–71 ; George Odger in that year ; and George Howell, afterwards M.P., from 1872–75.

The mantle of the Junta of 1867–71 had, by 1875, fallen upon a group of able organisers who, for many years, occupied the foremost place in the Trade Union world. Between 1872 and 1875 Allan and Applegarth were replaced by Henry Broadhurst, John Burnett, J. D. Prior, and George Shipton.[1] These leaders had moulded their methods and policy upon those of the able men who preceded them. It was they, indeed, aided by Alexander Macdonald and Thomas Burt, who had actually carried through the final achievement of 1875. Like Allan, Applegarth, and Guile, they belonged either to the iron or the building trades, and were permanent officials of Trade Union organisations. A comparison of the private minutes of the Parliamentary Committee between 1875 and 1885 with those of the Conference of Amalgamated Trades of 1867–71 reveals how exactly the new " Front Bench " carried on the traditions of the Junta. We see the same shrewd caution and practical opportunism. We notice the same assiduous lobbying in the House of Commons, and the same recurring deputations to evasive Ministers. For the first few years, at least, we watch the Committee in frequent consultation with the same devoted legal experts and Parliamentary friends.[2]   Through

---

Henry Broadhurst was for fourteen years annually re-elected secretary without a contest, temporarily ceding the post, whilst Under Secretary of State for the Home Department in 1886, to George Shipton. He was succeeded by Charles Fenwick, M.P., from 1890–93; then followed S. Woods, M.P., from 1894–1904; W. C. Steadman, M.P., from 1905–10; and the Right Honourable C. W. Bowerman, M.P., from 1911 onwards.

[1] Odger died in 1877, Guile in 1883, and Coulson (who had retired many years before) in 1893.

[2] To the counsels of Frederic Harrison, E. S. Beesly, H. Crompton, and A. J. Mundella was, from 1873, frequently added that of Mr. (afterwards Justice) R. S. Wright, who rendered invaluable service as a draughtsman. Henry Crompton supplied us with the following account of the subsequent separation between the Positivists and the Trade Union leaders :

" In the year 1881 the connection of the Parliamentary Committee with the Positivists was modified. There was not the same occasion for their services as there had been. After 1883, in which year Mr. F. Harrison and Mr. H. Crompton attended the Congress by invitation, the connection ceased altogether, though there was no breach of friendly relations. Till 1881 there had been entire agreement between them both as to policy and means of action. The policy of the Positivists had been to secure complete

the skilful guidance and indefatigable activity of Henry Broadhurst the political machinery of the Trade Union Movement was maintained and even increased in efficiency. If during these years the occupants of the " Front Bench " failed to give so decisive a lead to the Labour Movement as their predecessors had done, the fault lay, not in the men or in the machinery, but rather in the programme which they set themselves to carry out.

This programme, laid before all candidates for the House of Commons at the General Election of 1874, was based, as John Prior subsequently declared, on the principle " that all exceptional legislation affecting working men should be swept away, and that they should be placed on precisely

---

legal independence for workmen and their legitimate combinations ; to make them more respected and more conscious of their own work ; to lift them to a higher moral level ; that they should become citizens ready and desirous to perform all the duties of citizenship. The means employed was to consolidate and organise the power of the Trades Societies, through the institutions of the annual Congress and its Parliamentary Committee ; to use this power, as occasion served, for the general welfare as well as for trade interests. That the measures adopted or proposed by the Congress should be thoroughly discussed in the branches, and delegates well posted in the principal questions. To express it shortly—organisation of collective labour and political education of individual workmen.

" The condition of this effective force was that, while it was being used in furtherance of political action, it should be kept quite clear and independent of political parties. The divergence came with the advent of the Gladstonians to office. The Liberal Government began a policy of coercion in Ireland. Combination was to be put down by the very same mechanism which had been invented to repress labour combinations—by the law of conspiracy. The very ruling of Baron Bramwell as to the Tailors' strike was employed to concoct a law to convict Mr. Parnell and his coadjutors. As a result law was laid down by the Irish judges as to political combinations, which is binding in England, and has still to be resisted or abolished. The Positivists endeavoured to the utmost of their ability to rouse the working classes to a sense of the danger of these proceedings, and to offer an uncompromising resistance to the suspension of the Habeas Corpus Act. The Parliamentary Committee would have none of it. They no doubt believed that the interests of their clients would be best served by a narrower policy, by seeking the help and favour of the eminent statesmen in office. Instead of a compact, powerful force, holding the balance between the parties and the key of the situation, dictating its terms, they preferred to be the tag end of a party. In the end they did not get much, but the Congress was successfully captured and muzzled by the Gladstonian Government."

the same footing as other classes of the community." [1]   Its main items were the repeal of the hated Criminal Law Amendment Act of 1871, and the further legalisation of Trade Unionism.   The sweeping triumphs of 1875, and the acceptance by the Conservative Government of the proposals of the Junta, denuded the programme for subsequent years of its most striking proposals.   There remained over in this department certain minor amendments of law and procedure which occupied the attention of the Committee for the next few years, and were gradually, by their exertions, carried into effect. [2]

But one great disability still lay upon working men as such.   By the common law of England a person is liable for the results, not only of his own negligence, but also for that of his servant, if acting within the scope of his employment.   The one exception is that, whereas to a stranger the master is liable for the negligence of any person whom he employs, to his servant he is not liable for the negligence of a fellow-servant in common employment.   By this legal refinement, which dates only from 1837, and which successive judicial decisions have engrafted upon the common law, a workman who suffered injury through the negligence of some other person in the same employment was precluded from recovering that compensation from the common employer which a stranger, to whom the same accident had happened, could claim and enforce. [3]   If by the error of a signalman a railway train met with an accident, all the

[1] Report of Trades Union Congress, Dublin, 1880, p. 15.

[2] The working of the Trade Union Act of 1871 revealed some technical defects in the law, which were remedied by an amending Act in 1876 (39 and 40 Vic. c. 22).   Rules for the execution of the Employers and Workmen Act were framed by the Lord Chancellor in the same year.

[3] This defence of "common employment," which practically deprived the workman in large undertakings of any remedy in case of accidents arising through negligence in the works, was first recognised in the case of Priestly *v.* Fowler in 1837 (3 Meeson and Welby).   Not until 1868 did the House of Lords, as the final Court of Appeal, extend it to Scotland.   The growth of colossal industrial undertakings, in which thousands of workmen were, technically, "in common employment," made the occasional harshness of the law still more invidious.

injured passengers could obtain compensation from the railway company ; but the engine-driver and guard were expressly excluded from any remedy. What the workman demanded was the abolition of the doctrine of " common employment," and the placing of the employee upon exactly the same footing for compensation as any member of the public.

By the influence of the Miners' National Union and the Amalgamated Society of the Railway Servants (established in 1872) the removal of this disability was, from the first, placed in the foreground of the Trade Union programme. Year after year Employers' Liability Bills were brought in by the Trade Union representatives in the House of Commons, only to be met by stubborn resistance from the capitalists of both parties. Through the pertinacity of Henry Broadhurst a partial reform [1] was obtained from Gladstone's Government in 1880, in spite of the furious opposition of the great employers of labour sitting on both sides of the House. The responsibility of the employer for insuring his workmen against the risks of their calling was, for the first time, clearly recognised by Parliament. The report of the Parliamentary Committee for 1880 claimed that the main battle on the subject had been fought, and that " time and opportunity only were now wanting for the completion of this work." Since then the promotion of claims for compensation for accidents has been one of the most important functions of Trade Unions ; and many of the societies, such as the Bricklayers and Boilermakers, have recovered thousands of pounds for injured members or their relatives.[2] But the doctrine of " common employ-

[1] Act 43 and 44 Vic. c. 52 (1880).

[2] The annual Parliamentary returns for the next fifteen years showed that between three and four hundred cases came into court every year, the amount of compensation actually awarded reaching between £7000 and £8000. But a large number of cases were compromised, or settled without litigation. Meanwhile the relative number of accidents diminished. Whereas in 1877 one railway employee in 95 was more or less injured, in 1889 the proportion was only one in 195. Whereas between 1873 and 1880 one coal-miner in 446 met his death annually, between 1881 and 1890 the proportion was only one in 519 ; although there was apparently less improvement, if any, as regards non-fatal accidents in the mine.

ment," modified by this Act, was by no means abolished. Employers, moreover, were allowed to induce their workpeople to " contract out " of the provisions of the Act.[1] An Employers' Liability Bill, the last remnant of the demands of the Junta, remained, therefore, from 1872 onward a permanent item in the Trade Union programme down to 1896.

With the exception of this one proposal the Parliamentary programme of the Trade Union world was framed, in effect, by the New Front Bench. Curiously devoid of interest or reality, it is important to the political student as showing to what extent the thoughtful and superior workman had, at this time, imbibed the characteristic ideas of middle-class reformers.

The programme of the Parliamentary Committee between 1875 and 1885 falls mainly under three heads. We have first a group of measures the aim of which was the democratisation of the electoral, administrative, and judicial

---

[1] By " contracting out " was meant an arrangement between employer and employed by which the latter relinquish the rights conferred upon them by the Act, and often also their rights under the Common Law. The Act was silent on the subject ; but the judges decided, to the great surprise and dismay of the Trade Union leaders, that contracting out was permissible (see Griffiths *v*. Earl of Dudley, 9, Queen's Bench Division, 35). The usual form of " contracting out " was the establishment of a workman's insurance fund to which the workmen were compelled to subscribe, and to which the employer also contributed. Among the coal-miners, those of Lancashire, Somerset, and some collieries in Wales generally contracted out. The employees of the London and North-Western, and London and Brighton Railway Companies also contracted out. In one or two large undertakings in other industries a similar course was followed. But in the vast majority of cases employers did not resort to this expedient. Particulars are given in the *Report and Evidence of the Select Committee on Employers' Liability*, 1866 ; the publications of the Royal Commission on Labour, 1891–94; and *Miners' Thrift and Employers' Liability*, by G. L. Campbell (Wigan, 1891) ; and our *Industrial Democracy*.

In 1893–94 a further amending Bill passed the House of Commons which swept away the doctrine of common employment, and placed the workman with regard to compensation on the same footing as any other person. A clause making void any agreement by which the workman forewent his right of action, or " contracted out," was rejected by the House of Lords, and the Bill was thereupon abandoned. The question was settled in 1896 by the passage, under the Unionist Government, of the Workmen's Compensation Act, giving compensation in all cases, irrespective of the employers' default.

machinery of the State. Another set of reforms had for their end the enabling of the exceptionally thrifty or exceptionally industrious man to rise out of the wage-earning class. A third group of proposals aimed at the legal regulation of the conditions of particular industries.

Complete political Democracy had been for over a century the creed of the superior workmen. It was therefore not unnatural that it should come to the front in the Trades Union Congress. What appears peculiar is the form which this old-standing faith took in the hands of the Front Bench. The Trade Union leaders of 1837–42 had adopted enthusiastically the " Six Points " of the Charter. Even the sober Junta of 1867–71 had sat with Karl Marx on the committee of the " International," in the programme of which Universal Suffrage was but a preliminary bagatelle. To the Front Bench of 1875–85 Democracy appeared chiefly in the guise of the Codification of the Criminal Law, the Reform of the Jury System, the creation of a Court of Criminal Appeal, and the Regulation of the Summary Jurisdiction of the Magistracy—a curious group of law reforms which it is easy to trace to the little knot of barristers who had stood by the Unions in their hour of trial.[1] We do not wish to depreciate the value of these proposals, framed in the interests of all classes of the community ; but they were not, and probably were never intended to be, in any sense a democratisation of our judicial system.[2] When the Con-

---

[1] The legal advisers of the Junta realised that the triumph of 1875, though it resulted in a distinct strengthening of the Trade Union position, was mainly a moral victory. Though Trade Unions were made legal, the law of conspiracy was only partially reformed, whilst that relating to political combinations, unlawful assemblies, sedition, etc., remained, as it still remains, untouched. Expert lawyers knew in how many ways prejudiced tribunals might at any time make the law oppressive. The legal friends of Trade Unionism desired, therefore, to utilise the period of political quiet in simplifying the criminal law, and in removing as much of the obsolete matter as was possible. And though State Trials recommenced in Ireland in 1881, and criminal prosecutions of Trade Unionists continued in England down to 1891, the interval had been well spent in clearing away some of the grosser evils.

[2] In the proposed reform of the Jury laws, for instance, the Parliamentary Committee for several years did not venture to ask explicitly for

gress dealt with electoral reform it got no further than the
assimilation of the county and borough franchise—already
a commonplace of middle-class Liberalism.   The student of
Continental labour movements will find it difficult to believe
that in the representative Congress of the English artisans,
amendments in favour of Manhood Suffrage were even as
late as 1882 and 1883 rejected by large majorities.[1]   Nor
did the Parliamentary Committee put even the County
Franchise into their own programme until it had become
the battle-cry of the Liberal party at the General Election
of 1880.   The Extension of the Hours of Polling becomes a
subject of discussion from 1878 onward, but the Payment
of Election Expenses does not come up until 1883, and
Payment of Members not until 1884.

Scarcely less significant in character were the measures
of social reform advocated during these years.   The prominent Trade Unionists had been converted, as we have
already had occasion to point out, to the economic Individualism which at this time dominated the Liberal party.
A significant proof of this unconscious conversion is to be
found in the unanimity with which a Trades Union Congress
could repeatedly press for such " reforms " as Peasant
Proprietorship, the purchase by the artisan of his own
cottage, the establishment of " self-governing workshops,"
the multiplication of patents in the hands of individual
workmen, and other changes which would cut at the root
of Trade Unionism or any collective control of the means of
production.   For whatever advantages there might be in
turning the agricultural labourer into a tiny freeholder, it is
obvious that under such a system no Agricultural Labourers'

---

that payment of jurymen which alone would enable working men to serve,
and contented themselves with suggesting a lowering of the qualification
for juryman.   In 1876, indeed, John Burnett, then a prominent member
of the Committee, strongly opposed the Payment of Jurymen on the ground
that it might create a class of professional jurors (Trades Union Congress
Report, 1876, p. 14).

[1] See, for instance, the report of the 1876 Congress, p. 30 ; that of the
1882 Congress, p. 37 ; that of the 1883 Congress, p. 41 ; and *History of the
British Trades Union Congress*, by W. J. Davis, vol. i., 1910.

Union could exist. However useful it may be to make the town artisan independent of a landlord, it has been proved beyond controversy that wage-earning owners of houses lose that perfect mobility which enables them, through their Trade Union, to boycott the bad employer or desert the low-paying district. And we can imagine the dismay with which the leaders of the Nine Hours Movement would have discovered that any considerable proportion of the engineering work of Newcastle was being done in workshops owned by artisans whose interests as capitalists or patentees conflicted with the common interests of all the workers.

In no respect, however, does the conversion of the Trade Union leaders to middle-class views stand out more clearly than in their attitude to the clamour from the workers in certain industries for the legal protection of their Standard of Life. From time immemorial one of the leading tenets of Trade Unionism has been the desirability of maintaining by law the minimum Standard of Life of the workers, and it was still steadfastly held by two important sections of the Trade Union world, the Cotton Operatives and the Coalminers. But to the Parliamentary Committee of 1875–85, as to the Liberal legislators, every demand for securing the conditions of labour by legislation appeared as an invidious exception, only to be justified by the special helplessness or incompetency of the applicants. Nevertheless, many of the trades succeeded in persuading Congress to back up the particular sectional legislation they desired. The Tailors asked, on the one hand, for the extension of the Factory Acts to home workers, and, on the other, for compensation out of public funds when interfered with by the sanitary inspector. The Bakers complained with equal pertinacity of the lack of public inspection of bakehouses, and of the hardships of their regulation by the Smoke Prevention Acts. The London Cabmen sought the aid of Congress, not against their employers, the cab proprietors, but against the public. The men in charge of engines and boilers demanded that no one should be allowed to work at their trade without obtaining from the Government a certificate of competency.   In the absence of any fixed or consistent idea of the collective interest of the wage-earning class, or of Trade Unionists as such, every proposal that any section demanded for itself was accepted with equanimity by the Congress, and passed on to the Parliamentary Committee to carry out, however inconsistent it might be with the general principles that swayed their minds.[1]

It is not difficult to understand why, with such a pro-gramme, the Trade Union world failed, between 1876 and 1885, to exercise any effective influence upon the House of Commons.   A few concessions to the wage-earners were, indeed, obtained from the Government.   The Employers' Liability Act of 1880, to which we have already referred, represented, in spite of all its deficiencies, a new departure of considerable importance.   Useful little clauses protecting the interests of the wage-earners were, through Broadhurst's pertinacity, inserted in Chamberlain's Bankruptcy Act and in his Joint Stock Companies Act.[2]   But it was left to Charles Bradlaugh, who had never been a Trade Unionist, to initiate the useful law prohibiting the payment of wages in public-houses, though when it was introduced the Parlia-mentary Committee (observing that it was unnecessary in

---

[1] In this connection may be mentioned the extensive agitation pro-moted by Samuel Plimsoll for further legislation to prevent the loss of life at sea.   At the 1873 Trades Union Congress Plimsoll distributed copies of his book, *Our Merchant Seamen*, and enlisted, during the next three years, practically the whole political force of the Trade Union Movement in support of his Merchant Shipping Acts Amendment Bill.   The " Plimsoll and Seamen's Fund Committee," of which George Howell became secre-tary, received large financial help from the Unions, the South Yorkshire Miners' Association voting, in 1873, a levy of a shilling per member, and contributing over £1000.   The Parliamentary Committee gave Plimsoll's Bill a place in their programme for the General Election of 1874, and this Trade Union support contributed largely to Plimsoll's success in passing a temporary Act in 1875, and permanent legislation in 1876, against the combined efforts of a strong Conservative Government and the shipowners on both sides of the House.   (See *Labour Legislation, Labour Movements, and Labour Leaders*, by G. Howell, 1902.)

[2] Congress Reports, 1882 and 1883.

respect of organised trades) gave it a mild support. Brad-laugh it was, too, who in 1887 got passed the amendment of the law against Truck—a subject which the Parliamentary Committee had, in 1877, dismissed from their programme on the ground that they were unable, in the trades of which they had knowledge, to find sufficient evidence of its necessity.[1] But the failure of the Parliamentary Committee to induce the Government of the day to legislate for wage-earners as such was naturally most patent in that group of reforms which dealt with the legal regulation of the conditions of labour. To the great consolidating Factory Bill of 1878 they found only four small amendments to propose ; and of these only one was carried.[2] The " Sweating System " of home work against which the Tailors and Bootmakers were suggesting stringent but, as we venture to think, ill-considered legislation was permitted to expand free from all regulation. The bakehouses, too, were allowed to slip virtually out of inspection. Deputation after deputation waited on the Home Secretary to press for an increase in the number of factory inspectors, only to be met with the apparently unanswerable argument that it would cost money which the poor taxpayers could ill spare, until the astute and practical leaders of the Lancashire Cotton Operatives grew tired of the monotonous regularity with which their resolutions in favour of further factory inspection and more stringent regulations of the conditions of their trade were passed by Congress, and the little assistance which this endorsement procured for them. A " Northern Counties Factory Act Reform Association " was established in 1886, to do the work which the Trades Union Congress and its Parliamentary Committee had failed to accomplish. We have, in fact, only one important achievement of the Parliamentary Committee to record in this department of social reform. For years Congress had passed emphatic resolu-

[1] Parliamentary Committee's Report, September 17, 1877.
[2] That extending to factory scales and measures the provisions of the Weights and Measures Act relating to inspection, etc.

tions in favour of the selection of practical working men as
Factory Inspectors.   Great was the jubilation at the appoint-
ment, in 1882, of J. D. Prior, General Secretary of the
Amalgamated Society of Carpenters, and a member of the
Parliamentary Committee, to the post of Inspector.[1]

In matters of more general interest the Trade Union
leaders were not more successful, though the attempt to
reform the law and its administration resulted in some
minor improvements.   The first outcome of the projects
for law reform so dear to the Congresses of 1876–80 was
the Justices' Clerks Act of 1877, which enabled magistrates
to remit costs.   The passing of the Summary Jurisdiction
Act of 1879, which gave defendants the right to claim trial
before a jury whenever the penalty exceeded three months'
imprisonment, was, Howell observes, " materially aided by
the action of Congress."   But it is needless to inform the
reader that the Criminal Law never got itself codified.   To
this day juries continue to be drawn exclusively from the
upper and middle classes.   The long agitation for the
abolition of the unpaid magistracy ended in an anti-climax.
The Liberal Government of 1884 left the system unaltered,
but, on the nomination of Henry Broadhurst,[2] placed four
Trade Union leaders upon the magisterial bench in certain
Lancashire boroughs, a precedent since followed by successive Lord Chancellors.

In one direction the Parliamentary Committee saw their
hopes fully accomplished.   Their adoption of the particular
projects of electoral reform advocated by the Liberal party
enabled them to render effective help in the passing of the
Acts of 1885, which assimilated the County and the Borough
Franchise, effected a redistribution of seats, and made the
extended hours of polling universal.   But the desire of
successive Congresses for effective labour representation

---

[1] The appointment was first offered to Broadhurst, who elected to
continue his work as Secretary of the Parliamentary Committee, and who
suggested Prior (*Henry Broadhurst, the Story of his Life*, by himself, 1901).
[2] *Ibid.* p. 136.

continued to be baulked by the extortion from candidates of heavy election expenses, and by the refusal to provide payment for service in Parliament and other public bodies. On the burning question of the land the Parliamentary Committee supported with conscientious fervour Gladstone's Irish policy of creating small freeholds, and enthusiastically endorsed the proposals of Chamberlain for the extension of similar legislation to Great Britain. The same spirit no doubt entered into their support of the provisions of Chamberlain's Patent Act, designed to facilitate the taking out of patents by poor inventors. To sum up the situation, we may say that the resolutions of the Trades Union Congress on questions of general politics between 1880 and 1884 were successfully pressed on the Legislature only in so far as they happened to coincide with the proposals of the Liberal party. With the one great exception of the Employers' Liability Act, nothing seems really to have called out the full energies of the leaders. The manifestoes and published memoranda of the Parliamentary Committee during these years do not differ either in tone or in substance from the speeches and articles in which Chamberlain and other Radical capitalists were propounding a programme of individualist Radicalism. In fact, the draft " Address to the Workmen of the United Kingdom," which the Parliamentary Committee, in anticipation of the General Election, submitted to the Congress of 1885, fell far short of Chamberlain's " Unauthorised Programme." It occurred neither to the Parliamentary Committee nor to the Congress to suggest the obvious answer to Sir William Harcourt's financial objection to increased factory inspection. No trace is to be discovered of any consciousness on the part of the Trade Union leaders of the existence of a very substantial tribute annually levied upon the industrial world under the names of rent and interest. And even Chamberlain's modest and tentative proposals of these years, relating to the payment, by the recipients of that tribute, of some contribution by way of " ransom," found no echo in the official programme of the Trade Union world. Finally, though the Congress had adopted Payment of Election Expenses in 1883, and Payment of Members in 1884, the Parliamentary Committee omitted both these propositions from its draft, and, like Gladstone, could not even bring itself to ask for Free Education. The three latter points were added to the draft by the Congress.

The assimilation of the political creed of the Trade Union leaders with that of the official Liberal party was perfectly sincere. We have already described, in the preceding chapter, how the Junta had begun to be unconsciously converted from the traditional position of Trade Unionism to the principle of Administrative Nihilism, then dominant in the middle class. It is unnecessary for us to argue whether this conception of the functions of law and government is or is not an adequate view of social development. The able and conscientious men who formed the Front Bench of the Trades Union Congress of 1876–85 had grown up without any alternative political theory, and had accordingly erected the objection to legislative interference or Governmental administration into an absolute dogma.[1]

Laisser-faire, then, was the political and social creed of the Trade Union leaders of this time. Up to 1885 they undoubtedly represented the views current among the rank and file. At that date all observers were agreed that the Trade Unions of Great Britain would furnish an impenetrable barrier against Socialistic projects. Within a decade we find the whole Trade Union world permeated with Collectivist ideas, and, as the *Times* recorded as early as

---

[1] It may be mentioned that the Trades Union Congress, which at first had welcomed addresses from the middle and upper class friends of Trade Unionism, was, between 1881 and 1883, gradually restricted to Trade Unionists. At the Nottingham Congress in 1883, where Frederic Harrison read a paper on the " History of Trade Unionism," and Henry Crompton one on the " Codification of the Law," when Frederic Harrison proposed to take part in the discussion on the Land Question, he was not permitted to do so; and this rule has since been rigidly adhered to. At the Aberdeen Congress of 1884 Lord Rosebery was allowed to deliver an address on the " Federalism of the Trades Union Congress," but this was the last time that any one has been invited to read a paper.

1893, the Socialist party supreme in the Trades Union Congress.[1] This revolution in opinion is the chief event of Trade Union history at the close of the nineteenth century ; and we propose to analyse in some detail the various influences which in our opinion co-operated to bring it about. We shall trace the beginnings of a new intellectual ferment in the Trade Union world. We shall watch this working on minds awakened by an industrial contraction of exceptional character. We shall see it resulting in the revelation of hideous details of poverty and degradation, for which deepening social compunction imperatively demanded a remedy. We shall describe the recrudescence of a revolutionary Utopianism like the Owenism of 1833–34. We shall trace the gradual schooling of the impracticable elements into a sobered and somewhat bureaucratic Collectivism ; and finally, we shall watch the rapid diffusion of this new faith throughout the whole Trade Union world.[2]

If we had to assign to any one event the starting of the new current of thought, we should name the wide circulation in Great Britain of Henry George's *Progress and Poverty* during the years 1880–82. The optimist and aggressive tone of the book, in marked contrast with the complacent quietism into which the English working-class movement had sunk, and the force of the popularisation of

---

[1] *Times* leader on the Congress of Belfast, September 11, 1893, which deplores the remarkable " subservience to Mr. John Burns and his friends " manifested by the Congress—a subservience marked by the election of Mr. Burns for the Parliamentary Committee at the head of the poll, and by the adoption of a programme which included the nationalisation of the land and other means of production and distribution.

[2] The following description of the rise of the " New Unionism " of 1889 is based on minutes and reports of Trade Union organisations, the files of *Justice*, the *Labour Elector*, the *Trade Unionist*, the *Cotton Factory Times*, the *Workman's Times*, and other working-class journals. The documentary evidence has been elucidated and supplemented by the reminiscences of most of the principal actors in the movement, and by the personal recollections of the authors themselves, one of whom, as a member of the Fabian Society, observed the transformation from the Socialist side, whilst the other, as a disciple of Herbert Spencer and a colleague of Charles Booth, was investigating the contemporary changes from an Individualist standpoint.

the economic Theory of Rent, sounded the dominant note alike of the " New Unionism " and of the British Socialist Movement. Henry George made, it is true, no contribution to the problems of industrial organisation ; nor had he, outside of the " Single Tax " on land values, any intention of promoting a general Collectivist movement. But he succeeded, where previous writers had failed, in widely diffusing among all classes a vivid appreciation of the nature and results of the landlord's appropriation of economic rent. It is, in our judgement, the spread among the town artisans of this conception of rent which has so largely transformed the economic views of the Trade Union world, and which has gone far to shift the lines of politics. The land question in particular has been completely revolutionised. Instead of the Chartist cry of " Back to the Land," still adhered to by rural labourers and belated politicians, the town artisan is thinking of his claim to the unearned increment of urban land values, which he now watches falling into the coffers of the great landlords.

But if Henry George gave the starting push, it was the propaganda of the Socialists that got the new movement under way. The Socialist party, which became reorganised in London between 1881 and 1883, after practically a generation of quiescence, merged the project of Land Nationalisation in the wider conception of an organised Democratic community in which the collective power and the collective income should be consciously directed to the common benefit of all.[1] Whilst Henry George was, almost in his own despite, driving Peasant Proprietorship and Leasehold Enfranchisement out of the political field, the impressive description which Karl Marx had given of the effects of the Industrial Revolution was interpreting to the thoughtful workman the every-day incidents of industrial life. It needed no Socialist to convince the artisan in any of the great industries that his chance of rising to be a successful employer was becoming daily more remote. It required no

[1] See Mr. H. M. Hyndman's *England for All*, 1881.

agitator to point out that amid an enormous increase in wealth production the wages of the average mechanic remained scarcely sufficient to bring up his family in decency and comfort, whilst whole sections of his unskilled fellow-workers received less than the barest family maintenance. Even the skilled mechanic saw himself exposed to panics, commercial crises, and violent industrial dislocations, over which neither he nor his Trade Union had any control, and by which he and his children were often reduced to destitution. But it was the Socialists who supplied the workman with a plausible explanation of these untoward facts. Through the incessant lecturing of H. M. Hyndman, William Morris, and other disciples of Karl Marx, working men were taught that the impossibility of any large section of the working class becoming their own employers was due, not to lack of self-control, capacity, or thrift, but to the Industrial Revolution, with its improvement of mechanical processes, its massing of capital, and the consequent extinction of the small *entrepreneur* by great industrial establishments. In this light the divorce of the manual workers from the ownership of the means of production was seen to be no passing phase, but an economic development which must, under any system of private control of industry, become steadily more complete. And it was argued that the terrible alterations of over-production and commercial stagnation, the anomaly that a glut of commodities should be a cause of destitution, were the direct result of the management of industry with a view to personal profit, instead of to the satisfaction of public wants.

The economic circumstances of the time supplied the Socialist lecturers with dramatic illustrations of their theory. The acute depression of 1878–79 had been succeeded by only a brief and partial expansion during 1881–83. A period of prolonged though not exceptional contraction followed, during which certain staple trades experienced the most sudden and excessive fluctuations. In the great industry of shipbuilding, for instance, the bad times of 1879 were succeeded by a period during which trade expanded by leaps and bounds, more than twice the tonnage being built in 1883 than in 1879. In the very next year this enormous production came suddenly to an end, many shipbuilding yards being closed and whole towns on the north-east coast finding their occupation for the moment destroyed. The total tonnage built fell from 1,250,000 in 1883 to 750,000 in 1884, 540,000 in 1885, and to the still lower total of 473,000 in 1886. Thousands of the most highly skilled and best organised mechanics, who had been brought to Jarrow or Sunderland the year before, found themselves reduced to absolute destitution, not from any failure of their industry, but merely because the exigencies of competitive profit-making had led to the concentration in one year of the normal production of two. " In every shipbuilding port," says Robert Knight in the Boilermakers' Annual Report for 1886, " there are to be seen thousands of idle men vainly seeking for an honest day's work. The privation that has been endured by them, their wives and children, is terrible to contemplate. Sickness has been very prevalent, whilst the hundreds of pinched and hungry faces have told a tale of suffering and privation which no optimism could minimise or conceal. Hide it—cover it up as we may, there is a depth of grief and trouble the full revelations of which, we believe, cannot be indefinitely postponed. The workman may be ignorant of science and the arts, and the sum of his exact knowledge may be only that which he has gained in his closely circumscribed daily toil ; but he is not blind, and his thoughts do not take the shape of daily and hourly thanksgiving that his condition is not worse than it is ; he does not imitate the example of the pious shepherd of Salisbury Plain, who derived supreme contentment from the fact that a kind Providence had vouchsafed him salt to eat with his potatoes. He sees the lavish display of wealth in which he has no part. He sees a large and growing class enjoying inherited abundance. He sees miles of costly residences, each occupied by fewer people than are crowded into single rooms of the tenement in which he lives. He cannot fail to reason that there must be something wrong in a system which effects such unequal distribution of the wealth created by labour."

Other skilled trades had, between 1883 and 1887, a similar though less dramatic experience. At the International Trades Union Congress of 1886, James Mawdsley, the cautious leader of the Lancashire cotton-spinners, speaking as a member of the Parliamentary Committee on behalf of the British section, described the state of affairs in England in the following terms : " Wages had fallen, and there was a great number of unemployed. . . . Flax mills were being closed every day. . . . All the building trades were in a bad position ; . . . ironfoundries were in difficulties, and one-third of the shipwrights were without work. . . . Steam-engine makers were also slack, except those manufacturers who exported to France, Germany, and Austria. With a few rare exceptions, the depression affecting the great leading trades was felt in a thousand-and-one occupations. Seeing that there was a much larger number of unemployed, the question naturally presented itself as to whether there was any chance of improvement. He considered there was no chance of improvement so long as the present state of society continued to exist. . . . He did not understand their Socialism ; he had not studied it as perhaps he ought to have done. The workmen of England were not so advanced as the workmen of the Continent. Nevertheless they, at least, possessed one clear conception : they realised that the actual producers did not obtain their share of the wealth they created." [1] We see the same spirit spreading even to the most conservative and exclusive trades. " To our minds," writes the Central Secretary of the powerful Union of Flint Glass Makers, " it is very hard for employers to attempt to force men into systems by which they cannot earn an honourable living. These unjust attempts to

---

[1] *Report of the International Trades Union Congress at Paris, 1886*, by Adolphe Smith, 1886.

grind down the working men will not be tolerated much longer, for revolutionary changes are beginning to show themselves, and important matters affecting the industrial classes will speedily come to the front.   Why, for example, should Lord Dudley inherit coal-mines and land producing £1000 a day while his colliers have to slave all the week and cannot get a living ? " [1]

The discontent was fanned by well-intentioned if somewhat sentimental philanthropists, who were publishing their experiences in the sweated industries and the slums of the great cities.   The *Bitter Cry of Outcast London* and other gruesome stories were revealing, not only to the middle class, but also to the " aristocracy of labour," whole areas of industrial life which neither Trade Unionism nor Co-operation could hope to reach.   With the middle class the compunction thus excited resulted in elaborate investigations issuing in inconclusive reports.   A Royal Commission on the Housing of the Poor produced nothing more effectual than a slight addition to the existing powers of vestries and Town Councils.   Another on the Depression of Trade was absolutely barren.   A Select Committee of the House of Lords on the Poor Law failed even to discover the problems to be solved.   Another on the Sweating System ended, after years of delay, in an accurate diagnosis of the evil, coupled with a confession of inability to cope with it.   In 1885 an Edinburgh philanthropist provided a thousand pounds for a public conference to inquire whether some more equitable system of industrial remuneration could not be suggested : a conference which served only to cast doubt on such philanthropic schemes as profit-sharing and the " self-governing workshop," whilst bringing into prominence the Socialist proposals.[2]   And, more important than all these, Charles Booth, a great merchant and shipowner, began in 1886, at his own expense, a systematic statistical inquiry into the actual social condition of the whole popula-

---

[1] *Flint Glass Makers' Magazine,* November 1884.
[2] *Report of the Industrial Remuneration Conference,* 1885.

tion of London, the impressive results of which eventually reverberated from one end of the kingdom to the other.[1] The outcome of the investigations thus set on foot was an incalculable impetus to social reform. They had, for the most part, been undertaken in the expectation that a sober and scientific inquiry would prove the exceptional character of the harrowing incidents laid bare by the philanthropists, and unsparingly quoted by the new agitators. But to the genuine surprise alike of the economists and the Trade Union leaders, the lurid statements of the sensationalists and the Socialists were, on the whole, borne out by the statistics. The stories of unmerited misery were shown to be, not accidental exceptions to a general condition of moderate well-being, but typical instances of the average existence of great masses of the population. The " sweater " turned out to be, not an exceptionally cruel capitalist, but himself the helpless product of a widespread degeneration which extended over whole industries. In the wealthiest and most productive city in the world, Charles Booth, after an exhaustive census, was driven to the conclusion that a million and a quarter persons fell habitually below his " Poverty Line." Thirty-two per cent of the whole population of London (in some large districts over 60 per cent) were found to be living in a state of chronic poverty, which precluded not only the elementary conditions of civilisation and citizenship, but was incompatible with physical health or industrial efficiency. Moreover, Charles Booth's figures and the report of the House of Lords Committee on Sweating disproved, once for all, the comfortable assumption that all

[1] The results of twenty years of patient labour by Charles Booth and his assistants are embodied in the magnificent work, *Labour and Life of the People* (London, 1st edition, 2 vols., 1889–91 ; 2nd edition, 4 vols., 1893), reissued in greatly enlarged form as *Life and Labour in London*, 18 vols. ; *Pauperism and the Endowment of Old Age* (London, 1893) ; *The Aged Poor* (1894)   *Old Age and the Aged Poor* (1899) ; *Industrial Unrest and Trades Union Policy* (1913). In *Charles Booth : a Memoir* (1918) Mrs. Booth has given a personal biography (1840–1914) of a tireless investigator who, merely by the instrument of social diagnosis, got accomplished reforms of a magnitude that seemed at first wholly impracticable.

destitution originated in drink or vice. It was impossible, to use the well-known phrase of Burke, to draw an indictment against a third of the people of London, or against two-thirds of the East End.

The daily experience of whole sections of the wage-earners during these years of depression, and the statistical inquiries of the middle class, appeared, therefore, to justify the Socialist indictment of the capitalist system. What was perhaps of more effect was the fact that the Socialists alone seemed inspired by faith in a radical transformation of society, and that they alone offered a solution which had not yet been tried and found wanting. Prior to 1867 it had been possible to ascribe the evil state of the wage-earners to the malignant influence of class government and political exclusion. Cobden and Bright had eloquently described the millennium to be reached through untaxed products. For a whole generation the leaders of a consolidated Trade Unionism had demonstrated the advantageous terms that the artisan might, through collective bargaining and a reserve fund, wring from his employers. But in face of a protracted lack of employment, the extended suffrage, Free Trade, and well-administered Trade Unions proved alike helpless. Twenty years of the franchise had left the town artisan still at the mercy of commercial gamblers and exposed to the extortions of the slum landlord. A Liberal Government was actually in power, wielding an enormous majority, but manifesting no keen desire to remedy the results of economic inequality. No attempt was being made to redress even the admitted wrongs of the necessitous taxpayer. The Tea Duty remained untouched; the Land Tax was left unreformed; whilst the larger question of using some of the nation's wealth to provide decent conditions of existence for the great bulk of the people was not even mooted. A further Extension of the Franchise, Free Trade, and Popular Education were still the only social and economic panaceas that the Liberal party had to offer. But cheapness of commodities was of no use to the workman who was thrown out of employment ; and the spread of education served but to increase his discontent with existing social conditions and his ability to understand the theoretic explanations and practical proposals of the new school of reformers.

The working man found no more comfort in Trade Unionism than in party politics. The mason, carpenter, or ironfounder saw, for instance, his old and powerful Trade Society reduced to little more than a sick and burial club, refusing all support to strikes even against reductions of wages and increase of hours, and only maintaining its out-of-work benefit by running heavily into debt to its more prosperous members.[1] As the lean years followed one on another, he saw the benefits reduced, the contributions raised, and numbers of staunch Unionists left high and dry as members " out of benefit." The trade friendly society—the " scientific Trade Unionism " of the Front Bench—was in fact becoming rapidly discredited. John Burns and Tom Mann, young and energetic members of the Amalgamated Society of Engineers, were, between 1884 and 1889, vigorously denouncing, up and down the country, the supineness of their great amalgamated Union. " How long, how long," appeals Tom Mann to the Trade Unionists in 1886,[2] " will you be content with the present half-hearted policy of your Unions ? I readily grant that good work has been done in the past by the Unions ; but, in Heaven's name, what good purpose are they serving now ? All of them have large numbers out of employment even when

[1] The funds of the Stonemasons had been completely exhausted by the great strike of 1878. In January 1879 the Society determined, on a proposition submitted by the Central Executive, to close all pending disputes (including a general strike at Sheffield against a heavy reduction without due notice) ; and between that date and March 1885, though many of the branches struggled manfully, and in some cases successfully, against repeated reductions of wages, increases of hours, or infringements of the local bye-laws, no strike whatever was supported from the Society's funds. The case of the Stonemasons is typical of the other great trade friendly societies.

[2] *What a Compulsory Eight Hours Working Day means to the Workers,* by Tom Mann (1886), 16 pp.

their particular trade is busy. None of the important societies have any policy other than that of endeavouring to keep wages from falling. The true Unionist policy of *aggression* seems entirely lost sight of : in fact, the average Unionist of to-day is a man with a fossilised intellect, either hopelessly apathetic, or supporting a policy that plays directly into the hands of the capitalist exploiter. . . . I take my share of the work of the Trade Union to which I belong ; but I candidly confess that unless it shows more vigour at the present time (June 1886) I shall be compelled to take the view—against my will—that to continue to spend time over the ordinary squabble-investigating, do-nothing policy will be an unjustifiable waste of one's energies. I am sure there are thousands of others in my state of mind." [1]

[1] Mr. Tom Mann, one of the outstanding figures in the New Unionist Movement, was born at Foleshill, Warwickshire, in 1856, and apprenticed in an engineering shop at Birmingham, whence he came to London in 1878, and joined the Amalgamated Society of Engineers. Eagerly pursuing his self-education, he became acquainted first with the Co-operative Movement, and then with the writings of Henry George. In 1884 he visited the United States, where he worked for six months. On his return he joined the Battersea Branch of the Social Democratic Federation, and quickly became one of its leading speakers. His experience of the evils of overtime made the Eight Hours Day a prominent feature in his lectures, and in 1886 he published his views in the pamphlet, *What a Compulsory Eight Hours Working Day means to the Workers* (1886, 16 pp.), of which several editions have been printed. In the same year he left his trade in order to devote himself to the provincial propaganda of the Social Democratic Federation, spending over two years incessantly lecturing, first about Tyneside, and then in Lancashire. Returning to London early in 1889, he assisted in establishing the Gasworkers' Union and in organising the great dock strike, on the termination of which he was elected President of the Dockers' Union. For three years he applied himself to building up this organisation, deciding to resign in 1892, when he became a candidate for the General Secretaryship of the Amalgamated Society of Engineers. After an exciting contest, during which he addressed meetings of the members in all the great engineering centres, he failed of success only by 951 votes on a poll of 35,992. In the meantime he had been appointed, in 1891, a member of the Royal Commission on Labour, to which he submitted a striking scheme for consolidating the whole dock business of the port of London, by cutting a new channel for the Thames across the Isle of Dogs. On the establishment in 1893 of the London Reform Union he was appointed its secretary, a post which he relinquished in 1894 on being elected secretary of the Independent Labour Party. This he presently relinquished to emigrate to New Zealand ; and there and in Australia he threw himself energetically into Trade Union agitation. Returning to England in 1911, he became a

" Constituted as it is," writes John Burns in September
1887,[1] " Unionism carries within itself the source of its own
dissolution. . . . Their reckless assumption of the duties
and responsibilities that only the State or whole community
can discharge, in the nature of sick and superannuation
benefits, at the instance of the middle class, is crushing out
the larger Unions by taxing their members to an unbearable
extent. This so cripples them that the fear of being unable
to discharge their friendly society liabilities often makes
them submit to encroachments by the masters without
protest. The result of this is that all of them have ceased
to be Unions for maintaining the rights of labour, and have
degenerated into mere middle and upper class rate-reducing
institutions." [2]

---

fervent advocate of Syndicalism; and then became an organiser for
various General Labour Unions. In 1919 he was elected General Secretary
of the Amalgamated Society of Engineers, after an exhaustive ballot of
its great membership.

[1] Article in *Justice*, September 3, 1887.

[2] Mr. John Burns, in many respects the most striking personality in
the Labour Movement, was born at Battersea in 1859, and was apprenticed
to a local engineering firm. Already during his apprenticeship he made his
voice heard in public, in 1877 being actually arrested for persistently
speaking on Clapham Common, and in 1878 braving the " Jingo " mob at
a Hyde Park demonstration. As soon as he was out of his time (1879) he
joined the Amalgamated Society of Engineers, and became an advocate
of shorter hours of labour. An engagement as engineer on the Niger,
West Africa, during 1880–81, gave him leisure to read, which he utilised by
mastering Adam Smith and J. S. Mill. Returning to London, he worked
side by side with Victor Delahaye, an ex-Communard, who was afterwards
one of the French representatives at the Berlin Labour Conference, 1891,
and with whom he had many talks on the advancement of labour. In
1883 he joined the Social Democratic Federation, and at once became its
leading working-class member, championing its cause, for instance, in an
impressive speech at the Industrial Remuneration Conference in 1885. In
the same year he was elected by his district of the Amalgamated Society
of Engineers as its representative at the quinquennial delegate meeting of
the Society, where he found himself the youngest member. At the General
Election of 1885 he stood as Socialist candidate for West Nottingham,
receiving 598 votes. For the next two years he became known as the
leader of the London " unemployed " agitation. His prosecution for
sedition in 1886 (with three other prominent members of the Social Democratic Federation) aroused considerable interest, and on his acquittal his
speech for the defence, *The Man with the Red Flag*, had a large sale in
pamphlet form (1886; 16 pp.). At the prohibited demonstration at

O

Here we see the beginning of that agitation against the combination of friendly benefits with trade protection aims which subsequently became, for a short time, one of the characteristics of the " New Unionism." But if the trade friendly society withered up during these years into a mere benefit club, the purely trade society showed no greater vitality. The great depression of 1878–79 had swept out of existence hundreds of little local Unions which lacked the cohesion given by the friendly society side. The Lancashire and Midland Miners' organisations, which gave no benefits, had either collapsed altogether, or had dissolved into isolated pit clubs, incapable of combined action. The Lancashire cotton operatives, the Northumberland and Durham miners, and a few other essentially trade societies, held together only by surrendering to the employers one concession after another. With capitalists ready at any moment to suspend a profitless business, collective bargaining proved as powerless to avert reductions as the individual contract. In face of a long-continued depression of trade, marked by frequent oscillations in particular industries, both types of Trade Unionism, it seemed, had been tried and found wanting.

These were the circumstances under which the disillusioned working-class politician or Trade Unionist was reached by the lectures and writings of the Socialists, who

---

Trafalgar Square on " Bloody Sunday " (November 13, 1887), in conjunction with Mr. Cunninghame Graham, M.P., he broke through the police line, for which they were both sentenced to six weeks' imprisonment. In January 1889 he was elected for Battersea to the new London County Council, on which he became one of the most useful and influential members. His magnificent work in the dock strike and in organising the unskilled labourers is described in the text. At the General Election of 1892 he was chosen, by a large majority, M.P. for Battersea, and at the Trades Union Congress in 1893 he received the largest number of votes for the Parliamentary Committee, of which he accordingly became Chairman. In 1906 he was appointed President of the Local Government Board in Sir H. Campbell-Bannerman's Government, with a seat in the Cabinet—thus becoming the first working-man Cabinet Minister—a post which he held until August 1914, when he resigned on the outbreak of war. He retained his seat in Parliament until 1918, when he retired.

offered him not only a sympathetic explanation of the ills from which he suffered, but also a comprehensive scheme of social reform, extending from an Eight Hours Bill to the Nationalisation of the Means of Production. In a purely historical essay it is unnecessary for us to discuss the validity of the optimistic confidence with which the Socialists of these years declared that under a system of collective ownership the workers would not only be ensured at all times a competent livelihood, but would themselves control the administration of the surplus wealth of the nation. But in tracing the causes of the New Unionism of 1889–90, and the transformation of the Trade Union Movement from an Individualist to a Collectivist influence in the political world, we venture to ascribe a large share to the superior attractiveness of this buoyant faith over anything offered by the almost cynical fatalism of the old school.

The Socialist agitation benefited between 1886 and 1889 by a series of undesigned advertisements. Meetings of " the unemployed " in February 1886 led to unexpected riots, which threw all London into a panic, and were followed by a Government prosecution for sedition. Hyndman, Burns, Champion, and Williams, as the leaders of the Social Democratic Federation, were indicted at the Old Bailey, and their trial, ending in an acquittal, attracted the attention of the whole country to their doctrines. The " Unemployed " gatherings went on with ever-increasing noise until November 1887, when the Chief Commissioner of Police issued a proclamation prohibiting meetings in Trafalgar Square, which had for a whole generation served as the forum of the London agitator. This " attack on free speech " by a Conservative Government, coming after several minor attempts to suppress open-air meetings by its Liberal predecessor, rallied the forces of London artisan Radicalism to those of the Socialists. A gigantic demonstration on Sunday, November 13, 1887, was held in defiance of the police, only to be repulsed from Trafalgar Square by a free use of the police bludgeon and the calling out of both cavalry and infantry. John Burns and Cunninghame Graham, M.P., were imprisoned for their share in this transaction. A similar agitation on a smaller scale was going on in the provinces. On Tyneside and in the Midlands numerous emissaries of the Social Democratic Federation and the Socialist League were spreading the revolt against the helpless apathy into which the Trade Unions had sunk. In every large industrial centre the indefatigable lecturing of branches of Socialist organisations was stirring up a vague but effective unrest in all except the official circle of the Trade Union world.

To the great army of unskilled, or only partially skilled, workmen concentrated in London and other large cities the new crusade came as a gospel of deliverance. The unskilled labourer was getting tired of being referred, as the sole means of bettering his condition, to the " scientific Trade Unionism " alone recognised by the Front Bench. Trade Societies which admitted only workmen earning a high standard rate, which exacted a weekly contribution of not less than a shilling, and which frequently excluded all but regularly apprenticed men, were regarded by the builders' labourer, the gas stoker, or the docker, as aristocratic corporations with which he had as little in common as with the House of Lords. " The great bulk of our labourers," writes John Burns, " are ignored by the skilled workers. It is this selfish, snobbish desertion by the higher grades of the lower that makes success in many disputes impossible. Ostracised by their fellows, a spirit of revenge alone often prompts men to oppose or remain indifferent to Unionism, when if the Unions were wiser and more conciliatory, support would have been forthcoming where now jealousy and discontent prevails." [1] Even among the skilled workers, the younger artisans, if they had joined their Unions at all, were discontented with the exclusive and apathetic policy of the older members. Thus we find rising up, in such " aristocratic " Unions as the Amalgamated Society of

[1] Address to Trade Unionists in *Justice*, January 24, 1885.

Engineers and the London Society of Compositors, a " New Unionist " party of young men, who vigorously objected to the degradation of a Trade Union into a mutual insurance company, who protested against the exclusion of the lowly paid sections from the organisation of the trade, and who advocated the use of the political influence of the Society in the interests of Social-Democracy. By 1888 the Socialists had not only secured the allegiance of large sections of the unskilled labourers in London and some other towns, but had obtained an important body of recruits in the great " Amalgamated " societies.

At this pass nothing short of strangulation could have kept the new spirit out of the Trade Union Congress. It is interesting to notice that the first sign among the delegates is to be ascribed to the direct influence of Karl Marx. At the 1878 Congress at Bristol we find Adam Weiler, an old member of the " International," and a personal friend of the great Socialist, reading a paper in which he advocated legislation to limit the hours of labour.[1] At the next Congress Weiler took exception to the resolution in favour of establishing a Peasant Proprietorship moved on behalf of the Parliamentary Committee. But in that year his amendment in favour of Land Nationalisation did not even find a seconder. Three years later the effect of Henry George's propaganda becomes visible. In 1882, when the land question was again raised, the two ideals were sharply

---

[1] Weiler was the delegate of the Alliance Cabinetmakers' Society, and came from London. The Congress Report gives the following account of his paper : " After reviewing the position of the working classes under the present system, and comparing it with the state of things eighty years ago, he contended that the best means of bettering their position was to reduce the hours of toil. The result of this would be, first, to give every worker a better chance of employment, and thus lessen that sort of competition which was caused by hunger and want ; secondly, it would give them time and opportunity for rest and amusement, and that cultivation of their minds which would enable them to prepare themselves for the time when the present system of production would collapse, and the time of this collapse was not so distant as some supposed." The paper was received with much applause, and Weiler received the thanks of Congress. No resolution was passed.

contrasted, and in spite of protests against " communistic principles," a rider declaring for nationalisation was adopted by 71 votes to 31. The Parliamentary Committee made no change in their attitude on the question, contending that the vote had been taken in the absence of many delegates, and that it did not represent the opinion of the Congress as a whole. This contention was to some extent borne out by the votes of the next five Congresses, at all of which amendments in favour of the principle of nationalisation were rejected, though by decreasing majorities. At length, in 1887, at the Swansea Congress, the tide turned, and a vague addendum in favour of Land Nationalisation was accepted.[1] At the Bradford Congress in 1888 the very idea of Peasant Proprietorship had disappeared. The representatives of the agricultural labourers now asked only for individual occupation of publicly owned allotments. Ultimately the Congress adopted by 66 votes to 5 a distinct declaration in favour of Land Nationalisation, coupled with an instruction to the Parliamentary Committee to bring the proposal before the House of Commons.

Meanwhile Weiler had made another and more successful attempt to enlist the aid of the Congress in the legal regulation of the hours of labour. At the 1883 Congress he moved a resolution which instructed the Parliamentary Committee to obtain the legal limitation to eight hours of the maximum day of all workers in the employment of public authorities, or companies exercising Parliamentary powers. This was seconded by Edward Harford, the General Secretary of the Amalgamated Society of Railway Servants, and carried, in a thin meeting, by only 33 to 8. In 1885 the movement had so far gained weight that the Parliamentary Committee thought it expedient to temporise by promoting an investigation into the amount of overtime worked in Government departments, with the result of demonstrating how completely the practice of

[1] *History of the British Trades Union Congress*, by W. J. Davis, vol. i. p. 133.

systematic overtime had neutralised the Nine Hours victory.[1] At the 1887 Congress at Swansea the Parliamentary Committee were instructed to take a vote of the Trade Union world upon the whole question, a vote which revealed the unexpected fact that Applegarth's own Union, the Amalgamated Society of Carpenters and Joiners, had been converted to an Eight Hours Bill.[2] A second plebiscite, taken at the instance of the following year's Congress, showed that such old Unions as the Compositors, the Ironfounders, and the Railway Servants were swinging round.[3]

In the meantime the growing divergence of policy among the coal-miners, which we foreshadowed in the last chapter, had brought a powerful contingent of organised workmen to the support of the new party. We have already described the conversion of the leaders of the Northumberland and Durham miners to the principle of the Sliding Scale, involving, as it did, the dependence of the worker's standard of comfort upon the market price of his product. On another point, too, the two northern counties had broken away from the traditional policy of the Miners' organisation. Already in 1863 we noted that Crawford, one of the ablest of their leaders, was vigorously objecting, at the Leeds Conference, to an Eight Hours Bill for boys, on the ground that in Northumberland and Durham, where the hewers often worked in two shifts, such a restriction would interfere with the men's convenience. This resistance to a particular

---

[1] The Return moved for by George Howell regarding the Woolwich and Enfield engineering works showed that, during 1884 and 1885, more than half the artisans worked overtime, the average per week for each man varying from 9.4 hours in some shops to 17.8 in others.

[2] 11,966 of its members voted for an Eight Hours Day, and of these 9209 declared in favour of the enforcement of the eight hours limit by law. The total votes given for an Eight Hours Law was 17,267 ; against it, 3819.

[3] The votes in favour of an Eight Hours Day were 39,656 ; against it, 67,390, of which 56,541 were cast on behalf of the Cotton-spinners and Weavers. In favour of an Eight Hours Law, 28,511 ; against it, 12,283. The votes of the different trades, and a summary of the Congress proceedings on this subject, are given in *The Eight Hours Day*, by Sidney Webb and Harold Cox, 1891 ; see also *History of the British Trades Union Congress*, by W. J. Davis, vol. ii. pp. 7-8.

interference with the exceptional circumstances of the local industry gradually developed into a general objection to legal regulation of the hours of adult men. We find, therefore, the Northumberland and Durham miners from 1875 onwards ranging themselves more and more with the leaders of the iron and building trades, who, as we have seen, had become largely converted to the economic conceptions then current among the middle class. The fact that the Northumberland and Durham Associations, almost alone among Miners' Unions, had successfully weathered the bad times of 1877–79, and the constant presence of one or other of their leaders on the Parliamentary Committee, caused these opinions to be accepted as those of the whole industry.

But the miners elsewhere did not long rest content with the new policy of Durham and Northumberland. In December 1881 the amalgamated South and West Yorkshire Miners' Associations formally terminated the then existing Sliding Scale, and passed a resolution in favour of the policy of restricting the output. During the following years the Yorkshire employers several times proposed the re-establishment of a scale, but the men insisted on its being accompanied by an agreement for a minimum below which wages should in no event fall—a condition to which the coal-owners uniformly refused their assent. The lead given by the Yorkshire miners was quickly followed by other districts, notably by Lancashire. In this county Trade Unionism among the miners had, as we have seen, gone to pieces in the bad years. Reorganisation in local Unions came in 1881 ; and a Lancashire Miners' Federation was successfully established in the following year. At their Conference of 1883 the delegates of the Lancashire miners resolved, " That the time has come when the working miners shall regulate the production of coal ; that no collier or other underground worker shall work more than five days or shifts per week ; and that the hours from bank to bank be eight per shift." Finding it impossible to secure their object by strikes, the Lancashire men turned to that policy of legislative regulation which had marked the proceedings of the Conference of 1863.

With the improvement in trade which began in 1885, the membership and influence of the Lancashire and Yorkshire organisations rapidly increased, and new federations were started throughout the Midlands. The Scotch miners, too, had in 1886–87 a short outburst of organisation, when a national federation was formed with a membership of 23,000. All these Associations adopted the policy of regulating the output, and the Scotch miners, in particular, conducted, in 1887, a vigorous agitation in support of the clause limiting the day's work to eight hours, which two Scottish members endeavoured to insert in the Mines Regulation Act of 1887.[1] But the Executive of the National Union had, since Macdonald's death in 1881, fallen entirely into the hands of the Northumberland and Durham leaders. Under their influence it maintained its adherence to the principle of the Sliding Scale and its hostility to the Eight Hours Bill, thereby alienating, not only the new federations, but also the old-established and powerful Yorkshire Miners' Association. From 1885 to 1888 the battle between the contending doctrines ranged at every miners' conference.[2] During the latter year the combatants withdrew to separate camps. In September 1888 a conference of the representatives of non-sliding scale districts was called together in

[1] The clause was moved by S. Williamson, Liberal Member for Kilmarnock, and seconded by J. H. C. Hozier, Conservative Member for South Lanarkshire. It received no support from the " Labour Members," and was rejected by 159 to 104. See the *Eight Hours Day*, by Webb and Cox, 1891, p. 23.

[2] The " National Conferences " of the miners are a feature peculiar to the industry. Besides the periodical gatherings of the separate federations, the miners, since 1863, have had frequent conferences of delegates from all the organised districts in the kingdom. These conferences were, until 1889, held under the auspices of the National Union; subsequently they were summoned by the Miners' Federation. The meetings, from which reporters are now excluded, are consultative only, and their decisions are not authoritative until adopted by the separate organisations. See *Die Ordnung des Arbeitsverhältnisses in den Kohlengruben von Northumberland und Durham*, by Dr. Emil Auerbach (Leipzig, 1890, 268 pp.).

Manchester, when arrangements were made for the establishment of a new federation, into which no district governed
by a sliding scale was to be allowed to enter.   From this
time forth the old National Union on the one hand, and
the new Miners' Federation on the other, became rivals for
the allegiance of the various district associations, and somewhat unsympathetic critics of each other's policy and actions.
The issue was not long doubtful.   The National Union
gradually shrank up to Northumberland and Durham,
whilst the Miners' Federation, with its aggressive policy
and its semi-Socialistic principles of a minimum wage and
a legal day, grew apace.   From 36,000 members in 1888, it
rose to 96,000 in 1889, 147,000 in 1891, and over 200,000 in
1893, overshadowing in its growth all existing Trade Union
organisations.   The Socialist advocates of the legal limitation of the hours of labour accordingly enjoyed from 1888
onward, both in the Trade Union Congress and at the polling-
booths, the support of a rapidly growing contingent of
organised miners, whose solid adhesion has done more than
anything else to promote the general movement in favour
of an Eight Hours Bill.

It is easy at this distance to recognise, in the altered
tone of the rank and file of Congress delegates, a reflection
of the wider change of opinion outside.   But to the Trade
Union Front Bench, as, in fact, to most of the politicians
of the time, it was incredible that the new ideas should gain
any real footing among the skilled artisans.   The Parliamentary Committee regarded the innovations with much
the same feeling as that with which they had met the proposals of a little gang which had, in 1882, vainly attempted
to foist the principles of fiscal protection upon the Congress.[1]   When Congress insisted on passing a resolution
with which the Parliamentary Committee found themselves

---

[1] The " Fair Trade " attack had arisen in the following manner.   At
the Bristol Congress in 1878, certain delegates, who were strongly suspected
of being the paid agents of the organisation then agitating for the abolition
of the foreign bounties on sugar, attempted to force this question upon
the Congress, and made a serious disturbance.   These delegates afterwards

in disagreement, this expression of opinion was sometimes ignored as being nothing more than the fad of particular delegates. It was in vain that the Congress of 1888, after ten years' deliberation, definitely decided in favour of the principles of Land Nationalisation instead of Peasant Proprietorship. The Parliamentary Committee contented itself with promising that " a well-considered measure " would be put forward by the Committee. The Eight Hours question could not be treated so cavalierly. Direct resolutions in favour of legislative action were therefore staved off by proposals for inquiry. When a vote of the Trade Union world was decided upon, the Parliamentary Committee, in conjunction with many of the General Secretaries, were able practically to baulk the investigation. The voting paper was loaded with warnings and arguments against legislative action. No attempt was made to ensure a genuine vote of the rank and file. In some cases the Executive Committees were allowed to take upon themselves the responsibility of declaring the opinions held by the members of their societies, the total membership of which was then reckoned in the voting. In other instances the Executives were permitted without remonstrance simply to burke the question. The

---

became the paid representatives of the " Fair Trade League," an association avowedly composed of landlords and capitalists with the object of securing a reimposition of import duties. The Front Bench steadfastly refused to allow the Congress to be used for promotion of this object, and were exposed in return to what the Congress in 1882 declared to be " a cowardly, false, and slanderous attack, . . . an attempt at moral assassination." Instead of fighting the question of Free Trade *versus* Protection, the emissaries of the Fair Trade League developed an elaborate system of personal defamation, directed against Broadhurst, Howell, Shipton, and other leaders. For instance, Broadhurst's administration of the Gas Stokers' Relief Fund in 1872 was made the pretext for vague insinuations of malversation which were scattered broadcast through the Trade Union world. At the Congress of 1881 the " Fair Trade " delegates were expelled, on it being proved that their expenses were not paid by the Trade Union organisations which they nominally represented. A renewed attack on the Congress of 1882 ended in the triumphant victory of the Parliamentary Committee, the complete exoneration of Broadhurst and his colleagues, and the final discomfiture of the " Fair Trade " delegates. See *Henry Broadhurst : the Story of his Life,* by himself, 1901 ; *History of the British Trades Union Congress,* by W. J. Davis, vol. i., 1910.

inquiry failed to elicit any trustworthy census of the opinion of the Trade Union world.

An equal lack of sympathy was shown in connection with the growing feeling of the Congress in favour of the participation of British Trade Unionists in International Congresses. At the express command of Congress, the Parliamentary Committee sent delegates to the International gatherings of 1883 and 1886. But though these instructions were complied with, the Parliamentary Committee made it clear, in their annual reports, that far from favouring International action, " the position they assumed was that they were so well organised, so far ahead of foreign workmen, that little could be done until these were more on a level " with the skilled workers of England.[1] The Congress of 1886 nevertheless instructed the Parliamentary Committee to summon an International Conference in London in the following year. Instead of complying with this instruction, the Committee published, in May 1887, a lengthy pamphlet explaining that, owing to the indisposition of foreign workmen to make any pecuniary sacrifices for their Trade Unions, and the consequent lack of any stable working-class organisations, they had decided to refer the whole question again to the forthcoming Trade Union Congress. When the Congress met at Swansea in September 1887, it soon became evident that the Parliamentary Committee, on this question as on others, was quite out of touch with its constituents. In spite of the influence of the Front Bench, a resolution in favour of an International Congress was adopted ; and the Committee succeeded only in inducing Congress to impose restrictions which were intended to exclude the delegates of the German Social-Democratic party. The International Congress was held in London in November 1888. Notwithstanding every precaution, a majority of the representatives proved to be of Socialist views, Mrs. Besant, John Burns, Tom Mann, and Keir Hardie appearing among

---

[1] Report to Congress of 1884. This is another instance of the abandonment of the more generous views of Applegarth and Odger.

the British delegates. The stiff and unsympathetic attitude of the Parliamentary Committee led to heated and,
at times, unseemly controversies; and the resolutions
passed were treated by the Committee as of no account
whatsoever.

The net result of these proceedings was the loss by the
Parliamentary Committee of all intellectual leadership of
the Trade Union world. They failed either to resist the
new ideas or to guide them into practicable channels. The
official Trade Union programme from 1885 to 1889 became
steadily more colourless, in striking contrast with the rapid
march of politics in the country, which was sweeping the
Liberal party forward year by year until in 1891 it adopted
the so-called " Newcastle Programme." This programme
formulated, though very inadequately, the national side of
that semi-collectivist policy which under the name of Pro-
gressivism had superseded Liberalism in the London County
Council. All that the Parliamentary Committee did was to
abandon, one by one, the proposals for the democratisation
of the civil and judicial administration which the Front
Bench had so much at heart, without replacing them by
the more robust resolutions which the Congress in these
years was passing. The Land Question, on which a vigorous
advocacy of the creation of small freeholders had been
formerly maintained, dwindled to a meaningless demand for
undefined reform of the land laws, and finally disappeared
altogether on the adoption by the Congress of the principle
of nationalisation. The maintenance of the Nine Hours
Day, and the further reduction of the hours of labour by
means of voluntary combination (a frequent item in the
official agenda from 1875 to 1879) gradually dropped out
altogether as the new demand for legal regulation gathered
strength. In short, the Parliamentary Committee had perforce to give up those items in their programme which were
contrary to the new ideas of Congress, whilst they silently
abstained from incorporating the new resolutions with which
they were personally not in agreement.

It would, however, be unfair to assume that the stock of official Trade Unionism was, during these years, absolutely barren of new developments. To Mr. C. J. Drummond,[1] then Secretary to the London Society of Compositors, and a friend of the Parliamentary Committee, belongs the credit of having taken the first step towards the enforcement, through the Government, of a standard minimum wage. On the revision of the Government printing contract in 1884, Mr. Drummond secured the support of the Parliamentary Committee in an attempt to induce the Stationery Office to adopt, as the basis for the contract, the Trade Union rates of the London compositors. This attempt was, in the main, successful ; but the new contract was nevertheless given to a " closed " house, in which no member of the Union could work. The compositors did not let the matter rest. When the President of the Local Government Board (Joseph Chamberlain) issued a circular in January 1886, as to the effects of the depression in trade, Mr. Drummond replied by explicitly demanding the Government's recognition of the Standard Wage in all their dealings. The idea spread with great rapidity. A general demand was started that public authorities should present a good example as employers of labour by themselves paying Trade Union rates, and insisting on their contractors doing the same. Candidates for Parliament at the General Election of 1886 found themselves, at the instance of the London Society of Compositors,[2] for the first time " heckled " as to their willingness to insist on " Fair Wages " ; and it began slowly to dawn upon election agents that it might be prejudicial for their election literature to bear the imprint of " rat houses." In October 1886 the action of the London School Board in giving its printing contract to an " unfair " house was bitterly resented by the London compositors, who in-

---

[1] Mr. Drummond, who resigned his secretaryship in 1892, was in the following year appointed to the staff of the Labour Department of the Board of Trade, from which he retired in 1918.

[2] See its Circular of June 1886.

duced the London Trades Council to go on a vain deputation of protest. When, in November 1888, the London School Board election came round, A. G. Cook, a member of the London Society of Compositors, secured election for Finsbury, avowedly as a champion of Trade Union wages ; and two members of the Fabian Society, Mrs. Annie Besant and the Rev. Stewart Headlam, won seats as Socialists. By their eloquence and tactical skill these members induced the Board, early in 1889, to declare that it would henceforth insist on the payment of " Fair Wages " by all its contractors, a policy in which the Board was promptly followed by the newly established London County Council.[1] This new departure by the leading public bodies in the Metropolis did much to bring about a common understanding between the official Trade Unionists and the new movement. It is needless to describe in this place how, since that date, the principle of " Fair Wages " has developed. By 1894 a hundred and fifty local authorities had adopted some kind of " Fair Wages " resolution. In 1890, and more explicitly still in 1893, successive Governments found it necessary to repudiate the old principle of buying in the cheapest market, in favour of the now widespread feeling that public authorities as large employers of labour, instead of ignoring the condition of their employees, should use their influence to maintain the Standard Rate of Wages and Standard Hours of Labour recognised and in practice obtained by the Trade Unions concerned.

Though the Front Bench as a whole maintained during these years its policy of contemptuous inactivity, there were, as we have seen, some signs of the permeation of the new ideas. It was under these circumstances a grave misfortune

[1] Some isolated protests against the employment of non-Unionists are of earlier date. Thus, the minutes of the Birmingham Trades Council show that, on July 3, 1880, at the instance of a painters' delegate, it passed a resolution protesting against the employment of " non-Union and incompetent men " by the local hospital. And in the same month the Wolverhampton Trades Council had successfully protested against the employment of non-Unionist printers upon a new Liberal newspaper about to be established.

that the inevitable criticism on the Parliamentary Committee began by a scurrilous attack upon the personal character and conduct of its leaders.[1]   During the years 1887–89 the conscientious adhesion to the Liberal party of most of the Parliamentary Committee was made the occasion for gross charges of personal corruption. The General Secretaries of the great Unions, men who had for a lifetime diligently served their constituents, found their influence undermined, their character attacked, and themselves denounced, by the circulation all over the country of insidious accusations of treachery to the working classes. These charges found a too ready acceptance among, and were repeated by, those young and impatient recruits of the new movement who knew nothing of the history and services of the men they were attacking. In the year 1889 the friction reached its climax. During the summer the attacks upon the personal character of the Front Bench were redoubled. As the date of the Trade Union Congress approached, it became known that a determined attempt would be made by the Socialist delegates to oust the Parliamentary Committee from office. The Congress met at Dundee, and plunged straight into an angry conflict in which the Socialists were completely routed. The regular attenders of the Congress had, as we have seen, been gradually absorbing many of the new ideas, and were not altogether satisfied with the way their resolutions had been ignored by the Parliamentary Committee. But all discontent or criticism was swept away by the anger which the character of the attack had excited. A great majority of the delegates came expressly pledged to support Broadhurst and his colleagues, and when the division was taken only 11 out of a meeting of 188 delegates were found

---

[1] The chief medium for the attack was the *Labour Elector*, a penny weekly journal published, from September 1888 to April 1890, by Mr. H. H. Champion, an ex-officer of the Royal Artillery, who (prosecuted in 1886, as we have seen, with H. M. Hyndman, J. Burns, and Williams, for sedition) had at one time been a leading member of the Social Democratic Federation, from which he was excluded on a difference of policy. He afterwards emigrated to Melbourne, where he still (1920) resides.

to vote against him. The Cotton Operatives who had at all times supported factory legislation, the Miners who were demanding an Eight Hours Bill, the Londoners who came from the centre of the Socialist agitation—all rallied to defend the Parliamentary Committee. The little knot of assailants were thoroughly discredited ; and the triumph of the " old gang " was complete.[1]

The victory of the Parliamentary Committee was hailed with satisfaction by all who were alarmed at the progress of the new ideas. For a moment it looked as if the organised Trade Unions of skilled workers had definitely separated themselves from the new labour movement growing up around them. Such a separation would, in our opinion, have been an almost irreparable disaster. The Trade Union Congress could claim to represent less than 10 per cent of the wage-earners of the country. Many of the old societies were already shrinking up into insignificant minorities of superior workmen, intent mainly on securing their sick and superannuation benefits. Any definite exclusion of wider ideals might easily have reduced the whole Trade Union organisation to nothing more than a somewhat stagnant department of the Friendly Society movement. This danger was averted by a series of dramatic events which brought the new movement once more inside the Trade Union ranks. At the moment that Henry Broadhurst was triumphing over his enemies at Dundee, the London dock-labourers were marching to that brilliant victory over their employers which changed the whole face of the Trade Union world.

The great dock strike of 1889 was the culmination of an attempt to organise the unskilled workers which had begun in London two or three years before. The privations suffered by the unemployed labourers during the years of depression of trade, and the new spirit of hopefulness due to the Socialist propaganda, had led to efforts

[1] *Henry Broadhurst : the Story of his Life*, by himself, 1901, pp. 218-24 ; *History of the British Trades Union Congress*, by W. J. Davis, vol. i., 1910.

being made to bring the vast hordes of unskilled workmen in the Metropolis into some kind of organisation. At first this movement made very little progress. In July 1888, however, the harsh treatment suffered by the women employed in making lucifer matches roused the burning indignation of Mrs. Besant, then editing *The Link*, a little weekly newspaper which had arisen out of the struggle for Trafalgar Square. A fiery leading article had the unexpected result of causing the match-girls to revolt ; and 672 of them came out on strike. Without funds, without organisation, the struggle seemed hopeless. But by the indefatigable energy of Mrs. Besant and Herbert Burrows public opinion was aroused in a manner never before witnessed ; £400 was subscribed by hundreds of sympathisers in all classes ; and after a fortnight's obstinacy the employers were compelled, by sheer pressure of public feeling, to make some concessions to their workers.

The match-girls' victory turned a new leaf in Trade Union annals. Hitherto success had been in almost exact proportion to the workers' strength. It was a new experience for the weak to succeed because of their very weakness, by means of the intervention of the public. The lesson was not lost on other classes of workers. The London gas-stokers were being organised by Burns, Mann, and Tillett, aided by William Thorne, himself a gas-worker and a man of sterling integrity and capacity. The Gas-workers and General Labourers' Union, established in May 1889, quickly enrolled many thousands of members, who in the first days of August simultaneously demanded a reduction of their hours of labour from twelve to eight per day. After an interval of acute suspense, during which the directors of the three great London gas companies measured their forces, peaceful counsels prevailed, and the Eight Hours Day, to the general surprise of the men no less than that of the public, was conceded without a struggle, and was even accompanied by a slight increase of the week's wages.[1]

[1] The men employed by two of the gas companies in London, and

The success of such unorganised and unskilled workers as the Match-makers and the Gas-stokers led to renewed efforts to bring the great army of Dock-labourers into the ranks of Trade Unionism. For two years past the prominent London Socialists had journeyed to the dock gates in the early hours of the morning to preach organised revolt to the crowds of casuals struggling for work. Meanwhile Benjamin Tillett, then working as a labourer in the tea warehouses, was spending his strength in the apparently hopeless task of constituting the Tea-workers and General Labourers' Union. The membership of this society fluctuated between 300 and 2500 members ; it had practically no funds ; and its very existence seemed precarious. Suddenly the organisation received a new impulse. An insignificant dispute on the 12th of August 1889 as to the amount of " plus " (or bonus earned over and above the five-pence per hour) on a certain cargo, brought on an impulsive strike of the labourers at the South-West India Dock. The men demanded sixpence an hour, the abolition of sub-contract and piecework, extra pay for overtime, and a minimum engagement of four hours. Tillett called to his aid his friends Tom Mann and John Burns, and appealed to the whole body of dock labourers to take up the fight. The strike spread rapidly to all the docks north of the Thames. Within three days ten thousand labourers had, with one accord, left the precarious and ill-paid work to get which they had, morning after morning, fought at the dock gates. The two powerful Unions of Stevedores (the better-paid, trained workmen who load ships for export) cast in their lot with the dockers, and in the course of the

---

most of those engaged by provincial municipalities, have retained this boon. But in December 1889 the South Metropolitan Gas Company insisted, after a serious strike, on a return to the twelve hours' shift. A scheme of profit-sharing was used to break up their men's Union and induce them to accept individual engagements inconsistent with Collective Bargaining. This example (which is not unique) confirmed the Trade Unions in their objection to schemes of " Profit-sharing " or " Co-partner-ship."

next week practically all the river-side labour had joined the strike. Under the magnetic influence of John Burns, who suddenly became famous as a labour leader on both sides of the globe, the traffic of the world's greatest port was, for over four weeks, completely paralysed. An electric spark of sympathy with the poor dockers fired the enthusiasm of all classes of the community. Public disapproval hindered the dock companies from obtaining, even for their unskilled labour, sufficient blacklegs to take the strikers' place. A public subscription of £48,736 allowed Burns to organise an elaborate system of strike-pay, which not only maintained the honest docker, but also bribed every East End loafer to withhold his labour ; and finally the concentrated pressure of editors, clergymen, shareholders, ship-owners, and merchants enabled Cardinal Manning and Sydney (afterwards Lord) Buxton, as self-appointed mediators, to compel the Dock Directors to concede practically the whole of the men's demands, a delay of six weeks being granted to allow the new arrangements to be made. As in the case of the matchgirls in the previous year, the most remarkable feature of the dockers' strike was the almost universal sympathy with the workers' demands. A practical manifestation of that sympathy was given by the workmen of Australia. The Australian newspapers published telegraphic accounts of the conflict, with descriptions of the dockers' wrongs, which produced an unparalleled and unexpected result. Public subscriptions in aid of the London dockers were opened in all the principal towns on the Australian continent ; and money poured in from all sides. Over £30,000 was remitted to London by telegraph—an absolutely unique contribution towards the strike subsidy which went far to win the victory ultimately achieved.[1]

---

[1] This strike had the good fortune to find contemporary historians who were themselves concerned in all the phases of the struggle. *The Story of the Dockers' Strike*, by Mr. (afterwards Sir) Hubert Llewellyn Smith and Vaughan Nash (1890, 190 pp.), gives not only a detailed chronicle of the highly dramatic proceedings, but also a useful description of the organisation of the London Docks.

The immediate result of the dockers' success was the formation of a large number of Trade Unions among the unskilled labourers. Branches of the Dock, Wharf, and Riverside Labourers' Union (into which Tillett's little society was now transformed) were established at all the principal ports. A rival society of dockers, established at Liverpool, enrolled thousands of members at Glasgow and Belfast. The unskilled labourers in Newcastle joined the Tyneside and National Labour Union, which soon extended to all the neighbouring towns. The Gas-workers' Union enrolled tens of thousands of labourers of all kinds in the provincial cities. Organisation began again among the farm labourers. The National Union of Agricultural Labourers, which had sunk to a few thousand scattered members, suddenly rose in 1890 to over 14,000. New societies arose, which took in general as well as farm labourers ; such as the Eastern Counties Labour Federation, which, by 1892, had 17,000 members ; and the smaller societies centring respectively on Norwich, Devizes, Reading, Hitchin, Ipswich, and Kingsland in Herefordshire.[1] The General Railway Workers' Union, originally established in 1889 as a rival to the Amalgamated Society of Railway Servants, took in great numbers of general labourers. The National Amalgamated Sailors and Firemen's Union,[2] established in 1887, expanded during 1889 to

[1] This movement was much assisted by the " Red Van " campaigns of the English Land Restoration League, 1891–94, which coupled Land Nationalisation propaganda with the formation of local unions of the labourers in the Southern and Midland Counties of England. In the agricultural depression of 1894–95, when staffs were further reduced and wages again lowered, nearly all these new Unions sank to next to nothing, or entirely dissolved. Most information as to them is to be gained from *The Church Reformer* for 1891–95 ; *History of the English Agricultural Labourer*, by W. Hasbach, 1907 ; and Ernest Selley's *Village Trade Unions of Two Centuries*, 1919.

[2] Short-lived and turbulent combinations among seamen have existed at various periods for the past hundred years, notably between 1810 and 1825, on the north-east coast, where many sailors' benefit clubs were also established. In 1851, again, a widespread national organisation of seamen is said to have existed, having twenty-five branches between Peterhead and London, and numbering 30,000 members. This appears to have been a loose federation of practically autonomous port Unions, which for some years

a membership of 65,000. Within a year after the dockers' victory probably over 200,000 workers had been added to the Trade Union ranks, recruited from sections of the labour world formerly abandoned as incapable of organisation. All these societies were marked by low contributions and comprehensive membership. They were, at the outset, essentially, if not exclusively, devoted to trade protection, and were largely political in their aims. Their character-istic spirit is aptly expressed by the resolution of the Con-gress of the General Railway Workers' Union on the 19th of November 1890 : " That the Union shall remain a fighting one, and shall not be encumbered with any sick or accident fund." " We have at present," reports the General Secre-tary of the National Union of Gas-workers and General Labourers in November 1889, " one of the strongest labour Unions in England. It is true we have only one benefit attached, and that is strike pay. I do not believe in having sick pay, out-of-work pay, and a number of other pays. . . . The whole aim and intention of this Union is to reduce the hours of labour and reduce Sunday work." [1]

A wave of Trade Unionism, comparable in extent with those of 1833–34 and 1873–74, was now spreading into every corner of British industry. Already in 1888 the revival of trade has led to a marked increase in Trade Union member-ship. This normal growth now received a great impulse from the sensational events of the Dock strike. Even the

kept up a vigorous agitation against obnoxious clauses in the Merchant Shipping Acts of 1851–54, and fought the sailors' grievances in the law-courts. In 1879 the existing North of England Sailors and Sea-going Firemen's Friendly Association was established, but failed to maintain itself outside Sunderland. In 1887 its most vigorous member, J. Havelock Wilson, convinced that nothing but a national organisation would be effective, started the National Amalgamated Sailors and Firemen's Union, which his able and pertinacious " lobbying " made, for some years, an effective Parliamentary force.

[1] Address to members in First Half-Yearly Report (London, 1889). The spirit of the uprising is well given in *The New Trade Unionism*, by Tom Mann and Ben Tillett, 1890 ; on which George Shipton was moved to write *A Reply to Messrs. Tom Mann and Ben Tillett's Pamphlet entitled "The New Trade Unionism*," 1890.

oldest and most aristocratic Unions were affected by the revivalist fervour of the new leaders. The eleven principal societies in the shipbuilding and metal trades, which had been, since 1885, on the decline, increased from 115,000 at the end of 1888 to 130,000 in 1889, 145,000 in 1890, and 155,000 in 1891. The ten largest Unions in the building trades, which between 1885 and 1888 had, in the aggregate, likewise declined in numbers, rose from 57,000 in 1888 to 63,000 in 1889, 80,000 in 1890, and 94,000 in 1891. In certain individual societies the increase in membership during these years was unparalleled in their history. We have already referred to the rapid rise between 1888 and 1891 of that modern Colossus of Unions, the Miners' Federation. The Operative Society of Bricklayers, established in 1848, grew from a fairly stationary 7000 in 1888, to over 17,000 in 1891. The National Society of Boot and Shoe Operatives, established in 1874, went from 11,000 in 1888 to 30,000 in 1891. And, to turn to quite a different industry, the Amalgamated Society of Railway Servants, a trade friendly society of the old type, established in 1872, rose from 12,000 in 1888 to 30,000 in 1891. Nor was the expansion confined to a mere increase in membership. New Trades Councils sprang up in all directions, whilst those already existing were rejoined by the trades which had left them. Federations of the Unions in kindred trades were set on foot, and competing societies in the same trade sank their rivalry in the formation of local joint committees.

The victory of the London Dockers and the impetus it gave to Trade Unionism throughout the country at last opened the eyes of the Trade Union world to the significance of the new movement. It was no longer possible for the Parliamentary Committee to denounce the Socialists as a set of outside intriguers, when Burns and Mann, now become the representative working-men Socialists, stood at the head of a body of 200,000 hitherto unorganised workmen. The general secretaries of the older Unions, forming a compact official party behind the Front Bench, were veering around towards the advanced party. Their constituencies were becoming permeated with Socialism. In many instances the older members now supported the new faith. In other cases they found themselves submerged by the large accessions to their membership which, as we have already seen, resulted from the general expansion. The process of conversion was facilitated by the genuine admiration felt by the whole Trade Union world for the great organising power and generalship shown by the leaders of the new movement, and by the cessation of the personal abuse and recrimination which had hitherto marred the controversy. At the Dundee Congress of 1889, as we have seen, Henry Broadhurst, and his colleagues on the Parliamentary Committee, had triumphed all along the line. Within a year the situation had entirely changed. The Stonemasons, Broadhurst's own society, had decided, by a vote of the members, to support an Eight Hours Bill, and Broadhurst, under these circumstances, had perforce to refuse to act as their representative. The Executive Council of the Amalgamated Society of Engineers chose Burns and Mann as two out of their five delegates, impressing upon them all a recommendation to vote for the legal limitation of the hours of labour. Both the old-established societies of Carpenters gave a similar mandate. The Miners' Federation this time led the attack on the old Front Bench, and the resolution in favour of a general Eight Hours Bill was carried, after a heated debate, by 193 to 155. Broadhurst resigned his position as Secretary of the Parliamentary Committee on the ground of ill-health. George Shipton, the secretary of the London Trades Council, publicly declared his conversion to the legal regulation of the hours of labour. The Liverpool Congress was as decisive a victory for the Socialists as that of Dundee had been for the Parliamentary Committee. The delegates passed in all sixty resolutions. " Out of these sixty resolutions," said John Burns, " forty-five were nothing more or less than direct appeals to the State and Municipalities of this country to do for the workman what

Trade Unionism, ' Old ' and ' New,' has proved itself incapable of doing. Forty-five out of the sixty resolutions were asking for State or Municipal interference on behalf of the weak against the strong. ' Old ' Trade Unionists, from Lancashire, Northumberland, and Birmingham, asked for as many of these resolutions as the delegates from London ; but it is a remarkable and significant fact that 19 out of 20 delegates were in favour of the ' New ' Trades Union ideas of State interferences in all things except reduction of hours, and even on this we secured a majority that certainly entitles us Socialists to be jubilant at our success." [1]

But whilst the new faith was being adopted by the rank and file of Trade Unionists the character of the Socialist propaganda had been undergoing an equal transformation. The foremost representative of the Collectivist views had hitherto been the Social-Democratic Federation, of which Burns and Mann were active members. Under the dominant influence of Mr. H. M. Hyndman, this association adopted the economic basis and political organisation of State Socialism. Yet we find, along with these modern views, a distinct recrudescence of the characteristic projects of the revolutionary Owenism of 1833–34. The student of the volumes of *Justice* between 1884 and 1889 will be struck by the unconscious resemblance of many of the ideas and much of the phraseology of its contributors, to those of the *Poor Man's Guardian* and the *Pioneer* of 1834. We do not here allude to the revival, in 1885, of the old demand for an Eight Hours Bill, a measure regarded on both occasions as a " mere palliative." Nor need we refer to the constant assumption, made alike by Robert Owen and the Social-Democratic lecturers, that the acceptance of the Labour-value theory would enable the difficulty of the " unemployed " to be solved by organising the mutual exchange of their unmarketable products. But both in *Justice* and the *Pioneer* we see the same disbelief in separate action by

[1] *Speech delivered by John Burns on the Liverpool Congress, September 21, 1890* (1890, 32 pp.).

particular Trade Unions, in contrast to an organisation
including " every trade, skilled and unskilled, of every
nationality under the sun." [1] " The real emancipation of
labour," says the official manifesto of the Social-Democratic
Federation to the Trade Unions of Great Britain in September 1884, " can only be effected by the solemn banding
together of millions of human beings in a federation as wide
as the civilised world." [2] " The day has gone by," we read
in 1887, " for the efforts of isolated trades. . . . Nothing is
to be gained for the workers as a class without the complete
organisation of labourers of all grades, skilled and unskilled.
. . . We appeal therefore earnestly to the skilled artisans
of all trades, Unionists and non-Unionists alike, to make
common cause with their unskilled brethren, and with us
Social-Democrats, so that the workers may themselves take
hold of the means of production, and organise a Co-operative
Commonwealth for themselves and their children." [3] And
if the " scientific Socialists " of 1885 were logically pledged
to the administration of industry by the officials of the community at large, none the less do we see constantly cropping
up, especially among the working-class members, Owen's
diametrically opposite proposal that the workers must
" own their own factories and decide by vote who their
managers and foremen shall be." [4] Above all we see the
same faith in the near and inevitable advent of a sudden
revolution, when " it will only need a compact minority
to take advantage of some opportune accident that will
surely come, to overthrow the present system, and once and
for all lift the toilers from the present social degradation." [5]
" Noble Robert Owen," says Mr. Hyndman in 1885," seventy
years ago perceived ' the utter impossibility of succeeding

---

[1] *Justice*, November 7, 1885.

[2] Printed in *Justice*, September 6, 1884.

[3] " The Decay of Trade Unions," by H. M. Hyndman, *Justice*, June 18,
1887.

[4] " The Trade Union Congress," by John Burns, *Justice*, September 12,
1885.

[5] *Justice*, July 11, 1885.

in permanently improving the condition of our population by any half-measures.' We see the same truth if possible yet more clearly now. But the revolution which in his day was unprepared is now ripe and ready. . . . Nothing short of a revolution which shall place the producers of wealth in control of their own country can possibly change matters for the better. . . . Will it be peaceful ? We hope it may. That does not depend upon us. But, peaceful or violent, the great social revolution of the nineteenth century is at hand, and if fighting should be necessary the workers may at least remember the profound historical truth that ' Force is the midwife of progress delivering the old society pregnant with the new,' and reflect that they are striving for the final overthrow of a tyranny more degrading than the worst chattel slavery of ancient times." [1] " Let our mission be," he writes in 1887, " to help to band together the workers of the world for the great class struggle against their exploiters. No better date could be chosen for the establishment of such international action on a sound basis than the year 1889, which the classes look forward to with trembling and the masses with hope. I advocate no hasty outbreak, no premature and violent attempt on the part of the people to realise the full Social-Democratic programme. But I do say that from this time onwards we, as the Social-Democratic Labour Party of Great Britain, should make every effort to bear our part in the celebration by the international proletariat of the First Centenary of the great French Revolution, and thus to prepare for a complete International Social Revolution before the end of the century." [2]

The year 1889, instead of ushering in a " complete International Social Revolution " by a universal compact of the workers, turned the current of Socialist propaganda from revolutionary to constitutional channels. The advent

---

[1] *Justice*, July 18, 1885. The identity of purpose and methods between the two movements is indeed elsewhere directly asserted ; see " Socialism in '34," *ibid.*, April 19, 1884, and the extracts from the Owenite journals in the issue for July 25, 1885.

[2] *Ibid.*, August 6, 1887.

of political Democracy had put out of date the project of
" a combined assault by workers of every trade and grade
against the murderous monopoly of the minority." [1]   For
a moment, at the very crisis of the dockers' struggle, the
idea of a " General Strike " flickers up, only to be quickly
abandoned as impracticable.   When the problems of administration had actually to be faced by the new leaders the
specially Owenite characteristics of the Socialist propaganda
were quietly dropped.   In January 1889 John Burns was
elected a member of the London County Council, and
quickly found himself organising the beginnings of a bureaucratic municipal Collectivism, as far removed from Owen's
" national companies " as from the conceptions of the
Manchester School.   Tom Mann, as president of the Dockers'
Union, could not help discovering how impracticable it was
to set to work his unemployed members, accustomed only
to general labour, in the production for mutual exchange
of the bread and clothing of which they were in need.   And
whether working in municipal committees, or at the head
office of a great Union, both Burns and Mann had perforce
to realise the impossibility of bringing about any sudden
or simultaneous change in the social or industrial organisation of the whole community, or even of one town or trade.

Under these circumstances it is perhaps not surprising
that Burns and Mann left the Social Democratic Federation, and found themselves hotly denounced by their old
comrades. [2]   With the defection of the New Unionists,
revolutionary Socialism ceased to grow ; and the rival propaganda of constitutional action became the characteristic
feature of the British Socialist Movement.   Far from abusing
or deprecating Trade Unionism or Co-operation, the constitutional Collectivists urged it as a primary duty upon

---

[1] *Justice*, July 25, 1885.

[2] From 1889 onwards the columns of *Justice* abound in abuse and
denunciation of the leaders of the New Unionism.   We may cite, not so
much because it summarises this denunciation and abuse, but because of
the details of the movement that it incidentally gives, *The Rise and Progress of a Right Honourable*, by Joseph Burgess (1911).

every working-class Socialist to become a member of his Trade Union, to belong to the local Co-operative Society, and generally to take as active a part as possible in all organisations. Instead of denouncing partial reforms as mischievous attempts to defeat " the Social Revolution," the New Unionist leaders appealed to their followers to put their own representatives on Town Councils, and generally to use their electoral influence to bring about, in a regular and constitutional manner, the particular changes they had at heart. Instead of circulating calumnies against the personal character of Trade Union leaders, they flooded the Trade Union world with Socialist literature, dealing not so much in rhetorical appeals or Utopian aspirations as in economic expositions of the actual grievances of industrial life. The vague resolutions of the Trades Union Congresses were worked out in practical detail, or even embodied in draft bills which the local member of Parliament might be invited to introduce, or driven to support.

The new policy, adopted as it was by such prominent Socialists as Burns, Mann, and Tillett, and Mrs. Besant, appeared, from 1889 onward, increasingly justified by its success. The Collectivist victories on the London School Board and County Council, the steady growth of municipal activity, and the increasing influence exercised by working-men members of representative bodies, went far to persuade both Socialists and Trade Unionists that the only practicable means of securing for the community the ownership and control of the means of production lay in a wide extension of that national and municipal organisation of public services towards which Parliament and the Town Councils had already taken the first steps. In those industries in which neither national nor municipal administration was yet possible, the Socialists demanded such a regulation of the conditions of employment as would ensure to every worker a minimum Standard of Life. The extension of the Factory Acts and the more thorough administration of the Sanitary Law accordingly received a new impulse. In another direction the drastic taxation of Rent and Interest, pressed for by Land Nationalisers and Socialists alike, was justified as leading eventually to the collective absorption of all unearned incomes.   In short, from 1889 onward, the chief efforts of the British Socialist Movement have been directed, not to bringing about any sudden, complete, or simultaneous revolution, but to impregnating all the existing forces of society with Collectivist ideals and Collectivist principles.[1]

With the advent of the " New Unionism " of 1889-90 we close this chapter.   We shall see, in subsequent chapters to what extent, and in what way, the Trade Union Movement was permanently affected by the new movement. But we append at this point a brief account of what seem to us, first, the ephemeral features and, secondly, the more durable results of an impulse which did not wholly spend its force for a whole decade.

If we were to believe some of the more enthusiastic apostles of the " New Unionism," we should imagine that the aggressive trade society of unskilled labourers, un-encumbered with friendly benefits, was an unprecedented

---

[1] In this development some share is to be attributed to the work of the Fabian Society, which, established in 1883, began in 1887 to exercise a growing influence on working-class opinion.   The publication, in 1889, of *Fabian Essays in Socialism*, the circulation between 1887 and 1893 of three-quarters of a million copies of its series of " Fabian tracts," and the delivery of several thousand lectures a year in London and other industrial centres, contributed largely to substitute a practical and constitutional policy of Collectivist reform for the earlier revolutionary propaganda.   Tom Mann, Ben Tillett, and other Trade Union leaders were, from 1889 onwards, among the members of the parent Fabian Society, whilst the ninety independent local Fabian Societies in the provincial centres usually included many of the delegates to the local Trades Councils.   Some account of the Society and its work will be found in *Zum socialen Frieden*, by Dr. von Schulze Gaevernitz (Leipzig, 1891, 2 vols.) ; in *Englische Socialreformer*, by Dr. M. Grunwald (Leipzig, 1897) ; in *La Société Fabienne*, by Edouard Pfeiffer (Paris, 1911) ; in *Geschichte des Socialismus in England*, by M. Beer (Stuttgart, 1913), republished in different English form as *History of British Socialism* (vol. i., 1918 ; vol. ii., 1920) ; in *Socialism, a Critical Analysis*, by O. D. Skelton, 1911 ; and in *Political Thought in England from Herbert Spencer to the Present Day*, by Ernest Barker, 1915.   A superficial survey of the development of opinion is given in *Socialism in England*, by Sidney Webb (1st edition, 1889 ; 2nd edition, 1893). See *History of the Fabian Society*, by Edward R. Pease (1915).

departure in the history of labour organisation. Those who have followed our history thus far will know better than to entertain such an illusion, itself an old characteristic of Trade Unionist revivals. The purely trade society is as old as Trade Unionism itself. Throughout the whole history of the movement we find two types of societies co-existing. At special crises in the annals of Trade Unionism we see one or other of these types taking the lead, and becoming the " New Unionism " of that particular period. Both trade society and friendly society with trade objects were common in the eighteenth century. Legal persecution of trade combination brought to the front the Union cloaked in the guise of a benefit club ; and it was mainly for organisations of this type that Place and Hume won the emancipation of 1824–1825. In 1833–34 we find Place deploring as a mischievous innovation the growth of the new " Trades Unions " without friendly benefits. Twenty years later we see the leadership reverting to the " new model " of an elaborate trade friendly society which, for a whole generation, was vehemently denounced by employers as a fraud on the provident workman. The " New Unionism " of 1852, described by so friendly a critic as Professor Beesly as a novel departure, became, in its turn, the " Old Unionism " of 1889, when the more progressive spirits again plumed themselves on eliminating from their brand-new organisations the enervating influences of friendly benefits.

A closer examination of the facts shows that this almost rhythmical alternation of type has been only apparent. The impartial student will notice that whilst the purely trade society has been persistently adhered to by certain important industries, such as the Coal-miners and the Cotton-spinners, other trades, like the Engineers and the Iron-founders, have remained equally constant to the trade friendly society ; whilst others, again, such as the Compositors and the Carpenters, have passed backwards and forwards from one model to the other. But besides this adaptation of type to the circumstances of particular industries, we see also a preference for the purely trade society on no higher ground than its cheapness. The high contributions and levies paid by the Cotton-spinners to their essentially trade society are as far beyond the means of the Agricultural Labourer or the Docker as the weekly premiums for superannuation, sick, and other benefits charged to the Amalgamated Engineer. When, as in 1833–34, 1872, and 1889, a wave of enthusiasm sweeps the unskilled labourers into the Trade Union ranks, it is obviously necessary to form, at any rate in the first instance, organisations which make no greater tax upon their miserable earnings than a penny or twopence per week. The apparent rhythm of alternations between the two types of organisation is due, therefore, not to any general abandonment of one for the other, but to the accidental prominence, in certain crises of Trade Union history, of the Unions belonging to particular trades or classes of wage-earners. When, for instance, the cotton-spinners, the builders, and the unskilled labourers of 1834 loomed large to Francis Place as a revolutionary force, the purely trade society appeared to him to be the source of all that was evil in Trade Unionism. When, in 1848–52, the iron trades were conspiring against piecework and over-time, it was especially the illicit combination of trade and friendly society which attracted the attention of the public, and called forth the denunciations of the capitalist class. And when in 1889 the dockers were stopping the trade of London, and the coal-miners and cotton-spinners were pressing upon both political parties their demands for legislative interference, we see George Howell voicing the opposition to exclusively trade societies as dangerously militant bodies.[1]

If the purely trade society is no new thing, still less is the extension of Trade Unionism to the unskilled labourer an unprecedented innovation. The enthusiasm which, in 1872, enrolled a hundred thousand agricultural labourers in a few months, produced also numerous small societies

---

[1] *Trade Unionism Old and New,* 1891, *passim.*

of town labourers, some of which survived for years before absorption into larger organisations. The London and Counties Labour League, established as the Kent and Sussex Agricultural and General Labourers' Union in 1872, has maintained its existence down to the present day. The expansion of 1852 led to the formation in Glasgow of a Labourers' Society, which is reputed to have enrolled thousands of members. But it is with the enthusiasm of 1833–34 that the movement of 1889–90 has in this respect the greatest analogy. The almost instantaneous conversion to Trade Unionism after the dock strike of tens of thousands of the unskilled labourers of the towns recalls, indeed, nothing so much as the rapid enrolment of recruits among the poorest wage-earners by the emissaries of the Grand National Consolidated Trades Union.

But however strongly the outward features of the wave of 1889–90 may remind the student of those of 1833–34, the characteristics peculiar to the new movement significantly measure the extent of the advance, both in social theory and social methods, made by the wage-earners in the two intervening generations. Time and experience alone will show how far the empirical Socialism of the Trade Unionist of 1889, with its eclectic opportunism, its preference for municipal collectivism, its cautious adaptation of existing social structure, and its modest aspirations to a gradually increasing participation of the workmen in control, may safely be pronounced superior in practicability to the revolutionary and universal Communism of Robert Owen. In truth, the radical distinction between 1833–34 and 1889–90 is not a matter of the particular social theories which inspired the outbursts. To the great majority of the Trade Unionists the theories of the leaders at either date did but embody a vague aspiration after a more equitable social order. The practical difference—the difference reflected in the character and temper of the men attracted to the two movements, and of the attitude of the public towards them—is the difference of method and immediate

P

action. Robert Owen, as we have seen, despised and rejected political action, and strove to form a new voluntary organisation which should supersede, almost instantaneously and in some unexplained way, the whole industrial, political, and social administration of the country. In this disdain of all existing organisations, and the suddenness of the complete " social revolution " which it contemplated, the Owenism of 1833–34 found, as we have seen, an echo in much of the Socialist propaganda of 1884–89. The leaders of the New Unionists, on the contrary, sought to bring into the ranks of existing organisations—the Trade Union, the Municipality, or the State—great masses of unorganised workers who had hitherto been either absolutely outside the pale, or inert elements within it. They aimed, not at superseding existing social structures, but at capturing them all in the interests of the wage-earners. Above all, they sought to teach the great masses of undisciplined workers how to apply their newly acquired political power so as to obtain, in a perfectly constitutional manner, whatever changes in legislation or administration they desired.

The difference in method between the " New Unionism " of 1833–34 and that of 1889–90 may, we think, be ascribed in the main to the difference between the circumstances under which the movements arose. To Robert Owen, whose path was blocked on the political line by the disfranchisement of five out of six of the adult male population, open voting under intimidation, corrupt close corporations in the towns and a Whig oligarchy at the centre, the idea of relying on the constitutional instrument of the polling-booth must have appeared no less chimerical than his own programme appears to-day. The New Unionists of 1889–90, on the other hand, found ready for their use an extensive and all-embracing Democratic social structure, which it was impossible to destroy, and would have been foolish to attempt to ignore. The efforts of two generations of Radical Individualists and " Old Trade Unionists " had placed the legislative power and civil administration of the

country in the hands of a hierarchy of popularly elected
representative bodies. The great engine of taxation was,
for instance, now under the control of the wage-earning
voters instead of that of the land-owning class. The Home
Secretary and the factory inspector, the relieving-officer
and the borough surveyor, could be employed to carry out
the behests of the workers instead of those of the capitalists.
And thus it came about that the methods advocated by the
New Unionists of 1889–94 resemble, not those of the Owenites
of 1833–34, but much more the practical arts of political
warfare so successfully pursued by the Junta of 1867–75.

We shall see the change which had come over the English
working-class movement in the course of sixty years if we
compare the leaders of the two movements which we have
been contrasting. To Owen himself we may allow the
privilege of his genius, which did not prevent him from
being an extravagantly bad captain for a working-class
movement. But in his leading disciples ignorance of industrial conditions, contemptuous indifference to facts and
figures, and incapacity to measure, even in the smallest
actions, the relation between the means and the end, stand
in as marked contrast to the sober judgment of men like
John Burns as they did to the cautious shrewdness of Allan
and Applegarth. It would indeed be easy to find many
traits of personal likeness between Burns and Mann on the
one hand, and Allan and Applegarth on the other. High
personal character, scrupulous integrity, dignity or charm
of manner, marked all four alike, and the resemblance of
character is heightened by a noticeable resemblance in the
nature of their activity. The day's work of Tom Mann at
the head office of the Dockers' Union from 1889 to 1892,
and that of John Burns in the London County Council and
the lobby of the House of Commons from 1892 to 1906,
were close reproductions of Allan's activity at the general
office of his Engineers, and Applegarth's assiduous attendance to Parliamentary Committees and Royal Commissions.
In short, the ways and means of the leaders of the " New

Unionism " remind the student, not of the mystic rites and skeleton mummery of the Owenite movement, but rather of the restless energy and political ingenuity of the Junta or the Trades Union Congress Parliamentary Committee in those early days when the old Trade Unionists were fighting for legislative reforms with a faith which was as wise as it was fervent and sincere.

Some of the secondary characteristics of the New Unionism of 1889 promptly faded away.   The revulsion of feeling against the combination of friendly benefits with Trade Union purposes quickly disappeared, though the difficulty of levying high contributions upon ill-paid workers prevented the complete adoption of the contrary policy.[1]   The expansion of trade which began in 1889 proved to be but of brief duration, and with the returning contraction of 1892 many of the advantages gained by the wage-earners were lost.   Under the influence of this check the unskilled labourers once more largely fell away from the Trade Union ranks.   But just as 1873–74 left behind it a far more permanent structure than 1833–34, so 1889–90 added even more than 1873–74.   The older Unions retained a large part, at any rate, of the two hundred thousand members added to their ranks between 1887 and 1891.   But this numerical accession was of less importance than what may, without exaggeration, be termed the spiritual rebirth of organisations which were showing signs of decrepitude.   The selfish spirit of exclusiveness which often marked the relatively well-paid engineer, carpenter, or boilermaker of 1880–85, gave place to a more generous recognition of the essential solidarity of the wage-earning class.   For example, the whole constitution of the Amalgamated Society of Engineers was, in 1892, revised for the express purpose of opening the

---

[1] Thus the Dock, Wharf, and Riverside Labourers' Union soon gave Funeral Benefit—usually the first to be added ; whilst many of the branches started their own sick funds.   Some of the branches of the National Union of Gas-workers and General Labourers promptly added local benefit funds, and the addition of Accident Benefit by the whole society was presently adopted.

ranks of this most aristocratic of Unions to practically all
the mechanics in the innumerable branches of the engineering trade. Special facilities, moreover, were offered by this
and the other great societies to old men and artisans earning wages insufficient to pay for costly friendly benefits.
Nor was this all. The plumber vied with the engineer, the
carpenter with the shipwright, in helping to form Unions
among the labourers who work with or under them. And
the struggling Unions of women workers, which had originally some difficulty in gaining admittance to Trades Councils
and the Trade Union Congress, gratefully acknowledged a
complete change in the attitude of their male fellow-workers.
Not only was every assistance now given to the formation
of special Unions among women workers, but women were,
in some cases, even welcomed as members by Unions of
skilled artisans. A similar widening of sympathies and
strengthening of bonds of fellowship was shown in the very
general establishment of local joint committees of rival
societies in the same trade, as well as of larger federations.
Robert Knight's failures to form a federal council representing the different Unions concerned in shipbuilding were
retrieved in 1891 by his successful establishment of the
Federation of the Engineering and Shipbuilding Trades, which
maintained a permanent existence. The increased sense of
solidarity among all sections of wage-earners, moreover, led
to a greatly increased cordiality in international relations.
The Coal-miners, the Glass Bottle Makers, and the Textile
Operatives established more or less formal federations with
their fellow-workers on the Continent of Europe. At the
frequent international Congresses of these trades, as well as
at the Socialist Congress of the workers of all countries,
the representatives of the British Trade Unions largely laid
aside that insular conceit which led the Parliamentary Committee of 1884 to declare that, owing to his superiority, the
British Trade Unionist derived no benefit from international
relations. All this indicates a widening of the mental
horizon, a genuine elevation of the Trade Union Movement.

CHAPTER VIII

THE TRADE UNION WORLD

[1890–1894]

WHEN we were engaged, between 1890 and 1894, in investigating the history and organisation of all the several Unions, no complete statistics as to the extent of the membership were in existence. We accordingly sought to obtain, not only an analysis of the Trade Union world as it then was, but also a complete census of Trade Unionism from one end of the kingdom to the other. We retain this analysis practically as it stood in the first edition of the book in 1894, as a record of the position as it then was— in subsequent chapters tracing the principal changes and developments of the last thirty years.

To deal first with the aggregate membership, we were convinced in 1894 that, although a certain number of small local societies might have escaped our notice, we had included every Union then existing which had as many as 1000 members, as well as many falling below that figure. From these researches we estimated that the total Trade Union membership in the United Kingdom at the end of 1892 certainly exceeded 1,500,000 and probably did not reach 1,600,000. Our estimate was presently confirmed. Working upon the data thus supplied, the Labour Department of the Board of Trade extended its investigations, and now records a Trade Union membership for 1892 of

1,502,358.[1] The Trade Unionists of 1892 numbered, therefore, about 4 per cent of the Census population.

But to gauge the strength of the Trade Union world of 1892 we had to compare the number of Trade Unionists, not with the total population, but with that portion of it which might conceivably be included within its boundaries. Thus at the outset we had to ignore the propertied classes, the professions, the employers and the brain-workers of every kind, and confine our attention exclusively to the wage-earners engaged in manual work. Even of the working-class so defined we could exclude the children and the youths under twenty-one, who are not usually eligible for Trade Union membership. The women present a greater

[1] During the whole course of the nineteenth century the Government failed to ascertain, with any approach to accuracy, how numerous the Trade Unionists were. Until the appointment of Mr. John Burnett as Labour Correspondent of the Board of Trade in 1886, no attempt was made to collect, officially, any information about Trade Unionism. The five annual volumes published by Mr. Burnett between 1886 and 1891 contained a fund of information on Trade Union statistics, and the returns became year by year more complete. The report for 1891 gave particulars of 431 Unions with 1,109,014 members, whilst that for 1892 covered a slightly larger total. But, restricted as he was to societies making returns in the precise form required, Mr. Burnett was unable to get at many existing Unions, whilst a considerable deduction had to be made from his total for members counted both in district organisations and in federations. The Chief Registrar of Friendly Societies gave particulars, in his Report for 1892 (House of Commons Paper, 146—II. of March 28, 1893), of 1,063,000 members in 442 registered Trade Unions alone, after deducting organisations which are not Trade Unions, and many duplicate entries. A large number of societies, such as the Northern Counties Amalgamated Weavers' Association, many of the Miners' Unions, the English and Scottish Typographical Associations, the United Kingdom Society of Coachmakers, the Flint Glass Makers, the Yorkshire Glass Bottle Makers, and others were than (as most of them still are) unregistered. Thus our own statistics revealed a 50 per cent greater Trade Union membership than the Government figures. It is difficult to state with exactness the number of separate organisations included, as this must depend upon the manner in which federal bodies are regarded. These exhibit almost infinite variations in character, from the mere " centre of communication " maintained by the thirty-two completely independent local societies of Coopers, to the rigid unity of the forty district organisations which make up the Amalgamated Association of Operative Cotton-spinners. The number of independent societies may be reckoned at either 930 or at anything up to 1750, according to the view taken of federal Unions and federations. We put it approximately at 1100.

difficulty to the statistician. The adult female wage-earners engaged in manual labour in 1891 were estimated to number between two and three millions, of which only about 100,000 were even nominally within the Trade Union ranks. To what extent the men's Trade Unionism was weakened by its failure to enrol the women workers was a matter of dispute. From the industrial point of view the answer depends on complicated economic considerations, such as the extent to which women compete with men in particular industries, or women's trades with those in which men are employed. Owing to the exclusion of women from the Parliamentary franchise until 1918 their absence from the Trade Union world detracted little from its political force. We have dealt elsewhere [1] with the relation of women workers to the Trade Union organisation. Meanwhile we omit the women as well as the young persons under twenty-one from our estimate of the place occupied by Trade Unionism in working-class life.

We know of no exact statistics as to the total numbers of the manual-working class. The figures collected by Leone Levi, and those of Sir Robert Giffen, together with the inferences to be drawn from the census and from Charles Booth's works, led us to the conclusion—at best only hypothetical—that of the nine millions of men over twenty-one years of age in 1891, about seven millions belonged to the manual-working class. Out of every hundred of the population of all ages we could roughly estimate that about eighteen are in this sense working men adults. Accepting for the moment this hypothetical estimate, we arrived at the conclusion that the Trade Unionists numbered at this date about 20 per cent of the adult male manual-working class, or, roughly, one man in five.

But this revised percentage is itself misleading. If the million and a half Trade Unionists were evenly distributed

---

[1] See our *Industrial Democracy* and *Problems of Modern Industry*: also *Men's and Women's Wages, should they be Equal?* by Mrs. Sidney Webb, 1919.

among all occupations and through all districts, a movement which comprised only 20 per cent of working men
would be of slight economic or industrial importance, and
of no great weight in the political world. What gave the
Trade Union Movement its significance even thirty years
ago and transformed these million and a half units into an
organised world of their own, was the massing of Trade
Unionists in certain industries and districts in such a way
as to form a powerful majority of the working-class world.
The Trade Unionists were aggregated in the thriving industrial districts of the North of England. The seven
counties of England north of the Humber and the Dee contained at least 726,000 members of trade societies, or almost
half of the total for the United Kingdom. At a considerable distance from these followed the industrial Midlands,
where the seven counties of Leicester, Derby, Notts, Warwick,
Gloucester, Northampton, and Stafford included a total
Trade Union membership of at least 210,000, whilst South
Wales, including Monmouthshire, counted another 89,000
members of trade societies. The vast agglomeration of the
London district, in which we must reckon Middlesex, the
subsidiary boroughs of West Ham, Croydon, Richmond, and
Kingston, as well as Bromley in Kent, yielded not more
than 194,000 Trade Unionists.

These four districts, comprising nearly 21,000,000 inhabitants, or rather more than two-thirds of the population
of England and Wales, possessed in 1892 twelve-thirteenths
of its Trade Unionists. The total Trade Union membership
in the remainder of the country, with its 8,000,000 of population, did not exceed 105,000, largely labourers. The only
county in England in which in 1892 we found no trace of
Trade Union organisation was Rutland, which did not, at
this date, contain a single branch of any Union whatsoever.
But Huntingdonshire, Herefordshire, and Dorsetshire, containing together over 350,000 inhabitants, included, according to our estimate, only about 710 Trade Unionists between
them. Scotland, with four millions of population, had

147,000 Trade Unionists, nearly all aggregated in the narrow industrial belt between the Clyde and the Forth, two-thirds of the total, indeed, belonging to Glasgow and the neighbouring industrial centres. Ireland, with three-quarters of a million more population, counted but 40,000, nine-tenths of whom belonged to Dublin, Belfast, Cork, and Limerick.

Of particular counties, Northumberland and Durham at that date took the lead, closely followed by Lancashire. The table on following page supplies particulars of this date for the strongest Trade Union counties in England and Wales.

This superficial investigation shows us at once that Trade Unionism coincided in 1892, as it does in 1920, in the main with density of population. The thinly peopled plains of Dorsetshire, the Highlands of Scotland, the West of Ireland, the Cumberland and Westmorland Hills, were practically devoid of Trade Unionism ; the valleys of the Tyne and Tees, Lancashire and London, and the busy industrial villages of the Midlands showed a comparatively high percentage. But the correspondence of Trade Unionism with density of population is by no means exact. Oldham, for instance, with a population of 201,153, had 25,000 male Unionists,[1] or 12.43 per cent, whereas Birmingham (including the suburbs of Aston, Handsworth, and Solihull), with 621,253, had only 26,000, or 4.19 per cent. Newcastle (including Gateshead), with 328,066 inhabitants, had 26,500 Trade Unionists, or 8.08 per cent, whilst Leeds (including Wortley, Hunslet, and Burley) had but 16,000 to a population of 415,243, or 3.85 per cent. And, most striking exception of all, the crowded five and a half millions of the Metropolitan area had but 194,000 Trade Unionists, or only 3.52 per cent of its population, whilst Lancashire, even including its northern moorlands and its wide agricultural districts, had 332,000 for less than four millions of people,

[1] There were, at this date, altogether about 45,000 Unionists in Oldham, but of these some 20,000 were women.

or 8.63 per cent of its population. Reckoning that 18 out of every 100 of the population are adult male workmen, Trade Unionism thus counted among its adherents in some counties over 50 per cent of the total number of working men.

Table showing, for certain counties in England, and for South Wales, the total population in 1891, the ascertained number of Trade Unionists in 1892, and the percentage to population in each case. (In the first edition of this book the student will find a coloured map of England and Wales, showing, in five tints, the percentage of Trade Union membership to Census population in 1891 in the several counties, as estimated in this table.)

County.	Total Population in 1891.	Ascertained Number of Members of Trade Societies in 1892.	Percentage of Trade Unionists to Population.
Northumberland	506,030	56,815	11.23
Durham	1,024,369	114,810	11.21
Lancashire	3,957,906	331,535 *	8.63
Yorkshire, E. Riding . . .	318,570	23,630	7.42
Leicestershire	379,286	27,845	7.34
Derbyshire	432,414	29,510	6.82
South Wales and Monmouth-shire	1,325,315	88,810	6.70
Nottinghamshire . . .	505,311	31,050	6.14
Yorkshire, W. Riding . .	2,464,415	141,140	5.73
Gloucestershire	548,886	26,030	4.74
Cheshire	707,978	32,000	4.52
Staffordshire	1,103,452	49,545	4.49
Suffolk	353,758	14,885	4.21
Warwickshire	801,738	33,600	4.19
Northampton	308,072	12,210	3.96
Cumberland	266,549	10,280	3.86
London District (including Middlesex, Croydon, West Ham, Richmond, Kingston, and Bromley)	5,517,583	194,083	3.52
Yorkshire, N. Riding with York City.	435,897	15,215	3.49
Totals	20,957,529	1,232,993	5.89

No other county had 15,000 Trade Unionists, nor as much as 3 per cent of its population in trade societies.

* Of these, some 80,000 were women. Fully four-fifths of all the organised women workers were, at this date, included in the Lancashire textile Trade Unions.

But this percentage itself fails to give an adequate idea of the extent to which Trade Unionism, even in 1892, dominated the industrial centres in which it was strongest. Within the concentration by localities, there was a further concentration by trades—a fact which to a large extent explains the geographical distribution. The following table shows in what proportion the leading industries contributed to the total Trade Union forces :

Table showing the approximate number of members of trade societies in 1892 according to industries, in the different parts of the United Kingdom.

Trade.	England and Wales.*	Scotland.	Ireland.	Total.
Engineering and Metal Trades	233,450	45,300	8,250	287,000
Building Trades . . .	114,500	24,950	8,550	148,000
Mining	325,750	21,250	. .	347,000
Textile Manufactures .	184,270	12,330	3,400	200,000
Clothing and Leather Trades	78,650	8,400	2,950	90,000
Printing Trades . . .	37,950	5,650	2,400	46,000
Miscellaneous Crafts .	46,550	7,450	4,000	58,000
Labourers and Transport Workers	302,880	21,670	10,450	335,000
Totals	1,324,000	147,000	40,000	1,511,000 †

* Including the Channel Islands and the Isle of Man, which contained together about 1285 Trade Unionists.

† Included in the above total were 99,650 women in 52 Unions, distributed among the groups as follows :

Engineering and Metal Trades	2,850
Building and Furniture Trades	300
Mining	. .
Textile Manufactures	80,900
Clothing and Leather Trades	8,650
Printing Trades	400
Miscellaneous Crafts	3,450
Labourers and Transport Workers	3,100
	99,650

We may add that the subsequently published Board of Trade statistics

For the general reader, this table, together with the fore-going one showing the geographical distribution of Trade Unionism, completes our statistical survey of the Trade Union world of 1892. To the student of Trade Union statistics a more particular enumeration may be useful. Before we attempt to picture Trade Union life, we shall therefore devote a dozen pages (which the general reader may with a clear conscience skip) to the dry facts of organisation in each of the eight great divisions into which we distributed the Trade Union membership of 1892.

The first division, comprising all the numerous ramifications of the engineering, metal-working, and shipbuilding trades, was then characterised by old-established and highly developed national Unions, with large membership, centralised administration, and extensive friendly benefits. The 287,000 Trade Unionists in this division were enrolled in over 260 separate societies, but almost one-half belonged to one or other of four great national organisations, the Amalgamated Society of Engineers (established 1851), the United Society of Boilermakers and Iron Shipbuilders (established 1832),[1] the Friendly Society of Ironfounders of England, Ireland, and Wales (established 1809), and the Associated Society of Shipwrights, a belated amalgamation

---

for 1892, arranged on a slightly different classification, gave the following totals by industrial groups :

Metal, Engineering and Shipbuilding	279,534
Building .	157,971
Mining and Quarrying	315,272
Textile .	204,022
Clothing .	83,299
Transport	154,947
Other Trades .	307,313
	1,502,358

See Report on Trade Unions for 1901 (Cd. 773).

---

[1] The Boilermakers claim only to have been established since 1834, but there is evidence of the existence of the Society in 1832. In a few other cases, notably those of the Stonemasons, Plumbers, and Bricklayers, we have been able to carry the history of the organisation further back than has hitherto been suspected.

formed in 1882 by the many ancient local Unions of wooden shipbuilders. Of these great Unions, that of the Boiler-makers, with 39,000 members, was incomparably the strongest, having no rival for the allegiance of its trade and including practically the whole body of skilled work-men engaged in iron shipbuilding and boilermaking from one end of the United Kingdom to the other. The great Unions of Ironfounders and Shipwrights, with respectively 15,000 and 14,000 members, were not quite so universal as the Boilermakers. The Associated Society of Ironmoulders (Ironfounders) of Scotland (established 1831), with 6000 members and a few minor Unions of less skilled ironfounders, maintained separate organisations ; whilst the Shipwrights' Provident Union of the Port of London (established 1824, 1400 members), the Liverpool Trade and Friendly Associa-tion of Shipwrights (established 1800, 1400 members), and a few other old-fashioned port Unions still held aloof from the Shipwrights' amalgamation.[1] The Amalgamated Society of Engineers, the largest centralised Trade Union in the kingdom, with 66,000 members at home and 5000 abroad, towered over all its rivals, but had to compete with compact sectional or local Unions, admitting one or more of the numerous classes of workmen in the engineering and machine-making trade.[2] Among the actual producers of iron and steel, the British Steel Smelters' Association (estab-lished 1886), with 2400 members, originally a Scotch Union, was extending all over the kingdom ; whilst the Associated Society of Iron and Steel Workers (established 1862), with

[1] The equally archaic port Unions of the Sailmakers, dating, like those of the Shipwrights, from the last century, were united in the Federation of Sailmakers of Great Britain and Ireland (established 1890), with 1250 members.

[2] Of these the most important were the Steam-Engine Makers' Society (established 1824, 6000 members), the Associated Blacksmiths' Society (a Scottish organisation, established 1857, 2300 members), the United Kingdom Pattern Makers' Association (established 1872, 2500 members), the National Society of Amalgamated Brassworkers (established 1872, 6500 members), the United Journeymen Brassfounders' Association of Great Britain and Ireland (established 1866, 2500 members), and the United Machine Workers' Association (established 1844, 2500 members).

7800 members, occupied a unique position in the Trade Union world from its long and constant devotion to the sliding scale. The tin and hollow - ware workers,[1] the chippers and drillers, the Sheffield cutlers, and the craftsmen in precious metals were split up into innumerable local societies, with little federal union.

It is interesting to notice the large proportion which this division of Trade Unionists in Scotland bore to the total for that country. Whilst in England and Wales it formed only one-sixth of the aggregate number, in Scotland it measured nearly one-third, almost entirely centred about Glasgow.

Table showing the approximate number of Trade Unionists in each group of the Engineering and Shipbuilding Trades.

Trade.	England.	Scotland.	Ireland.	Total.
Engineers and Machine Makers	74,000	8,250	2,750	85,000
Smiths and Farriers . .	7,350	2,250	300	9,900
Brass and Copper Workers	13,350	2,000	150	15,500
Sheet Metal Workers . .	16,000	1,300	200	17,500
Ironfounders and Core-makers	15,500	7,250	500	23,250
Shipbuilding and Boiler making	45,500	13,250	3,600	62,350
Iron and Steel Smelters .	23,500	1,500	..	25,000
Workers in Precious Metals	3,500	..	..	3,500
Sundry Metal Workers .	34,750	9,500	750	45,000
Totals	233,450	45,300	8,250	287,000

The organisation of Builders and Furniture Makers resembled in many respects that of the Engineers and Shipbuilders. The 148,000 Trade Unionists in this division were sorted into 120 separate Unions; but again we find one-half of them belonging to one or other of three centralised

[1] The makers of tin plates had a Union in South Wales (established 1871, and reorganised 1887) which claimed a membership of 10,000. The National Amalgamated Tinplate Workers' Association of Great Britain (established 1876) had 3000 members, and the General Union of Sheet Metal Workers (established 1861) had 1250 members.

Trade Friendly Societies of national scope. Of these the Friendly Society of Operative Stonemasons (established 1832, 16,000 members) was the most powerful, having practically no rival throughout England or Ireland, and maintaining friendly relations with the corresponding United Operative Masons' Association of Scotland (established 1831, 5000 members). But the largest and richest Union in this division was the Amalgamated Society of Carpenters and Joiners (established 1860, 34,000 members at home and 4000 abroad). Although this Society could count but a small proportion of the total number of carpenters in the kingdom, it included three-fourths of those who were Trade Unionists, the remaining fourth being divided between the Associated Carpenters and Joiners of Scotland (established 1861, 6000 members), the old General Union of Carpenters and Joiners of England (established 1827, 4000 members), and a few tiny trade clubs in the Metropolis which had refused to merge themselves in either of the national organisations. The Bricklayers were in much the same position as the Carpenters. The Operative Bricklayers' Society (established 1848, 22,000 members) included three-fourths of the Trade Unionists, the remainder being found either in the United Operative Bricklayers' Trade, Accident, and Burial Society (established 1832, 2500 members), or in a few isolated local trade clubs in Scotland and Ireland. Of the other Unions in the Building Trades, the United Operative Plumbers' Association of Great Britain and Ireland (established 1832, reorganised 1865, 6500 members) was by far the most effective and compact, and was specially interesting as retaining practically the federal constitution of the Builders' Union of 1830–34. With the exception of the United Operative Plumbers' Association of Scotland (established 1872, 700 members), a small society resulting from a secession, no rival organisation existed. On the other hand, the Painters, Slaters, Packing-case Makers, Upholsterers, and French Polishers were split up into numberless small Unions, whilst the Cabinetmakers and Plasterers had each one considerable organisation [1] and several smaller societies, which, however, included but a small proportion of the trade.

Table showing the approximate number of Trade Unionists in the various branches of the Building and Furniture Trades.

Trade.	England.	Scotland.	Ireland.	Total.
Stonemasons	16,750	8,250	250	25,250
Bricklayers	24,000	700	2,300	27,000
Carpenters	33,000	7,850	3,250	44,100
Cabinetmakers	7,200	2,000	300	9,500
Sawyers and other Woodworkers	4,250	350	150	4,750
Plasterers	7,500	1,000	500	9,000
Painters	12,400	2,150	1,000	15,550
Plumbers	5,400	1,200	400	7,000
Upholsterers and French Polishers	2,500	450	300	3,250
Sundry Building Trades .	1,500	1,000	100	2,600
Totals.	114,500	24,950	8,550	148,000

The Miners and Quarrymen, comprising about sixty-five societies, were in 1892 the best organised of the eight great divisions into which we classified the Trade Union forces. Among the coalminers the "county," or district Union, without friendly benefits, was the predominating type. Nearly two-thirds of the whole 347,000 Trade Unionists in this division were gathered into the Miners' Federation of Great Britain (established 1888), a federal Union comprising about twenty independent organisations, some of which, like the Yorkshire Miners' Association (established 1858, 55,000 members), were highly centralised, whilst others, like the Lancashire Miners' Federation (established 1881, 43,000 members), were themselves federal bodies. The Miners' Federation, whilst not interfering with the financial autonomy or internal administration of its constituent bodies,

[1] The Alliance Cabinetmakers' Association (established 1865, 5500 members) and the National Association of Operative Plasterers (established 1862, 7000 members).

effectively centralised the industrial and Parliamentary policy of the whole army of its members from Fife to Somerset. Outside the Federation at this date stood the powerful and compact Northumberland Miners' Mutual Confident Association (established 1863, 17,000 members), and Durham Miners' Association (established 1869, 50,000 members), together with the solid little Mid and West Lothian Miners' Association (established 1885, 3600 members), and the loose organisations of Sliding Scale contributors which then figured as Trade Unions in South Wales.[1] The coal and iron miners of the West of Scotland had scarcely got beyond the ephemeral pit club and occasional Strike Union. Among the tin, lead, and copper miners Trade Unionism, as far as we can ascertain, was absolutely unknown.

Table showing the approximate number of Trade Unionists among the persons engaged in or about Mines and Quarries.

Trade.	England.	Scotland.	Ireland.	Total.
Coal and Iron Miners . .	301,000	17,500	..	318,500
Colliery Enginemen . .	5,000	1,500	..	6,500
Cokemen, Overmen, Colliery Mechanics, &c. . . .	9,250	500	..	9,750
Quarrymen	10,500	..	..	10,500
Shale Oil Workers . . .	..	1,750	..	1,750
Totals	325,750	21,250	..	347,000

The salient fact of Trade Unionism among the textile operatives in 1892 was that effective organisation was nearly confined to the workers in cotton, who contributed at least two-thirds of the 200,000 Trade Unionists in this division. Like the Miners the Cotton Operatives have always shown

[1] The South Wales miners were, at this date, in a transition state. The Miners' Federation had gained a considerable following in Monmouthshire and Glamorgan, but the bulk of the men still adhered to the Sliding Scale machinery, claiming 36,000 members, for the maintenance of which a fortnightly contribution was usually deducted by the employers from the miners' earnings. The Forest of Dean Miners' Association (4000 members) seceded from the Federation in 1893. A small Miners' Union (2250 members) at West Bromwich also held aloof.

a strong preference for federal Associations with exclusively trade objects. The powerful Amalgamated Association of Operative Cotton-spinners (established 1853), a federal Union of 19,500 members comprising forty separate district associations, joined with its sister federations, the Northern Counties Amalgamated Association of Weavers (established 1884, 71,000 members) and the Amalgamated Association of Card and Blowing Room Operatives (31,000 members, established 1886), in the United Textile Factory Workers' Association (established 1886). This Association, formed exclusively for Parliamentary purposes, focussed the very considerable political influence of 125,000 organised cotton operatives in Lancashire, Cheshire, and Yorkshire, and was, next to the Miners' Federation, by far the most powerful Trade Union organisation in the country.[1]

The highly developed organisation of the Cotton Operatives contrasted with the feebleness of the Woollen-workers. In the other branches of textile manufacture the extreme localisation of the separate industries had given rise to isolated county or district organisations of lace, hosiery, silk, flax, or carpet-workers usually confined to small areas, and exercising comparatively little influence in the Trade Union world. Incomparably the strongest among them was the Amalgamated Society of Operative Lace-makers (3500 members), which comprised practically all the adult male workers in the Nottingham machine-lace trade. If we exclude the constituent organisations of the United Textile Factory Workers' Association, the separate Unions in the various branches of the textile industry numbered 115.

---

[1] The Cotton-spinners' Union was then composed exclusively of adult males, the boy " piecers " being brigaded in subordinate organisations. In the Cotton-weavers and Card-room Operatives' Unions women formed a large majority of the members.

[TABLE

Table showing the approximate number of Trade Unionists in the various branches of the Textile Manufacture.

Trade.	England.	Scotland.	Ireland.	Total.
Cotton-spinners	19,500	..	..	19,500
Cotton-weavers	82,500	500	..	83,000
Cotton Card-room Operatives	31,000	..	..	31,000
Woollen-workers . . .	6,000	9,500	..	15,500
Woolsorters, Combers, &c.	2,500	..	..	2,500
Silkworkers	2,500	..	60	2,560
Flax and Linen-workers .	150	300	2,940	3,390
Carpet-weavers	2,600	400	..	3,000
Hosiery-workers . . .	6,350	100	50	6,500
Lacemakers	4,500	..	..	4,500
Elastic Webworkers. . .	700	..	..	700
Dyers, Bleachers, and Finishers	11,820	180	100	12,100
Overlookers	4,850	200	200	5,250
Calico-printers and Engravers	1,950	500	50	2,500
Miscellaneous Textiles . .	7,350	650	..	8,000
Totals	184,270	12,330	3,400	200,000

The large section of workers engaged in the manufacture of clothing and leather goods was, perhaps, the least organised of the skilled trades. One society, indeed, the National Union of Boot and Shoe Operatives (established 1874), counted almost 43,000 members, and exercised a very real control over the machine boot trade. And although the hand industry was in this case rapidly declining, the Amalgamated Association of Boot and Shoemakers (established 1862) maintained and even increased the earnings of this body of 4700 skilled handicraftsmen. The Tailors, on the other hand, had succeeded neither in controlling the new machine industry, nor in upholding the standard earnings of the handworkers. The Amalgamated Society of Tailors (established 1866, 17,000 members), together with the Scottish National Operative Tailors' Society (established 1866, 4500 members), had absorbed all the local Unions.

but included only a small proportion of those at work in the trade. The Felt Hatters and Trimmers' Union (established 1872) had 4300 members, together with a women's branch (established 1886) numbering nearly as many. In other branches of this division some strong organisations existed in the smaller industries, but the workers for the most part formed only feeble local clubs or else were totally unorganised. There were altogether over sixty separate Unions in this division.

Table showing the approximate number of Trade Unionists in the Clothing and Leather Trades.

Trade.	England.	Scotland.	Ireland.	Total.
Boot and Shoemakers . .	46,250	2,250	500	49,000
Other Leather Workers .	5,900	550	100	6,550
Tailors and other Clothing Makers	16,100	5,500	2,300	23,900
Hatmakers, Glovers, &c. .	10,400	100	50	10,550
Totals	78,650	8,400	2,950	90,000

The 46,000 Trade Unionists in the paper and printing trades were divided between four considerable Unions with 27,000 members, and forty-five little societies numbering not more than 19,000 altogether. The compositors lead off with three extensive organisations, the London Society of Compositors, confined to the Metropolis (established 1848, 9800 members), the Typographical Association (established 1849, 11,500 members), which had absorbed all but four of the Irish and four of the English local societies outside the Metropolis, and the Scottish Typographical Association (established 1852, 3000 members). The Bookbinders and Machine Rulers' Consolidated Union (established 1835, 3000 members), mainly composed of provincial workers, far exceeded the London Consolidated Bookbinders' Society, the largest of half-a-dozen Metropolitan Unions in this trade.

Table showing the approximate number of Trade Unionists in the various branches of the Paper and Printing Trades.

Trade.	England.	Scotland.	Ireland.	Total.
Compositors and Press and Machine Men	27,250	4,000	2,000	33,250
Bookbinders	5,150	700	300	6,150
Papermakers	3,150	500	...	3,650
Miscellaneous Printing Trades	2,400	450	100	2,950
Totals	37,950	5,650	2,400	46,000

There remained a number of trades which it was difficult to classify. These miscellaneous crafts furnished over 130 societies and 58,000 Trade Unionists. Some, like the Coopers, Cigarmakers, Brushmakers, Basketmakers, and Glassworkers, were usually well organised ; others, like the Coachbuilders, Potters, Bakers, and Ropeworkers, included but a small percentage of their trades.[1]

Table showing the approximate number of Trade Unionists in the Miscellaneous Trades.

Trade.	England.	Scotland.	Ireland.	Total.
Basket and Brushmakers	2,800	350	100	3,250
Coach and Waggon Builders	6,000	400	600	7,000
Coopers	4,400	1,300	300	6,000
Glassworkers	7,350	500	150	8,000
Millers and Bakers . . .	7,000	2,500	2,500	12,000
Potters	6,250	1,650	...	7,900
Sundry Trades . , . .	12,750	750	350	13,850
Totals	46,550	7,450	4,000	58,000

The great army of labourers, seamen, and transport workers of every kind we enclosed in a single division. Out of the 120 organisations belonging to this group the

[1] The United Kingdom Society of Coachmakers (established 1834) had 5500 members. The Mutual Association of Coopers (established 1878) was then a loose federation of old-fashioned local Unions, with about 6000 members.

Amalgamated Society of Railway Servants (established 1872), with its permanent membership of 31,000, its high contributions, extensive friendly benefits, and large accumulated funds, resembled in character the large national societies of the engineering and building trades. Alongside this stood the Associated Society of Locomotive Engineers and Firemen (established 1880, 7000 members). Some other Unions in this group, such as the London and Counties Labour League (established 1872, 13,000 members), and the National Agricultural Labourers' Union (established 1872, 15,000 members), had become essentially friendly societies. But the predominating type in this division was, as might have been expected, the new Union, with low contributions, fluctuating membership, and militant trade policy. Of these the strongest and apparently the most stable was the National Union of Gasworkers and General Labourers (established 1889), with 36,000 members on the books. Next in membership came the Dock, Wharf, and Riverside Labourers' Union (established 1889), the Tyneside and National Labour Union (established 1889), and the National Amalgamated Sailors and Firemen's Union (established 1887), each with a membership fluctuating between 20,000 and 40,000. Other prominent Unions in this division were the General Railway Workers' Union (established 1889), the National Union of Dock Labourers (established 1889), the National Amalgamated Coalporters' Union (established 1890), and the Navvies, Bricklayers' Labourers, and General Labourers' Union (established 1890). The builders' labourers and the carmen were organised in numerous local Unions, which, in some cases, such as the Mersey Quay and Railway Carters' Union (established 1887), and the Leeds Amalgamated Association of Builders' Labourers (established 1889), were effective trade societies. The chief exponent of New Unionism among the agricultural labourers was then the Eastern Counties Labour Federation (established 1890), which had enrolled 17,000 members in Suffolk and the neighbouring counties. But any statistical estimate of the

ill-defined and constantly fluctuating membership of the
Unions in this division must necessarily be of less value
than in the more definitely organised trades.[1]

*Table showing the approximate number of Trade Unionists among the
Labourers and Transport Workers of every kind.*

Trade.	England.	Scotland.	Ireland.	Total.
Seamen, Fishermen, Water-				
men, &c.	33,850	3,900	1,500	39,250
Railway Traffic Workers .	43,500	1,500	3,000	48,000
Enginemen, &c. (other than				
Colliery or Railway) . .	6,300	370	100	6,770
Carmen, &c.	19,000	3,500	1,000	23,500
Miscellaneous Labourers .	200,230	12,400	4,850	217,480
Totals	302,880	21,670	10,450	335,000

It would have been an interesting addition to our
statistics if we could have added to these tables a column
showing the proportion which the Unionists in each trade
bore to the total number of workers in it. Unfortunately
the classification of the census [2] is not sufficiently precise to
enable this to be done. We were therefore thrown back
upon such information on the point as we can obtain from
other sources. We knew, for instance, that in Lancashire

[1] We did not include in the above statistics the Unions in classes not
included among the manual workers. The National Union of Teachers,
established 1870, was, already in 1892, a powerful organisation with
23,000 members. The Telegraph Clerks, Life Assurance Agents, and
Shop Assistants also had Unions varying from 1000 to 5000 members,
and there were two organisations of postal employees. The National
Unions of Clerks and Domestic Servants were less definitely established.
There were also small societies among the London Dock Foremen and
Clerks and the Poplar Ships' Clerks.

Nor did we include such essentially benefit societies as the Marine
Engineers' Union (9500 members) and the United Kingdom Pilots'
Association, which were composed largely of workmen belonging for trade
purposes to particular Trade Unions.

[2] The census figures for 1891 merge, for each trade, " workmen, assistants, apprentices, and labourers." They do not, for instance, distinguish
between Bricklayers and Bricklayers' Labourers, who belong to very
different Trade Unions. Under Hosiers or Hatters are included shopkeepers and their assistants, as well as the manufacturing operatives.

the Amalgamated Association of Cotton-spinners included practically every competent workman engaged in the trade. The same might be said of the Boilermakers' Society in all the iron shipbuilding ports, though not in some of the Midland districts. And to turn to an even larger industry, 80 per cent of the coalminers were in union, some districts, such as Northumberland and parts of the West Riding of Yorkshire, having practically every hewer in the society. And in other industries and localities the Union was sometimes equally inclusive. Among the Dublin Coopers or the Midland Flint Glass Makers, the Nottingham Lacemakers or the Yorkshire Glass Bottle Makers, non-Unionism was practically unknown. We see, therefore, that instead of numbering only 4 per cent of the total population, the Trade Union world was in certain districts and in certain industries, already in 1892 practically coextensive with the manual labour class. On the other hand, there were many occupations in which Trade Unionism was non-existent. Whole classes of manual workers were practically excluded from the Trade Union ranks by the fact that they were not hired workers at wages. In the nooks and crannies of our industrial system were to be found countless manual workers who obtained a precarious livelihood by direct service of the consumer. Every town and village had its quota of hawkers, costermongers, tallymen, and other petty dealers ; of cobblers, tinkers, knifegrinders, glaziers, chairmenders, plumbers, and other jobbing craftsmen ; of cab-runners, " corner boys," men who " hang about the bridges," and all the innumerable parasites of the life of a great city. When we passed from these " independent producers " to the trades in which the small master survived, or in which home work prevailed, we saw another region almost barren of Trade Unionism. The tailors and cabinetmakers, for instance, though often highly-skilled craftsmen, had only a small minority of their trades in Union, whilst the chain and nailmakers were almost unorganised. The effect upon Trade Unionism of a backward type of industrial organisation was well seen in the manufacture of boots and shoes. In Leicestershire and Stafford, where the work was done in large factories, practically every workman was in the Union. In the Midland villages, where this was carried on as a domestic industry, and in East London, where it was only passing out of that phase, the National Society of Boot and Shoe Operatives counted but a small proportion of members. And in those districts in which the small master system still held its own it cast a blight even on other trades. Thus the Birmingham district and East London were bad Trade Union centres, not only for the sweated trades, but also for those carried on in large establishments. But the great bulk of non-Unionism was to be found in another field. The great army of labourers, as distinguished from mechanics, miners, or factory operatives, were in normal times as unorganised as the women workers. Except in certain counties, such as Kent, Suffolk, Norfolk, Oxfordshire, Wiltshire, and the Fen districts, Trade Unionism among the farm labourers could scarcely be said to exist. Of the three-quarters of a million of agricultural labourers in the United Kingdom, not more than 40,000 were then in union. Nor were the other classes of labour in much better plight. The two hundred thousand workers in the traffic department of the railways contributed only 48,000 Trade Unionists, mostly from such grades as guards and engine-drivers. The large class of tramway and omnibus workers had, after a brief rally, reverted to a state of disorganisation. The great army of warehousemen, porters, and other kinds of city labourers counted only a few hundred Trade Unionists in all the kingdom.

The Trade Union world was, therefore, in 1892, in the main composed of skilled craftsmen working in densely populated districts, where industry was conducted on a large scale. About one-half of the members belonged to the three staple trades of coalmining, cotton manufacture, and engineering, whilst the labourers and the women workers were, at this date, on the whole, non-Unionists.

But the influence of Trade Unionism on working-class life cannot be measured by the numbers actually contributing to the Union funds at any one time. Among the non-Unionists in the skilled trades a large proportion have at one time or another belonged to their societies. Though they have let their membership lapse for one reason or another, they follow the lead of the Union, and are mostly ready, on the slightest encouragement from its members, or improvement in their own position, to rejoin an organisation to which in spirit they still belong. In the Labour Unions the instability of employment and the constant shifting of residence caused the organisation, in 1892, to resemble a sieve, through which a perpetual stream of members was flowing, a small proportion only remaining attached for any length of time. These lapsed members constitute in some sense a volunteer force of Trade Unionism ready to fight side by side with their old comrades, provided that means can be found for their support. Moreover, the Trade Unionists not only belong to the most highly-skilled and best-paid industries, but they include, as a general rule, the picked men in each trade. The moral and intellectual influence which they exercise on the rest of their class is, therefore, out of all proportion to their numbers. In their ranks are found, in almost every industrial centre, all the prominent leaders of working-class opinion. They supply the directors of the co-operative stores, the administrators of clubs and friendly societies, and the working-class representatives on Parish, District, and Town Councils. Finally we may observe that the small but rapidly increasing class of working-men politicians invariably consists of men who are members of a trade society. We may safely assert that, even in 1892, no one but a staunch Trade Unionist would have had any chance of being returned as a working-class member to the House of Commons, or elected to a local governing body as a Labour representative.

It is therefore impossible by a statistical survey to give any adequate idea of the Trade Union world of 1892. We may note the fact that the thousand separate unions or branches between Blyth and Middlesborough numbered some 200,000 members. We may ascertain that within fifteen miles of the Manchester Exchange at least as many Trade Unionists lived and worked. But no figures can convey any real impression of the place which the Trade Union, even then, filled in the every-day life of the skilled artisans of the United Kingdom. We are therefore fortunate in being able to supplement our statistics by a graphic description of Trade Union life supplied to us in 1893 by a skilled craftsman, who joined his Union on the expiration of his apprenticeship, and served for some time in various official capacities.

To an apprentice, Trade Unionism is little more than a name. He may occasionally overhear the men in his shop discussing their Union and its work ; and he knows that after " club night " a number of stories of the incidents of the meeting will be related ; whilst, if he works in a strong Society shop, he may even hear heated discussions on resolutions submitted to the meeting. But the chief topic will always be the personal one— who was at the meeting, and what old chums were met ; for the " club " is generally the recognised meeting-place for " old cronies " in the trade. If he works in a shop where any of the Trade Union officials are also employed he may sometimes receive a word of advice and exhortation " to be sure to join the Society when he is a man." On the whole, however, his knowledge of, and interest in, the Society will be very slight. But should a strike occur at his shop whilst he is yet a lad, the presence and power of the Trade Union will be brought very vividly home to him ; and as he works by himself or with the other lads in an otherwise deserted shop he will form some opinions of his own. He will naturally feel a violent antipathy to the " Blacks " brought into his shop, for the sense of comradeship is strong among boys ; and he will notice with considerable pleasure that they are usually inferior workmen. But in spite of this, if the employer is " a good sort," who treats him well and kindly, he will probably still think that the men are wrong to strike. For the boy regards the employer as the one " who finds work for the men to do," and hence looks upon a strike as an act of ingratitude ; and further, he has also a vague idea that the men are in the position

of being many to one, and hence he promptly sides with the
weaker party.

As the youth draws near the end of his apprenticeship he finds
that he is frequently spoken to by Union men and urged to join
the Society.   He notices, too, that more attention is paid to him,
and that his opinions are frequently asked upon trade matters.
Finally he is invited round to the little public in which the
club meetings are held, and introduced to the Lodge officials, and
to a number of his fellow-tradesmen.   The advantages offered by
the Society are freely dilated upon, great stress being laid upon
the friendly benefits—the sick, superannuation, funeral, and,
above all, the out-of-work pay.   For the Trade Society is the
only institution which provides an out-of-work benefit.   Against
sickness and death he may already be insured in one or other of
the numerous Friendly Societies ; but the out-of-work pay is
never provided except by a Trade Society, since only there is it
possible to know whether a claimant is out of work by reason of
bad trade, or bad character, or inefficiency, or even if he is really
out of work at all.   And as the advantages of this provision are
pointed out to him he recollects the time when his father, a staid,
steady-going mechanic, was thrown out of work by slack times ;
and the memory of that bitter experience clings very closely to
him.   Perhaps he is also in love.   The thought of seeing " her "
miserable and their children hungry whilst he himself is helpless
to assist, must always be one of the most harrowing things to
a careful young artisan, with visions of a happy little home in
the near future.   There is, however, another view of the club
which appeals with almost equal force to our young artisan just
out of his apprenticeship and finding himself in possession of an
income nearly double that to which he has been accustomed.
The Trade Union Meeting House is the recognised club for the
men in the craft, and thus presents many social attractions.
Friendships are made—numerous " sing-songs " and smoking
concerts arranged ; and the joke and friendly glass, the good
cheer and the conviviality, all present great attractions to the
young workman.

The club is also a centre for obtaining the latest trade news.
Here come the unemployed from other towns ; here are to be
heard reports of reductions or advance of wages, increased or
diminished working hours, stories of tyranny, or the first rumours
of that bug-bear to the men—the invention of new machines,
with its probable displacement of their labour ; or even worse,
the introduction of women and boys at reduced prices.   There

is also an occasional visit from an important official of the central office to look forward to, and his words to digest afterwards. All these attractions incline the young artisan to enrol himself in the Lodge, but it is mainly personal considerations which in the end decide him to take the step. Are the good men in his trade —those whom he likes, who have treated him well, helped him out of his difficulties and given him coppers when a lad ; the powerful men, the foremen, and those whose words carry most weight with their fellows—are these men members of the Union ? If they are, and if, as is most probable in a Society shop, he has formed friendships with other young fellows who are already members, it is not long before he consents, and allows himself to be duly proposed as a candidate for membership.

The next club night sees him at the door of the club-room waiting anxiously, and perhaps timorously, whilst the formalities go on inside. Usually the ordinary business of the evening is all disposed of before the election of new members takes place. At the first mention by the President of the fact that a candidate is waiting to be elected, the doorkeeper (hitherto posted inside the door to see that no one comes in or goes out surreptitiously, and that none of the " worthy brothers " are in an unfit state to enter the room) slips rapidly outside, and holding the door firmly, refuses admission to any one while the ceremony lasts. The President then rising, calls for order, and having read out the name of the candidate and those of his proposer and seconder, asks those members to tell the Lodge what they know about him. Then the proposer rises, and addressing " Mr. President and worthy brothers," states what he knows—that the candidate is a young man, apprenticed in his shop and duly served his time— a good workman and a steady young fellow—anxious to join the Society and sure to be a credit to the Lodge. He resumes his seat amid applause ; and the seconder rises and repeats the same eulogy. Then the candidate is called into the room, the door-keeper admitting him with some ceremony. He enters in fear and trembling ; for the formality of admission, though shorn of its former mysterious rites, is still conducted with sufficient solemnity to make it loom as something rather terrible. At once he finds himself the object of the friendly curiosity of the members, and the cause of applause, all of which adds considerably to his nervousness and trepidation. But he is agreeably surprised to find the ceremony a very meagre one. The President, rising, calls upon all the members to do likewise, and then, all standing, he reads out an initiatory address, and a portion of the Rules of the Society. Then in a simple affirmation the candidate pledges himself to abide by the Rules, to study the interests of the Society, and neither to do, nor, if he can prevent it, allow to be done, anything in opposition thereto. He has then to formally sign this pledge. That being done, his name is entered as a member, and upon paying his entrance fee, he is presented with a card of membership and a book of Rules of the Society.

He is now an ordinary member of the Lodge, and this newly acquired dignity is fully brought home to him in the course of a week or so, when he receives his first summons to attend a Lodge meeting. He wends his way to the little public-house in the dirty back street where the Lodge is held, and arriving shortly before eight o'clock, the time fixed for the opening of business, finds a number of his fellow-workmen congregated round the bar discussing the evening's programme and trade matters generally. The men come in by twos and threes, and he notices that, with few exceptions, all are neat and clean, having been home and had their tea and a wash in the interval between then and working hours.[1] The officers of the Lodge arriving, are greeted with a general recognition as they pass upstairs to prepare the club-room for the business of the evening. Shortly after the hour fixed for commencing, the President takes the chair, and, as the men slowly straggle up into the room, rises and declares the meeting open for business. The club-room is a long, low-ceilinged room which constitutes the first floor of the public-house. Down the centre of the room runs a trestle table with forms along the sides, on which the members are seating themselves. At the top a shorter table is placed crosswise, forming a letter T, and here sits the group of officers. The room is decorated with the framed "emblems" of various trade societies, interspersed with gilt mirrors and advertising almanacs. At one end is a throne and canopy, showing that it is used also as a club-room by one or other of the friendly societies which still maintain the curious old rites of their orders. In a corner stands a cottage pianoforte, indicating that the room is also used for concerts, sing-songs, and convivial gatherings.

The first business of the evening is the payment of contributions. The Secretary, aided by the "Check Secretary," the

---

[1] Old members often recall the days when the men used to come to the club straight from work, and "in their dirt." They frequently ascribe the orderly behaviour at club meetings at the present time, as compared with the rowdiness of the past, largely to this change of habit, itself a direct result of the reduction of the hours of labour.

Money Steward, and Treasurer, receives the subscriptions from the men as they come, one by one, up the room, enters the payment in the books, and signs the members' cards. In many cases women and children come to pay the subscriptions of their husbands or fathers ; and he will feel a sense of shame at the idea of these having to come through the public bar to perform their errand. When the subscriptions are all received, the unemployed members, and the wives or other relatives of those who are sick, present themselves to draw their respective benefits. General inquiries are made after the health and hopes are expressed for the speedy recovery of the sick ones ; and the sums due are paid out by the officials with considerable formality. During these proceedings there has been a constant hum of conversation in the room, and a continual running in and out of members to the bar, and back again. But all this now comes to an end. The President rises and calls for order. Strangers and non-members are cleared out of the room. The doorkeeper takes up his position inside the door to watch the comers-in and goers-out ; and the drink-stewards make ready to attend to the members' wants, and act as waiters, in order to dispense with strangers in the room, and to prevent any unnecessary bustle and confusion.[1] The business of the evening opens with the reading of the minutes of the last meeting. Questions concerning the enforcement of some resolution, or the result of some instructions given to the officers, are asked and answered, and the minutes are confirmed by a show of hands and signed by the President. Then letters received, and copies of those despatched by the Secretary since the last meeting are read. These include letters from the General Office interpreting some rule as to the payment of benefits, from the District Committee giving notice of a trade regulation, and from other branch secretaries asking for particulars as to the character and ability of some candidate for admission. Then follows the excitement of the evening—the report of delegates appointed to interview an employer on some grievance. They will explain how they waited on Mr. So-and-so, who at first refused to see them, and ordered them off his premises ; how presently he came round and listened to their complaints ; how he denied the existence of the alleged evil, and demanded the names of the men who complained, which the delegates of course refused to give ; and how at last, after much dispute, he temporised, and gave them to understand that the grievance would be

---

[1] Many Unions forbid all drinking during the branch meeting.

remedied. Then the members present from the shop in question are called upon to explain what improvements, if any, have been made in the matters of which they complained. If their report is satisfactory, the subject is allowed to drop. If not, there is a heated discussion. Our friend, seated with the young fellows at the back of the room, finds himself clamouring for a strike. The officers do their best to hold the meeting back. They suggest that the District Committee [1] ought first to be communicated with ; or if the grievance is one against which the General Rules or District Bye-laws permit the men to strike without superior sanction, they urge further negotiations with the employer. The discussion is eventually closed by an order to the Secretary to write to the District Committee for advice, or by an instruction to the delegates to again interview the offending employer, and if he " bamboozles " them a second time, to strike the shop.

This excitement over, the interest of the meeting flags, and members drop out one by one. Perhaps there is an appeal by a member to whom the Committee has refused some benefit to which he thinks himself entitled. Against this decision he appeals to his fellow-members in Lodge assembled, urging his long membership, his wife and family, and his work for the Union as reasons why he should be leniently dealt with. Eloquent speeches are made on his behalf by personal friends. But the Committee and the officers declare that they have acted according to the Rules, and remind the Lodge that if they are ordered to pay an illegal benefit, the Central Office will disallow the amount, and order the members to repay it to the Union funds. With a strong Committee the vote will be against the man ; with a weak one, and especially if the man is a jovial and " free-and-easy " comrade, his friends will turn up in sufficient numbers to carry the appeal. It being now ten o'clock, all other business—such as resolutions proposed by individual members— gets adjourned to the next club night, and the President declares the Lodge duly closed. The Secretary hastens home, to sit up burning midnight oil in balancing the books, entering the minutes, making reports to the Central Executive or District Committee, and writing the letters ordered by the meeting.

The Lodge meeting soon plays an important part in the life of our active-minded artisan. He feels that he is taking part in the

---

[1] In the great Amalgamated Societies District Committees, composed of representatives of local branches, are formed in the great industrial Centres, and decide on the trade policy to be adopted by their constituent branches. These decisions must be confirmed by the Central Executive.

Q

actual government of a national institution. Special meetings are held to discuss and vote on questions submitted by the Executive to the whole body of the members, such as the alteration of a rule, the election of some central official, or a grant in aid of another trade. But primarily the Lodge is his Court of Appeal against all industrial tyranny, a court in which he is certain of a ready and sympathetic hearing. There he takes complaints of fines and deductions, of arbitrary foremen, of low piecework prices—of anything, in short, which affects his interest or comfort as a wage-earner.

The tendency of this ever-present power and actuality of the Lodge and its officials is to overshadow in the mind of the member the larger functions and responsibilities of the Central Executive. To him they are something far away in the vast outside world, and their powers are very vague and shadowy. They are, however, brought home to him in some of the incidents of his Trade Union and working life. There is, for instance, the " emblem " of his Society, a large and generally highly-coloured representation of the various processes of the trade in which he is engaged, often excellently designed and executed. This, purchased for a few shillings soon after his admission to the Society, or more probably at the time of his marriage, is hung, gaily framed, in his front parlour. On it is recorded his name, age, and date of admission to the Society, and it bears the signatures, and perhaps the portraits, of the general officers. To him it is some slight connecting link with the other men in his trade and Society. To his wife it is the charter of their rights in case of sickness, want of work, or death. As such it is an object of pride in the household, pointed out with due impressiveness to friends and casual visitors.

But more important is the Monthly Circular, now a recognised feature in most of the large Unions. Here the member feels himself brought into direct contact with the outside world of his trade. Has he been ill or out of work and drawn relief, his name and the amount of money drawn are duly recorded. If he has not himself been so unfortunate, he here learns the names of those who have, and perhaps hears from this source for the first time of such a calamity having befallen some friend in another and distant town. Here also are reports of the state of trade and the number of unemployed in every place where a branch of the Society exists ; of alterations in hours and rates of wages effected during the month, by friendly negotiations or by a lock-out or a strike. Finally, there are letters from lodges or from individual members on all sorts of topics, including spicy abuse of the Central Executive, and tart rejoinders from the General Secretary. As his interest in the Society increases, our artisan himself writes letters to the Circular, explaining some grievance, suggesting a remedy for some grievance already explained, or answering criticisms upon the conduct and policy of his District Committee or his Lodge.

In addition to the Monthly Circular there is the Annual Report. This is a large volume of some hundreds of pages, containing, in a summarised form, the progress and doings of the Society for the whole year, with the total income and expenditure and the balance in hand, the proportionate cost of all the various benefits, a statement of the accounts of each branch, and many other figures of interest and importance. He feels a glow of pride as the growth of his Society in funds and members is recorded, and perhaps also a longing to see his own name printed as one of the officers of one of the Lodges, and thus be even distantly associated with the success of the Society.

But after a year or two of the comparative freedom of the journeyman's life he begins to feel strongly the desire for change and adventure. The five or seven years' apprenticeship through which he has just passed has kept him chained in one place, and a period of unrest now begins. Moreover, he has heard as a commonplace among his fellow-workmen, that no man knows his own ability or what he is worth until he has worked in more towns or shops than one. They have also expatiated to him upon the delights of " the road " ; and finally he determines to take advantage of his membership of the Society to go on tramp on the first opportunity. He is therefore not altogether displeased when some temporary contraction in his trade causes his employer to turn him adrift, and thus gives him a right to draw his travelling card.[1]

At the close of his first day's tramp, footsore and weary, he seeks the public-house at which the local Lodge is held, and having refreshed himself, starts off to find the Secretary. To him he presents his tramp card. When, on examination, the dates upon it are found to be correct, and the distance traversed

---

[1] The travelling card, formerly called a " blank," is now, in most cases, a small book of receipt forms. On it is recorded the particulars of his membership, and the date to which he has paid his contributions. Along with it he receives a complete list of the public-houses which serve as the Society's Lodge-houses, and also a list of the names and addresses of the Lodge secretaries.

is sufficient to entitle the traveller to the full benefit of sixpence and a bed, the Secretary writes an order to the publican to provide this relief. The date and place are then clearly marked on the travelling card, and the Secretary retains the corresponding half of the receipt form to serve as his own voucher for the expenditure. Should he know of any suitable situation vacant in the town, he will tell the tramp to repair there in the morning. But if no such post offers itself, the wayfarer must start off again in the morning, in time to arrive before night at the next Lodge town, at which alone he can receive any further relief.

If our friend takes to the road during the summer months and finds a situation within a few weeks, he will have had nothing worse than a pleasant holiday excursion. But if his tramp falls during the winter, or if he has to remain for months on the move, he will be in a pitiable plight. Whilst he is in the thickly-populated industrial districts, where " relief towns " in his trade are frequently to be met with, he finds his supper and bed at the end of every fifteen or twenty miles. But as he one by one exhausts these towns, he will, by the rule forbidding relief from the same Lodge at less than three months' interval, be compelled to go further afield. He presently finds the Lodges so far apart that it is impossible for a man to walk from one to another in a day. The relief afforded becomes inadequate for his maintenance, and many are the shifts to which he has to resort for food and shelter. Finally, after a specified period, usually three months, his card " runs out " ; he has become " box-fast," and can draw no more from the Society until he has found a job, and resumed payment of his contributions.

But our artisan, being an able-bodied young craftsman, has found a job. Settled in a new town, his tramping for the present at an end, and himself recovered from the evils, moral and physical, which that brief period has wrought upon him, his interest in his Society revives. He attends his new Lodge regularly, at first because it is the only place in the town where he meets friends. Presently his old desire to figure as an official of the Society returns to him. He cultivates the acquaintance of the officers of the Lodge, mixes freely with the members, and takes every occasion to speak on exciting questions. At the next election he is appointed to some minor post, such as auditor or steward. He makes himself useful and popular, and in the course of the year finds himself a member of the Lodge Committee.

From membership of the Branch Committee he succeeds to

the position of Branch Secretary, the highest to which his fellow-tradesmen in his own town can elect him. On the night of the election he is somewhat surprised to find that there is no keen competition for the post. The pay of a Branch Secretary is meagre enough—from ten to fifty shillings per quarter. Most of his evenings and part of his Sundays are taken up with responsible clerical work. Besides attending the fortnightly or weekly committee meeting, lasting from eight to eleven or twelve at night, he has to prepare the agenda for the special and general meetings of the members, conduct the whole correspondence of the Lodge, draw up reports for the District Committee and Central Executive, keep the accounts, and prepare elaborate balance-sheets for the head office. Even his working day is not free from official duties. At any moment he may be called out of his shop to sign the card of a tramp, or he may have to hurry away in the dinner-hour to prevent members striking a shop without the sanction of the Lodge. When a deputation is appointed to wait on an employer, he must ask for a day off, and act as leading spokesman for the men. All this involves constant danger of dismissal from his work, or even boycott by the employers, as an " agitator." Nor will he always be thanked for his pains. Before he was elected to the Secretaryship, he was probably " hail, fellow, well met " with all the other members. Now he has constantly to thwart the wishes and interests of individual members. He must be always advising the Committee to refuse benefits to members whose cases fall outside the Rules of the Society, and counselling Lodge meetings to refuse to sanction strikes. Hence he soon finds little cliques formed among the malcontents, who bitterly oppose him. He is charged with injustice, pusillanimity, treachery, and finally with being a " master's man." But after a while, if he holds steadfastly on his course, and abides strictly to the Rules of the Society, he finds himself backed up by the Executive Committee, and gaining the confidence of the shrewd and sensible workmen who constitute the bulk of the members, and who can always be called up to support the officers in Lodge meetings.

One of the duties or privileges thrust on our Secretary is that of representing his trade on the local Trades Council. He is not altogether gratified to find that the Branch has elected, as his co-delegates, some of the more talkative and less level-headed of its members. Some older and more experienced men decline to serve, on the ground that they have no time, and " have seen enough of that sort of thing." Nevertheless our Secretary at the outset takes his position very seriously. To the young Trade Unionist the Trades Council represents the larger world of labour politics, and he has visions of working for the election of labour men on the local governing bodies, and of being himself run by the Trades Council for the School Board, or the Town Council, or perhaps even for Parliament itself. When the monthly meeting of the Council comes round, he therefore makes a point of arriving punctually at eight o'clock at the Council Chamber. He finds himself in the large and gaudily decorated assembly room, over the bar of one of the principal public-houses of the town. A low platform is erected at one end, with chairs and a small table for the Chairman and Secretary. Below the platform is placed a long table at which are seated the reporters of the local newspapers, and the rest of the room is filled with chairs and improvised benches for the delegates. Here he meets the thirty or sixty delegates of the other Unions. He notices with regret that the salaried officials of the Societies which have their head-quarters in the town, and the District Delegates of the great national Unions who are located in the neighbourhood—the very men he hoped to meet in this local " Parliament of Labour "—are conspicuous by their absence. The bulk of the delegates are either branch officials like himself, or representatives of the rank and file of Trade Unionism like his colleagues. The meeting opens quietly with much reading of minutes and correspondence by the Secretary. Then come the trade reports, delegate after delegate rising to protest against some encroachment by an employer, or to report the result of some negotiations for the removal of a grievance. A few questions may perhaps be asked by the other delegates, but there is usually no attempt to go into the merits of the case, the Council contenting itself with giving a sympathetic hearing, and applauding any general denunciation of industrial tyranny. If a strike is in progress, the delegates of the trade concerned ask for " credentials " (a letter by the Secretary of the Council commending the strikers to the assistance of other trades), and even appeal for financial assistance from the Council itself. This brings about difference of opinion. The whole Council has applauded the strike, but when it comes to the question of a levy, the representatives of such old-established Unions as the Compositors, Engineers, Masons, and Bricklayers get up and explain that the Rules of their Societies do not allow them to pledge themselves. On the other hand, the enthusiastic delegates from a newly-formed Labour Union promptly promise the assistance of their Society, and vehemently accuse the Council of apathy. Then follows a still more serious business—a complaint by one of the several Unions in the engineering or building trades that the members of a rival Union have lately " blacklegged " their dispute. The delegates from the aggrieved Society excitedly explain how their men had been withdrawn from a certain firm which refused to pay the Standard Rate, and how, almost immediately afterwards, the members of the other Society had accepted the employer's terms and got the work. Then the delegates from the accused Society with equal warmth assert that the work in question belonged properly to their branch of the trade ; that the members of the other Society had no business to be doing it at all ; and that as the employers offered the rates specified in their working rules, they were justified in accepting the job. At once an angry debate ensues, in which personal charges and technical details are bandied from side to side, to the utter bewilderment of the rest of the members. In vain the Chairman intervenes, and appeals for order. At last the Council, tired of the wrangle, rids itself of the question by referring it to a Committee, and an old member of the Council whispers to our friend a fervent hope that the Committee will shirk its job, and never meet, since its report would please neither party, and probably lead to the retirement of one if not both trades from the Council.

The next business brings the Council back to harmony. The delegates appointed at the last meeting to urge on the Town Council or the School Board the adoption of a " fair wage clause " now give in their report. They describe how Mr. Alderman Jones, a local politician of the old school, talked about wanton extravagance and the woes of the poor ratepayer ; and the Council will be moved to laughter at their rejoinder, " How about the recent increase in the salary of your friend, the Town Clerk ? " They repeat, with pleasure, the arguments they used on the deputation, and their final shot, a bold statement as to the number of Trade Unionists on the electoral register, is received with general applause. But in spite of all this they report that Alderman Jones has prevailed, and the Town Council has rejected the clause. Our new member notes with satisfaction that the Council is not so ineffective a body as he has been fearing. After a good deal of excited talk the Secretary is instructed to write to the local newspapers explaining the position, and calling attention to the example set by other leading municipalities. The members, new and old alike, undertake to heckle the retiring Town Councillors who voted against the interests of labour ; and the best men of the Council, to whichever political party they belong, join in voting for a Committee to run Trade Union candidates against their most obdurate opponents.

Passing, rejecting, or adjourning resolutions, of which notice has been given at a previous meeting, takes up the remainder of the evening. First come propositions submitted on behalf of the Executive Committee, composed of five or seven of the leading men in the Council. The Secretary explains that an influential member of the Trade Union Congress Parliamentary Committee has intimated that if they want a certain measure passed into law, they had better carry a particular resolution, which is thereupon read to the meeting. It is briefly discussed, carried unanimously, and handed to the reporters, the Secretary being ordered to send copies to the local M.P.'s and possibly to the Cabinet Minister concerned. Resolutions by other members are not so easily disposed of. The delegate from the Tailors, a fanatical adherent of the Peace Society, proposes a strong condemnation of increased armaments, ending up with a plea for international arbitration. But the engineer and the shipwright vehemently object to the resolution as impracticable, and one of them moves an amendment calling on the Government to find employment for hardworking mechanics in times of industrial depression by building additional ironclads. The Socialist Secretary of a Labour Union submits a resolution calling on the Town Council to open municipal workshops for the unemployed—a project which is ridiculed by the Conservative compositor (who is acting also as one of the reporters). During the debate the Chairman, Secretary, and Executive Committeemen lie low and say nothing, allowing the discussion to wander away from the point. The debate drops, and if a vote on a popular but impracticable resolution becomes imminent, some " old Parliamentary hand " suggests its adjournment to a fuller meeting. For the next few evenings our friend finds all this instructive and interesting enough. Before the year is up he has realised that, except on such simple issues as the Fair Wages Clause, and the payment of Trade Union wages by the local authorities, the crowded meeting of tired workmen, unused to official business, with knowledge and interest strictly limited to a single industry, is useless as a Court of Appeal, and ineffective even as a joint committee of the local trades. At the best the Council becomes the instrument, or, so to speak, the sounding-board, of the experienced members, who are in touch with the Trade Union Parliamentary leaders, and who (at a pay of only a few shillings a quarter) conduct all the correspondence and undertake all the business which the Trade Unions of the town have really in common.

But our friend receives a sudden check in his career. One pay-day he is told by his employer that he will not be wanted after next week. It may be that he has had some words with the foreman over a spoilt job, or that he has been making himself too prominent in Trade Union work, or simply that his employer's business is slack. But whatever the cause he is discharged, and must seek employment elsewhere. At once he declares himself on the funds of the Society, sending notice to the President and Treasurer of his position and signing the out-of-work book at the club daily, like any other unemployed member. For the next two or three weeks he tramps from shop to shop in his district seeking work, and eagerly scans the daily papers in hopes of finding an advertisement of some vacant situation. Then comes the news from a friend of a vacancy in a distant town. He resigns his position as Secretary of the Lodge, draws the balance of out-of-work pay due to him, and departs regretfully from the town where he has made so many friends to start upon a new situation.

On arriving at his new place he is surprised to find that there is no branch of his Society in the town. There are a few odd members, but not enough to support a branch—hence they send their contributions to the nearest Lodge town. As soon as he has settled down he takes steps to alter this. In his own work-shop he argues and cajoles the men into a belief in Trade Unionism. At night he frequents their favourite haunts, and by dint of argument, promises and appeals, finally gets enough of them to agree to join a Lodge to make it worth while opening one in the town. He forthwith communicates with the Central Executive Committee, and they, knowing his previous work, appoint him Secretary *pro tem.* A meeting of all the trade is then called by handbills sent round to the shops, and posted in the men's favourite public-houses. On the eventful night the General Secretary and perhaps another Central officer, come down to the town. They bring a Branch box containing sets of Rules and cards of membership, a full set of cash and other books, a number of business papers, and even a bottle of ink—in fact all that is needful to carry on the business of a Lodge. The room will be crammed full of the men in the trade interested in hearing what the Society is and what it wants to do. Speeches are made, the advances of wages and reduction of hours gained by the Society are enumerated, the friendly benefits are explained, and instances are given of men disabled from working at their trade, receiving £100 accident benefit from the Society, and setting up in a small business of their own. Then the General Secretary opens the Lodge, and entrance fees and contributions are paid by a large number of those present, and the meeting changed from a public to a private one. Officers are elected, our friend again finds himself chosen as Secretary, a friendly foreman accepts the post of Treasurer, while the other old members present at the meeting are elected to the remaining offices. Addresses from the Central officials start the Lodge on its way, and the meeting breaks up at a late hour with cheers for the Society and the General Secretary.

Within the next three months the Branch Secretary finds that all that glitters is not gold. At least half of those who joined at the beginning have lapsed, and at times the branch looks like collapsing altogether. But by dint of much hard work, persuasion, and perhaps the formation of friendships, it is kept together until a time of prosperity for the trade arrives. This is the Secretary's opportunity to make or break his Lodge, and being a wise man he takes it. He puts a resolution on the agenda paper for the next Lodge meeting in favour of an advance of wages, or a reduction of hours, or both. The next meeting carries it unanimously, and it at once becomes the talk of the whole trade in the town. Men flock down and join the club in order to assist and participate in the proposed improvements. Then the Secretary appeals to the General Executive for permission to ask for the advance. They consider the matter seriously, and want to know what proportion of the men in the town are members, and how long they have been so ; what is the feeling of the non-Unionists towards the proposed movement, and whether there is any local fund to support non-Unionists who come out, or buy off tramps and strangers who come to the town during the probable strike. All these questions being more or less satisfactorily answered, permission to seek the improvement is at length given, and now comes the Secretary's first taste of " powder " in an official capacity.

During this agitation the number of members in the Lodge has been steadily increasing, until it comes to include a good proportion of the trade in the town. The non-Unionists have also been approached as to their willingness to assist the movement, and the bulk of them readily agree to come out with the Society men if these undertake to maintain them. A special Committee is formed to conduct the " Advance Movement," including delegates from the non-Society shops prepared to strike. A local levy is put on the members of the Lodge, in order to form a fund from which to pay such strike expenses as may not be charged to the Union. At length all is ready, and our Secretary is instructed to serve notices upon all the employers in the town, asking for the advance in wages or the reduction of hours claimed by the men.

Meanwhile the employers have not been idle. They have heard rumours of the coming storm and have met together and consulted as to what should be done, and have formed a more or less temporary association to meet the attack. Upon receiving the notices from the men's Secretary they invite a deputation of the men to wait upon them and discuss the matter. To this the men of course agree, and on the appointed night the Secretary and the " Advance Committee " appear at the joint meeting. The leading employer having been elected to the chair, asks the men to open their case for an advance of wages and reduction of hours. This they do, emphasising the facts that wages are lower and hours longer here than in the same trade in neighbouring towns ; that the cost of living is increasing ; and that some men are always unemployed who would be absorbed by the proposed change. The employers retort by urging the smallness of their profits and the difficulty of securing orders in competition with other towns where wages are even less than they are here ; and also by urging that the cost of living is decreasing and not increasing— an assertion which they support by statements of the price of various articles at different times compared with the present. The men's Secretary has as much as he can do to keep his men in order. The new members—the " raw heads " of the Committee—are almost hoping that the employers will not agree, for to them a strike means merely a few weeks' " play," at the expense of the Union. And the ordinary workman is so little used to discussing with his adversaries that any statement of the other side of the case is apt to arouse temper. The employers, too, unaccustomed to treating with their men, and still feeling it somewhat derogatory to do so, are not inclined to mince matters, or smooth over difficulties. Hence the meeting becomes noisy ; discussion turns into recrimination ; and the conference breaks up in confusion.

Meanwhile the Central Executive has watched with anxiety the approach of a dispute which will involve the Union in expense, and end possibly in defeat. The General Secretary, accompanied by one of the Executive Council, appears on the scene, and endeavours to mediate. But as the town has been a non-Union one, the employers refuse to see any but their own workmen, and thus lose the chance of the very moderate compromise which the General Secretary is almost sure to offer. This slight to their Official naturally incenses the local Unionists, and on the following Saturday, when their notices have expired, they " pick up " their tools as they leave the works and the strike is begun.

Then follows a period of intense excitement and hard work for the men's officials. The employers advertise in all directions for men at " good wages " to take " steady employment," and counter advertisements are inserted giving notice of the strike. All the streets are closely picketed by men, who take it in turns to do duty in twos and threes outside a factory or workshop for so many hours each day ; pickets are sent to meet all trains, and by dint of promises, bribes, and appeals to their " manliness and brotherhood," workmen who have been attracted to the town by the employers' advertisements are induced to depart. Perhaps a few " blacks " may escape their vigilance and get into some shop. Every time they come out they are followed and urged to abandon their dirty calling and join their fellows in the good work. Some give way, and their fares are at once paid to the place whence they came. Subscription boxes and sheets are sent out to raise the funds necessary for the extra expenses, which must not be taken from the Society's funds. If the strike drags on for many weeks delegates go from town to town addressing meetings of Trade Unions and Trades Councils soliciting aid, and usually succeed in getting a good deal more than their own expenses, the surplus being remitted to the Lodge. There are the non-Unionists who have come out on strike to be supported ; " blacks " to bribe and send away ; printing and delivering of bills and placards to be paid for, and numerous other subsidiary expenses to be met, all of which must be defrayed from the local fund.

But even the most protracted strike comes to an end. If trade is good and the men are well organised, the employers will not have succeeded in getting any good workmen, and not even sufficient bad ones, to continue their works, and their plant and reputation are alike suffering from unskilled workmanship. So one by one they give in, and accept the men's terms, until at length the men are again at work. On the other hand, if business be slack the strike may end in another way. One by one the employers obtain enough men of one sort or another to carry out what orders they have in hand. As week succeeds week the strikers lose heart, until at last the weak ones suddenly return to work at the old terms. The officers and committeemen and a few dogged fighters may remain out, hoping against hope that something will turn up to make the employers give in. But the Central Executive will probably object to the continued drain of strike-pay, and may presently declare the strike closed. This will cause some little resentment among the local stalwarts, but the strike-pay being now at an end, those who are still unemployed must tramp off to another town in search of work.

If the strike results thus in failure the newly formed Lodge will soon disappear and the men in the trade remain unorganised until the advent of another leader of energy and ability. But if it has resulted in victory the prosperity of the Lodge is assured. The workmen in the trade flock to the support of an institution which has shown such practically beneficial results. Meanwhile the Secretary, to whom most of the credit is due, begins to be known throughout the trade, and spoken of as the man who changed such and such a place from a non-Union to a Union town. Short eulogistic notices of his career appear in the Monthly Circular, and thus the way is paved for his future advancement.

Having thus succeeded in organising his own trade, he finds an outlet for his energies in doing the same for others in his town. Perhaps there are other branches of his own industry without organisations, and if so he begins among them exactly the same work as he pursued among his own members. When the time is ripe a meeting is called and a branch of the society, which embraces the particular body of men, opened, and he accepts the post of President to help it along until its members have gained some experience. Then he will begin again with other trades and go through the same process, and thus in the course of time succeed in turning a very bad Trade Union town into a very good one. When that is accomplished he determines to start a Trades Council. He attends meetings of all the Unions and branches in the town and explains the objects and urges the importance of such a body. He writes letters to the local Press, and agitates among his own personal following until his object is well advertised. Finally a joint meeting of delegates from the majority of the local societies and branches is got together. The Rules of a neighbouring Trades Council are discussed and adopted, and at length a Trades Council is definitely established, if only by the two or three branches which he has himself organised. He is of course appointed its Secretary, and gradually by hard work, and perhaps by successfully agitating for some concession to labour by the Town Council or local School Board, he wins the approval of all the societies, and the Council then becomes a thoroughly representative body. As Secretary of a newly established Trades Council he becomes rapidly well known. He is in constant request as a speaker in both his own and neighbouring towns ; and he is sent to the Trade Union Congress and instructed to move some resolution of his own drafting. But as the work gradually increases, our friend, who has all the time to be earning a livelihood at his trade, finds that he must choose between the Trades Council and his own Lodge. Through the Trades Council he can become an influential local politician, and may one day find himself the successful " Labour Candidate " for the School Board or the Town Council. But this activity on behalf of labour generally draws him ever further away from the routine duties of Branch Secretary of a National Society, and he will hardly fail to displease some of the members of his own trade. He may therefore prefer to resign his Secretaryship of the Trades Council, take a back seat in politics, and spend all his leisure in the work of his own Society, with the honourable ambition of eventually becoming one of its salaried officers. In this case he not only conducts the business of his Lodge with regularity, but also serves on the District Committee. Presently, as the most methodical of its members, he will be chosen to act as its Secretary, and thus be brought into close communication with the Central Executive, and with other branches and districts.

All this constitutes what we may call the non-commissioned officer's service in the Trade Union world, carried out in the leisure, and paid for by the hour, snatched from a week's work at the bench or the forge. But now the fame of our Secretary and his steady work for the Society have spread throughout the district, and when it is decided to appoint a District Delegate with a salary of £2 or £2 : 10s. per week, many branches request him to run for the post. His personal friends and supporters among them raise an election fund for him, and for a few weeks he dashes about his district and attends all the branch meetings to urge his candidature upon the members. Finally the votes are taken in the Lodges by ballot and sent to the general office to be counted, and he finds himself duly elected to the post. Again he moves his home, this time to some central town, so that he can visit any part of his district with ease and rapidity. His district stretches over three or four counties, and includes many large industrial centres, and he finds himself fully occupied. Let us see how he spends his days, and what is the work he will do for his Society.

Every morning he receives a whole batch of letters on Society business. The General Secretary orders him immediately to visit one of the branches in his district and inspect the books, a report having reached the office of some irregularity. A Branch Secretary telegraphs for him to come over at once and settle a dispute which has broken out with an important firm. Another writes asking him to summon a mass meeting of the trade in the district to take a vote for or against a general strike against some real or fancied grievance. The Secretary of the Employers' Association in another town fixes an appointment with him to discuss the piecework prices for a new sort of work. Finally the Secretary of his District Committee instructs him to attend a joint meeting which they have arranged with the District Committee of another Union to settle a difficult question of overlap or apportionment of work between the members of the two societies.

Our friend spends the first half an hour at his correspondence, fixes a day for a special audit of the accounts of the suspected branch, drops a hasty line to the General Secretary informing him of his whereabouts for the next few days, and writes to the Branch Secretary strongly objecting to the proposed mass meeting to vote on a strike on the ground that " an aggregate meeting is an aggravated meeting," and appointing, instead, a day for a small conference of representatives from the different branches. Then he is off to the railway station so as to arrive promptly on the scene of the dispute just reported to him. Here he finds that a number of his members have peremptorily struck work and are hanging about the gates of the works. He will half persuade, half order them to instantly resume work, whilst he goes into the office to seek the employer. If it is a " Society shop " in a good Trade Union district he is heartily welcomed, and the matter is settled in a few minutes. The next train takes him to the neighbouring town, where he spends two or three hours with the Employers' Secretary, using all his wits to manipulate the new prices in such a way as at least to maintain, if not to increase, the weekly earnings of his members. In the evening he has to be back at the centre of his district, thrashing out, in the long and heated debate of a joint meeting, the difficult question of whose job the work in dispute between the two Unions properly is, and what constitutes a practical line of demarcation between the two trades. Thus he rushes about from day to day, finishing up at night with writing reports on the state of trade, organisation, and other matters to the Executive Committee sitting at the headquarters of his Union.

He has now been for many years the devoted servant of his fellow-workmen, re-elected at the end of each term to his post of District Delegate. Upon the removal by resignation or death of the General Secretary he is pressed on all sides to put up for the post. The members of the District Committee, and all the secretaries of the local branches, urge on him his fitness, and the advantages the district will derive from his election as General Secretary. Again a committee of his friends and supporters raises a fund to enable him to travel over the whole country and visit and address all the branches of the Society. Meanwhile the Executive Committee prepares for the election of the new General Secretary. At the removal of the late head officer they at once meet to appoint one of their number to carry on the duties *pro tem.*, and to issue notices asking for nominations for the post (generally confined to members who have been in the Society a certain number of years and are not in arrears with their subscriptions). Printed lists of candidates are forthwith sent to the branches in sufficient numbers to be distributed to all the members. A ballot-box is placed in the club-room, the election standing over at least two meeting nights in order to allow every member full opportunity to record his vote. The boxes are then sent from the branches to the central office, where the members of the Executive Committee count the papers and declare the result.

Our District Delegate having been declared duly elected to the post of General Secretary is again compelled to remove. This time it is to one of the great cities—London, Manchester, or Newcastle—the headquarters of his Society. He is now entitled to a salary ranging from £200 to £300 per annum, and has attained the highest office to which it is in the power of his fellow-tradesmen to appoint him. We will there leave him to enjoy the dignity and influence of the position, to struggle through the laborious routine work of a central office, and to discover the new difficulties and temptations which beset the life of the general officer of a great Trade Union.

The foregoing narrative gives us, in minute detail, the inner life of Trade Union organisation of thirty years ago. But this picture, on the face of it, represents the career of an officer, not a private soldier, in the Trade Union army. Nor must it be supposed that the great majority of the million and a half Trade Unionists rendered, even as privates,

any active service in the Trade Union forces. Only in the
crisis of some great dispute do we find the branch meetings
crowded, or the votes at all commensurate with the total
number of members. At other times the Trade Union
appears to the bulk of its members either as a political
organisation whose dictates they are ready to obey at
Parliamentary and other elections, or as a mere benefit
club in the management of which they do not desire to take
part. In the long intervals of peace during which the constitution of the Society is being slowly elaborated, the
financial basis strengthened, the political and trade policy
determined, less than a half or perhaps even a tenth of the
members will actively participate in the administrative and
legislative work. Practically the whole of this minority
will, at one time or another, serve on branch committees or
in such minor offices as steward, trustee, auditor or sick-
visitor. These are the members who form the solid nucleus
of the branch, always to be relied on to maintain the
authority of the committee. From their ranks come the
two principal branch officers, the President and the Secretary, upon whom the main burden of administration falls.
Though never elected for more than one year, these officers
frequently remain at their posts for many terms in succession ; and their offices are in any case filled from a narrow
circle of the ablest or most experienced members.

Besides the active soldiers in the Trade Union ranks,
to be counted by hundreds of thousands, we had therefore,
in 1892, a smaller class of non-commissioned officers made
up of the Secretaries and Presidents of local Unions, branches
and district committees of national societies, and of Trades
Councils. Of these we estimate that there were, in 1892,
over 20,000 holding office at any one time. These men form
the backbone of the Trade Union world, and constitute the
vital element in working-class politics. Dependent for their
livelihood on manual labour, they retain to the full the
workman's sense of insecurity, privation, and thwarted
aspirations. Their own singleness of purpose, the devotion

with which they serve their fellows in laborious offices with only nominal remuneration, and their ingenuous faith in the indefinite improvement of human nature by education and better conditions of life, all combine to maintain their enthusiasm for every kind of social reform. Thus they are always open to new ideas, provided these are put forward in a practical shape, by men whose character and intelligence they respect. This class of non-commissioned officers it is which has, in the main, proved the progressive element in the Trade Union world, and which actually determines the trend of working-class thought. Nevertheless these men are not the real administrators of Trade Union affairs except in the little local Unions, run by men working at their trade, which are fast disappearing. In the great national and county Unions the branch or lodge officials are strictly bound down by detailed rules, and are allowed practically no opportunity of acting on their own initiative. The actual government of the Trade Union world rests exclusively in the hands of a class apart, the salaried officers of the great societies.

This Civil Service of the Trade Union world, non-existent in 1850, numbered, in 1892, between six and seven hundred.[1] Alike in the modern organisation of industry, and in the machinery of Democratic politics, it was, even in 1892, taking every day a position of greater influence and importance. Yet if we may judge from the fact that we have not met with a single description of this new governing

---

[1] We did not include in this figure a large class of men who are indirectly paid officials of Trade Unions, such as the checkweighers among the coal-miners, and the " collectors " among the cotton-weavers, cardroom-workers, etc. The checkweigher, as we have stated (p. 305), is elected and paid weekly wages, not by the members of the Trade Union, but by all the miners in a particular coal-pit. But as Trade Unionism and the election of a checkweigher are practically coincident, he frequently serves as lodge secretary, etc. The collectors employed by certain Trade Unions to go from house to house and collect the members' contributions are remunerated by a percentage on their collections. Though not strictly salaried officials, they serve as Trade Union recruiting agents, as well as intermediaries between members and the central office, for complaints, appeals, and the circulation of information.

class, the character of its influence, and even its existence, had hitherto remained almost unobserved. To understand the part played by this Civil Service, both in the Trade Union Movement and in the modern industrial State, the reader must realise the qualities which the position demands, the temptations to which its holders are exposed, and the duties which they are called upon to perform.

The salaried official of a great Trade Union occupies a unique position. He belongs neither to the middle nor to the working class. The interests which he represents are exclusively those of the manual working class from which he has sprung, and his duties bring him into constant antagonism with the brain-working, property-owning class. On the other hand, his daily occupation is that of a brain-worker, and he is accordingly sharply marked off from the typical proletarian, dependent for his livelihood on physical toil.

The promotion of a working man to the position of a salaried brain-worker effects a complete and sudden change in his manner of life. Instead of working every day at a given task, he suddenly finds himself master of his own time, with duties which, though laborious enough, are indefinite, irregular, and easily neglected. The first requisite for his new post is therefore personal self-control. No greater misfortune can befall an energetic and public-spirited Trade Unionist, who on occasions takes a glass too much, than to become the salaried officer of his Union. So long as he is compelled, at least nine days out of every fourteen, to put in a hard day's manual work at regular hours, his propensity to drink may not prevent him from being an expert craftsman and an efficient citizen. Such a man, elected General Secretary or District Delegate, is doomed, almost inevitably, to become an habitual drunkard. Instead of being confined to the factory or the mine, he is now free to come and go at his own will, and drink is therefore accessible to him at all hours. His work involves constant travelling, and frequent waiting about in strange towns, with little choice of resort beyond the public-house. The regular periods of monotonous physical exertion are replaced by unaccustomed intellectual strain, irregular hours, and times of anxiety and excitement, during which he will be worried and enticed to drink by nearly every one he meets. And in addition to this the habitual drunkenness of a Trade Union official, though it involves discredit, seldom brings dismissal from his post. No discovery is more astounding to the middle-class investigator than the good-natured tolerance with which a Trade Union will, year after year, re-elect officers who are well known to be hopeless drunkards. The rooted dislike which working men have to " do a man out of his job " is strengthened, in the case of a Trade Union official, by a generous recognition of the fact that his service of his fellows has unfitted him to return to manual labour. Moreover, the ordinary member of a Trade Union overlooks the vital importance of skilled and efficient administration. He imagines that the drunkenness and the consequent incompetency of his General Secretary means only some delay in the routine work of the office, or, at the worst, some small malversation of the Society's funds. So long as the cash keeps right, and the reports appear at regular intervals, it seems never to occur to him that it is for lack of headship that his Society is losing ground in all directions, and forgoing, in one week, more than a dishonest Secretary could steal in a year.

Fortunately the almost invariable practice of electing the salaried officials from the ranks of the non-commissioned officers tends to exclude the workman deficient in personal self-control. The evenings and holidays spent in clerical duties for the branch do not attract the free liver, whilst the long apprenticeship in inferior offices gives his fellow-workmen ample opportunity of knowing his habits. Thus we find that the salaried officials of the old-established Unions are usually decorous and even dignified in their personal habits. An increasing number of them are rigid teetotalers, whilst many others resolutely refuse, at the risk of personal unpopularity, all convivial drinking with their members.

But another danger—one which would not immediately have occurred to the middle-class investigator—besets the workman who becomes a salaried official of his Union. The following extract, taken from the graphic narrative we have already quoted, explains how it appears to a thoughtful artisan :

And now begins a change which may possibly wreck his whole Trade Union career. As Branch Secretary, working at his trade, our friend, though superior in energy and ability to the rank and file of his members, remained in close touch with their feelings and desires. His promotion to a salaried office brings him wider knowledge and larger ideas. To the ordinary Trade Unionist the claim of the workman is that of Justice. He believes, almost as a matter of principle, that in any dispute the capitalist is in the wrong and the workman in the right. But when, as a District Delegate, it becomes his business to be perpetually investigating the exact circumstances of the men's quarrels, negotiating with employers, and arranging compromises, he begins more and more to recognise that there is something to be urged on the other side. There is also an unconscious bias at work. Whilst the points at issue no longer affect his own earnings or conditions of employment, any disputes between his members and their employers increase his work and add to his worry. The former vivid sense of the privations and subjection of the artisan's life gradually fades from his mind ; and he begins more and more to regard all complaints as perverse and unreasonable.

With this intellectual change may come a more invidious transformation. Nowadays the salaried officer of a great Union is courted and flattered by the middle class. He is asked to dine with them, and will admire their well-appointed houses, their fine carpets, the ease and luxury of their lives. Possibly, too, his wife begins to be dissatisfied. She will point out how So-and-so, who served his apprenticeship in the same shop, is now well-off, and steadily making a fortune ; and she reminds her husband that, had he worked half as hard for himself as he has for others, he also might now be rich, and living in comfort without fear of the morrow. He himself sees the truth of this. He knows many men who, with less ability and energy than himself, have, by steady pursuit of their own ends, become foremen, managers, or even small employers, whilst he is receiving only £2 or £4 a week without any chance of increase. And so the remarks of his wife and her relations, the workings of his own mind, the increase of years, a growing desire to be settled in life and to see the future clear before him and his children, and perhaps also a little envy of his middle-class friends, all begin insidiously, silently, unknown even to himself, to work a change in his views of life. He goes to live in a little villa in a lower middle-class suburb. The move leads to his dropping his workmen friends ; and his wife changes her acquaintances. With the habits of his new neighbours he insensibly adopts more and more of their ideas. Gradually he finds himself at issue with his members, who no longer agree to his proposals with the old alacrity. All this comes about by degrees, neither party understanding the cause. He attributes the breach to the influences of a clique of malcontents, or perhaps to the wild views held by the younger generation. They think him proud and " stuck-up," over-cautious and even apathetic in trade affairs. His manner to his members, and particularly to the unemployed who call for donation, undergoes a change. He begins to look down upon them all as " common workmen " ; but the unemployed he scorns as men who have made a failure of their lives ; and his scorn is probably undisguised. This arouses hatred. As he walks to the office in his tall hat and good overcoat, with a smart umbrella, curses not loud but deep are muttered against him by members loitering in search of work, and as these get jobs in other towns they spread stories of his arrogance and haughtiness. So gradually he loses the sympathy and support of those upon whom his position depends. At last the climax comes. A great strike threatens to involve the Society in desperate war. Un-consciously biased by distaste for the hard and unthankful work which a strike entails, he finds himself in small sympathy with the men's demands, and eventually arranges a compromise on terms distasteful to a large section of his members. The gathering storm-cloud now breaks. At his next appearance before a general meeting cries of " treachery " and " bribery " are raised. Alas ! it is not bribery. Not his morality but his intellect is corrupted. Secure in the consciousness of freedom from out-ward taint, he faces the meeting boldly, throws the accusation back in their faces, and for the moment carries his point. But his position now becomes rapidly unbearable. On all sides he finds suspicion deepening into hatred. The members, it is true, re-elect him to his post ; but they elect at the same time an Executive Committee pledged to oppose him in every way.[1] All this time he still fails to understand what has gone wrong, and probably attributes it to the intrigues of jealous opponents eager for his place. Harassed on all sides, distrusted and thwarted by his Executive Committee, at length he loses heart. He looks out for some opening of escape, and finally accepting a small appointment, lays down his Secretaryship with heartfelt relief and disappears for ever from the Trade Union world.

The Trade Union official who became too genteel for his post was, like the habitual drunkard, an exception. The average Secretary or District Delegate was too shrewd to get permanently out of touch with his constituents. Nevertheless the working man who became a salaried officer had to pick his way with considerable care between the dangers attendant on the *rôle* of boon companion and those inseparable from the more reputable but more hated character of the superior person. To personal self-control he had to add strength and independence of character, a real devotion to the class from which he had sprung, and a sturdy contempt for the luxury and " gentility " of those with whom he was brought in contact. All this remains as true to-day as it was in 1892, but the general advance in education and sobriety, and the steady tendency towards an assimilation of manners among all classes, render the contrasts of the social nineteenth century daily less marked. The Trade Union official of 1920 finds it much easier to maintain a position of self-respecting courtesy both among his own members and among the employers, officials, and middle-class politicians with whom he is brought in contact.

We break off now to describe, in the following chapters, the development of the Trade Union Movement from 1890 to 1920, and to discuss some of its outstanding features.

[1] We have here another instance of the deeply rooted objection on the part of workmen to " sack " their officials. A Society will make the life of an unpopular official unbearable, and will thwart him in every direction ; but so long as he hangs on he has a safe berth.

CHAPTER IX

[1890–1920]

IN 1892, after more than two centuries of development, Trade Unionism in the United Kingdom numbered, as we have seen, little more than a million and a half of members, in a community approaching forty millions ; or about 4 per cent of the census population and including possibly 20 per cent of the adult male manual-working wage-earners. At the beginning of 1920, as we estimate, the number of Trade Unionists is well over six millions, in a community that does not quite reach forty-eight millions ; being over 12 per cent of the census population and including probably as many as 60 per cent [1] of all the adult male manual-working wage-

---

[1] It is doubtful whether, in any country in the world, even in Australia or Denmark, there is in 1920 so large a proportion of the adult male manual workers enrolled in Trade Unions as in the United Kingdom ; and—Ireland being still relatively unorganised industrially—certainly not so large a proportion as in Great Britain alone.

The Trade Union Movement in Ireland has, apart from the Irish branches of British Unions, largely concentrated in the Belfast area, little connection with that in Great Britain, but its progress during the past thirty years has been scarcely less remarkable. The Irish railwaymen have abandoned their attempts at organisation in an Irish Union, and have lately swarmed into the National Union of Railwaymen to the number of over 20,000. The engineers in Ireland, whether at Belfast or elsewhere, are, to the number of 9000, in the Amalgamated Society of Engineers and other British Unions. The other great Unions have nearly all their Irish branches. But the great transformation has been in the foundation and remarkable development of the Transport and General Workers' Union, built up by James Connolly and James Larkin, which

earners in the kingdom. With the exception of slight pauses in 1893–95, 1902–4, and 1908–9, this remarkable growth in aggregate membership has been continuous during the whole thirty years.

It is important to notice the continuous acceleration of this increase. For a few years after the high tide of 1889–92 the aggregate membership dropped slightly. When in 1897 it started to rise again it took a whole decade to add half a million to the total of 1892–96. Three years more brought a second half million : a total growth in the eighteen years from 1892 to 1910 of about a million, or only about 66 per cent. It then took only three or four years to add another million ; whilst during the last few years the increase has not fallen far short of half a million a year, or of the order of 10 per cent per annum. Trade Union membership has, in fact, doubled in the last eight years.[1]

---

has survived both its tremendous Dublin strike of 1913 and the loss of both its leaders, and claims in 1920 over 100,000 members in 400 branches, being half the Trade Unionists in all Ireland. The only other Irish Trade Unions exceeding 5000 members are the Flax Roughers' Union, included with other Unions in an Irish Textile Workers' Federation, and the Clerical Workers' Union, together with the Irish Teachers' Society, which (unlike the National Union of Teachers in England and the Educational Institute of Scotland) is frankly affiliated with the (Irish) Labour Party. Scores of other Irish Trade Unions exist, practically all small, local, and sectional in character, and almost confined to the ten towns of Dublin, Belfast, Cork, Limerick, Waterford, Dundalk, Derry, Clonmel, Sligo, and Kilkenny. The total Trade Union membership in Ireland, which thirty years ago was only put at 40,000, may now exceed 200,000, about one-fifth of which is in and about Belfast. The Irish Trades Union Congress, established in 1894, and the Irish Labour Party meet annually.

The Irish Trade Union Movement, emerging from handicraftsmen's local clubs, some of them dating from the middle of the eighteenth century, and monopolist and sectional in policy, has, during the present century, become fired with nationalist spirit and almost revolutionary fervour. Its heroes are Michael Davitt, James Connolly, and James Larkin. The story of the Transport and General Workers' Union, with its extraordinary extension to all grades of wage-earners all over Ireland, and its sensational strikes in Dublin in 1913–14, is an epic in itself. Some idea of this development may be gathered from *The Irish Labour Movement*, by W. P. Ryan, 1919 ; *Labour in Irish History*, by James Connolly ; *Socialism Made Easy*, by the same (about 1905) ; the Annual Reports of the Irish Trades Union Congress since 1895 ; and those of the Irish Labour Party.

[1] Statistics of aggregate membership in the past are lacking. But we

No less significant is the fact that the increase has not been confined to particular industries, particular localities, or a particular sex, but has taken place, more or less, over the whole field. It is common in varying degrees to the skilled, the semi-skilled, and the unskilled workers. Even the women, still much less organised than the men, have in 1920 five or six times as many Trade Unionists as they had thirty years previously; and have trebled or quadrupled the then proportion of Trade Union membership to the adult women manual-working wage-earners. Financially, too, the Trade Unions have, on the whole, greatly advanced; and their aggregate accumulated funds in 1920 (apart from the assets of their Approved Society sections under the National Insurance Act) exceed fifteen millions sterling; being about ten times as much as in 1890, and constituting a " fighting fund " unimaginably greater than ever entered the mind of Gast or Doherty, Martin Jude or William Newton, or any other Trade Union leader of the preceding century. It is the stages and incidents of this past thirty years' growth that we have now to describe. We shall refer incidentally to half-a-dozen of the more important strikes of the generation; but nowadays it is not so much industrial disputes that constitute landmarks of Trade Union history as the steps, often statutory or political in character, by which the Movement advances in public influence and in a recognised participation in the government of industry. During the present century, at any rate, the action of Trade Unionism on legislation, and of legislation on Trade Unionism, has been incessant and reciprocal. The growing strength of the Movement has been marked by a series of legislative changes which have ratified and legalised the increasing influence of the wage-earners' com-

---

suggest that after the transient mass enrolments of 1833–34 had lapsed, the total membership in Great Britain of such Trade Unions as survived probably did not reach 100,000. It is doubtful whether, as late as 1860, there were half a million Trade Unionists. We give in an Appendix such past statistics as we have found.

binations in the government both of industry and political relations. And every one of these statutes—notably the Trade Disputes Act of 1906, the Trade Boards Act of 1908, the Coal Mines Regulation (Eight Hours) Act of 1908, the National Insurance Act of 1911, the Trade Union Act of 1913, the Corn Production Act of 1917, and the Trade Boards Extension Act of 1918—have been marked by immediate extensions of Trade Union membership and improvements in Trade Union organisation in the industries concerned.

During the thirty years which have elapsed since 1890 the progress of the Trade Union Movement, enormous as it has been, has been accompanied by relatively little change in the internal structure of the several Unions. What has occurred has been a marked change in the relative position and influence of the different sections of the Trade Union world, and even in its composition. Some sections have declined relatively to others. Even more significant is the vastly greater consolidation of the Trade Unionism of 1920 than that of 1890. Not only have many more of the societies grown into organisations of numerical and financial strength, but there has also been developed, especially during recent years, an interesting network of federations among Unions in the same industry, and often among cognate or associated industries, some of which, undertaking negotiations on a national scale for a whole industry, have become more influential and important than any but the largest Unions.

THE COTTON OPERATIVES

The most notable of these changes is the decline in relative influence of the cotton operatives. It is not that the Unions of Spinners, Weavers and Cardroom Operatives have decreased in membership or in accumulated funds. On the contrary, they have in the aggregate during the past thirty years more than doubled their membership ; and the

Amalgamated Association of Operative Cotton Spinners, with three-quarters of a million pounds belonging to its 25,000 members (exclusive of 26,000 piecers), is, now as formerly, the wealthiest Trade Union of any magnitude. Nor have these Unions in any sense lost their hold on their own trade, at least in its central district of Lancashire and Cheshire, though its outlying areas in Derbyshire, Yorkshire, and Glasgow are still somewhat neglected. But the growth of Trade Unionism in other industries has reduced the " Cotton Men " from ten or twelve to four or five per cent of the Trades Union Congress ; and, owing partly to internal differences, their leading personalities no longer dominate the counsels of the Movement. The excellent organisation of the Cotton Trade Unions has been maintained ; but it has not been copied by other trades, and their internecine dissensions have detracted from the influence of their various federations. There has been, in fact, during the whole thirty years, only two or three important incidents. A general strike of cotton-spinners took place in 1893, when all the mills were stopped for no less than twenty weeks. The employers had demanded a reduction of 10 per cent, whilst the Trade Union urged that the depression should be met by placing all the mills on short time. This stoppage was at last brought to an end by agreement between the employers and the Trade Union, arrived at without external intervention in a fourteen hours continuous session, which made the reduction in rates only 7d. in the £ (2·916 instead of 10 per cent), and included elaborate arrangements for future adjustment of wages and other differences by mutual discussion without cessation of work.[1] This " Brooklands Agreement," which we described in our *Industrial Democracy*, governed the spinning trade from 1893 to 1905, but was in the latter year formally terminated by the Unions concerned, on the ground that the machinery worked both slowly and in such a way as to hamper the operatives in obtaining the advantage of

[1] *Industrial Democracy*, pp. 38, 92, 103, 123, 258, etc.

good times. Provisional arrangements were made, but these did not prevent a strike of seven weeks in 1908, which ended in a compromise advantageous to the operatives. Apart from minor and local disputes, frequently about bad material or refusal to work with a non-Unionist, there was, however, no forward movement, notably with regard to the hours of labour. In 1902 a slight amendment of the Factory Act was secured by agreement with the employers, by which the factory week was reduced from 56½ to 55½ hours ; and with this the trade remained contented. Right down to 1919 there was no important trade movement, but in February of that year all sections of the cotton operatives claimed their share in the general reduction of hours that was proceeding ; and, after prolonged negotiations, 300,000 operatives struck in June. When it was seen that the stoppage of the mills had become general, the employers gave way and conceded a Forty-eight Hours week, which has not yet been embodied in law, accompanied by a 30 per cent advance in piece rates so as to involve no reduction of earnings.

The organisation of the cotton operatives, whilst remaining essentially as described in our *Industrial Democracy*, has gone on increasing in federal complexity. The various sections—notably spinners with their attendant piecers ; weavers, including winders, and in some towns also warpers, beamers, and reelers ; card, blowing and ring-room operatives ; warp-dressers and warpers ; tape-sizers ; beamers, twisters and drawers ; and overlookers—continue to be organised in very autonomous local bodies, which are styled sometimes societies or associations, and sometimes merely branches, and which vary in number in the different sections from half-a-dozen to ten times as many. But these are nearly all doubly united, first in a federal body for the whole of each section (which may be styled an amalgamation, a federation, an association, or a General Union of the section), and also in a local " Cotton Trades Federation " or " Textile Trades Federation," which combines the local organisations of the weavers and sometimes other sections in each of a couple of dozen geographical districts in Lancashire and Cheshire. The weavers' " amalgamation," and other sections of the " manufacturing " trade, are further united in the Northern Counties Amalgamated Association, with 175,000 members. Finally, all the federal organisations of the several sections are brought together in the United Textile Factory Workers' Association, which focuses the opinion of all the cotton operatives, including the Amalgamated Association of Bleachers and Dyers, on those fundamental issues on which they are conscious of a common and an equal interest.[1]

The officials of the Cotton Trade Unions—herein differing from those of the greatly developed General Union of Textile Workers, which has organised the (principally women) woollen weavers—have remained predominantly technicians, devot-

---

[1] The Amalgamated Association of Card and Blowing Room Operatives is (1920) once more a member. A further development of federal complexity is the formation of a Federation of Kindred Trades connected with the Export Shipping Industry of Manchester.

An invidious feature, in which the textile industry is unique, is the appearance during the present century, as the result of a quarrel as to " political action," of half-a-dozen separate local Trade Unions of weavers, largely Roman Catholic, at one time united in the Lancashire Federation of Protection Societies. These, which are neither numerous nor of extensive membership, remain outside the Amalgamated Association of Weavers ; and are watchful critics of any proposals, at the Trades Union Congress (to which they do not seek admission) or elsewhere, that offend the Roman Catholic Church (notably any suggestion of " Secular Education," or educational changes deemed inimical to the Roman Catholic schools). There is a National Conference of Catholic Trade Unionists having similar objects.

There was, in 1919, also a Jewish National Labour Council of Great Britain ; and from time to time Unions are formed, especially in the clothing trade (such as the Amalgamated Jewish Tailors, Machinists, and Pressers, established 1893), and in baking and cabinetmaking, aiming at enrolling Jewish workers. But this is not really a religious, or even primarily a racial, cleavage, but merely sectional organisation, usually transient, among particular branches of industry which happen to be principally carried on by Jews. At present most such societies in the clothing trade have been absorbed in the United Garment Workers' Trade Union, which, with upwards of 100,000 members, is actively negotiating for a merger with the older Amalgamated Society of Tailors and Tailoresses (established 1865) and the effective Scottish Operative Tailors' and Tailoresses' Association, with 5000 members, under the title of the United Tailors and Garment Workers.

ing themselves almost entirely to the protection of their members' trade interests, without taking much part in the wider interests now largely influencing the Trade Union world, and showing little sympathy either in larger federations or in the new spirit. They have been slow to take an active part in the political development of the Trade Union world, which has manifested itself, as we shall describe in a subsequent chapter, in the organisation of the Labour Party. This backwardness may be ascribed, in some degree, to the political history of Lancashire, where an ancestral Conservatism still lingers, and where it was possible, even in the twentieth century, for so prominent a Trade Union official as the late James Mawdsley, the able leader of the cotton-spinners, to stand for Parliament in 1906 as a member of the Conservative Party. The influence of an exceptionally large proportion of Roman Catholics among the cotton operatives must also be noted. It is a unique feature of the technical officials of the Cotton Unions that they have frequently been willing to serve the industry as the paid officials of the Employers' Associations when they have been offered higher salaries. Their main duty, whether acting for the employers or the workmen, is to secure uniformity in the application of the Collective Agreements as between mill and mill ; and such a duty, it is argued, like that of the valuer or accountant, is independent of personal opinion or bias, and can be rendered with equal fidelity to either client. This was not at first resented by the workmen, who even saw some advantage in the Employers' Association being served by officers thoroughly acquainted with the complicated technicalities as the operatives saw them. There has, however, latterly been a change of feeling; and though such transfers of services cannot be prevented (the Employers' Associations constantly finding the Trade Union official the best man available), they are now resented.[1]

---

[1] A recent case in which the Trade Union Assistant Secretary left the weavers for the employers, in the midst of a crisis, with the Union affairs in confusion, was stigmatised as desertion.

It is felt in some quarters that many of the " cotton men " have fallen out of harmony with the newer currents of thought in the Trade Union world. It is alleged that they accept too implicitly the employers' assumptions, and do not sympathise with aspirations of more fundamental change than a variation of wages or hours. But the influence of the " cotton men " is, in the Trade Union world, still important for their specific contribution, to Trade Union theory and practice, of equal piecework rates for both sexes ; of a rigid refusal to allow an employer to make the inferiority either of any workers or of any machines that he chooses to employ an excuse for deductions from the Standard Rate, and of the utmost possible improvement of machinery so long as the piecework rates are strictly controlled by Collective Bargaining and firmly embodied in rigidly enforced lists—points on which many Trade Unionists who would deem themselves " advanced " have not yet attained the same level.[1]

[1] The workers in the woollen and worsted trades, whose organisation went to pieces early in the nineteenth century on the extensive introduction of women and the successive transformations of the industry by machinery, have, during the past thirty years, developed extensive Trade Unions, which have steadily gained strength. In 1892 we could count only 18,000 Trade Unionists in the whole industry. In 1920, whilst the National Society of Woolcombers and Kindred Trades has 12,000 members and there are strong organisations of wool-sorters, warp-dressers, and over-lookers, the General Union of Textile Workers, established in 1881, now includes a membership, in the West of England as well as in Yorkshire, principally male and female weavers, numbering more than 100,000 (*The Heavy Woollen District Textile Workers' Union*, by Ben Turner, 1917). During the war these Unions were accorded equal representation with the employers and with the Government on the Wool Control Board, by which the Government supplies of wool were " rationed " among the manufacturers, and the prices fixed.

In the dyeing and finishing branch of the textile industry the Amalgamated Society of Dyers, Bleachers, Finishers, and Kindred Trades (established 1878), with 30,000 members, has outstripped the older National Society of Dyers and Finishers (established 1851 ; 12,000 members), and has entered into remarkable agreements with the monopolist combination of employers. (The Amalgamated Association of Bleachers and Dyers, centred at Bolton, which has over 22,000 members, occupies a similar leading position as regards the dyeing of cotton goods.) A recently formed National Association of Unions in the Textile Trades seeks to co-ordinate the influence of all the woollen workers and dyers, and counts a member-

The Building Trades

The Building Trades have lost their relative position in the Trade Union world to nearly as great an extent as the cotton operatives. Thirty years ago their representatives stood for 10 per cent of the Trades Union Congress, whereas to-day they probably do not represent 3 per cent of its membership. They have, for a whole generation, supplied no influential leader. The only large society in this section, the Amalgamated Society of Carpenters, Cabinetmakers, and Joiners (133,000 members), has more than doubled its membership since 1890, drawing in various small societies of cabinetmakers, and carpenters, but not yet the older General Union of Carpenters and Joiners, which counts 15,000 members ; and so, too, has the small but solid United Operative Plumbers' Society, with 14,000 members—neither of them, however, commanding the allegiance of anything like the whole of its craft. The numerous small societies of painters have, for the most part, drawn themselves together in the National Amalgamated Society of Operative House and Ship Painters and Decorators (30,000 members) ; whilst the National Amalgamated Furnishing Trades Association (12,500 members) represents a union of many small societies. Altogether the Trade Unions in the building trades, including all the little local societies, have probably done no more than double their membership of 1892, and the increase has been relatively least in the most skilled grades. This is due, in part, to an actual decline in the trade, the total numbers enumerated in the 1911 census being actually less than in that of 1901, the fall being even greater down to 1919, when it was estimated that only seven-twelfths as many men were at work at building as in 1901.

The story of the Building Trade Unions during the

---

ship of about 150,000, in 35 societies, which are grouped in four sections (" Raw Wool," " Managers and Overlookers," " Textile Workers," and " Dyers' Societies ").

thirty years is one of innumerable small sectional and local disputes with their employers—taking the form, during 1913, of repeated sudden strikes in the London area against non-Unionists, forced on by the " hot-heads " and discountenanced by the Executive Committees, and leading, in 1914, to a general lock-out by the London Master Builders' Association. The employers demanded that the Trade Unions should penalise members who struck without authority, and that the Unions should put up a pecuniary deposit which might be forfeited when a strike occurred in violation of the Working Rules. They also insisted on each workman signing a personal agreement to work quietly with non-Unionists, under penalty of a fine of 20s. In the lock-out that ensued the whole building trade of the Metropolis was stopped for over six months. Efforts at a settlement in June were rejected on ballot of the operatives ; and whilst signs of weakening occurred among the operatives the National Federation of Building Trade Employers had decided on a national lock-out throughout the kingdom in order to secure the employers' terms, when the outbreak of war brought the struggle to an end, and work was resumed practically on the old conditions.

During the war, when the bulk of the operatives were enrolled in the army, and building was restricted to the most urgently needed works, disputes remained in abeyance. At the beginning of 1918 a new start was made in the organisation of the industry by the establishment of a National Federation of Building Trade Operatives, itself a development from a previous National Building Trades Council, in which all the national Trade Unions, 13 in number, for the first time joined together. Notwithstanding great differences in numerical strength, the Unions agreed to constitute the Federation Executive of two representatives from each national union. The Federation is formed of local branches, each of which is composed of the branches in the locality of the nationally affiliated Unions, governed by the aggregate of the " Trades Management Committee " of such branches, acting under the direction and control of the Federation Executive. A significant new feature, recalling an expedient of the Trade Unionism of 1834, is the establishment of " Composite Branches " of individual building trades operatives in localities where no branch of the separate national unions exists. What success may attend this renewed effort at unified national organisation of the whole industry it is impossible to predict ; there are signs of a movement for actual amalgamation. The four principal Builders' Labourers' Unions are on the point of uniting in a strong amalgamation with 40,000 members. Other attempts at amalgamation, including one among the " house builders," the societies of bricklayers, masons and plasterers, have been voted. The Furnishing Trades Association was only prevented from merging in the Amalgamated Society of Carpenters by technical difficulties. On the other hand the separate Scottish and Irish Unions (except for the merging of the Associated Carpenters) stubbornly maintain their independence. Down to the present it must be said that combination in the building trades, torn by internecine conflicts and financially weakened by unsuccessful strikes, has, on the whole, been falling back. The gradual change of processes, and the introduction of new materials, with an actual decline in the numbers employed, has not been met by any improvement in the organisation of the older craft unions, whilst the workers in the new processes have failed to achieve effective union. With the great demand for building since the Armistice, the Building Trades Unions have, however, shown increased vitality ; and the position in the negotiating Joint Boards, at which they are now regularly meeting the employers' representatives, has considerably improved. The latest achievement of the industry is the establishment, jointly with the employers, of a " Builders' Parliament "—largely at the instance of Mr. Malcolm Sparkes—which is the most noteworthy example of the " Whitley Councils," to which we shall refer later.

ENGINEERING AND THE METAL TRADES

The large and steadily increasing army of operatives in the various processes connected with metals (who are combined in Germany in a single gigantic Metal Workers' Union) can be noticed here only in its three principal sections, the engineering industry, boilermaking and shipbuilding, and the production of iron and steel from the ore.

Trade Unionism in the engineering industry, though it has, during the past thirty years, greatly increased in aggregate membership, notably among the unskilled and semi-skilled workmen employed in engineering shops, can hardly be said to have grown in strength, whether manifested in effect upon the engineering employers, who have become very strongly combined throughout the whole kingdom, or in influence in the Trade Union world. This relative decline must be ascribed to the continued lack of any systematic organisation of the industry as a whole ; to a failure to cope with the changing processes and systems of remuneration which the employers have introduced ; and to the persistence of internecine war among the rival Unions themselves.

The trouble in the engineering world came to a head in 1897, precipitated perhaps by the employers, who wanted, as they said, to be " masters in their own shops." The Amalgamated Society of Engineers, which had maintained its predominant position among the engineering workmen, but only commanded the allegiance of a part of them, after a series of bickerings with the employers about the technical improvement of the industry, in which the workmen had shown themselves, to say the least, very conservative, found itself involved in a general strike and lock-out in all the principal engineering centres, nominally about the London engineering workmen's precipitate demand for an Eight Hours Day, but substantially over the employers' insistence on being masters in their own workshops, entitled to introduce what new methods of working they chose, and whatever new systems of remuneration according to results that they could persuade the several workmen to accept. The Union, to which apparently it did not occur to use the methods of publicity on which William Newton and John Burnett would have relied, failed to make clear its case to the public ; and public opinion was accordingly against the engineering workmen, believing them to be at the same time obstructive to industrial improvements and unable to formulate conditions that would safeguard their legitimate interests. The result was that the prolonged stoppage, which reduced the funds of the A.S.E. down to what only sufficed to meet the accrued liabilities for Superannuation Benefit, ended in a virtual victory for the employers. The A.S.E. quickly resumed its growth and stood, in the autumn of 1919, at 320,000 members, or over five times its membership of 1892. But the sectional societies also increased in size, and down to 1919 they counted in the aggregate, as in 1892, about half as many members as the A.S.E. itself.[1] Meanwhile, the great development of the engineering industry, and the successive changes in the machinery employed, have been accompanied by the introduction of various forms of " Payment by Results," in which the engineering Trade Unions have not known how to prevent the reintroduction of individual bargaining. Owing to its quarrels with the various sectional societies in the industry, the A.S.E. has been alternately in and out of the Trades Union Congress ; and, on general issues, has seldom sought to influence the Trade Union world as much as its magnitude and position would have entitled it to do. The same may be said of the other Trade

[1] The history of the struggles in the engineering industry may be gathered from the monthly *Journal* of the A.S.E. and the Annual Reports of this and other engineering Trade Unions ; from the references in *Engineering* and other employers' periodicals. For the lock-out of 1897, see also the *Times* and *Labour Gazette* for that year, and also an anonymous volume, *The Engineering Strike*, 1897. See also for some of the points at issue, *Industrial Democracy*, by S. and B. Webb, 1897 ; *An Introduction to Trade Unionism*, by G. D. H. Cole, 1917, and *The Works Manager To-day*, by Sidney Webb, 1918.

Unions in the engineering industry, which were contented to hold their own against their greater rival, and to see their membership progress with the growth of the industry itself.

The elaborate constitution of the Amalgamated Society of Engineers, which we described in a preceding chapter, has been, during the past thirty years, repeatedly tinkered with by delegate meetings, but without being substantially changed. There has been a perpetual balance and deadlock of opinion, which has led to successive modifications and reactions. Alongside the skilled engineering craftsmen, of different specialities in technique, there has grown up a vast number of unapprenticed and semi-skilled men, whom the Union has failed to exclude, not only from the workshops but also from the jobs formerly monopolised by the legitimate craftsmen. Should these interlopers be admitted to membership ? At one delegate meeting (1912) the rules were altered so as to admit (" Class F ") not only all varieties of skilled engineering craftsmen, but also practically any one working in an engineering shop. This was counteracted by the tacit refusal of most branches to carry out the decision of their own delegates ; and " Class F," which never obtained as many as 2000 members, was abolished by the next delegate meeting (1915.) The method of remuneration has been another bone of contention. Especially since the disastrous conflict of 1897, the employers have more and more insisted on the adoption of systems of " payment by results " instead of the weekly time rates, to which the engineering operatives, like those of most of the building trades, devotedly cling. What is to be the Union policy with regard to these varieties of piecework and " premium bonus " systems ? Failing to discover any device by which (as among the cotton operatives, the boot and shoe makers, and the Birmingham brassworkers) " payment by results " can be effectively safeguarded by being subjected to collective bargaining, the Amalgamated Society of Engineers has wavered, in its decisions and in the policy of its various districts, between (*a*) refusing to allow any other system than timework ; (*b*) limiting systems of payment by results to " those shops in which they have already been introduced " ; (*c*) insisting, as a condition of permitting payment by results, on the " Principle of Mutuality," which amounts to no more than the claim that the workman shall not have the piecework rates or " bonus times " arbitrarily imposed upon him, but shall be permitted individually to bargain with the foreman or rate-fixer for better terms. The result is a chaos of inconsistent customs and practices varying from shop to shop ; and withal, a tendency to a continuous decline in piecework rates (mitigated only by the greater or less extent to which collective " shop bargaining " prevails, and by its efficiency) which leads, in sullen resentment, to " ca' canny," or slow working. The third bone of contention has been how to deal with the competing Trade Unions, which are either societies of varieties of skilled engineers who prefer to remain unabsorbed in the A.S.E., or societies of new classes of operatives such as machine workers, workers in brass and copper, electrical craftsmen, and others, with whom the A.S.E. found itself disputing the control of the industry. Should these much smaller organisations be (*a*) ignored and their members treated as non-unionists ; or (*b*) admitted to joint deliberation and action in trade matters with the view to formulating a common policy ; or (*c*) dealt with by amalgamation on a still broader basis than that of the A.S.E. ? It would be useless to trace the results of the ebb and flow of these contrary views, which were, in the autumn of 1919, for the time being, partly reconciled by an agreement by which six of the competing Unions [1] are in 1920, with the A.S.E.,

---

[1] The Unions which, along with the A.S.E., ratified the agreement were the Steam Engine Makers' Society, the United Machine Workers' Association, the United Kingdom Society of Amalgamated Smiths and Strikers, the Associated Brassfounders and Coppersmiths' Society, the North of England Brass Turners' Society, and the London United Metal Turners, Fitters and Finishers, having an aggregate membership of 70,000.

The societies which failed to secure ratification on the members' vote, in some cases merely by the failure to obtain a sufficiently large poll, were to be merged in the Amalgamated Engineering Union with a membership of 400,000 and accumulated funds amounting to nearly four millions sterling. It remains to be seen whether this wider amalgamation will bring to engineering Trade Unionism the formulation of a systematic policy, national organisation, and competent leadership.

Underlying all these issues, and aggravating all the disputes to which they give rise, is the fundamental divergence between those who insist on an extreme local autonomy— the district being free to strike, and free to refuse to settle a local strike,—and those who maintain the importance of a national unity in trade policy, and the necessity, with centralised funds, of centralised control. Still more keen is the controversy between those who wish to maintain the present craftsmen's organisation, and those who seek to enlarge it into an organisation comprising all the workers in the industry, whether skilled or unskilled. During the past decade the discontent against the Central Executive, especially on the Clyde, has led to a so-called " rank and file " movement ; the development of the shop steward from a mere " card inspector " and membership recruiting officer into an aggressive strike leader ; and the joining together of the shop stewards (as at Glasgow, Sheffield, and Coventry) into such new forms of organisation as the " Clyde Workers' Committee," actively promoting their own local trade policies irrespective of the views of the Union as a whole.

---

the Amalgamated Toolmakers' Society, the Electrical Trades Union, the United Brass Founders and Finishers' Association, the Amalgamated Instrument Makers' Society, the United Pattern Makers' Association, the Associated Smiths and Strikers, the National Brassworkers and Metal Mechanics, the Association of Engineering and Shipbuilding Draughtsmen, and the Scale and Beam Makers' Society, with something like 100,000 members in the aggregate. Probably some of these will take another vote in the near future.

The old-established Friendly Society of Ironfounders (35,000 members) continues quite apart, though joining freely in engineering trade movements. An unusually protracted national strike in 1919, which is likely to end in a compromise, may possibly lead to proposals for closer union.

The " Shop Stewards' Movement," which assumed some importance in the engineering industry in 1915–19, was a new development of an old institution in Trade Unionism— we have referred elsewhere to the " Father of the Chapel " among the compositors, and to the checkweighman among the coal-miners — which acquired a special importance owing to the growing lack of correspondence between the membership of the Trade Union Branch or District Council and the grouping of the workmen in the different establishments, and also from the fact that the workmen in each establishment found themselves belonging to different Trade Unions. " The shop steward," it has been pointed out, " was originally a minor official appointed from the men in a particular workshop and charged with the duty of seeing that all the Trade Union contributions were paid. He had other small duties. But gradually, as the branch got more and more out of touch with the men in the shop, these men came to look to the official who was on the spot to represent their grievances. During the war the development of the shop steward movement was very rapid, particularly in the engineering industry. In some big industrial concerns, composed of a large number of workshops, the committees of stewards from the various shops very largely took over the whole conduct of negotiations and arrangement of shop conditions. Further, a national organisation of shop stewards was formed, at first mainly for propagandist purposes. The existing unions have considered some of the activities of shop stewards to be unofficial, and there has been a good deal of dissension within the unions on this score. Attempts have been made to reach an agreement by which Shop Stewards' Committees shall be fully recognised at once by the unions and by the managements. So far there has been no final settlement. An agreement was made in the early summer of 1919 between the Engineering Employers' Federation and the Unions ; how this will work in practice is not yet certain." [1]

[1] *Trade Unionism : a New Model*, by R. Page Arnot, 1919 ; and

R 2

It must, in fact, be said that although the Engineering Trade Unions have during the past thirty years not taken much part in general Trade Union issues, they have (in contrast with some other sections) contributed freely in both men and ideas. We have already dwelt upon the activities of Mr. John Burns and Mr. Tom Mann. We shall mention the political progress of Mr. George Barnes, who is also of the A.S.E. ; whilst the Friendly Society of Iron-founders has given Mr. Arthur Henderson to the Movement. And, in the long run possibly more important even than men, the ideas emanating from the engineering workshops have had a more than proportionate share in the ferment of these years. The vacancy in the office of General Secretary, occasioned by the election to the House of Commons of Mr. Robert Young, was filled in the autumn of 1919 by the election of Mr. Tom Mann ; and this election, together with the great amalgamation of competing Unions brought about at the same time, may perhaps open up a new era in engineering Trade Unionism.

In contrast with the failure of Trade Unionism in the engineering trades either to develop a systematic organisation or to cope with the changes in processes and methods of remuneration, the two powerful Unions of boilermakers and shipwrights have gone from strength to strength, doubling their numbers, absorbing practically all the remaining local societies in their industry, and closely combining with each other in policy and other activities, concluding, indeed, in the autumn of 1919 an agreement to submit to their respective memberships a proposal for a

---

various pamphlets printed at Glasgow, etc.. Some " extremist " thinkers among workmen have put their hopes of achieving the " Industrial Democracy " that they desire upon a development of the Shop Stewards' Movement, which should become, together with a " Works Committee," the instrument of transferring the management of each undertaking from its present capitalist owners and directors to the elected representatives of the persons employed. See *The Workers' Committee, an Outline of its Principles and Structures*, by J. T. Murphy (1918), and *Compromise or Independence, an Examination of the Whitley Report* (1918), by the same, both published by the Sheffield Workers' Committee.

formal amalgamation which may be joined by the strong society of Associated Blacksmiths. This would mean the consolidation, in one powerful Union of 170,000 members, of practically all the skilled craftsmen working in the construction of the hulls of ships, of boilers and tanks, and of steel bridge-work of all sorts. Concentrated largely in the ports of the north-east coast and those of the Clyde, with strong contingents in the relatively small number of other shipbuilding centres, the boilermakers and shipwrights have held their own in face of all the changes in their industry, and have known how to maintain a fairly uniform national policy.

Passing from engineering and shipbuilding to the smelting of the iron and steel from the ore, the one marked advance in organisation is that of the British Steel Smelters, which, established in 1886, and in 1892 having still only 2600 members, had by 1918, under the prudent leadership of Mr. John Hodge, drawn to itself over 40,000. The British steel smelters have the credit of equipping themselves with the most efficient office in the Trade Union world, with a real statistical department and a trained staff, including, for all their legal business, especially that connected with compensation for accidents, a qualified professional solicitor. Already before the outbreak of war a far-seeing policy of amalgamation had been virtually decided on ; and in 1915 a scheme was prepared for the merging of all the six important Unions in the industry of obtaining the metal from the ore, including the operatives in the tinplate and rolling mills. The plan for surmounting the legal and other difficulties of amalgamation, of which we may ascribe the authorship to Mr. John Hodge, Mr. Pugh, and Mr. Percy Cole, the able officials of the British Steel Smelters' Union, was one of extreme ingenuity as involving no more than a bare majority of the members voting, which deserves the attention of other societies as a " New Model." Three only out of the six societies (the British Steel Smelters' Association, the Associated Iron and Steel Workers of Great Britain, and the National Steel Workers' Association) were able to go forward in 1917,[1] when a new society, the British Iron, Steel, and Kindred Trades Association, was formed. The four societies then created the Iron and Steel Trades Confederation, to which they formally ceded powers and functions affecting the members of more than one of the constituent bodies, and therefore all general negotiations with the employers. The three old societies continued formally in existence, but they bound themselves not to enrol any new members, who were all to be taken by the new society, to which all the existing members were to be continuously urged to transfer themselves voluntarily. This process has already gone so far that the new society has swallowed up the British Steel Smelters' Society, which has been wound up and completely merged in the new body, into which the empty shells of the other two old bodies will presently fall. The Iron and Steel Trades Confederation will then be composed of one society only, and may be kept alive only to serve the same transitional purpose for other incoming societies.

THE COMPOSITORS

The printing trades have remained, during the past thirty years, curiously stationary so far as Trade Unionism is concerned, the London Society of Compositors, the Typographical Association, the Scottish Typographical Association, and the Dublin Typographical Society having, in the aggregate, increased their membership by three-fifths and steadily increased their rates of pay and strategic strength against their own employers, but commanding little influence in the Trade Union Movement as a whole, and in many small towns still leaving a considerable portion of the trade out-

---

[1] The Amalgamated Society of Steel and Ironworkers and the Tin and Sheet Millmen's Association failed to secure their members' ratification by vote, whilst the National Association of Blastfurnacemen withheld its adhesion. These may be expected to adhere in due course.

side their ranks. The less-skilled workers in the papermaking and printing establishments have greatly improved
their organisation ; and the National Union of Printing and
Paper Workers and the Operative Printers Assistants' Society
—both of them including women as well as men—have
become large and effective Trade Unions. All the societies
are united in the powerful Printing and Kindred Trades
Federation, to which the National Union of Journalists,
now a large society, has recently affiliated.

Boot and Shoemaking

Among the other constituents of the Trade Union world
in which a relative decline in influence is to be noted, is
that of the boot and shoemakers. Thirty years ago the
National Union of Boot and Shoe Operatives had achieved
a position of great influence in the trade. It had joined
with the Employers' Associations in building up, as described in our *Industrial Democracy*, an elaborate system
of Local Boards of Conciliation and Arbitration, united
in a National Conference of dignity and influence, with
resort to Lord James of Hereford as umpire, by means of
which stoppages of work were prevented, and, more important still, the illegitimate use of boy labour was restrained
and standard piecework rates were arrived at by collective
bargaining, and authoritatively imposed on the whole trade.
In 1894 the whole machinery was broken up, at the instance
of the very employers who had agreed to it, and had co-
operated for years in its working, because they found that,
under the rules and at the piecework rates prescribed, the
men were " making too much."

After a prolonged stoppage in 1894 the dispute was
patched up by the intervention of the Labour Department
of the Board of Trade ; and the National Union of Boot
and Shoe Operatives, with 80,000 members, has, on the
whole, held its own with the employers, with less elaborate
formal relations ; but the work of the Union is impaired

by the weakness of the organisation in the smaller workshops and the less important local centres of the trade.

On the other side, we have the rise to influence, not only in the Trade Union counsels but also in those of the nation, of the Women Workers, the General Labourers, the " black-coated proletariat " of shop assistants, clerks, teachers, technicians, and officials, the miners and the railwaymen, which has been the outstanding feature of the past thirty years.

Women Workers

In no section of the industrial community has the advance of Trade Unionism during the last thirty years been more marked than among the women workers. For the first half of this period, indeed—though the aggregate women membership of Trade Unions approximately doubled —this meant only a rise from about 100,000 in 1890 to about 200,000 in 1907, mostly in the textile industries ; and the number of women Trade Unionists outside those industries was in the latter year still under 30,000. But the long-continued patient work of the Women's Trade Union League was having its effect ; and the idea of Trade Unionism was being established among the women workers in many different industries. Much is to be ascribed to the efforts during these years of Sir Charles and Lady Dilke, who were unwearied in their assistance. In 1909, largely at the instance of Sir Charles Dilke and the women's leaders, especially Miss Mary Macarthur, Miss Gertrude Tuckwell, and Miss Susan Lawrence, Mr. Winston Churchill, as President of the Board of Trade, carried through Parliament the Trade Boards Bill, which enabled a legal minimum wage to be prescribed by joint boards in four specially low-paid industries, in which mainly women were employed. This measure not only considerably improved the position of the sweated workers in the chain and nail trades, the slop tailoring trade, paper box making and machine lace-making, but—as had been predicted on one side and denied on the other—greatly stimulated independent organisation among the women whose industrial status was raised. The extension of the Trade Boards and of the legal minimum wage in 1913 to half a dozen other trades had like effects, and the further extension of 1918 is already promising in the same direction. Trade Union membership was further greatly increased during 1912–14 as a result of the National Insurance Act, which brought many thousand recruits to the Approved Society sections of the Unions. It was, however, the Great War, with its unprecedented demand for women workers, and their admission, in " dilution " of or in substitution for men, to all sorts of occupations and processes into which they had not previously penetrated, at earnings which they had never before been permitted to receive, that brought the women into Trade Unionism by the hundred thousand. The National Federation of Women Workers—the largest exclusively feminine Union—rose from 11,000 in 1914 to over 60,000 in 1919. A small number of new Trade Unions exclusively for women were established in particular sections, such as the interesting little society of Women Acetylene Welders. The bulk of the women, however, continued to be organised in Trade Unions admitting both sexes. Besides the various Textile Unions, there are now thousands of women in the National Union of Railwaymen, the Railway Clerks' Association, Boot and Shoe Operatives, and the Iron and Steel Trades Confederation. Most of the general labour Unions, and others like the National Union of Printing and Paper Workers, the National Union of Shop Assistants, Warehousemen and Clerks, the Amalgamated Union of Co-operative and Commercial Employees and Allied Workers, had for a couple of decades been enrolling women members ; and the female membership of these societies now grew by leaps and bounds. But the greater part of the field of women's employment is still uncovered. In 1920, though it may be estimated that the total women membership of Trade Unions is nearly three-quarters of a million, this still represents less than 30 per cent of the adult women wage-earners.

The outstanding feature in women's Trade Unionism during the past decade has been its advance, not merely in numbers and achievements, but also in status and influence. This has come with accelerating speed. To the first Treasury Conference in 1915, at which the Government sought the help of the Trade Unions in the winning of the war, it apparently did not occur to any official to invite the National Federation of Women Workers ; but in all subsequent proceedings of the same nature Miss Mary Macarthur and Miss Susan Lawrence, on behalf of the women Trade Unionists in this and other societies, occupied a leading position. Whether before the Munitions Act Tribunals, the Committee on Production, or the Special Arbitration Tribunal set up by the Government to deal with the conditions of employment of women munition-workers, the women's case, whether put by the representatives of the Women's Unions, or by those of the principal Unions of general workers that included women, was so ably conducted as to secure for the women workers, almost for the first time, something like the same measure of justice as that which the men had wrested from the employers for themselves. The result was not only a marked rise in the standard of remuneration for women, the opening up to them of many fields of work from which they had hitherto been excluded, and a general improvement in their conditions of employment, but also a rapid development of Trade Unionism among them—nine-tenths of the women Trade Unionists being in societies enrolling both men and women—and the winning, for women's Trade Unions, of the respect of the Trade Union world. For the first time a woman was elected in 1919 by the Trades Union Congress to its Parliamentary Committee, Miss Margaret Bondfield, of the National Federation of Women Workers, receiving over three million votes. On the reconstitution in 1918 of the Labour Party, in which women had always been accorded equal rights, provision was made so that there should always be at least four women elected to the Executive Committee. A Standing Joint Committee of Women's Industrial Organisations, established in 1916, now initiates and co-ordinates the action of the principal women's Trade Unions, the Women's Co-operative Guild (which organises the women of the Co-operative movement), the Railway Women's Guild, composed of the wives of railwaymen, and the Women's Labour League, now the women's section of the Labour Party itself.

The General Workers

In 1888 the leaders of the skilled craftsmen and better-paid workmen were inclined to believe that effective or durable Trade Unionism among the general labourers and unskilled or nondescript workmen was as impracticable as it had hitherto proved to be among the mass of women wage-earners. The outburst of Trade Unionism among the dockers and gasworkers in 1888–89 was commonly expected to be as transient as analogous movements had been in 1834 and 1871. In 1920 we find the organisations of this despised section, some of them of over thirty years' standing, accounting for no less than 30 per cent of the whole Trade Union membership, and their leaders—notably Mr. Clynes, Mr. Thorne, and Mr. Robert Williams—exercising at least their full share of influence in the counsels of the Trade Union Movement as a whole. For a few years after 1889, indeed, the aggregate membership of the newly-formed labourers' Unions declined, and some of the weaker ones collapsed, or became merged in the larger societies. But the Gasworkers' and General Labourers' Union (established 1889), which changed its name in 1918 to the National Union of General Workers; and the Dock, Wharf, Riverside and General Workers' Union (established 1887) maintained themselves in existence; and already in 1907 there were as many as 150,000 organised labourers in half-a-dozen well-established societies. The outburst of Trade Unionism among the farm labourers in 1890 gradually faded away. But in 1906 a new society, the National Agricultural Labourers and Rural Workers' Trade Union, was formed, which at once made headway in Norfolk and the adjacent counties ; to be followed in 1913 by the energetic Scottish Farm Servants' Trade Union. Organisation was, between 1904 and 1911, steadily extending in all directions, when the passing of the National Insurance Act, which practically compelled every wage-earner to join an " Approved Society " of some kind, led to a dramatic expansion of Trade Union membership, from which the various Unions of general workers, as they now prefer to be styled, obtained their share of advantage. The Workers' Union, in particular, which had been established in 1898, for the enrolment of members among the nondescript and semi-skilled workers of all sorts not catered for by the craft Unions, had, after twelve years' existence, only 5000 members in 111 branches in 1910, but grew during 1911–13 to 91,000 members in 567 branches. In three years more it stood at 197,000 members in 750 branches, and by the end of 1919 its membership had risen to about 500,000 in nearly 2000 branches, comprising almost every kind and grade of worker, of any age and either sex, from clay-workers and tin miners to corporation employees and sanitary inspectors, from domestic servants and waiters to farm labourers and carmen, and every kind of nondescript worker in the factory, the yard, or on the road. The organising of the rural labourers has been shared by nearly all the principal Unions of General Workers. The passing of the Corn Production Act in 1917, with its incidental establishment of Joint Boards in every county of the United Kingdom, empowered to fix a legal minimum wage for a prescribed normal working day, had the result of greatly extending Trade Union membership among all sections of agricultural labourers, who are now (1920), for the first time in history, more or less organised in every county of Great Britain—partly in the very successful Agricultural

Labourers' Union, which had, at the end of 1919, 180,000 members in no fewer than 2700 branches ; partly in the Workers' Union, which has a large number of agricultural branches ; partly in the National Union of General Workers, the Dock, Wharf and Riverside Labourers' Union, and the National Amalgamated Union of Labour ; in all the Scottish counties, in the powerful Scottish Farm Servants' Union ; whilst in Ireland the agricultural wage-earners have been enrolled in the Transport and General Workers' Union. The total number of agricultural labourers in Trade Unions in 1920 probably reaches more than three hundred thousand, being about one-third of the total number of men employed in agriculture at wages.

Throughout the years of war the membership of the various Unions classified under the head of Transport and General Labour (including the dockers and seamen), which in 1892 was only 154,000, continued to increase by leaps and bounds until, in 1920, their aggregate membership considerably exceeds that of the entire Trade Union world of 1890, and does not fall far short of a couple of millions.

Of recent years there has been a steady pressure towards amalgamation and consolidation of forces. Many small and local Unions have been merged, and several of the larger bodies seem to be on the point of union. Meanwhile the movement towards closer federation is strong. In 1908 all the big general Labour Unions became associated in the General Labourers' National Council, a useful consultative body, having for its principal function the prevention of overlapping and conflict among the different Unions. It was successful in arranging for freedom of transfer and mutual recognition of each other's membership among its constituent Unions, and in promoting a certain amount of demarcation of spheres, and even of amalgamation. This Council in May 1917 developed into a National Federation of General Workers, which includes eleven important general Unions of General Workers, having an aggregate member-ship of over 800,000. This important federation took a significant step towards unification in November 1919, in appointing ten District Committees, consisting of two representatives of each of the affiliated societies, charged to consult with regard to any local trade dispute involving more than one society. Recent years have seen the rise of a new grouping. The several Unions of seamen, lightermen, dock and wharf labourers, coal-porters and carmen have asserted themselves as Transport Workers, seeking not merely to take common action in matters of wages and hours, but also to formulate regulations for the government of the whole industry of transport (apart from that of railways), which is one more example of the tendency to create "industrial" federations on a national basis. The organisation for the purpose is the National Transport Workers' Federation, comprising three dozen of the Unions having among their members men engaged in waterside transport work, including seamen, dockers, and carters. It was formed in November 1910 at the instance of the Dockers' Union, and came at once into prominence during the London strike of 1911, which it handled with great vigour.[1] This was the first great fight in the Port of London since the upheaval of 1889. The National Union of Sailors and Firemen, which had in vain appealed to the Shipping Federation to unite in constituting a Conciliation Board, in June 1911 struck for a uniform scale at all ports and various minor ameliorations of their conditions. Largely as a result of the excitement caused by the seamen's strike, the dockers in July came out for a rise from 6d. to 8d. per hour, with 1s. per hour for overtime. The stevedores, the gasworkers, the carmen,

---

[1] The London dock labourers found themselves in 1911, with an increased cost of living and the virtual abandonment of attempts to improve their method of employment, little better off than in 1889. See *Casual Labour at the Docks*, by H. A. Mess, 1916; and, for the position at other ports, *Le Travail casuel dans les ports anglais*, by J. Malégue, 1913; *The Liverpool Docks Problem*, 1912, and *The First Year's Working of the Liverpool Dock Scheme*, 1914, both by R. Williams (of the Labour Exchange); and "Towards the Solution of the Casual Labour Problem," by F. Keeling, in *Economic Journal*, March 1913.

the coal-porters, the tug-enginemen, the grain porters, and various other bodies of men engaged in or about the port, put forward their own claims. Amid great excitement the whole port was stopped, great meetings on Tower Hill were held daily, and processions of strikers, said to have been as many as 100,000 in number, paraded through the City. The unrest spread to most other ports, and there were some local disturbances. The Port of London Authority, under Lord Devonport, refused all parley, and the Government for some time practically supported this great corporate employer, which had failed (and has to this day failed) to comply with the section of the Act of Parliament by which it was constituted directing it to institute a scheme for more civilised conditions of employment for its labourers. The War Office, at the request of Mr. Winston Churchill, who was then at the Home Office, accumulated troops in London, and actually threatened to put 25,000 soldiers to break the strike by doing the dockers' work—a step which would undoubtedly have led to bloody conflict in the streets. Finally, however, the Cabinet gave way, and persuaded Lord Devonport and his colleagues, together with shipowners, wharfingers, and granary proprietors, to meet the representatives of the Unions with a view to agreement. For three whole days they sat and argued, ultimately arriving at an agreement under which the men returned to work on the immediate concession of about half their demand and the remission of the other half to arbitration. This was undertaken by Sir Albert Rollit, M.P., at the instance of the London Chamber of Commerce, his award eventually conceding to the men substantially their whole claim ; summed up in 8d. per hour for the dockers, with 1s. per hour for overtime, other trades, and the men at other ports, obtaining, in one or other form, analogous advantages.[1] In May 1912 the dispute flared up again in the Thames and Medway,

---

[1] *History of the London Transport Workers' Strike*, by Ben Tillett, 1911 ; *The Great Strike Movement of 1911 and its Lessons*, by H. W. Lee, 1911 ; *The Times* for June–August 1911 ; *Labour Gazette*, 1911–12.

when a combined strike and lock-out, in which 80,000 men were involved, stopped the work of the port for six weeks. Sympathetic strikes in other ports led to some 20,000 men being idle for a few days. The men asserted that the employers had not in all cases fulfilled the agreement of the previous year, and were discriminating against Trade Unionists. The employers seem to have been concerned, in the main, to avoid recognition of the Transport Workers' Federation, and to check its growing authority. In spite of the vigorous support of the *Daily Herald* ; of pecuniary help, not only from Australia and the United States, but also from the German Trade Unions ; and of the mediation of the Government, the strike failed owing to the men breaking away, and to the stubborn obstinacy of Lord Devonport, as Chairman of the Port of London Authority, who insisted on a resumption of work upon the employers' assurance that they would respect all agreements and consider any grievances put forward by the representatives of any section. Notwithstanding the failure of this somewhat premature effort of the Transport Workers' Federation, its formation, together with that of the National Federation of General Workers, have gone far to transform the position. For a couple of decades the efforts of the General Labourers' Unions took the form of innumerable local and sectional demands, not merely for higher rates of pay, though advances of several shillings per week have continually been secured, but for mutual agreement of piecework rates, a reduction of working hours, insistence on compensation for accidents, the provision of better accommodation or greater amenity in work, and extra allowances for tasks of peculiar strain or discomfort. The efforts of the federations have raised these local and sectional arrangements to the level of national questions ; and the agreements now concluded with the employers' national representatives amount to an increasingly effective control over the industry.

The " Black-Coated Proletariat "

If Trade Unionism has, in the past thirty years, successfully progressed downward to the women and the unskilled labourers, its advance, in a sense upwards, among the various sections of the " black-coated proletariat," has been no less remarkable. In 1892 there were only the smallest signs of Trade Union organisation among the clerks and shop assistants, the various sections of Post Office and other Government employees, the municipal officers, and the life assurance agents. Among wage-earners in these various occupations, numbering in the United Kingdom possibly several millions — badly paid, working under unsatisfactory conditions, and sometimes subject to actual tyranny—there were, thirty years ago, a few dozen small and struggling Trade Unions, with only a few tens of thousands of aggregate membership. In 1920 these have developed into powerful amalgamations in most of the several sections, nearly all fully recognised by their employers, whether private or public, with whom they enter into collective agreements ; and enrolling a total membership falling not far short of three-quarters of a million.

We may note first the army of shop assistants, warehousemen, and other employees in the distributive trades, wholesale and retail.[1] The National Amalgamated Union of Shop Assistants, Warehousemen, and Clerks, established in 1891, made at first slow progress, and counted in 1912, after a couple of decades of growth, fewer than 65,000 members. Partly as a result of the National Insurance Act, which practically compelled all employees under £160 to join some organisation, the Union went ahead by leaps and bounds, multiplying its branches and swelling its numbers, until it counts now over 100,000 members. Meanwhile

[1] *The Working Life of Shop Assistants*, by Joseph Hallsworth and R. J. Davis, 1913.

the Amalgamated Union of Co-operative Employees (also established in 1891)—in 1918 adding to its title also " Commercial Employees and Allied Workers "—has benefited by a similar expansion, counting, in 1920, also about 100,000 members. This society started on the basis of enrolling all employees of the Co-operative Societies, whatever their crafts, and no other persons, a constitution now disapproved of by the Trades Union Congress. It is, however, not now confined to persons employed by co-operative societies ; and whilst it includes a number of carmen, tailors, bakers, bootmakers, and others in co-operative employment who should more appropriately belong to other Unions, the negotiations that have been for some time in progress for the merging of both organisations in a single great Union of persons employed in the distributive trades, and the transfer of those belonging to specific crafts to their own societies, may probably presently be successful.

Of clerks, the most effective organisation is that of the clerical service of the railway companies, the Railway Clerks' Association, which takes in also stationmasters, inspectors, and superintendents (who are all eligible also for the National Union of Railwaymen, which some of them have joined). Established in 1897, it continued for a decade insignificant in magnitude, and had not by 1910 enrolled as many as 10,000 members. After the railway strike of 1911 it began to forge ahead, passing from 30,000 in 1914 to 42,000 in 1915—a total doubled by 1920, and with increasing strength it obtained gradually increasing recognition from the railway companies, successfully maintaining its right to enrol, not only clerks in the General Managers' offices, but also inspectors and stationmasters. As its membership grew, it was able successfully to contest the elections for representatives on the committees of the various superannuation funds instituted by the companies, and thereby to demonstrate its right to speak for the whole body of railway clerks. Whilst acting in friendly association with the National Union of Railwaymen, the Railway Clerks'

Association has latterly drawn to itself an ever-increasing proportion of the inspectors and stationmasters ; and in 1920, when it can count on a membership of nearly 90,000, it is claiming to speak for all grades of the Railway Clerical Administrative and Supervisory Staff. Since 1913, at least, it has been asserting a claim, as soon as the railways are nationalised, to some participation in their management ; and at the end of 1919, it is understood, some promise was made by the Minister of Transport that, in any Railway Board or National Advisory Committee that may be constituted, the Railway Clerks' Association would, with the National Union of Railwaymen and the Associated Society of Locomotive Engineers and Firemen, be accorded its due share of representation.

The great army of clerks in commercial offices has made less progress in organisation than the shop assistants and the railway clerks. For years, indeed, it seemed as if commercial clerks would not form a Trade Union ; and the National Union of Clerks (established 1890) made little headway. In 1912 it had still under 9000 members. In the past seven years it has bounded up to 55,000 members.[1] There is also a small Irish Clerical Workers' Union, principally in Dublin, resulting from a secession from the National Union. Most remarkable of all has been the formation, during the war, of a Bank Officers' Guild and an Irish Bank Officials' Association, having definitely Trade Union objects (though not yet seeking to join the Trades Union Congress), both of them being independent of the Bankers' Institute, which retains the character of a scientific and educational society. There is now even a Guild of Law Court Officials, having definitely Trade Union objects.

The great body of teachers of all kinds and grades, numbering altogether about 300,000 men and women in the United Kingdom, have, during the past thirty years, become strongly and very elaborately organised in many

[1] A separate Association of Women Clerks and Secretaries, long small in membership, has also risen to 4500 members.

different societies.[1] What is significant is the extent to which many of these professional associations have latterly adopted the purposes, and even the characteristic methods, of Trade Unionism. The largest of these bodies, the National Union of Teachers, established in 1890, has now over 102,000 members, and exercises great influence upon the conditions of employment of the teachers in elementary schools. During the past few years it has supported various district or county strikes for better salary-scales. The teachers in secondary schools are organised in four societies, for headmasters, headmistresses, assistant masters, and assistant mistresses respectively, united in a Federal Council of Secondary School Associations, which, though it has not yet fomented or supported a strike, has of late organised effective pressure to obtain greater security of tenure for assistants, better salary-scales, and a universal superannuation scheme.

Equally significant is the recent development of organisation among the industrial technicians, whether engineers, electricians, chemists, or merely foremen and managers ; among the workers in scientific laboratories, whether for research, medical, teaching, or administrative purposes ; and among the junior lecturers and assistants at University institutions. These organisations overlap in their spheres, if not also in their memberships, and are not yet stabilised, but most of them are united in the National Federation of Professional Workers of even wider scope. What is important is the growing divergence between what are essentially Trade Unions of the brain-working professionals and the purely " scientific societies " to which such persons have, until recent years, restricted their tendency to professional association. Some of the new bodies (such as the Society of Technical Engineers) have actually registered themselves as Trade Unions, a step taken also by the Medico-Political

[1] See *English Teachers and their Professional Organisations*, by Mrs. Sidney Webb, published as supplements to *The New Statesman* of September 25 and October 2, 1915.

Union, a vigorous association of medical practitioners; whilst the newly formed Actors' Association, like the National Union of Journalists, has applied for affiliation to the Trades Union Congress.

The life assurance agents—principally those employed in " industrial " insurance—number 100,000, and they have become organised in a score of societies, restricted to the staffs of particular companies. These organisations vary in their nature and in their degree of independence, from mere " welfare societies," dominated by the management, up to aggressive Trade Unions—the strongest being the National Association of Prudential Assurance Agents. They are mostly united in two different federations. Another, and perhaps wholesomer, basis of organisation is adopted by the National Union of Life Assurance Agents, which has now some thousands of members.

But the greatest development of Trade Unionism among the " black-coated proletariat " has been among the employees of the National and Local Government. This has been entirely a growth of the past thirty years. Beginning among the manual working staff of the Postmaster-General, and among the artisans and labourers of the Government dockyards, arsenals, and other manufacturing departments, there are now a hundred and seventy separate Trade Unions of State employees, from the crews of the Customs launches and the boy clerks, up to the Admiralty Constructive Engineers and the Superintendents of Mercantile Marine Offices. Of recent years, organisation has spread to the higher grades of the Civil Service, even to the " Class I." clerks ; and practically no one below the rank of an Under-Secretary of State is held to be outside the scope of the Society of Civil Servants. All the various societies are grouped in federations, from the " Waterguard Federation " and the Prison Officers' Federation of the United Kingdom ; through the United Government Workers' Federation and the Federal Council of Government Employees, combining the various kinds of manual working operatives ; up to the

Customs and Excise Federation, the Civil Service Federation, the Civil Service Alliance, and even the "National Federation of Professional Workers," which includes also teachers. The strongest of all these bodies is probably that of the various employees of the Postmaster-General, whose fight to secure "recognition" and the opportunity for "Collective Bargaining" has extended over a couple of decades. There are about fifty separate Unions of Post Office employees, mostly small and sectional bodies ; but the three principal societies (the Postal and Telegraph Clerks' Association, the Postmen's Federation, and the Fawcett Association) were amalgamated in 1919 into one powerful Union of Post Office Workers, with 90,000 members with eleven salaried officers, and affiliated both to the Trades Union Congress and the Labour Party, which can now meet the managing officials of the Post Office on something like equal terms.

The employees of the Local Authorities—thirty years ago entirely without organisation—are still not so well combined as those of the National Government. A score of different societies, from such grades as school-keepers, police and prison officers and asylum attendants, up to municipal clerks, share the work with the National Union of Corporation Workers and the Municipal Employees' Association. A large proportion of the wage-earners employed by Local Authorities are to be found in the Unions of General Workers. The National Association of Local Government Officers and Clerks is a large and powerful body, composed mainly of the clerical and supervisory grades.

Trade Unionism in the public service received a great fillip after 1906, when Mr. Sydney Buxton at the Post Office, together with some other Ministers, "recognised" the Unions of their employees, considered their corporate representations, and agreed to meet their officials. It was still further promoted when, in 1917, the Government consented to the establishment of an independent Arbitration

Tribunal for determining the terms of employment in the Civil Service for all grades and sections under £500 a year. Before this tribunal, whose awards were definitively authoritative, the representatives of any association could appear as plaintiffs, those of the Treasury appearing always as defendants. Finally, after the promulgation in 1917 of the " Whitley Report," which the Government, in impressing on other employers, found itself constrained to adopt in its own establishments, there was established during 1919 an elaborate series of joint councils (including even the civil departments of the War Office and the Admiralty) for particular branches of establishments; for whole departments, and for whole grades of the service throughout all departments, in which equal numbers of persons nominated by the employees' associations, and of superior officers chosen by the Government, representing the management, meet periodically to discuss on equal terms questions of office organisation, professional training, conditions of service, methods of promotion, and what not.[1]

[1] From 1913 onward a persistent attempt to establish a Trade Union was made by many of the Police and Prison Officers, which was resisted by the Home Secretary, as responsible for the Metropolitan Police, and by all the Local Authorities. In 1913 the Police and Prison Officers' Union was formed by ex-Inspector Symes, and in 1917 it was reorganised, without securing either recognition or sanction. Cases of " victimisation " having occurred, there was a sudden strike on August 29, 1918, which was participated in by nearly the whole of the police in many London divisions. This took the world (and also the criminal population) by surprise ; but through good-humoured handling by the Prime Minister (who received the Executive Committee of the Union and told them that " the Union could not be recognised during the war "), the Government persuaded the men promptly to resume their duties, with a cessation of " victimisation " for joining the Union and a substantial increase of pay. When hostilities ceased, the Union expected some measure of official sanction, but none was accorded, and grievances remained unredressed. On July 31, 1919, a second strike was suddenly called, which resulted in failure, only a couple of thousand men coming out in London, and a few hundred in Liverpool, Birkenhead, and elsewhere, together with a small number of prison warders. At Liverpool and Birkenhead there was serious looting of shops and public-houses by turbulent crowds. The authorities stood firm, the Home Secretary refusing all sanction for the establishment of a Trade Union in the police force and prison staff, and summarily dismissing all the strikers, at the same time announcing large concessions in the way of wages, promotion, and pensions, and conceding, not a Trade Union, but the establish-

THE MINERS

The outstanding feature of the Trade Union world between 1890 and 1920 has been the growing predominance, in its counsels and in its collective activity, of the organised forces of the coal-miners. Right down to 1888, as we have seen, the coal-miners of England, Scotland, and Wales, though sporadically forming local associations and now and again engaging in fierce conflicts with their employers, first in this coalfield and then in that, had failed to maintain any organisation of national scope. Though their representatives participated from time to time in the general activities of the Trade Union Movement, and sat in the Trades Union Congress; though with the guidance of W. P. Roberts in the 'forties, and under the successive leadership of Alexander Macdonald and Thomas Burt in the 'sixties and 'seventies, they exercised intermittently a considerable influence on its Parliamentary action—the miners, for the most part, kept to themselves, framed their own policy, and fought their own battles, in which, owing to an apparently incurable " localism," their success was not commensurate with their strength. The change came with the growing dissatisfaction with the policy of the Sliding Scale. This device for making the rate of wages vary in proportion to the selling price of coal, the adoption of which between 1874 and 1880—against the wish of Alexander Macdonald, and contrary to the advice of such friends as Professor Beesly and Lloyd Jones—we have already described, produced in the 'eighties an ever-increasing discontent. In 1881 the miners of Yorkshire merged their two Unions of South and West Yorkshire into the Yorkshire Miners'

---

ment of an elective organisation of the police force, by grades, entitled to make formal representations and complaints. This concession was embodied in the Police Act, 1919, which explicitly prohibited to the police either membership of, or affiliation to, any Trade Union or political organisation. The dismissed policemen were not reinstated, but the Government informally assisted some of them to obtain other employment.

Association, which began its successful career by terminating the local Sliding Scale agreement, and resolutely refused all future attempts to make wages depend on selling prices. The Lancashire and Cheshire Miners' Federation, a less well-organised body, presently followed its example. In 1885 a Midland Federation was formed by a number of smaller local associations for the purpose both of abolishing the Sliding Scale and of promoting the movement for an Eight Hours Day by legislative enactment. Three years later, at a conference at Manchester, the associations of Yorkshire, Lancashire and Cheshire, the Midlands, and Fifeshire, with a nascent local organisation in South Wales, established the Miners' Federation of Great Britain.[1] The aggregate membership of all these bodies was amazingly small—at the start only 36,000—but the new Federation had, from the first, a definite policy and great driving force. Outside it there remained the solid and numerically strong Durham Miners' Association and the Northumberland Miners' Mutual Confident Association, which (together with a surviving remnant of the Amalgamated Association in South Stafford-shire, and the purely nominal Sliding Scale Associations which then characterised most of the South Wales coalfield) still clung together as the National Union. It was the

---

[1] For the history of the Miners' Federation of Great Britain and the contemporary District Unions, we have drawn on the voluminous printed minutes of proceedings and reports which are seldom seen outside the Miners' Offices ; the various publications of the Labour Department of the Board of Trade (now the Ministry of Labour) and the Home Office ; *The British Coal Trade*, by H. Stanley Jevons (1915) ; *The British Coal Industry*, by Gilbert Stone (1919) ; *Labour Strife in the South Wales Coalfield, 1910–11*, by D. Evans (1911) ; *The Adjustment of Wages*, by Sir W. J. Ashley ; *Miners' Wages and the Sliding Scale*, by W. Smart (1894) ; *Miners and the Eight Hours Movement*, by M. Percy ; *History of the Durham Miners' Association*, by J. Wilson (1907) ; *A Great Labour Leader* [Thomas Burt], by Aaron Watson (1908) ; *Memoirs of a Miners' Leader*, by J. Wilson (1910) ; *Industrial Unionism and the Mining Industry*, by George Harvey (1917) ; *A Plan for the Democratic Control of the Mining Industry*, by the Industrial Committee of the South Wales Socialist Society (1919) ; the Reports and evidence of the Coal Industry Commission, 1919, and the voluminous newspaper discussion to which it gave rise, together with *Facts from the Coal Commission* and *Further Facts from the Coal Commission*, both by R. Page Arnot (1919).

National Union which played the leading part in securing reforms in the Coal Mines Regulation Act of 1887, which firmly established the checkweigher in practically every colliery of any importance. But this was its last constructive effort. Its subsequent history is little more than the long-drawn-out resistance of the able and respected leaders of the Northumberland and Durham miners to the new ideas of Labour policy which were, as we have described, becoming dominant in the Trades Union Congress, and which were from the first adopted, if not by all the leaders, at least by the successive delegate conferences of the Miners' Federation.

The establishment of the Federation coincided with a period of rapid expansion in the coal-mining industry. The number of persons employed rose considerably year after year, and Trade Unionism spread rapidly among them. An effective local organisation was built up in district after district, everywhere based on the autonomy in local concerns of the " lodge " or branch, consisting of the workers at a given colliery, and governed by mass meetings of the members, who elect a committee, which usually meets at least weekly. But although the National Union declined steadily in influence, it took twenty years to bring all the district associations into the Miners' Federation, the aggregate membership of which did not reach 200,000 until 1893, and seven years later was still only 363,000. Even so, the miners were, as we described them in 1892, in some ways the most effectively organised of the industrial groups into which we divided the Trade Union world of that date. With the adhesion of Northumberland and Durham in 1908, when the National Union came finally to an end, the membership of the Federation rose to nearly 600,000, whilst the next twelve years' growth of the industry, and the inclusion of a large proportion of the sectional unions among different grades of mine-workers,[1] have brought it in 1920 to nearly 900,000.

[1] The enginemen, boilermen and firemen, colliery mechanics, cokemen,

Meanwhile issue was joined by the mine-owners, who insisted everywhere in 1893 on considerable reductions in the wage-rates, on the plea that selling prices had fallen. The great strike that followed involved 400,000 men, and lasted from July to November. In the end the men had to submit to reductions, though they gained the important point of the practical though not explicit recognition of a minimum below which there was to be no fall. The next great achievement of the Federation was the carrying into law of the Eight Hours Bill, which, mainly owing to the opposition of the leaders of the Northumberland and Durham Miners, was not accomplished until 1908 ; and their influence in improving the Mines Regulation Act of 1911. Their third success, the outcome of a decade of successful organisation and intellectual leadership by Mr. Robert Smillie, who since 1912 has been annually elected to the presidency, was attained only at the cost of the greatest industrial struggle that Great Britain had yet experienced.

The national strike of miners in 1912, when practically every mine was stopped, and nearly a million miners suspended work for more than a month, arose out of the failure of the colliery companies to make adequate provision for repeated cases of individual hardship and injustice. The piece-work rates of the hewers or getters of coal might be satisfactorily adjusted to the agreed day-wage standard of the district, though the arrangements for this adjustment vary from district to district, and even from mine to mine, and are very far from complete or satisfactory. But what was to happen when, from circumstances beyond his own control, the miner found himself unable to get enough coal to produce a subsistence wage ? If he is assigned an " abnormal place "—where the seam is thin or crushed

---

under-managers, deputies, overmen and other officials, colliery clerks and various kinds of surface-workers about the mines have all their own Unions, which have greatly developed of recent years, and are in many districts not very willing to join the county miners' associations, though they often act in conjunction with these. Their own federations are referred to on p. 550.

Their own federations are referred to on p. 550.

S

into small coal (for which, in South Wales, the hewer is not paid at all) ; or where exceptional timbering is required to prevent dangerous falls ; or where there is much " stone " or water : or if, in " normal places," the colliery management does not keep him regularly supplied with " trams " or " tubs " into which to load the coal ; or with a sufficient provision of timber for props and sleepers ; or of rails— no amount of skill, strength, or assiduity will prevent his earnings from falling away, it may be to next to nothing. What had long been customary was, in some coalfields, the casting of lots for " places," and thus a periodical exchange of opportunities ; and in others the granting of an allowance, or " consideration," to hewers who complained of insufficient earnings. These allowances were granted irregularly, without the protection of Collective Bargaining, with insufficient provision for ensuring the avoidance of injustice ; and it is not now denied that, in some collieries, particularly in South Wales, the owners resorted to the simple expedient of restricting the manager to a fixed maximum sum each " measuring-up day," irrespective of the number and extent of the men's reasonable claims. These sums, moreover, were much reduced in times of bad trade, when profits were at a minimum, especially in collieries which were actually working at a loss. The agitation for securing a prescribed minimum of daily earnings for all the piece-workers continued for a whole decade without much result, producing not a few local stoppages, especially in South Wales. These flared up, in the latter part of 1910, in the Aberdare and Rhondda valleys, into an almost continuous series of disputes. The Miners' Federation found itself compelled in July 1911 to take the matter up as a national question ; and a ballot of its whole membership decided for a national strike if the universal adoption of the principle of a prescribed daily minimum, not merely for hewers but for all grades, was not conceded. The owners quibbled and eventually refused ; and after a further ballot a national strike was decided on.

which the Government negotiations failed to avert, and which, after long and repeated notice, began at the end of February 1912, and rapidly extended to practically every colliery in the kingdom. As neither the employers nor the workmen would give way, the Government then announced its intention of introducing a Bill to provide for the payment, to all underground workers in the mine, not of the prescribed minimum rates which the several districts had formulated, nor yet of the overriding national minima of 5s. for a man and 2s. for a boy which were being demanded, but of district minima, to be prescribed in each coalfield by a Joint Board of employers and workmen, presided over by an impartial chairman. These provisions were bitterly opposed, not only by the coal-owners, who objected to any legal minimum, but also by the workmen's representatives in the House of Commons, who demanded a prescribed national minimum ; but they were carried into law by substantial majorities. The Federation Executive was perplexed as to the line to take, as half the membership wanted to carry on the struggle ; but it was eventually decided to give the Act and the Joint Boards a chance, and the strike was declared at an end. The district minima and the rules applicable thereto had, in most cases, to be decided by the impartial chairmen ; and they varied considerably from district to district, being usually a little less than the workmen had claimed. But when the working of the system was understood, and it was got smoothly into operation, it was recognised that the Miners' Federation had achieved a very substantial victory. The miners had brought to their aid, in enforcing the payment of a periodically prescribed Minimum Day Wage to all underground workers, the strong arm of the law—not, it is true, as under the Mines Regulation Acts and the Factory and Workshop Acts, the criminal law, enforced by Government inspectors and prosecutions, but the civil law of contract, which they could themselves enforce by actions in the County Court. What the Federation extorted from the Government and the Legislature was " an extraordinary piece of hastily prepared legislation rushed through Parliament in the shadow of an unprecedented national calamity."[1] It has been found by experience that this Act, which is nominally only temporary, does secure to the hewers a substantial minimum of day wages, however unremunerative their conditions of work ; and the fixing of rates by the Joint Boards has, on the whole, considerably increased the wages of the various grades of the less skilled workers. But more important than these immediate results was the demonstration and the consolidation of the national strength of the Miners' Federation itself ; and the respect which its great power henceforth secured for it, alike in the Trade Union Movement, with the employers, and at the hands of the Government and the House of Commons.

The miners' organisations were fully occupied for a year or two in putting into operation the Act of 1912, and in enforcing the determinations of the Joint Boards. But in 1913 the delegate conference made a new move in authorising the Executive Committee to enter into relations with other Trade Unions with a view to joint action for mutual assistance. A formal alliance had been made between the Miners' Federation, the National Union of Railwaymen, and the Transport Workers' Federation—commonly referred to as the Triple Alliance—when everything was suddenly changed by the breaking out of the Great War. The 1500 colliery companies and individual colliery owners, most of whom are united in the Mining Association of Great Britain, as well as in district associations, have, throughout, steadfastly refused to meet the Miners' Federation for the negotiation of any national agreement, or the concession of national advances ; although there has long been elaborate machinery for negotiation in each district.

During the four and a quarter years that the world conflict lasted (1914–18), the miners, like the rest of the British working class, patriotically subordinated their interests to those of the nation as a whole. They volun-

[1] *The British Coal Trade* (by H. Stanley Jevons, 1915), p. 599.

teered for military service in such numbers that they had to be forbidden to leave the mines, and numbers of them were sent back from the armies in order to maintain the output of coal. Where, as in Durham, they had agreements securing them advances of wages in proportion to the rise in the selling price, they forewent these advances ; and they contented themselves everywhere with less substantial percentages of rise in rates, and with the two successive war bonuses of eighteen pence a day each—much below the rise in the cost of living—which the Government accorded to them in 1917 and 1918. With the cessation of hostilities at the end of 1918, as the cost of living continued to advance, the Miners' Federation (which had elected for its new secretary a young South Wales miner, Mr. Frank Hodges, who had educated himself at Labour Colleges ; and had also converted its presidency into a full-time salaried post, and for the first time acquired an office in London) again took up the forward movement which it had been concerting five years before ; and in February 1919, after balloting its whole membership, and giving elaborate notice, it demanded from the employers a general advance of wages of 30 per cent, the reduction of the hours of labour by an average of one-fourth (the nominal Eight Hours Day to be made a nominal Six Hours Day), and—most momentous of all— the elimination of the profit-making capitalist from the industry by the Nationalisation of the Mines, for which the Trades Union Congress had been vainly asking for over twenty years. As the railwaymen and the transport workers were at the same time in negotiation for improvements in their condition, there seemed, in March 1919, every prospect of the outbreak of a general strike on a scale even greater than that of 1912, the " Triple Alliance " uniting a membership of more than a million and a half, and wielding in combination the adult male labour of something like one-sixth of the whole nation. The Government, which was still, under war powers, directing both the mines and the railways, responded by the offer of a Statutory Commission, under a Judge of the High Court, with practically unlimited powers of investigation and recommendation ; at the same time giving the Federation publicly to understand that, whilst a strike would be suppressed with all the powers of the State, the recommendations of the Commission would be accepted by the Cabinet. The conference of the Miners' Federation spent many hours in deliberation. A large section of the delegates was for an immediate strike. The men had, indeed, an extraordinarily advantageous strategic position. The nation's stocks of coal were at a minimum, London having only three days' supply in hand. Ultimately the advice of the leaders prevailed ; and it was decided to postpone the withdrawal of labour for three weeks, and to take part in the Statutory Commission, on the express condition that this body presented an Interim Report within that time ; and—most revolutionary of all—that the Federation should be allowed to nominate to the Commission, not only three of its own members to balance the three coal-owners who had been informally designated by the Mining Association of Great Britain, but also three out of the six professedly disinterested members, so as to balance the three capitalists whom the Government had already chosen as representing the principal industries dependent on the supply of coal at a moderate price. To these terms the Prime Minister acceded. The Miners' Federation, setting a new precedent of far-reaching effect, thereupon nominated, along with its President, Vice-president, and Secretary, not three other workmen, but three economists and statisticians belonging to the Fabian Society, known to them by their lectures and writings.

The proceedings of this Commission, which sat daily in public in the King's Robing-Room at the House of Lords, created an immense sensation. Instead of the Trade Union, it was the management of the industry that was put upon its trial. The large profits of the industry under war conditions were revealed, and especially the enormous gains of the most advantageous mines ; and although the Govern-

ment itself had benefited through the Excess Profits'
Duty by 50, 60, and eventually 80 per cent of these gains,
it became apparent to every one that, but for this abstraction, the price of coal might have been reduced and the
miners' conditions improved to an extent never before
suspected. It was seen, too, that it was the separate
ownership of the mines which stood in the way of the
national sharing of the advantages of the best among them.
The chaotic state of the industry, with 1500 separately
working joint-stock companies operating at very different
costs—with no co-ordination of production, and with
extremely wasteful arrangements for transport and retail
distribution—was vividly presented. At the same time
the unsatisfactory conditions under which the miners lived
were impressively demonstrated, the scandalously bad
housing of the mining community in Lanarkshire and elsewhere making a national sensation. Prompt to the
appointed day the Commission presented three Reports.
The three mine-owners proposed no improvement in the
organisation of the industry, and offered an advance of
eighteen pence a day and a reduction of hours by one per
day, being only half what was demanded. The six representatives of the miners presented a long and reasoned
justification of the men's case ; arguing that, with a unification of the industry in national ownership, with the
adoption in all the mines of the mechanical improvements
already in use in the best-managed among them, with a
more carefully concerted transport system, and with a
municipal organisation of retail distribution, it was practicable to concede the men's full claim of 30 per cent advance
and a two hours' shortening of the working day without any
increase in the price of coal to the consumer. The Chairman of the Commission presented a third report, intermediate in its tenour, in which he was joined by the three
disinterested capitalist members, proposing an immediate
advance of two shillings per day, or 20 per cent, and an
immediate reduction of one hour per day, with a promise

of a further reduction by an hour in 1920, if the condition of the industry warranted it. With regard to nationalisation, this Report declared that, as there had not been sufficient time to investigate the proposal, the Commission would continue its sittings, and promptly present a further report ; but that it was plain, even on the evidence so far submitted, that the present system stood condemned, and that some other system must, by national purchase of the mines, be substituted for it—either State administration, or some plan by which the mines could be placed under a joint control in which the miners would share. This impressive declaration by the judicial Chairman, supported by the three capitalist members who were not mine-owners, made a great public sensation. The Cabinet immediately accepted the Chairman's Report, pledging itself to carry it out " in the letter and in the spirit." The Miners' Federation hesitated, but ultimately, in consideration of the offer of an immediate further examination of nationalisation, in the light of Mr. Justice Sankey's significant findings, decided to ballot its members, who, to the great relief of the public, by large majorities agreed to accept the Government proposal.

The Coal Industry Commission accordingly continued its sittings, now concentrating upon the issue of Nationalisation and the participation of the miners in control. The dramatic feature of the inquiry was the summoning of a succession of peers and other magnates owning mining royalties to the witness-chair, there to explain to the Commission and the public, under the sharp cross-examination of the Miners' Federation officials, how they or their ancestors had become possessed of these property rights, how much they yielded in each case, and what social service the recipients performed for their huge incomes. Much evidence was taken for and against State administration. Within a couple of months of almost incessant daily sittings this indefatigable Commission presented its further Report, again hopelessly divided. On the question of ownership of minerals, indeed, the whole thirteen Com-

missioners were unanimous—a momentous decision—in
recommending that the royalty owners should be at once
expropriated in favour of the State. All thirteen Commissioners were unanimous, too, in recommending the
admission of the workmen to some degree of participation
in the management by Pit and District Committees. But
there the Commissioners' agreement ended. What was
significant was that not the miners' representatives only,
but eight out of the thirteen (including the Chairman)
reported in favour of expropriating all the existing colliery
companies and other coal-owners. The Chairman, supported (in general terms and subject to additional suggestion) by the six miners' representatives, proposed an
elaborate scheme of Nationalisation, with administration
under a Minister of Mines by joint District Councils and
Pit Committees, in which the men would be largely represented. The other expropriating Commissioner preferred
to vest the mines in a series of District Coal Corporations
of capitalist shareholders, limited as to dividend, and
working under public control, with a restricted participation of the men in the administration. Five Commissioners,
including all three coal - owners, whilst agreeing to the
Nationalisation of Minerals, refused to contemplate any
substantial change in the working of the mines, least of
all any effective sharing of the workmen in the administration ; though even this capitalist minority gave lip-homage
to the principle by recommending the formation of purely
Advisory Pit and District Committees.

The Government, which had continued in administrative
and financial control of all the collieries of the United
Kingdom, whilst agreeing to adopt, in the spirit and in the
letter, the terms of Mr. Justice Sankey's first Report, took
no steps to bring it into effect, and left the local mine-owners
and miners' Unions to adjust for themselves the hours and
new rates of pay which it involved. Suddenly, a few weeks
before the new arrangements were to come into force, the
Coal Controller issued an order that no increase of rates was to

exceed 10 per cent—a patent blunder, as it was the average reduction of output that Mr. Justice Sankey had estimated at 10 per cent, and it was the actual reduction in each district that had to be compensated for. The Yorkshire Miners' Association had almost completed its arrangements with the Yorkshire mine-owners for a higher percentage of increase when the Government prohibition was received. The result was an angry strike which stopped the whole Yorkshire coalfield for several weeks, and spread to Nottinghamshire. In the end the Government had to withdraw its mistaken prohibition ; and the increase of rates, in Yorkshire as elsewhere, was, as the miners had asked, made as nearly as possible proportionate to the expected local reduction in output caused by the reduction of hours. The hasty action on both sides and the misunderstandings due to imperfect knowledge, or imperfect expression, lost the nation some four million tons of coal, and cost the Yorkshire Miners' Association about £356,000.

In October 1919 Mr. Lloyd George announced that whilst the Government would propose the nationalisation of mining royalties, and some undefined " trustification " of the mines by districts, there would be no adoption of Mr. Justice Sankey's Report. The Miners' Federation refused to accept anything in the nature of capitalist " trustification," and called in vain on the Government to fulfil its pledge to carry out the Report. In December 1919 the Federation, in conjunction with the Labour Party, the Parliamentary Committee of the Trades Union Congress, and the Co-operative Union, began a campaign of propaganda in favour of the Nationalisation of the Coal Supply, the effect of which, industrially and politically, has yet to become manifest. We have to break off the story in the middle of a critical period.

The Railwaymen

Another great industry, that of the operating staff of the railway system—scarcely mentioned in the first edition of our *History*—has come forcibly to the front. Right down to the end of the nineteenth century, indeed, the railway guards and signalmen, engine-drivers and firemen, shunters and porters, mechanics and labourers—though they numbered something like 5 per cent of all the male manual-working wage-earners—played hardly any part in the Trade Union Movement. Scattered in small numbers all over the country, and divided among themselves by differences of grade, conditions, and pay, they long seemed incapable of organisation as a vocation. For a whole generation after the establishment of railways no one appears to have thought Trade Unionism any more permissible among their employees than among the soldiers or the police. In 1865 an attempt to establish " The Railway Working Men's Provident Benefit Society "—which soon became virtually a Trade Union—by Charles Bassett Vincent, a clerk in the Railway Clearing House, was ruthlessly crushed by summary dismissals. In the same year an Association of Engine-drivers and Firemen on the North-Eastern Railway actually started a strike, but perished of the attempt. Not until the end of 1871 was a lasting Trade Union established, and then only by the assistance of Michael Bass, M.P., a large railway shareholder, by whose long-continued and entirely disinterested financial and other help the Amalgamated Society of Railway Servants struggled into being, with Frederick Evans as its first effective secretary. Other societies followed, of local or sectional character ; but even in 1892, after twenty years of organisation, and various abortive strikes, there were fewer than 50,000 railwaymen in any sort of Trade Union, or less than one in seven of the persons employed.[1]

[1] The other railwaymen's Unions are the Belfast and Dublin Locomotive Engine-drivers' and Firemen's Trade Union, founded in 1872, and still existing (1920) with a few hundred members ; the Associated Society of Locomotive Engineers and Firemen, founded in 1880, a powerful sectional society with 33,000 members, which long maintained a jealous rivalry with the Amalgamated ; the Railway Clerks' Association, founded in 1897, remaining very small for a whole decade, absorbing in 1911 the Railway Telegraph Clerks' Association, founded 1897, with 85,000

The objects of such railwaymen's societies as existed were for many years confined to the protection of members from " victimisation " or other tyranny ; to the provision of friendly benefits ; and to spasmodic attempts to get accidents prevented or compensated for, and hours of labour reduced. Wages questions took up little of the attention of the railway Unions of these years ; but strikes on particular railways—sometimes of particular grades or at particular centres only of a single railway—now and then occurred ; usually in resentment of some act of tyranny, or against some specially oppressive hours of labour, and often without the prior approval of the Executive Committee. In 1890 the Amalgamated Society for the first time launched an aggressive policy, mainly as regards the hours of labour, which were indeed scandalous.[1] A prolonged strike for a shorter working day on the Scottish lines at Christmas 1890 ended in failure, and the merging of the remnant of

members ; the Irish Railway Workers' Trade Union, founded in 1910, tiny and insignificant ; the National Union of Railway Clerks, formed in 1913, a tiny local body, arising out of the suspension of the Sheffield Branch of the Railway Clerks' Association, temporary only.

We may mention the Scottish Society of Railway Servants, founded in the eighteen-eighties, merged in the Amalgamated Society in 1892 ; the United Signalmen and Pointsmen, founded in 1880, merged in the N.U.R. in 1913 ; the General Railway Workers' Union, founded in 1889, merged in the N.U.R., 1913.

For the development of Trade Unionism in the railway world, and the various controversies, we have drawn mainly on the numerous reports and other publications of the Unions themselves ; the *Railway Review* and the *Railway Clerk* (the pleading for the Companies being found in the *Railway News*, subsequently incorporated in the *Railway Gazette*) ; *Trade Unionism on the Railways, its History and Problems*, by G. D. H. Cole and R. Page Arnot (1917) ; the *Souvenir History*, published by the Amalgamated Society of Railway Servants (1910) ; *Men and Rails*, by Rowland Kenney (1913) ; *Der Arbeitskampf der englischen Eisenbahner im Jahre 1911*, by C. Leubuscher, 1913; the various publications on the legal proceedings, for which see the next chapter ; the Reports of the Board of Trade on Railway Accidents, hours of labour, etc., of the Select Committee of 1892, and the Special Committee of Inquiry of 1911 ; *An Introduction to Trade Unionism*, by G. D. H. Cole (1918) ; *From Engine-cleaner to Privy Councillor* [J. H. Thomas], by J. F. Moir Bussy (1917).

[1] *Slavery on Scottish Railways* (1888); *The Scottish Railway Strike*, by James Mavor (1891).

the Scottish Society of Railway Servants in the larger Union. But it aroused public attention and led to an effective exposure by a Select Committee of the House of Commons in 1891–92. As a result the Board of Trade was given certain statutory powers in 1893 to remedy this tyranny—powers of which, unfortunately, little use was made. Not for nine years afterwards did the Board of Trade even call upon the railway companies for a return showing in how many cases men were kept on duty in excess of twelve hours at a stretch. Four-fifths of the railwaymen were still outside the ranks of Trade Unionism and could therefore be both oppressed by their employers and flouted by the Government Department. Their very right to combine was denied. Sir George Findlay, the General Manager of the London and North-Western Railway, voiced the common opinion of the Companies when he declared that " you might as well have a Trade Union or an ' Amalgamated Society ' in the Army, where discipline has to be kept at a very high standard, as have it on railways."

In December 1896, indeed, a determined attempt was made to root out Trade Unionism in Sir George Findlay's own railway company by the dismissal of men discovered to be Trade Unionists. Through the activity of the Society these victims found influential friends, who by public and private pressure compelled their reinstatement. The excitement caused by this incident had some share in swelling the membership of the Amalgamated Society, which doubled its numbers during the year 1897 ; and made its first big stride in the " All Grades Movement " in that year. Previous movements had been local and sectional, and nearly always in the interests of particular grades. For the first time all the railway companies were approached simultaneously, with a request for improvements in all grades from one end of the service to the other—a reduction of the time of duty, so as to bring the working day down to ten, and for some grades eight hours ; extra payments for overtime, and a uniform advance of 2s. per week for all grades except those for whom an eight hours day was sought. The Companies refused even to consider this very moderate request, and nearly a decade was to pass—a decade of slow building up of the organisation, first under Mr Richard Bell and Mr J. E. Williams, and then under Mr. J H. Thomas—before the Trade Unions of railwaymen were able to compel a hearing for their case.[1]

Meanwhile the Amalgamated Society of Railway Servants, and with it the whole Trade Union Movement, suffered in the law courts a temporary set-back. An impulsive strike on the Taff Vale Railway in South Wales, accompanied by extensive and successful picketing, was not countenanced by the Executive, but was eventually endorsed by its decision to take up the men's case ; and the Railway Company sued the Society for the loss occasioned by what were alleged to be the unlawful acts of its officers. To the surprise of the lawyers, as well as of the public, the judges held that—in spite of what had seemed the explicit provisions of the Trade Union Acts of 1871–76—a Trade Union could be made answerable in damages for all the acts of its officials, central or local, as if it were a corporate body, whilst still being denied the privileges of a corporate body. The strike and legal proceedings cost the Society from first to last nearly £50,000, whilst the danger to the corporate funds of all Trade Unions that the decision revealed put a damper on even the best justified strikes until, under persistent Trade Union pressure, strengthened by the entry into the House of Commons of a reinforced Labour Party, the Trade Disputes Act of 1906 restored the law to its state prior to the judicial decisions of 1902.

The railwaymen could then renew their " All Grades Movement " which the Companies in January 1907 again declined to consider, steadfastly refusing any recognition of the men's Trade Unions, and callously denying their

[1] The North Eastern Railway Company was so far an exception that, already in 1890, it was willing to receive representations from the Trade Union.

grievances.[1] Ballots of the membership of the Amalgamated Society and the General Union decided on a strike by 80,026 to 1857 votes, and in November 1907 a national stoppage was at hand when Mr. Lloyd George intervened as President of the Board of Trade, compelled the Companies to listen to reason, and persuaded both parties to accept an elaborate scheme of Local and Central Conciliation Boards, composed of equal numbers representing management and men, with an impartial chairman and authority to decide on wages and hours. These Conciliation Boards, unsatisfactory as they proved, represented a real triumph. For the first time the autocracy of the railway management was broken. There was, it is true, still no express recognition of the Trade Unions, but the men's representatives were to be freely elected on each railway by all the employees grouped according to their grades; and these elected representatives met the management on professedly equal terms. The elections showed how thoroughly justified was the claim of the Railwaymen's Trade Unions that they were voicing the wishes of practically the whole body of railwaymen. In spite of strenuous efforts by the management on most of the lines, and of the unfortunate jealousies among the different societies, in nearly all cases the nominees of one or other of the Unions were elected, often by large majorities. For the next few years the Amalgamated Society and the Associated Society of Locomotive Engineers and

---

[1] A notable feature was a statistical census of the wages of the railwaymen, compiled by the Amalgamated Society through its membership, for the presentation of which Mr. Richard Bell, the Secretary, obtained the services of a Cambridge graduate, Mr. W. T. Layton. This " Green Book " revealed that 38 per cent received 20s. per week or under, and 49.8 per cent between 21s. and 30s. ; with atrocious hours. Attempts to discredit these statistics were made by the Companies, it being in particular constantly suggested that nearly all the 100,000 paid under £1 per week were boys. It took the Board of Trade four years to compile and publish an official wage-census for October 1907, which eventually revealed that 96,000 adult railwaymen were receiving 19s. per week or less (Board of Trade Report, February 1912), an extraordinarily exact confirmation of the much-abused census taken by the Union. See *Men and Rails*, by Rowland Kenney, 1913.

Firemen were busy in fighting the cases of the various grades through the Conciliation Boards, and in securing thereby many small increases of wages and reductions of hours. But matters did not go smoothly. The Companies, for the most part, pursued a policy of obstruction and postponement, delaying the awards, quibbling about their application, and in some cases deliberately evading their terms, notably by inventing new grades to which men could be appointed at lower rates of pay than those prescribed. The " impartial " chairmen, moreover, differed among themselves in the assumptions on which they proceeded, and some of the awards caused great resentment. Meanwhile the cost of living was steadily rising, and railwaymen as a whole were falling further behind other organised workers. Progress was delayed in 1909–10 by a new set-back which the Amalgamated Society suffered in the law courts, in the prolonged litigation carried by one of its members, with capitalist assistance, right up to the House of Lords, by which the participation of any Trade Union in political activity was declared invalid—a piece of " judge-made law " to which we shall recur, and for which the Government and Parliament at first refused all redress. Suddenly, in August 1911, the pot boiled over. There was a spirit of revolt in the Labour world. In June and July the seamen and the dockers had struck, and stopped the port of London. There was an outburst of " unauthorised " railway strikes at Manchester, Liverpool, and some other big towns, and a general demand for a national strike. The Executives of the four principal railwaymen's Unions, for once acting closely in concert, gave the Companies twenty-four hours to decide whether they would consent to meet the men's representatives, or face a national stoppage. Once more the Government intervened, Mr. Asquith offering a Royal Commission of indefinite duration and issue, merely to propose amendments in the scheme of Conciliation Boards, and at the same time definitely informing the men—a fact which they judiciously refrained from publishing—that the Government would not hesitate to use the troops to prevent the commerce of the country from being interfered with.[1] The Unions refused the illusory offer, and a national strike began, which, although far from universal, was sufficient to disorganise the whole railway service—as many as 200,000 men stopping work—and was rapidly bringing industry to a standstill. At the instance of Mr. Winston Churchill, who was then Home Secretary, an overpowering display was made with the troops, which were sent to Manchester and other places, without requisition by the civil authorities, at the mere request of the Companies. In fact, a policy of repression had been decided on, and bloodshed was near at hand. In vain did the Union leaders ask Mr. Asquith, as Prime Minister, to take steps to obtain a meeting between the Companies' managers and the Union representatives. Wiser counsels seem to have prevailed in the Cabinet, which peremptorily instructed the Companies to let their General Managers meet the men's representatives face to face at the Board of Trade. For just upon twelve hours these managers, thus coerced, negotiated with four representatives of the Unions, together with Mr. Henderson and Mr. J. R. MacDonald of the Parliamentary Labour Party. At last an agreement was made—the first ever concluded between the Railway Companies as a whole and the Trade Unions of their employees—for an ending of the strike, on terms of complete reinstatement of the strikers ; an immediate consideration by the Conciliation Boards of all grievances ; and a prompt investigation by a bipartite Royal Commission of the dissatisfaction with these Boards, and the best way of amending the scheme.[2] When the

[1] This intimation undoubtedly meant that the Government had decided, as the *Times* expressly said, to use the Royal Engineers to run trains—a decision to be compared with that at once announced in the national railway strike of 1919, that no use would be made of the troops actually to run trains, nor would the Post Office officials be asked to do railwaymen's work, nor persons on State Unemployment Benefit be called upon to accept employment on the railways. The change in attitude of the Government in eight years is significant.

[2] The committee consisted, for the first time, of equal numbers of persons appointed as being representative of employers and workmen

Commission reported—it was ultimately termed a Special Committee of Inquiry—the Railwaymen's Union once more asked the Companies to meet them for negotiation, which the Companies again refused to do. On the Unions resolving to ballot their members as to a national strike, the House of Commons set a new precedent by passing, at the instance of the Government, a resolution formally recommending a joint meeting, whereupon the Companies gave way. At the meeting that ensued a new scheme of Conciliation Boards was jointly agreed to, amending the 1907 scheme generally on the line of the Special Committee's report, but introducing most of the other modifications that the Unions thought necessary. The machinery was made more rapid in action, and the scope of the Boards was extended. Most important of all, the men's side of each Board was allowed to choose as secretary a person not in the employ of the Company ; and it accordingly became possible for a Trade Union official to take up this work, and that not only for a single grade but, by acting for several Boards, simultaneously for all grades. This was not " recognition " in form, but at any rate the Trade Union official was let in. During the next two years, in spite of incredible obstructions, quibblings, and evasions by the Companies, a number of small improvements in the terms of service were obtained from the Boards for all the grades on practically all the lines. A result of this joint working of even greater importance was the merging, in 1913, after prolonged negotiations, of three out of the four principal societies of manual railway workers[1]—the Amalgamated, the General Union, and the

respectively—two on each side—none of them directly concerned with the industry, with an " impartial chairman," all five being selected by the Government. For the Companies, Sir T. Ratcliffe Ellis and Mr. C. G. Beale ; for the workmen, Mr. Arthur Henderson, M.P., and Mr. John Burnett ; the Chairman was Sir David Harrel, K.C.B., an official of the Irish Government.

[1] The Associated Society of Locomotive Engineers and Firemen, having now 51,000 members, unfortunately stood aloof ; and the annals of railway Trade Unionism were, down to 1918, largely made up of the wrangling between this society and the National Union of Railwaymen.

United Pointsmen and Signalmen—into a new Trade Union upon a carefully revised basis, under the title of the National Union of Railwaymen.

The " New Model " for Trade Union structure thus deliberately adopted merits attention. In contrast with what we have called the " New Model," in 1851 of the Amalgamated Society of Engineers, that of 1913 represents an attempt to include, in a single " amalgamated " Union, all the various " crafts " and grades of workers engaged in a single industry throughout the whole kingdom. The declared object of the National Union of Railwaymen is " to secure the complete organisation of all workers employed on or in connection with any railway in the United Kingdom." It thus definitely negatives both " sectionalism " and " localism " in favour of " Industrial Unionism." Indeed, it may be suggested that the new constitution passes, by definition, even beyond the " Industrial Unionism," to which the most advanced section of Trade Unionists were aspiring, into what has been termed " Employmental Unionism," in that it seeks to enrol in one Union, not merely all sections of railway workers, but actually all who are employed by any railway undertaking— thus including, not only the engineering and wood-working mechanics in the railway engineering workshops,[1] but also

---

[1] The mechanics and labourers in the railway companies' engineering and repairing shops, though many of them have always been members of the various engineering and other craft Unions, long remained relatively unorganised. Many of the less skilled were enrolled by the General Railway Workers' Union in 1889-1913; and when this was merged in the National Union of Railwaymen, with its broadened constitution, many more of the mechanics and labourers in the railway workshops were recruited, and the N.U.R. sought to obtain for them the advances and other benefits for which it was pressing. The railway companies disputed the right of the N.U.R. to speak for the " shopmen," and the claim provoked the resentment of the craft Unions, which were now paying increased attention to the organisation of men of their crafts in the railway workshops. Repeated attempts have been made to arrive at some " line of demarcation " or other compromise, by which this rivalry between Unions could be brought to an end ; but hitherto without success. The quarrel is inflamed by a conflict of Trade Union doctrine. The engineers, boilermakers, carpenters, and other trades assert that organisation should be

the cooks, waiters, and housemaids at the fifty-five railway hotels ; the sailors and firemen on board the railway companies' fleets of steamers, and (though no trouble has actually arisen about them) the compositors, lithographers, and bookbinders whom the railway printing works employ in the production of tickets, time-tables, office stationery, and advertisement posters ; even the men whom one, at least, of the largest companies keeps in constant employment at the manufacture of crutches and wooden legs for the disabled members of its staff. This all-inclusiveness has, since 1913, brought the National Union of Railwaymen into conflict with many other Trade Unions ; and the question of the proper lines of demarcation has so far remained unsettled. The principal new feature in constitutional structure was the establishment of a distinct legislature—the Annual General Meeting—consisting, in addition to the President and General Secretary, of sixty representatives elected by the membership in geographical constituencies of approximately equal size. Subordinate to the Annual General Meeting (which can be summoned specially when required) is the Executive Committee of the President, General Secretary, and twenty-four other members, the latter being severally elected by the device of the Single Transferable Vote by each of four prescribed departments of members in each of six gigantic geographical constituencies ; one-third of such representatives retiring annually, and after each triennial term of service, becoming ineligible for three years, whilst the Branches to which they belong also become unable to nominate representatives for a like term. The Executive Committee, which, like the Annual General Meeting, consists of working railwaymen, paid only for their days of service, meets quarterly and

---

by craft, whatever may be the industry in which the craftsman is working. The advocates of the " New Model " of the N.U.R. assert the superiority of organisation by industry, including in each industry all the crafts actually concerned. See *Trade Unionism on the Railways, its History and Problems*, by G. D. H. Cole and R. Page Arnot, 1917.

appoints four sectional sub-committees, which must also meet at least quarterly. Noteworthy, too, is the District Council, which—constitutionally only a voluntary federation of geographically adjacent Branches for propagandist and purely consultative purposes—has, with an unofficial National Federation of District Councils, developed into an active " caucus " of the more energetic members for discussing and promoting " forward movements " in the Annual General Meeting, and " organising " the elections to the Executive Committee.

With such a constitution, and the administration of extensive friendly benefits in a society now approaching half a million members, it is inevitable that the Executive Committee should wield extensive powers. It initiates and conducts all trade movements, and can therefore call a national strike, even without a ballot vote ; and whilst it may take a ballot vote at any time on any question, the rules expressly provide that it is not to be bound by the members' decision. Originally the Executive Committee had power also " to settle " any dispute ; but this was withdrawn by resolutions of the Annual General Meetings of 1915 and 1916, which required all settlements to be reported to itself for ratification. In practice very large powers, both of office management and of negotiation, are necessarily exercised by the six salaried officers, the President, the General Secretary, and the four Assistant Secretaries, each of whom is responsible for a separate branch of the Union's work. They have, however, not been able to prevent a series of " unauthorised " strikes, local or sectional in character.

At the beginning of 1914 everything pointed to a further forward movement by the N.U.R. Its Annual General Meeting cordially accepted the Miners' proposal to unite with them and the Transport Workers in the so-called Triple Alliance. Moreover, its desires now began to go beyond improvements in wages and hours. Its representatives had, for twenty years, sometimes moved and always supported the resolutions of the Trades Union Congress in favour of the Nationalisation of Railways. In 1913 the Railway Clerks' Association had gone a step further, and had asked also for participation in control. In 1914 the resolution intended to be submitted on behalf of the N.U.R. declared that " no system of State Ownership of the railways will be acceptable to organised railwaymen which does not guarantee to them their full political and social rights, allow them a due measure of control and responsibility in the safe and efficient working of the railway system, and assure to them a fair and equitable participation in the increased benefits likely to accrue from a more economical and scientific administration." Here we have the first expressions of the desire for participation in the management of the railways.[1] From that time forward the demand has become ever more explicit and determined. Meanwhile, however, the first step was plainly the drastic amendment of the scheme of Conciliation Boards ; and proposals were under consideration when war broke out. In marked contrast with their previous action, the Railway Companies were actually meeting the Union representatives in a joint committee of seven a side. The growth in membership of the National Union of Railwaymen at that date to over 300,000, and its entry into the " Triple Alliance " of miners, railwaymen, and transport workers, had, in fact, at last compelled the Companies, in fact, to concede " recognition," although they denied at the time that they were so doing. During the war the actual alteration of the scheme was to remain in abeyance, but the Executive Committee came in 1915 to a provisional agreement with the Companies as to certain amendments, which the Annual General Meeting of that year considered inadequate and refused to sanction. Meanwhile, in view of the rising cost of living, successive war

---

[1] The Presidential Address at the Annual Conference of the Railway Clerks' Association in 1913 had suggested that the representatives of the railway workers should constitute one-third of a National Railway Board —a proposal that did not content the larger Union.

bonuses, uniform throughout the Kingdom for all grades of the traffic staff, were obtained from the President of the Board of Trade—the cost, in effect, falling on the Government under its arrangement for guaranteeing to the shareholders the net revenue of 1913—amounting altogether to 33s. per week for men, 16s. 6d. per week for women and boys, and 8s. 3d. per week for girls, thus more than doubling the average pre-war wages. The Government, moreover, promised sympathetic consideration of the men's demand for an Eight Hours' Day immediately on the termination of the war.

When the Armistice in November 1918 brought hostilities to an end, negotiations were at once begun for a settlement of the outstanding questions. The National Union of Railwaymen, in more friendly conjunction with the Associated Society of Locomotive Engineers and Firemen, whilst gaining advances fully equivalent to the increase in the cost of living, had secured in principle not only recognition, but also the valuable right of entering into negotiation with the united management of all the railways, instead of always being referred to the several companies ; and even more important, it had obtained, in the uniform war bonuses, the basis of national rates of wages for the several grades, instead of rates and classes of workers varying from company to company. It was now to secure, without an effort, the Eight Hours' Day, to come into operation on February 1, 1919, which the Government, not even consulting the Railway Companies, singly or collectively, in December 1918, conceded in principle without reduction of wages, whilst the necessary reclassification of workers and adjustment of times and wages on a national system became the subject of prolonged and difficult negotiations between the Railway Executive Committee and the two principal Unions.

The negotiations for " standardisation " which necessarily involved the amalgamation of the uniform war bonus with the varying basic rate, were dragged out by the Government from February to the end of August, to the growing irritation of the railwaymen. What occurred, as Ministers subsequently confessed, or rather boasted, was that, beginning actually in February, the Government made extensive secret preparations to break the strike which it was foreseen would occur when the Government's decisions were made known. The railwaymen themselves confidently expected, seeing that the cost of living had not fallen, but was officially certified, in September 1919, at 115 per cent above that of July 1914, that their rates would be " standardised upwards," so as both to adopt the scales of the best companies for all the staff, and to include the whole of the war bonus. But this automatic inclusion of the war bonus in the Standard Rate, which some trades had already secured, was exactly what the leading industrial employers were, for their own trades, anxious to prevent. They counted, indeed, on bringing about throughout British industry, during 1919 or 1920, irrespective of any change in the cost of living, a general reduction of the " swollen " wages of war-time ; and there was a prevalent feeling among them, which is known to have been shared by some, at least, of the Ministers, and quite frankly expressed, that a big "fight with the Trade Unions " was inevitable, and that it would be " better to get it over " before industry had generally restarted under peace conditions. How far Sir Auckland Geddes, who as President of the Board of Trade was responsible for the negotiations, and his brother, Sir Eric Geddes, who as Minister of Transport took over the work, shared this view, and allowed it to inspire their official action, has not been revealed. The historian can only note that the Government proceedings appear consistent with this hypothesis. The Government deliberately separated from the mass of railwaymen the locomotive drivers and firemen, whose services were regarded as specially indispensable, and whose allegiance was divided between the two rival Unions. In August acceptable terms were proposed for these two classes, which conceded not only the absorption of the whole war bonus in the new scale of wages, but also certain further increases of pay, coming near to the Union's full claims. Such a concession, it was subsequently noted, was admirably calculated, in the event of a strike, to detach the drivers and firemen from their fellow-members ; to divide the two Unions, and to arouse expectations in the other grades which would make it practically certain that they would indignantly refuse the offer that was to be made in a few weeks. When the " definite " decision of the Government was sent to the Union, in a letter in which Sir Auckland Geddes with his own hand altered the word to " definitive," as if in order to ensure an explosion, it was found that by the new scale, beginning on January 1, 1920, every grade was to suffer a reduction off existing earnings, varying from only a shilling or two per week in some cases up to as much as sixteen shillings per week—the new standard rate of the porter, for instance, being fixed at 40s., as compared with the 51s. or 53s. that he was actually receiving, or with the 60s. per week for which the Union had asked. No explanation was given by the brothers Geddes that what was intended was that there should be on January 1, 1920, no reduction whatever in the men's earnings, and that the Government's policy was (as subsequently stated by Mr. Lloyd George, but only on the very morning of the strike, which was the first revelation of it) that there should never be any reduction at all unless the cost of living fell for over three months below 110 per cent in excess of pre-war prices, and that (as was announced only in the Government advertisements on the eighth day of the strike) the future " sliding scale," which had never been definitely formulated, would be allowed to work upwards as well as downwards. Unless the intention of the " definitive " offer was then and there to provoke an indignant strike, why was no hint of this " policy for 1920 " included ; why was it left to be only incidentally revealed, in such a way as not to be easily understood, in the final personal discussion with the Prime Minister ; and, seeing that the Minister of Food himself had publicly announced that what was probable, from January

1920, was not a fall but a further rise in the cost of living, why was the alarming suggestion of a reduction to 40s. per week ever made at all ? It is almost impossible to avoid the inference that the Government, which certainly decided the date and the issues, decided also the strike itself, with a view to " beating the Union," in order to get a free hand for railway reorganisation without the necessity of consulting the operatives ; in order, probably, to fit in with the general capitalist project of a scaling down of the " swollen " war-wages ; and, as some say, in order to supply Mr. Lloyd George with a useful " election stunt," with which, in the eyes of the middle class, irretrievably to damage the Labour Party.

Whether intentionally on the part of the Ministers, or by reason of an amazing maladroitness in their negotiations, what had been foreseen and expected by the Government, and for six months secretly prepared for, actually came to pass. On Wednesday, September 24, the Executive Council of the National Union of Railwaymen issued orders for a national strike to begin at midnight on Friday, September 26, unless countermanded by telegraph. So little had the Union intended or contemplated such action that absolutely no notice of the crisis had been given to the Miners' Federation or the Transport Workers' Federation, who were the railwaymen's colleagues in the Triple Alliance ; and the Union had only some £3000 available in cash. Efforts were made by the men to avert the stoppage, which it was recognised would be a national calamity. The Executive Council sought and obtained long interviews with the Prime Minister himself on Thursday, and even on the Friday morning ; and the verbatim reports of these discussions reveal (a) that the Government showed no inclination to meet the men's case—Sir Eric Geddes peremptorily intervening at one point even to prevent a criticism of the " definitive " new scale being adduced ; (b) that the Government did not even then set forth what subsequently turned out to have been the proposal that the Ministry of Transport had really intended to make (unless, indeed, we are to assume that the " definitive " offer was silently changed in the course of the strike). Again, it can only be inferred that Mr. Lloyd George either did not wish to prevent the strike or else was quite exceptionally below his usual level of lucidity in explanation of any scheme that he wished to have accepted. What the Prime Minister did was immediately to denounce to the public the National Union of Railwaymen as engaged in an anarchist conspiracy !

The nine days' stoppage that ensued was, in many respects, the most remarkable industrial conflict that we have yet seen. Half a million railwaymen left their work at midnight on the 26th of September, the Associated Society of Locomotive Engineers and Firemen at once joining loyally with the N.U.R., and very nearly every member of either Union coming out. The men on the Irish railways were directed to remain at work. Never before had there been so nearly a complete stoppage of the railway service from one end of Great Britain to the other. It is to be noted that the third Union, the Railway Clerks' Association (which had come to include the Clerical, Administrative, and Supervisory Staffs), directed its members to remain absolutely neutral, and not to do any of the strikers' work. The various Unions of Post Office employees sought and obtained an official decision that they were not to be called upon to do any service hitherto done by men on strike. The Government, which sent soldiers to guard some of the railway stations,[1] hastened to announce publicly—in significant contrast with its decision of 1912—that in no case would the troops be employed to run trains. For the first time the Government found itself liable to pay unemployment benefit to all other workers who were stopped as a result of the strike ; and for the enormous extension of the State Unemployment Benefit that was expected to be required, arrangements were promulgated under which the

---

[1] It was reported that in some cases the soldiers fraternised with the pickets and were promptly withdrawn to barracks ; and the Cabinet was certainly warned, by high military authority, against attempting to use the troops.

Benefit would be issued by each employer to his own wage-earners, when these were thrown idle by the strike ; and that whilst such persons might be called upon to take temporary employment in handling food supplies, they would not be required to accept service on the railways themselves.

There was, in spite of wild newspaper exaggerations, practically no disorder and no attempt to injure property. Except in a very few cases, in which local mishandling of the situation by the authorities led to resentment and misunderstanding, the Executive Council's order that the horses were not to be allowed to suffer was cordially acted on by the men. The Government was allowed, without attempt at obstruction, to bring at once into operation the elaborate arrangements it had long been preparing, for ensuring the regular supply of London and other large towns with milk and other foodstuffs by means of an extensive motor-lorry service. Volunteers for railway work were called for, and with the aid of the small remnant of non-unionists a tiny trickle of trains was set going, which provided for the local passenger service in London and some other cities ; and gradually accomplished one or two long-distance trains per day, which carried the mails and were crowded with venturous passengers. What stopped almost completely was the mineral and heavy goods traffic, and by the end of the week so many industries had come to the end of their fuel, and so many coalpits were short of waggons and of room at the pithead, that, whilst nearly 400,000 workmen in collieries and factories were already idle, the next week would have seen literally millions unemployed. Meanwhile, in spite of press reports to the contrary, the Union Executives knew that, whilst a few men returned to work, each day more joined the strikers, so that there were actually a greater number signing the book at the end than at the beginning of the struggle. But the National Union of Railwaymen found considerable difficulty in realising from its investments, and in making locally available at a couple of thousand centres, sufficient cash to pay immediately the half a million pounds of strike pay that was required ; and only the prompt and cordial assistance of the Co-operative Wholesale Society's printing department, which got out the necessary supply of cheques in marvellously quick time, and of the Co-operative Wholesale Society's Bank, which made the N.U.R. cheques payable at the several Co-operative Societies themselves, averted a breakdown. Food was in some cases refused to the strikers by shopkeepers ; and it may be that it was only the prompt assistance of the Co-operative Societies, which agreed to honour vouchers issued by the local strike committees, that prevented the Government from putting in operation a project of starving out the railwaymen's families by withdrawing their ration cards or withholding the food supplies under Government control. One blow below the belt the Government did strike in arbitrarily commanding the withholding from the strikers of a whole week's pay which they had earned by their service prior to the stoppage, and which it was the custom of the companies always to keep in hand for a week by way of security against theft or embezzlement. This had never been done in any previous railway strike. Whether or not the railwaymen had broken any legal contract of service by giving only three days' notice of their strike, is not clear—the point appears never to have been raised or decided,—but in any case the companies had only a right to sue each man for any damages that might be shown to be caused by such a breach of contract ; and the Government had plainly no legal warrant for becoming the judge in its own cause, and itself arbitrarily assessing the damages due from each man at precisely one week's earnings. This action, coupled with the evasive and ever-changing terms of the Government's wage proposals, and the campaign of abuse that the Government organised throughout the press—personally directed by Sir William Sutherland, one of the Prime Minister's secretaries—had a great influence in rallying the Trade Union world in support of the railwaymen.

The " publicity campaign," by which, for the first time in an industrial struggle, a persistent organised appeal was made by both sides to public opinion, was, indeed, the most remarkable feature of the struggle. At the outset the Government, in spite of the outspoken advocacy of the *Daily Herald*, had it all its own way. The public, seriously inconvenienced by the stoppage, was told by nearly every newspaper in the Kingdom—daily supplied by a Government office with a lengthy bulletin of " Strike News "—that the strike was the result of an " anarchist " conspiracy among the railwaymen ; that the Union had wantonly broken off negotiations without cause because it positively wished to " hold up " the whole community ; that the Government had not really intended any reduction of wages at all, and that the figure of 40s. had reference only to the contingency of the cost of living reverting to what it was before the war ; that, in fact, the Government were positively doubling the railwaymen's wages, and that the men, realising this, and discovering how they had been deceived by their Executive Council, were resuming their duties at all points. To counteract this Government propaganda, the *Daily Herald* made the most enterprising arrangements for getting its issue distributed all over England, and more than doubled its circulation, whilst the National Union of Railwaymen employed its own Publicity Department, utilising for this purpose the Labour Research Department.[1] A number of competent writers, cartoonists, and statisticians belonging to the Labour Party placed their services in this way at the Research Department's disposal, so that the Executive Council was able, within a couple of days, to pour forth a stream of articles, letters, speeches, and cartoons, for which the newspapers generally accorded space.[2] Every move of the Government, and every statement that it issued,

[1] For an account of this Department see pp. 571-2.
[2] A notable feature was a revolt of the compositors and printers' assistants, who threatened to strike and stop the newspapers altogether unless the railwaymen were allowed to present their case and unless abusive posters were abandoned.

was immediately countered by an appropriate answer. When Mr. Lloyd George supplied a message denouncing the strikers which appeared on the film in every cinema, Mr. J. H. Thomas was himself filmed in the act of delivering a cogent reply. But the Union's Publicity Department found the space given by the newspapers inadequate, and started placing full-page advertisements in the *Times* and other newspapers, in which the Government's equivocations and evasions as to the wages offered were effectively exposed. The Government followed suit, and presently the two advertisements appeared on successive pages, with the unforeseen result that the Government's statement of its proposals to the men was detected in changing from day to day as the strike continued, growing progressively more favourable to the men, but professing still to be the " definitive " decision of Sir Auckland Geddes which had provoked the strike. The outcome of a week's skilfully organised " publicity " was a steady shifting of public opinion, and even a distinct change in the newspaper editorials. By the end of the week the men's case was winning.

Meanwhile, the leaders of the principal Trade Unions indirectly affected by the railway stoppage, notably the various sections of Transport Workers, together with officials or representatives of the Miners, the Parliamentary Committee, and the Labour Party, had been meeting in anxious conclave—summoned, it should be stated, by the Executive of the National Transport Workers' Federation— with a view to restraining their own members from impetuous action in support of the railwaymen, and to bringing pressure to bear on both parties to secure a settlement. At first the prospect seemed hopeless. The Government took up an attitude of defiance. Mr. Lloyd George declared that he would not enter into any negotiations with the railwaymen's Unions until the men had unconditionally returned to their duty. A national appeal was made to all the Local Authorities—not to strengthen the police force by special constables, as is the constitutional procedure, but to institute a " Citizen Guard," in order to repel the forces of disorder ; a wild use of a term of bad omen, which was calculated, if not intended, to bring the " class war " into the streets. It was known that measures of arbitrary confiscation of the Union funds were seriously under consideration, together with discriminatory issues of food supplies. On the other side, the feeling of the Trade Unionists was rising to anger. The position could not well have been more serious. But the " eleven "—afterwards the " fourteen "—Trade Union mediators were patient and persistent. They had long interviews with the railwaymen's Executive. They had long discussions with the Prime Minister, the Chancellor of the Exchequer, and the Minister of Transport. They cleared up misunderstandings. They eliminated provocative expressions. They brought the Government to admit that there was no present chance of reducing wages. They got the railwaymen to see that merely to postpone the issue was to strengthen their grip upon what they were actually receiving. Notwithstanding the Government's defiant words, the Trade Union mediators got the railwaymen's Executive Council into prolonged and repeated discussions at 10 Downing Street with the Prime Minister and his colleagues.[1] At last, on Sunday morning, October 3, Mr. Lloyd George and Mr. Thomas were closeted together for the final stage ; the news was immediately flashed all over the kingdom that the strike was settled, and in the evening Mr. Thomas announced to a mass meeting of railwaymen in the Albert Hall the terms of settlement. These included an immediate resumption of work without victimisation or recrimination ; payment of the impounded arrears of wages ; " stabilisation " of existing earnings of all rates (except where improved) until September 30, 1920 ; negotiations as to " standardisation " and settlement of wage scales to be begun again, and a settlement to be come to before

---

[1] *Railway Dispute, 1919: Report to the Labour Movement of Great Britain by the Committee appointed at the Caxton Hall Conference* (National Transport Workers' Federation).

December 31, 1919 ; and the lowest adult railwayman to be raised forthwith to 51s. per week as a minimum. Before the end of 1919 it was announced that the Government had agreed to concede, for the future, that all questions relating to the conditions of service should be dealt with, not by the railway companies but by a Central Board of ten members (with power to increase by a further one on each side), five nominees of the National Union of Railwaymen and the Associated Society of Locomotive Engineers and Firemen, and five representatives of the railway management. In case of disagreement, reference will be made to an Appeal Board of twelve members, four nominated by these Trade Unions, four representing the management, and four the general public, with a chairman nominated by the Government. What is specially significant is that it is recognised that " the public " does not consist merely of the upper and middle, or of the capitalist and professional classes. Of the four representatives of the public, two are to be nominated, respectively, by the Associated Chambers of Commerce and the Federation of British Industries, and two, respectively, by the Parliamentary Committee of the Trades Union Congress and the Co-operative Union, who are thus taken to represent the four-fifths of the population (and therefore of the railway users) who are manual working wage-earners. At the same time it was conceded that the Advisory Committee for Railway Management, which replaces under the Minister of Transport the Railway Executive Committee, is to include, from the start, three representatives of the railwaymen's Unions, all the members having equal and identical functions and rights.

We do not yet know what agreement will be reached about " standardisation " or the future scale of wages, but the Ministry of Transport is not likely to try another fall with the railwaymen's Trade Unions. The strike has had, indeed, results of the first importance. The Government has learnt that Trade Unionism is not easily beaten, even when all the resources of the State are put forth against it,

T

and when public opinion is incensed. The great capitalist organisations have seen the warning against their projects of a general reduction of wages ; and this is postponed, at least, for a year. On the other hand, the railwaymen's Unions have realised the magnitude of the struggle into which they so precipitately entered, or into which they were so artfully inveigled. The need for, and the potency of, skilled publicity work, and the possibilities of a highly organised and adequately supported Labour Research Department, are commonly recognised. Finally, it is seen that national industrial conflicts of such a magnitude are matters of wider concern to the Trade Union world than any one Union can appreciate ; and an attempt was made, to be subsequently described, if not to continue in existence the group of " Fourteen Mediators," at least to get established some authoritative standing Council, by which the approach of an impending industrial crisis of national scope could be closely watched, so that all the necessary steps may be taken in time to deal with the situation in the best possible way. The Trade Union world realised its need for what was called a General Staff.

Amalgamations and Federations

Whilst the numerical strength and industrial and political influence of the several Trade Unions have thus steadily increased during the past thirty years, it is less easy to characterise the changes in the relations of Trade Unions with each other.

The multiplicity of separate organisations in which the six or seven million Trade Unionists are grouped, and the complication and diversity of the relations among the various societies, continue to-day, as they did thirty years ago, to baffle classification, and almost to defy analysis. It remains as impossible as it was in 1890 to state precisely how many distinct Trade Unions are in existence, because the endless variety of their federal organisations makes it uncertain which of the local or sectional Unions are to be counted as independent societies. We estimate, however, that upon any computation the number of financially distinct organisations, which we may put at about 1100, remains approximately what it was thirty years ago. The tendency to amalgamation, that is to say, has just about kept pace, arithmetically, with the starting of new organisations, whilst the average membership of each unit has more than quadrupled.

Such a statement fails, however, to do justice to the change that has come over the Trade Union world. Thirty years ago it was, on the whole, a congeries of numerically small units, only two or three of which counted as many as 50,000 members. To-day there are nearly a dozen which severally manage memberships of a quarter of a million, and probably fifty which deal with more than 50,000 each. A few other national societies of smaller membership are of some importance. Scattered up and down the United Kingdom a thousand other local or sectional societies exist, with memberships from a few dozen to a few thousand, but these play no part and exercise no influence in the movement as a whole. Probably five-sixths of all the Trade Union membership, and practically all its effective force, are to be found among the hundred principal societies to which the Ministry of Labour has long confined its detailed statistics.[1]

The movement for the amalgamation of competing societies has, during the past decade, been specially energetic and persistent. This has arisen, partly spontaneously, from the obvious disadvantages attendant both on rivalry

---

[1] British Trade Unionism has often been contrasted, to its disadvantage, with the more scientifically classified German Trade Unionism before the Great War. It was, for instance, often pointed out that the three millions of German Trade Unionists were grouped in no more than 48 Unions. This, however, ignored the numerous competing Hirsch-Duncker and Christian Unions, which were far more destructive of unity than are the crowd of minor societies in Great Britain and Ireland. At present (1920) the 48 largest Trade Unions of this country concentrate a larger membership than the much-praised 48 Trade Unions of Germany did in 1914.

between Trade Unions seeking to enrol the same classes of members throughout the kingdom—such as that between the various societies of railway employees—and on the division of workmen of the same craft among a number of independent local societies, such as the Coopers, the Chippers and Drillers, and the Painters and other branches of the Building Trades. But during the past decade the movement has been reinforced by the desire for an organisation based on the whole of an industry, such as engineering, housebuilding, mining, or the railway service, in which all the co-operating crafts and grades of workers would be associated in a single Industrial Union ; in contrast with the earlier conception of the separate organisation of each craft throughout the whole kingdom ; such as that of the carpenters, the enginemen, the engineering mechanics, the clerks, and by analogy the general labourers, in whatsoever industry they may be working. The case for the Industrial Union in such an industry as mining, for example, merely from the standpoint of Collective Bargaining, and for the sake of getting effective Common Rules, has always been a strong one ; but the movement for the substitution of " Industrial " for " Craft " Unionism has been strengthened since about 1911 by the aspirations of those who saw in Trade Unionism something more than an organisation for raising wages and shortening the working day. If the wage-earners were ever to obtain, through their own voluntary associations, the control of their own working lives, and to obtain a steadily increasing participation in the direction of industry ; if a Vocational Democracy were to be superimposed on a Democracy based on geographical constituencies ; it seemed as if this could be done only by Trade Unions co-extensive with each separate industry. The influence of the movement known as " Guild Socialism " has accordingly been exercised, on the whole, in favour of Industrial Unionism, not so much for the sake of its immediate advantages in improving the conditions of the wage-contract, as because it was only in this form that

Trade Unionism could become the vehicle of aspirations to the control of each industry by the whole mass of the workers employed therein.

Except in the way of industrial federations, to be hereafter referred to, it is only in mining and the railway service that any great progress has been made in this direction. The Miners' Federation of Great Britain, established, as we have seen, only in 1888, with no more than 36,000 members, has attracted to itself, year by year, an almost continuous stream of local or sectional organisations among the 1,200,000 workers in and about the coal and iron-stone mines ; successively absorbing into one or other of its local units or affiliating directly to itself, not only all the district associations, old or new, of coal-hewers and other underground workers, but also some of the separate organisations of enginemen and firemen, mine mechanics, deputies and overmen, colliery clerks, cokemen, and others employed in or about the mines, until its aggregate membership in 1920 is somewhere about 900,000. And though the Miners' Federation is still only a Federation of fully autonomous district associations—some of these, too, being themselves federations of the organisations of lesser localities ; and although it still depends for its funds almost entirely upon specific levies upon its constituents, it has found means, by its frequently meeting delegate conferences, controlling the strong Executive Committee which they elect, to centralise very effectively the general policy of the whole mining industry, notably with regard to the hours of labour, the conditions of safety, the percentage of general advances of wages and the amount of the national war bonuses, and last, though not least, on the burning issue of nationalisation of the mines and the participation of the miners in their administration. But although the Miners' Federation embodies in its constitution the principles of federalism and an extreme local autonomy, it takes no account of sectional differences, and makes no provision for the representation at its delegate conferences, or upon its Executive Committee, of any distinct grades or sections. Perhaps, for this reason, the Federation does not yet speak directly for all the organised manual working wage-earners in the industry. There are at least forty separate Trade Unions of enginemen, boilermen and firemen, colliery mechanics, cokemen, under-managers, deputies, overmen and other officials, colliery clerks, and surface-workers of various kinds, not yet affiliated to the Miners' Federation, either locally or nationally; these have formed National Federations, parallel with the Miners' Federation of Great Britain, of enginemen, deputies, colliery mechanics and under-managers respectively; and in February 1917 seventeen of the societies drew together to form the National Council of Colliery Workers other than Miners, for the purpose of maintaining their separate influence.

In the railway service, as we have already described, the merging in the Amalgamated Society of Railway Servants, first of the Scottish Society in 1892, and then of the General Railway Workers' Union, and the United Signalmen and Pointsmen's Society in 1913, made possible the establishment of the National Union of Railwaymen on the basis of an organisation co-extensive with the industry, with the embodiment in the constitution of sectional representation. The four " departments " into which the members are divided vote separately in the elections. Under these provisions the National Union of Railwaymen, though hampered by the continuance of the separate Associated Society of Locomotive Engineers and Firemen, has been able to make effective not only its claims for higher remuneration, but also its demands for a normal Eight Hours Day, a national system of classification, and national wage scales for the several grades; though still not its aspirations (expressed since 1914) to participation in management, or those (expressed for over a decade) to the elimination from industry of the capitalist profitmaker by the scheme of Railway Nationalisation.

In other industries, too, the concentration of Trade

Union forces during the past decade has increasingly taken the form of an amalgamation of rival sectional organisations, sometimes in response to a demand from the rank and file. Thus the Ship Constructors' and Shipwrights' Association, established in 1888, has successfully absorbed not only the very old Shipwrights' Provident Union of London, but also all the remaining local Trade Unions of shipwrights that long lingered in Liverpool, Dublin, etc. The National Amalgamated Furnishing Trades Association has taken over a number of small societies of French polishers, gilders, and upholsterers. The United Garment Workers' Trade Union was formed in 1915 by the amalgamation of a number of societies in the various sections of the tailoring trade ; and in 1919 it was agreed that this, together with the Scottish Society of Tailors and Tailoresses, should be merged in the old Amalgamated Society of Tailors and Tailoresses, which would then include practically all the organised workers in the making of men's and women's clothing in Great Britain. Many small Unions of machine workers, minor craftsmen, and general labourers have been absorbed in one or other of the half-a-dozen large Labour Unions. The Amalgamated Card and Blowing-Room Operatives have taken over various small sectional societies in the Cotton trade. In Sheffield thirteen small Unions, catering for different sections of the gold and silver workers, joined together in 1910 in the Gold, Silver, and Kindred Trades Society, which in 1913 absorbed several more societies in this industry. In the autumn of 1919, as we have already mentioned, six of the sectional societies in the engineering industry decided to merge themselves, with the Amalgamated Society of Engineers, in a new and more gigantic amalgamation with 400,000 members ; the United Pattern Makers' Society, the Electrical Trades Union, and many small and specialised societies of mechanics in iron still standing aloof. In the same month three of the principal Unions of postal and telegraph employees united in a single Union of Post Office Workers, with 90,000 members. Other amalgamations among small or local societies took place among the Basket-makers, the Block Printers, the Leather-workers, the Dyers, the various sections in the Pottery Trade, etc.

Such amalgamation is greatly obstructed by legal requirements. Down to 1917 the law demanded that each society desiring to unite should ratify the decision by a two-thirds majority not merely of those voting, but of the entire membership. Such a poll is almost impossible of attainment by Trade Unions, whose members cannot usually be individually communicated with, owing not only to their frequent changes of residence and the absence of many of them abroad, but also to the lack, in most cases, of any complete register of addresses. In 1917 the Government at last permitted the passage of an Amending Act for which Trade Unionists had often pressed; but even then insisted on any amalgamation being carried, at a 50 per cent poll of the whole membership, by at least 20 per cent majority, conditions which make amalgamation everywhere difficult, and in some Unions (such as those of seamen) quite impossible. In several cases Unions in which the general opinion has been in favour of amalgamation have failed to get the necessary vote. We have already described the ingenious device by which the British Steel Smelters' Society and the Iron and Steel Trades Confederation surmounted this difficulty.

Meanwhile, of federations as distinct from amalgamations the Trade Union world has a variety more bewildering than ever, some of which have already been referred to. We have to note that the Engineering and Shipbuilding Trades Federation, the establishment of which in 1889 we described in *Industrial Democracy*, has continued in existence, doing useful work from time to time in connection with demarcation disputes and other subjects of inter-union controversy, especially on the North-East Coast, notably contributing also in 1905 to the successful claim of the Clyde trades to weekly instead of fortnightly pays, which the employers had stubbornly resisted for a whole decade, but continuing to be weakened by the abstention, except for a few years, of the Amalgamated Society of Engineers, which, however, now frequently consents to act in conjunction with it in general trade questions.

What is significant is the change in type and purpose of these multifarious industrial federations, which have now come to form an important element in the Trade Union world.[1] Federation, in fact, has undergone a subtle change of character. Instead of loose alliances for mutual support in disputes, or for the adjustment of mutual differences as to " demarcation " and transfer of members, the federations of all the craft or sectional Unions engaged in particular industries—notably those of the Building Trades, the Transport Workers, and, though not yet to the same extent, the Printing Trades and the Woollen Workers, like the older organisation of the Cotton Operatives—have become increasingly, themselves negotiating bodies, recognised by the equally organised employers, and concerting with these what are, in effect, national regulations governing their industries throughout the whole kingdom. The later development of the Engineering and Shipbuilding Trades Federation has been in the same direction. In the case of the Miners' Federation of Great Britain the development has gone still further ; and this great organisation, whilst retaining the federal form, and, even now, not completely admitted to " recognition " by the Mining Association of Great Britain, unquestioningly acts for the whole industry in national issues, as if it were an " amalgamated " Union. Whether or not we are to see all the rival and sectional Unions in each industry amalgamating into a single " Industrial Union," as many Trade Unionists desire, it must be recognised that the development, during the past decade, of active negotiating federations for the several industries goes far to supply the most urgent need. In short, although financially distinct Trade Unions remain, on the whole, as numerous as ever, the number of separate negotiating

[1] See *An Introduction to Trade Unionism*, by G. D. H. Cole, 1917.

T 2

bodies, so far as concerns matters relating to an industry as a whole, becomes steadily smaller.

We pass now to federal bodies of a different character.

THE GENERAL FEDERATION OF TRADE UNIONS

In 1899, arising out of the losses caused by the costly engineering dispute of 1897–98, the Trades Union Congress established a General Federation of Trade Unions, largely at the instance of Robert Knight, the able secretary of the Boilermakers, designed exclusively as a mutual reinsurance agency against the heavy financial burden to which, in the form of Strike Pay, or Dispute or Contingent Benefit, labour disputes subject every active trade society.[1]   By means of a small contribution from a large aggregate membership (1s. or 2s. per year per member), the General Federation is able to recoup to its constituent societies 2s. 6d. or 5s. per week per member affected towards their several expenditures upon disputes.   Beginning with 44 societies, having a total membership of 343,000, it steadily increased the number of its adherents until, in 1913, it had affiliated as many as 150 societies, having at that date 884,291 members.   Since that time the number of societies has dropped to 141 in 1919 ; but their increase in membership had raised the aggregate affiliation to 1,215,107, the largest ever recorded.   The General Federation, whilst suffering for the past seven years from an arrest of growth, has to its credit twenty years' success in surmounting the difficulties which have destroyed every previous attempt of the kind, and its prudent management is shown by the fact that it was able, from its normal revenue, to discharge all its obligations down to 1905, and to accumulate a reserve of £119,656.   In that year the members rashly insisted on a reduction of the contribution by one-third, not foreseeing the outburst of disputes in 1908–9,

---

[1] See the *History of the British Trades Union Congress* (by W. J. Davis), vol. ii. (1916), p. 156 ; and the successive *Annual Reports* of the General Federation of Trade Unions from 1900 onward.

which caused the Federation to pay out for 638 disputes no less than £122,778, and necessitated in 1913 the doubling of the contribution. Since that date, in spite of payments to societies averaging £1500 every week of the year, the Federation has not only met its engagements, but also built up a reserve exceeding a quarter of a million sterling. In 1911 it formed an Approved Society under the National Insurance Act, with the object of relieving the separate Trade Unions, and notably the thousand small ones, from the onerous task of separately administering the Act, and to ensure that their members did not go off to the Industrial Insurance Companies, an effort which has failed to attract more than a few thousand members. An extension of the effort to the provision of death benefits, by the formation of a Friendly Society section in 1913, has proved scarcely more successful.

It must be recognised that during the past six or seven years the Federation has lost favour with important sections of the Trade Union world. It was probably inevitable that its inclusion of small sectional societies should eventually bring it into conflict with the larger Unions by whom such societies are often regarded as illegitimate competitors. Grounds of this kind may be assigned for the secession of the Amalgamated Society of Engineers and the Amalgamated Society of Tailors in 1915 ; and for the powerful hostility shown since 1913 by the Miners' Federation of Great Britain. But this feeling has been accentuated by a growing resentment of the part played by the General Federation— not unconnected with the forceful personality of the General Secretary—first in international relations, and secondly in the representation of Trade Union opinion to the Government and to the public.

The General Federation, from its very establishment, affiliated itself to the International Trade Union Federation, which aimed at the collection and publication of statistics of Trade Unionism all over the world by an International Trade Union Secretariat, and at the mutual interchange of Trade Union information. For the first fifteen years of its existence this action of the General Federation was not objected to, although the fact that it represented only 25 to 30 per cent of British Trade Unionism impaired the value of its statistical contributions. The Parliamentary Committee of the Trades Union Congress, which might well have undertaken the task, long ignored its international interests ; but during the Great War increasingly resented the appearance of the General Federation as the representative of British Trade Unionism, and especially the almost continuous negotiations between its secretary, Mr. Appleton, and Mr. Gompers, the Secretary of the American Federation of Labor, and with M. Jouhaux, the Secretary of the *Confederation Générale du Travail* of France, along lines not consistent with those of the Labour Party and the Trades Union Congress. When, in 1918, attempts were made to reconstitute the International Federation of Trade Unions, the Parliamentary Committee claimed at first to be itself the representative of Great Britain ; but presently compromised on a joint and equal representation by the two bodies.

But more serious than the question of international representation was the resentment at the ever-widening range of subjects at home on which Mr. Appleton, the Management Committee, and the Conferences of the General Federation claimed to voice the feelings of Organised Labour. It was urged that the Federation was formed exclusively for the purpose of mutually reinsuring Strike Benefit, and that it had accordingly no mandate, and did nothing but weaken the Trade Union forces, both in the narrow field of the conditions of the wage contract, and on the broader issues of Labour's political aspirations, whenever it entered into rivalry with the Parliamentary Committee of the Trades Union Congress on the one hand, or with the Labour Party on the other. It looks as if the General Federation must in future either restrict itself to the limited range of its original purpose, or else run the risk of being financially weakened by the secession of influential Trade Unions, which will not permanently remain affiliated to all three national bodies, when finding these speaking on the same subjects with different voices.

TRADES COUNCILS

Of another form of loose federation of the branches of all the Trade Unions within a given area we have already described the origin and the development in the local Trades Councils. These have gone on increasing in number, much more than in strength, until in 1920 we estimate that more than 500 are in existence, with an aggregate affiliated membership running into several millions of Trade Unionists. The character of their active membership, their functions, and their proceedings have remained much as we described them thirty years ago ; but they have, on the whole, increased in strength and local influence, as well as in numbers and membership. They were, as we shall presently mention, somewhat arbitrarily excluded in 1895 from the Trades Union Congress, of which they were actually the originators ; and although they have since joined in various provincial federations of Trades Councils,[1] these have never acquired any great strength, and do little more than arrange for co-operation in local demonstrations. An attempt to form a National Federation of Trades Councils did not succeed. On the other hand, as we shall describe in Chapter XI., the Trades Councils were, from its establishment in 1900, admitted, equally with Trade Unions, as constituents of the Labour Representation Committee (now the Labour Party), and whether as Trades Councils, or (notably with the smaller ones) in their new form of " Trades Councils and Local Labour Parties," they are coming slowly to form its geographical basis. It is more and more on the political side that they are in some degree succeeding in uniting the energies of the Trade Unions of a particular town. This is especially the case so far as municipal politics are concerned.

[1] Such as those for Kent, Lancashire and Cheshire, North Wales, the South-Western Counties, and Yorkshire.

They have, for instance, been the main force in securing the general adoption of the Fair Wages Clause, and in furthering the election of Labour Candidates to local governing bodies. But they are rigidly excluded from all participation in the government or trade policy of the Unions ; and, so far as Trade Unionism itself is concerned, their direct influence on questions of national scope is not great. Consisting, as in the main they do, of the delegates elected by branches of national societies, they are hampered by the narrow limits of the branch autonomy. For in trade matters the branch can bring to the Council no power which it does not itself possess, whilst towards any action involving expense by the Council it can, in many Unions, contribute only the voluntary extra-subscriptions of its members. During the present century, however, many Unions have started paying from central funds the affiliation fees of their branches to Trades Councils. Down to the end of the Nineteenth Century, however, the resources of the Councils accordingly seldom sufficed for more than the hire of a room to meet in,[1] the necessary postage and stationery, and the payment of a few pounds a year for the " loss of time " of their principal officers. In no case except London does a Trades Council as such, even in 1920, pay a " full-time " salary, so as to command the whole time of a single salaried official, though the Trades Councils of cities like Glasgow, Manchester, and Bradford have salaried secretaries who have other duties ; and where the Trades Council is combined with the Local Labour Party it is more and more coming to have the services of a Registration Officer or Election Agent, whose salary is usually provided as part of the election expenses of the Labour candidate.

For a long time it could hardly be said that the Trades Councils enjoyed even the moral support of the great

---

[1] At Nottingham, Leicester, Brighton, Hanley, Manchester, Worcester, and some other towns, the Trades Council has at times been allowed the use of a room in the Town Hall, or other municipal building. The Local Government Board in 1908 suggested to Local Authorities that this assistance should be generally afforded to them.

Unions. The central executives of the national societies were apt to view with suspicion and jealousy the existence of governing bodies in which they were not directly represented. The local branches, if not actually forbidden, were not encouraged to adhere to what might conceivably become a rival authority. The strong county Unions frequently stood aloof unless they were allowed an overwhelming representation. One of the notable changes of the present century has been the diminution of this jealousy of the Trades Councils. We know of no case in which branches are now forbidden to join a Trades Council. In most cases, although permission may have to be obtained from the Executive Council or Committee, it is nowadays readily granted, and with the recognition of the need for political action, between 1901 and 1913, came positive encouragement to the branches to affiliate to the Trades Councils of their localities.[1]

It remains, however, true in 1920 as in 1890 that the Trades Councils do not include the national leaders of the Trade Union world. The salaried officials of the old-established societies seldom take part in their proceedings. The London Trades Council, for instance, the classic meeting-place of the Junta, has long since ceased to be able to count among its delegates the General Secretaries of the Engineers, Bricklayers, Railwaymen, Steel-smelters, or of any other of the great Societies having their head offices in London. The powerful coterie of cotton officials forms no part of the Manchester Trades Council. Of the boilermakers, neither the General Secretary nor any one of the nine District

---

[1] One of the most active supporters of the Trades Council Movement is the National Union of Railwaymen, which has been largely responsible for the valuable help rendered by the Trades Councils in the organisation of agricultural labourers. The Amalgamated Union of Co-operative Employees, that of Operative Bakers of Great Britain and Ireland, and the Municipal Employees' Association are also outstanding supporters of the Trades Councils, whilst the Oldham Operative Cotton-spinners, and the Operative Lace Makers of Nottingham make branch affiliation compulsory. In many of the principal Unions branch affiliation fees are contributed wholly, or in large proportion, from Central Funds.

Delegates is usually to be found on a Trades Council. The Miners' Agents are notorious for abstention from the Councils in their localities. This, however, is due nowadays, whatever may once have been the reason, principally to the enormous additions to the work of all the salaried officials of the Trade Union world, which make it impossible for the majority of them to attend Trades Council meetings. The Trades Councils now serve as a useful training-ground, wider than that of the Trade Union Branch, for those whom we have elsewhere described as the non-commissioned officers of the Movement, from whose ranks nearly all the Trade Union leaders emerge.

Apart from their constant activity in municipal politics, and their energetic support of the Labour Party in all elections, the Trades Councils have, in the present century, considerably increased in usefulness. They have given valuable assistance in Trade Union propaganda, alike within their own districts and in the adjacent rural districts. No small part of the increase in Trade Union membership, notably among nondescript workers in the towns, and the agricultural labourers in the country, is to be ascribed to the constant work and support of some of the more active among them. They have done much to appease quarrels among the local branches of different Unions, and they are occasionally able to intervene successfully as arbitrators.[1] Even without formal arbitration they bring warring parties together. They nominate working-class representatives to many local committees and conferences, and serve, in this way, as useful links with public administration. Some of them have, of recent years, done a great deal to promote the better education of the artisan class. They affiliate to the Workers' Educational Association or the Labour College, and support its classes ; they arrange public meetings and

[1] The Manchester Trades Council, and especially its Chairman, Mr. Purcell, of the Amalgamated Furnishing Trades Association, successfully brought to a compromise the very serious strike of the Amalgamated Union of Co-operative Employees against the Lancashire and Yorkshire Co-operative Societies in 1919.

obtain outside speakers ; they affiliate to the Labour Research Department, which has a special " Trades Councils and Local Labour Parties Section " ; they subscribe to the travelling library of book-boxes maintained by the Fabian Society ; they frequently issue their own monthly bulletin of Trade Union and Labour news, or journal of local government information, or at least their annual *Year-Book* ; and they act as distributing centres for the nationally published pamphlets and leaflets — sometimes even for the more popular books on Labour questions.[1] They have come, in several centres, to form, by Joint Councils, an indispensable connecting link between the Trade Union and Co-operative Movements, and they serve, more than any other agency, as the cement between the local branches of these two movements and the Labour Party itself. To what extent they are destined, in their character of constituent members of the Labour Party, sometimes actually combined with Local Labour Parties (in the latter cases with the inclusion, since 1918, of a section of individual members, Trade Unionists or others, " workers by hand or by brain "), to develop an effective political organisation, drawing together the whole of the supporters of the Labour Party in each Parliamentary constituency, remains yet to be demonstrated.

THE TRADES UNION CONGRESS

But the most extensive federation of the Trade Union world is to-day, as it has always been, the Trades Union Congress, which could count in September 1919 an affiliated membership of more than five and a quarter millions, a number never paralleled in this or any other country. We have described in previous chapters the origin and development of this federal body, its uses in drawing together the scattered Trade Union forces, and its failure either to help

---

[1] The Gateshead Trades Council and Local Labour Party holds an " Information Bureau meeting " once a week, devoted to answering inquiries and affording information on Local Government affairs.

in the solution of the problems of industrial organisation or to give an intellectual lead to the rank and file.[1]

We drew attention in the first edition of this book in 1894 to the weakness of the organisation of this imposing annual Congress ; and, from 1895 onward, certain changes have been successively made in its constitution and procedure, not always, as we think, for the better. At the Norwich Congress in 1894 the Parliamentary Committee, which the Congress annually elects as its executive, was charged by a resolution proposed by W. J. Davis to consider the amendment of the Standing Orders, and to make the amended orders applicable to the next Congress. On the authority of this ambiguous resolution, which seems to have had in view only the establishment of Grand Committees to deal with the multiplicity of resolutions on the annual agenda, the Parliamentary Committee, of which the Chairman was then John Burns, M.P., decided forthwith to expel all the Trades Councils from the Congress, to make obligatory the " vote by card " according, not to the number of delegates, but to the aggregate membership of each Union, and to confine the delegates rigidly to the contemporary salaried officers and the members of Trade Unions actually working at their crafts—thereby excluding not only the veteran Henry Broadhurst, M.P., with John Burns himself, but also Keir Hardie, Tom Mann, and other leaders of the new movement that was seeking to make Trade Unionism a political force. Who, exactly, was responsible for this *coup d'état* was not officially revealed. It was said, with some authority, that James Mawdsley, the rough and forceful secretary of the Cotton-spinners, was at the bottom of the move, and that he made use of the personal rivalry between Henry Broadhurst and John Burns to get them both, and also the

---

[1] The Trades Union Congress has, since 1873, published a long and detailed *Annual Report* ; and the Parliamentary Committee has, for some years past, issued a *Quarterly Circular* to its constituent bodies. Besides these, there should be consulted the *History of the British Trades Union Congress*, by W. J. Davis, of which two volumes have been issued (1910 and 1916) ; *Henry Broadhurst, the Story of his Life*, by himself, 1901.

rebellious element from the Trades Councils, which all three disliked, excluded from future Congresses.[1] The Congress at Cardiff in 1895 was very angry, and, in effect, rebuked the Parliamentary Committee, but allowed the new Standing Orders to be confirmed on the newly adopted " card vote." In so far as the intention was to keep the new ideas out of Congress, the result was plainly a failure, as within four years (to be described in Chapter XI.) there was a majority in Congress for the creation of the independent organisation entitled the Labour Representation Committee, which became in due course the present Labour Party. The effect was merely to weaken the intellectual influence on the Trade Union world of the Congress and its Parliamentary Committee.

With this exception of the exclusion of the Trades Councils, and of the outstanding personalities whom they occasionally sent as delegates, the visitor to the Trades Union Congress in 1919 would have found very little difference between it and the Congresses of thirty years before, except for an increase in the size of the gathering and in the number of members represented ; and, as must be added, an all-round improvement in the education and manners, especially of the younger delegates. As an institution it can hardly be said to have shown, between 1890 and 1917 at least, any development at all.

It must be admitted that, with all its shortcomings, the Congress, which has now for over fifty years continued to meet annually in some industrial centre, serves many useful purposes. It is, to begin with, an outward and visible sign of that persistent sentiment of solidarity which has throughout the whole of the past century distinguished the working class. Composed of delegates from all the great national and county Unions and an increasing number of local societies, and largely attended by the salaried officials, the Congress, unlike the Trades Councils, is really representative

[1] See the significant comments in *History of the British Trades Union Congress*, by W. J. Davis, vol. ii., 1916, pp. 102-8.

(except for the absence of most of the political side of its organisation) of all the elements of the Trade Union world. Hence its discussions reveal, both to the Trade Union Civil Service and to party politicians, the movement of opinion among all sections of Trade Unionists, and, through them, of the great body of the wage-earners. Moreover, the week's meeting gives a unique opportunity for friendly intercourse between the representatives of the different trades, and thus leads frequently to joint action or wider federations. Nevertheless the Congress remains, as we have described it in its early years, rather a parade of the Trade Union forces than a genuine Parliament of Labour.[1]

All the incidental circumstances tend to accentuate the parade features of Congress at the expense of its legislative capacity. The Mayor and Corporation of the city in which it is held are frequently permitted to give a public welcome to the delegates, and to hold a sumptuous reception in their honour. The Strangers' Gallery is full of interested observers, Distinguished foreigners, representatives of Government departments, " fraternal delegates " from America and the Continent, and from the Co-operative Union and the National Union of Teachers, inquisitive politicians, and popularity-

---

[1] In the early period of its history the middle-class friends of Trade Unionism read papers and took part in debates. But for many years no one has been allowed to participate in its proceedings in any capacity except duly elected delegates who have worked at the trade they represent, or are actually salaried officials of affiliated Trade Unions. In 1892 and 1893 admission was further limited to those societies which contributed a specified amount per thousand members to the funds of the Congress. The Parliamentary Committee consists of seventeen members, elected by ballot of the whole of the delegates on the fifth day of the Congress. The successful candidates are usually the salaried officers of the great societies, the Standing Orders expressly providing that no trade shall have more than one representative except the miners, who may now have two. The Secretary receives, even in 1920, only £500 a year, and the post has nearly always been filled by an officer enjoying emoluments for other duties. For the last forty years the holder has almost constantly been a member of Parliament, with prior obligations to his constituents, which are not always consistent with the directions of his fellow Trade Unionists ; and with onerous Parliamentary duties, which often hamper his secretarial work. For many years he had to provide whatever clerical assistance he required ; but in 1896 a clerk, and in 1917 an Assistant Secretary, were added to the staff.

hunting ministers sit through every day's proceedings.
The press-table is crowded with reporters from all the
principal newspapers of the kingdom, whilst the local
organs vie with each other in bringing out special editions
containing verbatim reports of each day's discussions. But
what more than anything else makes the Congress a holiday
demonstration instead of a responsible deliberative assembly
is its total lack of legislative power. The delegates are well
aware that Congress resolutions on " subjects " have no
binding effect on their constituents, and therefore do not
take the trouble to put them in practicable form, or even
to make them consistent one with another. From the
outset the proceedings are unbusiness-like. Much of the
first day is consumed in pure routine and a lengthy inaugural
address from the President, who has been since 1900 always
the Chairman of the Parliamentary Committee of the
preceding year. The rest of the agenda consists of resolutions sent in by the various Unions and brought higgledy-
piggledy before the Congress in an order determined by
the chances of the ballot. These resolutions are subjected
to no selection or revision beyond an attempt by sub-
committees to merge in one the several proposals on each
subject. The delegates have at their disposal about twenty-
five hours to discuss every imaginable subject, ranging
from the nationalisation of the means of production down
to the prohibition of one carter driving two vehicles at a
time. To enable even a minority of those present to
speak for or against the proposals, each speaker is limited
to five, or perhaps to three minutes, a rule which is more
or less rigidly enforced. But, in spite of this vigorous
application of the closure, the President is seldom able to
get the business through, and has frequently as much as
he can do to maintain order. The Standing Orders Committee is entirely taken up with its mechanical business,
and is not authorised, any more than is the Parliamentary
Committee itself, to formulate a programme for the consideration of the delegates. Nor does the Congress receive

much guidance from experienced officials of the old-established Unions. Whether from a good-natured desire to let the private members have their turn at figuring in the newspapers, or from a somewhat cynical appreciation of the fruitlessness of Congress discussions, many of them habitually lie low, and seldom speak except to defend themselves against attacks. Moreover, they are busily engaged, both in and out of Congress hours, in arranging for the election of themselves or their friends on the Parliamentary Committee, which has hitherto always been governed by mutual " bargaining " for votes.[1] When the four days' talk draws near to an end, many of the resolutions on the agenda are still undisposed of. On the Saturday morning, when most of the delegates have started for home, a thin meeting hurries rapidly through the remainder of the proposals, speeches are reduced to sixty seconds each, and the Congress adopts a score of important resolutions in a couple of hours. From first to last there is no sign of a " Front Bench " of responsible leaders. As a business meeting the whole function of the Congress is discharged in the election of the Parliamentary Committee, to which the representation of the Trade Union world for the ensuing year is entrusted.

In the first edition of this book, in 1894, we gave a description of the work of the Parliamentary Committee which it is interesting to recall :

The duties of the Parliamentary Committee have never been expressly defined by Congress, and it will easily be understood that resolutions of the kind we have described afford but little guidance for practical work. But there is a general understanding that the Committee is to watch over the political interests

---

[1] Each Union casts votes in proportion to its affiliated membership, but can divide them as it pleases among the candidates. Between 1906 and 1915 the delegates were divided into ten groups of allied industries, and each group chose its own member. At the 1919 Congress a resolution was carried directing that the election should henceforth be by the transferable vote ; and it remains to be seen whether this will upset the " dickering for votes."

of its constituents, in much the same way as the Parliamentary Committee of a town council or a railway company. It is obvious that, in the case of the Trade Union world, such a mandate covers a wide field. The right of Free Association, won by Allan, Applegarth, Odger, and their allies, is now a past issue, but the Trade Union interest in legislation has, with the advance of Democracy, extended to larger and more complicated problems. The complete democratisation of the political machinery, the duty of the Government to be a model employer, the further regulation of private enterprise through perfected factory legislation, the public administration of monopolies, are all questions in which the Trade Union world of to-day considers itself keenly interested. To these distinctly labour issues must be added such interests of the non-propertied class as the incidence of taxation, the public provision for education and recreation, and the maintenance of the sick and the aged. We have here an amount of Parliamentary business far in excess of that falling upon the Parliamentary Committee of any ordinary town council or railway company. To examine all bills, public or private, introduced into Parliament that may possibly affect any of the foregoing Trade Union interests; to keep a constant watch on the administration of the public departments; to scrutinise the Budget, the Education Code, and the Orders of the Local Government Board; to bring pressure to bear on the Ministry of the day, so as to mould the Queen's Speech into a Labour Programme; to promote independent Bills on all the subjects upon which the Government refuses to legislate; and, lastly, to organise that 'persistent " lobbying " of Ministers and private members which finally clinches a popular demand—all this constitutes a task which would tax the energies of half a dozen highly trained Parliamentary agents devoting their whole time to their clients. This is the work which the Trade Union Congress delegates to a committee of busy officials, all absorbed in the multifarious details of their own societies, and served only by a Secretary who is paid for a small part of his time, and who accordingly combines the office with other duties.[1]

---

[1] The situation was for years further complicated by the fact that C. Fenwick, M.P., who in 1890 succeeded Henry Broadhurst in the office, was one of the Parliamentary representatives of the Durham miners, a majority of whom were not in accordance with the decision of the Congress on the crucial question of an Eight Hours' Bill. It was in vain that Fenwick, with most engaging candour, explained to each successive

The whole organisation is so absurdly inadequate to the task, that the Committee can hardly be blamed for giving up any attempt to keep pace with the work. The members leave their provincial headquarters fifteen or twenty times a year to spend a few hours in the little offices at 19 Buckingham Street, Strand, in deliberating upon such business as their Secretary brings before them. Preoccupied with the affairs of their societies, and unversed in general politics, they either confine their attention to the interests of their own trades, or look upon the fortnightly trip to London as a pleasant recreation from hard official duties. In the intervals between the meetings the Secretary struggles with the business as best he can, with such clerical help as he can afford to pay for out of his meagre allowance. Absorbed in his own Parliamentary duties, for the performance of which his constituents pay him a salary, he can devote to the general interests of the Trade Union world only the leavings of his time and attention. It is therefore not surprising to learn that the agenda laid before the Parliamentary Committee, instead of covering the extensive field indicated by the resolutions of the Congress, is habitually reduced to the barest minimum. The work annually accomplished by the Committee during the last few years has, in fact, been limited to a few deputations to the Government, two or three circulars to the Unions, a little consultation with friendly politicians, and the drafting of an elaborate report to Congress, describing, not their doings, but the legislation and other Parliamentary proceedings of the session. The result is that the executive committee of the United Textile Factory Workers' Association and the Miners' Federation exercised a far more potent influence in the lobby than the Committee representing the whole Trade Union world; whilst such expert manipulators as Mr. John Burns, Mr. Havelock

---

Congress that his pledge to his constituents, no less than his own opinions, would compel him actively to oppose all regulation of the hours of adult male labour. The Congress nevertheless elected him for four successive years as Secretary to the Parliamentary Committee, replacing him only in 1894 by an officer who was prepared to support the policy of the Congress. This is only another example of the extraordinary constancy (referred to at p. 471) with which a working-class organisation adheres to a man who has once been elected an officer—a constancy due, as we think, partly to a generous objection to " do a man out of his job," and partly to a deep-rooted belief that any given piece of work can be done as well by one man as another. Much the same situation has recurred frequently in the record of the Parliamentary Committee.

Wilson, or Mr. George Howell, can point to more reforms effected in a single session than the Parliamentary Committee has lately accomplished during a whole Parliament.

It is therefore not surprising that there exists in the Trade Union world a growing feeling of irritation against the Parliamentary Committee. In each successive Congress the Committee, instead of taking the lead, finds itself placed on its defence. But it is obvious that Congress itself is to blame. The members of the Committee, including the Secretary, are men of quite as sterling character and capacity as a board of railway directors or a committee of town councillors. But whereas a railway company or a town council places at the disposal of its Parliamentary Committee the whole energies of a specially trained town clerk or solicitor, and allows him, moreover, to call to his aid as many expert advisers as he thinks fit, the Trades Union Congress expects the Parliamentary affairs of a million and a half members to be transacted by a staff inferior to that of a third-rate Trade Union. At one period, it is true, the leaders of the Trade Union world as a whole successfully conducted a long and arduous Parliamentary campaign. We have described in a previous chapter the momentous legislative revolution in the status of Trade Unionism which was effected between 1867 and 1875. But the Conference of Amalgamated Trades, and its successors the Parliamentary Committee, had in these years at their command the freely given services of such a galaxy of legal and Parliamentary talent as Mr. Frederic Harrison, Professor E. S. Beesly, Mr. Henry Crompton, Mr. Thomas (now Judge) Hughes, Messrs. Godfrey and Vernon Lushington, and Mr. (now Justice) R. S. Wright. The objection felt by the present generation of Trade Unionists to be beholden to middle-class friends is not without a certain validity. But if the Trade Union Congress wants its Parliamentary business done it must, at any rate, provide such a salary as will secure the full services of the ablest man in the movement, equip his office with an adequate number of clerks, and authorise the Parliamentary Committee to retain such expert professional assistance as may from time to time be required.

Such was the position as we saw it in 1894. The Trades Union Congress did not in any important respect improve its organisation, nor equip its Parliamentary Committee with any adequate staff. Its failure to cope with the Parliamentary business in which the Trade Union world was interested became more and more manifest ; and the discontent was increased by the disinclination felt by many of the leading members of the Committee for the larger aspirations and more independent attitude in politics that marked the active spirits of the rank and file of Trade Union membership. All this co-operated to produce the vote of the 1899 Congress in favour of some definite step to increase the number of Labour Members in the House of Commons, out of which sprang the independent organisation subsequently known as the Labour Party, which we shall describe in Chapter XI. But although the Trades Union Congress thus created, at the very end of the nineteenth century, a separate political organisation for the Trade Union world, into which the steadily increasing political activity of the Trade Unions has since flowed, the Congress and its Parlia- mentary Committee made no change in their own work. There has accordingly continued to be the same stream, year after year, of miscellaneous resolutions before Congress, 99 per cent of them dealing with political issues, involving either legislation or a change of Government policy, resolu- tions which have continued to be presented and discussed without any regard to their place in any consistent programme for the Trade Union world as a whole. The Parliamentary Committee has continued to regard itself almost entirely as a Parliamentary Committee, just as if the Trade Unions had not united in a distinct political organisation and had not created their own Parliamentary Labour Party. The futile annual deputations to Ministers have continued to present to them the crude resolutions of the Trades Union Congress, without regard to the contemporary situation in the House of Commons, or the action taken by the Parlia- mentary Labour Party, and without taking into account in what relation they stand to the political programme of the Trade Union world as formulated, year by year, in the Conferences of the Labour Party. Meanwhile the essentially industrial work of the national organisation of Trade Unions has continued to be neglected. Both the Trades Union Congress and the Parliamentary Committee have shown the greatest disinclination to tackle such essentially Trade Union problems as those presented by the existence in the same trade of competing Trade Unions ; [1] by the formation of separate Unions on overlapping and mutually inconsistent bases ; by the growing rivalry between the warring conceptions of organisation by craft and organisation by industry ; by the increasing failure of the membership of each branch to correspond with the staffs of the separate gigantic establishments characteristic of the present day ; by the " rank and file movement," demanding a greater direct control of workshop conditions than can easily be made compatible with the centralisation of policy in the national executives ; by the development of the " Shop Stewards' " organisation ; by the spread in different industries of systems of " payment by results," unsafeguarded by the necessary adaptations of the Standard Rate and Collective Bargaining ; by the tendency of the employers to make deductions from the Standard Rate when it suits them to take on individuals or new classes of workers whom they declare to be inferior, whether women or boys, old men or partially incapacitated workers of any sort ; and by the introduction of " Scientific Management." [2]

[1] One such case may be mentioned. In 1898 a small Trade Union of old standing (Co-operative Smiths' Society, Gateshead) formally complained that the Amalgamated Society of Engineers had allowed its members to take the places of men who had struck. The Parliamentary Committee, acting under Standing Order No. 20, appointed three of its members as arbitrators, who, after elaborate inquiry, found the charge proved, and requested the A.S.E. to withdraw its members from the place in dispute. The A.S.E. refused to accept the award, and withdrew from the Congress (Annual Report of Trades Union Congress, 1899 ; *History of British Trades Union Congress*, by W. J. Davis, vol. ii., 1916, pp. 161-62, 165-67).

Another case, in 1902, was adjudicated on in a similar way, where the United Kingdom Amalgamated Smiths and Strikers complained of the Associated Blacksmiths' Society, which was found to blame (*ibid.* p. 208).

[2] In view of the failure of the Trades Union Congress to equip its Parliamentary Committee with any staff that would enable it to deal with these problems, the Fabian Society started in 1912 the Fabian Research Department, to investigate and supply information upon these and other questions. This organisation has now become the Labour

During the whole of this century, in fact, the Parliamentary Committee of the Trades Union Congress, and the Congress itself, have failed to grapple with the work that calls out to be done by some national organisation of the Trade Union world. After allowing to be created, on the one hand, the General Federation of Trade Unions, abandoning to it the whole function of insurance, together with the representation of British Trade Unionism in the International Federation of Trade Unions, and, on the other, the Labour Party, with its inevitable absorption of the political activity of the Trade Union world, the Parliamentary Committee of the Trades Union Congress has failed to recognise, and to concentrate upon, the sphere that it had left to itself, namely, to become the national organ for the improvement and development of British Trade Unionism in its industrial aspect. Whilst the Trades Union Congress has continued anxiously and nervously to abstain from any attempt to demarcate the spheres of rival Unions or to improve their mutual relations, action which would have brought the Parliamentary Committee dangerously into conflict with one or other of its constituents, and has confined its attention as much as ever to the statutory and governmental reforms which its various sections desired, it has been progressively overshadowed, on the political side, by the rise of the Labour Party, to be described in a subsequent chapter.

Research Department, an independent federal combination of Trade Unions, Co-operative and Socialist societies, and other Labour bodies (including the Labour Party, the English, Scottish, and Irish Trades Union Congresses, the Co-operative Union, the *Daily Herald*, most of the big Trade Unions, and some hundreds of Trade Councils, Local Labour Parties, etc.), with individual students and investigators. It has its offices at 34 Eccleston Square, London, S.W.1, next door to those of the Trades Union Congress and the Labour Party; issues to its members a monthly bulletin of information, and has published many useful books, pamphlets, and monographs. It answers a stream of questions from Trade Unions all over the country on every conceivable point of theory or practice; it supplies particulars of rates of pay, hours of labour, and conditions of employment in other trades; and it is frequently employed in helping to prepare cases for submission to Joint Boards or Arbitration Tribunals. Its influential conduct of the " publicity " of the National Union of Railwaymen in the 1919 strike has already been described.

Towards the end of 1919 the discontent of the Trade Union world with the position and attitude of the Parliamentary Committee came to a head. The sudden railway strike, described in this chapter, revealed the lack of any organ of co-ordination in industrial movements which inevitably affected the whole Trade Union Movement. The Parliamentary Committee itself laid before a special Trades Union Congress in December 1919 a report declaring that " the need has long been recognised for the development of more adequate machinery for the co-ordination of Labour activities, both for the movement as a whole, and especially for its industrial side. Again and again the lack of co-ordination has resulted, not only in the overlapping of administrative work, but also in unnecessary internal and other disputes, involving vast financial and moral damage to the whole Labour Movement. To do away with some of this overlapping and to provide means of co-ordinating the work of certain sections was the object with which the Triple Industrial Alliance was founded by the Miners, Railwaymen, and Transport Workers, and the same object is behind the numerous steps towards closer unity which have been taken in various industries and groups. The Negotiating Committee, hastily improvised to deal with the situation created by the railway strike this autumn, was generally felt to have fulfilled, however imperfectly, a vital need of Labour ; but it is clear that it ought not to have been necessary to create a new and temporary body to do this work ; the necessary machinery should have been already in existence in the form of a really effective central co-ordinating body for the movement as a whole.

" It appears to us that the body which is required should and must be developed out of the existing organisation of the Trades Union Congress and out of its closer co-operation with other sections of the working-class movement. At present, the Standing Orders do not permit the Parliamentary Committee to undertake the work which is required. Indeed, its functions, as they are now defined, are in great measure a survival from a previous period, when the chief duties of the Congress were political, and there existed no separate political organisation to express the policy and objects of Labour. We accordingly suggest that the whole functions and organisation of the Parliamentary Committee demand revision, with a view to developing out of it a real co-ordinating body for the industrial side of the whole Trade Union Movement. It is also necessary to take into account the relation of the reorganised Central Industrial Committee to the other sections of the movement, and especially to the Labour Party and to the Co-operative Movement.

" If a better central organisation could be developed both on the industrial side and by the closer joint working with the other wings of the working-class movement, a vast development of the very necessary work of publicity, information, and research would at once become possible. The research, publicity, and legal departments now working for the movement require co-ordination and extension equally with its industrial and political organisation. The research, publicity, and legal work now done by the Trades Union Congress, the Labour Party, and the Labour Research Department must be co-ordinated and greatly enlarged in close connection with the development of the executive machinery of the movement."

The proposal did not secure the approval of the Miners' Federation, but the special Congress, by a very large majority, passed the following resolution :

" That in view of the imperative need and demand for a central co-ordinating body representative of the whole Trade Union Movement and capable of efficiently dealing with industrial questions of national importance, the Parliamentary Committee be instructed to revise the Standing Orders of Congress in such manner as is necessary to secure the following changes in the functions and duties of the Executive body elected by Congress :

" (1) To substitute for the Parliamentary Committee a

Trades Union Congress General Council, to be elected annually by Congress.

" (2) To prepare a scheme determining the composition and methods of election of the General Council.

" (3) To make arrangements for the development of administrative departments in the offices of the General Council, in the direction of securing the necessary officials, staff, and equipment to secure an efficient Trade Union centre.

" Further, in order to avoid overlapping in the activity of working-class organisations, the Parliamentary Committee be instructed to consult with the Labour Party and the Co-operative Movement, with a view to devising a scheme for the setting up of departments under joint control, responsible for effective national and international service in the following and any other necessary directions :

" (a) *Research* : To secure general and statistical information on all questions affecting the worker as producer and consumer by the co-ordination and development of existing agencies.

" (b) *Legal advice* on all questions affecting the collective welfare of the members of working-class organisations.

" (c) *Publicity*, including preparation of suitable literature dealing with questions affecting the economic, social, and political welfare of the people ; with machinery for inaugurating special publicity campaigns to meet emergencies of an industrial or political character."

THE OFFICERS OF THE TRADE UNION MOVEMENT

If we survey the growth of the British Trade Union Movement during the past thirty years, what is conspicuous is that, whilst the Movement has marvellously increased in mass and momentum, it has been marked on the whole by inadequacy of leadership alike within each Union and in the Movement itself, and by a lack of that unity and persistency of purpose which wise leadership alone can give. Hence, in our opinion, the organised workers, whilst steadily advancing, have not secured anything like the results, either in the industrial or in the political field, that the individual sacrifices and efforts in their cause might have brought about. This deficiency in the brain-work of successful organisation is very marked in the various sections of the building trades, with their chaos of separate societies, and in the engineering industry, with its persistence of competing Unions formed on inconsistent bases, its lack of uniformity in Standard Rates, and its failure to devise any plan of safeguarding Collective Bargaining in the various systems of " Payment by Results." But it has been equally apparent in the incapacity of the Trade Union Movement as a whole to establish any central authority to prevent overlapping organisations and demarcation disputes, and to co-ordinate the efforts of the various sections of workers towards a higher standard of life and greater control over the conditions of their working lives. The British workmen, it must be said, have not become aware of the absolute need for what we may call Labour Statesmanship. They have not yet learnt how, either in their separate Trade Unions or in the Labour Movement as a whole, to attract and train, to select and retain in office, to accord freedom of initiative to and yet to control, a sufficient staff of qualified officials capable not merely of individual leadership, but also of well devised " team play " in the long-drawn-out struggle of the wage-earning class for its " place in the sun." To this constant falling short of the reasonably expected achievements is, we think, due the perpetual see-saw in Trade Union policy : the Trade Unionists of one decade relying principally on political action, to the neglect of the industrial weapon, whilst those of a succeeding decade, temporarily disillusioned with political action, rush wildly into strikes and neglect the ballot-box. This change of feeling is due each time to the failure of the results to come up to expectation. We shall understand some of the reasons for this shortcoming if we examine how the Trade Union Movement is, in fact, officered.

The affairs, industrial and political, of the six million Trade Unionists, enrolled in possibly as many as fifty thousand local branches or lodges (including a thousand independent small local societies), are administered by perhaps 100,000 annually elected branch officials and shop stewards. These may be regarded as the non-commissioned officers of the Movement ; and it is fundamentally on their sobriety and personal integrity, combined with an intimate knowledge of their several crafts and a steadiness of judgement, that the successful conduct of the branch business depends. They continue to work at their trades, and receive only a few pounds a year for all their onerous and sometimes dangerous work. It is these non-commissioned officers of the Trade Union army who keep the Trade Union organisation alive. But they have neither the training, nor the leisure, nor even the opportunity, so long as they remain non-commissioned officers, working at their trades, to formulate a detailed policy, or to supply the day-by-day executive leadership to the particular Trade Union, or to the Trade Union Movement. For the work of translating into action, industrial or political, the desires or convictions of the whole body of the members, the Trade Union world necessarily depends, in the main, on its salaried officers, who devote the whole of their time to the service of the Movement, in one or other capacity. Such a whole-time salaried staff was slow to be formed. In 1850 it did not exist at all. It probably did not in 1860 number as many as a hundred throughout the whole kingdom. In 1892, in the first edition of this book, we put it approximately at 600. In 1920, with a fourfold growth in membership, and (under the National Insurance Act) a vast increase in the office and financial business of the Trade Unions, we estimate the total number of the salaried officers of all the Trade Unions

U

and their federations (not including mere shorthand typists and office-boys) at three or four thousand, of whom perhaps one-tenth, in or out of Parliament, are engaged exclusively on election and other political work. But even on the industrial side, Trade Union officials differ considerably in the work they have to do, and the differences in function result in marked varieties of type.

We have first the salaried officials of the skilled trades. They are broadly distinguished from the officers of the Labourers' Unions by the fact that they are invariably men who have worked at the crafts they represent, and who have usually served their society as branch secretaries. We may distinguish among them two leading types, the Administrator of Friendly Benefits, and the Trade Official.

To the type of Administrator of Friendly Benefits, the school of William Allan, belong most of the General and Assistant Secretaries at the head offices of the great Trade Friendly Societies organisations in which the mass of routine, financial, and other office business has become so great that only the ablest men succeed in rising above it. Owing to the continued increase in membership of the principal Unions, to their tendency to amalgamate into larger and larger aggregations, to the constant extension of friendly benefits, and since 1911 to the enormous addition to the work made by the National Insurance Act, the administrative staffs of the Unions have had to be doubled and quadrupled. But the Trade Union official of this type, however great may be his nominal position, has, during the past thirty years, come to exercise less and less influence on the Trade Union world. Rigidly confined to his office, he becomes in most cases a painstaking clerk, and rises at the best to the level of the shrewd manager of an insurance company. He passes his life in investigating the claims of his members to the various benefits, and in upholding, at all hazard of un-popularity, a sound financial system of adequate contribu-tions and moderate benefits. Questions of trade policy interest him principally so far as they tend to swell or diminish the number of his members in receipt of " Out of Work Pay." He is therefore apt to be more intent on getting unemployed members off the books than on raising the Standard Rate of wages or decreasing the length of the Normal Day. For the same reason he proves a tenacious champion of his members' rights in all quarrels about overlap and demarcation of work ; and it may happen that he finds himself more often engaged in disputes with rival Unions than with employers. He represents the most conservative element in Trade Union life. On all occasions he sits tight, and votes solid for what he conceives to be the official or moderate party.

More influential in Trade Union politics is the salaried officer of the other type. The Trade Official, as we have called him, is largely the result of the prevalence, in certain industries, of a complicated system of " Payment by Results." We have already described how the cotton lists on the one hand and the checkweigher clause on the other called into existence a specially trained class, which has since been augmented by the adoption of piecework lists in boot and shoemaking and other industries. The officers of this type are professionals in the art of Collective Bargaining. They spend their lives in intricate calculations on technical details, and in conducting delicate negotiations with the employers or their professional agents. It matters little whether they are the general secretaries of essentially trade societies, such as the federal Unions of Cotton-spinners and Cotton-weavers, or the exclusively trade delegates of societies with friendly benefits, such as the Steel-smelters, the Boilermakers, and the Boot and Shoe Operatives. In either case their attention is almost entirely devoted to the earnings of their members. Alert and open-minded, they are keen observers of market prices, employers' profits, the course of international trade, and everything which may affect the gross product of their industry. They are more acutely conscious of incompetency, whether in employer or employed, than they can always express. Supporters of improved processes, new machinery, and "speeding up," they would rather see an antiquated mill closed or an incompetent member discharged than reduce the Standard Rate. Nor do they confine themselves exclusively to the money wages of their clients. Among them are to be found the best advocates of legislative regulation of the conditions of employment, and whilst they have during the present century fallen somewhat into the background when wider political issues have come to the fore, the elaboration of the Labour Code during the past fifty years has been due, in the main, to their detailed knowledge and untiring pertinacity.

The Trade Official, however, has the defects of his qualities. The energetic workman, who at about thirty years of age leaves the factory, the forge, or the mine, to spend his days pitting his brains against those of shrewd employers and sharp-witted solicitors, has necessarily to concentrate all his energies upon the limited range of his new work. As a Branch Secretary, he may have taken a keen interest in the grievances and demands of other trades besides his own. Soon he finds his duties incompatible with any such wide outlook. The feeling of class solidarity, so vivid in the manual working wage-earner, tends gradually to be replaced by a narrow trade interest. The District Delegate of the Boilermakers finds it as much as he can do to master the innumerable and constantly changing details of every variety of iron-ship, boiler, and bridge building in every port, and even at every yard. The Investigator of the National Union of Boot and Shoe Operatives is often hard put to it to estimate accurately the labour in each of the thousand changing styles of boots, whilst at the same time keeping pace with ever-increasing complexity both of machinery and division of labour. The Cotton Official, with his bewildering lists, throws his whole mind into coping with the infinite variety of calculations involved in new patterns, increased speed, and every alteration of count and draw and warp and weft. The Miners' Agents can seldom travel beyond the analogous problems of their own industry. Such a Trade Official, if he has any leisure and energy left at the end of his exhausting day's work, broods over larger problems, still special to his own industry. The Secretary of a Cotton Union finds it necessary to puzzle his head over the employers' contention that Bimetallism, or a new Indian Factory Act, deserves the operatives' support ; or to think out some way of defeating the evasions of the law against over-steaming or of the " particulars clause." The whole staff of the Boilermakers will be absorbed in considering the effect of the different systems of apprenticeship in the shipyards, or the proper method of meeting the ruinously violent fluctuations in shipbuilding. The Miners will be thinking only of the technical improvement of the conditions of safety of the mine, or of the way to protect the interests of the hewer in an " abnormal place." And the modern Knight of St. Crispin racks his brains about none of these things, but is wholly concerned with the evil of home work, and whether the inspection of small workshops would be more rigidly carried out under the Home Office or under the Town Council. It is not surprising, therefore, that the Trade Officials are characterised by an intense and somewhat narrow sectionalism. The very knowledge of, and absorption in, the technical details of one particular trade, which makes them such expert specialists, prevents them developing the higher qualities necessary for the political leadership of the Trade Union world.

In another class stand the organisers and secretaries of what used to be called the Labourers' Unions, and are now styled Unions of General Workers — a less stable class, numbering in 1892 about two hundred, and in 1920 possibly ten times as many. In contrast with the practice of the old-established societies these officers have at no time been always selected from the ranks of the workers whose affairs they administer.[1] In " revivalist " times the cause of the

---

[1] For instance, Henry Taylor, the coadjutor of Joseph Arch in organising the agricultural labourers in 1872, was a carpenter ; Tom Mann,

unskilled workers attracts, from the ranks of the non-commissioned officers of other industries, men of striking capacity and missionary fervour, such as John Burns and Tom Mann, who organised and led the dock labourers to victory in 1889. But these men regarded themselves and were regarded more as apostles to the unconverted than as salaried officers, and they ceded their posts as soon as competent successors among their constituents could be found. In the main the unskilled workmen have had to rely for officers on men drawn from their own ranks. In not a few cases a sturdy general labourer has proved himself a first-rate administrator of a great national Union. But it was a special drawback to these Unions in the early days of their development that the " failures," who drift from other occupations into the ranks of general labour, frequently got elected, on account of their superior education, to posts in which personal self-control and persistent industry are all-important. Nor were the duties of an organiser of unskilled labourers in old days such as developed either regular habits or business capacity. The absence of any extensive system of friendly benefits reduced to a minimum the administrative functions and clerical labour of the head office. The members, for the most part engaged simply in general labour, and paid by the day or hour, had no occasion for elaborate piecework lists, even supposing that their Unions had won that full recognition by the employers which such arrangements imply. On the other hand, the branches of a Labourers' Union in those days were, for one reason or another, always crumbling away ; and the total membership was only maintained by perpetually breaking fresh ground. Hence the greater part of the

for two years salaried President of the Dock, Wharf, and Riverside Labourers, has always been a member, and is now General Secretary, of the Amalgamated Society of Engineers ; whilst Edward M'Hugh, for some time General Secretary of the National Union of Dock Labourers, is a compositor ; Mr. Charles Duncan, President of the Workers' Union, is an engineer ; Mr. R. Walker, General Secretary of the Agricultural Labourers' Union, was successively a shopkeeper and a railway clerk, and so on.

organiser's time was taken up in maintaining the enthusiasm of his members, and in sweeping in new converts. This involved constant travelling, and the whirl of excitement implied in an everlasting round of missions in non-Union districts. The typical organiser of a Labourers' Union in 1889-94 approximated, therefore, more closely than any other figure in the Trade Union world, to the middle-class conception of a Trade Union official. He was, in fact, a professional agitator. He might be a saint or he might be an adventurer ; but he was seldom a man of affairs.[1]

During the past quarter of a century these Unions of Labourers, which are now better styled Unions of General Workers, have changed in character, and are now often huge national organisations of financial stability, administered by

[1] The fervent energy of the typical official of the Labour Union of that day was well described in 1894 in the following sketch by Mrs. Bruce Glasier (Katherine Conway), a member of the " Independent Labour Party." " He has his offices, but is generally conspicuous there from his absence. Walter Crane's ' Triumph of Labour ' hangs on the wall, and copies of *The Fabian Essays*, and the greater proportion of the tracts issued by the Manchester or Glasgow Labour Presses, lie scattered over the room. In England, Byron and Shelley, in Scotland, Byron and Burns, are the approved poets. Carlyle and a borrowed Ruskin or two are also in evidence, and a library edition of Thorold Rogers' *Work and Wages*. John Stuart Mill's *Political Economy*, side by side with a *Student's Marx*, giᵛ ᵉ proof of a laudable determination to go to the roots of the matter, and to base all arguments on close and careful study. But the call to action is never-ceasing, and train-travelling, if conducive to the enormous success of new journalism, affords but little opportunity for serious reading. ' The daily newspapers are continually filled with lies, which one ought to know how to refute,' and the situation all over the globe ' may develop at any moment.'

" Yet, unlike the old Unionist leader, he is ever ready for the interviewer or the sympathetic inquirer, of whatever class or sex. Right racily he will describe the rapid growth of the movement since the great dock strike of 1889, and show the necessity in dealing with such mixed masses of men as fill the ranks of unskilled labour to-day, of continually striking while the iron is hot, and of substituting a policy of *coup d'état* for the deliberate preparation of the older Unions. ' Lose here, win there,' is our only motto, he says, resolutely determined to look at defeat from the point of view of a general-in-chief, and not from the narrower range of an officer in charge of a special division. At the moment of surrender he may have been white to the lips, but the next day will find him cheery and undaunted in another part of the country, carrying on his campaign and enrolling hundreds of recruits by the sheer energy of his confident eloquence." (*Weekly Sun*, January 28, 1894.)

men as competent as any in the Trade Union world. Their
officers, who have greatly increased in number, have elaborated a technique of their own, combining an efficiency in
recruiting with an effective representation of their members'
case in negotiations with the employers, and before arbitration tribunals, which, particularly in such influential bodies
as the National Union of General Workers, the Dock, Wharf
and Riverside Labourers' Union, the Workers' Union and
the National Federation of Women Workers, brings them
much nearer what we have described as the Trade Official
than the typical labourers' organiser of 1889. The exclusively women's Unions, among which the National
Federation of Women Workers is the only one of magnitude,
have been exceptionally fortunate in attracting and retaining women of outstanding capacity—good organisers and
skilled negotiators—who have not only obtained for their
members a remarkable improvement in the conditions of
employment, but have, by their statesmanship, won a
position of outstanding influence in the Trade Union Movement. It is, indeed, important to note that the accomplished officials of the larger Unions of General Workers,
and not those of women only, have become aware of a
diversity of view between the skilled craftsman with a
" vested interest " in his trade, and the unskilled or, as,
they prefer to call them, the semi-skilled or general workers,
bent on being considered qualified for any work which the
employer has to give. Hence these officials sometimes
take a larger view of Labour questions than the trade
officials of the skilled crafts. They tend to be in favour of
the amalgamation of separate societies into " One Big
Union " ; of much more equality of remuneration among
all manual workers ; of the " open door " to capacity ; of
equal rates for men and women on the same job ; and of a
levelling up of the Standard of Life of the lowest section of
the workers. This leads them instinctively to a co-ordinated
use of the industrial and the political weapons.

Some of these officials, however, are paid in a manner

which may exercise an adverse influence on their activity. A new method of remuneration of the officers of a Trade Union has been devised. In one case the very able General Secretary of a Union of skilled craftsmen, whose services have been in the past most valuable to the trade, is reputed to be paid so much per member per annum, and with the great increase in membership to be making an income four times as large as the salaries of the General Secretaries of great Trade Unions. In another very extensive Union of unskilled and semi‑skilled workers, practically the whole staff is paid " by results," the Branch Secretaries, for instance, by rule retaining for themselves " six per cent on the contributions, levies and fines received from the members of the Branch on behalf of, and remitted to, the Chief Office " ; and being paid also " a procuration fee of 1s." for " introducing new members " into the Approved Society ; and for the extra work involved in disputes, a further " 6d. when under 25 members are affected, and 1s. for the first 25 or over ; 2s. for the first 50 ; 6d. per 50 or part thereof afterwards." This method of remunerating Trade Union officials—analogous to that successfully employed by the Industrial Insurance Companies for their agents—has certain attractions. A fairly adequate remuneration for the position and work can thus be allotted to the officer, without its amount being specifically voted by the members or appearing in the accounts in such a way as to offend the rank and file by a contrast between their weekly wage for manual labour and the Standard Rate of what is essentially a different occupation. It is, however, rightly regarded as a pernicious system. The practice of " paying by results " is alleged to lead sometimes to reckless recruiting, to " in and out " Trade Unionism, and even to wholesale poaching among the membership of other Unions ; and it produces in the Trade Union world a type of " business man " more concerned for numbers than for raising the Standard of Life of the members he has enrolled, or for co‑operation with other Trade Unions for their common ends.

U 2

Quite another type, of more recent introduction, is the Political Officer of the Trade Union world. He may be merely the Registration Officer or Election Agent serving the local Labour Party and the Labour Candidate in a particular constituency ; he may be simply a Labour M.P. ; he may be the secretary or staff officer of a great Trade Union or powerful federation, or, indeed, of the Labour Party itself, devoting himself to political functions ; he may combine with one or other of these posts, or some other Trade Union office, that of a Member of Parliament ; but he is distinguished from the typical General Secretary, Trade Official or Labour Organiser—from one or other of which he has usually developed—by his absorption in the political work of the Movement, either inside the House of Commons or outside it, within one constituency or in a wider field. He may not always hold a political office. A marked feature of the past decade has been the frequency and the amount of the calls upon the time of the Trade Union leaders who are not in Parliament, for public service in which their own Unions have no special concern. The Trade Union official has to serve on innumerable public bodies, nearly always without pay of any kind, from local Pension or Food or Profiteering Act Committees, or the magisterial bench, up to National Arbitration Tribunals, official Committees of Enquiry or Royal Commissions. Such a man is perpetually devoting hours every day to the consideration and discussion, and sometimes to the joint decision, of issues of public character, in which it is his special function to represent, not the opinions and interests of the particular Trade Unionists by whom he is paid, but the opinions and interests of the whole wage-earning class. All this important work, a twentieth century addition to the functions of the Trade Union staff, and not alone the increasing calls of Parliament, is tending more and more to the development of what we have called the Political Officer of the movement.

These three or four thousand salaried officials of the

Trade Union world, whatever their several types, and whatever the duties to which they are assigned, are, with insignificant exceptions, all selected in one way, namely by popular election by the whole body of members, either of their respective Unions, or of particular districts of those Unions. They are, in the skilled trades, required to be members of the Union making the appointment ; and in order to gain the suffrages of their fellow-members they must necessarily have made themselves known to them in some way. They are, accordingly, selected almost invariably from among what we have described as the non-commissioned officers of the Movement, those who are serving or who have served as Branch Secretaries, or other local officers. They have thus all essentially the same training—a training which has no more reference to the work of an administrator of Friendly Benefits than to that of a Political Officer. What happens is that the popular workman is, by the votes of his fellow-workers, taken suddenly from the bench, the forge or the mine, at any age from 30 to 50, with no large experience than that of a Branch Official, and put to do the highly specialised work of one or other of the types that we have described.[1] It is a further difficulty that such training and experience that an individual Trade Unionist may have had, and such capacity as he may have shown, whilst they may secure his election to a salaried office, or his promotion from one such office to another, will be held to have no bearing on the question of which office he will be chosen to fill. The popular Branch Secretary, who has led a successful strike, may be elected as General Secretary in a head office where his work will be mainly that of the manager of an insurance company. The successful Trade Official, expert at negotiating complicated changes in piece-work lists, may find himself elected as the Union's candidate

---

[1] It is, we think, only the Iron and Steel Trades Confederation that had laid down and acted on the principle of entrusting the appointment of salaried officials to the Executive Committee, on the express ground that popular election by ballot is not the right way to select administrative officers.

for Parliament ; and will, in due course, be sent to the
House of Commons to deal on behalf of the whole wage-
earning class, with political issues to which he has never
given so much as a thought. The Trade Union secretary,
whose daily work has trained him to the meticulous supervision of the friendly benefits, may find himself perpetually
called away from his office to represent the interests of
Labour as a member of Royal Commissions and Committees
of Enquiry on every imaginable subject.

With such imperfect methods of selection for office, and
with so complete a lack of systematic training for their
onerous and important functions, it is, we think, a matter
for surprise that Trade Union officials should have won a
well-deserved reputation for knowledge and skill in negotiations with employers. But their haphazard selection and
inadequate training are not the only difficulties that they
have to overcome. Trade Union officials are nearly always
overworked and expected to become specialist experts in
half-a-dozen techniques ; they are exposed to harassing
and demoralising conditions of life, and they are habitually
underpaid. The conditions of employment and the terms
of service which the Trade Unions, out of ignorance, impose
on those who serve them, far from being conducive to
efficient administration and wise leadership, are often
disgracefully poor. In November 1919 the National Union
of Railwaymen set a notable example in raising the salaries
of their two principal officers to £1000 a year each. But
this is wholly exceptional. Even now, after the great rise in
the cost of living, the salary of the staff officer of an important
and wealthy Trade Union rarely exceeds £400 or £500 a
year, without any provision for any other retiring allowance
than the Union's own Superannuation Benefit of ten or
twelve shillings per week, if such a benefit exists at all.
The average member forgets that what he has to compare
the Secretary's salary with is not the weekly wage of the
manual working members of the Union, but—on the very
doctrine of the Standard Rate in which they all believe—

the remuneration given by " good employers " for the kind
of work that the Secretary has to perform. When we
remember that the modern Trade Union official has to be
constantly travelling and consorting with employers and
officials of much higher standards of expenditure than his
own, and when we realise the magnitude and financial importance of the work that he performs, the smallness of
the salary and the lack of courtesy and amenity accorded
to the office is almost ludicrous. The result is that the
able and ambitious young workman in a skilled trade is not
much tempted by the career, even if he regards it as one
of Trade Union leadership, unless he is (as so many are) an
altruistic enthusiast ; or unless his ambitions are ultimately
political in character. The able young workman will both
rise more rapidly and enjoy a pleasanter life by eschewing
any ostensible service of his fellow-workmen, and taking
advantage of the eagerness of intelligent employers to
discover competent foremen and managers, nowadays not
altogether uninfluenced by the sub-conscious desire to divert
from Trade Unionism to Capitalism the most active-minded
of the proletariat. Nor does the danger to the Trade Union
world end with the refusal of some of its ablest young
members to become Trade Union officials. The inferiority
of position, alike in salary, in dignity and in amenity, to
which a Trade Union condemns its officers, compared
with that enjoyed by men of corresponding ability and
function in other spheres, puts a perpetual strain on the
loyalty of Trade Union officials. They are constantly being
tempted away from the service of their fellows by offers of
appointments in the business world, or by Employers'
Associations, or in Government Departments. And there
are other evils of underpayment. A Trade Union official
whose income is insufficient for his daily needs is tempted to
make unduly liberal charges for his travelling expenses, and
may well find it more remunerative to be perpetually multiplying deputations and committee meetings away from home
than to be attending to his duties at the office. He may

be driven to duplicate functions and posts in order to make a living wage. The darkest side of such a picture, the temptation to accept from employers or from the Government those hidden bribes that are decorously veiled as allowances for expenses or temporary salaries for special posts, is happily one which Trade Union loyalty and a sturdy sense of working-class honour have hitherto made it seldom necessary to explore. But such things have not been unknown; and their underlying cause—the unwise and mean underpayment of Trade Union officials—deserves the attention of the Trade Union world.

We have so far considered the officials of the Trade Union world merely as individual administrators. This, indeed, is almost the only way in which their work is regarded by their members. It is remarkable how slow the Trade Union world is to recognise the importance, to administrative or political efficiency, of the constitution of a hierarchy, a group or a team. Where a great society has a salaried staff of half-a-dozen to a score of officials—under such designations as General Secretary, Assistant Secretaries, President, Members of Executive Council or District Delegates, Organisers or Investigators—it is almost invariable to find them all separately elected by the whole body of members, or what is even more destructive of unity, by different district memberships. We only know of one example in the Trade Union world—that of the Iron and Steel Trades Confederation—in which the responsible Executive Committee itself appoints the official staff upon which the performance of the work depends. All the salaried officers of a Trade Union, whatever their designations or functions, can usually claim to have the same, and therefore equal authority, namely, their direct election by the members. This results in the lack of any organic relation not only between the Executive Committee and the District Officers who ought to be its local agents, but even between the Executive Committee and the General Secretary and Assistant Secretaries. The Executive Committee can shunt to purely routine work a General Secretary whom it dislikes, and an unfriendly General Secretary can practically destroy the authority of the Executive Committee. In some cases the work of the office is in practice divided up amongst all the salaried staff, Executive Councillors, General Secretary, and Assistant Secretaries indiscriminately, each man doing his own job in the way he thinks best, and any consultation or corporate decision being reduced to a minimum. There is, in fact, no guarantee that there will be any unity of policy within an Executive Committee elected by a dozen different districts, or between an Executive Committee and its leading officials, who are elected at different times for different reasons. The members may choose a majority of reactionary Executive Councillors and simultaneously a revolutionary General Secretary. In nearly all Unions any suggestion as to the desirability of adopting the middle-class device of entrusting a responsible Executive Committee with the power of choosing its own officers has been resented as undemocratic.[1] In some Unions the indispensable amount of unity is secured, not without internal friction, by the presence of some dominant personality, who may be a secretary or president, or merely a member of the Executive Committee. The same drawback is seen in the constitutions of such wider federations as the Trades Union Congress and the Labour Party.

[1] It would clearly be an advantage if the distinction between those responsible for policy (whether designated Executive Councillors, President or otherwise) and those whose function should be executive only, were fully borne in mind. Whilst the former should certainly be elected by, and held responsible to, the membership, it is submitted that experience shows the advantage of purely executive officers—which may be what the secretaries and district delegates should become—being appointed by, and held responsible to, those who are elected.

At least, a separation should be made between persons elected to be responsible for policy, and officers employed for tasks requiring specialised training (such as the whole of the insurance work of the Union and of its Approved Society ; its constantly increasing statistical requirements, and its legal business). Such officers should certainly be appointed, not elected ; and should take no part in the decision of issues of policy, even as regards their own department. Speaking generally, much more specialisation of functions and officers should be aimed at in all Unions of magnitude.

The result is that the Trade Union Movement has not yet evolved anything in the nature of Cabinet Government, based on unity of policy among the chief administrators, nor do we see any approach to the Party System, which in our national politics alone makes Cabinet Government possible. It looks as if any Democracy on a vocational basis must inevitably be dominated by a diversity of sectional interests which does not coincide with any cleavage in intellectual opinions. From the standpoint of corporate efficiency the drawback is that the sectional divergencies are always interfering with the formulation and unhesitating execution of decisions on wider issues, on which it would be advantageous for the Movement as a whole, in the interests of all, to have an effective general will, even if it be only that of a numerical majority.

Finally, it is a great drawback to the Trade Union world that it possesses no capital city, and no central headquarters even in London. Its salaried officials, on whom it depends for leadership and policy, are scattered all over the country. The General Secretaries of the great Trade Friendly Societies and of the Unions of General Workers are dispersed between London, Manchester, Newcastle, Glasgow, Aberdeen, Liverpool, and Leicester. The officials of the Cotton Operatives are quartered in a dozen Lancashire towns, and those of the Miners in every coalfield. The District Delegates of the Engineering and Shipbuilding Trades and the organisers of the Dockers and the Seamen are stationed in all the principal ports. We have seen how little the Trades Union Congress, meeting once a year for less than a week, supplies any central organ of consultation or direction. The meeting in London, every few weeks, of the two or three dozen members of the Parliamentary Committee and the Executive Committee of the Labour Party is wholly inadequate for the constant consultation upon policy, the mutual communication of each other's immediate projects, and the taking of decisions of common interest that the present stage of the Trade Union Movement requires. Probably no single thing would do so much to increase the efficiency of the Trade Union world as a whole as the provision of an adequate Central Institute and general office building in Westminster, at which could be concentrated all the meetings of national organisations, federations and committees; and which would make at any rate possible the constant personal communication of all the different headquarters.[1]

[1] Such a building was decided on in 1918–19 by joint and separate conferences of the Trades Union Congress and Labour Party, as a " Memorial of Freedom and Peace," in memory of those who lost their lives in the Great War. It is, however, by no means certain that the necessary large cost will be subscribed.

CHAPTER X

THE PLACE OF TRADE UNIONISM IN THE STATE

[1890–1920]

In 1890 Trade Union organisation had already become a lawful institution; its leading members had begun to be made members of Royal Commissions and justices ·of the peace; they were, now and then, given such Civil Service appointments as Factory Inspectors; and two or three of them had won their way into the House of Commons. But these advances were still exceptional and precarious. The next thirty years were to see the legal position of Trade Unionism, actually in consequence of renewed assaults, very firmly consolidated by statute, and the Trade Union claim to participation in all public enquiries, and to nominate members to all governmental commissions and committees, practically admitted. Trade Union representatives have won an equal entrance to local bodies, from Quarter Sessions and all the elected Councils down to Pension and Food and Profiteering Act Committees; an influential Labour Party has been established in Parliament; and most remarkable of all, the Trade Union itself has been tacitly accepted as a part of the administrative machinery of the State.

It is a characteristic feature of Trade Union history, at the end as at the beginning of the record of the past hundred years, that we have to trace the advance of the Movement through a series of attacks upon Trade Unionism itself. It is in this light that we regard the Royal Commission on Labour set up by the Conservative Government of 1891. Its professed purpose was to enquire into the relations between Capital and Labour, with a view to their improvement. But its composition was significantly weighted against the wage-earners. It is true that, in the large total membership, seven Trade Union officials were included, among them being Mr. Tom Mann ; but whilst the great employers who sat on the Commission were supported by legislators, lawyers, and economists of their own class, having substantially their own assumptions and opinions, the Trade Unionist minority was allowed no expert colleagues. From the start the Commission set itself—probably quite without any consciousness of bias—to discredit alike the economic basis of the workmen's combinations, the methods and devices of Trade Unionism, and the projects of social and economic reform that were then making headway in the Trade Union world. In the end, after two years' exhaustive enquiry, which cost the nation nearly £50,000, the majority of the Commissioners either found it impossible, or deemed it inexpedient, to report anything in the nature of an indictment against Trade Unionism in theory or practice ; and could not bring themselves to recommend any, even the slightest, reversal of what had, up to the very date of the report, been conceded or enacted, whether with regard to the recognition of Trade Unions, the collective regulation of wages, the legal prescription of minimum conditions of employment or the political activities of the workmen's combinations. The majority of the Commissioners—it is significant that they were joined by three out of the seven Trade Unionists—contented themselves with deprecating, and mildly arguing against, every one of the projects of reform that were then in the air. What is interesting is the fact that the most reactionary section of the Commission nearly persuaded their colleagues of the majority to recommend putting Trade Unions compulsorily into the strait-jacket of legal incorporation, involving them in corporate liability for the acts of their officers or agents, with the object of inducing the Unions to enter—not, as is usual in Collective Bargaining, into treaties defining merely *minimum* conditions—but into legally binding obligations with the employers, in which the Unions would become liable in damages if any of their members refused to work on the collectively prescribed terms. At the last moment the majority of the Commissioners recoiled from this proposal, which was left to be put forward as a separate report over the names of seven Commissioners. The Labour Minority Report, signed by four [1] out of the seven Trade Unionist Commissioners, whilst protesting strongly against any interference with Trade Union freedom, took the form of a long and detailed plea for a large number of immediately practicable industrial, economic, and social reforms, envisaged as step by step progress towards a complete transformation of the social order.[2]

The Commission had no direct results in legislation or administration ; but the Board of Trade set up a Labour Department, appointed a number of Trade Unionists as its officials or correspondents, and started the admirably edited monthly *Labour Gazette*. The next move came in the form of an assault on the legal position of Trade Unionism, which, in one or other manifestation, held the stage for more than a decade.

For a quarter of a century the peculiar legal status which had been conferred upon a Trade Union by the Acts of 1871–76 was not interfered with by the lawyers. At the

[1] William Abraham (South Wales Miners), J. Mawdsley (Cotton-spinners), Michael Austin, M.P. (Irish Labour), and Tom Mann (Amalgamated Society of Engineers).

[2] For the Labour Commission see its Report and Evidence, published in 1892–94 in many volumes, the Report itself being C. 2421 of 1894. An epitome was published as *The Labour Question*, by T. G. Spyers, 1894 ; see also " The Failure of the Labour Commission," by Mrs. Sidney Webb, in *Nineteenth Century*, 1893. The Trade Unionist Minority Report had a wide circulation as an Independent Labour Party pamphlet. It reads, in 1920, curiously prophetic of the actual legislative and administrative changes that have taken place.

close of the nineteenth century, when Trade Unionism had by its very success again become unpopular among the propertied and professional classes, as well as in the business world, a new assault was made upon it.

ACTIONS FOR DAMAGES

The attempt to suppress Trade Unionism by the criminal law was practically abandoned.[1] But officers of Trade Unions found themselves involved in civil actions, in which the employers sued them for damages caused by Trade Union activity which the judges held to be, although not criminal, nevertheless wrongful. What could no longer be punished by imprisonment with hard labour might at any rate be penalised by heavy damages and costs, for which the Trade Unionist's home could be sold up. The Trade Unions in 1875-80, though, as we have described, warned

---

[1] For half a century after the repeal of the Combination Acts in 1824–25 the controversy as to the legal position of Trade Unionism was always muddled up, in the minds of lawyers as well as economists and the public, with that of physical violence. Because angry strikers here and there committed assaults, and occasionally destroyed property, it was habitually assumed, as it still is by some people thinking themselves educated, that Trade Unionism practically depended on, and inevitably involved, personal molestation of one sort or another. This led magistrates, right down to 1891, occasionally to regard as a criminal offence, under the head of "intimidation," any threat or warning uttered by a Trade Unionist to an employer or a non-unionist workman, even if the consequences alluded to were of the most peaceful kind. In 1891 a specially constituted Court of the Queen's Bench Division definitely laid it down that "intimidation," under the Act of 1875, was confined to the threat of committing a criminal offence against person or tangible property (Memorandum by Sir Frederick Pollock in Appendix to Report of Royal Commission on Labour, C. 7063 ; see also *Law Quarterly Review*, January 1892 ; *Industrial Democracy*, by S. and B. Webb, Appendix I., 1897 ; Gibson *v*. Lawson, and Curran *v*. Treleaven, 1891, 2 Q.B. 545).

Magistrates continued, however, for some time to treat unfairly such breaches of public order as " obstructing the thoroughfare " or committing acts of annoyance to the public, when committed in connection with a strike of which they disapproved, which would not be proceeded against as criminal if they had been done by an excited crowd of stockbrokers in the City, by the audience of a street-corner preacher, or by a gathering of the Primrose League. Such discrimination by the police or the magistrate is unjust.

by their friendly legal advisers, had not realised the importance of insisting that the elastic and indeterminable law of conspiracy should be put on a reasonable footing; and though they were, by 1891, fairly safe from its use to reinforce the criminal law, the lawyers found means, under the figment of " conspiracy to injure," to bring under the head of torts or actionable wrongs the most ordinary and non-criminal acts of Trade Union officers which would have been, if done by one person only, without conspiracy, no ground for legal proceedings. After-ages will be amazed at the flagrant unfairness with which the conception of a " conspiracy to injure " was applied at the close of the nineteenth century. The greatest possible injury to other people's income or business, not involving the violation of a recognised legal right, if committed by employers for the augmentation of their profits (even in " restraint of trade," by means of the deliberate conspiracy of an association), was held not to be actionable.[1] But it was held to be an actionable wrong to the employer for a couple of men to wait in the street, in a town many miles distant, for the purpose of quite quietly and peacefully persuading a workman not to enter into a contract of service. The most pacific " picketing " of an employer's premises, though admittedly no longer a criminal act, was, if done in concert, held to be an actionable wrong. If a Trade Union Secretary published a perfectly accurate list of firms which were " non-Union," with the intention of warning Trade Unionists not to take service with them, this gave each of the " blacklisted " firms the right to sue him for damages. It was held to be ground for damages for a Trade Union official merely to request one firm not to supply goods to another; or to ask an employer not to employ any particular person; or even to urge the members of his own Union quite lawfully to come out on strike on the termination of their engagement

---

[1] Mogul Steamship Company *v.* M'Gregor, Gow & Co. (1892), A.C. 25 ; Scottish Co-operative Wholesale Society *v.* Glasgow Fleshers' Trade Defence Association (1897), 35 Sc.L.R. 645 ; see *History of Co-operation in Scotland*, by William Maxwell, 1910, p. 349.

of service, if the object of the strike was considered by the Court to be to put pressure on the will of some other employer or some other workman. And whilst any solicitation or persuasion to break a contract of service by a Trade Union official was certainly actionable, it became doubtful whether he would not be equally liable if he had carefully abstained from, and had really not intended, any such suggestion, whenever the members of his Society became so influenced by his action, or were thought by the Court to have been so influenced, that they, spontaneously and against his desires, impetuously came out on strike before their notices had expired.[1] It was a further aggravation, of which less advantage was actually taken by employers in this country than by those of the United States, that where the Court was convinced that an actionable wrong was threatened or intended, it was possible very summarily to obtain an injunction against its commission, any breach of which was punishable by imprisonment for contempt of Court. It became, therefore, at least theoretically possible that almost any action by a Trade Union by which an employer felt himself injured might be summarily prohibited by peremptory injunction ; and some things were thus prohibited, even in this country.

---

[1] For all these cases see *Industrial Democracy*, by S. and B. Webb, Appendix I., 1897 ; *Trade Union Law*, by H. Cohen and G. Howell, 1901 ; *The Law Relating to Trade Unions*, by D. R. C. Hunt, 1902 ; *Trade Unions and the Law*, by G. F. Assinder, 1905 ; *The Present and Future of Trade Unions*, by A. H. Ruegg and H. Cohen, 1906 ; Report of Royal Commission on Trade Disputes, Cd. 2825, 1906 ; Temperton v. Russell (1893), 1 Q.B. 715 ; 62 L.T.Q.B. 412 ; 62 L.T. 78 ; 41 W.R. 565. 57. J.P. 676 ; Trollope and Others v. The London Building Trades Federation and Others (1895), 72 L.T. 342 ; 11 T.L.R. 280 ; Pink v. The Federation of Trade Unions (1893), 67 L.T. 258 ; 8 T.L.R. 216, 711 ; 36 S.T. 201 ; J. Lyons and Son v. Wilkin (1896), 1 Ch. 811 ; the same again (1899), 1 Ch. 255 ; Allen v. Flood (1898), A.C. 1 ; 67 L.J.Q.B. 119 ; 77 L.T. 717 ; 14 T.L.R. 125 ; 46 W.R. 258 ; 47 S.J. 149 ; 62 J.P. 595 ; Quinn v. Leathem (1901), A.C. 495 ; 70 L.J.P.C. 76 ; 85 L.T. 289 ; 17 T.L.R. 749 ; 50 W.R. 139 ; 65 J.P. 708 ; W.N. 170. For foreign comments see *La Situation juridique des Trade Unions en Angleterre*, by Morin (Caen, 1907) ; *Le Droit d'Association en Angleterre*, by H. E. Barrault (Paris, 1908) ; *Das englische Gewerkvereinsrecht seit 1870*, by F. Haneld, 1909.

THE TAFF VALE CASE

All this development of the Law of Conspiracy and the Law of Torts, though it went far to render nugatory the intention of the Legislature in 1871–76 to make lawful a deliberately concerted strike, left unchallenged the position of the Trade Union itself as immune from legal proceedings against its corporate funds, an anomalous position which everybody understood to have been conceded by the Acts of 1871–76. In 1901, after thirty years of unquestioned immunity, the judges decided, to the almost universal surprise of the legal profession as well as of the Trade Union world, that this had not been enacted by Parliament. In 1900 a tumultuous and at first unauthorised strike had broken out among the employees of the Taff Vale Railway Company in South Wales, in the course of which there had been a certain amount of tumultuous picketing, and other acts of an unlawful character. In the teeth of the advice of the Company's lawyers, Beasley, the General Manager, insisted on the Company suing for damages, not the workmen guilty of the unlawful acts, but the Amalgamated Society of Railway Servants itself ; and on fighting the case through to the highest tribunal. After elaborate argument, the Law Lords decided that the Trade Union, though admittedly not a corporate body, could be sued in a corporate capacity for damages alleged to have been caused by the action of its officers, and that an injunction could be issued against it, restraining it and all its officers, not merely from criminal acts, but also from unlawfully, though without the slightest criminality, causing loss to other persons. Moreover, in their elaborate reasons for their judgement, the Law Lords expressed the view that not only an injunction but also a mandamus could be issued against a Trade Union, requiring it to do anything that any person could lawfully call upon it to do ; that a registered Trade Union could be sued in its registered name, just as if it were a corporation ;

that even an unregistered Trade Union could be made collectively liable for damages, and might be sued in the names of its proper officers, the members of its executive committees and its trustees ; and that the damages and costs could be recovered from the property of the Trade Union, whether this was in the hands of separate trustees or not. The effect of this momentous judgement, in fact, was, in flagrant disregard of the intention of the Government and of Parliament in 1871–76, to impose upon a Trade Union, whether registered or not, although it was still denied the advantages and privileges of incorporation, complete corporate liability for any injury or damage caused by any person who could be deemed to be acting as the agent of the Union, not merely in respect of any criminal offence which he might have committed, but also in respect of any act, not contravening the criminal law, which the judges might hold to have been actionable. The Amalgamated Society of Railway Servants, which had not authorised the Taff Vale strike nor any wrongful acts that were committed by the strikers, but which, after the strike had occurred, had done its best to conduct it to a successful issue, and had paid Strike Benefit, was compelled to pay £23,000 in damages, and incurred a total expense of £42,000.[1]

---

[1] Taff Vale Railway Company *v.* Amalgamated Society of Railway Servants (1901), A.C. 426 ; 70 L.J.K.B. 905 ; 85 L.T. 147 ; 17 T.L.R. 698 ; 65 J.P. 596 ; 50 W.R. 44 ; Report of Royal Commission on Trade Disputes, 1906, Cd. 2825 ; *The Law and Trade Unions : A Brief Review of Recent Litigation, specially prepared at the instance of Richard Bell, M.P.,* 1901 ; *Statement by the Parliamentary Committee on the Taff Vale Case,* 1902 ; *History of the British Trades Union Congress,* by W. J. Davis, vol. ii. 1916, pp. 201-2 ; *Trade Union Law,* by H. Cohen and George Howell, 1901 ; *The Legal Position of Trade Unions,* by H. H. Slesser and W. S. Clark, 1912 ; *Industrial Democracy,* by S. and B. Webb, Introduction to the 1902 edition, pp. xxiv-xxxvi. It does not appear that, in the strictly legal sense, the Taff Vale judgement was unwarranted. Though the Act of 1871 had been supposed to prevent a Trade Union from being proceeded against, it contained no explicit grant of immunity from being made answerable for any damage that might be wrongfully caused. In fact, both the 1871 Act and that of 1876 expressly provided that the registered Trade Union itself should be liable to be brought into Court for the petty penalties instituted for failure to supply the Registrar with copies of rules and balance-sheets ; and also that the trustees of a

It has been estimated that, from first to last, the damages and expenses in which the various Trade Unions were cast, owing to this, and the other judgements against Trade Unions and Trade Union officials personally, amounted to not less than £200,000.

The little world of Trade Union officials, already alarmed at the prospect of being individually sued for damages, was thrown into consternation by the Taff Vale judgement, which seemed to destroy, at a blow, the status that had been, with so much effort, acquired in 1871–76. The full extent of the danger was not at first apprehended. Why, it was asked, should not the Trade Union rules, and the instructions of Trade Union Executive Committees, expressly forbid the commission by officials of any wrongful acts? It was only gradually realised that, under the figment of " conspiracy to injure " that the lawyers had elaborated, even the most innocent acts, which an individual could quite lawfully commit, might be held wrongful and action-

---

registered Union should sue and be sued on its behalf. What the Act of 1871 did was to relieve the Trade Union from its character of criminality by reason of its purposes being in restraint of trade, and of its character of illegality from the same cause ; and to prohibit legal proceedings directly to enforce certain agreements among its members, or between it and its members, or among different Unions. These were assumed to be all the cases that could arise. It seems to have been taken for granted by the Minority of the Trade Union Commission of 1869, by the Home Office in 1870–71, by the Parliament of 1871–76, and the Royal Commission on Labour in 1893, that an unincorporated body could not be sued for damages in tort any more than for a civil debt. But in the following years, without any reference to Trade Unionism, the Courts successively enlarged their procedure so as to admit of any group of persons having a common interest being made parties to a " representative action " (Duke of Bedford *v.* Ellis, 1901, A.C. 1, where the tenants of shops in Covent Garden were parties). This enabled even an unregistered Trade Union to be sued (Yorkshire Miners' Association *v.* Howden, 1905, A.C. 256). In 1893, and again in 1895, actions against unregistered Trade Union organisations had been maintained in the lower Courts (Trollope and Others *v.* The London Building Trades Federation and Others, 1895, 72 L.T. 342 ; 11 T.L.R. 280 ; W.N. 45 ; Pink *v.* The Federation of Trades and Labour Unions, etc., 1893, 67 L.T. 258 ; 8 T.L.R. 216, 711 ; 36 S.J. 201). But these had not been noticed by the Trade Union Movement as a whole ; and they had not been seriously defended, not fully argued, and not carried to the highest tribunal.

able if they were committed by or on behalf of an association to the pecuniary injury of any other person ; and that there was no assignable limit, as the cases had shown, either to what might be held to be wrongful acts, or to the nature or amount of the damage that the Courts might hold to have been caused by such acts in the ordinary course of any extensive strike. Moreover, under the ordinary law of agency, the most explicit prohibition of unlawful acts in the rules of the association, coupled with the most scrupulous care in the Executive Committee in framing its instructions to its officials, would not prevent the Trade Union from being held liable for any pecuniary injury that might be caused, even in defiance of instructions and in disobedience to the rules, by any of its officers acting within the scope of their employment ; or, indeed, by any member, paid or unpaid, whom the Courts might hold to be acting as the agent of the Union. And as every stoppage of work, however lawful, necessarily involved financial loss to the employers, it could be foreseen that even the most carefully conducted strike might be made at least the occasion for costly litigation, and probably the opportunity for getting the Trade Union cast in swingeing damages. The immediate result was very largely to paralyse the Executive Committees and responsible officials of all Trade Unions, and greatly to cripple their action, either in securing improvements in their members' conditions of employment or in resisting the employers' demands for reductions. In particular, the general advances for which the railway workers were asking were delayed. The capitalists did not fail to use the opportunity to break down the workmen's defences. Trade Unionism had to a great extent lost its sting.[1]

[1] The number of stoppages through disputes known to the Labour Department of the Board of Trade, which between 1891 and 1899 had never been fewer than 700 in a year, did not again reach this figure for a whole decade ; and sank in 1903-5—years during which trade was checked, and some reduction of wages took place—to only half the number. Of the 135 claims to the Strike Benefit admitted by the General Federation of Trade Unions in 1903, we read that " no less than 130 have

Though it took some time for the Trade Union world to realise the peril, the effect on the Movement was profound. Up and down the country every society, great and small, and practically every branch, rallied in defence of its right to exist. The first result was to make the newly-formed Labour Party, which will be hereafter described, and which had hitherto hung fire, into an effective political force. The effect of the Taff Vale judgement was, in 1902–3, to double, and by 1906–7 to treble the number of adhering Trade Unions, and to raise the affiliated membership of the Party to nearly a million. As the Dissolution of Parliament approached, the Trade Unions organised a systematic canvass of all prospective candidates, making it plain that none would receive working-class support unless they pledged themselves to a Bill to undo the Taff Vale judgement and put back Trade Unionism into the legal position that Parliament had conferred upon it in 1871. When the General Election at last took place, in January 1906, the Labour Party (still known as the Labour Representation Committee) put no fewer than fifty independent candidates in the field, of whom, to the astonishment of the politicians, twenty-nine were at the head of the poll.[1]

THE TRADE DISPUTES ACT

The first claim of the Labour Party was for the statutory reversal of the Taff Vale judgement, which every one now admitted to be necessary. The question was what should be done. There were, substantially, only two alternatives. One was that, in view of the difficulty of effectually maintaining it against legal ingenuity, the Trade Unions should

---

been caused by attempts on the part of employers to encroach upon the recognised conditions prevailing in the particular trades " (*Fifth Annual Report of the Federation*, 1904, p. 11).

[1] In addition, twelve workmen, mostly miners, were elected under the auspices of the Liberal Party. Nearly all these came over to the Labour Party in 1910 (*History of Labour Representation*, by A. W. Humphrey, 1912).

forgo their position of being outside the law, and should claim, instead, full rights, not only of citizenship, but actually of being duly authorised constituent parts of the social structure, lawfully fulfilling a recognised function in industrial organisation. But for the Trade Union to become, not merely an instrument of defence, but actually an organ of government in the industrial world, required a great advance in public opinion. It assumed an explicit recognition of the legitimate function of the Trade Union, as the basis of a Vocational Democracy, exercising a definite share in the control and administration of industry. It involved a complete transformation of both the criminal and the civil law, so that workmen's combinations and strikes, together with peaceful picketing in its legitimate form, should be unreservedly and explicitly legalised; the law of civil conspiracy practically abrogated, so that nothing should be unlawful when done in concert with others which would not be unlawful if done by an individual alone; and reasonable limits set to liability for the acts of agents and to the scope for injunctions, so that a Trade Union Executive would be able both to know the law and to be ensured against its perversion. The alternative was to make no claim for the profound advance in Trade Union status that would be involved in such a policy; to forgo any hope of satisfactory or complete amendment of the law, and merely to re-enact the exceptional legislation of 1871, this time specifically insisting that a Trade Union, whether registered or not, should be put outside the law, and made expressly immune from legal proceedings for anything, whether lawful or unlawful, done by its officers or by itself. The outgoing Conservative Government had appointed in 1903 a small Royal Commission to consider the state of the law as to Trade Unionism, before which the Trade Unions had refused to give evidence, because the Commission, which was made up almost entirely of lawyers, included no Trade Unionist. This Commission, it is believed, was told privately not to report until after the General

Election, in order that the Conservative Government might not be embarrassed by the dilemma. Early in 1906 it reported in favour of the Trade Union accepting full responsibility for its own actions, subject to considerable, but far from adequate, amendments of the law.[1] This proposal was definitely rejected by the Labour Party, which introduced a Bill of its own, merely restoring the position of 1871. When the Liberal Government brought in a Bill very much on the lines of the Commission's Report, there was a dramatic exhibition of the electoral power that Trade Unionism, once it is roused, can exercise in its own defence. Member after member rose from different parts of the House to explain that they had pledged themselves to vote for the complete immunity which Trade Unions were supposed to have been granted in 1871. Nothing less than this would suffice ; and the most powerful Government hitherto known was constrained, in spite of the protests of lawyers and employers, to pass into law the Trade Disputes Act of 1906.[2]

The Trade Disputes Act, which remains (1920) the main charter of Trade Unionism, explicitly declares, without any qualification or exception, that no civil action shall be entertained against a Trade Union in respect of any wrongful act committed by or on behalf of the Union ; an extraordinary and unlimited immunity, however great may be the damage caused, and however unwarranted the act, which most lawyers, as well as all employers, regard as nothing less than monstrous.[3] At the same time the Act,

[1] *Report of Royal Commission on Trade Disputes and Trade Combinations*, Cd. 2825.

[2] 6 Edward VII. c. 47.

[3] Trade Unionists would be well advised not to presume too far on this apparently absolute immunity from legal proceedings. It must not be imagined that either the ingenuity of the lawyers or the prejudice of the judges has been exhausted. It has already been urged that the immunity of a Trade Union from being sued should be regarded as implicitly limited to acts done in contemplation or furtherance of a trade dispute ; but such a limitation has so far been negatived (Vacher *v.* London Society of Compositors, 29 T.R. 73). It is now suggested that the immunity might one day be held to be limited to acts committed by a Trade Union *in the exercise of its specifically Trade Union functions, or*

whilst not abrogating or even defining the law as to civil conspiracy, gives three exceptional privileges to Trade Union officials by declaring that, *when committed in contemplation or furtherance of a trade dispute*, (1) an act done in concert shall not be actionable if it would not have been actionable if done without concert ; (2) attendance solely in order to inform or persuade peacefully shall be lawful ; and (3) an act shall not be actionable merely by reason of its inducing another person to break a contract of employment, or of its being an interference with another person's business, or with his right to dispose of his capital or his labour as he chooses.   These exceptional statutory privileges for the protection of Trade Union officials in the exercise of their lawful vocation, and of " pickets " in the performance of their lawful function—in themselves a triumph for Trade Unionism—have ever since excited great resentment in most of those who are not wage-earners.   Some friends of the Trade Unions expressed at the time the doubt whether the policy thus forced upon Parliament would prove, in the long run, entirely in the interest of the Movement ; and whether it would not have been better to have chosen the bolder policy of insisting on a complete reform of the law,

---

for the " statutory objects " of Trade Unions as defined by the Act, and not to acts which the Court might hold to be beyond its legitimate scope, or not specifically connected with what they might in their wisdom consider to be the principal purpose of a Trade Union.   (But see Shinwell *v.* National Sailors' and Firemen's Union, 1913, a decision of the Scottish Court of Session, limiting the liability of a Union to reimburse its trustees for damages incurred by them.)   Thus, a new Taff Vale case, at a moment when public opinion was exceptionally hostile to Trade Unionism, is by no means impossible.   Similarly, Trade Union officials should remember that their privileged position is confined to a *trade dispute*, which, as specifically defined in the Act, *does not include all strikes* ; and what limits the Courts might set to the phrase is uncertain.   Moreover, the Trade Disputes Act does not repeal other statutes ; and Trade Union officials have been fined for persuading sailors not to embark, in contravention of the Merchant Shipping Acts.   The Trade Disputes Act does not protect officials committing illegalities other than those to which it expressly refers, or under circumstances other than those indicated.   See Valentine *v.* Hyde (1919) ; Conway *v.* Wade (1908), A.C. 506 ; Larkin *v.* Belfast Harbour Commissioners (1908), 2 Ir.K.B.D. 214 ; *Legal Position of Trade Unions*, by H. H. Slesser and W. S. Clark, 1912.

to which, when properly reformed, Trade Unions should be subject in the same way as any other associations. The lawyers, as it proved, were not long in taking their revenge.

THE OSBORNE JUDGEMENT

This time the legal assault on Trade Unionism took a new form. The result of the dramatic victory of the Trade Disputes Act, and of the activity of the Labour members in the House of Commons, was considerably to increase the influence of the Labour Party in the country, where preparations were made for contesting any number of constituencies irrespective of the convenience of the Liberal and Conservative parties. The railway companies, in particular, found the presence in Parliament of the secretary of the railwaymen's principal Trade Union very inconvenient. Within a couple of years of the passing of the Trade Disputes Act, on July 22, 1908, one of the members of the Amalgamated Society of Railway Servants took legal proceedings to restrain it from spending any of its funds on political objects, contending that this was beyond the powers of a Trade Union. Such a contention found no support among eminent lawyers, several of whom had formally advised that Trade Unions were undoubtedly entitled to undertake political activities if their rules authorised such action and a majority of their members desired it. W. V. Osborne, the dissentient member of the Amalgamated Society of Railway Servants, took a different view ; and, liberally financed from capitalist sources, carried his case right up to the highest tribunal. As a result, in December 1909, as in 1825, 1867–71, and 1901–6, every Trade Union in the land found its position and status once more gravely impugned. In what became widely known as the Osborne Judgement, the House of Lords, acting in its judicial capacity as the highest Court of Appeal, practically tore up what had, since 1871, been universally understood to be the legal constitution of a Trade Union.[1]

[1] A verbatim report of the proceedings (November 1908) in the Court

The decision of the judges in the Osborne case throws so much light, not only on the status of Trade Unionism in English law, but also on the animus and prejudice which the Trade Disputes Act and the Labour Party had excited, that we think it worth treating at some length. Formally this judgement decided only that W. V. Osborne, a member of the Walthamstow Branch of the Amalgamated Society of Railway Servants, was entitled to restrain that Trade Union from making a levy on its members (and from using any of its funds) for the purpose of supporting the Labour Party, or maintaining Members of Parliament. But in the course of that decision a majority of the Law Lords, therein following all three judges of the Court of Appeal, laid it down as law (and thereby made it law until Parliament should otherwise determine), (*a*) that although Parliament has always avoided any express incorporation of Trade Unions, these were all now to be deemed to be corporate bodies, formed under statute, and not unincorporated groups of individual persons ; (*b*) that it follows, by an undoubted principle of English law, that a body corporate, created under statute, cannot lawfully do anything outside the purposes for which the statute has incorporated it ; (*c*) that as the purposes for which Trade Unions are incorporated have to be found somewhere authoritatively given, the definition which Parliament incidentally enacted in the Trade Union Act of 1876 must be taken to enumerate, accurately and exhaustively, all the purposes which any group of persons falling within that definition can, as a corporate body, lawfully pursue ; and (*d*) that the payment of the salaries and election expenses of Members of Parlia-

---

of Appeal in Osborne *v.* Amalgamated Society of Railway Servants was published by the defendants (Unity House, Euston Road, London). The House of Lords' judgement was given on December 21, 1909, when it was widely commented on. The most convenient analysis is that by Professor W. M. Geldart, *The Osborne Judgment and After*, 1910, and *The Present Law of Trade Disputes and Trade Unions*, 1914. See " The Osborne Revolution," by Sidney Webb, in *The English Review* for January 1911 ; and *My Case*, by W. V. Osborne, 1910.

X

ment, and indeed, any political action whatsoever, not being mentioned as one of these purposes and not being considered by the judges incidental to them, could not lawfully be undertaken by any Trade Union, even if it was formed, from the outset, with this purpose duly expressed in its original rules, and even if all its members agreed to it, and continued to desire that their organisation should carry it out.

This momentous judgement destroyed, at a blow, the peculiar legal status which Frederic Harrison had devised for Trade Unionism in 1868, and which Parliament thought that it had enacted in 1871–76. The statutes of 1871 and 1876, which had always been supposed to have enlarged the freedom of Trade Unions, were now held to have deprived these bodies of powers that they had formerly enjoyed. It was not, as will be seen, a question of protecting a dissentient minority. Whether the members were unanimous, or whether they were nearly evenly divided, did not affect the legal position. Trade Unions found themselves suddenly forbidden to do anything, even if all their members desired it, which could not be brought within the terms of a clause in the Act of 1876, which Parliament (as Lord James of Hereford emphatically declared) never meant to be taken in that sense. " What is not within the ambit of that statute," said Lord Halsbury, " is, I think, *prohibited* both to a corporation and a combination." This was the new limitation put on Trade Unions. All their educational work was prohibited ; all their participation in municipal administration was forbidden ; all their association for common purposes in Trades Councils and the Trades Union Congress became illegal. The judges stopped the most characteristic and, as was supposed, the most constitutional of the three customary ways that (as we have shown in our *Industrial Democracy*) Trade Unions pursued of enforcing their Common Rules, namely, the Method of Legal Enactment ; grave doubt was thrown on the legality of some of the developments of their second way, the Method of Mutual

Insurance ; whilst the way that the House of Lords expressly prescribed was exactly that which used to give rise to so much controversy, namely, the Method of Collective Bargaining, with its concomitant of the Strike. So topsy-turvy a view of Trade Unionism, a view which seems to have arisen from the judges' ignorance of its two centuries of history, could not have survived open discussion, and therefore could hardly have been taken by even the most prejudiced Parliament.

THE DEVELOPMENT OF ENGLISH LAW

What was the explanation of the view of the Trade Union constitution that the judges took ? The English Courts of Justice, it must be remembered, have peculiar rules of their own for the construction of statutes. When the plain man wants to know what a document means, he seeks every available explanation of the intention of the author. When the historian inquires the purpose and intention of an Act of Parliament, he considers all the contemporary evidence as to the minds of those concerned. The Courts of Law, for good and sufficient reasons, debar themselves from going behind the face of the document, and are therefore at the mercy of all the unstudied ineptitudes of House of Commons phraseology. Along with this rigour as to the intention of a statute, the English and American judges combine a capacity for developments of doctrine in the form of legal principles which is, we believe, unequalled in other judicial systems. Now, the subject of corporations is one of those in which there had been, among the past generations of English lawyers, a silent and almost unself-conscious development of doctrine, of which, in Germany, Gierke had been the great inspirer, and Maitland in this country the brilliant exponent.[1] Our English law long rigidly refused to admit that a corporate entity could arise

---

[1] *Political Theories of the Middle Ages*, by O. Gierke, with introduction by F. W. Maitland, 1900 ; see also the works of J. N. Figgis.

of itself, without some formal and legally authoritative act of outside power. How, it was asked, except by some definite act of creation by a superior, could the *persona ficta* come into existence ?   How, otherwise (as Madox quaintly puts it), could this mere " society of mortal men " become something " immortal, invisible, and incorporeal " ? [1]   As a matter of fact, associations or social entities of all sorts always did arise, without the intervention of the lawyers, and nowadays they arise with amazing ease, without any act of creation by a superior ; and when the English lawyers refused to recognise them as existing, it was they who were irrational, and the common law itself that was at fault. Nowadays we live in a world of social entities of all sorts, and of every degree of informality, corporate entities that to the old-fashioned lawyers are still legally non-existent as such— clubs and committees of every possible kind ; groups and circles, societies and associations for every conceivable purpose ; unions and combinations and trusts in every trade and profession ; schools and colleges and " University Extension Classes," often existing and spending and acting most energetically as entities, having a common purse and a single will, in practice even perpetual succession, and (if they desire such a futile luxury) a common seal, without any sort of formal incorporation.   Gradually English lawyers (whom we need not suspect of reading Gierke, or even, for that matter, Maitland) were unconsciously imbibing the legally heterodox view that a corporate entity is anything which acts as such ; and so far from making it impossible for the *persona ficta* to come into existence without a formal act of creation, they had been, by little alterations of procedure and imperceptible changes in legal principles, sometimes by harmless little dodges and fictions of the Courts themselves, coming near to the practical result of putting every association which is, in fact, a social entity, however informal in its constitution, and however " spontaneous " in its origin, in the same position of a *persona ficta,* for the purpose

[1] *Firma Burgi,* by T. Madox, 1726, pp. 50, 279.

of suing and of being sued, as if it had been created by a formal instrument of incorporation, decorated by many seals, and procured at vast expense from the post-Reformation Pope himself ; or as if it had been expressly incorporated by the Royal Charter of a Protestant King or the private statute of a Victorian Parliament.

Now this development of legal doctrine to fit the circumstances of modern social life is, when one comes to think of it, only common sense. If twenty old ladies in the workhouse club together to provide themselves with a special pot of tea, and agree that one among them shall be the treasurer of their painfully-hoarded pennies as a common fund, they do, in fact, create a social entity just as real in its way as the Governor and Company of the Bank of England. Why should not the law, if it ever comes to hear of the action of the twenty old ladies in the workhouse, deal with the situation as it really is, according to their wishes and intentions, without inquiring by what formal act of external power a *persona ficta* has been created ; and therefore without demanding that the old ladies shall first procure a charter of incorporation from the Pope, from the King, or from Parliament ? And considering that Trade Unions were now in fact social entities, often having behind them more than a hundred years of " perpetual succession " ; counting sometimes over a hundred thousand members moving by a single will ; and occasionally accumulating in a common purse as much as half a million of money, the Law Lords might well think it absurd and irrational of Parliament to have decided in 1871–76, and again in 1906, to regard them as unincorporated groups of persons, having, in a corporate capacity, no legally enforceable obligations and hardly any legally enforceable rights. It may have been absurd and irrational, but what right— so the Trade Unionists asked — had the judges to change the law ?

Whatever may be the justification for the momentous change in the law which the Six Judges (namely, the three

members of the Court of Appeal, and three out of the five
Law Lords, all of whom agreed in the series of propositions
that we have cited) suddenly, without Parliamentary
authority, of their own motion effected, it created an intolerable situation.   There was, in the first place, the
application of the doctrine of *ultra vires* to corporate entities
quite unaware of its existence.   It was all very well, in
order to fit the law to the facts, to throw over the old legal
doctrine that the *persona ficta* of a corporation could only
come into existence by some formal act of incorporation by
an external authority.   But then it plainly would not do
to retain, as the Six Judges quite calmly retained, the
severe limitations on the action of statutory corporate
entities which is involved in the doctrine of *ultra vires*, and
which, as Lord Halsbury put it, was to *prohibit* them from
doing what they liked.   The argument for that principle is
that such a corporate entity owes its existence entirely to
the statutory authority by which it is created ; that the
legislature has brought it into being for certain definite
purposes ; that for those purposes and no others the exceptional powers of a corporation have been conferred upon
it ; that as such it is, in a sense, the agent whom the community has entrusted with the execution of these functions,
and who cannot therefore (even if all the constituent members of its body so agree and desire) assume any other
purposes or functions.   But any such doctrine of *ultra vires*
can have no rational application to the corporate entity
formed by the twenty old ladies in the workhouse for their
private pot of tea.   If we are going, in effect, to treat as
corporate entities all sorts of spontaneously arising associations, such as an unregistered Trade Union (and some of
the wealthiest and most powerful Trade Unions were still
unregistered), or such as an Employers' Association (which
was hardly ever a registered body)—corporate entities which
were, in fact, lawfully in existence long before the Act of
1876—we must give up the fiction that the purposes of these
associations have been authoritatively fixed and defined in

advance by Parliament in such a way that the members themselves, even when they are unanimous and when they are acting in strict accord with their constitution and rules, cannot add to or alter the objects or methods of their organisation. What was logically required, in fact, was not the arbitrary identification of spontaneously arising associative entities with legally created corporations, but the formulation of a new conception as to the functions and legal rights that such spontaneously arising associative entities—to which the limitations of legally created corporations could not be simply assumed to apply—should, as a class, be permitted to exercise.

THE MISCARRIAGE OF JUSTICE

We come now to the second cardinal feature of the decision of the Six Judges in 1909, in which they showed both prejudice and ignorance. Having found that the Trade Unions were, in fact, corporate entities, and that they had been, in various clumsy ways, dealt with by Parliament very much as if they were legally corporate entities—though Parliament had advisedly abstained from incorporating them, and had, indeed, always referred to them as being what in fact they were, namely already existing and spontaneously arising associations, not created by its will— the Six Judges took the view that some authoritative specification of the objects and purposes of a Trade Union had to be discovered by hook or by crook. It seems to have been by them inconceivable (though Lord James of Hereford, one of their own number, who had personally taken part in all the legislation, expressly told them it was in fact so) that no such specification should exist. They accordingly found it in an enumeration which Parliament had given in the Act of 1876 of all the various bodies which were to be entitled to the privileges conferred by the Act—a definition introduced, so a well-informed writer men-

tioned in 1878, for the special advantage of Trade Unions [1]
—principally to enable them to be registered by the Chief
Registrar of Friendly Societies. The Law Lords now held
that this definition must be deemed to be an exhaustive
enumeration, not merely of the kinds of societies to be
eligible for registration, but also of all the objects and purposes that Parliament intended any of those bodies, whether
registered or unregistered, to be free at any time to pursue.
The result was that all Trade Unions and Employers'
Associations, and, indeed, all informal groups of workmen
or employers falling within this definition, suddenly found
themselves (to the complete amazement of every one concerned, including the lawyers) rigidly confined in their
action, even if all their members otherwise wished and
agreed, to matters which were specified in an enumerating
clause of an Act of Parliament of a generation before, which
had never before been supposed to have that meaning, or
to have any restrictive effect at all. We ought to speak
with proper respect of the judges, though sometimes, by
their curious ignorance of life outside the Law Courts, and
especially of "what everybody knows," they try us hard.
But it is necessary to state plainly, with regard to this part
of the Osborne Judgement, that to the present writers, as to
the whole British working class and many other people,
including lawyers, it seemed an astounding aberration,
amounting to a grave miscarriage of justice. Again, let it
be noted that Lord James of Hereford, who knew what
Parliament had intended, and what Trade Unions actually
were, expressly dissented from his colleagues on this point,
saying that the enumeration clause in the Act of 1876 was
never intended to be "a clause of limitation or exhaustive
definition" of objects and purposes ; and arguing that it
did not prevent a Trade Union from having other purposes,
or pursuing other methods, not in themselves unlawful,
even though these were not enumerated in the definition

[1] *Conflicts of Capital and Labour*, by G. Howell, 1st edition, 1878,
2nd edition, 1890, p. 479.

clause and were not even incidental to the purposes therein enumerated. But what is the history of this definition clause ? As it stands in the Act of 1876 it runs as follows :

The term " Trade Union " means any combination, whether temporary or permanent, for regulating the relations between workmen and masters, or between workmen and workmen, or between masters and masters, or for imposing restrictive conditions on the conduct of any trade or business, whether such combination would or would not, if the principal Act had not been passed, have been deemed to have been an unlawful combination by reason of some one or more of its purposes being in restraint of trade.

Now, to the lay mind, this extremely loose enumeration[1] of kinds of societies seems plainly intended to bring within its net, and therefore to admit to the advantages of the Act, a wide range of existing or possible associations of different kinds. It was to include all sorts of Employers' Associations as well as Trade Unions. It was to include bodies already in existence as well as those to be formed in the future. It was to include bodies seeking to impose restrictive conditions " in restraint of trade," as well as those having no such unlawful objects. It was to include, therefore, bodies already enjoying a full measure of lawful existence and legal recognition, as well as those for the first time fully legalised by the legislation of 1871–76. To the logician it will be clear that we have here a case of classification by type, not by delimitation. " It is determined," says Whewell and J. S. Mill, " not by a boundary line without, but by a central point within ; not by what it strictly excludes, but by what it eminently includes ; by an example, not by a precept."[2] Accordingly the clause

---

[1] It should be recorded, as an instance of the prescience of Sir Charles Dilke, that he is reported to have declared at the time that " the trade union Acts were spoilt during their passage through the House by the insertion of obscure definition clauses " (*Conflicts of Capital and Labour*, by G. Howell, 1890, p. 479).

[2] Whewell, *History of Scientific Ideas*, vol. ii. p. 120 ; J. S. Mill, *System of Logic*, vol. ii. p. 276.

names specifically one by one the various attributes, any
one of which is to be typical of the class. It sufficed for the
purpose to name only one attribute belonging to each body
which it was desired to include. What its other attributes
might be was irrelevant. It does not occur to the ordinary
reader, any more than to the logician, that the effect of the
clause is, not merely to include associations of different
kinds, but also to limit the legal freedom of all those associations, with all their varied functions, exclusively to the
purposes specified in the definition, which were merely recited in order to bring a number of heterogeneous bodies
into one class. On the construction put upon this clause
by the Six Judges, the Act of 1876 was a measure which
deprived Trade Unions and Employers' Associations, many
of which had been for years lawfully in existence, without
any unlawful objects or methods, of a freedom that they
had up to then enjoyed; it was an Act rigidly confining·
their operations to a limited field, and for ever prohibiting
them (as Lord Halsbury expressly declared) from doing anything not included in the list of functions incidentally then
and there given. It is safe to say that, to any historical
student who knows anything of the circumstances of the
case, such a supposition is preposterous. No Trade Union
and no Employers' Association was aware in 1876 that its
freedom was being thus restricted. Thomas Burt, M.P.,
and Lord James of Hereford (then Sir Henry James, M.P.),
who took part in passing the Act, certainly never dreamed
that they were doing anything of the sort. The Home
Office officials who prepared it, and Lord Cross (then Home
Secretary) who introduced it, quite plainly had not the
remotest notion that they were taking away from Trade
Unions (which they were anxious to legalise) any of the
functions which these Unions were in fact exercising, and
which such Trade Unions as were lawful associations were
already *lawfully* exercising; or that they were prohibiting
these Trade Unions from doing anything not specified in
the incidental enumeration of attributes that was then,

merely for the purpose of including various kinds of associations, statutorily enacted. As a matter of fact, the definition clause in the Act of 1876 was enacted merely to correct
in one small particular the definition clause in the Act of
1871. That clause had defined a Trade Union as meaning
" such combination . . . as would, if this Act had not
passed, been deemed to have been an unlawful combination
by reason of some one or more of the purposes being in
restraint of trade." This was found in practice inconvenient,
because it had inadvertently excluded from registration and
all the benefits of the Act those Trade Unions and Employers'
Associations which were already lawful associations, free
from any unlawful purpose. A Trade Union had to prove
that it was (but for the Act) an unlawful body before it
could be admitted to the advantages of the Act. It was
also inexpedient, because it actually offered an inducement
to Trade Unions to have purposes or methods " in restraint
of trade," in order to obtain these advantages. Now, supposing that the Act of 1876 had not been passed, and that
the definition clause had remained in the terms of that of
the Act of 1871, would the Six Judges have equally construed it as offering a complete and exhaustive enumeration
of the permissible activities of a Trade Union, making it
actually illegal for the future for any association of workmen or employer to deal with the conditions of employment,
*except in ways that would (but for the 1871 Act) have been
unlawful* ? And if the definition clause in the 1871 Act
cannot be construed as (to use Lord James of Hereford's
words) " a clause of limitation or exhaustive definition " of
Trade Union activities, with what consistency can the
definition clause of the 1876 Act (which follows the same
wording, and merely extends the definition so as to take in
lawful as well as unlawful societies) be so construed ? Successive Chief Registrars of Friendly Societies, like every one
else, had always understood the definition clause to be an
enabling clause, not a restricting one ; and they had accordingly for a whole generation willingly registered rules pre-

sented to them by Trade Unions, including in their objects and purposes all sorts of things not enumerated in the definition, and not even incidental to any of the purposes therein enumerated. It was, in 1909, not at first realised—certainly the Six Judges did not realise—how extensive and how varied were the actually existing operations of Trade Unions that they were rendering illegal. Not political action alone, not municipal action alone, but any work of general education of their members or others; the formation of a library; the establishment or management of " University Extension " or " Workers' Educational Association " classes; the subscription to circulating book-boxes; the provision of public lectures; the establishment of scholarships at Ruskin College, Oxford, or any other College—all of which things were at the time actually being done by Trade Unions—were all henceforth to be *ultra vires* and illegal. The two hundred Trades Councils, local federations of different Trade Unions for the purpose of dealing with matters of general interest to workmen, which took no part in the collective bargaining of any particular Trade Union, were probably thereby equally made illegal; though they were in 1876 already a quarter of a century old, and in 1909 numbered nearly a million members. The annual Trade Union Congress itself, then in its fortieth year, and dealing almost exclusively with Parliamentary projects, came under the same ban. The active participation which Trade Unions had here and there taken in technical education, and their co-operation with the Local Education Authorities, which had sometimes been found so useful, were certainly *ultra vires*. One would suppose, strictly speaking, that a similar illegality was to attach to all the vast " friendly society " side of Trade Unionism, with its sick and accident and out-of-work benefits—not one of them being referred to in the definition which the Six Judges declared to contain an exhaustive enumeration of the purposes and objects that Parliament intended to permit Trade Unions to pursue. But here the Six Judges saved themselves—though in a way logically destructive of their claim that the definition clause itself was one of " exhaustive " enumeration of permissible Trade Union purposes—by holding that these friendly benefits, though not mentioned in the definition clause, were referred to elsewhere in the Act, and might be regarded as incidental to the purpose of regulating the conditions of employment. This, indeed, so far as benefits paid to the workman himself are concerned, was a plausible view. Strike Benefit, in particular, is plainly incidental to striking, and sick benefit might conceivably be held to protect the worker from industrial oppression whilst sick. But the same cannot be said of the most widely spread of all Trade Union benefits, the provision of funeral money on a member's death. In some cases the Trade Unions were actually paying for the funerals of their deceased members' widows and orphan children. This was a mere act of humanity to the deceased member's widow and orphans ; and it could not, by any stretch of imagination, be supposed to improve the workers' bargaining power, or to be in any way incidental to the regulation or restriction of the conditions of employment. Yet Funeral Benefit was in 1909 (as it was in 1876) the one among the so-called " friendly " benefits most universally adopted by Trade Unions. More than a million Trade Unionists were thus effecting through their societies a humble life insurance. This extensive life insurance business of Trade Unions could not be said to be in any way included in the definition clause of the 1876 Act, even if the sick and unemployment benefits were. If the judgements in the Osborne Case were correct, the whole of this life insurance business of Trade Unions (as distinguished from the sick and unemployment benefits), or at least the whole of that relating to widows and orphans, must be held to have been inadvertently prohibited by Parliament in 1871 and 1876, and to have been ever since *ultra vires* and illegal. It is impossible for the plain man to avoid the conclusion, even though the six other authorities take a contrary view, that Lord James of Hereford was right in declaring that the definition in the Act of 1876 was not meant by Parliament to be " a clause of limitation or exhaustive definition " of the permissible purposes of a Trade Union ; and, accordingly, that the Six Judges had —presumably following quite accurately the narrow technical rules of their profession—put upon the statute a construction which Parliament had in no way intended.

What then did Parliament intend to fix and define as the permissible objects and functions of a Trade Union ? The answer of the historical student is clear and unhesitating. Parliament quite certainly intended, in 1871 and 1876, to fix and define nothing of the sort ; but meant, whether wisely or not, to leave Trade Unions as they then were— as such of them, indeed, as had no unlawful purpose or method had long *legally* been—namely, as free as any other unincorporated groups of persons to take whatever action they might choose, subject only to their own contractual agreements, and to the general law of the land. From this position we venture, as historians, to say that Parliament did not, in 1871 or 1876, intentionally depart.

Finally, we have the argument of the Six Judges that, seeing that the sole lawful purposes of a Trade Union are " regulating the relations between workmen and masters, or between workmen and workmen, or between masters and masters," and " imposing restrictive conditions on the conduct of any trade or business," no action of a Parliamentary or political kind is within the definition, or even incidental to anything therein. This view, to put it bluntly, showed an ignorance of Trade Unionism, British industrial history, and the circumstances not only of 1871–76, but also of 1908–9, which was as remarkable as it was deplorable. On the face of it, to take first the words of the statute, the most usual and the most natural way of " regulating " the relations between people, and the most obvious expedient for " imposing " restrictive conditions on industry, is an Act of Parliament. It was to Acts of Parliament, as we have abundantly shown in *Industrial Democracy*, that the

Trade Unions had for a century been looking, and were in 1871-76, many of them, looking, for a very large part of the " regulating " of industrial conditions, and of the " restrictive conditions " that they existed to promote. What the judges apparently forgot is that conditions of employment include not merely wages, but also hours of labour, sanitary conditions, precautions against accident, compensation for injuries, and what not. If the Six Judges had remembered how, in fact, in Great Britain the great majority of industrial relations were regulated, and how the great mass of restrictive conditions were, in fact, imposed on industry ; or if they had had recalled to them the long and persistent struggle of the Trade Unions to get adopted the Factory Acts, the Mines Regulation Acts, the Truck Acts, the Shop Hours Acts, and so many more, they could hardly have argued that such actions as engaging in Parliamentary business, supporting or opposing Parliamentary candidates, and helping members of Parliament favourable to " regulating," and " imposing restrictive conditions "—actions characteristic of Trade Unions for generations—were not incidental to these legitimate purposes. As a matter of fact, the getting and enforcing of legislation is, historically, as much a part of Trade Union function as maintaining a strike.[1] One Trade Union at least, which no one ever dreamt to be illegal, the United Textile Factory Workers' Association, has existed exclusively for political action, and had no other functions.[2] This kind of Trade Union action is even antecedent in date to any corporate dealing with employers. During the whole two centuries of Trade Union history, as in *Industrial Democracy* we have described, the Unions have had at their disposal, and have simultaneously adopted, three different

---

[1] George Howell, in his *Conflicts of Capital and Labour*, 1890, gives a list, three pages long, of Acts which, as he expressly testifies from personal knowledge, were promoted or supported by the Trade Unions ; and in his *Labour Legislation, Labour Movements and Labour Leaders*, 1902, pp. 469-73, a still longer one.

[2] *Industrial Democracy*, pp. 124, 251, 258-60.

methods of imposing and enforcing the Common Rules which they sought to get adopted in the conditions of employment. From 1700 downwards they have used the Method of Mutual Insurance ; from the very beginning of the eighteenth century down to the present day the records show them to have been continuously employing the Method of Legal Enactment ; whilst only intermittently during the eighteenth century, and not openly and avowedly until 1824, could they rely on the Method of Collective Bargaining. The Miners' Unions, and the Agricultural Labourers' Unions, in particular, had been particularly active in support of the extension of the franchise between 1863 and 1884. Even the expenditure of Trade Union funds on Parliamentary candidatures was practised by Trade Unions at any rate as early as 1868, as soon, in fact, as the town artisans were enfranchised ; and the payment of Trade Union Members of Parliament was begun as early as 1874, and had lasted continuously from that date. Yet the Six Judges assumed, apparently without adequate consideration, and certainly on inaccurate information, that Parliament in 1876 intended to authorise Trade Unions to pursue their first and third methods, but intended to prohibit them, from that time forth, from using the Method of Legal Enactment, just at the moment when this latter was being most effectively employed. It is, indeed, almost comic to remember that the Bill which is supposed to have effected this revolution in the Trade Union position was brought in by Lord Cross, then Sir R. A. Cross, M.P., fresh from his election by a constituency in which the Trade Unionists had been, politically, the dominant factor ; that it was debated in a House of Commons in which the direct influence of the Trade Unions was at the highest point that it had hitherto reached ; that at the General Election of 1874, from which the members had lately come, the Trade Unions, as we have described in the present volume, had worked with might and main for the rejection of candidates opposed to their political claims, and had had a much larger share than political historians

usually recognise in the Gladstonian defeat; that two
Trade Union members were actually then sitting in the
House, one, at least (Thomas Burt), being openly maintained
as a salaried representative of his Union, by a salary avowedly
fixed on a scale to enable him to sit in Parliament; [1] that the
Conservative Government promptly introduced the particular
legal enactments to obtain which the Trade Unions had
spent their money, namely, the Nine Hours Bill, the Employer
and Workman Bill, and the Trade Union Bill; and that
the Six Judges ask us to believe that the latter Bill, which
the Trade Union members themselves helped to pass, was
designed and intended to prevent Thomas Burt from
drawing a salary from the Northumberland Miners' Mutual
Confident Society whilst sitting in the House of Commons;
to prohibit the Northumberland Miners' Mutual Confident
Society, just because it was a Trade Union, from taking any
part in future elections in the Morpeth Division, and to
make the action of this and all other Trade Unions in paying
for political work and Parliamentary candidatures, even
with the unanimous consent of their members, from that
time forth illegal.

We have thought it worth while to place on record this
analysis of the legally authoritative part of the Osborne
Judgement, which, though partly modified by a subsequent
statute, has not been overruled, and is still legally authoritative, because it is of historical importance. It is significant
as showing how far the Courts of Justice were, as lately as
1909, still out of touch, so far as Trade Unionism is concerned,
either with Parliament or with the political economists.
The case was, however, of even greater import. The bias
and prejudice, the animus and partiality—doubtless unconscious to the judges themselves—which were displayed
by those who ought to have been free from such intellectual
influences; the undisguised glee with which this grave miscarriage of justice was received by the governing class, and
the prolonged delay of a professedly Liberal and Radical

[1] *A Great Labour Leader* [Thomas Burt], by Aaron Watson, 1908.

Cabinet, and a professedly Liberal and Radical House of Commons in remedying it, had a great effect on the minds of the wage-earners, and contributed notably to the increasing bitterness of feeling against the " governing class," and against a State organisation in which such a miscarriage of justice could take place. We must, indeed, look behind the legal technicalities of the Six Judges, and consider what was the animus behind their extraordinary judgement. The " subservience " of Parliament to the Trade Unions in passing the Trade Disputes Act of 1906 had excited the deepest resentment of the lawyers. The progress of the Labour Party was causing a quite exaggerated alarm among members of the governing class. What lay behind the Osborne Judgement was a determination to exclude the influence of the workmen's combinations from the political field. This is really what the Osborne Judgement prohibited. One irreverent legal critic, indeed, went so far as to remark that the Law Lords were so anxious to make it clear that Trade Unions were not to be entitled to pay for Members of Parliament, that they failed to heed how much law they were severally demolishing in the process ! It is instructive to examine the arguments adduced by the Law Lords and the judges on this point, apart from their decision as to Trade Union status. These opinions could hardly be deemed to be law, as they all differed one from another, and none of them obtained the support of a majority of the Law Lords. Such as they are, however, they seem not to have been connected with Trade Unionism at all, but with the nature of the House of Commons. One of the Law Lords (Lord James of Hereford) merely objected to Trade Unions paying a Member of Parliament who was (as was quite incorrectly assumed) bound by a rule of the paying body requiring him to vote in a particular way, not on labour questions only, but on all issues that might come before Parliament. Another Law Lord (Lord Shaw), with whom Lord Justice Fletcher Moulton seemed to agree, held that what was illegal was not the payment of Members of Parliament, but their subjection, by whomsoever paid, to a " pledge-bound " party organisation (as the Labour Party was alleged to be). Another judge (Farwell, L.J.) took a different line, and held that it was illegal for a corporate body to require its own members to subscribe collectively towards the support of a Member of Parliament with whose views they might individually not agree. What the historian and the student of political science will say is that these were matters for legislation, not for the sudden intervention of the judiciary. The House of Commons is prompt enough to defend its own honour and its own " privilege " ; and the function of the judges will begin when any of the acts referred to has been made an illegal practice. In 1909, as now, the practices complained of, whether or not they were correctly described, and however objectionable to these particular gentlemen they might be, were all lawful ; and the judges and Law Lords were abusing the privileges of their office by importing them to prejudice the legal issue.

The Osborne Judgement received the support, not only of the great mass of property owners and professional men, but also, though tacitly, of the Liberal and Conservative Parties. A distinct challenge was thereby thrown down to the Trade Union world. Not only were the activities of their Unions to be crippled, not only was their freedom to combine for whatever purposes they chose to be abrogated, they were to be expressly forbidden to aspire to protect their interests or promote their objects by Parliamentary representation, or in any way to engage in politics. It was this challenge to Organised Labour that absorbed the whole interest of the Trade Union world for the next three or four years.

The experienced Trade Union leaders did not forget that it might well be a matter for Trade Union consideration how far it is wise and prudent for a Trade Union to engage in general politics. We have elsewhere pointed out [1] with some elaboration how dangerous it may become to the

---

[1] *Industrial Democracy*, by Sidney and Beatrice Webb, 1897, pp. 838-40,

strength and authority of a Trade Union if any large section of the persons in the trade are driven out of its ranks, or deterred from joining, because they find their convictions outraged by part of its action. Nothing could be more unwise for a Trade Union than to offend its Roman Catholic members by espousing the cause of secular education.[1] But this is a point which each Trade Union must decide for itself. It is not a matter in which outsiders can offer more than counsel. It is clearly not a matter in which the discretion of the Trade Union, any more than that of an individual employer, can properly be limited by law. For no Trade Union can nowadays abstain altogether from political action. Without co-operating with other Trade Unions in taking Parliamentary action of a very energetic and very watchful kind, it cannot (as long experience has demonstrated to practically all Trade Unionists) protect the interests of its members. Without taking a vigorous part in promoting, enforcing, and resisting all sorts of legislation affecting education, sanitation, the Poor Law, the whole range of the Factories, Mines, Railways, and Merchant Shipping Acts, the Shop Hours, Truck, Industrial Arbitration and Conciliation, and now even the Trade Boards' Act, the Trade Union cannot properly fulfil its function of looking after the regulation of the conditions of employment. But this is not all. The interests of its members require the most watchful scrutiny of the administration of every public department. There is not a day passes but something in Parliament demands its attention. On this point Trade Union opinion is unanimous. We have never met any member of a Trade Union—and Osborne himself is no exception—who has any contrary view. To suggest that there is anything improper, or against public policy, for a Trade Union to give an annual retaining fee to a Member of Parliament whom its members trust, or to take the necessary steps to get that member elected,

---

[1] For this reason the Trades Union Congress now refuses to entertain any motion on this subject.

in order to ensure that what the Trade Union conceives to be its own interests shall be protected, was to take up a position of extraordinary unfairness. When more than a quarter of the whole House of Commons habitually consists, not merely of individual employers, but actually of persons drawing salaries or stipends from capitalist corporations of one kind or another—when, in fact, the number of companies of shareholders in railways, banks, insurance companies, breweries, ocean telegraphs, shipbuilding yards, shipping companies, steamship lines, iron and steel works, coal mines, and joint stock enterprises of all sorts actually represented in the House of Commons by their own salaried chairmen, directors, trustees, managers, secretaries, or solicitors is beyond all computation—the claim that there is something improper, something inconsistent with our electoral system, something at variance with the honourable nature of the House of Commons, for the workmen's organisations to retain a few dozen of the Members whom the constituencies (knowing of this payment) deliberately elect, or to help such Members to provide their election expenses, is an argument so extraordinary in its unfairness that it drives the active-minded workman frantic with rage. It is no answer to say that these representatives of capitalist corporations are not expressly paid to sit in Parliament. They are at any rate desired by their employers to sit, and permitted by the law to receive their salaries notwithstanding that they do sit. This was forbidden to representatives of Trade Unions. That it should be illegal for the salaried President or Secretary of the Amalgamated Society of Railway Servants to sit in Parliament, when it is perfectly legal for the much more generously salaried Chairman or Director of a Railway Company to sit there, is an anomaly hard for any candid man to defend ; and the anomaly is all the greater in that the interests of the railway company come, almost every year, into conflict with those of the community at large, and the railway chairman is, on these occasions, quite frankly there to promote his own company's

Bill, and to defend the interests of the shareholders by whom he is paid. To say that the workmen's organisations shall not pay their representatives in the way that suits working-class conditions, whilst railway shareholders may pay their representatives in the way that suits capitalist conditions— to assume a great concern for the wounded conscience of a Liberal or Conservative Trade Unionist who finds his Union paying its Secretary or its President to sit as a Radical or Labour Member of Parliament, and no concern at all for the Socialist or Radical shareholder in a railway company who finds his company paying its Conservative Chairman M.P.—is to be guilty of an amazing degree of class bias, if not of hypocrisy. After all, it is not the Trade Union but the constituency that elects the Member of Parliament. The Trade Union payment only enables him to stand. Whatever may be thought of the policy of the Labour Party, or the particular form of its organisation, if we regard the Trade Union payment as a retaining fee for looking after what the Trade Union members as a whole conceive to be their own interest ; if the Trade Union members have the opportunity of choosing, by a majority, which among competing persons (or, for that matter, which among competing groups of persons) they will entrust with this Trade Union task ; if the Trade Union assumes no responsibility for and exercises no coercion upon its Parliamentary representative with regard to issues on which it has not voted, no Trade Unionist's political conscience need be wounded by the fact that, outside the range of the task that the Trade Union has confided to him, the Union's Parliamentary agent (who must have views of one sort or another) expresses opinions in accord with those of the constituency that elected him, or joins together with other members of like opinions to form a political party. When, three-quarters of a century ago, J. A. Roebuck was the salaried agent in the House of Commons for the Legislative Assembly of Lower Canada, no one complained that it was against the dignity of Parliament for him to be thus retained and paid ; and so long as he attended faithfully to Canadian business it was never contended that the tender conscience of any Canadian Conservative was offended by the ultra-Radical utterances or extremely independent political alliances of the Member for Bath.

THE TRADE UNION ACT OF 1913

It is an instance of the failure of both the governing class and the party politicians to appreciate the workman's standpoint, or to understand the temper of the Trade Union world, that this crippling judgement remained for nearly four years unreversed. The Liberal and Conservative Parties were, during 1910 and 1911, quarrelling about the Budget and the exact powers to be exercised by the House of Lords ; and two successive General Elections were fought without bringing the Trade Unions any redress. Meanwhile, up and down the country discontented or venal Trade Unionists were sought out by solicitors and others acting for the employers ; and were induced to lend their names to proceedings for injunctions against their own Unions, prohibiting them from subscribing to the Labour Party, from contributing towards the election expenses of candidates, from taking action in municipal elections, from subscribing to educational classes, and from taking shares in a " Labour " newspaper. It may have seemed a skilful political dodge, during the elections of 1910, to hamstring in this way the growing Labour Party ; but the resentment caused by such behaviour makes it doubtful whether action of this kind is, in the long run, politically advantageous. In the first place, the House of Commons, in 1911, felt itself compelled, as an alternative to restoring Trade Union liberties, to concede the payment of £400 a year to all Members of Parliament. Finally, in 1913, the Cabinet, after a severe internal struggle, brought itself to introduce a Bill giving power generally to any Trade Union to include in its constitution any lawful purpose whatever, so long as its principal objects were those of a Trade Union as defined in the 1876 Act ; and to spend money on any purpose thus authorised. It was, indeed, provided that before the financing of certain specified political objects could be undertaken, including the support of Parliamentary or Municipal candidates or members, or the publication or distribution of political documents,[1] a ballot of the members was to be held in a prescribed form, and a simple majority of those voting secured ; the payments were to be made out of a special political fund, and any member was to be entitled to claim to be exempt from the special subscription to that political fund. These restrictive provisions were opposed by the Labour Members in the House of Commons ; but with slight amendment the measure was passed into law as the Trade Union Act of 1913.[2]

It is not easy to sum up the whole effect of the legal assaults upon Trade Unionism between 1901 and 1913. Politically, the result was to exasperate the active-minded workmen, and greatly to promote, though with some delay, the growth of an independent Labour Party in the House of Commons. On the other hand, it must not be overlooked that the temporary crippling of Trade Unionism seemed to be of financial advantage to that generation of employers. It was, perhaps, not altogether an accident that the brunt of the attack had to be borne by the Amalgamated Society of Railway Servants, a Union then struggling for " recognition " in such a position as to make effective its claims to better remuneration and shorter hours of labour for the whole body of railwaymen. It may fairly be reckoned that the railwaymen were, by means of the two great pieces of litigation to which their Union was subjected, held at bay for something like a decade, during which the improvement in their conditions, in spite of a slowly-increasing cost of living, was (mainly through the evasions of the railway

---

[1] If the main object of a newspaper is political, any expenditure by a Trade Union upon it (including the purchase of shares) is itself political (Bennett *v.* National Amalgamated Society of Operative Painters (1915), 31 T.L.R. 203).

[2] 3 George V. c. 30.

companies by their silent " regrading " of their staffs)
extremely small.[1] A rise of wages to the extent of only
a penny per hour for the whole body of railwaymen would
have cost the railway companies, in the aggregate, something like five or six million pounds a year. If any such
advance was, by means of the Taff Vale Case and the
Osborne Judgement, staved off for ten years, the gain to the
whole body of railway shareholders of that generation might
be put as high as fifty or sixty millions sterling—a sum worth
taking a little trouble about and spending a little money
upon, in items not revealed in the published accounts. But
the crippling effect of the litigation was not confined to the
Amalgamated Society of Railway Servants, which spent,
altogether, nearly £50,000 in law costs in defending the pass
for the whole Trade Union Movement. If, in the temporary
set-back to trade in 1903–5, and in the revival that
immediately followed it ; or in the recurring set-back of
1908–9, and the great improvement of the ensuing years,
the whole body of wage-earners in the kingdom lost only
a penny per hour from their wages, or gained less than they
might otherwise have done to the extent of no more than
a penny per hour, their financial loss, in one year alone,
would have amounted to something like a hundred million
pounds. And whatever they forwent in this way, they
lost not during one year only, but during at least several
years, and many of them for a whole decade. There is no
doubt that the capitalist employers, thinking only of their
profits for the time being, regarded even a temporary
crippling of the Trade Union Movement as well worth all
that it might cost them. The historian, thinking more of
the secular effort upon social institutions, will not find the
balance-sheet so easy to construct. The final result of the
successive attempts between 1901 and 1913 to cripple Trade
Unionism by legal proceedings was to give it the firmest

---

[1] " The average weekly earnings of railway servants, as given by the
Board of Trade, were lower in 1910 than in 1907 " (*Trade Unionism on
the Railways*, by G. D. H. Cole and R. Page Arnot, 1917, pp. 21-22).

possible basis in statute law. The right of workmen to combine for any purpose not in itself unlawful was definitely established. The strike, with its " restraint of trade," and its interference with profits and business ; peaceful picketing even on an extensive scale ; the persuasion of workmen to withdraw from employment even in breach of contract, and the other frequent incidents of an industrial dispute were specifically declared to ˌbe, not only not criminal, but actually lawful. The right of Trade Unions to undertake whatever political and other activities their members might desire was expressly conceded. Finally, a complete immunity of Trade Unions in their corporate capacity from being sued or made answerable in damages, for any act whatsoever, however great might be the damage thereby caused to other parties, was established by statute in the most absolute form.[1] The Trade Unions, it must be remembered, had not asked for these sweeping changes in their position. They had been, in 1900, content with the legislation of 1871–76. It was the successive assaults made upon them by the legal proceedings of 1901–13 that eventually drove the Government and Parliament, rather than formally concede to Trade Unionism its proper position in the government of industry, and effect the necessary fundamental amendment of the law, once more to create for the workmen's organisations an anomalous status

THE RISE IN STATUS OF TRADE UNIONISM

So far we have described only the changes in the legal status of the Trade Unions and the consequent increase in their freedom of action and in their influence, alike in the industrial and political sphere. This advance in legal status

---

[1] *The Legal Position of Trade Unions*, by H. H. Slesser and W. Smith Clark, 2nd ed., 1914; *The Present Law of Trade Disputes and Trade Unions*, by Professor W. M. Geldart, 1914 ; *Entwicklung des Koalisationsrechts in England*, by G. Krojanker, 1914 ; *An Introduction to Trade Union Law*, by H. H. Slesser, 1919 ; *The Law of Trade Unions*, by H. H. Slesser and C. Baker (to be published in 1920).

has been accompanied by a still more revolutionary transformation of the social and political standing of the official representatives of the Trade Union world—a transformation which has been immensely accelerated by the Great War. We may, in fact, not unfairly say that Trade Unionism has, in 1920, won its recognition by Parliament and the Government, by law and by custom, as a separate element in the community, entitled to distinct recognition as part of the social machinery of the State, its members being thus allowed to give—like the clergy in Convocation—not only their votes as citizens, but also their concurrence as an order or estate.

Like all revolutionary changes in the British constitution, the recognition of the Trade Union Movement as part of the governmental structure of the nation began in an almost imperceptible way. Though Trade Union leaders had been, since 1869, appointed occasionally and sparsely on Royal Commissions and Departmental Committees, it was possible, as recently as 1903, for a Government to set up a Royal Commission on Trade Disputes and Trade Combinations without a single Trade Unionist member. Such a thing has not been repeated. It is now taken for granted that Trade Unionism must be distinctively and effectually represented, usually by men or women of its own informal nomination, on all Royal Commissions and Departmental Committees, whether or not these inquiries are concerned specifically with " Labour Questions "—excepting only such as are so exclusively financial or professional that the representatives of Labour do not seek or desire representation upon them.

In 1885–86, and again in 1892–95, Liberal Prime Ministers had appointed leading Trade Unionists (who were, it must be noted, also Liberal M.P.'s) to subordinate Ministerial positions, where they were permitted practically no influence.[1] In 1905 Sir Henry Campbell-Bannerman startled

[1] Henry Broadhurst (Friendly Society of Operative Stonemasons) was Under Secretary of State for the Home Department (1885–86) ; and Thomas Burt (Northumberland Miners' Mutual Confident Society) Parliamentary Secretary to the Board of Trade (1892–95).

some of his Whig associates by asking Mr. John Burns—who had presided over the Trades Union Congress as a representative of the Amalgamated Society of Engineers, but who had sat in Parliament since 1892 as a Liberal supporter—to join his Cabinet as President of the Local Government Board. This recognition of Labour in the inner councils of the Government was quickly followed by an explicit recognition of the Trade Unions as part of the machinery of State administration. In 1911, when the vast scheme of National Insurance was brought forward by Mr. Asquith's Government, and Parliament sanctioned the raising and expenditure of more than twenty million pounds a year for the relief of sickness and unemployment, the Trade Unions, equally with the universally praised Friendly Societies, were made the agents for the administration of the sickness, invalidity, and maternity benefits, and, parallel with the Government's own local organisation, and to the exclusion of the Friendly Societies, also for the administration of the State Unemployment Benefit to their own members. But it was during the Great War that we watch the most extensive advance in the status, alike of the official representatives of the Trade Unions and of the Trade Unions themselves, as organs of representation and government. It is needless to say that this recognition was not accorded to the Trade Union world without a *quid pro quo* from the Trade Union Movement to the Government. Hence the part played by the Trade Unions in the national effort, and its effect on their influence and status, demands explicit notice.

BRITISH TRADE UNIONISM AND THE WAR

Though theoretically internationalist in sympathy, and predominantly opposed to " militarism " at home as well as abroad, British Trade Unionism, when war was declared, took a decided line.[1] From first to last the whole strength

[1] For the facts as to Trade Unionism during the war, the most con

of the Movement—in spite of the pacifist faith of a relatively small minority, which included the most fervent and eloquent of the Labour members and was supported by the energetic propaganda of the fraction of the Trade Unionists who were also members of the Socialist Society known as the I.L.P.—was thrown on the side of the nation's effort. From every industry workmen flocked to the colours, with the utmost encouragement and assistance from their Trade Unions ; until the miners, the railwaymen, and the engineers, in particular, had to be refused as recruits, exempted from conscription, and even returned from the army, in order that the indispensable industrial services might be maintained. The number of workers in engineering and the manufacture of munitions of war had, indeed, to be largely increased ; and the Government found itself, within a year, under the necessity of asking the Trade Unions for the unprecedented sacrifice of the relinquishment, for the duration of the war, of the entire network of " Trade Union Conditions " which had been slowly built up by generations of effort for the protection of the workmen's Standard of Life. This enormous draft on the patriotism of the rank and file could only be secured by enlisting the support of the official representatives of the Trade Union world—by according to them a unique and unprecedented place as the diplomatic representatives of the wage-earning class. In the famous Treasury Conference of February 1915 the capitalist employers were ignored, and the principal Ministers

---

venient source is the *Labour Year Book* for 1916 and 1919 ; see also *Labour in War Time*, by G. D. H. Cole, 1915, and *Self-Government in Industry*, by the same, 1917 ; the large number of Government publications issued by the Local Government Board, the Board of Trade, the Ministry of Labour, and especially the Ministry of Munitions, together with the awards of the Committee on Production, most of which are briefly noticed in the monthly *Labour Gazette* ; the monthly Circular (since 1917) of the Labour Research Department ; the unpublished monthly journal of the Ministry of Munitions ; Reports of the Trades Union Congress, 1915–19, and of the Labour Party Conferences, 1914–19 ; publications of the War Emergency Workers' National Committee ; *The Restoration of Trade Union Conditions*, by Sidney Webb, 1916 ; *Women in the Engineering Trades*, by Barbara Drake, 1917.

of the Crown negotiated directly with the authorised representatives of the whole Trade Union world, not only in
respect of the terms of service of Government employees,
but also with regard to the conditions of employment of all
persons, men and women, skilled and unskilled, unionists
and non-unionists, engaged on any work needed for the
conduct of the war—a phrase which was afterwards stretched
to include four-fifths of the entire manual-working class.
The Trade Union Executives agreed, at this Conference or
subsequently, to suspend, for the duration of the war, all
their rules and customary practices restrictive of the output
of anything required by the Government for the conduct of
the war ; all limitation of employment to apprenticed men,
to Trade Unionists, to men of proved technical skill, to
adults and even to the male sex ; all reservation of particular
jobs or particular machines to workers of particular trades ;
all definition of a Normal Day, and all objection to overtime,
night-work, or Sunday duty ; and even many of the Factory
Act prohibitions by which the health and even the safety of
the operatives had been protected.   In order that the utmost
possible output of munitions of every kind might be secured,
elaborate schemes of " dilution " were assented to, under
which the various tasks were subdivided and rearranged, a
very large amount of automatic machinery was introduced,
and successive drafts of " dilutees " were brought into the
factories and workshops—men and boys from other occupations, sometimes even non-manual workers, as well as
women and girls—and put to work under the tuition and
direction of the minority of skilled craftsmen at top speed,
at time wages differing entirely from the Trade Union
rates, or at piecework prices unsafeguarded by Collective
Bargaining, for hours of labour indefinitely lengthened, sometimes under conditions such as no Trade Union would have
permitted.   It must be recorded to the credit of the Trade
Unions that not one of the societies refused this sacrifice,
which was made without any demand for compensatory
increase of pay, merely upon the condition—to which not

only the Ministry, but also the Opposition Leaders and the House of Commons as a whole, elaborately and repeatedly pledged themselves—that the abandonment of the " Trade Union Conditions " was only to be for the duration of the war, and exclusively for the service of the Government, not to the profit of any private employer ; and that everything that was abrogated was to be reinstated when peace came.

Under stress of the national emergency, the Government made ever greater demands on the patriotism of the Trade Unions, which accepted successively, so far as war-work was concerned, a legal abrogation of the employers' competition for their members' services by the prohibition of advertisement for employees, and of the engagement of men from other districts—an unprecedented interference with the " Law of Supply and Demand "—the suspension of the right to strike for better terms ; the submission of all disputes to the decision of a Government Department of arbitration, the awards of which, with the abrogation of the right to strike, or even freely to relinquish employment, became virtually compulsory ; the legal enforcement under penalties of the employer's workshop rules ; and even legally enforced continuance, not only in munition work, but actually in the service of a particular employer, under the penal jurisdiction of the ubiquitous Munitions Tribunals. The Munitions of War Acts, 1915, 1916 and 1917, by which all this industrial coercion was statutorily imposed, were accepted by overwhelming majorities at successive Trade Union and Labour Party Conferences. It was a serious aggravation of this " involuntary servitude " that the rigid enforcement of compulsory military service—extended successively from single men to fathers of families, from 18 years of age to 51—had the incidental effect of enforcing what was virtually " industrial conscription " on those who were left for the indispensable civilian employment ; and the individual workman realised that the penalty for any failure of implicit obedience to the foreman might be instant relegation to the trenches. Although this inevitable result of Compulsory Military Service was foreseen and deplored,[1] the successive Military Service Acts were—in view of the nation's needs—ratified, in effect, by great majorities at the workmen's National Congresses. The strongest protests were made, but as each measure was passed it was accepted without resistance, and proposals to resist were always rejected by large majorities. It speaks volumes, both for the patriotism of the Trade Unionists and for the strength of Trade Union loyalty and Trade Union organisation, that under such repressive circumstances the Trade Union leaders were able, on the whole, to prevent their members from hindering production by industrial revolts. A certain amount of friction was, of course, not to be avoided. Strikes, though greatly reduced in number, were not wholly prevented; and the South Wales coal-miners and the engineering workmen on the Clyde — largely through arbitrary and repressive action by their respective employers—broke into open rebellion ; which led, in the one industry, to the Government overriding the recalcitrant South Wales employers and assuming the direction and the financial responsibility of all the coal mines throughout the kingdom ; and, in the other, to the arbitrary arrest and deportation of the leaders of the unofficial organisation of revolt styled the " Clyde Workers' Committee." The Trade Union Executives and officials, whilst restraining their members and deprecating all stoppages of production, were able to put up a good fight against the unnecessary and unreasonable demands which, with a view to " after the war " conditions, employers were not unwilling to use the national emergency to put forward. These Trade Union spokesmen had to obtain for their members the successive rises in money wages which the steadily rising cost of living made necessary, and they had constantly to stand their

---

[1] *Compulsory Military Service and Industrial Conscription : what they mean to the Workers* (War Emergency Workers' National Committee, 1915) ; *Memorandum on Industrial and Civil Liberties* (Woolwich Joint Committee on Problems arising from the War).

ground in the innumerable mixed committees and arbitration proceedings into which the Government was always inveigling them. On the whole, whilst co-operating in every way in meeting the national emergency, the Trade Union organisation during the four and a-quarter years of war remained intact ; and Trade Union membership—allowing for the millions absent with the colours—steadily increased. Nor did the Trade Union Movement make any serious revolt when the Government found itself unable to fulfil, with any literal exactness, the specific pledges which it had given to Organised Labour. The complications and difficulties of the Government were, in fact, so great that the pledges were not kept. The first promise to be broken was that the abrogation of Trade Union Conditions and the removal of everything restrictive of output should not be allowed to increase the profits of the employers. The so-called " Munitions Levy " was imposed in 1916 on " controlled establishments," in fulfilment of this pledge, in order to confiscate for the Exchequer the whole of their excess profit, over and above a permitted addition of 20 per cent and very liberal allowances for increased capital and extra exertion by the employers themselves. It will hardly be believed that, in flagrant disregard of the specific pledge, within a year this Munitions Levy was abolished ; and the firms especially benefiting by the workmen's sacrifices were made merely subject, in common with all other trades where there had been no such abrogation of Trade Union Conditions, to the 80 per cent Excess Profits Duty, with the result of increasing the net income left to those employers whose profits had doubled, and of doing, with regard to all the employers, the very thing that the Trade Unions had stipulated should not be done, namely, giving the employers themselves a financial interest in " dilution." [1] As the war dragged on, and prices rose, the successive

[1] The Government seems to have hoodwinked the public into believing that 80 per cent of all the excess profits was the same thing as 100 per cent of the profits in excess of 20 per cent addition to the pre-war profits.

war-bonuses and additions to wages—especially those of the miners and the bulk of the women workers—in many cases fell steadily behind the rise in the cost of living ; and in 1917 the War Cabinet was actually guilty of a formal instruction to the presumedly impartial central arbitration tribunal that no further increase of wages was to be awarded—an instruction which, on its public disclosure, had to be apologised for and virtually withdrawn.   Even the pledge as to wages in the solemn " Treasury Agreement " of 1915, at which the " Trade Union Conditions " were surrendered, was not fulfilled, at any rate as regards the women workers ; and had to be made the subject of a subsequent serious investigation by the War Cabinet Committee on Women in Industry, in which all the " whitewashing " of a Government majority failed to convince the Trade Unionists, any more than it did the only unpaid member of the Committee, that the Government officials had not betrayed them.[1]   The solemnly promised " Restoration of Trade Union Conditions " was only imperfectly carried out.   What the Government did, and that only after long delay, was not what it had promised, namely, actually to see the pre-war conditions and practices reinstated, but to enact a statute enabling the workmen to proceed in the law courts against employers who failed to restore them ; continuance of any such restoration to be obligatory only for one year.[2]

[1] *Report of the War Cabinet Committee on Women in Industry*, Cmd. 135, 1919.   The Minority Report by Mrs. Sidney Webb was republished by the Fabian Society, under the title of *Men's and Women's Wages : Should they be equal ?*, 1919.

[2] Restoration of Pre-War Practices Act, 1919 (9 and 10 George V. c. 42). During the first year after the cessation of hostilities the problem of restoration did not assume so acute a form as had been expected.   A large part of the new automatic machinery which had been introduced in 1915–18 was found to have been greatly deteriorated by excessive working and had to be scrapped ; there was an immediate demand for ordinary engineering work of the old type ; and the British employers did not, in fact, set themselves at once to apply " mass production " to the making of steam engines and motor cars, agricultural implements and machinery generally, nor make any dramatic advances in its application to the production of sewing-machines, bicycles, and electrical apparatus.   During

The Trade Unionists, in fact, who had at the outset of the war patriotically refrained from bargaining as to the

1919 the extensive readaptation of the machine-shops, and the great demand for new tools (especially machine-tools) facilitated the absorption, often in new situations, of all the skilled engineers. There was, accordingly, little difficulty in finding employment at good wages for practically all the skilled workmen, and (except for temporary dislocations arising in consequence of the disputes in coalmining, ironfounding, and other trades) the percentage of members of the Amalgamated Society of Engineers and other Unions of skilled craftsmen remained throughout the year at a minimum. The great bulk of the "dilutees," including substantially all the women, received their discharge on the cessation of their jobs of "repetition work" on munitions of war, the employers preferring, in face of the immediate demand, to avoid trouble, to revert to the old methods and to get back their former staffs, rather than engage in the hazardous enterprise of reorganising their factory methods. Hence, taking the engineering industry as a whole, the men got back the work from the women ; though not without some attempts at resistance by individual employers, which were not persisted in ; and not without leaving the total number of women employed in 1920 in what might be deemed their own branches of the engineering industry apparently double that of 1913. Many of the male "dilutees" on discharge also reverted to other employment, but some proportion of them, who had acquired skill, and were members of various Unions admitting semi-skilled workers, found employment in engineering shops on particular machines or in particular jobs. There has apparently been a continuous increase in the proportion of machines demanding less than full skill (such as milling machines and small turret lathes), and therefore of "semi-skilled" men in employment, without (owing to the expansion of the industry as a whole) any reduction in the number of skilled men. In face of the great demand for output, and of the fact that hardly any members of the skilled Unions were unemployed, this fact did not evoke objection. The position as regards the Premium Bonus System or other form of "Payment by Results" was left unchanged. Few, if any, legal proceedings were actually taken against employers in the Munitions Courts under the Restoration of Pre-War Practices Act. The employers and the Government were, during the first half of the year, in a state of alarm lest there should be a Labour uprising, which would seriously interfere with the resumption of business ; and great care was exercised to avoid any disputes. Successive advances of wages were awarded to meet the rising cost of living, and all rates were "stabilised " by law, so as to prevent any employer from effecting a reduction, first until May 20, 1919, then until November 20, 1919, and finally until September 30, 1920; a new "Industrial Court" being set up by statute (Industrial Courts Act 1919) empowered to give non-obligatory decisions in any disputes that might be voluntarily referred to it—a measure from which the Parliamentary Labour Party succeeded in eliminating every implication of Compulsory Arbitration, Obligatory Awards, or the Abrogation of the Right to Strike. But the difficulties are not yet surmounted ; and when there comes a slump in business, and skilled engineers find themselves unemployed, the Government pledge will be heard of again.

price of their aid, were, on the whole, " done " at its close. Though here and there particular sections had received exceptionally high earnings in the time of stress, the rates of wages, taking industry as a whole, did not, as the Government returns prove, rise either so quickly or so high as the cost of living ; so that, whilst many persons suffered great hardship, the great majority of wage-earners found the product in commodities of their rates of pay in 1919 less rather than more than it was in 1913. During the war, indeed, many thousands of households got in the aggregate more, and both earned and needed more ; because the young and the aged were at work and costing more than when not at work, whilst overtime and night-work increased the strain and the requirements of all. When peace came, it was found that the Government, for all its promises, had made no arrangements whatever to prevent unemployment ; and none to relieve the unemployed beyond an entirely improvised and dwindling weekly dole, which (so far as civilians were concerned) was suddenly brought to an end on November 20, 1919, without any alternative provision being immediately made.

It would thus be easy to argue that the representatives of the Trade Union world made a series of bad bargains with the Government, and through the Government with the capitalist employers, at a time when the nation's needs would have enabled the organised manual workers almost to dictate their own terms. But this is to take a short-sighted view. It is a sufficient answer to say that the great mass of the Trade Unionists, like the leaders themselves, wanted above all things that the nation should win the war ; found it repugnant to make stipulations in the national emergency, and did not realise the extent to which they were being tricked and cheated by the officials. But apart from this impulsive and unself-regarding patriotism we think that, when it becomes possible to cast up and balance all the results of the innovations of the war period, the Trade Union Movement will be found to have gained and not lost. We may suggest, perhaps paradoxically, that the very ease with which the War Cabinet suppressed the civil liberties of the manual-working wage-earners during the war, and even continued after the Armistice a machinery of industrial *espionage*, with *agents provocateurs* of workshop " sedition," enormously increased the solidarity of the Trade Union Movement—an effect intensified during 1919 by the costly and futile intervention of the British Government in Russia on behalf of military leaders whom the Trade Unionists, rightly or wrongly, believed to be organising the forces of political and economic reaction. Sober and responsible Trade Unionists, who had taken for granted the easy-going freedom and tolerance characteristic of English life in times of peace, suddenly realised that these conditions could at any moment be withdrawn from them by what seemed the arbitrary fiat of a Government over which they found that they had no control. In this way the abrogation of Trade Union liberty during the war gave the same sort of intellectual fillip to Trade Unionism and the Labour Party in 1915–19 that had been given in 1901–13 by the Taff Vale Case and the Osborne Judgement. At the same time the Government found itself compelled, in order to secure the co-operation of the Trade Unions, both during the war and amid the menacing economic conditions of the first half of 1919, to accord to them, and to their leaders, a *locus standi* in the determination of essentially national issues that was undreamt of in previous times. The Trade Unions, in fact, through shouldering their responsibility in the national cause, gained enormously in social and political status. In practically every branch of public administration, from unimportant local committees up to the Cabinet itself, we find the Trade Union world now accepted as forming, virtually, a separate constituency, which has to be specially represented. We shall tell the tale in our next chapter of the participation of members of the Parliamentary Labour Party in the Coalition Governments of Mr. Asquith and Mr. Lloyd George. What is here relevant is that these Trade Union officials were selected in the main, not on personal grounds, but because they represented the Trade Union Movement. They accepted ministerial office with the approval, and they relinquished ministerial office at the request of the National Conference of the Labour Party, in which the Trade Unions exercised the predominant influence. A similar recognition of the Trade Union Movement has marked all the recently constituted Local Government structure, from the committees set up in 1914 for the relief of distress to those organised in 1917 for the rationing and control of the food supply, and the tribunals formed in 1919 for the suppression of " profiteering." In all these cases the Government specifically required the appointment of representatives of the local Trade Unions. Trade Unionists have to constitute half the members appointed to the Advisory Committees attached to the Employment Exchanges ; and Trade Unionist workmen sit, not only on the temporary " Munitions Courts " administering the disciplinary provisions of the Munitions of War Acts, but also on the local Tribunals of Appeal to determine whether a workman is entitled to the State Unemployment Benefit. In the administration of the Military and Naval Pensions Act of 1916 a further step in recognition of Trade Unionism was taken. Not only were the nominees of Labour placed upon the Statutory (Central) Pensions Committee, but, in the order constituting the Local Pensions Committees, the Trade Union organisations in each locality, which were named in the schemes, were expressly and specifically accorded the right to elect whom they chose as their representatives on these committees by which the pensions were to be awarded.[1] When, towards the close of the war, the Committee presided over by the Rt. Hon. J. H. Whitley, M.P., propounded its scheme of Joint Industrial Councils of equal numbers of representative employers and workers for the supervision and eventual

---

[1] See this noted in the report of the Parliamentary Committee in the *Annual Report of the Trades Union Congress*, 1917.

administration of many matters of interest in each industry throughout the kingdom—the " mouse " which was practically the whole outcome as regards industrial reorganisation of the Ministry of Reconstruction—it was specifically to the Trade Unions in each industry, and to them alone, that the election of the wage-earners' representatives was entrusted.[1]

[1] The " Whitley Report," published early in 1917, when possibilities of industrial and social " reconstruction " were much discussed, made a great stir, which was increased by the definite endorsement of its recommendations by the Government, and its energetic promotion of their adoption throughout British industry. Whilst significantly abstaining from any suggestion of " profit-sharing, copartnership, or particular systems of wages," the Report emphasised the importance of (a) " adequate organisation on the part of both employers and employed " ; (b) the imperative need for a greater opportunity of participating in the discussion about and adjustment of " those parts of industry by which they are most affected " of the work-people in each occupation; (c) the subordination of any decisions to those of the Trade Unions and Employers' Associations. Among the subjects to be dealt with by the hierarchy of National, District, and Works Councils or Committees were : (i.) " the better utilisation of the practical knowledge and experience of the work-people . . . and for securing to them a greater share in and responsibility for the determination and observance of the conditions under which their work is carried on " ; (ii.) " the settlement of the general principles governing the conditions of employment . . . having regard to the need for securing to the work-people a share in the increased prosperity of the industry " ; (iii.) the methods to be adopted for negotiations, adjusting wages, determining differences and " ensuring to the work-people the greatest possible security of earnings and employment " ; (iv.) technical education, industrial research, utilisation of inventions, and improvement of processes ; (v.) proposed legislation affecting the industry. After two years' propagandist effort, it seems (1920) as if the principal industries, such as agriculture, transport, mining, cotton, engineering, or shipbuilding are unlikely to adopt the scheme ; but two or three score trades have equipped themselves either with " Whitley Councils "—the District Councils and Works Committees are much more slow to form—or with " Interim Industrial Reconstruction Committees," which may be regarded as provisional Councils, in such industries as pottery, house-building, woollen manufacture, hosiery, heavy chemicals, furniture-making, bread-baking, matchmaking, metallic bedstead manufacturing, saw-milling, and vehicle building. The Government found itself constrained, after an obstinate resistance by the heads of nearly all the departments, to institute the Councils throughout the public service. We venture on the prediction that some such scheme will commend itself in all nationalised or municipalised industries and services, including such as may be effectively " controlled " by the Government, though remaining nominally the property of the private capitalist—possibly also in the Co-operative Movement ; but that it is not likely to find favour either in the well-organised industries (for which alone it was devised) or in those in which there are Trade Boards legally

When, in 1919, it seemed desirable to make a series of comprehensive reforms in the terms of employment, it was not to Parliament that the Prime Minister turned, but to a "National Industrial Conference," to which he summoned some five hundred representatives of the Employers' Associations and Trade Unions. It was by this body, through its own sub-committee of thirty employers' representatives and thirty Trade Union representatives, that were elaborated the measures instituting a Legal Maximum Eight Hours Day and a statutory Minimum Wage Commission that the Ministry undertook to present to Parliament. In the Royal Commission on Agriculture of 1919, the several Unions enrolling farm labourers were invited to nominate as many members (eight) as were accorded to the farmers, whilst of the four remaining members appointed as scientific or statistical experts—all landlords being excluded—two were chosen among those known to be sympathetic to Labour. In the statutory Coal Industry Commission of the same year, to which reference has already been made, the Miners' Federation made its participation absolutely conditional on being allowed to nominate half of the total membership, under a presumedly impartial Judge of the High Court, including not merely three Trade Union officials to balance the three mine-owners, but also three out of the six " disinterested " members by whom—all royalty owners being excluded—the Commission was to be completed.

---

determining wages, etc. ; or, indeed, permanently in any others conducted under the system of capitalist profit-making. See the series of " Whitley Reports," Cd. 8606, 9001, 9002, 9085, 9099, and 9153 ; the Industrial Reports, Nos. 1 to 4, of the Ministry of Reconstruction ; the able and well-informed article, " La politique de paix sociale en Angleterre," by Élie Halévy, in *Revue d'Économie Politique*, No. 4 of 1919 ; *Recommendation on the Whitley Report put forward by the Federation of British Industries*, 1917 ; *National Guilds or Whitley Councils ?* (National Guilds League), 1918. For the " Builders' Parliament," in many ways the most interesting of these Councils, though as yet achieving only schemes in which the employers, as a whole, do not concur, see *A Memorandum on Industrial Self-Government*, by Malcolm Sparkes ; *Masters and Men, a new Co-partnership*, by Thomas Foster ; and *The Industrial Council for the Building Industry*, by the Garton Foundation, 1919.

All this constitutional development is at once the recognition and the result of the new position in the State that Trade Unionism has won—a position due not merely to the numerical growth that we have described, but also to the uprise of new ideas and wider aspirations in the Trade Union world itself.

THE REVOLUTION IN THOUGHT

The new ideas which are to-day taking root in the Trade Union world centre round the aspiration of the organisations of manual workers to take part—some would urge the predominant part, a few might say the sole part—in the control and direction of the industries in which they gain their livelihood. Such a claim was made, as we have described in the third chapter of this work, in its most extreme form, by the revolutionary Trade Unionism of 1830–34 ; and it lingered on in the minds of the Chartists as long as any of them survived. But after the collapse, in 1848, of Chartism as an organised movement British Trade Unionism settled down to the attainment of a strictly limited end—the maintenance and progressive improvement, within each separate occupation or craft, of the terms of the bargain made by the wage-earner with the employers, including alike all the conditions of service and complete freedom from personal oppression. Hence the Trade Unionist as such, during the second half of the nineteenth century, tacitly accepted the existing organisation of industry. He discussed the rival advantages of private enterprise carried on in the interests of the capitalist profit-maker on the one hand, and of the Consumers' Co-operative Movement or State and Municipal enterprise on the other, almost exclusively from the standpoint of whether the profit-making employers or the representatives of the consumers or the citizens offered better conditions of employment to the members of his own organisation. Right down to the end of the nineteenth century this remained the dominant working-class view.

We find in the proceedings of the Royal Commission on Labour, 1891-94, a striking demonstration of the strictly limited purpose of British Trade Unionism at that date. Whether we study the elaborate collection of Trade Union rules and other documents made by the Commission, or the personal evidence given by the leaders or advocates of Trade Unionism, we find from beginning to end absolutely no claim, and even no suggestion, that the Trade Union should participate in the direction of industry, otherwise than in arranging with the employers the conditions of the wage-earner's working life.[1] One or two Unions included, among their published " objects," vague and pious references to the desirability of co-operative production ; but the assumption was always that any such co-operative produc-

---

[1] It must be remembered that the conditions of the manual worker's life dealt with by the Trade Unions up to 1894 included a wide range of material circumstances and moral considerations. Besides the maintenance of standard rates and methods of remuneration, the reduction of the normal day, and payment for overtime, we find among the objects of Trade Unions, as reported to the Commission, the prevention of stoppages from wages ; the maintenance of the apprenticeship system and the keeping out of the trade all who are not qualified ; the abolition of the character note ; the prevention of victimisation ; the provision of legal assistance to members in respect of compensation for accidents ; the establishment of an agency through which employers may obtain efficient men ; watching over the proceedings of local boards and law courts ; the enforcement of the Factory Acts and other protective legislative enactments ; the improvement of dietary scales and house and shop accommodation where workers have to live in ; the collection and circulation of information on trade matters ; the establishment of benefit funds for unemployment, disputes, sickness, accidents and death ; the assistance of members anxious to migrate or emigrate ; the establishment of " that reciprocal confidence which is so essential between workmen and masters," and the promotion of arbitration and conciliation ; the regulation of output ; the promotion of friendly intercourse with workers of other countries ; the assistance of other trades in times of difficulty ; and political action—the support of Parliamentary and Municipal Labour candidates, of Trades Councils, of the Trades Union Congress, and of Labour newspapers. Some Unions decide to promote co-operative enterprise, " to secure the legal recognition of the natural rights of labourers to the produce of their toil," whilst others promote the " moral, social, intellectual and professional advancement " of the working class. " Trade Societies," state the rules of the Associated Shipwrights, " must be maintained as the guard of workmen against capitalists until some higher effort of productive co-operation has been inaugurated which shall secure to workers a more equitable share of the product of labour."

tion would be carried out by the members of the Union working in and managing a particular establishment, which would take its place, like any private establishment, within the framework of the capitalist system. When a Trade Union leader was also a Socialist he assumed that the " Socialisation " of industry would be carried out by the Central or Local Government, or by the Consumers' Co-operative Movement. Hence, Mr. Tom Mann, himself a Royal Commissioner, who was called as a witness before the Commission, was a powerful advocate of nationalisation and municipalisation. " I am distinctly favourable, and am associated with those who are earnestly advocating," he stated from the witness-chair, " the advisability of encouraging the State to at once entertain the proposal of the State control of railways. I am also identified with those who are favourable to the nationalisation of the land, which means, of course, a State control of land in the common interest ; and I am continually advocating the desirability for statesmen and politicians and municipal councillors to try and understand in what particular departments of industry they can get to work and exercise their faculties in controlling trade and industry in the common interest where that interest would be likely to be secured better than under the present method." When asked by the Duke of Devonshire whether his advocacy of the nationalisation of the railways was in the interests of the public or mainly in the interests of the workmen employed on the railways, he replied : " Not mainly on behalf of the workers ; I would put it equally so. I believe it would serve the public interest, the general well-being of the community. . . . I do not believe that a Government Department will ever be healthy until the public themselves are healthy in this direction, and are keeping a watchful eye upon the whole governmental show and secure the general well-being by their watchfulness. I do not think that State control of industry will ever be brought about until that development on the part of the public themselves is brought about, and they desire to see it controlled in the common interest. . . . When a sufficient number of men are prepared to take the initiative, and educate public opinion to the desirability of a superior method of control in the common interest, then I believe it will be done, not all at once, but gradually." [1]

But Mr. Tom Mann did not stand alone. The Independent Labour Party, the largest and the most popular of Socialist societies in the United Kingdom, established in 1893, and largely recruited from the ranks of Trade Unionists, carried on, right down to the outbreak of the Great War, a vigorous propaganda in favour of an indefinite extension of State and Municipal administration of industrial undertakings, whilst the more doctrinaire Social Democratic Federation was, in its early days, outspokenly contemptuous of the whole Trade Union Movement as a mere " palliative " of the Capitalist system. This bias in favour of the communal organisation, in favour of the government of the people by and for the people organised in geographical areas, was, until the opening of the twentieth century, equally dominant among the most " advanced " Labour and Socialist thinkers on the Continent of Europe.[2]

---

[1] *Minutes of Evidence, Royal Commission on Labour:* "Report of Evidence from Co-operative Societies and Public Officials," 1893, C 7063—1 (Q 2098, 2117—8).

Mr. Tom Mann was also in favour of the Consumers' Co-operative Movement, and had in those days a distinct bias for legal enactment over direct action in determining the conditions of employment. " I should have said," he stated in the witness-chair, " that I, as a Trade Unionist, am of opinion that in my capacity of citizen I have just as full a right to use Parliament for the general betterment of the conditions of the workers, of whom I am one, as I have to use the Trade Union ; and when I could use the institution of Parliament to do that constructive work that I sometimes use the Trade Union for, and could use Parliament more effectively than I could the Trade Union, then I should favour the use of Parliament, not necessarily in order to enforce men to do something which they might not wish to do, but because it was the more effective instrument to use to bring about changed conditions " (*Ibid.* Q 2531).

[2] An interesting sidelight is afforded by the reprobation by the German Social Democratic Party, in 1894, of Eduard Bernstein for translating our *History of Trade Unionism*, on the ground that Trade Unionism had no place in the Socialist State, and that it was needless to trouble about it !

But in spite of the assumption that services and industries ought to be carried out by democracies of consumers and citizens, organised in geographical districts—that is, by the Central and Local Government of a Political Democracy—there always remained, in the hearts of the manual working class in Great Britain, an instinctive faith in the opposite idea of Associations of Producers owning, as such, both the instruments and the product of their labour. Throughout the whole of the second half of the nineteenth century it was pathetic to see this faith struggling on, in spite of the almost constant failure of the innumerable little manufacturing establishments carried on by Associations of Producers. What finally killed it as an ideal, in the eyes of the Trade Unionists of Great Britain, was the fact that Co-operative Production and its child, Co-partnership, were taken up by the most reactionary persons and parties in the State. Great peers and Conservative statesmen were always blessing " Co-operative Production," and always trying to stimulate the workers to undertake business on their own account. When the invariable failure of self-governing workshops became too obvious, the advocates of Co-operative Production fell back on " Labour Copartnership "—partnership in business with the capitalist class! This was so obviously, and almost avowedly, an attack on, or at least a proposal for the supersession of Trade Unionism, that it aroused the fiercest opposition ; and the very idea became anathema in the Trade Union world. In short, there was, from the collapse of Owenism and Chartism in the eighteen-thirties and -forties, right down to 1900, practically no sign that the British Trade Unions ever thought of themselves otherwise than as organisations to secure an ever-improving Standard of Life by means of an ever-increasing control of the conditions under which they worked. They neither desired nor sought any participation in the management of the technical processes of industry (except in so far as these might affect the conditions of their employment, or the selection of persons to be employed) ; whilst it never occurred to a Trade Union to claim any power over, or responsibility for, buying the raw materials or marketing the product. On the contrary, the most advanced Trade Union leaders were never tired of asserting that their members must enjoy the full standard conditions of employment, whatever arrangements the employers might make with regard to the other factors of production ; or however unskilful employers or groups of employers might prove to be in the buying of the raw material, or in the selling of the commodities in the markets of the world.

With the opening years of the twentieth century we become aware of a new intellectual ferment, not confined to any one country, nor even to the manual working class. We watch, emerging in various forms, new variants of the old idea of the organisation of industries and services by those who are actually carrying them on. We see it working among the brain-working professionals. Alike in England and in France the teachers in the schools and the professors in the colleges began to assert both their moral right to manage the institutions as they alone know how, and the advantage that this would be to the community. The doctors were demanding a similar control over the exercise of their own function. But the most conspicuous, and the most widely influential, of the forms taken by the idea was the revolutionary movement that spread among large sections of the wage-earners almost simultaneously in France, the classic home of associations of producers, and in the United States, with its large population of foreign immigrants. In both these countries any widespread Trade Unionism was of much more recent growth than in Great Britain, and was still regarded, alike by the employers and by the Government, as an undesirable and revolutionary force. The " *syndicats* " of France, and the Labour Unions among the foreign workers in the United States were, in fact, at the opening of the twentieth century, in much the same stage of development as the British Trade Unions were when they were swept into the vortex of revolutionary Owenism

in 1834. Alike in their constitutions and in their declared
objects, in the first decade of the new century, the General
Confederation of Labour in France and the Industrial
Workers of the World in the United States bear a striking
resemblance to the Grand National Consolidated Trades
Union that we have described in an earlier chapter; and,
like that organisation, both of them excited a quite exaggerated terror in the hearts of magistrates and Ministers
of State. Indeed, the doctrines and phraseology of the mass
of literature turned out by French Trade Unionists between
1900 and 1910 are remarkably like—allowing for the superior
literary power of the French—the pamphlets and leaflets
of the Owenite Trade Unionism.[1] There is the same conception of a republic of industry, consisting of a federation
of Trade Unions, local and central; the federation of shop
clubs, branches, or local unions forming the Local Authority
for all purposes, whilst a standing conference of the national
representatives of all the Trade Unions constitutes a co-
ordinating or superintending National Authority. There is
the same reliance, as a means of achievement, on continuous
strikes, culminating in a " general expropriatory strike."
There is the same denunciation of the political State as a
useless encumbrance, and the same appeal to the soldiers
to join the workers in upsetting the existing system.

We need not stay to inquire how this new ferment
crossed the Atlantic or the Channel. Between 1905 and
1910 we become aware of the birth, in some of the industrial
districts, of a number of new propagandist groups—more
especially among the miners and engineers—groups of
persons in revolt not only against the Capitalist System
but against the limited aims of contemporary Trade Unionism and the usual categories of contemporary Socialism.
The pioneer of the new faith in the United Kingdom seems
to have been James Connolly, afterwards organiser of the

---

[1] See, for convenient summaries, *Syndicalism in France*, by Louis
Levine, 1911, and *What Syndicalism Means*, by S. and B. Webb, 1912;
see also *American Syndicalism*, by J. Graham Brooks, 1913.

Irish Transport and General Workers Union, to which we have already referred, a man of noble character and fine intelligence, whose tragic execution in 1916, after the suppression of the Dublin rising, made him one of the martyred heroes of the Irish race.   Connolly, who was a disciple of the founder of the American Socialist Labour Party, Daniel De Leon, started a similar organisation on the Clyde in 1905.   In opposition to the contemporary Socialist propaganda in favour of the nationalisation and municipalisation of industries and services, to be brought about by political action, he advocated the direct supersession of the Capitalist System in each workshop and in every industry, by the organised workers thereof.   " It is an axiom," he said, " enforced by all the experience of the ages, that they who rule industrially will rule politically. . . . That natural law leads us as individuals to unite in our craft, as crafts to unite in our industry, as industries in our class ; and the finished expression of that evolution is, we believe, the appearance of our class upon the political battle-ground with all the economic power behind it to enforce its mandates. Until that day dawns our political parties of the working class are but propagandist agencies, John the Baptists of the New Redemption ; but when that day dawns our political party will be armed with all the might of our class ; will be revolutionary in fact as well as in thought."   " Let us be clear," he adds, " as to the function of Industrial Unionism.   That function is to build up an industrial republic inside the shell of the political State, in order that when that industrial republic is fully organised it may crack the shell of the political State and step into its place in the scheme of the universe. . . . Under a Socialist form of society the administration of affairs will be in the hands of representatives of the various industries of the nation ; . . . the workers in the shops and factories will organise themselves into unions, each union comprising all the workers at a given industry ; . . . said union will democratically control the workshop life of its own industry, electing all foremen, etc., and regulating the routine of labour in that industry in subordination to the needs of society in general, to the needs of its allied trades and to the department of industry to which it belongs. . . . Representatives elected from these various departments of industry will meet and form the industrial administration or national government of the country. In short, Social Democracy, as its name implies, is the application to industry, or to the social life of the nation, of the fundamental principles of Democracy. Such application will necessarily have to begin in the workshop, and proceed logically and consecutively upward through all the grades of industrial organisation until it reaches the culminating point of national executive power and direction. In other words, Socialism must proceed from the bottom upwards, whereas capitalist political society is organised from above downward ; Socialism will be administered by a committee of experts elected from the industries and professions of the land ; capitalist society is governed by representatives elected from districts, and is based upon territorial division."[1] A similar ferment waʋ to be seen at work amongst the South Wales miners, giving rise to a series of propagandist organisations, preaching the doctrine of Industrial Unionism as a revolutionary force, and culminating in the much-denounced pamphlet *The Miners' Next Step*, 1912, which created some sensation in the capitalist world.[2]

In 1910 we find Mr. Tom Mann, fresh from organising strikes in Australia, and inspired by a visit to Paris, preaching the new faith to large popular audiences in London and the principal provincial cities with the same sincerity and eloquence with which he had formerly advocated State and Municipal Socialism and the statutory regulation of the conditions of employment. " The Industrial Syndicalist," he explains, holds that " to run industry through Parliament, that is by State machinery, will be even more mischievous

[1] *Socialism made Easy*, by James Connolly, 1905, pp. 13, 16-17.
[2] *The Miners' Next Step*, 1912.

to the working class than the existing method, for it will assuredly mean that the capitalist class will, through Government Departments, exercise over the national forces, and over the workers, a domination that is even more rigid than is the case to-day. And the Syndicalist also declares that in the near future the industrially organised workers will themselves undertake the entire responsibility of running the industries in the interest of all who work, and are entitled to enjoy the result of labour." [1] " We therefore most certainly favour strikes; we shall always do our best to help strikes to be successful, and shall prepare the way as rapidly as possible for THE GENERAL STRIKE of national proportions. This will be the actual Social and Industrial Revolution. The workers will refuse to any longer manipulate the machinery of production in the interest of the capitalist class, and there will be no power on earth able to compel them to work when they thus refuse. . . . When the capitalists get tired of running industries, the workers will cheerfully invite them to abdicate, and through and by their industrial organisations will run the industries themselves in the interests of the whole community." [2] " Finally, and vitally essential it is," sums up Mr. Tom Mann in 1911, " to show that economic emancipation to the working class can only be secured by the working class asserting its power in workshops, factories, warehouses, mills and mines, on ships and boats and engines, and wherever work is performed, ever extending their control over the tools of production, until, by the power of the internationally organised Proletariat, capitalist production shall entirely cease, and the industrial socialist republic will be ushered in, and thus the Social Revolution realised." [3]

---

[1] *The Syndicalist*, January 1912. Column entitled, " What we Syndicalists are after " (by Tom Mann).

[2] *The Industrial Syndicalist*, March 1911. " The Weapon Shaping " (by Tom Mann; p. 5).

[3] *Ibid.*, April 1911. " A Twofold Warning " (by Tom Mann). We are concerned, in this volume, only with the effect of these new movements of working-class thought upon British Trade Unionism, and this is not the occasion for any complete appreciation of Syndicalism or Industrial

The revolutionary Industrial Unionism and Syndicalism preached by James Connolly and Tom Mann and other fervent missionaries between 1905 and 1912 did not commend itself to the officials and leaders of the Trade Unions any more than it did to the cautious and essentially Conservative-minded men and women who make up the rank and file of the British working class. But, like other revolutionary movements in England, it prepared the way for constitutional proposals. The ideal of taking over the instruments of production appealed to all intelligent workmen as workmen. To them it seemed merely Co-operative Production writ large, the ownership of the instruments and of the product of labour by the workers themselves. But the ownership and management was now to be carried out, not by small competing establishments doomed to failure, but in the industry as a whole by a " blackleg-proof " Trade Union. To the idealistic and active-minded Trade Union official in particular, weary of the perpetual haggling with employers over fractional changes in wages and hours, the prospect of becoming the representative of his fellow-workers in a self-governing industry, with all the initiative and responsibility that such a position would involve, was decidedly attractive. So long as this ideal was associated with violent and revolutionary methods, and left no room for the political democracy to which Englishmen are

Unionism. The Syndicalist Movement in this country had died down prior to the war, but the Industrial Unionist Movement simmered on in the Clyde district and in South Wales. Its chief organisation is the Socialist Labour Party, which is not, and has never been, connected either with any other Socialist organisation in this country or with the Labour Party that is described in the next chapter. It was, we think, the moving spirits of the Socialist Labour Party who were, as Trade Unionist workmen, mainly responsible for the aggressive action of the Clyde Workers Committee between 1915 and 1918, and also for the rise of the Shop Stewards Movement, and for its spread from the Clyde to English engineering centres. At the present moment (1920) the Socialist Labour Party, owing to the personal qualities of its leading spirits, J. T. Murphy and A. MacManus, holds the leading position in this school of thought, which received a great impulse from the accession of Lenin to power in Russia. But it remains a ferment rather than a statistically important element in the Trade Union world.

accustomed, or even for the Consumers' Co-operative Movement, it failed to get accepted either by responsible officials
or by the mass of sober-minded members. The bridge
between the old conception of Trade Unionism and the new
was built by a fresh group of Socialists, who called themselves National Guildsmen. This group of able thinkers,
largely drawn from the Universities, accepted from what
we may call the Communal Socialists the idea of the
ownership of the instruments of production by the representatives of the citizen-consumers, but proposed to vest the
management in national associations of the producers in
each industry—organisations which they declared ought to
include, not merely the present wage-earners, but all the
workers, by hand or by brain.[1] These guilds were to grow
out of the existing Trade Unions, gradually made co-extensive with each industry. We have neither the space, nor
would it be within the scope of this book, to describe or
criticise this conception of National Guilds, or the theories
and schemes of the Guild Socialists. These theories and
schemes are none the worse for being still in the making.
What we are concerned with, as historians of the Trade
Union Movement, is the rapid adoption between 1913 and
1920 by many of the younger leaders of the Movement, and
subject to various modifications, also by some of the most
powerful of the Trade Unions, of this new ideal of the develop-

---

[1] The revival of the Owenite proposal to develop existing Trade
Unions into great Associations of Producers for the carrying on of each
industry must be attributed perhaps to Mr. A. J. Penty (*The Restoration
of the Gild System*, 1906), who, however, aimed originally at a mediaeval
localism ; or to Mr. S. G. Hobson and Mr. A. R. Orage in a series of articles
in *The New Age* (afterwards published in a volume, *National Guilds*, 1913,
by S. G. Hobson). The idea was developed by Mr. G. D. H. Cole and
his associates, and widely promulgated in the Trade Union world. An
organisation for this propaganda, the National Guilds League, was started
in 1915, and attained a membership of several hundreds, amongst whom
were some of the younger leaders of the Trade Union Movement. See its
monthly, *The Guildsman* ; the various books by G. D. H. Cole (especially
The World of Labour, Self-Government in Industry, and *Labour in the
Commonwealth*), S. G. Hobson (*Guild Principles in Peace and War*), M. B.
Reckitt and C. E. Bechhofer (*The Meaning of National Guilds*), A. J.
Penty, and G. R. S. Taylor.

ment of the existing Trade Unions into self-organised, self-contained, self-governing industrial democracies, as supplying the future method of conducting industries and services. The schemes put forward by the National Union of Railwaymen, the Miners' Federation of Great Britain, and the Union of Postal Workers differ widely from the revolutionary Syndicalism of Mr. Tom Mann and the large visions of the Industrial Workers of the World. They do not even go so far as the projects of the National Guildsmen. In fact, they limit the claim of the manual workers merely to participation in the management, fully conceding that the final authority must be vested in the representatives of the community of citizens or consumers. Thus we see the Annual General Meeting of the National Union of Railwaymen in 1914 resolving unanimously: " That this Congress, while reaffirming previous decisions in favour of the nationalisation of railways, and approving the action of the Executive Committee in arranging to obtain and give evidence before the Royal Commission, declares that no system of State ownership of the railways will be acceptable to organised railwaymen which does not guarantee to them their full political and social rights, *allow them a due measure of control and responsibility in the safe and efficient working of the railway system,* and assure to them a fair and equitable participation of the increased benefits likely to accrue from a more economical and scientific administration." [1] In a modified form this resolution was brought forward by the Railway Clerks' Association, supported by the N.U.R., and passed by the Trades Union Congress of 1917.[2] A similar

---

[1] N.U.R. *Agenda and Decisions of the Annual General Meeting,* June 1914, p. 7.

[2] The resolution runs as follows : " That in view of the success which, in spite of unparalleled difficulties, has attended the working of the railways under State control, this Congress urge the Parliamentary Congress to press the Government to arrange for the complete nationalisation of all the railways, and to place them under a Minister of Railways, who shall be responsible to Parliament, and *be assisted by national and local advisory committees, upon which the organised railway workers shall be adequately represented*" (*Trades Union Congress Annual Report,* 1917, p. 345).

movement in favour of participation in management has
taken root among the postal workers of all kinds, in England
as also in France.   At the Annual Conference, in May 1919,
of the Postal and Telegraph Clerks' Association, which had
in previous years been passing resolutions on the subject, it
was emphatically pointed out that the control demanded by
the postal employees was not restricted to securing better
conditions of employment, but that they desired to participate in directing the technical improvement of the service
for the good of the community.[1]   The Conference resolved :
" That in view of the obstructive attitude of the Department
on the question of the development of the Post Office
Savings Bank, the modernising of the Post Office Insurance
System, and the expansion and improvement of the Post
Office Services generally, this Conference directs that
representatives of the Association be appointed to investigate
and report on the working of the postal cheque and transfer
services from both the national and international standpoint, and that the report be widely circulated, and propaganda work undertaken, so that this development of the
Post Office Savings Bank—giving a greatly improved trans-
mission of moneys system—be introduced throughout." [2]
Finally, we may cite the scheme for the Nationalisation of
the Coal-mines that the Miners' Federation brought formally
before the Coal Industry Commission in 1919.   Six years
previously the Miners' Federation had had a Bill drafted
and published, which provided merely for the vesting of the
collieries in a Ministry of Mines, and for the administration
of the whole industry by that department.[3]   All that the
Federation was then concerned to secure for the miners
themselves was the continuance of free and lawful Trade
Unionism.   The Bill of 1919 [4] imposed on the Minister of

---

[1] *Postal and Telegraph Record*, May 22, 1919, p. 237.
[2] *Ibid.*
[3] *The Nationalisation of Mines Bill* (Fabian Tract, No. 171, 1913).
[4] The Nationalisation of Mines and Minerals Bill, 1919, given in full in
Further Facts from the Coal Commission, by R. Page Arnot, 1919.   The
Miners' Federation Conference of 1918 had passed the following resolution :

Mines a whole series of National and District Councils, and Pit Committees, each of which was to consist, to the extent of one half, of members nominated by the Federation, the other half being nominated by the Minister; and the expectation was not concealed that it would be by these bipartite bodies that the administration would be conducted. We record these schemes, which are by the nature of the case only imperfect drafts prepared for propaganda, not so much for their importance as precisely defined industrial constitutions, but as being indicative of the change of spirit that has come over the Trade Union world.

The Increased Reliance on Direct Action

The acceptance, during the last decade, by Parliament, by the Executive Government, and by public opinion, of the Trade Union organisation as part of the machinery of government in all matters concerning the life and labour of the manual working class, has been coincident, some would say paradoxically coincident, with an increased reliance on the strike, commonly known as the method of Direct Action, and with an enlargement of the purposes for which this method is used by Trade Unionists. There is an impression in the public mind, which easily forgets its previous impressions of the same kind, that we are to-day (1920) living in an era of strikes. Although this impression

---

" That in the opinion of this Conference the time has arrived in the history of the coal-mining industry when it is clearly in the national interests to transfer the entire industry from private ownership and control to State ownership with joint control and administration by the workmen and the State. In pursuance of this opinion the National Executive be instructed to immediately reconsider the draft Bill for the Nationalisation of the Mines . . . in the light of the newer phases of development in the industry, so as to make provision for the aforesaid joint control and administration when the measure becomes law ; further, a Conference be called at an early date to receive a report from the Executive Committee upon the draft proposals and to determine the best means of co-operating with the National Labour Party to ensure the passage of a new Bill into law " (*Report of Annual Conference of the Miners' Federation of Great Britain,* July 9, 1918, p. 44).

is not justified by the number of strikes, as compared with those of 1825, 1833–34, 1857–60, 1871–74, and 1885–86, there is some basis for the feeling. The strikes and threats of strikes during the past decade (excluding the four years of war) have been on a larger scale, and, in a sense, more menacing, than those of previous periods. When we published, in 1897, our detailed analysis of the theory and practice of contemporary Trade Unionism (*Industrial Democracy*), the very term " direct action " was unknown in this country. The strike was regarded, not as a distinct method of Trade Union action, but merely as the culminating incident of a breakdown of the Method of Collective Bargaining.[1] The Trade Union plea for the right to strike has always been a simple one. It is a mere derivative of the right of Freedom of Contract. Whenever an individual workman had the right to refuse to enter or continue in a contract of service, any group of individuals might, if they chose, exercise a like freedom. After the collapse of Owenism and Chartism all thought of using the weapon of the strike, otherwise than as an incident in Collective Bargaining with the employers, seems to have left the Trade Union Movement in Great Britain. Indeed, during the last half of the nineteenth century, the use of the weapon of the strike was falling into disrepute, even as an incident of Collective Bargaining, not only among the officials of the great trade friendly societies, such as the Amalgamated Society of Engineers and Carpenters, but also among the younger and more militant members of the Trade Union movement. The " extremists " of the last decade of the

---

[1] At the end of our chapter on the "Method of Collective Bargaining" we cursorily dealt with the strike as a necessary incident of collective bargaining : " It is impossible to deny that the perpetual liability to end in a strike or a lock-out is a grave drawback to the Method of Collective Bargaining. So long as the parties to a bargain are free to agree or not to agree, it is inevitable that, human nature being as it is, there should now and again come a deadlock, leading to that trial of strength and endurance which lies behind all bargaining. We know of no device for avoiding this trial of strength except a deliberate decision of the community expressed in legislative enactment " (*Industrial Democracy*, p. 221).

nineteenth century, as we have described in a previous chapter, were out for the " capture " of Parliament and Local Authorities by an " independent " Party of Labour ; and political action was commonly regarded as the shortest and most convenient way of securing not only Socialist but also the distinctively Trade Union objects. It was at that time left to the " reactionaries " in the Trade Union Movement, who disliked the idea of a political Labour Party, to advocate reliance on " ourselves alone." [1]

But with the revolution of thought that we have described there has arisen, with regard to Direct Action, a change of practice. In 1913–14 there was an outburst of exasperated strikes designed, we may almost say, to supersede Collective Bargaining—to repudiate any making of long-term agreements, to spring demand after demand upon employers, to compel every workman to join the Union, avowedly with the view of building up the Trade Union as a dominant force. This spasm of industrial " insurrectionism " was abruptly stopped by the outbreak of war. The " political " element creeps in with the strikes and threats of strikes of the Miners' Federation in 1912 and 1919, designed, not to further Collective Bargaining with the employers, but to cause the Government and Parliament to alter the organisation of the industry, in the earlier case by the enactment of a Minimum Wage law, and in the other by the elimination of the capitalist profitmaker in favour of public ownership and workers' control. During the years of war Direct Action took another form. The weapon of a concerted refusal to work was used by some Trade Unions, in matters entirely unconnected with their conditions of employment, in order to prevent particular individuals from doing what they wished to do. The most sensational examples were afforded by the National Union of Sailors and Firemen in 1917–18, when its members, by refusing to work, at the dictation of Mr. J. Havelock Wilson,

[1] See, for instance, *Trade Unionism New and Old*, by George Howell, 1891.

the Secretary of the Union, prevented certain Labour Leaders [1] from proceeding to Petrograd, actually by direction of the Government ; and subsequently others [2] from going to Paris with Government passports, on the instructions of the Labour Party, because the Union, or at any rate Mr. Havelock Wilson, disapproved of these visits, and of their supposed object in arranging for an International Labour and Socialist Congress. Another case was the withdrawal by the Electrical Trades Union in 1918 of their members (taking with them the indispensable fuses) from the Albert Hall in London, when the directors of the Hall cancelled its letting for a Labour Demonstration, of the purposes and resolutions of which they disapproved, or thought that their patrons would disapprove. What the Electrical Trades Union intimated was that, unless the Hall was allowed, as heretofore, to be used for Labour meetings, it should not be used for a forthcoming demonstration of the supporters of the Coalition Government, or for any other meetings. The result was that (it is said on a hint from Downing Street) the directors of the Hall withdrew their objection to the Labour Demonstration, and have since continued to allow such meetings. Yet another example of Direct Action was given by the printing staffs of certain newspaper offices in London during the railway strike of 1919, when they threatened instantly to withdraw their labour, and thus absolutely to prevent the issue of the newspapers, unless the use of " lying posters " was given up, and unless the case of the National Union of Railwaymen was fairly treated in the papers, and accorded reasonable space. The gravest case of all was the threat by the Miners' Federation in 1919, that all the coal-mines might stop working unless Compulsory Military Service was immedi-

[1] Mr. G. H. Roberts (Typographical Society), then Parliamentary Secretary to the Board of Trade ; and Mr. J. Ramsay MacDonald, Treasurer of the Labour Party.

[2] The Rt. Hon. Arthur Henderson (Friendly Society of Ironfounders), and M. Camille Huysmans, Secretary of the International Socialist Congress.

ately brought to an end, and unless the policy of military intervention in Russia against the Bolshevik Government of Russia was abandoned. By what was perhaps a fortunate coincidence the Secretary of State for War was able to declare that all Compulsory Military Service was to cease at or before the end of the current financial year ; and the Prime Minister to announce that no more troops, and, after certain consignments already arranged for, no more military stores, would be sent in aid of those who were attacking the Bolshevik Government.

How far can these instances of Direct Action be deemed to indicate a change of thought in the Trade Union world with regard to the use of the strike weapon ? We must note that, in spite of the temporary lull in strikes in the latter part of the last century, there has been no change in Trade Union policy with regard to the strike in disputes with employers about the conditions of employment. The Trade Unions have always included in this term the dismissal of men for reasons other than their inefficiency as workmen, the engagement of non-Unionists, the presence of an obnoxious foreman or manager, or any interference with the conduct of employees outside the works. Nor has there been any development in the original Trade Union position with regard to sympathetic strikes in aid of other sections of workers in their struggles with their employers. It is possible that some of the insurrectionary strikes of 1911–14 were inspired by the new thought that we have described—the disillusionment as to the Parliamentary potency of a Labour Party, and the vision of a Democracy based on industrial organisation and secured by industrial action. But, in the main, the increased frequency and magnitude of strikes in these years are sufficiently accounted for by the continued fall in real wages due to rising prices, combined with the steadily improving organisation of the workers concerned. There was a new element in the proposal of the Miners' Federation in 1919 to strike if the Government did not fulfil its pledge to carry into effect the Sankey Report described in the last chapter. The significant and authoritative declaration in the first Report of March 20, 1919, that " the present system of ownership and working in the coal industry stands condemned, and some other system must be substituted for it, either nationalisation or a method of unification by national purchase and/or by joint control," and the explicit acceptance of this Report by the Government " in the spirit and in the letter," formed an integral part of the bargain between the Miners' Federation and the Government, on the strength of which they forewent the strike at the end of March 1919 on which they had decided. It can hardly be contended that the " present system of ownership and working " is not a necessary part of the conditions of employment, or that the Miners are not entitled to refuse to enter into contracts of service under a system that Mr. Bonar Law agrees with Mr. Justice Sankey, and nine out of the other twelve members of the Royal Commission, in holding to " stand condemned." On the other hand, though the Government controls the industry and dictates the wages, the alterations in the conditions of employment that the Miners' Federation asks for require not only one but probably several Acts of Parliament, which a majority of the members of the present House of Commons, notwithstanding the explicit Government pledge, refuses to pass. What the Miners' Federation threatens, by a stoppage of the coal industry, is to coerce into agreement with them not their employers, the colliery owners, not even the Ministry with whom they made the bargain, but, in effect, the recalcitrant capitalist majority of the House of Commons which cannot be displaced without a General Election.

But an entirely new development of Direct Action, alike in form and in substance, is the distinctly political, or, as we should prefer to call it, the non-economic strike—that is, the strike, not for any alteration in the conditions of employment of any section of the Trade Union world, but with a view to enforce, either on individuals, on Parliament, or on the Government, some other course of action desired by the strikers. So far as we know, there is, on this question, no consistent body of opinion in the Trade Union world ; all that we find are currents of opinion arising from different assumptions of social expediency. There is, first, a small section of Trade Unionists who are Syndicalists or extreme Industrial Unionists in opinion, and who look forward to the supersession of political Democracy, and the reconstitution of society on the basis of the suffrages of the several trades. Like the Sinn Feiners in Ireland, though on different grounds, they do not acknowledge the competency of the existing Parliament to undertake the government of the country, and they advocate Direct Action as the only weapon of revolt accessible to the workers organised as workers. But it was no such theory of social revolution that induced Mr. Havelock Wilson to prevent the visit of Mr. G. H. Roberts and Mr. MacDonald to Petrograd, when the Government wished them to go ; or to prevent Mr. Henderson and M. Camille Huysmans from using their passports to Paris. Nor were the electricians of the Albert Hall inspired by faith in an immediate revolution of the Russian type. It cannot even be suggested that the widespread approval by the more active spirits of the Trade Union world of the proposed strike to stop the intervention of Great Britain in support of the reactionary Russian leaders was accompanied by any desire to set up in Great Britain the constitution which is believed to obtain in Moscow and Petrograd. We must look elsewhere for the motive that underlies and is held by many to justify the non-economic or " political " strike.

We suggest that the explanation is a more complex one. We have first the impulsive tendency of some men in all classes to use any powers that they possess, whether over land, capital, or labour, to dictate to their fellow-men a course of conduct on any question on which they feel hotly, even if it is wholly unconnected with their several economic functions. This delight in an anarchic use of economic power is, it is needless to say, not peculiar to those whose economic power is that of labour. There have been innumerable instances, within our own memories, among landlords and capitalists, of actions no less arbitrary than that of Mr. Havelock Wilson (who, it must be remembered, had the general approval of the capitalist press ; and, in the case of the attempted internment in this country of a distinguished Belgian visitor, M. Huysmans, the connivance of the naval officers, if not of the Admiralty). We find within the last few decades many cases of landlords who have ejected persons, not because they were objectionable tenants, or had failed to pay their rent, but because they had supported a political candidate, or had led to action on the part of the Local Authority, to which the landlord objected. We have seen landed proprietors refusing sites for Nonconformist chapels, not because they objected to buildings of that character, or were dissatisfied with the price offered, but because they disliked the theology of the promoters. We have heard of banks refusing to the Trade Unions who were their customers any accommodation at all on the occasion of a strike, merely because they disliked the strike. We have seen employers dismissing workmen, not for their inefficiency, not even for their Trade Union activities, which might be held to affect the economic interest of the capitalist, but because the workmen held different political opinions from those of the employer. But these cases of the use of economic power to prevent individuals from pursuing or promoting their own religious or political creeds are emphatically condemned by the Trade Union Movement. Thus no Trade Union support was overtly given to Mr. Havelock Wilson, even by those Trade Union leaders who agreed with him in detesting any meeting between Britons and enemy subjects.

We have a quite different class of cases when Direct Action is taken in reprisal for the Direct Action of other persons or groups of persons. This was the case in the strike of the electricians at the Albert Hall. It was a reprisal for the

use by the directors of the Albert Hall of their power over
lettings to bann opinions that they happened to dislike,
whilst permitting the use of their hall to the other side.
A more difficult case is that of the threatened refusal to
work of the compositors against the newspapers who denied
fair play to the railwaymen. Here our judgement may
depend on what view is taken of the function of newspapers ;
how far are newspapers what their name implies, the public
purveyors of news ? Supposing that all the capitalist
press were deliberately to boycott all Labour news, whilst
deliberately giving currency to false statements about
Labour Leaders and the Labour Movement, would the
compositors, as representing the Trade Union world in this
industry, be justified in a strike ? The only conclusion we
can suggest is that, human nature being instinctively
militant, any anarchic use of the power given by one form
of monopoly will lead to a similar anarchic use of the power
given by another form of monopoly.

We come now to the third class of use of the method of
Direct Action, a general strike of the manual workers to
compel the Government of the country to abstain from
political courses distasteful to those who control a monopoly
of labour power, or to the majority of them. This form of
Direct Action is justified by a minority of Trade Unionists,
who consider that under the present constitution of Parliament the organised workmen have practically no chance
of getting their fair share of representation—an argument
strengthened by every election trick, and especially by the
partisan use of the capitalist press as an election instrument.
The majority of Trade Unionists, however, do not, at the
present time, seem to support this view. They reply that
the manual workers and their wives now constitute, in
every district, a majority of the electorate. They can, if
they choose, return to Parliament a Labour majority and
make a Labour Government. This very consideration,
indeed, seems to make any such general strike impracticable,
and, as a matter of fact, no such proposal of a general strike

has yet been endorsed by the Trades Union Congress. We can imagine occasions that might, in the eyes of the Trade Union world, fully justify a general strike of non-economic or political character. If, for instance, a reactionary Parliament were to pass a measure disfranchising the bulk of the manual workers, or depriving them of political power by such a device as the " Three Class Franchise " of Prussia and Saxony—if any Act were passed depriving the Trade Unions of the rights and liberties now conceded to them— if the Executive or the judges were to use against the Trade Unions, by injunction or otherwise, any weapon that might be fished up from the legal armoury, confiscating their funds or prohibiting their action—then, indeed, we might see the Trades Union Congress recommending a General Strike ; and it would be supported not only by the wage-earning class as a whole, but also by a large section of the middle class, and even by some members of the House of Lords. That is one reason why, short of madness, no such act would be committed by the Government or by Parliament. If any such act were perpetrated, it would probably involve a revolution not in the British but in the continental sense. It must be remembered that the " last word " in Direct Action is with the police and the army, and there not with the officers but with the rank and file.

To sum up, the vast majority of Trade Unionists object to Direct Action, whether by landlords or capitalists or by organised workers, for objects other than those connected with the economic function of the Direct Actionists. Trade Unionists, on the whole, are not prepared to disapprove of Direct Action as a reprisal for Direct Action taken by other persons or groups. With regard to a general strike of non-economic or political character, in favour of a particular home or foreign policy, we very much doubt whether the Trade Union Congress could be induced to endorse it, or the rank and file to carry it out, except only in case the Government made a direct attack upon the political or industrial liberty of the manual working class, which it seemed imperative to resist by every possible means, not excluding forceful revolution itself.

THE DEMAND FOR THE ELIMINATION OF THE CAPITALIST PROFIT-MAKER

It is interesting to note that this widening enlargement of the aspirations and purposes of Trade Unionism has been accompanied, not by any decline, but by an actual renewal of the faith in Communal Socialism, towards which we described the Trade Union Movement as tending in 1889–94. For the Trade Unionist objects, more strongly than ever, to any financial partnership with the capitalist employers, or with the shareholders, in any industry or service, on the sufficient ground that any such sharing of profits would, whilst leaving intact the tribute of rent and interest to proprietors, irretrievably break up the solidarity of the manual working class. To the new school of Trade Unionists the nationalisation or municipalisation of industry, or its assumption by consumers' co-operation, is a necessary preliminary to the partnership of Labour in its government. What they are after is to alter, not only the status of the manual worker, but also the status of the employer who is the director of industry ; they wish them both to become the agents of the community ; they desire that manual workers and brain workers alike should be inspired, not by the greed of gain made by profit on price, but by the desire to produce the commodities and services needed by the community in return for a sufficient livelihood, and the personal freedom and personal responsibility which they believe would spring from vocational self-government. Thus we find Mr. Hodges, the General Secretary of the Miners' Federation, in one of his numerous speeches in favour of the nationalisation of the mines, declaring that what they demanded was " a new status for the worker as a controller of his industry. Miners were not anarchists, although they had the power to be. They realised that

z

their interests were bound up with those of the community, and therefore they demanded conditions which would develop the corporate sense. . . . Education was carrying men along social rather than individualistic lines, and right throughout the mining industry there was the desire to be something different from what they were. This desire to be master of the work in which the man was engaged was the great thing that was vital in working-class life. . . . There had never been a movement born of greater moral aspiration than this movement for the nationalisation of the mines. The miner wanted to be in a position where it would be to him a point of honour not to allow even a piece of timber to be wasted, where he would want to do his work well. · He wanted a Social Contract." [1]

[1] These extracts from a speech by Mr. Hodges are put together from the separate imperfect reports in the *Times*, *Daily News*, and *Daily Herald* of October 27, 1919. A more explicit statement of Mr. Hodges' views will be found in his speech at the Annual Conference of the Miners' Federation in July 1918 : " For the last two or three years a new movement has sprung up in the labour world which deals with the question. of joint control of the industry by representatives from the side which represents, for the most part, the consumer, and representatives of the workmen, who are the producers. Nationalisation in the old sense is no longer attractive. As a matter of fact, you can have nationalisation, but still be in no better position than you are now under private ownership. That is the experience of institutions which have been State owned and State controlled for many years. The most remarkable scheme worked out during the last year is the theory worked out by the . . . Postmen's Federation. He has endeavoured to provide a scheme by which the postal workers should have a definite amount of control, a definite form of control, in the postal service, and in working it out he has demonstrated beyond all doubt how at every point he is up against the power of the bureaucrats, as exemplified by the State. Now, is it any good to have these mines nationalised unless we are going to exercise some form of control as producers ? If not, the whole tendency will be towards the power of bureaucracy. We shall be given no status at all in the industry, except to be the mere producers, as we have been in the past years. Under State ownership the workmen should be desirous of having something more than the mere question of wages or the mere consideration of employment ; the workmen should have some directive power in the industry in which they are engaged. Now, how are we going to have this directive power under State control ? I think we must admit that the side representing the consumers (the State) should have some form of control on property which will be State property, and when a national industry becomes State controlled you must have permanent officials to look after the consumers'

The demand for the nationalisation or municipalisation of industries and services, or their absorption by the Consumers' Co-operative Movement, was greatly strengthened by the experience, during the war and after the Armistice, of the failure of every alternative method of preventing " profiteering." The rapid development of capitalist combinations and price-agreements [1] ; the ill-success of the most stringent Government control in preventing alarming increases of price ; the inability of even legally fixed maximum prices to do anything more, under private ownership, than authorise the charge required to cover the cost at the least efficient and least well - equipped establishment of which the output was needed ; the enormous and even unprecedented profits made throughout the whole range of business enterprise ; the helplessness of the consumers, in the mere expectation of shortage, and their willingness to pay almost any price that was demanded rather than go without—combined with the obvious breakdown of capitalist competition as a safeguard of the public which the proceedings under the Profiteering Act revealed—all these things co-operated to convince the bulk of the wage-earning class, many of the families living on fixed incomes, and (in

interests, and from the purely producers' point of view the Miners' Federation must represent the producers in the central authority and in the decentralised authority, right down to the separate collieries. Are we ready to do this ? Are we prepared for this, starting at the separate collieries, indicating how the industry is to be developed locally? Men must take their share in understanding all the relations embodied in the export side of the trade ; they must take a share even in controlling the banking arrangements which govern the financial side of the industry, and with that comes a very great deal of responsibility. Now, are we prepared to assume that responsibility, a responsibility which is implied in the term workmen's control ? It is going to be a big task and a test of the educational attainments of the miners themselves if they assume control of the industry, and if it did not thrive under that control there is the possibility we should have to hark back to private ownership in order to make it successful. . . . I hold these views, and unless they are accompanied by an effective form of working-class control, I do not believe that nationalisation will do any good for anybody " (*Report of Annual Conference of the Miners' Federation of Great Britain, July 9, 1918*, pp. 49-51).

[1] Report of the Committee on Combinations and Trusts, 1919.

spite of the objection to " bureaucratic control ") some even among business men, that there was practically no other course open, in the industries and services that were sufficiently highly developed to render such a course practicable, than a gradual substitution of public for private ownership. This advance in public opinion is naturally reflected in the passionate support of public ownership, with participation of the workers in administration and control, given by the Trades Union Congress and Labour Party Conference.

It will have become clear from our review of the larger conception now current of the place of Trade Unionism in the State, that the Trade Unionist, as such, no longer retains the acquiescent and neutral attitude towards the two great parties of British politics, nor to the Capitalist System itself, which characterised the Trade Unionism of thirty or forty years ago. The object and purpose of the New Unionism of 1913–19 — not without analogy with that of 1830–34, but with a significant difference—cannot be attained without the transformation of British politics, and the supersession, in one occupation after another, of the capitalist profit-maker as the governor and director of industry. Meanwhile, as a result of the successive attacks upon the very existence of Trade Unionism, even in its most limited form, there has been growing up a distinct political organisation of the Trade Union Movement, aiming at securing the acceptance by the electorate, as a whole, of a definitely Socialist policy in the administration of both home and foreign affairs. It is this formation of a Labour Party, ready for the carrying into effect of the new ideas, that we have now to describe.

CHAPTER XI

POLITICAL ORGANISATION

[1900–1920]

FIFTY years ago, when Professor Brentano described the British Trade Union Movement with greater knowledge and insight than any one else had then shown,[1] nothing seemed more unlikely than that the Movement would become organised as an independent political party, appealing to the whole electorate on a general programme, returning its own contingent of members to the House of Commons, and asserting a claim, as soon as that contingent should become the strongest party in Parliament, to constitute a national administration. For nearly a quarter of a century more, as we have described in a previous chapter, though Trade Unionism was making itself slowly more and more felt in politics, it was still possible for economists and statesmen to believe that " Labour " in Great Britain would organise only to maintain its sectional industrial interests, and that it would impinge on politics, if at all, only occasionally, in defence of Trade Unionism itself, or in support of some particular project of industrial law. By 1894, when the first edition of this book was published, there was already

---

[1] See his *Arbeitergilden der Gegenwart*, 1871–72 ; his more generalised survey, *Das Arbeitsverhältniss gemäss den heutigen Recht* (Leipsic, 1877), translated as *The Relation of Labour to the Law of To-day* (New York, 1890) ; and his article on " The Growth of a Trades Union," in the *North British Review*, October 1870.

manifest, as we then stated, a great shifting of Trade Union opinion on the

" pressing question of the position to be taken by the Trade Union world in the party struggles of To-day and the politics of To-morrow. In our chapter on ' The Old Unionism and the New,' we described the rapid conversion of the superior workman to the general principles of Collectivism. This revolution of opinion in the rank and file has been followed by a marked change of front on the part of the salaried officials, and by a growing distrust of the aristocratic and middle-class representatives of both the great political parties. To the working-man politician of 1894 it seems inconceivable that either landlords or capitalists will actively help him to nationalise land and mining royalties, to absorb unearned incomes by taxation, or to control private enterprise in the interests of the wage-earner. Thus we find throughout the whole Trade Union world an almost unanimous desire to make the working-class organisations in some way effective for political purposes. Nor is this a new thing. The sense of solidarity has, as we have seen, never been lacking among those active soldiers and non-commissioned officers who constitute the most vital element in the Trade Union army. The generous aid from trade to trade, the pathetic attempts to form General Unions, the constant aspirations after universal federation, all testify to the reality and force of this instinctive solidarity. The Collectivist faith of the ' New Unionism ' is only another manifestation of the same deep-rooted belief in the essential Brotherhood of Labour. But, as we have seen, the basis of the association of these million and a half wage-earners is, primarily, sectional in its nature. They come together, and contribute their pence, for the defence of their interests as Boilermakers, Miners, Cotton-spinners, and not directly for the advancement of the whole working class. Among the salaried officers of the Unions, it is, as we have said, the Trade Official, chosen and paid for the express purpose of maintaining the interests of his own particular trade, who is the active force. The effect has been to intensify the sectionalism to which an organisation based on trades must necessarily be prone. The vague general Collectivism of the non-commissioned officers has hitherto got translated into practical proposals only in so far as it can be expressed in projects for the advantage of a particular trade. Some organised trades have known how to draft and to extort from Parliament a voluminous Labour Code, the provisions of which are exceptionally well adapted for the protection of the particular workers concerned. The ' particulars clause ' [1] and the law against the ' over-steaming ' of weaving sheds are, for instance, triumphs of collective control which could hardly have been conceived by any one except the astute trade officials of the Cotton Operatives. But there is no attempt to deal with any question as a whole. Trade Unionists are, for instance, unanimously in favour of drastic legislation to put down ' sweating ' in all trades whatsoever. But no salaried officer of the Trade Union world feels it to be his business to improve the Labour Code for any industry but his own. Thus, whereas the Factory Acts have been effectively elaborated to meet the special circumstances of a few trades, for all the rest they remain in the form of merely general prohibitions which it is practically impossible to enforce. How far it is possible, by the development of Trades Councils, the reform of the Trades Union Congress, the increased efficiency of the Parliamentary Committee, the growth of Trade Union representation in the House of Commons, or, finally, by the creation of any new federal machinery, to counteract the fundamental sectionalism of Trade Union organisation, to supplement the specialised trade officials by an equally specialised Civil Service of working-class politicians, and thus to render the Trade Union world, with its million of electors, and its leadership of Labour, an effective political force in the State, is, on the whole, the most momentous question of contemporary politics." [2]

The quarter of a century that has elapsed since these words were written has seen an extensive political development of the Trade Union Movement, taking the form of building up a separate and independent party of " Labour " in the House of Commons, which we have now to record.[3]

[1] Sec. 24 of the Factory Act of 1891 provides, as regards textile manufactures, that the employer shall supply every worker by the piece with certain particulars as to the quantity of work and rate of remuneration for it.

[2] *History of Trade Unionism*, by S. and B. Webb, 1st ed., 1894, pp. 476-78.

[3] The most important sources of information are the Annual Reports of the Trades Union Congress, 1874-1919, and other publications of its Parliamentary Committee; those of the Annual Conferences of the Labour Representation Committee, 1901-5, and of the Labour Party, 1906-19, together with the Party's other publications, especially *Labour and the New Social Order*, 1918 ; the reports and contemporary publica-

The continued propaganda of the Socialists, and of others who wished to see the Trade Union Movement become an effective political force, which we have described as active from 1884 onwards, did not, for nearly a couple of decades, produce a political " Labour Party." So strong was at that time the resistance of most of the Trade Union leaders to any participation of their societies in general politics, even on the lines of complete independence of both Liberal and Conservative Parties, that " Labour Representation " had still, for some years, to be fought for apart from Trade Unionism. The leaders, indeed, did not really care about Trade Union influence in the House of Commons.[1] Many

---

tions of the Socialist Societies, especially the Independent Labour Party from 1893, and the Fabian Society from 1884; *Labour Year Book* for 1916 and 1919; *History of British Socialism*, by M. Beer, vol. ii., 1920; *History of the British Trades Union Congress*, by W. J. Davis, 2 vols., 1910, 1916; *Die englische Arbeiterpartei*, by G. Guettler, 1914; *Aims of Labour*, by Rt. Hon. A. Henderson, 1918; *History of the Fabian Society*, by E. R. Pease, 1916; *History of Labour Representation*, by A. W. Humphrey, 1912; biographies of Joseph Arch, Henry Broadhurst, Robert Applegarth, Thomas Burt, John Wilson, J. H. Thomas, W. J. Davis, etc.

[1] The movement for " Labour Representation " (which " at that time meant working-men members of Parliament and nothing else," *History of Labour Representation*, by A. W. Humphrey, 1912) was first got under way by George Potter's London Working Men's Association in 1866, mentioned at the end of Chapter VI. At the second Trades Union Congress, at Birmingham in 1869, a paper had been read on " Direct Labour Representation in Parliament," but Congress took no action. A separate " Labour Representation League " was then formed under the presidency of R. M. Lathom, a Chancery barrister, to which many leading Trade Unionists belonged, of which Henry Broadhurst was secretary from 1872 to about 1878, and which sought from the Liberal Party opportunities for the return of a few working-class members; but (as formerly in the cases of William Newton's contest for the Tower Hamlets in 1852 and George Odger's at Southwark in 1870) in vain. At the General Election of 1874, as we have already described, fourteen workmen went to the poll; but in ten of the constituencies they were fought by both parties, and only in the other four did the Liberals allow them to be fought by Conservatives alone, with the result that two only (out of the latter four) were elected, namely, Alexander Macdonald and Thomas Burt. At the General Election in 1880, again with Liberal acquiescence, Henry Broadhurst was added to their number; and in 1885 this was raised to eleven (of whom six were miners). All these, whilst pushing measures desired by the Trade Unions, acted habitually with the Liberal Party. In 1886 —the Labour Representation League having faded away about 1881— the Congress appointed a " Labour Electoral Committee " to do the

of them, as we have described, remained for a whole generation averse even from legal regulation of the conditions of
employment.   In national politics they were mostly Liberals,
with the strongest possible admiration for Gladstone and
Bright ; or else (as in Lancashire) convinced Conservatives,
concerned to defend the Church of England or Roman
Catholic elementary schools in which their children were
being educated or carried away by the glamour of an
Imperialist foreign policy.   They asked for nothing more
than a few working-class members in the House of Commons,
belonging to one or other of the " respectable " parties, to
which they could thus obtain access for the adjustment of any
matters in which their societies happened to be interested.

In 1887, at his first appearance at the Trades Union
Congress, J. Keir Hardie,[1] representing a small Union of

---

same work ; but this was never able to free itself from subserviency to
the Liberal Party, and it achieved no success, dying away in 1893.   Some
personal reminiscences are given in " Labour Representation Thirty Years
Ago," by Henry Broadhurst, M.P., in the *Fourth Annual Report of General
Federation of Trade Unions*, 1903 ; see also *History of Labour Representation*, by A. W. Humphrey, 1912.

[1] In a " scribbling diary " of 1884 is the following entry :

" Written by Jas. K. Hardie, born August 15, 1856, married August 3,
1879, began work as a message boy in Glasgow when 8 years and 9 months
old, wrought for some time in a printing office in Trongate, in the
brass finishing shop of the Anchor Line Shipping Co., also as a rivet
heater in Thompson's heatyard.   Left Glasgow in the year 1866 and went
into No. 18 pit of the Moss at Newarthill, from thence to Quarter Iron
Works, and again to one or two other collieries in neighbourhood of
Hamilton.   Was elected Secretary to Miners' Association in 1878, and
for the same position in Ayrshire in 1879 ; resigned April, 1882, when got
appointment unsolicited as correspondent to *Cumnock News*.   Brought
up an atheist, converted to Christianity in 1878."

Keir Hardie, whose kindliness and integrity of character endeared him
to all who knew him, was from 1887 down to his death in 1915 the apostle
of " independency " in the political organisation of Labour.   He sat in
the Trades Union Congress from 1887 to 1895 as representative of the
Ayrshire Miners ; and in the House of Commons from 1892 to 1895 (for
West Ham), from 1906 to 1915 (for Merthyr).   He was Chairman of the
" I.L.P." from 1893 to 1898, and again in 1914.   Pending the publication
of a biography by W. Stewart, reference may be made to a biographical
sketch entitled *From Pit to Parliament*, by Frank Smith ; a character
sketch by F. Pethick Lawrence in the *Labour Record* for August 1905 ;
the issues of the *Labour Leader* for September 30 and October 7, 1915 ;

Ayrshire Miners, demanded a new start. He called upon
the Trade Unionists definitely to sever their connection
with the existing political parties, by which the workmen
were constantly befooled and betrayed, and insisted on the
necessity of forming an entirely independent party of Labour,
to which the whole working-class movement should rally.
On the Congress he produced no apparent effect.[1] But, six
months later, when a Parliamentary vacancy occurred in
Mid-Lanark, Keir Hardie was nominated, against Liberal
and Tory alike, on the principle of entire independence ;
and in spite of every effort to induce him to withdraw,[2] he
went to the poll, obtaining only 619 votes. A society was
then formed to work for independent Labour representation,
under the designation of the Scottish Labour Party, having
for chairman Mr R. B. Cunninghame Graham, M.P., who
had been elected as a Liberal but who had become a Socialist. The " new spirit " of 1889, which we have described,
put heart into the movement for political independence ;
and after much further propaganda by the Socialists,[3] at the
General Election of 1892 Keir Hardie was elected for West
Ham, avowedly as the first member of an independent Party
of Labour ; together with fourteen other workmen,[4] whose
independence of the Liberal Party, even where it was

---

and an article entitled " An Old Diary," by F. J. in the *Socialist Review*,
January 1919.

[1] *Annual Report of Trades Union Congress*, 1887.

[2] It is said that the Liberal Party agents attempted, in vain, to bribe
him to withdraw ; eventually offering as high a price as a safe Liberal
seat on the first opportunity, all his election expenses, and £300 a year—
if only he would wear the Liberal badge !

[3] See, for instance, the following " Fabian Tracts," which had a large
circulation among Trade Unionists : No. 6 of 1887, " The True Radical
Programme " ; No. 11 of 1890, " The Workers' Political Programme " ;
No. 40 of 1892, " The Fabian Election Manifesto " ; No. 49 of 1894, " A
Plan of Campaign for Labour " (*History of the Fabian Society*, by E. R.
Pease, 1916).

[4] These included John Burns (Amalgamated Society of Engineers),
J. Havelock Wilson (National Sailors' and Firemen's Union), Joseph
Arch (Agricultural Labourers' Union), W. R. (afterwards Sir William)
Cremer (General Union of Carpenters), G. Howell (Operative Bricklayers'
Society), J. Rowlands (an ex-watchcase-maker), and eight coalminers.

claimed, was less marked than their obvious jealousy of Keir Hardie. There was apparently still no hope of gaining the adherence of the Trade Unions as such ; and at the Glasgow Trades Union Congress of 1892 arrangements were made by a few of the delegates to hold a smaller conference, which took place at Bradford, in 1893, under the chairmanship of Keir Hardie, when those who were determined to establish a separate political party formed a society, made up of individual adherents, which was styled the Independent Labour Party. In this the Scottish Labour Party was merged, but it remained without the affiliation of Trade Unions in their corporate capacity. The Independent Labour Party, of which throughout his life Keir Hardie was the outstanding figure, carried on a strenuous propagandist campaign, and during the next two years put up independent candidates at by-elections, with uniform ill-success. At the General Election of 1895, no fewer than twenty-eight " I.L.P." candidates went to the poll, every one of them (including Keir Hardie himself at West Ham) being unsuccessful. With two or three exceptions, the Trade Unionist members in alliance with the Liberal Party successfully maintained their seats. The establishment of an aggressively independent Labour Party in Parliament still looked hopeless.

With the new century an effort was made on fresh lines. The continuous propaganda had had its effect, even on the Trades Union Congress. In 1898 it could be suggested in the presidential address [1] that a " committee should be appointed to draft a scheme of political organisation for the Trade Union world on the ground that just as trades federation is a matter of vital necessity for industrial organisation, so also will a scheme of political action be of vital necessity if we wish Parliament to faithfully register the effect of the industrial revolution on our social life." The very next year a resolution—which had been drafted in

---

[1] By J. O'Grady (Furnishing Trades), afterwards M.P. for Leeds ; *Annual Report of Trades Union Congress*, 1898.

London by the members of the Independent Labour Party
—was carried on the motion of the Amalgamated Society
of Railway Servants, against the votes of the miners as well
as of the textile workers, directing the convening of a
special congress representing Trade Unions, Co-operative
Societies, and Socialist organisations, in order to devise
means of increasing the number of Labour members.[1] It
was urged on the Parliamentary Committee that the Socialist
organisations had a right to be strongly represented on the
proposed Committee ; and the Parliamentary Committee,
which had no faith in the scheme and attached little importance to it, nominated four of its members (S. Woods, W. C.
Steadman, R. Bell, and W. Thorne), all of whom afterwards
became Members of Parliament, to sit with two representatives each from the Independent Labour Party (Keir Hardie
and J. Ramsay MacDonald), the Fabian Society (G. Bernard
Shaw and E. R. Pease), and the Social Democratic Federation (H. Quelch and H. R. Taylor). This Committee took
the business into its own hands, and drew up a constitution,
upon a federal basis, for a " Labour Representation Committee," as an independent organisation, including Trade
Unions and Trades Councils, along with Co-operative and
Socialist Societies ; and in February 1900 a specially summoned congress, attended by 129 delegates, representing
Trade Unions aggregating half a million members, and

[1] This was adopted in preference to what was considered a more
extreme proposal (moved by P. Vogel of the Waiters' Union, a Socialist),
appointing the Trades Union Congress itself the organisation for independent Labour representation in Parliament ; requiring every Union
to contribute a halfpenny per member per annum, and making the
Parliamentary Committee disburse the election expenses and the salaries
of the members returned to the House of Commons (*Annual Report of
Trades Union Congress*, 1899).

It was afterwards stated that the leaders of the Trades Union Congress had had in contemplation the subordination of the Labour Representation Committee to the Congress. But with a different constituency
the new body had necessarily to be an independent organisation ; and in
1904 the General Purposes Committee reported to the Trades Union
Congress, which endorsed the report, that any resolution to endorse or
amend the constitution of the Labour Representation Committee would
not be in order at the Trades Union Congress (*ibid.*, 1904).

Socialist societies claiming fewer than seventy thousand, adopted the draft constitution, established the new body, appointed its first executive, and gave it, in Mr. J. Ramsay MacDonald, not merely its first secretary but also a skilful organiser, to whose patient and persistent effort no small part of its subsequent success has been due.

For two years the Labour Representation Committee, in spite of diligent propaganda among Trade Union Executives, seemed to hang fire. The General Election of 1900 found it unprepared ; and, though it put fifteen candidates in the field, only two of them were successful. No Co-operative Society joined ; the Social Democratic Federation withdrew ; scarcely a score of Trades Councils were enrolled ; and though sixty-five separate Trade Unions gradually adhered—being only about five or six per cent of the total number—the aggregate affiliated membership of the Party did not reach half a million. Then the tide turned, mainly through the rally of Trade Unionism as it became aware of the full implications of the assault upon it made by the decision in the Taff Vale case, which we have already described. The miners stood aloof only because they preferred to use their own organisation. In 1901 the Miners' Federation voted a levy of a penny per month on all its membership in order to create a Parliamentary Fund ; and the running of as many as seventy candidates was then talked about. During the year 1902 the number of adhering Trade Unions and Trades Councils, and the total affiliated membership, were alike practically doubled. In the next two years the Committee contested no fewer than six Parliamentary by-elections, returning its members in half of them.[1] Meanwhile the Conservative Government obstinately refused to allow legislation restoring to Trade Unions the statutory

[1] D. J. (afterwards Sir David) Shackleton (Lancashire Weavers) was allowed a walk-over at Clitheroe in 1902 ; and in 1903 W. (afterwards the Rt. Honourable W.) Crooks (Coopers) carried Woolwich after an exciting contest, and Arthur (afterwards the Rt. Honourable Arthur) Henderson (Friendly Society of Ironfounders) won Barnard Castle in a three-cornered fight.

status of 1871–76, of which the judges' decision in the Taff
Vale case had deprived them. Careful preparation was
accordingly made for a successful appeal to Trade Unionists
at the General Election which was approaching ; and when
it came, in January 1906, no fewer than fifty independent
Labour candidates were put in the field against Liberals and
Conservatives alike. To the general surprise of the political
world, as many as twenty-nine of these were successful ;
besides a dozen other workmen, mostly miners, who again
stood with Liberal Party support and were still regarded as
belonging to that Party. The twenty-nine at once formed
themselves into, and were recognised as, a separate independent party in the House of Commons, with its own
officers and whips, concerned to push its own programme
irrespective of the desires and convenience of the other
political parties. At the same time the Labour Representation Committee changed its name to the Labour Party

We need not concern ourselves with the Parliamentary
struggles of the next three years, during which the Parliamentary Labour Party may claim to have indirectly secured
the passage, as Government measures, of the Trade Disputes
Act, the Miners' Eight Hours Act, and the Trade Boards
Act, and to have developed something like a Parliamentary
programme. It suffered, however, in the Trade Union
world, from its inevitable failure to impress its will on the
triumphant Liberal majority of these years. What saved
the Labour Party from decline, and gave it indeed fresh
impetus in the Trade Union movement, was the renewed
legal assault on Trade Unionism itself, which in 1909, as we
have described, culminated in the Osborne Judgement of
the highest Appeal Court, by which the Trade Unions were
prohibited from applying any of their funds to political
activities and to the support of the Labour Party in particular. The refusal of the Liberal Government for four
whole years to remedy this gross miscarriage of justice
though conscious that it was not permanently defensible ;
and the unconcealed desire of the Liberal Party politicians

to put the Labour Party out of action as an independent political force, swung over to its side the great bulk of active Trade Unionists, including many, especially in Lancashire, who had hitherto counted to the Conservative Party. By 1913, in spite of a large number of injunctions restraining Trade Unions from affiliating, the Labour Party could count on a membership of nearly two millions, and this number has since steadily grown. The two General Elections of 1910, though dominated by other issues, left the Parliamentary Labour Party unshaken ; whilst the accession to the Party of the Miners' members raised its Parliamentary strength to forty-two. Payment of members was secured in 1911, and the Mines (Minimum Wage) Act in 1912, but not until 1913 could the Government be induced to pass into law the Trade Union Act, which once more permitted Trade Unions to engage in any lawful purposes that their members desired. This concession was, even then, made subject to any objecting member being enabled to withhold that part of his contribution applicable to political purposes—an illogical restriction, because it applied only to the dissentient's tiny fraction of money, and he was not empowered to prevent the majority of members from using the indivisible corporate power of the Union itself. This restriction, not put upon any other corporate body, was universally believed to have been imposed, in the assumed interest of the Liberal Party, with the object of crippling the political influence of Trade Unionism ; and is still bitterly resented.[1]

Whilst it was very largely the successive assaults on Trade Unionism itself that built up the Labour Party, the ultimate defeat of these assaults, the concession of Payment of Members, and the attainment of legal security by the Trade Union Act of 1913, did nothing to stay its progress.

---

[1] In some Unions outside influence, notably that of the railway companies, went to the expense of printing and distributing hundreds of thousands of forms by which dissentient members could claim exemption from the tiny " political " contribution ; and in the Amalgamated Society of Railway Servants, in particular, thousands of such claims were made. The number has now greatly diminished (1920).

At the same time, the injunctions of the years 1909–12, and the fear of litigation, together with a certain disillusionment with Parliamentary action among the rank and file, led to the gradual falling away of some Trade Unions, mostly of comparatively small membership. The very basis of the Labour Party, upon which alone it has proved possible to build up a successful political force—the combination, within a political federation, of Trade Unions having extensive membership and not very intense political energy, and Socialist societies of relatively scanty membership but overflowing with political talent and zeal—necessarily led to complications. It needed all the tact and patient persuasion of the leaders of both sections to convince the Socialists that their ideals and projects were not being sacrificed to the stolidity and the prejudices of the mass of Trade Unionists ; and at the same time to explain to the Trade Unionists how valuable was the aid of the knowledge, eloquence, and Parliamentary ability contributed by such Socialist representatives as Keir Hardie, Philip Snowden, J. Ramsay MacDonald, and W. C. Anderson. Moreover, the complications and difficulties of Parliamentary action in a House of Commons where the Government continuously possessed a solid majority ; the political necessity of supporting the Liberal Party Bills relating to the Budget and the House of Lords, and of not playing into the hands of a still more reactionary Front Opposition Bench, were not readily comprehended by the average workman. What the militants in the country failed to allow for was the impotence of a small Parliamentary section to secure the adoption of its own policy by a Parliamentary majority. But it is, we think, now admitted that it was a misfortune that the Parliamentary Labour Party of these years never managed to put before the country the large outlines of an alternative programme based on the Party's conception of a new social order, eliminating the capitalist profit-maker wherever possible, and giving free scope to communal and industrial Democracy—notably with regard to the administration of the railways and the mines, the prevention of Unemployment, and also the provision for the nation's non-effectives, which the Government dealt with so unsatisfactorily in the National Insurance Act of 1911. The failure of the Parliamentary Labour Party between 1910 and 1914 to strike the imagination of the Trade Union world led to a certain reaction against political action as such, and to a growing doubt among the active spirits as to the value of a Labour Party which did not succeed in taking vigorous independent action, either in Parliament or on the platform and in the press, along the lines of changing the existing order of society. A like failure to strike the imagination characterised *The Daily Citizen*—the organ which the Labour Party and the Trade Union Movement had established with such high hopes—and its inability to gain either intellectual influence or adequate circulation did not lighten the somewhat gloomy atmosphere of the Labour Party councils of 1913–14.[1] This reaction did not appreciably affect the numerical and financial strength of the Labour Party itself, as the relatively few withdrawals of Unions were outweighed by the steady increase in membership of the hundred principal Unions which remained faithful, by the accession

---

[1] *The Daily Citizen* was started by a separate limited company, in which the control was permanently secured to representatives of the Trade Unions and the Labour Party, on November 8, 1912. The total capital raised from the Trade Unions from first to last was approximately £200,000. This important journalistic venture, starting under good auspices, met with untoward circumstances. It was crippled by a legal decision that Trade Unions had no power to subscribe to its cost, or even to make investments in its shares (an inference from the Osborne Judgement, which was reversed by the Trade Union Act of 1913, subject to compliance with the conditions as to political expenditure). Before this set-back could be got over, the outbreak of war upset all financial calculations, and made the conduct of a newspaper increasingly onerous. The paper stopped on June 5, 1915, and the company was wound up, all creditors being paid in full, but the shareholders losing practically all that they had ventured. The failure was a serious blow to the Labour Party, which has been badly in want of a daily newspaper—a lack supplied in 1919 by the energetic and adventurous *Daily Herald*, which, under the direction of Mr. George Lansbury, has drawn to itself an unusual amount of talent, and now needs only whole-hearted support from the Trade Unions.

of other Unions, and by the continual increase in the number and strength of the affiliated Trades Councils and Local Labour Parties. But the reaction in Trade Union opinion weakened the influence of the members of the Parliamentary Party, alike in the House of Commons and in their own societies. A wave of " Labour Unrest," of " Syndicalism," of " rank and file movements " for a more aggressive Trade Unionism, of organisation by " shop stewards " in opposition to national executives, and of preference for " Direct Action " over Parliamentary procedure swept over British Trade Unionism, affecting especially the London building trades, the South Wales Miners, and the engineering and shipbuilding industry on the Clyde. The impetuous strikes in 1911–13 of the Railwaymen, the Coal-miners, the Transport Workers, and the London Building Trades, which we have already described, were influenced, partly, by this new spirit. The number of disputes reported to the Labour Department, which had sunk in 1908 to only 399, rose in 1911 to 903, and culminated in the latter half of 1913 and the first half of 1914 in the outbreak of something like a hundred and fifty strikes per month. British Trade Unionism was, in fact, in the summer of 1914, working up for an almost revolutionary outburst of gigantic industrial disputes, which could not have failed to be seriously embarrassing for the political organisation to which the movement had committed itself, when, in August 1914, war was declared, and all internal conflict had perforce to be suspended.

During the war (1914–18) the task of the Labour Party was one of exceptional difficulty. It had necessarily to support the Government in a struggle of which five-sixths of its Parliamentary representatives and probably nine-tenths of its aggregate membership approved. The very gravity of the national crisis compelled the Party to abstain from any action that would have weakened the country's defence. On the other hand, the three successive Administrations that held office during the war were all driven by their needs, as we have already described, to impose upon the wage-

earners cruel sacrifices, and to violate, not once but repeatedly, all that Organised Labour in Britain held dear. The
Party could not refrain, at whatever cost of misconstruction,
from withstanding unjustifiable demands by the Government ; [1] protesting against its successive breaches of faith
to the Trade Unions ; demanding the conditions in the
forthcoming Treaty of Peace that, as could be already
foreseen, would be necessary to protect the wage-earning
class ; standing up for the scandalously ill-used " conscientious objectors," and doing its best to secure, in the eventual
demobilisation and social reconstruction, the utmost possible
protection of the mass of the people against Unemployment
and " Profiteering." In all this the Labour Party earned
the respect of the most thoughtful Trade Unionists, but
necessarily exposed itself to a constant stream of newspaper
misrepresentation and abuse. Any opposition or resistance
to the official demands was inevitably misrepresented as,
and mistaken for, an almost treasonable " Pacifism " or
" Defeatism "—a misunderstanding of the attitude of the
Party to which colour was lent by the persistence and
eloquence with which the small Pacifist Minority within the

[1] It was, for instance, only the determined private resistance of the
Trade Unionist leaders of the Labour Party that compelled the Government to abandon its project of introducing several hundred thousand
Chinese labourers into Great Britain ; a project which, if carried out,
not only might have been calamitous in its effect upon the Standard of
Life of the British workman—not to mention other evil consequences—
but would almost certainly have also led to a Labour revolt against the
continuance of the war. In this connection may be noted the valuable
work done throughout the war, not in the interests of Trade Unionism
only, but in those of the wage-earning class, and of the community as a
whole, by the War Emergency Workers' National Committee (J. S.
Middleton, Honorary Secretary), a body which included representatives
not only of the Parliamentary Committee, Labour Party, and General
Federation, but also of the Co-operative Union, the National Union of
Teachers, and other organisations. The valuable though often unwelcome
assistance which this Committee gave to the Government by insisting on
the redress of grievances that officialdom would have ignored, and by its
working out of policy and persistence in agitation on such matters as
pensions, limitation of prices, food-rationing, rent restriction, and other
subjects, on which its publications had marked results, deserve the attention of the historian.

Party—a minority which, it must be said, included some of the most talented and active of its leading members in the House of Commons—used every opportunity publicly to denounce the Government's conduct in the war. But although the Pacifist Group in Parliament was strenuously supported in the country by the relatively small but extremely active constituent society of the Labour Party styled The Independent Labour Party—the very name helping the popular misunderstanding—the Trade Unionists, forming the vast majority of the Labour Party, remained, with extremely few exceptions, grimly determined at all costs to win the war.

If Organised Labour had been against the war, it is safe to say that the national effort could not have been maintained. The need for the formal association of the Labour Party with the Administration was recognised by Mr. Asquith in 1915, when he formed the first Coalition Cabinet, into which he invited the chairman of the Parliamentary Labour Party, Mr. Arthur Henderson (Friendly Society of Ironfounders), who became President of the Board of Education. Later on, in 1916, Mr. G. N. Barnes (Amalgamated Society of Engineers) was appointed to the new office of Minister of Pensions. When, in December 1916, Mr. Asquith resigned, and Mr. Lloyd George formed a new Coalition Government, Mr. Henderson entered the small War Cabinet that was then formed, with the nominal office of Paymaster-General; whilst Mr. Barnes continued Minister of Pensions, Mr. John Hodge (British Steel Smelters' Society) was appointed to the new office of Minister of Labour, and three other members of the Party (Mr. W. Brace, South Wales Miners; Mr. G. H. Roberts, Typographical Society; and Mr. James Parker, National Union of General Workers) received minor ministerial posts.[1]

Throughout the whole period of the war all the several

[1] Subsequently Mr. J. R. Clynes (National Union of General Workers) was appointed Parliamentary Secretary to the Minister of Food; and on Lord Rhondda's death he succeeded him as Minister of Food.

demands of the Government upon the organised workers, the abrogation of " Trade Union Conditions " in all industries working for war needs, the first and second Munitions of War Acts, the subversion of individual liberty by the successive orders under the Defence of the Realm Acts, the successive applications of the Military Service Acts, the imposition of what was practically Compulsory Arbitration to settle the rates of wages—were accepted, though only after serious protest, by large majorities at the various Conferences of the Labour Party, as well as by the various annual Trades Union Congresses,[1] in spite of the resistance of minorities, including more than " pacifists." The entry of Mr. Henderson into Mr. Asquith's first Coalition Government, and that of Mr. Barnes into Mr. Lloyd George's War Cabinet, together with the acceptance of ministerial office by other leading members of the Labour Party—though any such ministerial coalition was in flagrant violation of the very principles of its existence, and was strenuously combated on grounds of expediency by many of its members who loyally supported the war—equally received the endorsement of large majorities at the Party Conferences. From the beginning of the war to the end, the Labour Party, alike in all its corporate acts and by the individual efforts of its leading members (other than the minority already mentioned), stuck at nothing in its determination to help the Government to win the war.

More controversial were the persistent efforts made by the Labour Party to maintain its international relations with the Labour and Socialist Movements of Continental Europe. From the first it was seen to be important to get the representatives of the Trade Unions and Socialist organisations of the Allied Nations, and not merely their Governments, united in a declaration of the aims and the justification of a war that was everywhere outraging working-class idealism. Such a unanimity was success-

[1] See the printed reports of Labour Party Conferences and Trades Union Congresses, 1914-19.

fully achieved in February 1915 at a conference, held in London at the instance of the Labour Party, of delegates from the working-class organisations of France, Belgium, and Great Britain, with Russian representatives, then allied in arms against the Central Empires.[1] Later on, when a Minority Party had been formed among the German Socialists, and when the Austrian and Hungarian working-class Movements were also in revolt against the militarism of their Government, repeated efforts were made by the Labour Party to encourage this revolt, and for this purpose to obtain the necessary Government facilities for a meeting, in some neutral city, of the working-class " International," at which the Allied Case could be laid before the neutrals, and a basis found for united action with all the working-class elements in opposition to the dominant military Imperialism. After the Russian revolution of March 1917, the Petrograd Workmen's and Soldiers' Council actually issued an invitation for a working-class " International " at Stockholm ; and the participation of the British Labour Party in this International Congress, which was not then favoured by Mr. Henderson, received at one time no small support from the Prime Minister, Mr. Lloyd George. In the end the Government despatched Mr. Henderson on an official mission to Petrograd (incidentally empowering him, if he thought fit, to remain there as Ambassador at £8000 a year). Meanwhile the proposal for an International Congress had been modified, first into one for a purely consultative gathering, and then into one for a series of separate interviews between a committee of neutrals and the representatives of each of the belligerents in turn, with a view to discovering a possible basis for peace—a project to which Mr. Henderson, from what he learnt at Petrograd, was converted. A National Conference of the Labour Party in August 1917 approved of participation in such a Congress at Stockholm ; but the French and Italian Governments would not hear of it,

[1] *Report of the Inter-Allied Socialist and Labour Conference,* February 15, 1915.

and Mr. Lloyd George went back on his prior approval, absolutely declining to allow passports to be issued. Amid great excitement, and under circumstances of insult and indignity which created resentment among the British working class, Mr. Henderson felt obliged to tender his resignation of his place in the War Cabinet, in which he was succeeded by Mr. Barnes, who was getting more and more out of sympathy with the majority of the Party.[1] The Labour Party Executive, in alliance with the Parliamentary Committee of the Trades Union Congress, then applied itself to getting agreement among the Labour and Socialist Movements of the Allied Nations as to the lines on which —assuming an Allied victory—the terms of peace should be drawn, in order to avert as much as possible of the widespread misery which, it could be foreseen, must necessarily fall upon the wage-earning class. In this effort, in which Mr. Henderson displayed great tact and patience, he had the implicit sanction of the British Government, and, with some reluctance, also of the Governments of the other Allied Nations by whom the necessary passports were issued for an Inter-Allied Conference in London in August 1917, which was abortive ; for provisional discussions at Paris in February 1918 ; and for a second Inter-Allied Conference at the end of the same month in London, which resulted in a virtually unanimous agreement upon what should be the terms of peace,[2] on a basis already approved on December 28, 1917, by a Joint Conference of the Trades Union Congress and the Labour Party, and widely published all over the world. The terms thus agreed were, in fact, immediately adopted in outline in a public deliverance by Mr. Lloyd George as those on which Germany could have peace at any time ; and the same proposals were promptly made the basis of President Wilson's celebrated " Fourteen Points "

[1] Mr. Hodge succeeded to Mr. Barnes as Minister of Pensions, Mr. Roberts to Mr. Hodge as Minister of Labour, and Mr. G. J. Wardle (National Union of Railwaymen) to Mr. Roberts as Parliamentary Secretary of the Board of Trade.

[2] *Memorandum on War Aims* (Labour Party), February 1918.

on which eventually (but only after another ten months' costly war) the Armistice of November 11, 1918, was concluded. Profound was the disappointment, and bitter the resentment, of the greater part of the organised Labour Movement of Great Britain when it was revealed how seriously the diplomatists at the Paris Conference had departed from these terms in the Treaty of Peace which was imposed on the Central Empires.[1]

We have already attempted to sum up the effect of the Great War on the industrial status of Trade Unionism. It is more difficult to estimate its effect on the political organisation of the movement. The outbreak of the war had found the Labour Party, in the see-saw of Trade Union opinion to which we have elsewhere referred, suffering from an inevitable disillusionment among Trade Unionists as to the immediate potency of Parliamentary representation—a disillusionment manifested in the outbreak of rebellious

[1] It is difficult not to be struck with the greater breadth of vision, the higher idealism, and (as we venture to say) the larger statesmanship of the Labour Party in its projects and proposals for the resettlement of the world after the Great War, compared with those which the statesmen and diplomatists of the capitalist parties of Great Britain, France, Italy, and, as we grieve to say, also the United States, with the acquiescence of deliberately inflamed popular electorates, succeeded in embodying in the Treaty of Peace. Apart from the indefensible redistributions of political sovereignty, not essentially differing in spirit from those of the Congress of Vienna in 1814–15 (and probably less stable even than these), against which Labour opinion had strongly protested in advance, it is impossible not to regret the failure to incorporate in the Treaty the proposals, for which the Labour Party had secured the support of the organised working-class opinion of the world, for (i.) the universal abandonment of discriminatory fiscal barriers to international trade ; (ii.) the administration of Colonial possessions exclusively in the interest of the local inhabitants, and on the basis of equality of opportunity for traders of all nations ; (iii.) concerted international control of the exportable surplus of materials and food-stuffs of all the several countries, so as to mitigate, as far as possible, in the general world-shortage which the Labour Party foresaw, the inevitable widespread starvation in the most necessitous areas, whether enemy, allied, or neutral ; (iv.) deliberate Government action in each country for the prevention of unemployment, instead of letting it occur and then merely relieving the unemployed. In questions of foreign policy the Labour Party, inspired by its idealism, has shown itself at its best, instead of this department of politics being, as is often ignorantly assumed, altogether beyond its capacity.

strikes that characterised the years 1911–14. The achievements of the Labour Party in the House of Commons had fallen short of the eager hopes with which the new party had raised its standard on its triumphant entry in 1906. In 1914, it may be said, the Labour Party was at a dead point. The effect upon it of the Great War was to raise it in proportion to the height of the vastly greater issues with which it was compelled to deal. Amid the stress of war, and of the intensely controversial decisions which it had necessarily to take, the Labour Party revised its constitution, widened its aims, opened its ranks to the " workers by brain " as well as the workers by hand, and received the accession of many thousands of converts from the Liberal and Conservative Parties. It made great progress in its difficult task of superimposing, on an organisation based on national societies, the necessary complementary organisation of its affiliated membership by geographical constituencies. It equipped itself during the war, for the first time, with a far-reaching and well-considered programme not confined to distinctively " Labour " issues, but covering the whole field of home politics, and even extending to foreign relations.[1] The formulation of such a programme,

---

[1] The new constitution and enlarged programme which the Labour Party adopted at its Conferences of 1917–18, after six months' consideration and discussion by the constituent organisations, were little more than a ratification for general adoption of what had become the practice of particular districts. Thus, the more active Local Labour Parties, such as those of Woolwich and Blackburn, had long welcomed the adhesion of supporters who were not manual workers. The successive annual Conferences had passed resolutions which, taken together, amounted to a pretty complete programme of constructive legislation, wholly Collectivist in principle. Hence the deliberate and formal opening of the Party, through the Local Labour Parties, to " workers by brain " as well as " workers by hand "; and the explicit adoption, as a programme, of *Labour and the New Social Order* were not such innovations as the newspapers made out and as the public generally supposed. But they created a sensation, not only in the United Kingdom, but also in the United States and in the British Dominions ; and they led to a considerable accession of membership, largely from the professional and middle classes, which was steadily increased as the unsatisfactory character of the Treaty of Peace, the continued " militarism " of the Government, and the aggression of a " Protectionist ' capitalism became manifest.

from beginning to end essentially Socialist in character, and including alike ideals of social reconstruction and detailed reforms of immediate practicability, together with the whole-hearted adoption of this programme, after six months' consideration by the constituent societies and branches, was a notable achievement, which placed the British Labour Party ahead of those of other countries. Moreover, the formulation of a comprehensive social programme and of " terms of Peace," based on the principles for which the war had ostensibly been fought—principles which were certainly not carried in the Treaty of Peace—transformed the Labour Party from a group representing merely the class interests of the manual workers into a fully constituted political Party of national scope, ready to take over the government of the country and to conduct both home and foreign affairs on definite principles. Taken together with the intellectual bankruptcy of the Liberal Party and its apparent incapacity to formulate any positive policy, whether with regard to the redistribution of wealth within our own community or with regard to our attitude towards other races within or without the British Empire, the emergence of the Labour Party programme meant that the Party stood forth, in public opinion, as the inevitable alternative to the present Coalition Government when the time came for this to fall. The result was that, aided by the steady growth of Trade Unionism, the Party came near, between 1914 and 1919, to doubling its aggregate membership. When hostilities ceased, it insisted on resuming the complete independence of the other political parties, which it had, by joining the successive Coalition Governments, consented temporarily to forgo ; and such of its leaders as refused to withdraw from ministerial office [1] were unhesitatingly shed from the Party. Meanwhile, the extension of the franchise and redistribution of seats, which had been carried by general consent in the spring of 1918, turned out to raise the

---

[1] Messrs. Barnes, Roberts (who became Minister of Food), Parker, and Wardle.

electorate to nearly treble that of 1910, whilst the new constituencies proved to have been so adjusted as greatly to facilitate an increase in the number of miners' representatives. When the General Election came, in December 1918, though the Labour Party fought under great disadvantages and it was seen that most of the soldier electors would be unable to record their votes, it put no fewer than 361 Labour candidates in the field against Liberal and Conservative alike, contesting two-thirds of all the constituencies in Great Britain. In face of a " Lloyd George tide " of unprecedented strength these Labour candidates received nearly one-fourth of all the votes polled in the United Kingdom ; and though five-sixths of these numerous Labour candidatures were unsuccessful (including, unfortunately, most of its ablest Parliamentarians such as Messrs. Henderson,[1] MacDonald, Anderson, and Snowden), the Party increased its numerical strength in the House of Commons by 50 per cent, and, to the universal surprise, returned more than twice as many members as did the remnant of the Liberal Party adhering to Mr. Asquith—becoming, in fact, entitled to the position of " His Majesty's Opposition."

It can hardly be said that during the session of 1919 the Parliamentary Labour Party, considerably strengthened in numbers but weakened by the defeat of its ablest Parliamentarians, has, under the leadership of the Right Honourable W. Adamson (Scottish Miners), made as much of its opportunities as the Labour Party in the country expected and desired. The political organisation of the Trade Union world remains, indeed, very far from adequate to the achievement of its far-reaching aims. It is not merely that the average British Trade Unionist, unlike the German, the Danish, Swedish, or the Belgian, has learnt so little the duty of subordinating minor personal or local issues, and of voting with his Party with as much loyalty as he shows in striking with his fellow-unionists, that by no means all

---

[1] Mr. Henderson was re-elected to Parliament in 1919 at a bye-election, capturing a strong Conservative seat at Widnes (Lancashire).

the aggregate British Trade Union membership can steadfastly be relied on to vote for the Labour candidates. Nor is it only that the British Labour Party still fails to command the affiliation of as many Trade Unions as the Trades Union Congress, and that the great majority of the smaller and the local societies—less from dissent than out of apathy—remain aloof from both sides of the national organisation. The Trades Union Congress itself, after engendering, as independent organisations, first the General Federation of Trade Unions, and then the Labour Party, has not yet resigned itself to limiting its activities. The General Federation of Trade Unions may be said, indeed, to have now disappeared from the Trade Union world as an effective force in the determination of industrial or political policy. There remain three separate organisations of national scope : the Parliamentary Committee of the Trades Union Congress which it is now proposed to transform into a General Council, the Executive Committee of the Labour Party, and the members of the House of Commons who form the Parliamentary Labour Party. Unfortunately, between these three groups there has been some lack of mutual consultation, and an indefiniteness if not a confusion of policy which stands in the way of effective leadership.[1] This has prevented the bringing to bear upon the political field of the full force, now almost a moiety of the whole registered electorate of Great Britain, that the Trade Union world may (including the wives of Trade Unionist electors) fairly claim to include. Fundamentally, however, the shortcomings of the political organisation of the Trade Union world are to be ascribed to its failure, down to the present, to develop a staff of trained political officers at all equal to those of the Trade Union organisers and Trade Union negotiators in the industrial field. The Labour

---

[1] A " Joint Board "—from which the General Federation of Trade Unions was afterwards excluded—and, later on, joint meetings of the Parliamentary Committee of the Trades Union Congress and the Executive Committee of the Labour Party, did something to remove friction.

Party, which can as yet rely only on the quite inadequate contribution from its affiliated societies of no more than twopence per member annually, has, so far, not succeeded in obtaining and keeping the services, as Registration Officers and Election Agents, of anything like so extensive and so competent a staff as either of the other political parties ; and Labour Party candidatures are still run, occasionally with astonishing success, very largely upon that transient enthusiasm of the crowd upon which experienced electioneers wisely decline to rely for victory. What is, however, much more crippling to the Labour Party than the scanty funds with which its constituent societies supply it, and this insufficiency in the staff of trained election organisers, is the scarcity of trained Parliamentary representatives. Down to to-day the great bulk of Labour Members of Parliament have been drawn from the ranks of the salaried secretaries and other industrial officers of Trade Unions, who are nearly always not only men of competence in their own spheres, but also exceptionally good speakers for popular audiences, and, generally, in many respects above the average of middle-class candidates. But as Members of Parliament they have serious shortcomings. They can, to begin with, seldom devote the necessary time to their new duties. They usually find themselves compelled to strive to combine attendance at the House of Commons with the onerous industrial service of their societies. The Trade Unions have, as yet, only in a few cases realised the necessity of setting free from the constant burden of Trade Union work—as they might by promotion to some such consultative office as that of a salaried President —such of their officials as secure election to Parliament ; whilst these officers, unable to maintain themselves and their families in London on their Parliamentary allowance for expenses of £400 a year, and afraid lest the loss of their seats may presently leave them without incomes, dare not resign their Trade Union posts. The result is an imperfect and always uncertain attendance of the Labour Members at the House of Commons ; a fatal division and diversion of their attention ; and an inevitable failure on their part to discharge with the fullest efficiency the duties of their two offices. Equally destructive of Parliamentary efficiency is the omission of the Trade Union world to provide or secure any training in the duties of a Member of Parliament for those whom they select as candidates and whose election expenses they defray with unstinted liberality. The life-long training which these candidates have enjoyed as Branch and District Secretaries, as industrial organisers and nego-tiators, and as administrators of great Trade Unions, valuable as it is for Trade Union purposes, does not include, and indeed tends rather to exclude, the practical training in general politics, the working acquaintance with the British Con-stitution, the knowledge of how to use and how to control the adroit and well-equipped Civil Service, and the ability to translate both the half-articulate desires of the electorate to the House of Commons, and the advice of the political expert to the electorate, which, coupled with the general art of " Parliamentarianism," constitutes the equipment of the really efficient Member of the House of Commons. Add to this that the very training which the life of the successful Trade Union official has given him, his perpetual struggle to rise in his vocation in competitive rivalry, not with persons of opposite views but actually with personal acquaintances of the same craft and the same political opinions as himself, is, in itself, not a good preparation for the incessant mutual consultation and carefully planned " team-work " which contributes so much to the effective-ness of a minority party in the House of Commons. Add to this again the personal rivalries among members of the Party, the jealousies from which no party is free, and the almost complete lack of opportunity for the constant social intercourse with each other away from the House of Commons that the members of the other parties enjoy—and it will be realised how seriously the Parliamentary Labour Party is handicapped by being made up, as it is at present, almost entirely of men who are compelled also to serve as Trade Union officials. Already, however, there are signs of improvement. Some Trade Unions, whilst willing to spend large sums on Parliamentary candidatures, are demurring to their salaried officials going to Westminster. The Workers' Educational Association, Ruskin College, and other educational agencies are doing much to provide a wider political training than Trade Unionists have heretofore enjoyed. And as the Parliamentary Labour Party, claiming to-day to represent, not the Trade Unionists only, but the whole community of " workers by hand or by brain," expands from sixty to four or six times that number—as it must before it can be confronted with the task of forming a Government—it will necessarily come to include an ever-increasing proportion of members drawn from other than Trade Union ranks ; whilst even its Trade Union members cannot fail to acquire more of that habit of mutual intercourse and that art of combined action which, coupled with the Parliamentary skill and capacity for public administration of those who rise to leadership, is the necessary basis of successful party achievement.

Meanwhile, the political organisation of the Trade Union Movement, and the enlargement of its ideas on Communal and Industrial Democracy, have been manifesting themselves also in the important sphere of Local Government. After the " Labour " successes at the elections of Local Authorities, which continued for a whole decade from 1892, and placed over a thousand Trade Unionists and Socialists on Parish, District, Borough and County Councils, there ensued another decade in which, in the majority of districts, this active participation in local elections was impaired by the diversion of interest, both to Parliament and to industrial organisation. From 1914 to 1919 local elections were suspended. On their resumption in the latter year, they were energetically contested by the Labour Party, all over Great Britain, on its new and definitely Socialist programme, with the unexpected result that, up and down the country, the Labour candidates frequently swept the board, polling in the aggregate a very substantial proportion of the votes, electing altogether several thousand Councillors (five or six hundred in Scotland alone), and being returned in actual majorities in nearly half the Metropolitan Boroughs, several important Counties and Municipalities, and many Urban Districts and Parishes.

It must be apparent that any history of Trade Unionism that breaks off at the beginning of 1920 halts, not at the end of an epoch, but—we may almost say—at the opening of a new chapter. British Trade Unionism, at a moment when it is, both industrially and politically, stronger than ever before, is seething with new ideas and far-reaching aspirations. At the same time, its most recent advances in status and power are by no means yet accepted by what remains the governing class; its political and industrial position is still precarious, and within a very brief space it may again find itself fighting against a frontal attack upon its very existence. And in face of the common enemy— now united as an autocratic capitalism—Industrial Democracy is uncertain of itself, and almost blindly groping after a precise adjustment of powers and functions between Associations of Producers and Associations of Consumers.

Let us elaborate these points in detail. One result of the Great War has been, if not the actual enthronement of Democracy, a tremendous shifting of authority to the mass of the people. Of this shifting of the basis of power the advance in the status of Trade Unionism and the advent,

In British politics, of the Labour Party, are but preliminary manifestations. As yet the mass of the people, to whom power is passing, have made but little effective use of their opportunities. At least seven-eighths of the nation's accumulated wealth, and with it nearly all the effective authority, is still in the hands of one-eighth of the population ; and the seven-eighths of the people find themselves in consequence still restricted, as regards the means of life, to less than half of that national income which is exclusively the product of those who labour by hand or by brain. The " leisure class "—the men and women who live by owning and not by working, a class increasing in actual numbers, if not relatively to the workers—seem to the great mass of working people to be showing themselves, if possible, more frivolous and more insolent in their irresponsible consumption, by themselves and their families, of the relatively enormous share that they are able to take from the national income. It is coming to be more and more felt that the continued existence of this class involves a quite unwarranted burden upon their fellow-citizens working by hand or by brain. Very naturally there is widespread discontent, and the emergence of all sorts of exasperated criticisms and extravagant schemes.

The truth is, of course, that Democracy, whether political or industrial, is still in its infancy. The common run of men and women, who have only just been enfranchised politically, and are even yet only partially organised industrially, are as yet unable to make full use of Democratic institutions. The majority of them cannot be induced, in the economic pressure to which Capitalism subjects them, to take the trouble or give the continuous thought involved in any effective participation in public affairs. The result is that such Democratic institutions as we possess are, of necessity, still inefficiently managed ; and neither the citizen-consumers nor the Trade Unionist producers find themselves exercising much effective control over their own lives. The active-minded minority sees itself submerged

2 A

by the " apathetic mass " ; the individual feels enslaved by the " machine." The complaint of the " rank and file "— using that term to mean, not any " extremist " minority, but merely the majority, the " common run of men "— comes to no more than that they do not find themselves obtaining the results in their daily lives which they expected, and which they were, as they understood, promised. This, we think, is the explanation of the perpetual " see-saw " within the Labour Movement, decade after decade, between an infatuation for industrial or " direct " action and an equal infatuation for political or Parliamentary and Municipal action—each, unfortunately, to the temporary neglect of the other. Or to state the Democratic problem in a more fundamental form, the see-saw is between the aspiration to vest the control over the instruments of production in Democracies of Producers, and the alternating belief that this control can best be vested in Democracies of Consumers. But it is abundantly clear, alike from history and economic analysis, that in any genuine Democracy both forms of organisation are indispensably required. In the modern State every person throughout his whole life consumes a great variety of commodities and services which he cannot produce ; whilst men and women, occupied in production, habitually produce a single commodity or service for other persons to consume. Their interests and desires as producers, and as producers of a single commodity or service, are not, and can never be, identical with the interests and desires of these same people as consumers of many different commodities and services—just as their interests and desires as citizens of a community, or as members of a race which they wish to continue in independent existence, are not necessarily identical with those of which they are conscious either as producers or as consumers.

It is, in fact, now realised that Democratic organisation involves the acceptance, not of a single basis—that of the undifferentiated human being—but of various separate and distinct bases : man as a producer ; man as a consumer ;

man as a citizen concerned with the continued existence and independence of his race or community ; possibly also other bases, such as man as a scientist or man as a religious believer. What is wrong in each successive generation is the intolerant fanaticism of the enthusiasts which leads them to insist on any one form of this multiplex Democracy to the exclusion of the other forms. We see to-day uppermost a revival of faith in Associations of Producers, as being, in an industrial community, the form of Democratic organisation most important to the working people. To some one-sided minds, as was inevitable, the all-embracing Association of Producers seems the only form that Democratic organisation can validly take. Interesting to the historian is the intellectual connection of this revival with the previous manifestations, in the Trade Union Movement, of the idea of " Co-operative Production," whether in the revolutionary Owenism of 1830–34, the Christian Socialism of 1848–52, or the experiments of particular Unions in 1872. As we have explained, the Trade Union, being essentially an Association of Producers, has never quite lost the idea that, so far as industry is concerned, this form of association, and no other, is Democracy. But the new form in which the faith in Associations of Producers is now expressing itself is concerned less with the ownership of the instruments of production (it being to-day commonly taken for granted that this must be vested in the community as a whole) than with the management of industry. According to the most thoroughgoing advocates of this creed, the management of each industry should be placed, not separately in the hands of those engaged in each establishment, any more than in the hands of private capitalist employers, but in the hands of the whole body of persons throughout the community who are actually co-operating in the work of the industry, whether by hand or by brain ; this management being shared, by Workshop or Pit Committees, District Councils and National Boards, among all these " workers."

This conception seems to us too one-sided to be adopted

in its entirety, or to be successful if it were so adopted. We venture to give, necessarily in a cursory and generalised form, the results of our own investigations into the management of industries and services by Democracies of Producers and Democracies of Consumers respectively. In so far as we may draw any valid inferences from previous experiments of different kinds, we must note that the record of the successive attempts, in modern industry, to place the entire management of industrial undertakings in the hands of Associations of Producers has been one of failure. In marked contrast, the opposite form of Democracy, in which the management has been placed in the hands of Associations of Consumers, has achieved a large and constantly increasing measure of success. We do not refer merely to the ever-growing development throughout the civilised world, in certain extensive fields of industrial operation, of Municipal and National Government, though from this some valuable lessons may be learnt. Even more instructive is the continuous and ever-widening success, in the importing, manufacturing, and distributing of household supplies, of the voluntary Associations of Consumers known as the Co-operative Movement, which is almost entirely made up of the same class of men and women—often, indeed, of the very same individuals—as we find in the abortive " self-governing workshops " and in the Trade Union Movement. Why, for instance, is it possible for the manual workers, organised as consumers, to carry on successfully the most extensive establishments for the milling of flour, the baking of bread, the making of boots and shoes, and the weaving of cloth, when repeated attempts to conduct such establishments by the same kind of members organised as Associations of Producers have not succeeded ? [1]

[1] For the successive experiments in Co-operative Production by Associations of Producers the student is referred to *The Co-operative Movement in Great Britain*, by Beatrice Potter (Mrs. Sidney Webb) (1891) ; *Co-operative Production*, by Benjamin Jones (1894) ; and, for a more recent survey, the supplement to *The New Statesman* of February 14, 1914, entitled "Co-operative Production and Profit Sharing."

The Democracy of Associations of Consumers, whatever its shortcomings and defects, has, we suggest, the great advantage of being demonstrably practicable. The job can be done. It has also the further merit that it solves the problem presented by what the economists call the Law of Rent. It does not leave to any individual or group of individuals the appropriation and enjoyment of those advantages of superior sites and soils, and other differential factors in production, which should be, economically and ethically, taken only by the community as a whole. Moreover, management by Associations of Consumers, whether National, Municipal, or Co-operative, gives one practical solution to the problem of fixing prices without competition, by enabling every producer to be paid at his own full Standard Rate, and distributing the various products at prices just over cost, the whole eventual surplus being returned to the purchasers in a rebate or discount on purchases, called " dividend " ; or otherwise appropriated for the benefit and by direction of the consumers themselves. Hence there is no danger of private monopoly ; no opportunity for particular groups of producers to make corners in raw materials ; to get monopoly prices for commodities in times of scarcity, or to resist legitimate improvements in machinery or processes merely because these would interfere with the vested interests of the persons owning particular instruments of production or possessing a particular kind of skill. In short, the control of industries and services by Democracies of Consumers realises the Socialist principle of production for use and not for exchange, with all its manifold advantages. The most significant of these superiorities of Production for Use over Production for Exchange is its inevitable effect on the structure and working of Democracy. Seeing that the larger the output the smaller the burden of overhead charges—or, to put it in another way, the greater the membership the more advantageous the enterprise— Associations of Consumers are not tempted to close their ranks. This kind of Democracy automatically remains always open to new-comers. On the other hand, Associations of Producers, whether capitalists, technicians or manual workers, exactly because they turn out commodities and services not for their own use, but for exchange, are perpetually impelled to limit their numbers, so as to get, for the existing membership, the highest possible remuneration. This kind of Democracy is, therefore, instinctively exclusive, tending always to become, within the community, a privileged body. All this amounts to a solid reason in favour of " nationalisation," " municipalisation," and the consumers' Co-operative Movement, which is reflected in the continuous and actually accelerating extension of all of them, not in one country only, but throughout the civilised world.[1]

But the Democracy based on Associations of Consumers, whether in the National Government, the Municipality, or the Co-operative Society, reveals certain shortcomings and defects, some transient and resulting only from the existing Capitalism, and others needing the remedy of a complementary Democracy of Producers. So long as we have a society characterised by gross inequalities of income, it is inevitable that the conduct of industries and services by Associations of Consumers should be even more advantageous to the rich than to the poor, and of little or no use to those who are destitute. The same trail of a Capitalist environment affects also the conditions of employment. The Co-operative Society, the Municipality or the Government Department cannot practically depart far from the normal conditions of the rest of the community ; and thus avails little to raise the condition of the manual working class. If, however, the Associations of Consumers were co-extensive with the community, they would themselves fix the standard. But there is a more fundamental criticism. The Democracy

---

[1] See *Towards Social Democracy ?* by Sidney Webb (1916) ; and for recent surveys, the supplements to *The New Statesman* of May 30, 1914, and May 8, 1915, entitled, respectively, " The Co-operative Movement " and " State and Municipal Enterprise."

of Consumers, in Co-operative Society, Municipality or State—however wide may be the franchise, however effective may be the Parliamentary machinery, and however much the elected executive is brought under constituency control—has the outstanding defect to the manual-working producer that, so far as his own working life is concerned, he does not feel it to be Democracy at all ! The management, it is complained, is always " government from above." It is exactly for this reason that in the evolution of British Democracy the conduct of industries and services by Associations of Consumers—whether in the voluntary Co-operative Society or in the geographically organised Municipality or State—has had, for a correlative, the organisation of Associations of Producers, whether Professional Societies or Trade Unions. Their first object was merely to maintain and improve their members' Standard of Life. Without the enforcement of a Standard Rate and protection against personal tyranny, government by Associations of Consumers is apt to develop many of the evils of the " sweating " characteristic of unrestrained capitalism. It is not now denied, even by the economists, that Trade Unionism, in its establishment of the Doctrine of the Common Rule, and the elaboration of this into the Standard Rate, the Normal Day, and the Policy of the National Minimum, has to its credit during the past three-quarters of a century no small measure of success, with more triumphs easily within view. Trade Unionism among the manual workers, like Professional Association among the brain-workers,[1] has emphatically justified itself by its achievements.

But Trade Unionism, though it has gone far to protect the worker from tyranny, has not, as yet, gained for him any

[1] For a recent survey of Professional Association in England and Wales—the only general study of it known to us—see the supplements to the *New Statesman* of September 25 and October 2, 1915 (" English Teachers and their Professional Associations "), and April 21 and 28, 1917 (" Professional Associations "). The student will note the distinction between two types of associations among professional brain-workers, one having essentially Trade Union purposes, the other (which we distinguish as the Scientific Society) concerned only for the increase of knowledge.

positive participation in industrial management.   To this
extent the complaints of the objectors among the manual-
working class are justified.   In the perpetual see-saw of
opinion in the Labour world the movement towards Parliamentary action and in favour of what we may call Communal Socialism became, at one time, almost an infatuation,
in that its most enthusiastic advocates thought that it would,
by itself, solve all problems.   A reaction was inevitable.
The danger is that this reaction may itself take on the
character of an infatuation—this time in favour of the
universal domination of Associations of Producers, and the
" Direct Action " to which they are prone—against which,
in the perpetual see-saw, there will come, in its turn, a
contrary reaction, in the course of which Trade Unionism
itself may suffer.

This is not to say that the legitimate and desirable movement, specially characteristic of the present century, for
increased direct participation in "management" of the
Associations of Producers—whether of Professional Societies
or of Trade Unions, of doctors and teachers, or of miners and
railwaymen—has been, in this or any other country, anything like exhausted.   In our view, in fact, it is along these
lines that the next developments are to be expected.   But,
unless we are mistaken in our analysis, this does not mean
that the Trade Unions or Professional Societies will take
over the entire management of their industries or services,
for which, in our opinion, no Association of Producers can
be fitted.[1] Democracies of Producers, like Democracies of
Consumers, have their peculiar defects, and develop certain
characteristic toxins from the very intensity of the interests
that they represent.   The chief of these defects is the
corporate exclusiveness and corporate selfishness habitually
developed by associations based on the common interest of
a particular section of workers, as against other sections of

---

[1] We add as an Appendix an extract from the concluding chapter of
our *Industrial Democracy*, published in 1897, in which we dealt with this
point.

workers on the one hand, and against the whole body of consumers and citizens on the other. When Democracies of Producers own the instruments of production, or even secure a monopoly of the service to be rendered, they have always tended in the past to close their ranks, to stereotype their processes and faculties, to exclude outsiders and to ban heterodoxy. We see this tendency at work alike in the ancient and modern world, in the castes of India and the Gilds of China, in the mediaeval Craft Gilds as well as in the modern Trade Unions and Professional Associations. So long as the Trade Union is an organ of revolt against the Capitalist System—so long as the manual workers are fighting a common enemy in the private owner of land and capital—this corporate selfishness is held in check ; though the frequency of demarcation disputes, even in the Trade Union Movement of to-day, gives some indication of what might happen if the Trade Union became an organ of government. We see no way of securing the community of consumers and citizens against this spirit of corporate exclusiveness, and against the inherent objection of an existing generation of producers to new methods of working unfamiliar to them, otherwise than placing the supreme control in the Democracies of Consumers and citizens. There is a further and more subtle defect in Democracies of Producers, the very mention of which may perhaps be resented by those Industrial Unionists who seek to curb the " corporateness " of National Gilds by the " self-government " of the workshop. The experience of self-governing workshops shows that the relationship between the indispensable director or manager (who must, like the conductor of an orchestra, decide the tune and set the time) and the workers whom he directs becomes hopelessly untenable if this director or manager is elected or dismissible by the very persons to whom he gives orders. Over and over again, in the records of the almost innumerable self-governing workshops that have been established in Great Britain or on the Continent, we find their failure intimately

2 A 2

connected with the impracticable position of a manager directing the workers during the day, and being reprimanded or altogether superseded by a committee meeting of these same workers in the evening ! Finally, there is the difficult question of the price to be put on the article when it passes to the consumer. Normally the price of a commodity must cover the cost of production, and this cost is, in the main, determined by the character of the machinery and process employed. Hence, if the organised workers are given the power to decide not only the number and qualifications of the persons to be employed but also the machinery and process to be used, they will, in fact, determine the price to be charged to the consumer—not always to the consumer's advantage, or consistently with the interests of other sections of workers.[1]

To sum up, we expect to see the supreme authority in each industry or service vested, not in the workers as such, but in the community as a whole. Any National Board may well include representatives of the producers of the particular product or service, and also of its consumers, but they must be reinforced by the presence of represent-

---

[1] We do not discuss here all the difficulties inherent in the government of a large and populous community — such, for instance, as that of combining a large measure of local autonomy (which is what many people mean by freedom) with the necessary unity of national policy and central control (without which there would be gross inequality, internecine strife, and chaos). This difficulty has to be faced alike by Industrial Unionists, Gild Socialists, and the advocates of Democracy based on geographical constituencies. Nor have we mentioned the problems, in which the Trade Unions have their own wealth of experience, as to the relationship between elected representatives and their constituents ; between representative assemblies and executive committees ; and between executive committees and the official staff. These problems and difficulties (on which we have written in our *Industrial Democracy*) are common to all democratic systems of administration, whether based on constituencies of producers, consumers, or citizens. It seems to us that constituencies of producers present special difficulties of their own, such as (i.) that of defining the boundaries between industries or services, and (ii.) the problem, within an industry or a service, of. how to provide for the representation of. numerically unequal distinct sections, groups, or grades, each with its own *technique*. The further we go in Democracy the more complicated it becomes, and the greater the need for knowledge.

atives of the community organised as citizens, interested in the future as well as the present prosperity of the community. The management of industry, a complex function of many kinds and grades, will, as we see it, not be the sole sphere of either the one or the other set of partners, but is clearly destined to be distributed between them—the actual direction and decision being shared between the representatives of the Trade Union or Professional Society on the one hand, and those of the community in Co-operative Society, Municipality, or National Government on the other. And this recognition of the essential partnership in management between Associations of Producers and that Association of Consumers which is the community in one or other form, will, we suggest, take different shapes in different industries and services, in different countries, and at different periods ; and, as we must add, will necessarily take time and thought to work out in detail. One thing is clear. There will be a steadily increasing recognition of a fundamental change in the status both of the directors and managers of industry (who are now usually either themselves capitalists, or hired for the service of capitalist interests), and of the technicians and manual workers. The directors and managers of industry, however they may be selected and paid, will become increasingly the officers of the community, serving not their own but the whole community's interests. The technicians and manual workers will become ever less and less the personal servants of the directors and managers ; and will be more and more enrolled, like them, in the service, not of any private employer, but of the community itself, whether the form be that of State or Municipality or Co-operative Society, or any combination or variant of these. To use the expression of the present General Secretary of the Miners' Federation (Frank Hodges), manager, technician, and manual worker alike will become parties to a " social " as distinguished from a commercial contract. All alike, indeed, whatever may be the exact form of ownership of the instruments of production, will, so far as function is concerned, become increasingly partners in the performance of a common public service.

We see in this evolution a great future for the Trade Unions, if they will, in organisation and personal equipment, rise to the height of their enlarged function. They will need, by amalgamation or federation, and by affording facilities for easy admission and for a simple transfer of membership, to make themselves much more nearly than at present co-extensive with their several industries. They will have to make special provision in their constitutions to secure an effective representation, on their own executive and legislative councils, of distinct crafts, grades, or specialisations, which must always form small minorities of the whole body. They will find it necessary to make the local organisation of their members, in branch or district, much more coincident than at present with their members' several places of employment, so as to approximate to making identical the workshop and the branch. There would seem to be a great development opening up for the Works Committees and the " Shop Stewards," brought effectively into organic relation with the nationally settled industrial policy. At any rate, in industries already passing under the control of Associations of Consumers, whether by nationalisation or municipalisation, or by the spread of consumers' co-operation, there will be great scope for District Councils and National Boards, as well as for Advisory and Research Committees representative of different specialities, in which managers and foremen, technicians and operatives, will jointly supersede the capitalist Board of Directors. But the management of each industry is very far from being the whole of the task. In Parliament itself, and on Municipal Councils, the World of Labour, by hand or by brain, will need to give a continuous and an equal backing to its own political party, in order to see to it that it has its own representatives—specialised and trained for this supreme political function—not by ones and twos, but in force ; gradually coming, in fact, to predominate over the representatives of the surviving capitalist and landlord parties. Trade Unionists, in the mass, will not only have to continue and extend the loyalty and self-devotion which have always been characteristic of successful Trade Unionism, but also to acquire a more comprehensive understanding of the working of democratic institutions, a more accurate appreciation of the imperative necessity of combining both the leading types of democratic self-government—on the one hand the self-government based on the common needs of the whole population divided into geographical constituencies, and on the other the self-government springing from the special requirements of men and women bound together by the fellowship of a common task and a common technique. The Trade Unions and Professional Societies, if they are increasingly to participate in the government of their industries and services, will in particular have to provide themselves with a greater number of whole-time specialist representatives, better paid and more considerately treated than at present, and supplied with increased opportunities for education and training.

We end on a note of warning. The object and purpose of the workers, organised vocationally in Trade Unions and Professional Associations, and politically in the Labour Party, is no mere increase of wages or reduction of hours.[1] It comprises nothing less than a reconstruction of society, by the elimination, from the nation's industries and services, of the Capitalist Profitmaker, and the consequent shrinking up of the class of functionless persons who live merely by

---

[1] This is well put by an American economist. "The Trade Union programme, or rather the Trade Union programmes, for each Trade Union has a programme of its own, is not the unrelated economic demands and methods which it is usually conceived to be, but it is a closely integrated social philosophy and plan of action. In the case of most Union types the programme centres indeed about economic demands and methods, but it rests on the broad foundation of the conception of right, of rights, and of general theory peculiar to the workers ; and it fans out to reflect all the economic, ethical, juridical, and social hopes and fears, aims, attitudes, and aspirations of the group. It expresses the workers' social theory and the rules of the game to which they are committed, not only in industry but in social affairs generally. It is the organised workers' conceptual world " (*Trade Unionism in the United States*, by R. F. Hoxie, p. 280).

owning. Profit-making as a pursuit, with its sanctification of the motive of pecuniary self-interest, is the demon that has to be exorcised. The journey of the Labour Party towards its goal must necessarily be a long and arduous one. In the painful " Pilgrim's Progress " of Democracy the workers will be perpetually tempted into by-paths that lead only to the Slough of Despond. It is not so much the enticing away of individuals in the open pursuit of wealth that is to be feared, as the temptation of particular Trade Unions, or particular sections of the workers, to enter into alliances with Associations of Capitalist Employers for the exploitation of the consumer. " Co-partnership," or profit-sharing with individual capitalists, has been seen through and rejected. But the " co-partnership " of Trade Unions with Associations of Capitalists—whether as a development of " Whitley Councils " or otherwise— which far-sighted capitalists will presently offer in specious forms (with a view, particularly, to Protective Customs Tariffs and other devices for maintaining unnecessarily high prices, or to governmental favours and remissions of taxation) is, we fear, hankered after by some Trade Union leaders, and might be made seductive to particular grades or sections of workers. Any such policy, however plausible, would in our judgement be a disastrous under-mining of the solidarity of the whole working class, and a formidable obstacle to any genuine Democratic Control of Industry, as well as to any general progress in personal freedom and in the more equal sharing of the National Product.

APPENDICES

APPENDIX I

In Dublin the Trade Union descent from the Gilds is embodied
in the printed documents of the Unions themselves, and is
commonly assumed to be confirmed by their possession of the
Gild charters. The Trade Union banners not only, in many
cases, bear the same arms as the old Gilds, but often also the
date of their incorporation. Thus, the old society of " regular "
carpenters (now a branch of the Amalgamated) claims to date
from 1490; the " Regular Operative House-painters' Trade
Union " connects itself with the Guild of St. Luke, 1670; and
the local unions of bricklayers and plasterers assume the date
of the incorporation of the Bricklayers' and Plasterers' Company
by Charles II. (1670). The box of the Dublin Bricklayers'
Society does, in fact, contain a parchment which purports to
be the original charter of the latter Company. How this document, given to the exclusively Protestant incorporation of
working masters, which was abolished by statute in 1840, came
into the possession of what has always been a mainly Roman
Catholic body of wage-earners, dating certainly from 1830, is
not clear. The parchment, which is bereft of its seal and bears
on the back, in the handwriting of a lawyer's clerk, the words
" Bricklayers, 28th June, 1843," was probably thrown aside as
worthless after the dissolution of the Company.

A search among contemporary pamphlets brought to light
an interesting episode in the history of the Dublin building
trades. It appears that, after the dissolution of the Company,
Benjamin Pemberton, who had been Master, and who was
evidently a man of energy and ability, attempted to form an

alliance between the then powerful journeymen bricklayers' and plasterers' societies and the master bricklayers and plasterers, in order to resist the common enemy, the " foreign contractor." This had long been a favourite project of Pemberton's. Already in 1812 he had urged the rapidly decaying Company to resist the uprising of " builders," and to admit Roman Catholic craftsmen. But the Company, which then included scarcely a dozen practising master bricklayers or plasterers, took no action. In 1832 Pemberton turned to the men, and vainly proposed to the " Trades Political Union," a kind of Trades Council, that they should take common action against " the contract system." At last, in 1846, six years after the abolition of the Company, he seems to have succeeded in forming some kind of alliance. The journeymen bricklayers and plasterers were induced to accept, from himself and his associates, formal certificates of proficiency. Several of these certificates, signed by Pemberton and other employers, are in the possession of the older workmen, but no one could explain to us their use. The alliance probably rested on some promise of preference for employment on the one part, and refusal to work for a contractor on the other. This close connection between a leading member of the Company and the Trade Unionists may perhaps account for the old charter, then become waste paper, finding its way into the Trade Union chest.

Particulars of Pemberton's action will be found in the pamphlet entitled *An Address of the Bricklayers and Plasterers to the Tradesmen of the City of Dublin on the necessity of their co-operating for the attainment of their corporate rights and privileges*, by Benjamin Pemberton (Dublin, 1833, 36 pages), preserved in Vol. 1567 of the *Haliday Tracts* in the Royal Irish Academy. In no other case, either in Dublin or elsewhere, have we found a Trade Union in possession of any Gild documents or relics.

The absolute impossibility of any passage of the Dublin Companies into the local Trade Unions will be apparent when we remember that the bulk of the wage-earning population of the city are, and have always been, Roman Catholics. The Dublin Companies were, to the last, rigidly confined to Episcopalian Protestants. Even after the barriers had been nominally removed by the Catholic Emancipation in 1829, the Companies, then shrunk up into little cliques of middle-class capitalists, with little or no connection with the trades, steadfastly refused to admit any Roman Catholics to membership. A few well-to-do Roman Catholics forced themselves in between 1829 and 1838 by mandamus. But when inquiry was made in 1838 by the Commissioners appointed under the Municipal Corporations Act, only half a dozen Roman Catholics were members, and the Companies were found to be composed, in the main, of capitalists and professional men. There is no evidence that even one wage-earner was in their ranks. Long before this time the Trade Unions of Dublin had obtained an unenviable notoriety. Already, in 1824, the Chief Constable of Dublin testified to the complete organisation of the operatives in illegal associations. In 1838 O'Connell made his celebrated attack upon them in the House of Commons, which led to a Select Committee. In short, whilst the Dublin Companies were, until their abolition by the Act of 1840, in much the same condition as those of London, with the added fact of religious exclusiveness, the Dublin Trade Unions were long before that date at the height of their power.

The adoption by the Dublin Trade Unions of the arms, mottoes, saints, and dates of origin of the old Dublin Gilds is more interesting as a trait of Irish character than as any proof of historic continuity. Thus, in their rules of 1883, the brick-layers content themselves with repeating the original preface common to the Trade Societies which were formed in the beginning of this century, to the effect that " the journeyman bricklayers of the City of Dublin have imposed on themselves the adoption of the following laudable scheme of raising a Fund for friendly society purposes." A card of membership, dated 1830, bears no reference to the Gild or Company of Bricklayers and Plasterers from whom descent is now claimed. The rules of 1883 are entitled those of the " incorporated " brick or stone layers' association, and in the edition of 1888 this had developed into the " Ancient Gild of Saint Bartholomew." Finally, the coat of arms of the old company with the date of its incorporation (" A.D. 1670 ") appear on the new banner of the society. Similarly, the old local society of " Regular Carpenters," which was well known as a Trade Union in 1824, and was engaged in a strike in 1833 (seven years before the abolition of the " Company of Carpenters, Millers, Masons, and Tylers, or Gild of the fraternity of the Blessed Virgin Mary, of the house of St. Thomas the Martyr," established by Henry VIII. in 1532), adopted for the first time, in its rules of 1881, the coat of arms and motto of the Gild, but retained its own title of " The United Brothers of St. Joseph." The card of membership, printed in 1887, boldly gives the date of establishment as 1458, whilst other printed matter places it at 1490. The Dublin painters now inscribe 1670 on their new banner, but the earliest traditions of their members date only from 1820. In short, the Irish Trade Unionist, with his genuine love for the picturesque, and his reverence for historical association, has steadily " annexed " antiquity, and has embraced every opportunity for transferring the origin of his society a few generations further back.

APPENDIX II

RULES AND REGULATIONS OF THE GRAND NATIONAL CONSOLIDATED TRADES UNION OF GREAT BRITAIN AND IRELAND, INSTITUTED FOR THE PURPOSE OF THE MORE EFFECTUALLY ENABLING THE WORKING CLASSES TO SECURE, PROTECT, AND ESTABLISH THE RIGHTS OF INDUSTRY (1834). (Goldsmiths' Library, University of London.)

I. Each Trade in this Consolidated Union shall have its Grand Lodge in that town or city most eligible for it ; such Grand Lodge to be governed internally by a Grand Master, Deputy Grand Master, and Grand Secretary, and a Committee of Management.

II. Each Grand Lodge shall have its District Lodges, in any number, to be designated or named after the town or city in which the District Lodge is founded.

III. Each Grand Lodge shall be considered the head of its own particular trade, and to have certain exclusive powers accordingly ; but in all other respects the Grand Lodges are to answer the same ends as the District Lodges.

IV. Each District Lodge shall embrace within itself all operatives of the same trade, living in smaller towns or villages adjacent to it ; and shall be governed internally by a President, Vice-President, Secretary, and a Committee of Management.

V. Each District Lodge shall have (if necessary) its Branch Lodge or Lodges, numbered in rotation ; such Branch Lodges to be under the control of the District Lodge from which they sprung.

VI. An unlimited number of the above described Lodges shall form and constitute the Grand National Consolidated Trades Union of Great Britain and Ireland.

VII. Each District shall have its Central Committee, composed of a Deputy, or Deputies, from every District Lodge of the different trades in the district; such Central Committee shall meet once in every week to superintend and watch over the interests of the Consolidated Union in that District, transmitting a report of the same, monthly, to the Executive Council in London, together with any suggestions of improvements they may think proper.

VIII. The General government of the G.N.C.T.U. shall be vested in a Grand Council of Delegates from each of the Central Committees of all the Districts in the C.U., to be holden every six months, at such places as shall be decided upon at the preceding Council; the next Meeting of the Grand Council of the C.U. to be held on the first day of September 1834, and to continue its sitting so long as may be requisite.

IX. During the recess of the Grand Council of Delegates, the Government of the C.U. shall be vested in an Executive Council of Five; which Executive will in future be chosen at the Grand Delegate Council aforesaid.

X. All dispensations or grants for the formation of new Lodges shall come from the Grand Lodge of each particular trade, or from the Executive Council. Applications for dispensations to come through the Central Committee of the District or by memorial, signed by at least 20 Operatives of the place where such new Lodge is proposed to be founded.

XI. The Executive Council shall act as trustees for all Funds provided by the C.U., for the adjustment of strikes, the purchasing or renting of land, establishing provision stores, workshops, etc.; or for any other purposes connected with the general benefit of the whole of the Union.

XII. All sums for the above purposes to be transmitted from the Lodges to the Executive Council through some safe and accredited medium.

XIII. District and Grand Lodges shall have the control of their own funds, subject to the levies imposed upon them by the Executive Council.

XIV. The ordinary weekly subscriptions of members be threepence each member.

XV. No strike or turn out for an *advance* of wages shall be made by the members of any Lodge in the Consolidated Union without the consent of the Executive Council; but in all cases of a *reduction* of wages the Central Committee of the District shall have the power of deciding whether a strike shall or shall not take place; and should such Central Committee be necessitated to order a levy in support of such strike brought on by such reduction of wages, such order shall be made on all the Lodges; in the first instance, in the District in which such reduction hath taken place; and on advice being forwarded to the Executive they shall consider the case, and order accordingly.

XVI. No higher sum than 10s. per week each shall be paid to members during a strike or turn out.

XVII. All Lodges shall be divided into local sections of 20 men each, or as near that number as may be.

Miscellaneous and Auxiliary Lodges

XVIII. In all cases where the number of operatives in a particular Trade, in any District, is too limited to allow of such Trade forming a Lodge of itself, the members of such Trade shall be permitted to become Unionists by joining the Lodge of any other Trade in the District. Should there be several Trades in a District thus limited with respect to the number of their Operatives, they shall be allowed to form together a District Miscellaneous Lodge, with permission, in order to extend the sphere of the brotherhood, to hold out the hand of fellowship to all really useful Labourers employed productively.

XIX. And, in order that all acknowledged Friends to the Productive Classes may attach themselves to the C.U., an Auxiliary Lodge may be established in every City or Town in the Kingdom. The members of each Lodge shall conform to all the Rules and Regulations herein contained, and be bound in the same manner, and subject to all the Laws of the G.U.C.T.U.; and shall not, in any manner, or at any time or place, speak or write *anything* in opposition to these Laws or the interests of the Union aforesaid. The Auxiliary Lodge shall be liable to be dissolved according to Article XXII.

XX. Lodges of Industrious Females shall be instituted in every District where it may be practicable; such Lodges to be considered, in every respect, as part of, and belonging to, the G.N.C.T.U.

Employment of Turn Outs

XXI. In all cases of strikes or turn outs, where it is practicable to employ Members in the making or producing of such commodities or articles as are in demand among their brother Unionists, or any other operatives willing to purchase the same, each Lodge shall provide a work-room or shop in which such commodities and articles may be manufactured on account of that Lodge, which shall make proper arrangements for the supply of the necessary materials ; over which arrangements the Central Committee of the District shall have the control, subject to the scrutiny of the Grand Lodge Committee of the Trade on strike.

XXII. The Grand Lodge of each Trade to have the power of dissolving any District Lodge, in that Trade, for any violation of these Laws, any outrage upon the Public Peace, or for gross neglect of Duty. All Branch, Miscellaneous, or Auxiliary Lodges to be subject to the same control.

XXIII. The internal management and general concerns of each Grand or District Lodge are vested in a Committee of Management, composed of at least Seven, and not more than 25 Members, each to be chosen by Ballot, and elected by having not less than three-fourths of the Votes of the Members present, at the time of his election, in his favour. The whole of this Committee to go out of office Quarterly, eligible, however, to re-election. The Grand Master, or President, and the Secretary, or Grand Secretary of a Grand or a District Lodge, to be considered Members of its Committee of Management by virtue of their Offices.

XXIV. Each Grand Lodge, in this C.U., to be considered the centre of information regarding the general affairs of its particular Trade ; each District Lodge to communicate with its Grand Lodge at the end of each month, and to give an account to it of the number of people Members in the District Lodge—the gross number of hours of labour performed by them in that district—the state of its funds—and any local or general intelligence that may be considered of interest to the Grand Lodge.

XXV. The Committee of Management in each Lodge shall sit at least on one evening in every week for the despatch of business—and oftener if necessary.

XXVI. Each Grand or District Lodge to hold its meetings on one evening in every month ; at which meeting a Report of the Proceedings of the Committee, during the past month, shall be laid before the Members, together with an Abstract of the state of the Funds, an account of the prospects of the Society, and any propositions or By-Laws which the Committee may have to suggest for adoption, and any other information or correspondence of interest to the Members. All nominations of fresh Officers to be made at Lodge meetings, and all complaints of Members to be considered and discussed therein.

XXVII. The Grand Master or Deputy Grand Master, President, or Vice-President, or both, shall preside at all meetings of Grand or District Lodges, to keep order, state and put questions according to the sense and intention of the Members, give effect to the resolutions, and cause them to be put in force ; and they shall be addressed by Members, during Lodge hours, by their proper titles.

XXVIII. No subject which does not immediately concern the interests of the Trade shall be discussed at any meetings of Committees or Lodges ; and no proposition shall be adopted in either without the consent of at least three-fourths of the members present at its proposal—the question to be decided by ballot if any Member demand it. Not less than five Members of Committee of Management to constitute a Quorum, provided the rest have all been duly summoned ; no Grand or District Lodge to be considered open unless at least 30 members be present.

XXIX. Each Grand or District Lodge shall have the power to appoint Sub-Committees to enquire into or manage any affair touching their interests, of which Committees the head officers of the Lodge are always to be considered Members.

Of Secretaries

XXX. The duties of a secretary to a Grand or District Lodge are :—To attend Lodge and Committee meetings and take minutes of the proceedings, entering the same in a book to be kept for that purpose.

To conduct all the correspondence of the Society. To take down the names and addresses of parties desirous of being initiated into the Order ; and upon receiving the initiation fee from each, and entering the amount into a book, he will give each party a card, by which they may be admitted into the place appointed for the ceremony.

To receive the subscriptions of members, entering the same into a small account book, numbering the Subscribers from No. 1, and following up the sequence in regulation order, giving to each Subscriber a card, on which his contribution or payment shall be noted.

To enter all additional weekly payments, and all levies, into separate small books; all subscriptions and payments to be afterwards copied into a ledger, ruled expressly for the purpose.

The Secretary to be paid an adequate weekly salary; and to be allowed an Assistant if the amount of business require it.

The Secretary of each Grand or District Lodge shall balance his books once every fortnight, and the Managing Committee shall audit them, going over each item of receipt and expenditure with strict attention, checking the same with scrupulous care; and if found correct, three of the Committee shall verify the same by affixing their signatures to the page on which the balance is struck.

Initiation

XXXI. Any of the Officers or Members of a Lodge may be appointed by the Committee of Management to perform the Initiation Service; and to have charge of the Robes, etc., for that purpose; for which the Committee may allow him a reasonable remuneration.

Any party applying to be initiated must bring forward two witnesses as to character and the identity of his trade or occupation.

Of Branch Lodges

XXXII. Branch Lodge Meetings shall be held on one evening in every week, in the respective localities; at which Lodges any motion, proposed by law, etc., may be discussed and considered by the Members previous to its being finally submitted to the Grand or District Lodge Committee.

XXXIII. The Members of each Branch may elect a President to preside at the Branch Lodge, and a Secretary to collect subscriptions or levies for their Grand or District Lodge; who shall also attend meetings of the Committee of Management for instructions and information, and to submit suggestions, complaints, etc., from his Branch Lodge. No salaries or fees to be allowed to officers of Branch Lodges, unless by the unanimous consent of their Members.

Wardens, Etc.

XXXIV. In addition to the Officers before mentioned in these regulations, there shall be, in each Grand and District Lodge a Warden, an Inside Tyler, an Outside Tyler, and a Conductor, whose principal duties are to attend Initiations, and see that no improper persons be admitted into the meetings. These officers to be elected in the same manner, and at the same periods, as other officers.

Miscellaneous Articles

XXXV. Any Member shall be liable to expulsion from the Lodges for any improper conduct therein ; and shall be excluded from the benefits of the Society if his subscriptions be more than six months in arrear, unless the Committee of Management shall see cause to decide otherwise.

XXXVI. The *G.U.C.T.U. Gazette* to be considered the official organ of the Executive Council, and the general medium of intelligence on the affairs of the Union.

XXXVII. Each Lodge shall, as soon as possible, make arrangements for furnishing the means of instituting Libraries or Reading-Rooms, or any other arrangements, affording them every facility for meeting together for friendly conversation, mutual instruction, and rational amusement or recreation.

XXXVIII. In all cases, where it be practicable, each Lodge shall establish within its locality one or more Depots for provisions and articles in general domestic use, in order that its Members may be supplied with the best of such commodities at little above wholesale prices.

XXXIX. Each District and Grand Lodge shall endeavour to institute a Fund for the support of sick and aged Members, and for defraying the funeral expenses of deceased Members, on a similar principle to that of Benefit Societies ; such fund to be kept up by small monthly contributions from those Unionists who are willing to subscribe towards it.

XL. Each Grand or District Lodge to have the power of

making its own By-Laws for purposes not comprised in these Regulations ; but such By-Laws or Laws must not be in opposition to, or in counteraction of, any of the Articles herein specified.

XLI. No Member can enter Lodge Meetings without giving the proper signs, and producing his card to prove his membership, and that he is not in arrears of subscription for more than one month, unless lenity has been granted by order of Committee.

XLII. That a separate Treasurer be appointed for every £20 of the funds collected ; and that such Treasurers shall not suffer any money to be withdrawn from their hands without a written order, signed by at least three of the Managing Committee and presented by the Secretary, or one of the other officers of the Society

XLIII. All sums under £30 shall be left in the hands of the Secretary for current expenses ; but no outlay shall be made by him without an express order from the Managing Committee, signed by at least three of its Members.

XLIV. That every Member of this Union do use his best endeavours, by fair and open argument, and the force of good example, and not by intimidation or violence, to induce his fellows to join the brotherhood, in order that no workmen may remain out of the Union to undersell them in the market of labour ; as, while that is done, employers will be enabled to resist the demands of the Unionists, whereas, if no operatives remain out of union, employers will be compelled to keep up the price of Labour.

XLV. That each Member of the C.U. pay a Registration Fee of 3d. to defray the general expenses ; which fee is to be transmitted to the Executive once in every month.

XLVI. That although the design of the Union is, in the first instance, to raise the wages of the workmen, or prevent any further reduction therein, and to diminish the hours of labour, the great and ultimate object of it must be to establish the paramount rights of Industry and Humanity, by instituting such measures as shall effectually prevent the ignorant, idle, and useless part of Society from having that undue control over the fruits of our toil, which, through the agency of a vicious money system, they at present possess ; and that, consequently, the Unionists should lose no opportunity of mutually encouraging and assisting each other in bringing about A DIFFERENT ORDER OF THINGS, in which the really useful and intelligent part of society only shall have the direction of its affairs, and in which well-directed industry and virtue shall meet their just distinction and reward, and vicious idleness its merited contempt and destitution.

XLVII. All the Rules and Regulations herein contained be subject to the revision, alteration, or abrogation of the Grand Delegate Council.

APPENDIX III

SLIDING SCALES

THE Sliding Scale, an arrangement by which it is agreed in advance that wages shall vary in a definite relation to changes in the market price of the product, appears to have been familiar to the iron trade for a couple of generations. " About fifty years ago Mr. G. B. Thorneycroft, of Wolverhampton, head of a well-known firm of iron-masters, suggested to certain other houses that wages should fluctuate with the price of ' marked bars ' —these words indicating a quality of iron that then enjoyed a high reputation. The suggestion was adopted to this extent, that when a demand was made by the men for an advance in wages, any advance that was given was proportionate to the selling price of ' marked bars.' The puddlers received, as a rule, 1s. for each pound of the selling price ; but on exceptional occasions, a special temporary advance or ' premium ' was conceded. The terms of this arrangement do not seem to have been reduced to writing, though they remained in force for many years, and were well known as the Thorneycroft scale." [1]

At the time of the great strike of Staffordshire puddlers, in 1865, a local understanding of a similar nature appears to have been in existence. The joint committee of iron-masters and puddlers, which was established at Darlington in 1869 as the " North of England Manufactured Iron Board," soon worked out a formal sliding scale for its own guidance. This scale, as well as that adopted by the Midland Iron Trade Board, has been repeatedly revised, abandoned, and again re-established ; but its working has, on the whole, commended itself to the repre-

[1] Statement furnished to Professor Munro by Mr. Daniel Jones, of the Midland Iron and Steel Wages Board, quoted in *Sliding Scales in the Coal and Iron Industries* (p. 141).

sentatives of the ironworkers, and has, so far as the principle is concerned, produced no important dissensions among them. " We believe," said Mr. Trow, the men's secretary, to the Labour Commission in 1892, " it would be most satisfactory if this principle were generally adopted. . . . In all our experience of the past we have had less trouble in the periods in which sliding scales have obtained." The cause of the exceptional satisfaction of the ironworkers with their Wages Boards and Sliding Scales is obscure, but it may be interesting to the student to note that the members of the Ironworkers Association are largely sub-contractors, themselves employing workmen who are usually outside the Union, and have no direct representation on the Board. For a careful statement of the facts as to these Wage Boards and Sliding Scales in the iron industry, see *The Adjustment of Wages* (by Sir W. J. Ashley, 1903), pp. 142-151, and specimen rules, reports, and scales, pp. 268-307. At present (1920) separate Sliding Scales of this nature are in force for the Cleveland and the North Lincolnshire Blast-furnacemen ; the Scottish Iron and the Consett Millmen ; Brown Bayley's No. 1 Mill ; the Scottish Enginemen and Steel Millmen ; the Staffordshire Sheet Trade ; the Midlands Puddling Mills and Forges ; and the South Wales and Monmouthshire Iron and Steel Trade.

Widely different has been the result of the Sliding Scale among the coal miners. Its introduction into this trade dates from 1874, though it was not until 1879 that its adoption became common. Since then it has been abandoned in all districts, and it is energetically repudiated by the Miners' Federation. The following table includes all the Sliding Scales in the coal industry known to us. Between 1879 and 1886 there were a number of informal Sliding Scales in force for particular collieries, which were mostly superseded by the more general scales, or otherwise came to an end. It is believed that no Sliding Scale is now in force in any coal district.

July 24,	1874	South Staffordshire I.	Revised	1877.
May 28,	1875	South Wales I.	,,	1880.
April 13,	1876	Somerset.	Ended	1889.
February 6,	1877	Cannock Chase I.	Revised	1879.
March 14,	1877	Durham I.	,,	1879.
November 1,	1877	South Staffordshire II.	,,	1882.
April 14,	1879	Cannock Chase II.	,,	1882.
October 11,	1879	Durham II.	,,	1887.
October 31,	1879	Cumberland I.	Ended	1881.

November 3,	1879	Ferndale Colliery I. (S. Wales).	Revised	1881.
November 10,	1879	Bedworth Colliery I. (Warwick).	„	1880.
November 15,	1879	Northumberland I.	„	1883.
December 19,	1879	Ocean Colliery I. (S. Wales).	„	1882.
January 17,	1880	South Wales II.	„	1882.
January 20,	1880	West Yorkshire.	Ended	?
January 26,	1880	North Wales.	„	1881.
February 14,	1880	Bedworth Colliery II.	„	?
January 1,	1881	Ashton and Oldham I.	Revised	1882.
December 31,	1881	Ferndale Colliery II.		?
January 1,	1882	South Staffordshire III.	Ended	1884.
April 29,	1882	Durham III.	Revised	1884.
June 6,	1882	South Wales III.	„	1889.
June 22,	1882	Cannock Chase, &c. III.	Ended	1883.
July 18,	1882	Ashton & Oldham II.	„	1883.
August 24,	1882	South Wales (Anthracite).		?
September 29,	1882	Cumberland II.	Revised	1884.
March 9,	1883	Northumberland II.	Ended	1886.
June 12,	1884	Durham IV.	„	1889.
November 28,	1884	Cumberland III.	Revised	1886.
March 12,	1886	Forest of Dean.	Ended	1888 ?
April 14,	1886	Altham Colliery (Northd.).	„	?
February 25,	1887	Cumberland IV.	Ended	1888 ?
May 24,	1887	Northumberland III.	„	1887.
June,	1887	Lanarkshire.	„	1889.
October,	1888	South Staffordshire IV.	„	?
January 18,	1890	South Wales IV.	„	?
September,	1893	Forest of Dean.	„	?

An exposition of the construction and working of Sliding Scales is contained in *Industrial Peace*, by L. L. Price. Details of numerous Scales are given in the report made by a Committee to the British Association, entitled *Sliding Scales in the Coal Industry*, which was prepared by Professor J. E. C. Munro (Manchester, 1885), and in the *Particulars of Sliding Scales, Past, Present, and Proposed*, printed by the Lancashire Miners' Federation in 1886 (Openshaw, 1886, 20 pp.). Supplementary information is given in Professor Munro's papers before the Manchester Statistical Society, entitled, " Sliding Scales in the Iron Industry " (Manchester, 1885), and " Sliding Scales in the Coal and Iron Industries from 1885 to 1889 " (Manchester, 1889). The whole question is discussed in *The Adjustment of Wages* (by

Sir William Ashley, 1903), pp. 45-71 ; and in our own *Industrial Democracy*, 1897.

The proceedings in the numerous arbitrations in the coal and iron trade in the North of England, as well as several others which are printed, furnish abundant information on the subject of their working. A table of the variations of wages under sliding scales was prepared by Professor J. E. C. Munro for the Royal Commission on Mining Royalties, and published as Appendix V. to the First Report, 1890 (C 6195).

APPENDIX IV

THE SUMMONS TO THE FIRST TRADE UNION CONGRESS

No copy of the invitation to the first Trade Union Congress has been preserved, either in the archives of the Congress, the Manchester Trades Council, or any other organisation known to us. Fortunately, it was printed in the *Ironworkers' Journal* for May 1868. But of this only one file now exists, and as the summons is of some historical interest we reprint it for convenience of reference.

" MANCHESTER, *April* 16, 1868.

" SIR—You are requested to lay the following before your Society. The vital *interests* involved, it is conceived, will justify the officials in convening a special meeting for the consideration thereof.

" The Manchester and Salford Trades Council having recently taken into their serious consideration the present aspect of Trades Unions, and the profound ignorance which prevails in the public mind with reference to their operations and principles, together with the probability of an attempt being made by the Legislature, during the present Session of Parliament, to introduce a measure which might prove detrimental to the interests of such Societies *unless some prompt and decisive action be taken by the working classes themselves*, beg most respectfully to intimate that it has been decided to hold in Manchester, as the main centre of industry in the provinces, a Congress of the representatives of Trades Councils, Federations of Trades, and Trade Societies in general.

" The Congress will assume the character of the Annual Meetings of the Social Science Association, in the transactions of which Society the artisan class is almost excluded ; and papers

738

previously carefully prepared by such Societies as elect to do so, will be laid before the Congress on the various subjects which at the present time affect the Trade Societies, each paper to be followed by discussion on the points advanced, with a view of the merits and demerits of each question being thoroughly ventilated through the medium of the public press. It is further decided that the subjects treated upon shall include the following :

" 1. Trade Unions an absolute necessity.
" 2. Trade Unions and Political Economy.
" 3. The effect of Trade Unions on foreign competition.
" 4. Regulation of the hours of labour.
" 5. Limitation of apprentices.
" 6. Technical Education.
" 7. Courts of Arbitration and Conciliation.
" 8. Co-operation.
" 9. The present inequality of the law in regard to conspiracy, intimidation, picketing, coercion, etc.
" 10. Factory Acts Extension Bill, 1867 : the necessity of compulsory inspection and its application to all places where women and children are employed.
" 11. The present Royal Commission on Trades Unions— how far worthy of the confidence of the Trade Union interests.
" 12. Legalization of Trade Societies.
" 13. The necessity of an Annual Congress of Trade Representatives from the various centres of industry.

" All Trades Councils, Federations of Trades, and Trade Societies generally are respectfully solicited to intimate their adhesion to this project on or before the 12th of May next, together with a notification of the subject of the paper that each body will undertake to prepare, and the number of delegates by whom they will be respectively represented ; after which date all information as to the place of meeting, etc., will be supplied.

" It is not imperative that all Societies should prepare papers, it being anticipated that the subjects will be taken up by those most capable of expounding the principles sought to be maintained. Several have already adhered to the project, and have signified their intention of taking up the subjects Nos. 1, 4, 6, and 7.

" The Congress will be held on Whit-Tuesday, the 2nd of June next, its duration not to exceed five days ; and all expenses in connection therewith, which will be very small, and as economical as possible, will be equalized amongst those Societies sending delegates, and will not extend beyond their sittings.

" Communications to be addressed to Mr. W. H. Wood, Typographical Institute, 29 Water Street, Manchester.

" By order of the Manchester & Salford Trades Council.

" S. C. NICHOLSON, President.
" W. H. WOOD, Secretary."

APPENDIX V

DISTRIBUTION OF TRADE UNIONISTS IN THE UNITED KINGDOM

WE endeavoured in 1893–94 to analyse the membership of all the Trade Unions of which we could obtain particulars, in such a way as to show the number and percentage to population in each part of the United Kingdom. The following table gives the local distribution of 1,507,026 Trade Unionists in 1892. The distribution was, in most cases, made by branches, special estimates being prepared for us in a few instances by the officers of the Unions concerned. With regard to a few Unions having about 4000 members no local distribution could be arrived at.

Table showing the distribution of Trade Union membership in 1892 in each part of the United Kingdom, with the percentage to population in each case.

County.	Population in 1891.	Ascertained Trade Unionists in 1892.	Number of Trade Unionists per 100 of population.
Bedfordshire	165,999	553	0·33
Berkshire	268,357	975	0·36
Buckinghamshire . .	164,442	720	0·44
Cambridgeshire . . .	196,269	2,855	1·45
Cheshire	707,978	32,000	4·52
Cornwall	318,583	630	0·20
Cumberland	266,549	10,280	3·86
Derbyshire	432,414	29,510	6·82
Devonshire	636,225	6,030	0·95
Dorsetshire	188,995	305	0·16

County.	Population in 1891.	Ascertained Trade Unionists in 1892.	Number of Trade Unionists per 100 of population.
Durham	1,024,369	114,810	11·21
Essex	396,057	3,370	0·85
(without West Ham, included in London).			
Gloucestershire	548,886	26,030	4·74
Hampshire	587,578	5,665	0·96
(without Isle of Wight, treated separately).			
Herefordshire	113,346	385	0·34
Hertfordshire	215,179	1,125	0·52
Huntingdonshire . . .	50,289	20	0·04
Isle of Wight	78,672	295	0·37
Kent	737,044	12,445	1·69
(without Bromley, included in London).			
Lancashire	3,957,906	331,535	8·63
Leicestershire	379,286	27,845	7·34
Lincoln	467,281	9,480	2·03
London	5,517,583	194,083	3·52
(including Bromley, Croydon, Kingston, Richmond, West Ham and Middlesex).			
Norfolk	460,362	4,880	1·06
Northamptonshire . . .	308,072	12,210	3·96
Northumberland	506,030	56,815	11·23
Nottinghamshire	505,311	31,050	6·14
Oxford	188,220	1,815	0·96
Rutland	22,123	0	0·00
Shropshire	254,765	3,225	1·26
Somerset . . . „ .	510,076	6,595	1·29
Staffordshire	1,103,452	49,545	4·49
Suffolk	353,758	14,885	4·21
Surrey	275,638	730	0·26
(without Croydon, Kingston, and Richmond, included in London).			
Sussex	554,542	2,810	0·51
Warwickshire	801,738	33,600	4·19
Westmoreland	66,215	530	0·80

County.	Population in 1891.	Ascertained Trade Unionists in 1892.	Number of Trade Unionists per 100 of population.
Wiltshire	255,119	3,680	1·44
Worcestershire	422,530	7,840	1·86
Yorkshire, East Riding . .	318,570	23,630	7·42
Yorkshire, North Riding . . (with York City).	435,897	15,215	3·49
Yorkshire, West Riding . .	2,464,415	141,140	5·73
Total, England	27,226,120	1,221,141	4·49
North Wales	451,090	8,820	1·96
South Wales and Monmouth .	1,325,315	88,810	6·70
Total, Wales and Monmouth	1,776,405	97,630	5·50
Total, England and Wales	29,002,525	1,318,771	4·55
Scotland	4,033,103	146,925	3·64
Ireland	4,706,162	40,045	0·85
Isle of Man	55,598	75	0·13
Guernsey	35,339	1,170	3·31
Jersey	54,518	40	0·07
Alderney and Sark . . .	2,415	0	0·00
Total, United Kingdom	37,889,660	1,507,026	3·98

APPENDIX

It is unfortunately impossible to present any complete statistics
appointment, in 1886, of John Burnett as Labour Correspondent
statistics of the movement ; and the old Unions seldom possess
of Ironfounders, it is true, has exact figures since its establish-
The following tables may be useful as placing on record such

1. Amalgamated Society of Engineers.
2. Friendly Society of Ironfounders.
3. Steam Engine Makers' Society.
4. Associated Ironmoulders of Scotland.
5. United Society of Boilermakers and Iron Shipwrights.
6. Operative Stonemasons' Friendly Society.
7. Operative Bricklayers' Society.
8. General Union of Operative Carpenters and Joiners.
9. Typographical Association.
10. London Society of Compositors.
11. Bookbinders' and Machine Rulers' Consolidated Union.
12. United Kingdom Society of Coachmakers.
13. Flint Glass Makers' Friendly Society.
14. Amicable and Brotherly Society of Machine Printers.
15. Machine, Engine, and Iron Grinders' Society.
16. Associated Blacksmiths' Society.
17. Amalgamated Society of Carpenters and Joiners.
18. Associated Carpenters and Joiners.
19. National Association of Operative Plasterers.
20. Northumberland Miners' Mutual Confident Association.
21. United Journeymen Brassfounders' Association of Great Britain and
    Ireland.
22. United Operative Plumbers' Association.
23. Alliance Cabinet Makers' Association.

VI

of Trade Union membership at different periods. Until the
to the Board of Trade, no attempt was made to collect any
a complete series of their own archives. The Friendly Society
ment in 1809. No total figures can be given with any confidence.
comparative figures as we have been able to collect:

24. United Operative Bricklayers' Trade, Accident, Sick, and Burial Society.
25. Amalgamated Society of Tailors.
26. Amalgamated Association of Operative Cotton Spinners.
27. Glass Bottle Makers of Yorkshire United Trade Protection Society.
28. Durham Miners' Association.
29. National Society of Amalgamated Brassworkers.
30. United Pattern Makers' Association.
31. National Union of Boot and Shoe Operatives.
32. Amalgamated Society of Railway Servants.
33. Yorkshire Miners' Association.
34. United Machine Workers' Association.
35. National Amalgamated Furnishing Trades Association.
36. Railway Clerks' Association.
37. Amalgamated Tramway and Vehicle Workers.
38. National Union of Dock Labourers.
39. British Steel Smelters.
40. National Amalgamated Union of Shop Assistants.
41. Amalgamated Union of Co-operative Employees.
42. National Union of Clerks.
43. Workers' Union.
44. Amalgamated Musicians' Union.
45. National Amalgamated Union of Labour.
46. Postmen's Federation.
47. Post Office Engineering Stores.

Table showing the Membership of certain Trade Unions at

Number of Society.	Year of Establishment.	1850.	1855.	1860.	1865.	1870.
1.	1851 *	5,000	12,553	20,935	30,984	34,711
2.	1809	4,073	5,685	7,973	10,604	8,994
3.	1824	2,068	1,662	2,050	2,521	2,819
4.	1831	814	1,381	2,084	3,046	2,766
5.	1832	1,771	3,500	4,146	8,621	7,261
6.	1832	4,671	8,093	9,125	15,483	13,965
7.	1848	340	924	1,641	4,320	1,441
8.	1827	535	1,180	2,228	6,986	8,008
9.	1849	603	1,288	1,473	1,992	2,430
10.	1848	1,800	2,300	2,650	2,800	3,350
11.	1835	420	340	500	748	915
12.	1834	1,567	3,040	4,086	4,599	5,801
13.	1849	500	897	1,355	1,606	1,776
14.	1841	375	452	508	530	570
15.	1844	200	110	330	449	280
		24,737	43,405	61,084	95,289	95,087
16.	1857	—	—	856	1,815	1,590
17.	1860	—	—	618	5,670	10,178
18.	1861	—	—	—	4,453	3,585
19.	1862	—	—	—	4,441	2,461
20.	1863	—	—	—	4,250	5,328
21.	1866	—	—	—	—	1,457
22.	1832	?	?	?	?	1,537
23.	1865	—	—	—	?	242
24.	1832	?		?	?	3,850
25.	1866	—	—	—	—	4,006
26.	1853	—	?	?	?	10,518
27.	1860	—	—	?	?	792
28.	1869	—	—	—	—	1,899
						142,530

* Established January 10, 1851. The membership given for 1850 is
† Merged in the National Union of Bookbinders and Machine Rulers,
‡ In 1902 joined with the Operative Cabinet and Chair Makers
Association.

Successive Periods, from 1850 to 1918 inclusive.

1875.	1880.	1885.	1890.	1900.	1910.	1918.
44,032	44,692	51,689	67,928	87,672	110,733	298,782
12,336	11,580	12,376	14,821	18,357	17,990	28,586
3,871	4,134	5,062	5,822	8,566	14,401	27,206
4,346	4,664	5,611	6,198	7,504	7,880	7,961
16,191	17,688	28,212	32,926	47,670	49,393	95,761
24,543	12,610	11,285	12,538	19,419	7,055	4,929
4,832	5,700	6,412	12,740	38,830	23,284	34,441
10,885	4,420	1,734	2,485	7,727	5,653	12,000
3,600	5,350	6,551	9,016	16,179	21,436	11,602
4,200	5,100	6,435	8,910	11,287	12,230	12,940
1,670	1,501	1,788	2,910	4,064	5,027	— †
7,251	4,989	4,560	5,367	6,536	6,854	15,118
2,005	1,963	1,985	2,123	2,409	916	775
650	690	740	860	963	983	228
390	258	277	304	433	703	746
140,802	125,339	144,717	184,948	277,616	284,538	551,075
2,113	2,002	2,335	2,300	2,933	2,953	17,238
14,917	17,764	25,781	31,495	65,012	55,785	} 124,841
6,642	4,673	4,535	4,742	9,808	3,964	}
3,742	3,211	2,110	4,236	11,009	6,522	4,110
17,561	10,707	13,128	16,961	23,950	37,361	40,000
1,821	1,890	2,344	2,162	—	5,241	7,500
1,679	2,232	2,666	5,350	11,186	10,907	13,000
1,965	1,346	1,246	4,298	5,270	—	— ‡
7,350	3,282	1,975	1,725	3,428	1,655	2,950
14,352	12,583	13,969	16,629	13,439	12,143	29,422
14,257	11,834	16,579	18,145	18,384	22,992	24,806
1,120	1,061	1,522	1,899	2,840	2,450	2,800
38,000	30,000	35,000	49,000	80,260	121,805	126,250
266,321	227,924	267,907	343,890	546,135	559,316	944,992

that with which the amalgamation started.
1911.
of Scotland to form the National Amalgamated Furnishing Trades

Number of Society.	Year of Establishment.	1850.	1855.	1860.	1865.	1870.
29.	1872	—	—	—	—	—
30.	1872	—	—	—	—	—
31.	1874	—	—	—	—	—
32.	1872	—	—	—	—	—
33.	1858	—	—	?	?	?
34.	1844	?	?	?	?	?
35.	1902	—	—	—	—	—
36.	1897	—	—	—	—	—
37.	1889	—	—	—	—	—
38.	1889	—	—	—	—	—
39.	1886	—	—	—	—	—
40.	1891	—	—	—	—	—
41.	1891	—	—	—	—	—
42.	1891	—	—	—	—	—
43.	1898	—	—	—	—	—
44.	1893	—	—	—	—	—
45.	1889	—	—	—	—	—
46.	1891	—	—	—	—	—
47.	1896	—	—	—	—	—

* Amalgamated in 1913 with the United Pointsmen and Signalmen Railwaymen.

† In 1917 the members of the British Steel Smelters were merged in

We have suggested that it is doubtful whether, in 1842, there A quarter of a century later George Howell and others could number was reached until the years of good trade that followed whether the aggregate of a million was again reached until the end of the century were two millions attained—a number increased by over fifty per cent.

1875.	1880.	1885.	1890.	1900.	1910.	1918.
5,271	4,633	3,582	7,958	8,675	7,373	25,000
418	824	1,241	2,205	4,604	7,214	10,290
4,311	6,404	10,464	23,459	27,960	30,197	83,017
13,018	8,589	9,052	26,360	62,023	75,153	— (*)
8,000	2,800	8,000	50,000	54,475	88,271	100,400
276	279	455	2,501	3,769	4,843	23,374
297,615	251,453	300,701	456,373	707,641	772,367	1,187,073
—	—	—	—	6,248 (1902)	6,685	47,220
—	—	—	—	1,550	9,476	66,130
—	—	—	?	9,214	17,076	40,564
—	—	—	?	13,388	14,253	45,000
—	—	—	?	10,467	17,491	40,000(?)†
—	—	—	—	7,551	22,426	83,000 (1919)
—	—	—	—	6,733	29,886	87,134
—	—	—	—	82	3,166	35,000
—	—	—	?	2,879	5,016	230,000
—	—	—	—	3,286	6,182	14,649
—	—	—	?	21,111	16,017	143,931
—	—	—	—	23,180	37,892	65,078
—	—	—	—	940	3,500	14,000
				106,629	189,046	911,706
				814,270	961,413	2,098,779

and the General Railway Workers' Union to form the National Union of

the Iron and Steel Trades Confederation.

were as many as 100,000 enrolled and contributing members.
talk vaguely of a million members, but we doubt whether this
1871. In 1878–80 there was a great falling off, and we doubt
1885. In 1892 we recorded a million and a half. Not until
doubled by 1915, and in the last four or five years again

Table showing the aggregate Trade Union Membership in groups of Industries at the end of each of the years 1892–1917 inclusive.[1]

Year.	Building.	Mining and Quarrying.	Metal, Engineering, and Shipbuilding.	Textile.	Clothing.	Transport.	Other Trades.			Total, all Unions.
							Printing, Paper, etc.	Wood-working.	Other Trades.	
1892	157,971	315,272	279,534	204,022	83,299	154,947	307,313			1,502,358
1893	172,870	318,112	266,813	205,546	80,768	142,084	293,224			1,479,417
1894	178,721	307,276	263,572	214,331	81,786	123,896	266,718			1,436,300
1895	179,283	280,065	269,169	218,805	78,560	120,475	261,479			1,407,836
1896	193,341	279,977	303,518	217,950	76,997	134,877	287,805			1,494,465
1897	215,603	283,054	319,745	218,619	75,852	183,994	317,131			1,613,998
1898	232,040	366,731	312,444	240,895	69,954	147,957	54,436	—	264,074	1,688,531
1899	249,988	445,706	335,746	245,301	66,777	163,685	56,727	—	284,640	1,848,570
1900	253,412	524,150	342,079	245,438	67,183	171,599	57,228	—	294,615	1,955,704
1901	248,967	530,953	338,468	243,474	65,660	169,199	58,274	—	311,766	1,966,761
1902	245,141	532,082	337,064	246,829	64,094	158,714	59,062	—	310,321	1,953,307
1903	238,141	529,028	337,122	244,081	61,713	159,051	60,138	—	301,769	1,931,043
1904	225,149	501,764	334,822	246,473	58,598	159,788	62,428	—	306,087	1,895,109
1905	205,179	496,828	340,364	266,416	60,394	167,017	62,368	—	321,807	1,920,373
1906	196,492	571,336	361,453	302,968	59,806	190,155	64,451	—	367,145	2,113,806
1907	193,190	703,344	376,805	354,427	68,810	238,813	68,221	—	403,136	2,406,746
1908	177,718	719,384	365,134	362,540	65,637	230,642	72,970	41,797	353,505	2,388,727
1909	162,278	722,639	359,838	366,445	65,882	224,037	71,531	39,240	357,177	2,369,067
1910	156,985	731,305	370,055	379,644	67,158	245,223	74,275	38,881	382,816	2,446,342
1911	173,182	752,419	415,176	436,927	74,423	513,538	77,252	45,474	530,512	3,018,903
1912	203,773	757,147	479,471	478,097	91,855	514,724	76,807	50,853	635,107	3,287,884
1913	248,647	915,734	538,541	515,684	105,929	699,952	84,414	64,442	813,772	3,987,115
1914	235,828	870,198	557,769	497,494	102,538	705,501	92,283	64,296	796,902	3,918,809
1915	228,475	857,183	633,502	507,731	114,085	737,290	97,290	65,210	886,313	4,126,793
1916	229,272	877,694	695,347	530,411	121,656	803,872	97,669	69,403	1,012,623	4,437,947
1917	257,286	941,120	847,202	627,919	149,756	903,109	109,586	83,369	1,360,165	5,287,522

[1] [From Labour Department's Reports on Trade Unions for 1900, 1905–7 and 1912, Cmd. 773, 4651 and 6109, and *Labour Gazette*.]

APPENDIX VII

PUBLICATIONS RELATING TO TRADE UNIONS

IN the first edition of this book we gave a list, 45 pages long, of books, pamphlets, reports, and other documents bearing on the workmen's combinations. In *Industrial Democracy*, 1897, we gave a supplementary list, 23 pages long. We do not reproduce these lists, to which the student can always refer ; nor have we attempted to bring them down to date. The really useful material for Trade Union study is to be found in the publications of the Trade Unions themselves—the innumerable editions of rules, the thousands of annual and monthly reports, the voluminous lists of piece-work prices, the intricate working agreements, the verbatim reports of conferences, delegate meetings and proceedings before Conciliation and Arbitration Boards—which are ignored by the British Museum, and are practically never preserved in local public libraries. We made an extensive collection in 1891–97, which we have deposited in the British Library of Political Science, attached to the London School of Economics and Political Science, where it has been, to some extent, kept up to date, and where it is accessible to any serious student. Some old pamphlets and reports of interest are in the Goldsmiths' Library at the University of London. Of Trade Union publications since 1913 the most extensive collection is that of the Labour Research Department, attached to the Labour Party, 34 Eccleston Square, London.

APPENDIX VIII

THE RELATIONSHIP OF TRADE UNIONISM TO THE GOVERNMENT OF INDUSTRY

IN our work on *Industrial Democracy*, published in 1897, we formulated the following tentative conclusions with regard to the participation of the workmen's organisations in industrial management, and the relation of Trade Unionism to political Democracy:

" This survey of the changes required in Trade Union policy leads us straight to a conclusion as to the part which Trade Unionism will be expected to play in the management of the industry of a democratic state. The interminable series of decisions, which together make up industrial administration, fall into three main classes. There is, first, the decision as to what shall be produced—that is to say, the exact commodity or service to be supplied to the consumers. There is, secondly, the judgement as to the manner in which the production shall take place, the adoption of material, the choice of processes, and the selection of human agents. Finally, there is the altogether different question of the conditions under which these human agents shall be employed—the temperature, atmosphere, and sanitary arrangements amid which they shall work, the intensity and duration of their toil, and the wages given as its reward.

" To obtain for the community the maximum satisfaction it is essential that the needs and desires of the consumers should be the main factor in determining the commodities and services to be produced. Whether these needs and desires can best be ascertained and satisfied by the private enterprise of capitalist profit-makers, keenly interested in securing custom, or by the public service of salaried officials, intent on pleasing associations of consumers (as in the British Co-operative Movement), or associations of citizens (the Municipality or the State), is at present the crucial problem of Democracy. But whichever way this issue may be decided, one thing is certain, namely, that the several sections of manual workers, enrolled in their Trade Unions, will have, under private enterprise or Collectivism, no more to do with the determination of what is to be produced than any other citizens or consumers. As manual workers and wage-earners, they bring to the problem no specialised knowledge; and as persons fitted for the performance of particular services, they are even biassed against the inevitable changes in demand which characterise progressive community. This is even more the case with regard to the second department of industrial administration—the adoption of material, the choice of processes, and the selection of human agents. Here, the Trade Unions concerned are specially disqualified, not only by their ignorance of the possible alternatives, but also by their overwhelming bias in favour of a particular material, a particular process, or a particular grade of workers, irrespective of whether these are or are not the best adapted for the gratification of the consumers' desires. On the other hand, the directors of industry, whether thrown up by the competitive struggle or deliberately appointed by the consumers or citizens, have been specially picked out and trained to discover the best means of satisfying the consumers' desires. Moreover, the bias of their self-interest coincides with the object of their customers or employers—that is to say, the best and cheapest production. Thus, if we leave out of account the disturbing influence of monopoly in private enterprise, and corruption in public administration, it would at first sight seem as if we might safely leave the organisation of production and distribution under the one system as under the other to the expert knowledge of the directors of industry. But this is subject to one all-important qualification. The permanent bias of the profit-maker, and even of the salaried official of the Co-operative Society, the Municipality, or the Government Department, is to lower the expense of production. So far as immediate results are concerned, it seems equally advantageous whether this reduction of cost is secured by a better choice of materials, processes, or men, or by some lowering of wages or other worsening of the conditions upon which the human agents are employed But the democratic state is, as we have seen, vitally interested in upholding the highest possible Standard of Life of all its citizens, and especially of the manual workers who form four-fifths of the whole. Hence the bias of the directors of industry in favor of cheapness has, in the interests of the community, to be perpetually controlled and guided by a determination to maintain, and progressively to raise, the conditions of employment.

" This leads us to the third branch of industrial administration —the settlement of the conditions under which the human beings are to be employed. The adoption of one material rather than another, the choice between alternative processes or alternative ways of organising the factory, the selection of particular grades of workers, or even of a particular foreman, may affect, for the worse, the Standard of Life of the operatives concerned. This indirect influence on the conditions of employment passes imperceptibly into the direct determination of the wages, hours, and other terms of the wage contract. On all these matters the consumers, on the one hand, and the directors of industry on the other, are permanently disqualified from acting as arbiters. In our chapter on ' The Higgling of the Market ' we described how, in the elaborate division of labour which characterises the modern industrial system, thousands of workers co-operate in the bringing to market of a single commodity ; and no consumer, even if he desired it, could possibly ascertain or judge of the conditions of employment in all these varied trades. Thus, the consumers of all classes are not only biassed in favour of low prices ; they are compelled to accept this apparent or genuine cheapness as the only practicable test of efficiency of production. And though the immediate employer of each section of workpeople knows the hours that they work and the wages that they receive, he is precluded by the stream of competitive pressure, transmitted through the retail shopkeeper and the wholesale trader, from effectively resisting the promptings of his own self-interest towards a constant cheapening of labour. Moreover, though he may be statistically aware of the conditions of employment his lack of personal experience of those conditions deprives him of any real knowledge of their effects. To the brain-working captain of industry, maintaining himself and his family on thousands a year, the manual-working wage-earner seems to belong to another species, having mental faculties and bodily needs altogether different from his own. Men and women of the upper or middle classes are totally unable to realise what state of body and mind, what level of character and conduct, result from a life spent, from childhood to old age, amid the dirt, the smell, the noise, the ugliness, and the vitiated atmosphere of the workshop ; under constant subjection to the peremptory, or it may be brutal, orders of the foreman ; kept continuously at the laborious manual toil for sixty or seventy hours in every week of the year ; and maintained by the food, clothing, house-accommodation, recreation, and family life which are implied by a precarious income of between ten shillings and two pounds a week. If the democratic state is to attain its fullest and finest development, it is essential that the actual needs and desires of the human agents concerned should be the main considerations in determining the conditions of employment. Here then we find the special function of the Trade Union in the administration of industry. The simplest member of the working-class organisation knows at any rate where the shoe pinches. The Trade Union official is specially selected by his fellow-workmen for his capacity to express the grievances from which they suffer, and is trained by his calling in devising remedies for them. But in expressing the desires of their members, and in insisting on the necessary reforms, the Trade Unions act within the constant friction-brake supplied by the need of securing employment. It is always the consumers and the consumers alone, whether they act through profit-making *entrepreneurs* or through their own salaried officials, who determine how many of each particular grade of workers they care to employ on the conditions demanded. . . . Thus we find no neat formula for defining the rights and duties of the individual in society. In the democratic state every individual is both master and servant. In the work that he does for the community in return for his subsistence he is, and must remain, a servant, subject to the instructions and directions of those whose desires he is helping to satisfy. As a Citizen-Elector jointly with his fellows, and as a Consumer to the extent of his demand, he is a master, determining, free from any superior, what shall be done. Hence, it is the supreme paradox of democracy that every man is a servant in respect of the matters of which he possesses the most expert proficiency, namely, the professional craft to which he devotes his working hours ; and he is a master over that on which he knows no more than anybody else, namely, the general interests of the community as a whole. In this paradox, we suggest, lies at once the justification and the strength of democracy. It is not, as is commonly asserted by the superficial, that Ignorance rules over Knowledge, and Mediocrity over Capacity. In the administration of society Knowledge and Capacity can make no real and durable progress except by acting on and through the minds of the common human material which it is desired to improve. It is only by carrying along with him the ' average sensual man,' that even the wisest and most philanthropic reformer, however autocratic his power, can genuinely change the face of things. Moreover, not even the wisest of men can be trusted with that supreme authority which comes from the union of knowledge, capacity, and opportunity with the power of untrammelled and ultimate decision. Democracy is an expedient—perhaps the only practicable expedient—for preventing the concentration in any single individual or in any single class of what inevitably becomes, when so concentrated, a terrible engine of oppression. The autocratic emperor, served by a trained bureaucracy, seems to the Anglo-Saxon a perilously near approach to such a concentration. If democracy meant, as early observers imagined, a similar concentration of Knowledge and Power in the hands of the numerical majority for the time being, it might easily become as injurious a tyranny as any autocracy. An actual study of the spontaneous democracies of Anglo-Saxon workmen, or, as we suggest, of any other democratic institutions, reveals the splitting up of this dangerous authority into two parts. Whether in political or in industrial democracy, though it is the Citizen who, as Elector or Consumer, ultimately gives the order, it is the Professional Expert who advises what the order shall be.

" It is another aspect of this paradox that, in the democratic state, no man minds his own business. In the economic sphere this is a necessary consequence of division of labour ; Robinson Crusoe, producing solely for his own consumption, being the last man who minded nothing but his own business. The extreme complication brought about by universal production for exchange in itself implies that every one works with a view to fulfilling the desires of other people. The crowding together of dense populations, and especially the co-operative enterprises which then arise, extend in every direction this spontaneous delegation to professional experts of what the isolated individual once deemed ' his own business.' Thus, the citizen in a modern municipality no longer produces his own food or makes his own clothes ; no longer protects his own life or property ; no longer fetches his own water ; no longer makes his own thoroughfares, or cleans or lights them when made ; no longer removes his own refuse or even disinfects his own dwelling. He no longer educates his own children, or doctors and nurses his own

tions into the larger and perhaps more significant types
democratic organisation."

In 1920, after nearly a quarter of a century of further expe
ence and consideration, we should, in some respects, put t
differently. The growth, among all classes, and especia
among the manual workers and the technicians, of what
may call corporate self-consciousness and public spirit, and t
diffusion of education—coupled with further discoveries
the technique of democratic institutions—would lead us t
day to include, and even to put in the forefront, certa
additional suggestions, which we can here only summari
briefly.

There is, in the first place, a genuine need for, and a rea
social advantage in giving recognition to, the contemporar
transformation in the status of the manual working wage-earner
on the one hand, and of the technicians on the other, as com
pared with that of the manager or mere " captain of industry.
This change of status, which is, perhaps, the most importan
feature of the industrial history of the past quarter of a century
will be most easily accorded its legitimate recognition in those
industries and services in which the profit-making capitalist
proprietor is dispensed with in favour of public ownership,
whether national, municipal, or co-operative. This is, incidentally, an important reason for what is called " nationalisation."
It is a real social gain that the General Secretary of the Swiss
Railwaymen's Trade Union should sit as one of the five members
of the supreme governing board of the Swiss railway administration. We ourselves look for the admission of nominees of the
manual workers, as well as of the technicians, upon the executive
boards and committees, on terms of complete equality with the
other members, in all publicly owned industries and services ;
not merely, or even mainly, for the sake of the advantages
of the counsel and criticism that the newcomers may bring
from new standpoints, but principally for the sake of both
inspiring and satisfying the increasing sense of corporate self-
consciousness and public spirit among all those employed in
these enterprises.

In the second place we should lay stress on the change that
is taking place in the nature (and in the conception) of authority
itself. In our analysis of 1897 we confined ourselves unduly to
a separation of spheres of authority. Whilst still regarding that
analytic separation of " management " into three classes of
judgements or decisions as fundamentally valid, we should

invalids. Trade Unionism adds to the long list of functions thus
delegated to professional experts the settlement of the conditions
on which the citizen will agree to co-operate in the national
service. In the fully-developed democratic state the Citizen
will be always minding other people's business. In his professional occupation he will, whether as brain-worker or manual
labourer, be continually striving to fulfil the desires of those
whom he serves ; whilst as an Elector, in his parish or his
co-operative society, his Trade Union or his political association, he will be perpetually passing judgment on issues in
which his personal interest is no greater than that of his
fellows.

" If, then, we are asked whether democracy, as shown by
an analysis of Trade Unionism, is consistent with Individual
Liberty, we are compelled to answer by asking, What is Liberty ?
If Liberty means every man being his own master, and following
his own impulses, then it is clearly inconsistent, not so much
with democracy or any other particular form of government, as
with the crowding together of population in dense masses,
with the division of labour, and, as we think, civilisation itself. What
particular individuals, sections, or classes usually mean by
' freedom of contract,' ' freedom of association,' or ' freedom
of enterprise ' is freedom of opportunity to use the power that
they happen to possess—that is to say, to compel other less
powerful people to accept their terms. This sort of personal
freedom in a community composed of unequal units is not
distinguishable from compulsion. It is, therefore, necessary to
define Liberty before talking about it ; a definition which every
man will frame according to his own view of what is socially
desirable. We ourselves understand by the words ' Liberty '
or ' Freedom,' not any quantum of natural or inalienable
rights, but such conditions of existence in the community as
do, in practice, result in the utmost possible development of
faculty in the individual human being. Now, in this sense
democracy is not only consistent with Liberty, but is, as it
seems to us, the only way of securing the largest amount of it.
It is open to argument whether other forms of government
may not achieve a fuller development of the faculties of particular
individuals or classes. To an autocrat, untrammelled rule over
a whole kingdom may mean an exercise of his individual
faculties, and a development of his individual personality, such
as no other situation in life would afford. An aristocracy or
government by one class in the interests of one class, may

conceivably enable that class to develop a perfection in physical grace or intellectual charm attainable by no other system of society. Similarly, it might be argued that, where the ownership of the means of production and the administration of industry are unreservedly left to the capitalist class, this 'freedom of enterprise' would result in a development of faculty among the captains of industry which could not otherwise be reached. We dissent from all these propositions, if only on the ground that the fullest development of personal character requires the pressure of discipline as well as the stimulus of opportunity. But however untrammelled power may affect the character of those who possess it, autocracy, aristocracy, and plutocracy have all, from the point of view of the lover of liberty, one fatal defect — they necessarily involve a restriction in the opportunity for development of faculty among the great mass of the population. It is only when the resources of the nation are deliberately organised and dealt with for the benefit, not of particular individuals or classes, but of the entire community; when the administration of industry, as of every other branch of human affairs, becomes the function of specialised experts, working through deliberately adjusted Common Rules; and when the ultimate decision on policy rests in no other hands than those of the citizens themselves, that the maximum aggregate development of individual intellect and individual character in the community as a whole can be attained.

"For our analysis helps us to disentangle from the complex influences on individual development those caused by democracy itself. The universal specialisation and delegation which, as we suggest, democratic institutions involve, necessarily imply a great increase in capacity and efficiency, if only because specialisation in service means expertness, and delegation compels selection. This deepening and narrowing of professional skill may be expected, in the fully-developed democratic state, to be accompanied by a growth in culture of which our present imperfect organisation gives us no adequate idea. So long as life is one long scramble for personal gain—still more, when it is one long struggle against destitution—there is no free time or strength for much development of the sympathetic, intellectual, artistic, or religious faculties. When the conditions of employment are deliberately regulated so as to secure adequate food, education, and leisure to every capable citizen, the great mass of the population will, for the first time, have any real chance of

expanding in friendship and family affection, and of satisfying the instinct for knowledge or beauty. It is an even more unique attribute of democracy that it is always taking the mind of the individual off his own narrow interests and immediate concerns, and forcing him to give his thoughts and leisure, not to satisfying his own desires, but to considering the needs and desires of his fellows. As an Elector—still more as a chosen Representative —in his parish, in his professional association, in his co-operative society, or in the wider political institutions of his state, the 'average sensual man' is perpetually impelled to appreciate and to decide issues of public policy. The working of democratic institutions means, therefore, one long training in enlightened altruism, one continual weighing, not of the advantage of the particular act to the particular individual, at the particular moment, but of those 'larger expediencies' on which all successful conduct of social life depends.

"If now, at the end of this long analysis, we try to formulate our dominant impression, it is a sense of the vastness and complexity of democracy itself. Modern civilised states are driven to this complication by the dense massing of their populations, and the course of industrial development. The very desire to secure mobility in the crowd compels the adoption of one regulation after another, which limit the right of every man to use the air, the water, the land, and even the artificially produced instruments of production, in the way that he may think best. The very discovery of improved industrial methods, by leading to specialisation, makes manual labourer and brain-worker alike dependent on the rest of the community for the means of subsistence, and subordinates them, even in their own crafts, to the action of others. In the world of civilisation and progress, no man can be his own master. But the very fact that, in modern society, the individual thus necessarily loses control over his own life, makes him desire to regain collectively what has become individually impossible. Hence the irresistible tendency to popular government, in spite of all its difficulties and dangers. But democracy is still the Great Unknown. Of its full scope and import we can yet catch only glimpses. As one department of social life after another becomes the subject of careful examination we shall gradually attain to a more complete vision. Our own tentative conclusions, derived from the study of one manifestation of the democratic spirit, may, we hope, not only suggest hypotheses for future verification, but also stimulate other students to carry out original investiga-

nowadays attach even more importance to the ways in which authority itself, in industry as well as in the rest of government, is being rapidly transformed, alike in substance and in methods of expression. The need for final decisions will remain, not merely in emergencies, but also as to policy ; and it is of high importance to vest the responsibility for decision, according to the nature of the case, in the right hands. But we suggest that a great deal of the old autocracy in industry and services, once deemed to be indispensable, is ceasing to be necessary to efficiency, and will accordingly, as Democracy becomes more genuinely accepted, gradually be dispensed with. A steadily increasing sphere will, except in matters of emergency, be found for consultation among all grades and sections concerned, out of which will emerge judgements and decisions arrived at, very largely, by common consent. This will, we believe, produce actually a higher standard of industrial efficiency than mere autocracy could ever hope for. Where knowledge is a common possession the facts themselves will often decide ; and though decisions may be short, sharp, and necessarily formulated by the appropriate person, they will not inevitably bear the impress of (or be resented as) the dictates of irresponsible autocracy. We may instance two large classes of considerations which will, we think, with great social advantage, come to be matters for mutual consultation in those committees and councils which already characterise the administration of all industry on a large scale, whether under private or public ownership, and which will, in the future, be increasingly representative of all grades of workers by hand or by brain. To such committees and councils there will come, as a matter of course, a stream of reports from the disinterested outside costing experts, which will carry with them no coercive authority, but which will graphically reveal the efficiency results, so far as regards cost and output, of each part of the enterprise, in comparison both with its own past, and with the corresponding results of other analogous enterprises. Similarly, there will come a stream of financial and merely statistical reports from equally disinterested outside auditors and statisticians, making graphic revelations as to the progress of the enterprise, in comparison with its own previous experience and with the progress of like enterprises elsewhere. Further, there will be a stream of what we may call scientific reports, also from disinterested outside experts, not only describing new inventions and discoveries in the technique of the particular enterprise, but suggesting, in the light of recent surveys of the work, how they could be practically applied to its peculiar circumstances. These three classes of reports, all of them by disinterested experts, engaged in keeping under review all analogous enterprises at home or abroad, and having neither interest in, nor authority over, any of them, will, we suggest, be discussed by the members of the committees and councils on terms of equality ; the decisions being taken, according to the nature of the case, by those in whom the responsibility for decision may be vested.

But there will be a second extensive class of reports of a different character, conveying not statements of fact but views of policy. There will, we must assume, be reports from those responsible, not merely or mainly for satisfying the existing generation of consumers, producers, or citizens, but for safeguarding the interests of the community as a whole, in the future as well as in the present. There will be the reports from the organs of the consumers or users of the particular commodity or service (such as the District Committees representing telephone users set up by the Postmaster-General as organs of criticism and suggestion for his telephone administration). Finally there will be reports conveying criticisms and suggestions from committees or councils representing other enterprises, or other sections of producers (whether technicians or manual workers), which may have something to communicate that they deem important. These reports will, none of them, come with coercive authority, but merely as conveying information, to be considered in the consultations out of which the necessary decisions will emerge.

Opinions may differ as to the competence to take part in such consultations of the selected representatives of the manual workers and the technicians respectively. We are ourselves of opinion that, taking the business as a whole, such representatives will be found to compare, in competence, quite favourably with the average member of a Board of Directors. But whether or not the counsels and decisions of great industrial enterprises are likely to be much improved by such consultations—and we confidently expect that they will be—we suggest that it is predominantly in this form that the principles of Democracy may, in practice, be applied to industrial administration ; and that it will be for the Professional Associations of the technicians and the Trade Unions of the manual workers to prove themselves equal to the transformation in their status that this or any other application of Democracy involves.

But here we must pause. In a future work on the achievements, policy, and immediate controversies of the British Labour and Socialist Movement we shall give the historical and the psychological analysis, in the light of the experience of the past few decades, upon which we base our present conclusions.

INDEX

765

Index 769

THE END

Printed in Great Britain by R. & R. CLARK, LIMITED, *Edinburgh.*

LIVERPOOL
JOHN MOORES UNIVERSITY
TRUEMAN STREET LIBRARY
15-21 WEBSTER STREET
LIVERPOOL L3 2ET
TEL. 051 231 4022/4023